China's Big Power Ambition under Xi Jinping

Instead of emphasizing China as a developing country, Chinese President Xi Jinping has identified China as a big power and accentuated China's big power status. This book explores the narratives and driving forces behind Chinas' big power ambition. Three narratives rooted in Sino-centralism are examined. One is China's demands for the reform of global governance to reflect the values and interests of China as a rising power. Another is China's Belt and Road Initiative to construct a nascent China-centred world order. The third is the China model and self-image promotion in the developing countries.

There are many forces that have driven or constrained China's big power ambition. This collection focuses on two sets of forces. One is China's domestic politics and economic incentives and disincentives. The other is China's geopolitical and geo-economic interests. These forces have both motivated and constrained China's big power ambition.

The chapters in this book were originally published in the *Journal of Contemporary China*.

Suisheng Zhao is Professor and Director of the Center for China-US Cooperation at Josef Korbel School of International Studies, University of Denver and Founding Editor of the *Journal of Contemporary China*.

China's Big Power Ambition under Xi Jinping

Narratives and Driving Forces

Edited by
Suisheng Zhao

Routledge
Taylor & Francis Group

LONDON AND NEW YORK

First published 2022
by Routledge
2 Park Square, Milton Park, Abingdon, Oxon OX14 4RN

and by Routledge
605 Third Avenue, New York, NY 10158

Routledge is an imprint of the Taylor & Francis Group, an informa business

© 2022 Taylor & Francis

British Library Cataloguing in Publication Data
A catalogue record for this book is available from the British Library

ISBN: 978-1-032-05721-7 (hbk)
ISBN: 978-1-032-05722-4 (pbk)
ISBN: 978-1-003-19887-1 (ebk)

DOI: 10.4324/9781003198871

Typeset in Myriad Pro
by Newgen Publishing UK

Publisher's Note
The publisher accepts responsibility for any inconsistencies that may have arisen during the conversion of this book from journal articles to book chapters, namely the inclusion of journal terminology.

Disclaimer
Every effort has been made to contact copyright holders for their permission to reprint material in this book. The publishers would be grateful to hear from any copyright holder who is not here acknowledged and will undertake to rectify any errors or omissions in future editions of this book.

Contents

Citation Information

The chapters in this book were originally published in various issues of the *Journal of Contemporary China*. When citing this material, please use the original citations and page numbering for each article, as follows:

Chapter 1
Rhetoric and Reality of China's Global Leadership in the Context of COVID-19: Implications for the US-led World Order and Liberal Globalization
Suisheng Zhao
Journal of Contemporary China, volume 30, issue 128 (2021), pp. 233–248

Chapter 2
China's Strategic Narratives in Global Governance Reform under Xi Jinping
Yi Edward Yang
Journal of Contemporary China, volume 30, issue 128 (2021), pp. 299–313

Chapter 3
China's Belt and Road Initiative as Nascent World Order Structure and Concept? Between Sino-Centering and Sino-Deflecting
Ray Silvius
Journal of Contemporary China, volume 30, issue 128 (2021), pp. 314–329

Chapter 4
Co-evolutionary Pragmatism: Re-examine 'China Model' and Its Impact on Developing Countries
Tang Xiaoyang
Journal of Contemporary China, volume 29, issue 126 (2020), pp. 853–870

Chapter 5
From 'Peaceful Rise' to Peacebuilder? How Evolving Chinese Discourses and Self-perceptions Impact Its Growing Influence in Conflict Societies
Pascal Abb
Journal of Contemporary China, volume 30, issue 129 (2021), pp. 402–416

For any permission-related enquiries please visit:
www.tandfonline.com/page/help/permissions

Notes on Contributors

Pascal Abb is Senior Researcher at the Peace Research Institute Frankfurt (PRIF), Germany. He is currently conducting a research project on the impact of Chinese agency on conflict states, as well as on emerging Chinese discourses on conflict mitigation.

Malte Brosig is Professor in the Department of International Relations at the University of the Witwatersrand in Johannesburg. He joined the Department in 2009 after receiving his PhD from the University of Portsmouth. His main research interests focus on issues of peace and security, international organizations, rising powers, and peacekeeping in Africa.

Jean-Pierre Cabestan is Professor at the Department of Government and International Studies at Hong Kong Baptist University. He is also Associate Research Fellow at Asia Centre in Paris and at the French Centre for Research on Contemporary China in Hong Kong.

Gustavo de L. T. Oliveira is Assistant Professor of Global and International Studies at the University of California Irvine, and Co-editor of a special issue in *Political Geography* on China's Belt and Road Initiative.

Narisong Huhe received his PhD in Political Science from Old Dominion University. Currently he is Senior Lecturer at University of Strathclyde. His recent publications have appeared in *Political Research Quarterly, Studies in Comparative International Development, British Journal of Political Science, Political Studies, Social Science Research*, and *Social Science Quarterly*.

Wonjae Hwang is Associate Professor in the Department of Political Science at the University of Tennessee. His main research interests include Korean politics and the link between globalization and domestic and international politics.

Lee Jones is Reader (Associate Professor) in International Politics at Queen Mary University of London. His research focuses on security, governance, and political economy, with an empirical focus on the Asia-Pacific. He is author of *ASEAN, Sovereignty and Intervention in Southeast Asia* (2012), *Societies Under Siege: Exploring How International Economic Sanctions (Do Not) Work* (2015) and, with Shahar Hameiri, *Governing Borderless Threats: Non-Traditional Security and the Politics of State Transformation* (2015).

Hongyi Lai is Associate Professor of the School of Politics and International Relations, University of Nottingham (UoN), UK. His previous posts included Associate Professor at the School of Contemporary Chinese Studies at UoN and Senior Research Fellow at East Asian Institute, National University of Singapore.

Yao Lin received his PhD in Political Science from Columbia University and then his JD from Yale Law School. He is currently Global Perspectives on Society Fellow at New York University Shanghai. His research interests include political and legal theory as well as contemporary Chinese social and political thought.

Xin Liu is Senior Lecturer and Chair of the China Research Center at the School of Humanities, Language and Global Studies, University of Central Lancashire, UK. She received her PhD and MBA at the same university. Her research interest lies in the multidisciplinary area covering public diplomacy, international relations, cultural studies, media and communications.

Margaret Myers is Director of the Asia & Latin America Program at the Inter-American Dialogue, and Co-editor of *The Political Economy of China-Latin America Relations* (2017).

Andrew Scobell holds the Bren Chair in Non-Western Strategic Thought at Marine Corps University and is Adjunct Professor of Asian Studies at the Walsh of Foreign Service at Georgetown University, USA.

Ray Silvius is Associate Professor in the Department of Political Science at the University of Winnipeg in Winnipeg, Canada. He is the author of *Culture, Political Economy and Civilisation in a Multipolar World Order: The Case of Russia* (2016).

Min Tang is Associate Professor in the School of Public Economics and Administration at Shanghai University of Finance and Economics. His research focuses on comparative democratization, political attitudes, and Chinese public opinions.

Steve Tsang is Professor of Chinese Studies and Director of the SOAS China Institute at SOAS University of London, UK. He is also an Associate Fellow at the Chatham House and an Emeritus Fellow of St Antony's College, Oxford, UK.

Tang Xiaoyang is Associate Professor and Vice Chair in the Department of International Relations at Tsinghua University. He is also the Deputy Director at the Carnegie-Tsinghua Center for Global Policy.

Yi Edward Yang is Professor of Political Science at James Madison University, USA. He specializes in foreign policy decision-making, political psychology, and Chinese foreign policy. His research has appeared in several edited volumes and peer-reviewed scholarly journals including the *Journal of Conflict Resolution*, *International Studies Quarterly*, *Political Psychology*, *Journal of Contemporary China*, and the *Chinese Journal of International Politics*.

Suisheng Zhao is Professor and Director of the Center for China-US Cooperation at Josef Korbel School of International Studies, University of Denver; and Editor of the *Journal of Contemporary China*.

Yang Zhong is visiting Changjiang Scholar at the School of International and Public Affairs and adjunct researcher at China Institute for Urban Governance of Shanghai Jiao Tong University and a professor of Political Science the University of Tennessee. His main research interests include political culture in China, local governance, and political participation in China.

Yizheng Zou is Associate Professor in the Institute for China's Overseas Interests at Shenzhen University, China. His past research focused on media, identity, and British imperialism in China. His current research focuses on China's Belt and Road Initiative, particularly the impact of major Chinese projects in Myanmar.

Part I

The Narratives

Rhetoric and Reality of China's Global Leadership in the Context of COVID-19: Implications for the US-led World Order and Liberal Globalization

Suisheng Zhao

ABSTRACT
When President Trump-led America abandoned the global leadership, China casted itself as the global leader in response to COVID-19, placing challenges to the US-led world order and liberal globalization. China's rhetoric, however, has not matched its actions in comprehensively providing global public goods and developing universally accepted values. As neither the US and China have taken the global leadership that most countries can trust and count on, the world is in the danger of moving toward the vicious power rivalry, hampering the multilateral responses to global crisis such as COVID-19.

The US response to COVID-19 was sadly emblematic. Spending more than a month to play down the threat, delaying the diagnostic testing and stockpiling essential equipment after the World Health Organization (WHO) declared the Public Health Emergency on 30 January 2020, the Trump administration was unprepared, ill-equipped and overwhelmed. Disdaining international cooperation and focusing the bulk of its efforts on blaming the WHO and China, President Trump astonished the world by suggesting disinfectant and ultraviolet light could possibly be used to treat Covid-19.

Containing the outbreak by strict confinement measures and coming out of the crisis in a stronger position than many other countries, the Chinese government wasted no time to launch a propaganda campaign, trumpeting its powerful state capacity in time of crisis in contrast to the contradictory and incoherent response of the US and European democracies. As the US faltered in its handling of the pandemic, China enhanced its influence across the world by exporting medical equipment, expertise, experience, and largesse to other hard-hit countries through the so-called coronavirus diplomacy.

In some scholar's eyes, the Trump administration's belated, self-centered, haphazard, and tone-deaf response marked the death of American competence and beginning of the "post-American' order.[1] Beijing moved quickly and adeptly to take advantage of the opening created by U.S. mistakes to fill vacuum of the global leadership.[2] The rest of the world was 'accommodating to a world of

---

[1] Stephen M. Walt,'The Death of American Competence. *Foreign Policy*,' March 23, 2020, accessed June 2, 2020, https://foreign policy.com/2020/03/23/death-american-competence-reputation-coronavirus/, Kevin D. Williamson, 'Pandemic: The First Great Crisis of the Post-American Era,' *National Review*, March 29, 2020, accessed June 2, 2020, https://www.nationalreview.com/2020/03/coronavirus-pandemic-first-great-crisis-post-american-era/.

[2] K. M. Campbell and R. Doshi, 'The Coronavirus Could Reshape Global Order. China Is Maneuvering for International Leadership as the United States Falters', *Foreign Affairs*, March 18, 2020, accessed June 2, 2020, https://www.foreignaffairs.com/articles/china/2020-03-18/coronavirus-could-reshape-global-order?utm_campaign=Foreign%20Policy&utm_content=85046008&utm_medium=email&utm_source=hs_email.

growing Chinese power, in the absence of any viable alternative.'[3] President Xi Jinping-led China actively contributed to world governance and human development and became a global leader in the 21st century.[4]

Is China ready to step into the breach left by the Trump administration and become a global leader in reconstructing the world order and globalization? This article argues that taking advantage of the US retreat from the liberal world order and globalization, China has indeed filled some vacuums by proposing Chinese vision for the world order, grasping increasing number of leadership positions in the international organizations, and launching Beijing-led multilateral institutions to advance Beijing's priorities and values. But China has pushed for an illiberal statist world order and appealed primarily to the authoritarian regimes. China's ambition for global leadership has entrenched the divide between democratic and authoritarian countries. But China is still a fragile big power and does not have enough resources to lead a crusade against liberal democracies and overtake the US global leadership in supplying the global public goods. Although COVID-19 affected more countries than any other single event in recent history, it was unfolded in a vacuum of global leadership and furious US-China blame game to shirk responsibilities, paralyzing the global cooperation in response to the pandemic.

The China Challenge to the US-led World Order

The US global leadership was established through the construction and maintenance of the Post-WWII world order and the promotion of Post-Cold War liberal globalization. Prospering in the US-led order and benefiting immensely from liberal globalization, China is no longer a revolutionary power seeking to 'the overthrow of the existing world order because as a big power, China occupies a pivotal position in the international organizations.'[5]

A rising China, however, has regarded the order unfair and unreasonable enough to reflect the interests and values of the emerging powers like China and become a revisionist power to advance its status as a rule-maker, expand its influence in the hierarchy, and change aspects of the order that it views as undermining its values and interests.[6] Blaming the US promotion of liberal values responsible for conflict, disruption and chaos worldwide, 'China' leaders see the post-1945 liberal international order as reflecting the worldview of the victorious white colonial powers that created it. Xi considers the world of 2020 to be radically different from that of the post-war era.'[7]

The US-led order worked well when American democracy functioned as a model for the rest of the world and America was able to defend and pay for the order. But America is no longer a beacon of liberal democracy and many Americans are no longer willing to pay for the global leadership. Bill Clinton was elected President in 1992 partially because he promised the arrival of a peace dividend after the Cold War to be invested in strengthening America at home. Barack Obama was elected President in 2008 because he promised to pull the US troops from the Middle East and Afghanistan.

Openly stating that the US would comply with the rules only if they are in its interest, the Trump administration spent great efforts on bilateral rather than multilateral diplomacy, favoring a sovereign normative order over a liberal order. Although the American leadership was essential to multinational agreements on trade, climate change, regional security and arms control, President

[3]Hal Brands and Jake Sullivan, 'China Has Two Paths to Global Domination,' *Foreign Policy*, May 22, 2020, accessed June 26, 2020, https://foreignpolicy.com/2020/05/22/china-superpower-two-paths-global-domination-cold-war/.

[4]周新民 (Zhou Xinmin), '大变局时代呼唤世界政治领袖' (The era of great changes calls for world political leaders), 网际谈兵 (Military Net), June 9, 2020, https://club.6parkbbs.com/military/index.php?app=forum&act=threadview&tid=15782581.

[5]吴正龙 (Wu Zhenglong), "解读当今世界"百年未有之大变局 (Interpretation of the world's big changes not seen in a century), 环球网 (Huangqiunet), September 25, 2018, accessed June 2, 2020, https://opinion.huanqiu.com/article/9CaKrnKcZDj.

[6]Suisheng Zhao, 'A Revisionist Stakeholder: China and the Post-World War II World Order,' *Journal of Contemporary China*, 27:113, 2018, accessed June 2, 2020, https://www.tandfonline.com/doi/full/10.1080/10670564.2018.1458029.

[7]Kevin Rudd, 'The Coronavirus and Xi Jinping's Worldview,' *Project Syndicate*, February 8, 2020, accessed June, 2 2020, https://www.project-syndicate.org/commentary/coronavirus-will-not-change-xi-jinping-china-governance-by-kevin-rudd-2020-02.

Trump has cut US global commitments and broken up alliances, withdrawing the US from the Trans-Pacific Partnership, Paris climate accord, and the United Nations Educational, Scientific and Cultural Organization (UNESCO), criticizing nearly every multilateral network the US was part of, and suggesting Japan and South Korea develop nuclear weapons of their own.

The Chinese, therefore, complained that while the Americans often asked China to follow the rules-based liberal international order, 'It has become harder and harder for foreign policy makers in China to discern what rules the Americans want themselves and others to abide by, what kind of world order they hope to maintain.'[8] 'The US accused China as revisionist, but the US as the main builder of the global order challenged it,' causing the world anxiety and leading to global trust deficit, governance deficit, peace deficit, and development deficit."[9]

A Chinese scholar warned that 'the post-WWII order has quickly become disorder and dangerous to fail, evidence from racial contradictions to regional conflicts, from refugee issues to climate change, from terrorism to financial crisis, and from arms race to nuclear weapons proliferation. World conflicts and contradictions have approached the new thresholds since 2019, leading to a more complicated, more severe and unpredictable turbulent future.'[10]

China has long taken an à la carte approach to the world order, supporting the international institutions such as the World Bank that served its interests, turning others such as the UN Peace Keeping to its own purposes, and weakening those such as the human rights regimes that might pose a challenge to its values. But the Chinese leadership has become increasingly proactive to shape the rules and norms forming the basis for the world order and created international institutions to better align with its values and interests.

Presenting the Chinese vision for the world order, President Xi put forwarded the Community of Shared Future for Mankind (CSFM) in 2013. The Chinese government managed to incorporate this phrase into the UN resolution on the 55th UN Commission for Social Development in 2017. It was also enshrined by the UN Security Council, the Human Rights Council and the First Committee of the UN General Assembly.

The Chinese term (人类命运共同体) was at first translated into English as the Community of Common Destiny for Mankind. As the term is increasingly used, the English translation is standardized as the CSFM because the word 'destiny' implies a lack of choice along a pre-determined trajectory, possibly generating resistance.

Promising to build an 'open, inclusive, clean and beautiful world that enjoys lasting peace, universal security and common prosperity,' the CSFM calls for all socio-political systems to be respected as equally valid, i.e. democracies are not a model superior to authoritarianism. All should peacefully coexist, not attempting to transform the others.[11] Claiming to boost the shared future for mankind, China's attempt to shaping the world order, however, is primarily to advance Chinese interests. In President Xi's words, 'it is to position China in the commanding heights of the international competition.'[12]

For this purpose, China has tried to increase its voting shares and leadership positions in the UN and other international organizations. China's voting shares in the International Monetary Fund (IMF) were increased from 3.994% to 6.390% to become the third largest share-nation in 2015, paving the way for Beijing to flex its muscle in the global economy. As a result of the reform, the share of

[8]Wang Jisi, 'Did America Get China Wrong: The View from China,' *Foreign Affairs*, July/August 2018, accessed June 2, 2020, https://www.foreignaffairs.com/articles/china/2018-06-14/did-america-get-china-wrong.

[9]寒 竹 (Han Zhu), '国际秩序与世界秩序的博弈与中国的位置' (The Game between International Order and World Order and China's Position), 复旦大学中国研究院 (The China Research Center, Fudan University, November 26, 2019, accessed June 2, 2020, http://www.cifu.fudan.edu.cn/24/91/c12233a205969/page.htm.

[10]周新民 (Zhou Xinmin), '大变局时代呼唤世界政治领袖' (The era of great changes calls for world political leaders), 网际谈兵 (Military Net), June 9, 2020, https://club.6parkbbs.com/military/index.php?app=forum&act=threadview&tid=15782581.

[11]Xiang Bo, 'China Keywords: Community with Shared Future for Mankind,' *Xinhua*, January 24, 2018, accessed June 2, 2020, http://www.xinhuanet.com/english/2018-01/24/c_136921370.htm.

[12]习近平 (Xi Jinping), '推动全球治理体制更加公正更加合理' (Pushing for a more just and reasonable global governance), *Xinhua*, 13 October 2015, accessed June 2, 2020, http://news.xinhuanet.com/politics/2015-10/13/c_1116812159.htm.

advanced economies was dropped from 60.5% to 57.7 while the share of emerging markets and developing countries rose from 39.5% to 42.3%.

Enjoying veto power as a permanent member in the UN Security Council, China's representation in the UN is enhanced immensely as Chinese officials have held the position of Under-Secretary-General for the UN Department of Economic and Social Affairs since 2007 and taken the helm in four of 15 UN specialized agencies, including the Food and Agriculture Organization (FAO), the International Telecommunication Union (ITU), the United Nations Industrial Development Organization (UNIDP), and the International Civil Aviation Organization (ICAO).

These leadership positions have helped advance China's economic influence. For example, the ITU, which establishes global technology specifications, has worked closely with Chinese companies to assist developing countries in Africa, the Middle East and Asia build their telecom infrastructure and cooperate in China's 'digital Silk Road' since a Chinese official took its top post in 2015. It received 20 standards proposals on the storage and analysis of footage for facial recognition cameras and recordings by audio surveillance devices from Chinese companies in 2016–2019. Half of the standards were approved, helping Chinese leadership in developing global technology standards.[13]

More importantly, these positions have helped advance China's political ends. The most well-known case is the refusal of Taiwan's attendance in the ICAO and WHO that involve universal aviation safety and public health. The ICAO has denied Taiwan's participation as an observer since China's Liu Fang became secretary-general in 2015. Headed by Margaret Chan, a Chinese national from Hong Kong in 2006–2017, WHO allowed Taiwan to participate as an observer with the title 'Chinese Taipei' after Ma Ying-jeou was elected the President in 2008. After President Tsai Ing-wen was elected in 2016, WHO suspended Taiwan's observer position in 2017 because Beijing was concerned about her pro-independence tendency. A Taiwan diplomat complained that WHO relegated decisions concerning Taiwan to Beijing.[14]

During the Director-General election in 2017, China supported Tedros Adhanom, former Ethiopian minister of health and minister of foreign affairs. The day after his electoral victory, Tedros reiterated adherence to the 'One China' principle, 'meaning that WHO would not invite Taiwan for participation without China's approval.'[15] After the eruption of COVID-19, WHO officials did not reply Taiwanese inquiries in December 2019 about whether the coronavirus could, contrary to Beijing's claim, be transmitted between humans. In late March 2020, assistant director-general Bruce Aylward, who led the WHO-China Joint Mission on Coronavirus, even disconnected a video interview to avoid a question about Taiwan, leaving the impression that 'WHO officials have acted like good soldiers in China's campaign to cut off Taiwan.'[16]

WHO was also criticized for hiding information at China behest in the initial response to COVID-19. Finding a scapegoat for his failure to contain the pandemic effectively, President Trump withdrew the US from WHO on ground that it was bought by China. President Trump obviously exaggerated China's influence. China contributed 40 USD million while the US 450 USD million WHO in 2019. China's influence was not because of money but because of its focused and strategic efforts to work with WHO. It was impossible that WHO hid information at China's behest because the US was well represented in the top ranks of WHO.[17] A week after the US suspension of funding, China pledged 30 USD million on top of its annual contribution to WHO, further advancing its influence.

---

[13]Anna Gross and Madhumita Murgia, 'China Shows its Dominace In Surveillance technology,' *Financial Times*, December 26, 2019, accessed June 2, 2020, https://www.ft.com/content/b34d8ff8-21b4-11ea-92da-f0c92e957a96.

[14]Vincent Yi-hsiang Chao, 'Why Taiwan Belongs in the World Health Organization (WHO)', *National Interest*, April 20, 2020, accessed June 2, 2020, https://nationalinterest.org/feature/why-taiwan-belongs-world-health-organization-who-146172.

[15]Yanzhong Huang, 'Tedros, Taiwan, and Trump: What They Tell Us About China's Growing Clout in Global Health,' *Council on Foreign Relations*, June 7, 2017, accessed June 2, 2020, https://www.cfr.org/blog/tedros-taiwan-and-trump-what-they-tell-us-about-chinas-growing-clout-global-health.

[16]John Pomfret, 'Taiwan must participate in the WHO. Global health is too important to play politics,' *Washington Post*, April 14, 2020, accessed June 2, 2020, https://www.washingtonpost.com/opinions/2020/04/14/taiwan-must-join-who-global-health-is-too-important-play-politics.

[17]Julian Borger, 'Caught in a superpower struggle: the inside story of the WHO's response to coronavirus,' *The Guardian*, April 18, 2020, accessed June 2 2020, https://www.theguardian.com/world/2020/apr/18/caught-in-a-superpower-struggle-the-inside-story-of-the-whos-response-to-coronavirus.

China's actions, therefore, raised the concern that China used its ample political and economic clout to politicize U.N. agencies.[18] Complaining about China's diplomatic muscle-flexing in U.N. agencies to skew them in China's favor, the U.S. coordinated with its allies and blocked the Chinese candidate from grabbing the Director-General position of the World Intellectual Property Organization (WIPO) in March 2020, accusing that China's intellectual property violations ran against WIPO's mandate to devise and enforce rules in preventing intellectual property theft and infringement. Had China won the position, China would have taken five or one-third of leadership positions of all UN agencies, establishing Chinese centrality in the UN agencies.

Outside of the UN, China has taken initiatives to create new institutions, notably the New Development Bank (NDB) headquartered in Shanghai and established by the BRICS countries of Brazil, Russia, India, China, and South Africa in 2014, a symbolic gesture to create a sort of IMF clone towards reshaping the international financial architecture. China also launched the Asian Infrastructure Investment Bank (AIIB) in 2015, headquartered in Beijing and headed by a Chinese national. The US dissuaded its allies from joining the AIIB, but the UK, France, Germany, Italy, Australia and South Korea applied as founding members, a powerful testament to China's influence in the international development finance.

The G-7 of the U.S. and its six closest allies has long been the leader in international economic affairs. But China is not included. President Hu Jintao accepted the invitation to attend the G-7 summit in 2003, the first and only Chinese leader presented. China, therefore, has promoted the G-20 established in 2009, given China's membership, as an alternative to the G-7. China has held BRICS leaders' meetings on the G-20 sidelines to coordinate their positions there. In addition, although China has never joined the G-77 of developing nations in the UN, Beijing supports the group and has formed G77+ China to advance their common interests.

China's Statist Response to the Retreat of Liberal Globalization

As the biggest beneficiary of globalization, China has been concerned about the backlash represented by the duel shocks of America First and Brexit. Entrenching their nativist approach, the Trump administration launched the trade wars against China and Britain left the EU, the strongest kind of institutionalized globalization the world has even seen. National borders become tighter and protectionism become the norm rather than the exception.

Positioning China as the torchbearer of globalization, even if its behavior at home painted a different picture, President Xi presented China as an unlikely champion of the globalization in his speech at the World Economic Forum in Davos in January 2017. Introducing Xi, Klaus Schwab, the founder of the Forum, said that 'In a world marked by great uncertainty and volatility, the international community is looking to China.'[19]

But the globalization that China has advocated is different from liberal globalization once promoted by the West. According to one Chinese scholar, each country must make a choice of globalization that is good to itself. China has promoted economic globalization supported by political multipolarization and multi-culturalism while liberal globalization emphasizes political democratization, economic privatization, and universalization of liberal values.[20]

---

[18]Editorial, 'China must not politicize international agencies,' *Nikkei Asian Review*, April 1, 2020, accessed June 2, 2020, https://asia.nikkei.com/Opinion/The-Nikkei-View/China-must-not-politicize-international-agencies.

[19]Shahid Javed Burki, China: the new champion of globalisation, *The Express Tribune*, February 26, 2018, accessed June 2, 2020, https://tribune.com.pk/story/1644956/6-china-new-champion-globalisation/.

[20]黄仁伟 (Huang Renwei), 从全球化、逆全球化到有选择的全球化 (From globalization and Anti-globalization to Selective Globalization), *探索与争鸣杂志(Exploration and Contention)*, March 21, 2017, accessed June 2, 2020, https://www.yicai.com/news/5251702.html.

China has pushed illiberal globalization that leaves more leeway for states to conduct themselves as they please, shelling off China's tightening state control over information flow and state-led economic growth. China has thus pursued a state-enhancing, not state-diminishing, globalization for statist ends through globalist means.

Taking the statist approach, China has competed with the US to make rules in governing the accesses to cyberspace. The US has championed open and decentralized multi-stakeholder model, in which corporations and civil society actors work together with states to regulate cyberspace. Beijing has insisted on the inter-governmental model based on the "cyberspace sovereignty, by which the Worldwide Web is no longer driven by a single set of standards and rules. Consumers no longer have the same access. Constructing its independent internet with a separate system of technology, standards, infrastructure, and supply chains, the Chinese state has built a vast human and electronic surveillance apparatus to access ubiquitous data gathered about Chinese citizens through social media and online shopping platforms and track their every move. China has made a seminal swing away from liberal globalization, drawing the world's largest group of Internet users away from interconnected global commons and living under cyber-totalitarianism.[21]

China has brought statist approach toward the international human rights governance. Claiming that the priority of human rights protection in developing countries is different from the priority in the West, the Chinese government has asserted that human rights are first the rights of economic development, not individual civil rights. A Chinese senior diplomat wrote that 'China has explored and blazed a distinctly Chinese path of human rights development tailored to its national circumstances.'[22] China has, therefore, deconstructed the notion of universal human rights with a concept that economic and social rights are more fundamental than civil and political rights, the proper balance is to be determined by the state according to national circumstances.

Forming a strong coalition consisting mostly of authoritarian governments in the UN Human Rights Council (UNHRC), China often put Western democracies in the voting minority. China's first two UNHRC resolutions were adopted in June 2017 and March 2018, respectively. Both treated human rights as primarily the rights of states and did not have any balancing reference to the rights of individuals, the role of civil society groups or the mandate of UNHRC to monitor abuses. Taking the individual out of the picture, China framed the human rights as purely a matter for states, focusing solely on intergovernmental cooperation.

China's victory in UNHRC challenged liberal human rights norms and universal human rights monitoring. While Western officials and rights organizations saw the resolutions as tools to make the world a safer place for autocrats, the Chinese government celebrated the setback to the West's monopoly on human rights discourse and 'a major shift in the global human rights conversation.'[23]

China's position has been enhanced after the US withdrawal from UNHRC in 2018. When the US was a member, it could work with European countries and tip the balance in favor of the agenda of democracies. Without the US, China has advanced its position. On 1 April 2020, China was appointed to the UNHRC influential panel of five nations in charge of picking UN human rights mandate-holders who investigate, monitor, and publicly report on either specific country situations, or on thematic issues in all parts of the world, such as freedom of speech and religion. Serving as a panelist nation, China could help vet candidates for the critical UN human rights posts and help decide whom to recommend for appointment. In most cases, the Council President appoints the experts selected by the five-nation panel.[24]

---

[21]Emile Simpson, 'Globalization Has Created a Chinese Monster,' *Foreign Policy*, February 26, 2018, accessed June 2, 2020, https://foreignpolicy.com/2018/02/26/globalization-has-created-a-chinese-monster/.

[22]张军 (Zhang Jun), '在发展进程中促进和保护人权' (Promote and Protect Human Rights in the Process of Development), 外交 (*Foreign Affairs Journal*), 130, (winter 2018), p. 8.

[23]'China's party paper trumpets U.N. rights resolution as combating West's monopoly,' *Reuters*, June 24, 2017, accessed June 2, 2020, https://www.reuters.com/article/us-china-rights-un-idUSKBN19F0A8.

[24]'China joins U.N. human rights panel, will help pick experts on free speech, health, arbitrary detention,' *UN Watch*, April 2, 2020, accessed June 2, 2020, https://unwatch.org/china-joins-u-n-human-rights-panel-will-help-pick-experts-on-free-speech-health-arbitrary-detention/.

Chinese Authoritarianism in Time of Crisis

China's statist approach gained momentum after China quickly contained the spread of COVID-19. The outbreak was initially predicted as China's Chernobyl moment, a mishandled disaster for the Chinese leadership to lose political legitimacy. But once the Chinese government realized the scale of the threat, it made the most consequential decision to quarantine the city of Wuhan on 23 January 2020, the epicenter of the epidemic and home to more than 11 million people, and then extended the quarantine to the entire country. Large swathes of the public transportation, factories, shops, and schools/universities were shut down. People were ordered to stay home. Two hospitals with a total capacity of 2,300 beds were built in Wuhan within 10 days. Requiring people to wear face masks, the government ordered factories into overdrive and produced millions of masks every day.

Launching an arsenal of propaganda campaign in the media and large street banners calling on people to be hygienic and follow order, the state used harsh control measures, including community policing by residents monitoring and reporting each other's violations. The state introduced big data and monitoring technology to track people's contacts with the virus. Temperature checkpoints were installed everywhere. In the high-tech country where privacy is limited, citizens were assigned health rating codes on their cellphones based on their medical history and tracking records in contacts with infected people or visits to high-risk places. An approved code was entrance requirement for many places to stop the spread of the virus.

The scale and speed of these measures were unseen in history, a testament to the untrammeled authoritarian state power in times of crisis. The rapid centralization of power by President Xi generated strong capacity for the state to take the zealous and heavy-handed actions and deliver results. China announced zero new domestic cases on March 18 and reported zero coronavirus deaths on April 7. The 76-day lockdown on Wuhan was lifted on April 8, an implicit pushback against some of the criticism about aggressive authoritarian measures. The WHO mission to China in late February reported that 'China's bold approach to contain the rapid spread of this new respiratory pathogen has changed the course of a rapidly escalating and deadly epidemic.'[25]

When China stabilized the outbreak, the pandemic went on a rampage in Europe and the US. China began to ship masks, surgical gowns, diagnostic tests, and sometimes doctors to the pandemic-ravaged foreign countries and position itself as the partner of choice. Jack Ma's Alibaba Foundation took a lead in distributing free masks around the world. Owning most of the global medical supply chain, the Chinese government send medical teams and supplies to more than a hundred countries around the world. Chinese media dutifully reported every delivery. One observer described the stunts at foreign airports designed to mark the arrival of Chinese aid. The plane landed; the receiving nation's dignitaries went out to meet it; the Chinese experts emerged, looking competent in their hazmat gear; and everyone uttered words of gratitude and relief.[26]

Boosting China's international image by publicizing its generosity, Beijing launched a propaganda campaign to buttress the claim in the superiority of the China's authoritarian system. COVID-19 tallies became a league table not only for public health management but also the state governance to overcome the crisis. China began at a low spot but soon overtook the US and European countries. From the vantage point, President Xi instructed the Chinese officials to take initiatives and effectively influence international public opinion (有效影响国际舆论) by telling the stories of China's fight against the epidemic and showing the spirit of the Chinese people united and working together."[27]

---

[25]"WHO Says China Actions Blunted Virus Spread, Leading to Drop,' Bloomberg News, February 24, 2020, https://www.bloomberg.com/news/articles/2020-02-24/who-says-china-lockdown-blunted-new-epidemic-leading-to-decline.

[26]Anne Applebaum, 'The Rest of the World Is Laughing at Trump: The president created a leadership vacuum. China intends to fill it,' *The Atlantic*, May 3, 2020, https://www.theatlantic.com/ideas/archive/2020/05/time-americans-are-doing-nothing/611056/.

[27]习近平 (Xi Jinping), '在中央政治局常委会会议研究应对新型冠状病毒肺炎疫情工作时的讲话' (Speech at the Politburo Standing Committee on the response to the coronavirus), *Qiush*, February 15, 2020, accessed June 2, 2020, http://www.gov.cn/xinwen/2020-02/15/content_5479271.htm.

In a gambit to turn the pandemic that started in China into a celebration of China's authoritarian system, the CCP propaganda machine highlighted the strong capacity of the authoritarian state in contrast to the spectacular incapacity of the democracies that could not cherish the precious time China won for them. The Chinese government succeeded not only in building a powerful economy but also in suppressing the spread of Covid-19, demonstrating the superiority of Chinese authoritarian system over Western democracy in effective mobilization of vast resources and willingness to undertake tough but necessary sacrifices in time of crisis. Creating the collective obedience, orderliness, and respect for life, China's unified leadership was said to have played the national chess game with remarkable coordination in resource allocation, personnel integration, and implementation of measures because of the institutional advantages of 'centralizing resources to do big things' (集中力量办大事) and 'strictly following orders and highly effective collaboration' (令行禁止高效协同).[28]

Many Chinese scholars contributed to the propaganda campaign. Wu Xinbo in Fudan University argued that it did not matter if a state was democratic or authoritarian. What it mattered was the governance. Winning the turnaround battle against COVID-19, China demonstrated its outstanding governance ability as a responsible big power. While the world's positive impression of China used to come from its economic performance, China's response to COVID-19 gave the world a new understanding of its governance capacity and sense of big power responsibility.[29]

Taking a victory lap to celebrate China's success in crisis management, Fang Yongpeng of Fudan University compared China's performance with other countries and concluded that this 'control group experiment' confirmed the superiority of China's system. The Western model of limited government could not cope with the crisis. A strong and decisive state is necessary. 'Because abnormality and normality are a pair of blurred concepts, a system that cannot deal with abnormal crisis is not a good system.'[30]

Trolling US serious misjudgment and incompetence, a *Global Times* editorial suggested that 'As a typical Western democracy, the US apparently had a huge loophole in its understanding of COVID-19 early.'[31] The US used to be known for the attractiveness of its values and the effectiveness of its institutions. But the charms were tarnished by its worst-in-class performance in the face of COVID-19, confirming the declining US and its faltering model.

Wang Yong of Beijing University claimed that the pandemic marginalized the US from the center of the world stage. 'In the past, people regarded the US economy, political system, ideas, and popular culture as the benchmark of the world. Through this pandemic, the world has a clearer understanding of the real situation in America. The US is no longer a model for the future of the world.'[32]

Beijing celebrated the superiority of the Chinese system not only because it quickly contained the virus but also because other countries, including liberal democracies, began to copy China to impose stringent quarantine and erect barriers to the movement of people. One article in *nature* described that 'As the new coronavirus marches around the globe, countries with escalating outbreaks are eager to learn whether China's extreme lockdowns were responsible for bringing the crisis there

[28]郝身永 (Hao Shengyong), "抗'疫'背后的中国之治 (China's Governance behind the success of combating the virus), Dongfangnet, April 8, 2020, accessed June, 2 2020, http://pinglun.eastday.com/p/20200408/u1ai20467098.html; 郭凯 (Guo Kai), 金信烨 (Jing Xinye), '疫情防控阻击战彰显中国制度优势' (the epidemic prevention highlighted the Chinese system advantage), Peoplenet, April 7, 2020, accessed June 2, 2020, http://dangjian.people.com.cn/n1/2020/0407/c117092-31663979.html; 吴家华, '战"疫"中国模式彰显制度优势' (Combating Virus China model highlights Institutional Advantages), Chinanet, April 7 2020, accessed June 2, 2020, http://opinion.china.com.cn/opinion_13_220613.html.
[29]吴心伯 (Wu Xinbo), 疫情加速世界后霸权时代到来 (COVID-19 has accelerated the the advent of post-hegemony era), 参考消息 (Reference News), June 16, 2020, accessed June 23, 2020, http://www.cankaoxiaoxi.com/china/20200616/2412828.shtml.
[30]范勇鹏 (Fan Yongpeng), '中央集权只适用于极端状态？这种观点忽略了一个问题,' (the Centralization of power only applies to extreme conditions? This view ignores a problem), 观察者网 (Guangcha-net), April 7, 2010, accessed June 2, 2020, https://www.guancha.cn/FanYongPeng/2020_04_07_545745.shtml.
[31]Editorial, 'WHO should probe US' virus misconduct,' *Global Times*, April 25, 2020, accessed June 2, 2020, https://www.globaltimes.cn/content/1186718.shtml.
[32]王勇 (Wang Yong), '疫情下的中美关系与国际大变局' (The Sino-US Relations and Global Great Changes under the Pandemic), 盘古智库 (Pangoal), April 16, 2020, accessed June 2, 2020, https://ishare.ifeng.com/c/s/v002gWw9LSxl9U-_xlbAYfxgjdOsRPZf3Nj6mlAR3GLLM2JY__.

under control. Other nations are now following China's lead and limiting movement within their borders, while dozens of countries have restricted international visitors.'[33]

France passed a decree that people must fill forms every time leaving home. America's borders with Canada and Mexico remained open during WWII but were closed this time. Many countries used surveillance technologies to enforce quarantines and track people's contacts with the virus, putting a twist on the tradeoff among privacy, accountability, and safety. For example, Israel used cellphone location data to track Israeli citizens. Greece established the short message service (SMS) system for people to send SMS declaration in advance for approval to leave home. Asian countries, including South Korea, Taiwan, and Singapore, were more successful than the US in limiting the spread of COVID-19 because they adopted smartphone app-tracking technology for contact tracing among its populations. The US refused to use high-tech tracing for the fear of the privacy incursions and became the epicenter of the pandemic.

Some democracies also copied China to strengthen the role of the state in the economy. After COVID-19 caused major disruptions in global supply chains, the US and some European governments enhanced the state role to rebuild a national economy instead of a global one and built redundancy in their manufacturing products regardless of cost and rationality, disrupting the global production chains. For Beijing and many Chinese, it is hypocritical of the US and European countries to blame China when they copied China in response to the devastating impact of the virus.

The statist approach regained popularity because liberal globalization that created so much opportunities for economic growth also made the world vulnerable. The growing global connectedness meant that when things went bad in one place, that trouble could be transmitted farther, faster, deeper and cheaper than ever. After coronavirus occurred in Wuhan, it moved quickly across borders, leaving national governments much less able to contain the virus.[34] Lives and livelihoods were destroyed but the government was either powerless to help them or did not care what happened to them. Resentment of liberal globalization on the rise, creating opportunities for a breed of China's statist governance as an alternative.

The Burden of Strategic Overdraft

As the US wrestled with the myriad distractions of coronavirus, recession, and racial upheavals, China has moved to a much more active profile to exploit the global leadership vacuum left by the US. But China has not filled the vacuum because it cannot afford the cost of providing sweeping global public goods without overtaxing its resources or diluting the impact of its efforts.

China is much more fragile and vulnerable than President Xi has presented to the world. China's per capita GDP was about 10,000 USD in 2019, ranking 72nd in the world, slightly better than Mexico's, but only one-fourth that of Japan and one-third that of South Korea, and about 15% of the US's 62,887. USD Still a middle-income country, it is not clear if China could become the first authoritarian regime to avoid the middle-income trap that keeps many emerging economies from entering the exclusive club of high-income countries. Riding the waves of economic globalization, China has not liberalized its political system. Removing presidential term limits, President Xi has reinforced ideological orthodox, rolled back civil liberties, and turned his back on all important political reforms, including free press, the rule of law and an independent judiciary essential for sustaining economic growth.

China has faced many structural weaknesses externally and internally. During the early decades of economic taking off, China enjoyed expanding access to foreign markets, resources and technology. Still depending on foreign technology in many areas, the exports of its products, and the imports of

---

[33]David Cyranoski, 'What China's coronavirus response can teach the rest of the world,' *Nature*, March 7, 2020, accessed June 2, 2020, https://www.nature.com/articles/d41586-020-00741-x.
[34]Thomas L. Friedman, 'Our New Historical Divide: B.C. and A.C.—the World Before Corona and the World After,' *New York Times*, March 17, 2020, accessed June 2, 2020, https://www.nytimes.com/2020/03/17/opinion/coronavirus-trends.html.

food and energy, the global rise of protectionism, particularly the trade war with the US and COVID-19, has deteriorated China external environment. Many governments began to re-think China relations and reconsider supply chain strategies to serve national security and public health goals. The Chinese leadership must act boldly to jump ahead on the technological curve, including 5 G, AI, biotech, and maintain good relations with foreign countries to continue economic growth and raise living standards as promised to the Chinese people.

Decimating its own natural endowments, China has suffered environmental destruction, entrenched industrial overcapacity, and huge local government debt. China's one-child policy hastened and exacerbated the slowdown in birthrates to 1.05% in 2019 (the U.S. was 1.73), leading to the swiftly aging crisis. The costs of social security and caring for the elderly are increasing. COVID-19 has compounded the damage. Chinese economy shrank by 6.8% in the first quarter of 2020, its first contraction since the end of the Cultural Revolution in 1976.

As the structural headwinds of foreign protectionism, resource depletion, and domestic problems take their toll, Chinese growth may have reached peak. China's economic slowdown put President Xi under pressure ahead of the CCP's centennial anniversary in 2021. When China's economy was booming, Presidents Jiang Zemin and Hu Jintao loosened political controls and announced to the world its peaceful rise. In the mid of an economic slump, large number of unemployment may emerge, and unrest roil the country's margins. While the authoritarian state does not hold democratic elections, it still faces internal pressures to deliver economic gains as a key source of the legitimacy. Warning the potential for a Soviet-style collapse, President Xi has doubled internal security spending and advanced propaganda, censorship, and surveillance systems, constructing a vast techno-security state to stop any kind of unrests.

Unease in a society where nobody under forty has experienced national economic setbacks, the Chinese government called the young people to make 'long-term preparation for hardship' in response to COVID-19, which 'may mean higher prices, no expected salary increases, and to withstand temporary unemployment.' Warning that 'young people cannot take the fast track of national development for grant,' the Chinese government called each of individuals to take the responsibility to bear the hardship.[35]

These warnings were not overstatement because the CCP regime saw itself as a besieged fortress during COVID-19. After the coronavirus started, Chinese social media were overflown with messages demanding accountability and transparency of the government. Although democracy was under attack in China, its basic ideas still aspired Chinese liberal intellectuals. The government's initial mismanagement, amplified by the death of a doctor who was reprimanded for speaking out about the virus, provided an opportunity for liberals to challenge President Xi's personal autocracy. Demanding freedom of speech, several liberals, such as Tsinghua University Professor Xu Zhangrun, private entrepreneur Ren Zhiqiang and political activist Xu Zhiyong, publicly denounced Xi's power concentration.

While they were rapidly silenced, some foreign organizations and governments filed lawsuits demanding Chinese compensation for their damages caused by the pandemic started in China. Although the case for Chinese liability was unlikely going anywhere, they made many Chinese nervous for a global scapegoating China shaped by the global geopolitics and strategic rivalries.

In response, Chinese diplomats stationed all over the world fought back against the so-called stigmatization of China, heaping scorn on anyone who criticized China. Chinese diplomats used to be known for their low profile and courtesy but now known as wolf warriors (战狼), derived from the 2018 Chinese movie 'Wolf Warrior' in which a Chinese special-operations fighter defeated Western-led mercenaries and became a national hero for defending China's overseas interests. No longer emphasizing diplomatic protocol, Chinese diplomats competed to demonstrate a tougher attitude,

---

[35]中央政法委 (Central Political and Law Commission), '做好艰苦奋斗的长期准备 不要涨价就骂娘' (make long-term preparations for hard work), *Tacent News*, June 1,2020, accessed June 2, 2020, https://xw.qq.com/cmsid/20190601A0HLM600?from=groupmessage&isappinstalled=0.

offensive tone, and more confrontational cruel and ruthless against foreign rivals. The emphasis on fighting highlighted one of the new features of Xi's foreign policy, conceiving diplomacy as a war against enemy forces that must be defeated.

Chinese diplomats inundated international newspapers with op-eds hailing the sacrifices Beijing made to buy time for other countries and pointing out US failure to deflect the blame on China and counter Western accusations that coronavirus originated in China. Zhao Lijian, Foreign Ministry Spokesperson famous for his sharp and abusive language, publicly floated a conspiracy theory crudely blaming that the American military brought the virus to China during the Military World Games in Wuhan. This unsubstantiated claim was supported by Chinese media and particularly the wild social media across China's tightly controlled internet. Demonstrating his fighting spirit, Foreign Minister Wang Yi blamed the 'political virus' spreading in the US alongside the coronavirus, slamming US politicians for 'jumping at any opportunity' to attack and scapegoated China for the consequences of their disastrous mismanagement of the crisis.[36]

China's aggressive diplomatic and propaganda offensive was aimed to divert attention from Beijing's poor early handling of the outbreak and play to a nationalist domestic audience. Depicting Beijing as a heroic leader in the global struggle against the pandemic, the Chinese government was to whitewashing China's culpability in initial cover-up and suppression of early warnings and then failing to arrest the transmission to other countries. Blaming all setbacks on Western meddling, the state propaganda made use of the shrill rhetoric from President Trump's blame on China to build solidarity and nationalist credentials.

Although President Trump failed U.S. leadership in response to COVID-19, China is far from matching the US in the major elements of global leadership. Spending enormous sums to modernize its military, China's military has become much stronger but still cannot project far beyond its home region. China's imperial outpost such as Piraeus harbour in Greece are useless without the regional assets as China's access to the outside is mainly over land through adjacent countries and its maritime vector is weak. The US trade routes do not cross adjacent countries and its access to the outside world is less costly, less difficult and poses less risks than the Chinese predicament. With the world's largest concentration of capital and technology, the US remains the only superpower that can project power into every region in the world.

Taking advantage of the US and others' preoccupation by COVID-19, China has advanced its interests in a spate of incidents that constituted a strategic blunder in China's relations with neighbors. Setting up new administrative districts in the South China Sea in the face of Vietnam's opposition in April 2020, Chinese ships sunk or harassed ships from Vietnam, Malaysia and Japan in areas they considered their exclusive economic zones, leading to a remarkable strategic reversal in the Philippines's relationship with Beijing. The deadly skirmish of Chinese forces against Indian troops in May 2020 triggered a powerful anti-Chinese sentiment in India. After Australia called for an inquiry into the origins of the novel coronavirus, China moved to restrict Australian imports and discourage tourism there. One commentator, therefore, concluded that 'Thanks to its actions over the past few years under Xi, China today finds itself in the same strategic situation as the Soviet Union did during the Cold War—surrounded by countries that are growing increasingly hostile to it.'[37]

Facing formidable rivals and confronting daunting internal difficulties, Chinese leaders must fight an uphill battle to mobilize resources for the costly global leadership. China's resources are finite. The increasing military expenses reduce the funds in domestic welfare. China can only take on so many geopolitical and geo-economic challenges. One Beijing strategist, therefore, warned about 'the risk

---

[36]'State Councilor and Foreign Minister Wang Yi Meets the Press,' PRC Ministry of Foreign Affairs, May 24, 2020, accessed May 24, 2020, https://www.fmprc.gov.cn/mfa_eng/zxxx_662805/t1782262.shtml.

[37]Fareed Zakaria, 'China has been bungling its post-coronavirus foreign policy,' Washington Post, June 25, 2020, accessed June 28, 2020, https://www.washingtonpost.com/opinions/global-opinions/china-has-been-bungling-its-post-coronavirus-foreign-policy/2020/06/25/5beac38c-b71b-11ea-a8da-693df3d7674a_story.html.

CHINA'S BIG POWER AMBITION

of China's strategic overdraft' (战略透支).[38] A Shanghai venture capitalist with strong official connections asserted that China 'will never seek to lead the current global system, let alone invent, and pay for, a new one to run the world.'[39] Kevin Rudd, former prime minister of Australia, argued that 'it is simply inconsistent with Beijing's political playbook, as well as China's perception of its still-limited national capabilities, for it to assume sweeping global leadership or drive an effective multilateral order that was not simply a direct expression of China's own national interests and hierarchical values.'[40]

It is easy to find examples of China's reluctance to take on the international obligations where Chinese interests are not immediately at stake. China was the largest polluter that emitted more carbon from burning fossil fuels than the US and Europe combined. But China proposed the principle of 'common but differentiated responsibilities' to press the US and other developed countries to commit financial pledges to poorer nations while China and other developing countries only needed to do what they could in the light of their national conditions.

China's face-mask diplomacy was not contributing to the global public goods. Manufacturing half of the world's medical masks, China hoarded its supply and banned exports after the outbreak. Beijing started shipping these supplies to other countries only after it contained the spread at home. But some of the equipment billed as aids was sold and expensive. Recipients in the Netherlands, Spain, Canada, and Turkey rejected Chinese-made testing kits and protective equipment as substandard. Finland's prime minister fired the head of the country's emergency supply agency for spending millions of euros on defective Chinese facemasks.

China's propaganda catered primarily to the domestic audience, acting as a constraint on the scale of its aid and leading to a tendency to frame the assistance in ways that highlight the benefit to China, perpetuating the perception that China's aid came with strings attached and targeted at furthering China's strategic objectives and interests.[41] Leaders in some countries, therefore, criticized China for eschewing its aid as the 'battle of narratives' and 'politics of generosity.' Public attention in Africa was riveted by stories of widespread discrimination and racism against African expats in southern China, triggering for the first time a large mobilization of African diplomats and governments protesting the way their nationals were treated in China. China's actions blurred the weak US response and increased the demand for US leadership, stoking fears that Beijing cannot be trusted.[42]

In this case, while the pandemic hurt the US's prestige and compounded global concerns about American competence and reliability, China was not able to demonstrate its global leadership in providing global public goods because it is less powerful, and its authoritarian political system makes it harder to exercise the enlightened, positive-sum leadership. The coronavirus crisis showed the darker sides of China, from covering up the initial outbreak to concocting an absurd story about how the virus originated in the US to selling defective tests to countries in grave need, encouraging resistance to Beijing's global ambitions. As the Western governments were faulted for mismanaging the pandemic or failing to galvanize an international response, China's standing took a hit. The wave of criticism, sometimes from friendly nations, underscored the challenge facing Beijing for global leadership.

All countries advance their own interests. It is nothing wrong that China does so rigorously and vigorously. But China has used the rhetoric of the global leadership to cover its attempts to advance

[38]Shi Yinhong, 'Amid Western uncertainties, China mustn't spread too thin', Global Times, October 26, 2016, accessed June 2, 2020, http://www.globaltimes.cn/content/1013884.shtml.
[39]Eric X. Li, 'The Middle Kingdom and the Coming World Disorder,' The World Post, February 4, 2014, accessed June 2, 2020, http://feedly.com/k/1e3JeDm.
[40]Kevin Rudd, The world after COVID-19," Economist, April 15, 2020, accessed June 2, 2020, https://www.economist.com/open-future/2020/04/15/by-invitation-kevin-rudd-on-america-china-and-saving-the-who.
[41]Tian Huileng, 'As China's cases dwindle, Beijing strives to take the lead in the coronavirus crisis,' CNBC News, April 3, 2020, accessed June 2, 2020, https://www.cnbc.com/2020/04/03/china-pursues-global-leadership-ambitions-in-coronavirus-response.html.
[42]Joel Wuthnow, 'China's Inopportune Pandemic Assertiveness,' PacNet #33, June 10, 2020, accessed June 28, 2020, https://mailchi.mp/pacforum/pacnet-33-chinas-inopportune-pandemic-assertiveness-1170041?e=19e05c85a8.

its own interests. Touting its gawky community of shared future for mankind, Beijing has yet to demonstrate the willingness to align and in some cases subordinate China's narrow interests to the greater global good and forge multilateral response to the global challenge. As a result, clear discrepancies between China's rhetoric and actions have persisted.

The Baggage of Pax-Sinica

For some observers, China's attempt for global leadership implies a desire to install the traditional Chinese tianxia (天下) order, in which China occupies the paramount position and those along its margins are expected to accept such dominance and show fealty to the center. The vision of the Shared Future for Mankind is often confused with the Tianxia order that is hardly accepted by other countries in the 21st century.[43] Many of China's neighbors, therefore, view China's power aspiration with a wary eye that, as China becomes ever more wealthy and powerful, China's imperial past can produce an undue pressure on its leaders to restore the old Chinese order in the name of the community for mankind.

But China has not articulated a universally accepted vision of the world order. Nor has China convinced other countries that its leadership would contribute to a better world rather than just a more powerful and autocratic China. Targeting primarily at authoritarian countries, China has hoped that its preferred rules, norms and values would be more readily accepted by these regimes. One American observer criticized that 'Xi's vision for a desired future is to appeal to the developing world elites who feel estranged, disaffected or threatened by the prospect of liberal democracy.' Therefore, 'At stake is not only the predominant position of the U.S. in the current system but more importantly the potential erosion of fundamental human rights, freedom of thought and expression, and self-government around the world.'[44]

The tensions surrounding China's rise, therefore, do not simply result from clashing economic and geopolitical interests but also the distrust that often afflicts relationships between democratic governments and powerful authoritarian regimes. This gulf between Beijing's political values and those of the democracies means that the US, Western Europe and other democratic countries would be unease about the rise of China's authoritarianism. China's global leadership is not politically or culturally inspirational or attractive if China is ruled by a regime with objectives and policies so deeply at odds with the liberal democracies.

Against the background of retreating democracy in the US and the advance of the Chinese state in economic development and response to COVID-19, China's authoritarianism may appeal to the leaders of some developing countries. From this perspective, 'the U.S. democratic system is facing one of the great stress tests of its history without any certainty about the outcome.'[45] But the liberal value of open and participatory politics with restraint in authority remains appealing to many countries. Over time, the US may well self-correct after exhausting all other options, as it has done so often in history.

Yan Xuetong, one prominent Chinese scholar, admits that although China's rise may help expand the influence of its traditional values of benevolence and righteousness in building a world order based on the norms of fairness, justice and civility, liberalism still wields greater influence than any other ideology.[46] One observer responded that Chinese traditional value is less appealing than liberalism because of its emphasis on the steep power hierarchies. No amount of win-win rhetoric in

[43]Wang Fei-ling, *The China Order: Centralia, World Empire, and the Nature of Chinese Power*, Albany, NY: SUNY Press, 2017, p. 4.
[44]Nadège Rolland, 'China's Vision for a New World Order,' NBR Special Report, no. 83 January 27, 2020, accessed June 2, 2020, https://www.nbr.org/publication/chinas-vision-for-a-new-world-order/.
[45]Frederick Kempe, 'Who China's Xi Jinping really wants to win the 2020 U.S. election,' CNBC, June 27, 2020, accessed June 27, 2020, https://www.cnbc.com/2020/06/27/op-ed-china-gains-political-influence-in-strategic-outpost-kiribati.html.
[46]Yan Xuetong, 'The winner of China–US conflict rides on national leadership,' *East Asia Forum*, April 2, 2019, accessed June 2, 2020, https://www.eastasiaforum.org/2019/04/02/the-winner-of-china-us-conflict-rides-on-national-leadership/.

international fora fully makes up for the appeal of how a government treats its own citizens. China's benevolent power is not compatible with the rule of the Communist Party.[47]

Although Chinese no longer refer to neighbors as barbarians, Chinese culture is closely linked to the framing of normative hierarchy. Chinese vision for a future order draws inspiration from its historical experiences based on power and hierarchy instead of freedom and equality. For most of history, China was either an imperial power dominating its neighbors or a victim of humiliation by Western powers. China has limited experiences in modern diplomacy as an equal player. Cultural and power hierarchy as well as victim narrative have colored the Chinese thinking of international relations. They have yet learned about the statecraft of treating others on equal footing.

The hierarchical order is normatively and practically at odds with the modern diplomacy. It would prevail only in an environment where China is the largest and most powerful state, its civilization superiority is widely acknowledged, and in the absence of a competing paradigm. None of these factors characterize today's world. There are number of powerful states claiming to have superior civilizations of their own, and there are alternative organizing principles for the component parts of the totality.[48]

Given the choice, most countries would rather navigate a US-led world order. A survey of public opinion in six Asian countries in May–October 2019 found a median of 64% had favorable views of the U.S. while opinions of China were negative. Majorities in Japan (85%), South Korea (63%) and Australia (57%) expressed an unfavorable opinion of the neighboring power. Around half in the Philippines (54%) and India (46%) said the same.[49] A regional *Pax Sinica* is not desirable for China's neighbors, not alone for the world.

Lacking universally accepted values to exert influence over the formulation of ideas underpinning the international order, the CCP's belief system is confusing to many people at home and abroad, with its mutating, idiosyncratic mix of canonical Marxist-Leninism, socialism 'with Chinese character-istics,' nationalism, and sprinkled elements of Confucianism. What China's domestic repression means for the world order is also a concern. U.S. Vice-President Mike Pence argued that 'A country that oppresses its own people rarely stops there.' China's repressive stance domestically and increasingly aggressive foreign policy were not coincidental developments, but different manifesta-tions of the same trend.[50] An American observer warned that China-led world order would be a 'macrocosm of its domestic political order,' emphasizing 'privileges rather than rights, power rather than law, fealty rather than alliance.'[51]

Leadership is not just about taking the titles in the UN organizations but also exercised through individuals who can confidently and freely express their opinions. Chinese representatives in the international organizations are reluctant to speak off the script because of afraid of getting into trouble at home. Chinese scholars have difficulty to work in the international organizations, private foundations and think-tanks that develop and advise on UN policy because they can hardly express their independent views. For the same reason, Chinese NGOs have rarely engaged in policy discus-sions in international forums.[52] Authoritarianism has undermined China's global influence.

---

[47]Pär Nyrén, 'Reviewing the noted Chinese foreign policy thinker's latest book,' *The Diplomat*, June 28, 2019, accessed June 2, 2020, https://thediplomat.com/2019/06/chinas-liberal-hawk-yan-xuetongs-vision-for-chinese-benevolent-dominance/.

[48]June Teufel Dreyer, 'The Tianxia Trope: Will China Change the International Order?' *Journal of Contemporary China*, vol. 24, no.96, November 2015,, accessed June 2, 2020, https://www.tandfonline.com/doi/full/10.1080/10670564.2015.1030951.

[49]Heremiah Cha, 'People in Asia-Pacific regard the U.S. more favorably than China, but Trump gets negative marks,' *Pew Research Center*, February 25, 2020, accessed June 2, 2020, https://www.pewresearch.org/fact-tank/2020/02/25/people-in-asia-pacific-regard-the-u-s-more-favorably-than-china-but-trump-gets-negative-marks/.

[50]'Remarks by Vice President Pence on the Administration's Policy Toward China,' US Embassy & Consulates in China, October 4, 2018, accessed June 2, 2020, https://china.usembassy-china.org.cn/remarks-by-vice-president-pence-on-the-administrations-policy-toward-china/.

[51]Kori Schake, 'How International Hegemony Changes Hands,' *Cato Unbound*, March 5, 2018, accessed June 2, 2020, https://www.cato-unbound.org/2018/03/05/kori-schake/how-international-hegemony-changes-hands.

[52]Elizabeth M. Lynch, 'Do Human Rights Restrictions At Home Undermine China's Role At the UN?' *China Law and Policy*, March 30, 2020, accessed June 2, 2020, https://chinalawandpolicy.com/2020/03/30/do-human-rights-restrictions-at-home-undermine-chinas-role-at-the-un/.

Until China builds a strong and free civil society at home and develops values that appeal universally, it misses one of the core features of global leadership. While US global influence has dropped under President Trump, it still holds much more soft power than China because its universal values of liberty and prosperity attract other nations. Beijing must overcome the internal and external challenges that stemmed from its authoritarian system and hierarchical perception to win trust of other nations.

Conclusion

While the world entangled with and exposed to America's incoherent and erratic power, China has not demonstrated more leadership than the US. The global leadership was absence when it was required most urgently. The Trump administration's slow reaction to COVID-19 gave China a golden opportunity to mitigate the growing tensions with the US and harness the multilateral institutions to smash through the pandemic and global macroeconomic responses.

But China missed the opportunity. The official speculations about US military bringing the virus to China triggered an eruption of anti-China sentiments in the US and enhanced the hands of the Trump administration to finger China as the culprit for America's woes. The aggressiveness and incoherence of China's narrative about the pandemic and its criticism of democratic governance complicated the relations with many countries. To make things worse, the infighting between the US and China eviscerated international cooperation and prevented the UN Security Council (UNSC) from passing a resolution to declare COVID-19 an international security threat. Such a designation would carry the binding force of international law to help mobilize global resources and deploy the entire multilateral arsenal against the pandemic.

The UNSC had a track record in response to pandemics under the US leadership. The U.S. chaired the meeting to pass UNSC Resolution 1308 in July 2000, transforming public health concern over the HIV/AIDS pandemic in Africa into a matter of international security to coordinate response and helping galvanize a multilateral response, including the establishment of the Global Fund for AIDS, Tuberculosis, and Malaria in 2002. The US also led the passage of UNSC Resolution 2177 in September 2014, designating the Ebola outbreak in West Africa a threat to international security and created the U.N. Mission for Ebola Emergency Response, the first U.N. emergency mission directed at a public health crisis.

Confronting a public health threat that dwarfs any pandemic since the Great Influenza of 1918, however, the UNSC failed to pass a resolution. China held the rotating presidency of the UNSC in March 2020 and insisted that COVID-19 did not fall within the UNSC's 'geopolitical' ambit. Washington also dragged the feet by demanding that any resolution specify the Chinese origins of the coronavirus. The Chinese blasted Washington for politicizing the outbreak.[53]

Estonia, a rotating member of the UNSC, proposed a statement on March 24, expressing growing concern about the unprecedented extent of the COVID-19 outbreak constituting a threat to international peace and security. China rejected the draft because it included a phrase that all countries show 'full transparency' in their reporting on the outbreak. Chinese interpreted it as a veiled attack on their lack of transparency in initial outbreak and blocked the statement to avoid embarrassment.[54]

While the absence of leadership paralyzed the UN response, the meeting of the G7 in March 2020 also failed to agree on a joint declaration because US Secretary of State Mike Pompeo insisted on describing COVID-19 as the 'Wuhan virus' and the others gave up in disgust. The G20 meeting on the

[53] Josh Lederman, 'US Insisting that the UN all out Chinese Origins of Coronavirus,' *NBS News*, March 25, 2020, accessed June 2, 2020, https://www.nbcnews.com/politics/national-security/u-s-insisting-u-n-call-out-chinese-origins-coronavirus-n1169111.
[54] Stewart M. Patrick, 'As COVID-19 Runs Rampant, the U.N. Security Council Must Act,' *World Politics Review*, March 30, 2020, accessed June 2, 2020, https://www.worldpoliticsreview.com/articles/28640/as-covid-19-runs-rampant-the-u-n-security-council-must-act.

following day was unable to coordinate a global economic strategy to protect critical global supply chains and avoid deepening the recession.

The WHO remains the focal point for COVID-19 response within the U.N. system. But its ability is undermined by the US withdrawal. It also lacks the authority to cut through the political obstacles ranging from trade barriers to border closures, travel restrictions, supply chain interruptions and impediments to sharing vaccines. Turning the tide on the global crisis requires international cooperation, including prompt collective decisions on matters that are fundamentally political, rather than purely technical.

COVID-19 is a non-traditional security threat transcending rivalry and enmity and diluting the concept of zero-sum military-led national security threat. Like earthquake or climate change, COVID-19 respects no borders and is non-discriminatory and unbiased in its effects regarding wealth and nationality as well as democracy versus autocracy. The crisis should have galvanized international cooperation led by big powers such as China and the US to fight against a common enemy. But instead, COVID-19 worsened the US-China geopolitical tensions.

The world is in danger of moving toward the jungle where it's everyone for themselves and the strong do what they can and the weak suffer what they must if the US cannot wake up to do the right thing and no one steps up to take the leadership in the way that America emerged at the sun set on the British Empire. Profound global crises, such as imposed by WW-II, often lead to cathartic changes. The world is waiting to see if and how COVID-19 would reshape global geopolitical and geo-economic contours and dynamics.

Disclosure Statement

No potential conflict of interest was reported by the author.

China's Strategic Narratives in Global Governance Reform under Xi Jinping

Yi Edward Yang

ABSTRACT

Beijing has long sought to shape global narratives about China. The Xi Jinping administration not only continued that effort but also added an entirely new dimension: it now seeks to use discourse power, particularly through formulating and promoting strategic narratives, to reshape the international system itself. Drawing upon social identity theory (SIT) and strategic narratives framework, this study shows that Beijing employs a multifaceted narrative strategy to redefine existing norms or create new ones in varied global governance domains. A theoretical framework is presented to explain the strategy and subsequently applied to illustrate China's strategic narratives at the international system level and in three global governance areas, i.e., climate change, human rights, and Internet governance.

Introduction

Since the Chinese Communist Party's (CCP) 18th Party Congress first convened in November 2012, President Xi Jinping has called for China's greater participation in the global governance system—the set of international rules, institutions, and enforcement mechanisms the global community uses to solve common problems. In his November 2014 speech at the Central Conference on Work Relating to Foreign Affairs, Xi stated that China would 'work to reform the international system and global governance' but carefully avoided calling for China to play a leading role.[1] In June 2018, in the context of the surging anti-globalist populism in the West and the U.S. retreat from global leadership, Xi stepped up from his previous rhetoric by calling for China to 'take an active part in leading the reform of the global governance system.'[2]

This article examines China's effort at achieving this goal by way of strengthening its discourse power (*hua yu quan*) to reshape the existing global governance system, a topic that has so far received few scholarly attentions.[3] Beijing has long sought to put out its own narratives about China

---

[1]Xinhua, 'Xi jin ping chu xi zhong yang wai shi gong zuo hui yi bing fa biao zhong yao jiang hua' [Xi Jinping attended the Central Foreign Affairs Working Conference and delivered an important speech], November 29, 2014, accessed November 20, 2019, http://www.xinhuanet.com/politics/2014-11/29/c_1113457723.htm. Previously, in his speech to the 19th Party Congress in November 2017, President Xi stated that China will 'take an active part in reforming and developing the global governance system, and keep contributing Chinese wisdom and strength to global governance'. Even on climate change, where China emerged as a global leader after 2015, Xi simply stated that 'we will get actively involved in global environmental governance and fulfill our commitments on emissions reduction'. See Xi Jinping, 'Secure a Decisive Victory in Building a Moderately Prosperous Society in All Respects and Strive for the Great Success of Socialism with Chinese Characteristics for a New Era', Xinhua, October 18, 2017, accessed November 20, 2019, http://www.xinhuanet.com/english/download/Xi_Jinping's_report_at_19th_CPC_National_Congress.pdf. For the Chinese version of this speech, see http://www.gov.cn/zhuanti/2017-10/27/content_5234876.htm, accessed November 20, 2019.

[2]Xinhua, 'Xi urges breaking new ground in major country diplomacy with Chinese characteristics', accessed November 20, 2019, http://www.xinhuanet.com/english/2018-06/24/c_137276269.htm.

to the world. State-sponsored efforts to acquire more discourse power in world affairs started in the Hu Jintao era, when Beijing established the Grand External Propaganda program and injected billions of dollars to internationalize state media outlets to 'tell the China story well'. Xi not only continued that effort but also added an entirely new component. Instead of only seeking to shape how the world sees China, now Beijing seeks to use discourse power, particularly through creating, disseminating, and promoting strategic narratives, to shape the international system itself.

Specifically, this article explores the following research questions: (1) Why is China emphasizing discourse power as a means to achieve its global governance reform ambitions? (2) How is the Xi Jinping administration deploying strategic narratives in its drive to lead the global governance reform? Drawing upon social identity theory (SIT) and strategic narratives framework, this article argues that, driven by its desire for a deserving great power status, Beijing is employing a multifaceted narrative strategy to influence existing norms and create new ones in varied global governance areas. A theoretical framework is presented to explain the strategy and is subsequently applied to illustrate China's strategic narratives at the international system level and in three global governance areas, i.e., climate change, human rights, and Internet governance. The conclusion section discusses the theoretical and policy implications of this study as well as the plan for future research.

The next section reviews the current literature on status seeking and discourse power in international relations (IR) within the context of China's foreign policy, thereby illustrating the empirical and theoretical relevance of the study.

The Quest for Great Power Status and Discourse Power

Since the founding of the People's Republic of China (PRC) in 1949, generations of Chinese leaders have sought to return the nation to its once held great power status on the world stage. President Xi Jinping is no exception. At the 19th Party Congress in October 2017, Xi spelled out his vision to transform China into a global power 'moving closer to center stage' in unprecedented clarity.[4] In his widely publicized concept 'Chinese dream', national rejuvenation—restoring China's previous standing as a great power—is a crucial element. Xi's vision marks a decisive shift from the approach captured in Deng Xiaoping's famous ethos that China should hide its capabilities and bide its time.

As Larson and Shevchenko noted, great power status delivers prestige, respect and concrete benefits to national interests.[5] Great powers expect to be consulted on important world and regional issues by other members of the 'great powers club'. Great powers have the advantage of participating in and, hence the opportunity to shape and make rules/norms for regional and/or international institutions. For state leaders, their nations' ability to achieve great power status also helps to legitimize the regime domestically, compensating for, when necessary, domestic failures such as economic weakness or personal scandals.[6] These benefits, at both national and leadership levels, motivate national elites to seek great power status on behalf of their states. China's quest for great power status is further reinforced by the historic narrative that China's standing was lost unjustifiably in what is known as the 'Century of

---

[3]Examples of published English language research on China's discourse power in international relations include: Lutgard Lams, 'Othering in Chinese Official Media Narratives during Diplomatic Standoffs with the US and Japan', *Palgrave Communications* 3(1), (2017), pp. 1–11; Lutgard Lam, 'Examining Strategic Narratives in Chinese Official Discourse under Xi Jinping' *Journal of Chinese Political Science* 23(3), (2018), pp. 387–411; Paul S.N. Lee. 'The Rise of China and Its Contest for Discursive Power', *Global Media and China* 1(1–2), (2016), pp. 102–120. https://journals.sagepub.com/doi/full/10.1177/2059436416650549; Rex Li, 'Contending Narratives of the International Order: US/Chinese Discursive Power and Its Effects on the UK', *Asian Perspective* 43(2), (2019), pp. 349–385, https://muse.jhu.edu/article/725800; Alice D. Ba, 'China's "Belt and Road" in Southeast Asia: Constructing the Strategic Narrative in Singapore', *Asian Perspective* 43(2), (2019), pp. 249–272, https://muse.jhu.edu/article/725796; Kejin Zhao, 'China's Rise and its Discursive Power Strategy', *Chinese Political Science Review* 1 (3), (2016), pp. 539–64.
[4]Xinhua, 'Full text of Xi Jinping's report at 19th CPC National Congress', accessed November 20, 2019, https://www.chinadaily.com.cn/china/19thcpcnationalcongress/2017-11/04/content_34115212.htm.
[5]Deborah Welch Larson and Alexei Shevchenko, 'Status Seekers: Chinese and Russian Responses to U.S. Primacy', *International Security* 34(4), 2010, pp. 63–95. https://www.jstor.org/stable/40784562; Deborah Welch Larson and Alexei Shevchenko, *Quest for Status: Chinese and Russian Foreign Policy* (New Haven, London: Yale University Press, 2019).
[6]Larson and Shevchenko, 'Quest for Status'.

Humiliation', stretching from defeat at the hands of the British in the First Opium War up to the proclamation of the People's Republic by Mao Zedong in 1949. As Yan Xuetong makes clear, 'the Chinese regard their rise as regaining China's lost international status rather than as obtaining something new'.[7] For the Chinese, it is only fair and logical to restore China to its 'rightful' place as a preeminent global power.

As China intensifies its effort to regain the great power status, will it try to delegitimize, overthrow, and replace the existing U.S.-led liberal international order (LIO)? This has been a central and profound question in the debate about the implications of China's rise.[8] Two mainstream IR theories provide contrastingly different predictions. The realist school generally predicts that China's growing strength will propel it to act more assertively in pursuing its interests and a 'revisionist' tendency would ensue to disrupt the international order.[9] Liberal theories, on the other hand, contend that because the current international order is defined by interdependence and openness, it can persuade rising powers such as China that the status quo serves its interests and that it should become a defender—not a challenger— of the existing international order's rules, norms, and institutions.[10] Scholarly debate aside, in recent years there has been an upsurge in U.S. media and policy characterization of China as a challenger to the existing rule-based international order.[11] The most notable examples include the reference of China, in the 2017 and 2018 U.S. National Defense Strategy respectively, as a 'revisionist' power, along with Russia, intending to reshape the existing international order in its own authoritarian image.[12]

A critical assessment shows that IR theories paint an overly simplistic depiction of China's trajectory as driven by system level variables. The alarming 'revisionist' characterization of China looming over the media and policy community is also not based on rigorous and systematic empirical assessment.[13] A more useful approach is to analyze the nexus between China's aspiration for the great power status and degree to which the existing international order satisfies that goal. Under President Xi Jinping, China's new foreign policy orientation, though more ambitious, contains a view of the existing international order that has been consistent in recent years. That is, it is neither completely satisfied with the existing international order nor determined to overthrow it. Beijing, as Oriana Skylar Mastro contends, does not intend to replace Washington at the top of the international system.[14] China has neither the interest nor capability in engaging in military and political adventures required of a dominant power that are costly and self-constraining.[15] Indeed, even after four decades of rapid growth, China is still far from the position of assuming global leadership and remaking the world order.[16] Even achieving dominance in its peripheral region is not an easy endeavor due to the presence of the U.S.-led military alliance structure

---

[7]Xuetong Yan, 'The Rise of China in Chinese Eyes', *Journal of Contemporary China* 10(26), (2001), pp. 33–39. http://www. tandfonline.com/doi/abs/10.1080/10670560123407.

[8]Alastair Iain Johnston, 'China in a world of orders: rethinking compliance and challenges in Beijing's international relations', *International Security* 44(2), (2019), pp. 9–60; Graham Allison, 'The Thucydides Trap: Are the U.S. and China Headed for War?' *The Atlantic*, September 24, 2015, accessed November 20, 2019, https://www.theatlantic.com/international/archive/2015/09/uni ted-states-china-war-thucydides-trap/406756/.

[9]Charles Glasser, 'Will China's rise lead to war', *Foreign Affairs*, Mar/Apr 2011, Vol. 90 Issue 2, pp. 80–91; Graham Allison, 'The Thucydides Trap: Are the U.S. and China Headed for War?'; Graham Allison, *Destined for War: Can America and China Escape Thucydides's Trap?* (Houghton Mifflin Harcourt, 2017).

[10]Charles Glasser, 'Will China's rise lead to war'; Robert Keohane and Lisa Martin, 'The Promise of Institutionalist Theory', *International Security* 20(1), (1995), pp. 39–51, https://www.jstor.org/stable/2539214; Robert Keohane and Joseph Nye, Jr., *Power and Interdependence* (Boston: Little Brown, 1977); Robert Keohane, *After Hegemony* (Princeton, NJ: Princeton University Press, 1984).

[11]Alastair Iain Johnston, 'China in a world of orders: rethinking compliance and challenges in Beijing's international relations', 2019.

[12]National Security Strategy of the United States of America (Washington, D.C.: White House, December 2017); and 2018 National Defense Strategy of the United States of America: Sharpening the American
   Military's Competitive Edge (Washington, D.C.: U.S. Department of Defense, February 2018).

[13]Alastair Iain Johnston, 'China in a world of orders: rethinking compliance and challenges in Beijing's international relations', 2019.

[14]Oriana Skylar Mastro, 'The Stealth Superpower: How China Hid Its Global Ambitions', *Foreign Affairs*, January/February 2019, accessed November 20, 2019, https://www.foreignaffairs.com/articles/china/china-plan-rule-asia.

[15]Ibid.

[16]Suisheng Zhao, 'China as a Rising Power versus the US-led World Order', *Rising Powers Quarterly* 1(1), (2016), pp. 13–21.

and the neighboring countries alignment with the U.S. to hedge against perceived 'China threat'. Moreover, Beijing has yet to be able to articulate a new vision of global order that is convincingly superior to the existing one in concrete and tangible ways. Chinese leaders also recognize that the existing international order's web of rules and institutions have provided (and will continue to do so in the foreseeable future) a stable and beneficial platform for its rise, hence China has a strong incentive not to seriously challenge the existing system.

What China is experiencing now is akin to what Steven Ward described as the 'distributive dissatisfaction' phase in which a rising power possesses 'a desire to acquire more of something—more influence, more territory, more wealth, more status'—largely within the context of the existing international order.[17] In other words, unsatisfied with its current status and associated privileges, the rising power seeks to reform and reshape, but not overthrow, the existing international order. Indeed, within the CCP elites, there is a clear dissatisfaction with the distribution of power in the major institutions of global governance, and some of the norms and principles underpin them.[18] Sources behind this satisfaction are multifaceted. First, Beijing feels a 'status deficit' in its role in global affairs. Some Chinese elites contend that the international order is intimately linked to the distribution and redistribution of power in the international system.[19] As Chinese economic and military power grows, they argue, it is time for China to make an effort to reshape the international order that has been driven and dominated by the United States.[20] It now demands to play a leadership role (and to be treated as such), commensurate with its power status, in global governance rule/norm making. Second, in Beijing's view, the liberal international order embodies the values and ideologies of the West, which it no longer finds agreeable or acceptable.[21] Third, China sees the existing order needs to be reformed as it is unequipped to accommodate the recent global changes (e.g., increasing multi-polarity and technological advancement) or interests of the developing countries, among which China counts itself.[22] It is against this backdrop that Xi Jinping called for China to take a leadership role in global governance, representing a clear departure from his predecessors.

Discourse Power and Global Governance Leadership

To achieve the ambition of leading the global governance reform, the Xi Jinping administration is keenly aware of the importance of increasing China's discourse power in world affairs. In his speech at a national propaganda-working meeting on 20 August 2013, Xi urged the cadres to 'create new concepts, new scopes, new narratives which integrate both Chinese and non-Chinese elements, so as to tell the Chinese story and spread Chinese voice well'.[23] The communique of the 5th Plenary Session of 18th CCP Central Committee specifically mentioned the determination 'to raise China's institutional discourse power in global economic governance'.[24]

Specifically, greater discourse power can help Beijing achieve its foreign policy goals in the following ways. First, as IR constructivist theorists contend, state identities and international order are constructed through discourse.[25] Thus, China's successful transition into the aspired new identity, i.e., the leader of

[17]Steven Ward, *Status and the Challenge of Rising Powers* (Cambridge: Cambridge University Press, 2017), http://dx.doi.org/10.1017/9781316856444.
[18]United Kingdom Parliament, *'China and the Rules-Based International System'*, 2019, accessed November 15, 2019, https://publications.parliament.uk/pa/cm201719/cmselect/cmfaff/612/61205.htm.
[19]Rex Li, 'Contending Narratives of the International Order: US/Chinese Discursive Power and Its Effects on the UK'.
[20]He Yafei, 'Cong quanqiu zhili gaige dao chong su guoji zhixu' [*From the reform of global governance to the reshaping of the international order*], FT Zhongwen wang [FTChinese.com], Jinrong Shibao [Financial Times], March 27, 2017, accessed November 15, 2019, https://ftchinese.com/story/001071929?full.
[21]Melanie Hart and Blaine Johnson, *'Mapping China's Global Governance Ambitions'*, Center for American Progress, February 2019, https://www.americanprogress.org/issues/security/reports/2019/02/28/466768/mapping-chinas-global-governance-ambitions/.
[22]United Kingdom Parliament, 'China and the Rules-Based International System', 2019.
[23]Xinhua, *'Xi Jinping: Ideological work is the party's extremely important task'*, Xinhuanet, August 20, 2013, accessed November 20, 2019, http://www.xinhuanet.com/politics/2013-08/20/c_117021464.htm.
[24]Caixin, 'zhong gong shi ba jie wu zhong quan hui gong bao (quan wen)', October 29, 2015, accessed November 20, 2019, http://www.caixin.com/2015-10-29/100867990_1.html.

global governance reform, must be explained and justified through effective and convincing narratives. Second, in the global governance arena, states with strong discourse power have advantages in agenda setting as well as rulemaking, both of which are essential for leading global governance reform. Third, Chinese leaders recognize that the existing international order is primarily based on Western liberal values (e.g., democracy, human rights, openness and rule of law), many of which conflict with CCP values.[26] By having stronger discourse power, Beijing can reshape how other nations define, interpret, and implement those values in ways more aligned with the Chinese perspective. Fourth, Chinese leaders are keenly aware of how powerful discourse can create favorable or unfavorable conditions for a state in world affairs. As a target of Western originated anti-China narratives such as the 'China threat'—which stains China's image, tarnishes its reputation, and reduces its attraction as a partner and great power— Beijing is determined to take the initiative in telling its own story to the world.[27]

Strategic Narratives, Social Identity Theory (SIT) and Chinese Strategy

China's aspiration for greater discourse power in global governance highlights the importance of strategic narratives, a concept recently advanced in the studies of IR. Narratives are frameworks or stories constructed to allow people to make sense of the world, policies, events, and interactions. Miskimmon et al. argue that narratives are not only 'representations of a sequence of events and identities,' but are also used as 'communicative tools through which political actors—usually elites—attempt to give determined meaning to past, present and future in order to achieve political objectives'.[28] Strategic narratives, intended specifically for achieving certain political objectives, are formulated and promoted by leaders to influence domestic and international audiences to drive them towards particular outcomes.[29] Strategic narratives thus are a useful tool for political actors to extend their influence, manage expectations, and change the discursive environment.[30] In the short term, Freedman writes, 'Narratives are designed or nurtured with the intention of structuring the responses of others to developing events'.[31] But in the long term, 'getting others at home and abroad to buy in to your strategic narrative can shape their interests, their identity, and their understanding of how international relations works and where it is heading'.[32] Hence, strategic narratives, properly employed, are particularly useful for China to communicate its new role/identity and vision of the global order to both domestic and international audiences. It is fair to say that strategic narratives are directly linked to the degree of success of Xi Jinping's new foreign policy ambition.

There are different ways to distinguish various types of strategic narratives. Miskimmon and colleagues distinguish three levels of strategic narratives.[33] International/system narratives describe how the world is structured, who the players are, and how it works.[34] It indicates a number of interrelated

[25] Alexander Wendt, 'Anarchy Is What States Make of It: The Social Construction of Power Politics', *International Organization* 46(2), (1992), pp. 391–425, www.jstor.org/stable/2706858.

[26] Nadège Rolland, 'China's vision for a new world order', NBR Special Report no. 83, January 27, 2020, accessed May 20, 2020, https://www.nbr.org/publication/chinas-vision-for-a-new-world-order/.

[27] Yi Edward Yang and Xinsheng Liu, 'The 'China Threat' through the Lens of US Print Media: 1992–2006 ', *Journal of Contemporary China* (21)76, (2012), pp. 695–711, DOI: 10.1080/10670564.2012.666838.

[28] Alister Miskimmon, Ben O'Loughlin, and Laura Roselle, *Strategic narratives: Communication Power and the New World Order* (New York: Routledge, 2013), p. 5.

[29] Ibid.

[30] Ibid.

[31] Lawrence Freedman, *The Transformation of Strategic Affairs* (Adelphi Paper 379) (London: IISS/Routledge, 2006).

[32] Ibid.

[33] Miskimmon et al., *Strategic narratives*; Classification of strategic narratives by Chinese scholars are similar to those of Miskimmon et al. For instance, they make a distinction between system and issue levels of narratives where the system level includes both Chinese vision of the international system as well as its own role/mission in it. See Jisheng Sun, 'zhong guo guo ji hua yu quan de su zao yu ti sheng lu jiu', [China's Approach to Shape and Improve its International Discursive Power: Diplomatic Practice Since the 8th Party Congress as an Example], shi jie jing ji yu zheng zhi [World Economics and Politics] 3, (2019), pp. 19–43; Guangbin Yang, 'you bi yao nong qing hua yu quan dao di shi shen me' [It is necessary to understand what is exactly discourse power], September 10, 2018, Beijing Daily.

[34] Miskimmon et al., *Strategic Narratives*.

attributes of the international order such as system polarity and the identification of great powers, alignment of interests, prospect for cooperation, integration, or confrontation in the order, and the scope for the socialization of political actors.[35] Examples include narratives such as the Cold War, the War on Terror, and the LIO. Identity narratives set out the story of a political actor (e.g., a nation state): what values it has, what role it should play in the world, what kinds of interests are worth pursuing, and its goals. A state's identity narrative is highly related to the actual (or desired) beliefs, place, reputation, prestige, credibility, etc. Examples of identity narratives include China's rise presents as either a threat or opportunity to the world. Issue narratives focuses on why a policy is needed and (normatively) desirable, and how to successfully implement it. Issue narratives set policies or actions in a context, with an explanation of who the important actors are, what the conflict or issue is, and how a particular course of action will resolve the underlying issue. Examples of issue narratives include justifications for China's Belt and Road Initiative (BRI) that provides connectivity and collective goods.

Empirically, as noted by Colley, the conceptualization of narrative has been broad and vague.[36] It has been used often interchangeably with concepts such as 'frame' or 'framework'. This study adopts Colley's definition of narrative—' ... text consists of a temporally, spatially, and causally connected sequence of events, selected and evaluated as meaningful for a particular audience'.[37] It is a 'socially constructed discourse often involving a logically plausible plot with actors, a beginning, middle, and end'.[38] For a narrative to be strategic, it needs to be constructed deliberately by political actors to achieve political objectives—typically involving selective interpretations of the past, present, and future designed to achieve political objectives through persuasion.

The next section discusses the strategic narratives that China has formulated and promoted in support of its bid for leading global governance reform.

Social Identity Theory (SIT) and China's Narrative Strategy

As aforementioned, China is not currently seeking to overthrow the existing international order. Instead, it intends to reform it to better suit its own values and interests. In both scholarly writings and popular media coverage, the concept of liberal, international order has been defined and operationalized in different ways.[39] The current study distinguishes China's interaction with the existing order on two levels. The first is the system level—the fundamental norms and institutions reflecting the power/authority structure of the existing order and the main actors and their primary interests.[40] The second level is defined by various, global. governance issues (e.g., climate change, international trade, etc.). As Alastair Iain Johnston noted, China's policies vis-à-vis global governance is issue/domain dependent.[41] There are issue areas where China supports the existing norms and rules such as climate change, nuclear nonproliferation, public health, etc. China opposes norms and institutions in some issue areas, such as human rights, primarily rooted in Western liberal values antithetical to those of Beijing. There also are emerging issue areas, such as Internet governance, where international norms are still developing, for which China is determined to play a significant role. Considering the cross-issue variation in China's interests, how does China deploy the tool of strategic narratives to achieve its goals in the complex landscape of global governance?

---

[35]Ibid.
[36]Thomas Colley, *Always at War: British Public Narratives of War* (Ann Arbor: University of Michigan Press, 2019).
[37]Ibid., p. 6.
[38]Ibid. Colley also notes that narratives may not always contain all these elements. In addition, there are 'habitual' narratives, which lack dramatic sequences of events but instead describe how thoughts typically occur over time. There are hypothetical narratives, suggesting possible future outcomes depending on what policy is pursued.
[39]Alastair Iain Johnston, 'China in a world of orders: rethinking compliance and challenges in Beijing's international relations', 2019, p. 12.
[40]This is similar to what Alastair Iain Johnston ('China in a world of orders: rethinking compliance and challenges in Beijing's international relations', 2019) refers to as the 'constitutive order'.
[41]Alastair Iain Johnston, *'China in a world of orders: rethinking compliance and challenges in Beijing's international relations'*, 2019, p. 12.

Drawing on Social Identity Theory (SIT), this study argues that China is utilizing a multi-pronged narrative strategy. In IR research, SIT has been employed and adapted by Deborah Welch Larson and Alexei Shevchenko to explain Chinese and Russian foreign policy in seek of status change.[42] The adapted SIT states that social groups strive to achieve a positively distinctive identity.[43] When a group is unsatisfied with its identity or feels it is threatened, it may pursue one of several identity management strategies: social mobility, social competition, or social creativity.[44] The choice of strategy depends on the 'permeability of dominant group (or "elite clubs")' and the 'legitimacy and stability of the status hierarchy'.[45] In the context of international relations, social mobility strategy requires a state to emulate the values and norms of the higher-status states in exchange for admission into elite clubs. For social mobility to be viable, the elite clubs need to be permeable to new members and the existing order is deemed legitimate. When the current elite club is permeable, but the state finds certain club norms unattractive, it may instead adopt the social creativity strategy, striving to retain and capitalize on its own unique characteristics. In practice, the state may reframe a negative attribute (according to the dominant norms) as positive or stresses achievement in a different domain. Social competition is adopted when a state deems the international status hierarchy as impermeable, unstable or illegitimate. In turn, the state engages in social competition, aiming to overtake the dominant group in areas it considers feasible. To summarize, SIT suggests that in international relations states may 'improve their status by joining elite clubs, trying to best the dominant states, or achieving preeminence outside the arena of geopolitical competition.'[46]

Insights from SIT and its applications in IR are particularly useful in elucidating how China uses carefully crafted strategic narratives to achieve its goals in global governance. At the international system level, the liberal international order by and large remains stable and legitimate and current elite members (i.e., U.S.-led liberal democratic states) welcome China's participation on the condition that it follows the existing rules and behaves like a responsible stakeholder. However, China harbors significant dissatisfactions towards the current order for reasons aforementioned. Its intentions vis-à-vis the current order are thus twofold: to enhance its own status as a rule/norm maker in general and to lead the reform of certain global governance areas it deems obsolete and unaligned with its own interests. In this context, China's strategic narratives at the international system level is best described as social creativity narrative, indicating its selected adoption of existing rules and norms and its aspiration for leadership in niche areas within the current system.

China's strategic narratives, at the issue area level, are much more complex and involves all three strategies laid out in SIT. As the world's second largest economy, China is heavily dependent on the global system. It is in China's interest to work collaboratively with other nations to address common challenges such as climate change, terrorism, pandemic disease, nuclear proliferation and global financial crises that threaten worldwide security and prosperity. Sharing common interests with the U.S. and other Western liberal democracies, China therefore has been a constructive supporter of relevant international rules and norms. These are also institutions that welcome China's participation without which major global challenges would be impossible to solve. For these issues where China's interests are aligned with the existing order, China's strategic narratives are likely echoing social mobility for which China strives to 'join the club' and be a contributing member. In other areas of global governance where Western liberal democratic norms promoting universal values such as freedom, human rights, and democracy pose unique political challenges for China. Beijing perceives them as politically threatening and do not intend to comply with these norms. In these areas, Beijing

---

[42]Deborah Welch Larson and Alexei Shevchenko, *Quest for Status*; Henri Tajfel, ed., *Social Identity and Intergroup Relations* (Cambridge University Press, 1982).

[43]Deborah Welch Larson and Alexei Shevchenko, *Quest for Status*. See a list of other IR research applying the SIT framework, see p. 822 in Steven Michael Ward, 'Lost in translation: Social identity theory and the study of status in world politics', *International Studies Quarterly* (2017), doi: 10.1093/isq/sqx042.

[44]Ibid.

[45]Ibid. What follows in the paragraph is a summary of Larson and Shevchenko's elaboration of the three strategies in their 2019 book, *Quest for Status*.

[46]Ibid., p.2.

strives to alter established norms by injecting strategic narratives legitimizing and promoting its own values. In these areas, China can find ample allies, particularly among developing countries, that would support its narratives so that China can carve out its own niche area. This corresponds to a strategy of social creativity. Finally, there are new areas of global governance (e.g., Internet governance) crucial to China's interests without established norms yet. Under these circumstances, China is expected to compete with other actors to ensure any norms/rules to be established will reflect China's values and interests. For these cases, strategic narratives are more likely to follow the social competition strategy.

The next section illustrates the explanatory power of the above theoretical framework with four short case studies. It begins with China's international system level strategic narrative under the Xi Jinping administration, i.e., a community of shared destiny for mankind. It is followed by tracing China's recent strategic narratives in three global governance issue areas, i.e., climate change, human rights, and Internet governance, to illustrate the application of the three narrative strategies (i.e., social mobility, social creativity, and social competition).

Illustrative Cases of China's Strategic Narratives in Global Governance

China's International System Level Strategic Narrative: A 'Community of Common Destiny for Mankind'

At the system level, Xi Jinping has encapsulated Beijing's long-term vision for transforming the international order and its emergence as a global leader in the strategic narrative coined as a 'community of common destiny for mankind'. Originally used by his predecessor, Hu Jintao, in 2007, it was Xi that brought this terminology into global attention and elevated it to a pillar of his foreign policy. This concept was first introduced in the report of the CCP's 18th National Congress in 2012. Since then, it has been mentioned more than 100 times in Xi's speeches and presented as China's core principle to deal with the numerous challenges in global affairs.

In March 2013, Xi proposed the idea internationally for the first time at the Moscow State Institute of International Relations. In September 2015, he delivered a major speech at the 70th United Nations (UN) General Assembly, in which Xi explained that the community of common destiny for mankind encompasses five dimensions including political partnership, security, economic development, cultural exchanges and environment. It shows Beijing's ambition in global governance reform is extraordinarily wide-ranging.[47] In January 2017, Xi reiterated the idea again in his speech to the World Economic Forum at Davos, noting that 'Mankind has become a community of common destiny that one is inseparable from the other, and their interest is highly inter-mingled and inter-dependent'.[48]

What does this narrative say about the new vision and China's role in it? According to the Chinese official interpretation, the 'community of common destiny' describes a 'new' approach to international relations that embodies the principles of equality and fairness. By definition, it is a community in which all countries should jointly shape the future of the world, write the international rules, manage global affairs and ensure that development outcomes are shared by all.[49] It distinguishes itself from the current model with its emphasis on 'win-win' relations. In a speech by China's Foreign Minister Wang Yi, he laid out China's role in the 'new model'—the building of a community with a shared future for mankind makes it necessary for China to make practical efforts and set an example, as well as unswervingly pursue a road to a great nation which is different from that of traditional.[50] In the context of the new model, Beijing offers 'Chinese wisdom' as a unique solution 'to the problems facing mankind'.

[47]Liza Tobin, 'Xi's Vision for Transforming Global Governance: A Strategic Challenge for Washington and Its Allies', *Texas National Security Review* 2(1), (2018), http://dx.doi.org/10.26153/tsw/863.

[48]Xi Jinping, *The Governance of China*, Vol. 2 (Beijing: Foreign Languages Press, 2017).

[49]Xinhua, 'Chinese president eyes shared, win-win development for mankind's future', January 19, 2017, http://www.xinhuanet.com/english/2017-01/19/c_135996080.htm.

As such, the 'community of common destiny' meets the criteria of a strategic narrative: China is its central actor; it has a plot with a beginning and end; it is produced by a political actor—China—to persuade other nations to support its vision of the world order. By highlighting the new model's differences from the existing order in terms of fairness and equality, China is clearly trying to establish itself as a leader primarily attractive to developing countries. This is an effort to succeed in a niche area without supplanting the current international order, hence an example of the strategy of social creativity.

China's Strategic Narratives in Global Governance Issue Areas: Climate Change

Climate change is a global challenge that requires collective effort from all major economies in the world. Existing international climate institutions are open to all participants, especially countries like China, the world's second largest economy and one of the biggest greenhouse gas emitters. Zhang and Orbie contend that China's climate strategic narratives have evolved in three phases (2009–2018).[51] During the early phases, China's strategic narratives depicted itself as a victim of an unfair climate regime dominated by developed countries who created the climate problem in the first place. Since then, however, China's domestic situation related to climate/environmental issues experienced profound changes. For example, the worsening air pollution greatly enhanced Chinese citizens' environmental awareness and demand for change. At the same time, Chinese economy started transitioning into a new model that increasingly relies on low emissions technologies.[52] These domestic factors, combined with international pressure, called for an updated strategic narrative to meet China's evolving interests on climate issues.[53]

The new strategic narrative was subsequently presented to the world in Xi Jinping's speech at the Paris climate conference (2015), in which the international climate institutions were narrated as a dimension of the 'community of a shared future of mankind', China's international system-level narrative. Following the logic of the 'community of a shared future of mankind', all countries, regardless of size or economy, should shoulder shared and differentiated responsibility for the win-win outcome of international climate governance. As for China's role in the new narrative, Xi announced that 'China upholds the values of friendship, justice and shared interests, and takes an active part in international cooperation on climate change'.[54] This new narrative shows that the climate change issue is now framed as "… a challenge for the whole world and no country can stand aloof."[55] Additionally, the narrative lays out the principle of the distribution of responsibility—'We should create a future of win-win cooperation, with each country making contribution to the best of its ability' and 'Given the difference between developed and developing countries in historical responsibility, developing stage and coping capability, the principle of common but differentiated responsibilities, instead of being obsolete, must continue to be adhered to'.[56] In sum, the promotion of this new strategic narrative facilitated and justified China's transformation from a victim of 'environmental imperialism' to a stakeholder of the climate change regime. This is clearly an example

---

[50]Ministry of Foreign Affairs of the People's Republic of China, 'Wang Yi Talks about General Goal of Major Country Diplomacy with Chinese Characteristics in New Era: To Promote the Building of a Community with Shared Future for Mankind', October 19, 2017, https://www.fmprc.gov.cn/mfa_eng/zxxx_662805/t1503758.shtml.

[51]Yunhan Zhang and Jan Orbie, 'Strategic narratives in China's climate policy: Analysing three phases in China's discourse coalition', The Pacific Review, (2019), DOI: 10.1080/09512748.2019.1637366.

[52]Ibid.

[53]Ibid.; Lin Xu and Ying Chen, 'quan qiu qi hou zhi li yu Zhong guo de zhan lue xuan ze' [Global Climate Governance and China's Strategic Choice], Shi jie jing ji yu zheng zhi [World Economics and Politics] 1, (2013), pp. 116–34.

[54]Yunhan Zhang and Jan Orbie, 'Strategic narratives in China's climate policy: Analysing three phases in China's discourse coalition'; China Daily, 'Full text of President Xi's speech at opening ceremony of Paris climate summit', December 1, 2015, http://www.chinadaily.com.cn/world/XiattendsParisclimateconference/2015-12/01/content_22592469.htm.

[55]Ministry of Foreign Affairs of the People's Republic of China, 'Foreign Ministry Spokesperson Hua Chunying's Regular Press Conference on June 1, 2017   , June 1, 2017, https://www.fmprc.gov.cn/mfa_eng/xwfw_665399/s2510_665401/2511_665403/t1467100.shtml.

[56]China Daily, 'Full text of President Xi's speech at opening ceremony of Paris climate summit', December 1, 2015, http://www.chinadaily.com.cn/world/XiattendsParisclimateconference/2015-12/01/content_22592469.htm.

of social mobility strategy which enables China to become a participant, contributor, and potentially a leader of the climate governance club.

Since the adoption of the new narrative, China became a staunch defender of the existing climate regime. In the aftermath of the U.S. withdrawal from the Paris Agreement under the Trump Administration, China reiterated its recognition of climate change as a global challenge and the need for multilateral cooperation. In response to Trump's decision, the spokesperson of China's Foreign Ministry stated that 'The Paris Agreement is a hard-won result which represents the broadest consensus of the international community and sets the target for the global campaign against climate change' and 'China will stay committed to upholding and promoting the global governance on climate change and take an active part in the multilateral process on climate change. We will work with all relevant parties to safeguard the outcomes of the Paris Agreement, press ahead with the negotiation and implementation of the enforcement rules, and promote green, low-carbon and sustainable growth of the world'.[57] Xi Jinping reiterated China's stance when delivering an address to the United Nations in Geneva in 2017. He referenced the Paris Agreement, and emphasized the role of governments around the world in ensuring the agreement is adhered to and upheld in upcoming years. 'The Paris agreement is a milestone in the history of climate governance. We must ensure this endeavor is not derailed', said Xi, 'All parties should work together to implement the Paris agreement. China will continue to take steps to tackle climate change and fully honor its obligations'.[58] These statements, among others, projected a clear strategic narrative that depicts China as a committed supporter of the existing international climate regime. Zhang and Orbie further argued that China's determination to back the Paris agreement and UNFCC is that Beijing views them as the platform to pursue 'institutional discourse power'.[59] The institutional discourse power is defined as 'the discourse power solidified by international institutions. It refers to an actor's ability to understand and apply discourse to persuade other actors and construct the rules and structure of the international governance system'.[60]

More significantly, at the 19th CCP National Congress in 2017, Xi Jinping took a striking further step by declaring the intention to position China as the next global leader taking on climate change. In his work report, Xi stated that China will be 'Taking a driving seat in international cooperation to respond to climate change. China has become an important participant, contributor, and torch-bearer in the global endeavor for ecological civilization'.[61] This milestone narrative signals that after becoming a member of the international climate institution, China now seized the opportunity to claim a leadership role when the U.S. withdrawal created a power vacuum.[62]

China's Strategic Narrative in Global Governance Issue Areas: Human Rights

The existing global human rights regime is dominated by norms and rules rooted in Western liberal democratic tradition which Beijing regards as politically threatening. The United Nations adopted the Universal Declaration of Human Rights in 1948.[63] That declaration sets a common human rights standard that applies to all UN member states. It treats human rights as inalienable and includes

---

[57]Ministry of Foreign Affairs of the People's Republic of China, 'Foreign Ministry Spokesperson Hua Chunying's Regular Press Conference on June 1, 2017   , n.d., https://www.fmprc.gov.cn/mfa_eng/xwfw_665399/s2510_665401/2511_665403/t1467100.shtml.

[58]Partnership for Action on Green Economy, 'China Tackles Climate Change and Honors Paris Agreement', January 28, 2017, https://www.un-page.org/china-tackles-climate-change-and-honors-paris-agreement.

[59]Yunhan Zhang and Jan Orbie, 'Strategic narratives in China's climate policy: Analysing three phases in China's discourse coalition'.

[60]The People's Daily, 'xie li ti gao zhi du xing hua yu quan', February 19, 2016, http://opinion.people.com.cn/n1/2016/0219/c1003-28134857.html. Original in Chinese, translated in Yunhan Zhang and Jan Orbie, 'Strategic narratives in China's climate policy: Analysing three phases in China's discourse coalition', p. 19.

[61]Xinhua, 'Full text of Xi Jinping's report at 19th CPC National Congress', November 3, 2017, http://www.xinhuanet.com/english/special/2017-11/03/c_136725942.htm.

[62]China later retreated from this narrative by claiming it does not yet have the capability to be the leader. For detailed discussions see Zhang and Orbie 2019.

rights and freedoms that are generally associated with liberal democracies such as freedom of assembly, freedom of expression, and the right to participate in government. Since 1948, a series of international human rights laws and conventions have expanded this standard and set forth specific obligations for nation states.[64]

This set of global governance norms and standards apply to all nations, and that creates a problem for Beijing. The Chinese political system does not recognize inalienable individual rights or any other limits on CCP authority.[65] The Chinese system puts the collective before the individual, and the CCP speaks on behalf of the collective. The party can either protect or deny individual rights as needed to balance against broader collective objectives (which are set and defined by the party). When Beijing takes actions that infringe on individual rights to pursue collective goals, those actions often violate the international human rights standard, triggering international censure. That creates political pressure for Beijing and can be economically costly if other nations impose sanctions against China.

Beijing realized, without discourse power, China could only engage in conversations within the conceptual framework of human rights established by the West. Therefore, to change the awkward and reactive situation, China has decided to play the offensive by promoting strategic narratives that highlight the differences in the conceptualization and practices of human rights between countries headed by China and the West. In this case, Beijing is using the social creativity narrative strategy: it is working to shift the prevailing international norm from a universal and inalienable human rights standard based on liberal, democratic values to an alternative standard that gives nation-states the right to balance individual rights against competing national objectives. In the narrative, Beijing states that human rights are culturally bound concepts. Whereas the West prioritizes individual rights, China, like many other Asian nations, focuses on the synthesis of individual and collective rights, prioritizing individual's responsibility towards family and society.[66]

Beijing is convening its own human rights forums to rally other nations to support this alternative approach to human rights, and it is also successfully passing UN Resolutions to normalize this more lenient approach within the United Nations. Those activities demonstrate how China is seeking to redefine the current norm. China hosted its first South-South Human Rights Forum in December 2017. President Xi Jinping delivered an opening message to the forum in which he stated that human rights 'can only be promoted in light of specific national conditions' and therefore cannot be addressed with a single universal standard.[67] Instead, he called for developing nations to follow a more nuanced and flexible standard that mixes 'universality and particularity'. The forum produced a Beijing Declaration—signed by 300 international representatives—that outlined a new human rights standard giving nation-states leeway to balance human rights against other needs, particularly economic development and national security needs.[68] It also declares that the international community should respect different political systems, rather than holding all nations to the

---

[63]United Nations, 'The Universal Declaration of Human Rights', Adopted December 10, 1948, https://www.un.org/en/universal-declaration-human-rights/index.html.

[64]The definitive document of the current international regimes of human rights is the International Bill of Human Rights. It consists of the Universal Declaration of Human Rights (adopted in 1948), the International Covenant on Civil and Political Rights (ICCPR, 1966) with its two Optional Protocols and the International Covenant on Economic, Social and Cultural Rights (ICESCR, 1966). The two covenants entered into force in 1976. For a general overview, see the United Nations Human Rights page, https://www.un.org/en/sections/issues-depth/human-rights/.

[65]China signed the ICESR in 1997 and ratified it in 2001. China signed the ICCPR in 1998, but has yet to ratify it.

[66]Zixia Zhang, 'zhong guo ren quan guan nian xia de hua yu quan' [Discourse Power in the context of China's Human Rights Concepts], xu lie lun [Theoretical Studies] 3, (2015), pp. 5–7; Danhong Ren and Yonghe Zhang, 'lun Zhong guo ren quan hua yu ti xi de jian gou yu guo ji hua yu quan de zheng qu' [On constructing the discourse system of China's human rights and striving for international right of speech], xi nan zheng fa da xue xue bao [Journal of Southwest University of Political Science and Law] 21(1), (2019), pp. 64–72.

[67]China.org, 'Congratulatory Message from President Xi Jinping to the "South-South Human Rights Forum', December 7, 2017, English translation available at http://p.china.org.cn/2017-12/07/content_50091431.htm.

[68]Xinhua, 'Full text of Beijing Declaration adopted by the First South-South Human Rights Forum', December 8, 2017, http://www.chinadaily.com.cn/a/201712/08/WS5a2aaa68a310eefe3e99ef85.html.

same human rights standard. The declaration specifically creates space for states to legitimately restrict or deny human rights. Article 5 states that:

> Restrictions on the exercise of human rights must be determined by law, and only for the protection of the human rights and fundamental freedoms of other members of society (including freedom from religious desecration, racism and discrimination) and meet the legitimate needs of national security, public order, public health, public safety, public morals and the general welfare of the people. Everyone is responsible to all others and to society, and the enjoyment of human rights and fundamental freedoms must be balanced with the fulfillment of corresponding responsibilities.

Within the UN Human Rights Council, China has successfully passed two resolutions that bring elements of this more lenient standard into the UN framework. In June 2017, the UNHRC passed a Chinese resolution suggesting that human rights must be balanced with economic development needs.[69] In March 2018, the UNHRC passed a Chinese resolution that calls for the international community to address human rights problems through 'mutually beneficial cooperation' and to take 'national and regional particularities and various historical, cultural and religious backgrounds' into account when determining what human rights standard a particular nation should meet.[70] In sum, Beijing is working—successfully—to build more maneuvering room into UN human rights doctrine.[71] Its creative strategic narratives has been working quite effectively.

China's Strategic Narrative in Global Governance Issue Areas: Internet Governance

Unlike the human rights domain, Internet governance is still an emerging and contested global governance issue area.[72] The global community has not yet rallied around a single set of norms and standards for cyberspace. This gives China an opportunity to engage in the social competition narrative strategy, striving to proactively lead the effort in crafting the cyber governance norms consistent with its own values and priorities. For instance, China championed and hosted twice the 'World Internet Conference' where discussions on global Internet rule/norm-making took place. Fully taking the host advantage, China wasted no time in promoting to the whole world its own vision of Internet governance. In July 2014, Xi Jinping for the first time mentioned Internet governance when addressing the Brazilian congress and reiterated such an expression in the congratulatory remarks to the first World Internet Conference. In Brazil, Xi laid out the initial strategic narrative that embodies, justifies, and propagates China's approach to Internet governance:

> In today's world, the development of the Internet raises new challenges to the national sovereignty, security and development interests of all countries. All countries have the right to safeguard their information security, and the international community should build a multilateral, democratic and transparent international Internet governance system based on the principle of mutual respect and mutual trust.[73]

China's Internet sovereignty narrative stands in clear contrast to those of western countries such as the United States. In 2011, the United States began to actively promote a liberal 'free and open' approach to Internet governance. That approach narrates Internet freedom—or the 'freedom to connect', as then Secretary of State Hillary Clinton phrased it in her seminal February 2011 speech— as a universal human right that cannot be legitimately restricted by nation-states.[74] The Trump Administration's 2018 *National Cyber Strategy* follows the same principle, stating that:

---

[69]UN General Assembly, 'Human Rights Council: Thirty-fifth session, Agenda item 3, A/HRC/35/L.33 , Geneva: 2017, https://undocs.org/A/HRC/35/L.33.

[70]UN General Assembly, 'Human Rights Council: Thirty-seventh session, Agenda item 3, A/HRC/37/L.36 , Geneva: 2018, https://undocs.org/A/HRC/37/L.36.

[71]Ted Piccone, 'China's Long Game on Human Rights at the United Nations', Brookings, September 2018, https://www.brookings.edu/research/chinas-long-game-on-human-rights-at-the-united-nations/.

[72]Alastair Iain Johnston, '*China in a world of orders: rethinking compliance and challenges in Beijing's international relations*', 2019.

[73]Ministry of Foreign Affairs of the People's Republic of China, 'Xi Jinping Delivers Important Speech at National Congress of Brazil-Carry Forward Traditional Friendship and Jointly Open up New Chapter of Cooperation', July 17, 2014, https://www.fmprc.gov.cn/mfa_eng/zxxx_662805/t1176214.shtml.

The United States stands firm on its principles to protect and promote an open, interoperable, reliable, and secure Internet. We will work to ensure that our approach to an open Internet is the international standard. We will also work to prevent authoritarian states that view the open Internet as a political threat from transforming the free and open Internet into an authoritarian web under their control, under the guise of security or countering terrorism.[75]

China however views Internet control as a critical and irreplaceable tool for maintaining political stability. If a 'free and open' Internet becomes the global standard, that will create problems for Beijing. China's Internet control practices would be deemed illegitimate by the global community; China would likely face new external pressures to relax those controls, and potential costs—such as sanctions or trade barriers—if China does not do so. To avoid that, China is pushing its own Internet governance norm—the Internet sovereignty approach—that recognizes a nation-state's authority to limit and control Internet activity within its own borders. The absence of established international norms in this emerging area further incentivized China to adopt a proactive social competition narrative strategy.

President Xi detailed China's Internet sovereignty approach in his speech to China's second World Internet Conference in 2015. He put forth four principles and five proposals that, in sum, calls for individual nations to take their own path on Internet governance rather than seeking to meet a common global standard and call for Internet freedom to be balanced with order, stating that 'cyberspace must be governed, operated and used in accordance with law'.[76] In 2017, the Cyberspace Administration of China (CAC) published an article in the Chinese Communist Party journal, *Qiushi*, detailing its interpretation of Xi Jinping's 'four principles and five proposals' and how the CAC is working to implement them. In that article, the CAC states that 'cyberspace has become a new field of competition for global governance, and we must comprehensively strengthen international exchanges and cooperation in cyberspace, to push China's proposition of Internet governance toward becoming an international consensus'.[77]

Towards that end, Beijing is actively pushing this Chinese-style Internet sovereignty norm on two fronts: bilaterally with nations that welcome China's guidance on Internet governance, and multilaterally within international institutions. Bilaterally, China's Belt and Road Initiative includes a 'Digital Silk Road' program that educates officials from Belt and Road partner nations about China's domestic approach to Internet governance and helps them implement similar policies at home. There is anecdotal evidence that this program is helping to spread China's Internet governance model to other nations. For example, after China ran digital training programs for Zimbabwe, then-President Robert Mugabe declared that his nation sought to follow China's example, stating in 2016 that 'the Chinese have put in place security measures and we will look at these so that we stop these abuses on the Internet'.[78] Zimbabwe subsequently adopted a cybercrime and cybersecurity bill that restricts Internet freedom.

At the multilateral level, China is focusing on the United Nations as the best forum to gain broad multilateral support for Internet sovereignty norms and push back against the U.S.-backed 'free and

---

[74]Hillary Clinton, 'Internet Rights &Wrongs: Choices and Challenges in a Networked World', delivered February 15, 2011, The George Washington University, Washington, D.C., accessed May 28, 2020, https://2009-2017.state.gov/secretary/20092013clinton/rm/2011/02/156619.htm.

[75]National Cyber Strategy of the United States of America, September 2018, https://www.whitehouse.gov/wp-content/uploads/2018/09/National-Cyber-Strategy.pdf.

[76]Ministry of Foreign Affairs of the People's Republic of China, 'Xi jin ping zai di er jie shi jie hu lian wang da hui kai mu shi shang de jiang hua (Quan wen)' [Speech by Xi Jinping at the opening ceremony of the second World Internet Conference (Full text)], December 16, 2015, https://www.fmprc.gov.cn/chn//gxh/tyb/zyxw/t1324843.htm. For the English version of this speech, see https://www.fmprc.gov.cn/mfa_eng/wjdt_665385/zyjh_665391/t1327570.shtml.

[77]Translation: 'Deepening the Implementation of General Secretary Xi Jinping's Strategic Thinking on Building China into a Cyber Superpower: Steadily Advancing Cybersecurity and Informatization Work', by the Cyberspace Administration of China Theoretical Studies Center Group, Qiushi, September 15, 2017, http://www.qstheory.cn/dukan/qs/2017-09/15/c_1121647633.htm. Translated by: Elsa B. Kania, Samm Sacks (Center for Strategic and International Studies), Paul Triolo (Eurasia Group), and Graham Webster (Yale Law School Paul Tsai China Center). Translation at https://www.newamerica.org/cybersecurity-initiative/blog/chinas-strategic-thinking-building-power-cyberspace/.

[78]Melanie Hart and Blaine Johnson, 'Mapping China's Global Governance Ambitions', Center for American Progress, February 2019, https://www.americanprogress.org/issues/security/reports/2019/02/28/466768/mapping-chinas-global-governance-ambitions/.

open' approach.[79] China submitted an *'International Code of Conduct for Information Security'* to the U.N. General Assembly in September 2011; in 2015 China submitted an updated version jointly with a group of Shanghai Cooperation Organization (SCO) nations. Both documents push China's Internet sovereignty concept and generally aim to legitimize Internet control.[80] China is also an active participant in the UN Group of Governmental Experts (GGE) process on cyberspace. Some nations view China's insistence on adding 'state sovereignty' to the GGE list of governance principles as a key factor in that group's inability to determine how international law should apply in the Internet domain.

As mentioned above, the CAC states that China's goal is to 'push China's proposition of Internet governance toward becoming an international consensus'. If that is correct, the Internet sovereignty narrative is helping China march towards that goal.[81] Beijing is blocking other nations' attempts to build consensus around the 'free and open Internet' approach. China is also rallying other authoritarian regimes around a common cyber sovereignty principle—as evidenced by the SCO code of conduct—and it is leveraging bilateral investments (particularly digital infrastructure investments) to expand the number of states that fall in that category.

Conclusion

Since becoming China's indisputable leader, Xi Jinping departed from the 'keeping a low profile' ethos that guided China's foreign policy during much of the reform era. His call for China to lead global governance reform has drawn much analytical attention. This article examined how Beijing is striving to achieve that goal by way of strengthening its discourse power, an important but under-investigated subject. The novel theoretical framework, synthesizing the social identity theory and strategic narratives framework, allowed us to look beyond the mainstream IR theories to dissect China's views of and strategic intentions towards the current international order and role it intends to play. By focusing on narratives, this study identified changes and continuities in China's foreign policy principles in different issue/policy domains across generations of leaders. Systematic tracking of narratives also enables researchers to compare rhetoric versus actions.

This study contributes to the broader discussion on China's role in global governance and its attitude toward current international order. China's growing power and confidence are certainly driving its revved-up ambition for a leadership role in global governance. However, analysis in this article shows its strategy for achieving that goal is complex and nuanced, varying across different issue areas determined by the attributes of the existing norms and China's own interests.[82] Hence, the combination of the SIT theory and strategic narratives should be a welcoming addition to the theoretical and methodological toolbox with which scholars can employ to examine Chinese foreign policy in particular and rising power behavior in general. This study also contributes to the SIT research program by underscoring that the same actor (a state or a group) may pursue a combination of various status-seeking strategies across issue/policy domains.

This study is a preliminary one and further studies can expand both theoretically and methodologically. Below are a few possibilities. First, the selection of the cases is for the purpose of illustrating

[79]Beijing's 2017 International Strategy of Cooperation on Cyberspace whitepaper states that 'the United Nations should play a key role in formulating international rules in cyberspace', International Strategy of Cooperation on Cyberspace, March 1, 2017, English version available at http://www.xinhuanet.com//english/china/2017-03/01/c_136094371.htm.

[80]Henry Rõigas, 'An Updated Draft of the Code of Conduct Distributed in the United Nations—What's New?', CCDCOE, https://ccdcoe.org/incyder-articles/an-updated-draft-of-the-code-of-conduct-distributed-in-the-united-nations-whats-new/. Ministry of Foreign Affairs of the P.R.C., 'International Code of Conduct for Information Security', September 12, 2011, English version available at https://www.fmprc.gov.cn/mfa_eng/wjdt_665385/2649_665393/t858323.shtml.

[81]Joe Uchill, 'Russia and China get a big win on internet "sovereignty"', November 21, 2019, Axios, https://www.axios.com/russia-china-united-nations-internet-sovereignty-3b4c14d0-a875-43a2-85cf-21497723c2ab.html.

[82]On this point, this study isin agreement with Alastair Iain Johnston's assessment (*'China in a world of orders: rethinking compliance and challenges in Beijing's international relations'*) that China's interaction with the international order is nuanced and varies by domain.

the logic of the theoretical framework, i.e., how and why China's strategic narratives strategies vary in different global governance domains. For a more robust test, future studies should include valid and rigorous measure of narratives. Second, each of the cases presented herein could be expanded to be a stand-alone investigation, featuring detailed analysis of the causal mechanisms (domestic and/or international) that drive the strategic narratives. Third, it is also important to look at the outcomes pertaining to the strategic narratives. Have the narratives achieved their intended objectives? How do we measure the effectiveness of narratives? What factors explain the successful narratives vs. unsuccessful narratives?

Acknowledgments

The author wishes to thank Nele Noesselt, Gregory Moore, and participants of the International Authors' Workshop on Governance Innovation and Policy Change under Xi Jinping (September 2019, Tutzing, Germany) for their helpful comments and suggestions on the earlier drafts of this article.

Disclosure Statement

No potential conflict of interest was reported by the authors.

China's Belt and Road Initiative as Nascent World Order Structure and Concept? Between Sino-Centering and Sino-Deflecting

Ray Silvius

ABSTRACT

This article considers Chinese state-sanctioned representations of the Belt and Road Initiative (BRI) as the conceptual apparatus of a Chinese state project with world order significance. The Chinese state organizes and produces ideational consistency and coherence for the BRI through publicly oriented documents and speeches. Such undertakings exhibit a Sino-centering and Sino-deflecting strategy with a dual temporal logic. First, the 'Silk Road' is extolled as an historical achievement of multiple civilizations under Chinese stewardship. Second, the BRI is presented as the contemporary manifestation of a Silk Road tradition: technically complex infrastructure and economic governance mechanisms designed as a 'win-win' endeavor for participating members. This article considers these representations of the BRI alongside the initiative's standing as an expansion of China's global economic structures.

Introduction

China's Belt and Road Initiative (BRI) is a comprehensive undertaking viewed by many pundits and academics alike as the centerpiece of Chinese diplomacy under President Xi Jinping.[1] The article considers the BRI as the culmination of an emerging institutional, governance, and ideational prism that is enmeshed by Chinese state decisions and economic relations. It builds upon previous work in which the author considers the discursive, conceptual, material and strategic components of emerging post (US) hegemonic world order structures.[2] Here, the BRI serves as an example of how Chinese 'state-sanctioned' discourse is forging world order concepts amid the unfolding of its attendant politics. The ideas behind the BRI can be understood as the latest development of a 'Sino-centric' world order conceptual apparatus that has accompanied China's spectacular, if uneven, economic development and its accompanying rise to global prominence during the 21st century.

The BRI is a multitudinous series of initiatives, involving state and non-state actors, capital, and labor at numerous geographical scales. While its solidity and coherence as a single undertaking should be scrutinized, the Chinese state serves as the primary agent in organizing and producing ideational consistency and coherence with the undertaking. Such ideational components of the initiative are not immune to change; however, once entered into the discursive field within which the BRI is articulated and understood, they persist *in spite of* the emergent politics of the project itself. Through state action, ideational components of emerging world order structures, replete with normative, political, and economic significance, are 'embedded' in thinking about the projects,

---

[1] Suisheng Zhao, 'China's Belt-Road Initiative as the signature of President Xi Jinping diplomacy: Easier said than done', *Journal of Contemporary China* 29(123), (2020), pp. 319–335.

[2] Ray Silvius, *Culture, Political Economy and Civilisation in a Multipolar World Order: The Case of Russia* (New York: Taylor & Francis, 2016).

imbuing BRI-related phenomena with a performative force that does extend naturally or automatically from the 'materiality' of the mega-project itself.

Nonetheless, Chinese state thinking and knowledge production on the BRI is not a pure act of political philosophy. And, despite its standing as a 'state project' organized in the main by the Chinese state (including Chinese state capital), the BRI cannot be *articulated* as being solely a Chinese affair, if it is to perform an integrative function beyond Chinese national space and if non-Chinese actors are expected to acknowledge the legitimacy of the Chinese state as a steward of the initiative.

The representation of the BRI has become its own reality generating its own momentum. Insofar as the Chinese state and Chinese officials represent the BRI, what are they representing and what function does this serve?

The intention of this article is to demonstrate state-sanctioned representations, which are cultivated to provide intelligibility and coherence to a Chinese state project with global aspirations. This state project involves coordination, material and governance capabilities among disparate social, political and economic forces, whose particular interests render them unable to articulate a project for society as a whole. It also involves ideas. With the BRI, the Chinese state endeavors to outline the contours of a project that is not reducible to Chinese interests but rather offers the possibility for mutual gain amongst Chinese and non-Chinese actors.

Indeed the BRI may be, and is, represented in countless ways; however, the cooperative, mutually beneficial aspects at the level of world order as *projected by* the Chinese state are the focus of analysis here. Such aspects are central to the Chinese state's public diplomacy efforts, which it deems necessary if the BRI is to be received as a project that is not reducible to the interests of Chinese state, capital, and citizen.

This article remains agnostic in assessing whether or not the Chinese state has been, or will be, successful in forging Sino-Centric world order structures or whether the BRI functions in a 'positive sum' manner. Instead, it outlines ideational, institutional and material components of the BRI as a project undertaken by the Chinese state. State-sanctioned BRI discourse embeds the twin qualities of *Sino-Centric and Sino-deflecting*, at once seeking to demonstrate the need for Chinese leadership and prominence while simultaneously deflecting these qualities. The syncretic quality of publicly oriented documents compiled by the Chinese state and speeches offered by Chinese officials, including President Xi, can be understood in the context of this dual quality, the intention of which is to legitimate Chinese stewardship over the BRI in two senses.

Contemporary Chinese state structures reference China's historical role in developing the Silk Road as a cooperative endeavor which provides positive sum gain for participating peoples and nations. Moreover, they assert China's *contemporary* ability to facilitate public goods across affected regions via a complex mega-initiative. The corresponding 'state-sanctioned' conceptual apparatus expressing the BRI at the level of world order blends this historically derived and contemporary identity while the organizing function of the Chinese state expands well beyond Chinese territory and national economy.

Running through the Sino-Centering and Sino-Deflecting approach, therefore, is a dual temporal logic. On the one hand, the 'Silk Road' is extolled as an historical achievement of multiple civilizations under Chinese stewardship. On the other, the BRI is presented as the contemporary manifestation of the Silk Road tradition, although it is delineated as an amalgam of mundane, although technically complex, contemporary infrastructure and governance mechanisms, also under Chinese stewardship but as a collaborative 'win-win' endeavor.

This article proceeds on the terrain of critical International Political Economy (IPE) and develops as follows: Section 2 examines how China's rise to global prominence in the 21st century has been accompanied by attempts to carve out 'ideational space' for a Sino-centric world order. Such attempts may be thought of as part of a larger 'state project' within which the contours of a Sino-centric world order have been articulated via select 'ideational' markers—motifs, language, and concepts derived from Chinese historical practices. The BRI is but a recent example of this larger shift in centering China in world order structures and adds tangible material content to more abstract historical discussions of identity, cultural particularity, and difference. Section 3 considers what political economy modes of analysis can contribute to the growing literature on the BRI. Section 4 illustrates how a particular form of BRI thinking—that which is both Sino-Centric and Sino-Deflecting —has been embedded in select core documents and statements. Section 5 serves as a conclusion.

Rendering World Order Intelligible through a Chinese Prism: The Belt and Road Initiative as Chinese State Project

Some words on how world order has been imagined and knowledge on it in twenty-first century China has been produced is warranted prior to considering how various scholars have approached analyzing the BRI and demonstrating how a syncretic vision of the BRI has been embedded in Chinese state documents and Chinese officials' statements about the BRI. To this end, in an attempt to provide the Chinese state with the conceptual apparatus through which the nature of Chinese world order may be communicated and comprehended, a range of 'world order concepts' have been produced in China by Chinese academics.

This undertaking follows from the author's previous scholarship[3] on how state-sanctioned ideational apparatuses within the post-(US)hegemonic global political economy. It follows from Robert Cox's methodology[4] for understanding changing world order structures over time according to the material capabilities undergirding them, the ideas by which hegemonic and counter-hegemonic world order visions are articulated, and the institutional matrixes that routinize, cement, or challenge such visions. Hence, hegemonic here is used in the broadly accepted manner found within 'Coxian' approaches to international political economy, implying degrees of both coercion and consent in establishing leadership over wider apparatuses of power and economy.[5]

State structures and officials selectively mine national histories and foster *intersubjective understandings*, or ideas that render the social and political worlds intelligible to particular groups—so as to articulate contemporary institutional and economic projects in the context of world order.

In order to cultivate consent amongst those parties from which legitimacy is sought, those aspiring to greater degrees of economic and political leadership must both offer material incentives, and, as is the subject of this article, develop a lexicon that conveys mutual gain for, and is rendered intelligible by, a wider array of social, economic and political forces. Considering the BRI as a world order project necessitates accounting for its economic, geographical and institutional dimensions, as well as how it is formulated as that in which the fates of multiple peoples, nations, and civilisations are cast as intertwined under the auspices of Chinese leadership.

Importantly, the BRI serves as the project through which Chinese state organs and personalities 'embed' common-sense understandings of a post-American global political economy,[6] vacillating between the technical requirements for contemporary economic 'connectivity' and the *universal* shared history of the Silk Road as a project for human betterment. Such understandings circumscribe the ideational field within which the BRI is to be imagined, eschewing aspects of a purely Sino-centric discourse for the purpose of a *global* project under the stewardship of Chinese state and society but neither reducible to it, nor for its benefit alone.

---

[3]Ray Silvius, 'The Russian state, Eurasianism, and civilisations in the contemporary global political economy', *Journal of Global Faultlines* 2(1), (2014), 44–69; Ray Silvius, 'Eurasianism and Putin's Embedded Civilizationalism', in *The Eurasian Project and Europe*, ed. David Lane and Vsevolod Samokhvalov (London: Palgrave Macmillan, 2015), pp. 75–88; Ray Silvius, 'Understanding Eurasian integration and contestation in the post-Soviet conjuncture: Lessons from geopolitical economy and critical historicism', *Research in Political Economy* 30, (2015), pp. 235–258; Silvius, *Culture, Political Economy, and Civilisation*.

[4]Robert W. Cox, 'Social forces, states and world orders: beyond international relations theory', *Millennium* 10(2), (1981), pp. 126–155; Robert W. Cox, *Production, Power, and World Order: Social Forces in the Making of History* (New York: Columbia University Press, 1987); Robert W. Cox and Timothy J. Sinclair, *Approaches to World Order* (Cambridge: Cambridge University Press, 1996).

[5]However, the author acknowledges that the term is fiercely debated within literature on Chinese foreign policy, including the extent to which China can and does have hegemonic aspirations.

[6]See *inter alia* Silvius, *Culture, Political Economy, and Civilisation*; and Silvius, 'Eurasianism and Putin's Embedded Civilizationalism.'

Sino-centering discourse holds that China possesses unique qualities making it fit for leadership under the auspices of the BRI. The first is China being positioned as an historical steward of 'positive sum' economic relations across non-Chinese space by incorporating disparate peoples into the orbit of Chinese civilization, but without compromising the integrity of other civilizations. The second is that it possesses competencies to integrate local, national, and regional economies according to financial and technical criteria associated with contemporary economic management. The third is that it possesses the political will to participate in, if not assume the cost of maintaining, multilateral fora for the purposes of maintaining the integrity of the BRI. The fourth is that it expresses current developments as a logical extension of Chinese history.

The state-sanctioned conceptual apparatus associated with the BRI is also *Sino-deflecting* in two important ways. First, the BRI and its historical antecedents are articulated as being not solely reducible to Chinese interests, nor a creation of China alone. Rather, it is a multi-civilizational endeavor. Second, it offers a world history that is replete with a co-prosperity that is not reducible to Chinese agency, albeit it is one with China assuming a significant role. A crucial aspect of the Sino-deflecting approach is to illustrate that a multi-party and multilateral institutional order sustains the BRI.

A state project, as articulated by Jessop, is a process-based account of the state that acknowledges state disunity and fragmentation and the corresponding drive to impose a functional unity upon state organs and society as a whole. In Jessop's formulation, the state imparts a degree of cohesion over social forces, including capital, which are incapable of exceeding their own direct interest to articulate a hegemonic project for society as a whole. State projects are animated by state-produced ideas: discursive practices couple with institutional practices that mold identities and subjectivities comprising the state system itself. The material components of these projects do not 'speak for themselves.' They are instead constantly interpreted and represented through conceptual apparatuses that are at least in part cultivated by state organs.[7]

One way of thinking about this for present purposes is how the BRI, through state organs and officials, has been cast as a world order structure that embodies cooperative values, 'positive sum gains', and multilateral fora rather than that which is reducible to Chinese interests. The BRI may be a project that has its material origins within the contours of the Chinese domestic political economy; however, in order to be rendered intelligible and relatable to a wider audience, a vocabulary and conceptual apparatus that appeals to a wider array of economic and social actors are required.

The BRI is the latest in a series of endeavors by the Chinese state to articulate China's place within world order structures. The following is a brief examination of this phenomenon.[8] Chinese foreign policy in the latter quarter of the twentieth century was characterized in part by a focus on multipolarity.[9] Womack suggests that multipolarity has been an explicit component of Chinese foreign policy analysis since 1986 but that it was implicit in a series of analogue concepts beginning in the early stages of the PRC from the 'Five Principles of Peaceful co-existence' (1953), through a 'non-aligned security stance' from 1982 to 1991 until the 1990s, during which time multipolarity became aspirational for Chinese foreign policymakers as a means to carve out space for Chinese influence amid American unipolarity.[10] According to Scott, multipolarity (*duojihua*) was part of a bundle of concepts featuring prominently in the PRC's public diplomacy in the first decade of the 2000s, appearing alongside 'democratization of international relations' (*guoji guanxi mingzhuhua*), 'peaceful rise' (*heping jueqi*), 'peaceful development' (*heping fazhan*) and 'harmonious world' (*hexie*

---

[7]Bob Jessop, and Stijn Oosterlynck, 'Cultural political economy: on making the cultural turn without falling into soft economic sociology', *Geoforum* 39(3), (2008), pp. 1155–1169; Bob Jessop, *State Theory: Putting the Capitalist State in its Place* (University Park: Penn State Press, 1990).

[8]This paragraph is derived from Ray Silvius, 'Chinese–Russian economic relations: developing the infrastructure of a multipolar global political economy?' *International Politics* 56(5), (2019), pp. 622–638.

[9]Kurt Radtke, 'China, Japan and multipolarity', *The China Quarterly* 80, (1979), pp. 846–856.

[10]Brantly Womack, 'Asymmetry theory and China's concept of multipolarity', *Journal of Contemporary China* 13(39), (2004), pp. 351–366; see also Wu Baiyi, 'The Chinese security concept and its historical evolution', *Journal of Contemporary China* 10(27), (2001), pp. 275–283.

shijie).[11] As such, it functioned in state-sanctioned representations of Chinese intentions in the global system and appeared in English language outlets as a means to signal Chinese intentions of working within, rather than upending or replacing, the existing institutional architecture at the level of world order.

As China developed rapidly during the end of the 1990s and the first decade of the 2000s, so too did interest in the contours of a *possible* Sino-centric world order. Early contributions to, or engagements with, a nascent school of Chinese International Relations (IR) scholarship could be read as offering a cultural, 'epistemological' and historical defense against the intellectual and practical hegemony of non-Chinese thinking. Attempts to explain previous Sino-centric world orders as constituted by endogenous Chinese practices of statecraft, culture, and diplomacy precede this period, but became more common during it.[12] Additional scholarship has contributed conceptual and epistemological fodder, including studies on China's historical *tianxia* ('all under heaven') and the possibilities of *tianxia* as the basis for a *contemporary* Sino-centric world order structure[13], and examinations of China's tributary system as an ordering principle for global relations that contrasts to modern European-Western practices of colonization, capitalism, and inter-state competition.[14] These endeavors would crystalize in the early 2000s as what may be referred to as International Relations Theory with Chinese Characteristics, borrowing from Deng Xiaoping's speech at the 14th Party Congress of the Communist Party of China, during which he proclaimed the veracity of 'socialism with Chinese characteristics'.[15]

Whether Chinese IR scholarship adheres more closely towards state objectives than does 'Western' IR scholarship certainly warrants discussion. Presently, it is sufficient to consider the extent to which such thinking has served as a form of intellectual production that has, to some degree, co-evolved with efforts by the Chinese state to articulate both its place within an existing world order and the possibilities of an emerging Sino-Centric world order.

Chinese IR theory sits under a broad umbrella and is now well established as an academic endeavour. The construction of the BRI, however, signifies the activation of Chinese world order concepts in real time for the purpose of public consumption. With the BRI comes a new stage of the application of Chinese state-sanctioned thinking about world order as an act of public diplomacy. In

---

[11]David Scott, 'China and the "responsibilities" of a "responsible" power—the uncertainties of appropriate power rise language', *Asia-Pacific Review* 17(1), (2010), pp. 72–96.

[12]See, *inter alia*, John Fairbank, *The Chinese World Order: Traditional China's Foreign Relations* (Cambridge: Harvard University Press, 1968); Florian Schneider, 'Reconceptualising world order: Chinese political thought and its challenge to International Relations theory', *Review of International Studies* 40(4), (2014), pp. 683–703; Yongjin Zhang, 'System, empire and state in Chinese international relations', *Review of International Studies* 27(5), (2001), pp. 43–63.

[13]June Teufel Dreyer, 'The 'Tianxia Trope': will China change the international system?", *Journal of Contemporary China* 24(96), (2015), pp. 1015–1031; Tingyang Zhao, 'Rethinking empire from a Chinese concept "All-under-Heaven"(Tian-xia,)', *Social Identities* 12(1), (2006), pp. 29–41.

[14]Hsiao-Ting Lin, 'The tributary system in China's historical imagination: China and Hunza, ca. 1760–1960   ', *Journal of the Royal Asiatic Society* 19(4), (2009), pp. 489–507; Su-Yan Pan and Joe Tin-Yau Lo, 'Re-conceptualizing China's rise as a global power: a neo-tributary perspective', *The Pacific Review* 30(1), (2017), pp. 1–25; Yongjin Zhang and Barry Buzan 'The tributary system as international society in theory and practice', *The Chinese Journal of International Politics* 5(1), (2012), pp. 3–36; Giovanni Arrighi, 'Reading Hobbes in Beijing. Great power politics and the challenge of the peaceful ascent,' in Mark Blyth (ed.), *Routledge Handbook of International Political Economy: IPE as a Global Conversation.* (New York: Routledge, 2009), pp. 163–179.

[15]Qingxin K. Wang and Mark Blyth, 'Constructivism and the study of international political economy in China', *Review of International Political Economy*, 20(6), (2013), pp. 1–24.

William A. Callahan, 'China and the globalisation of IR Theory: discussion of building International Relations Theory with Chinese characteristics", (2001), pp. 75–88; Gregory Chin, Margaret M. Pearson, and Wang Yong, 'Introduction–IPE with China's characteristics', *Review of International Political Economy* 20(6), (2013), pp. 1145–1164; Gustaaf Geeraerts and Men Jing, 'International relations theory in China', *Global Society*, 15(3), (2001), pp. 251–276; Nele Noesselt, 'Revisiting the debate on constructing a theory of international relations with Chinese characteristics', *The China Quarterly* 222, (2015), pp. 430–448; Lu Peng, 'Chinese IR Sino-centrism tradition and its influence on the Chinese School Movement', *The Pacific Review* 32(2), (2019), pp. 150–167; Yaqing Qin, 'Development of international relations theory in China: Progress through debates', *International Relations of the Asia-Pacific* 11(2), (2011), pp. 231–257; Hung-Jen Wang, 'Being uniquely universal: building Chinese international relations theory', *Journal of Contemporary China* 22(81), (2013), pp. 518–534; Hung-Jen Wang, *The Rise of China and Chinese International Relations Scholarship* (Lanham: Lexington Books, 2013); Qingxin K. Wang and Mark Blyth, 'Constructivism and the study of international political economy in China', *Review of International Political Economy* 20(6), (2013), pp. 1276–1299.

short, attempts to better understand historically constituted Chinese world order(s) and the rehabilitated role of Chinese political philosophy constitute part of the puzzle to understand *contemporary* aspirations towards a Sino-centric world order. The other is the demonstration of governance, managerial, political, and technocratic competence for twenty-first century economic management as the 'Chinese economy' is well beyond a strictly 'national' affair. The BRI as an actually existing undertaking, replete with its own ideational dimensions, is a logical place to consider the 'material' and 'ideational' components of China's foremost contemporary state project with aims at world order significance.

Parameters of BRI and Existing BRI Scholarship

Following from Jessop's idea of state projects and Cox's world order methodology, the conceptual apparatus embedded within state articulations of the BRI can be understood in the context of hegemonic strategy—whereby leading power blocs cultivate buy-in and consent from multiple parties for a larger initiative.[16] This hegemonic strategy is part of a larger state project meant to facilitate the extension of Chinese economic practices beyond Chinese borders, and critical International Political Economy (IPE) scholarship is particularly well suited to explore this phenomenon.

The intention of this section is to consider what analytical value a critical IPE approach—sensitive to the material and ideational components of the BRI as a Chinese state project cast at the level of world order—can add to the increasingly crowded field of studies on the BRI. One prominent tendency within foreign policy-oriented BRI studies is to consider the BRI as a reorientation of Chinese foreign policy towards a more activist position in its immediate region and beyond. Chinese foreign policy was characterized by the practice of *taoguangyanghui* ('keeping a low profile') beginning with Deng Xiaoping in 1990–1991 until Xi Jinping formally presented the strategy of *fenfayouwei* ('striving for achievement') during a speech at the Chinese Communist Party's foreign affairs conference in October 2013, with the BRI comprising a more active initiative in line with the latter.[17] The BRI has been considered as a key component of China's grand strategy in Eurasia, portending a shift from China positioning itself as a 'rule-taker' to a 'rule-maker' via regional institutions.[18]

Nonetheless, as it is more concerned with the BRI as an outgrowth of Chinese economic practices, this article is less concerned with BRI scholarship that views the BRI predominantly through a foreign policy prism and the way in which the BRI reflects strategic executive-level decision-making within the Chinese state.[19] Instead, it is intended to consider the economic 'roots' of the BRI and the relationship between the Chinese economy and the nascent Sino-centric multilateral order. The suggestion here is that the former is analytically prior to the latter, whereby the emerging institutional order is designed to govern an increasingly, complex, networked, economic structure that exceeds the boundaries of China.

Scholars have emphasized that the BRI serves to realize numerous *domestic* Chinese economic objectives. For example, it is the latest iteration of the Chinese state's concern to address the economic imbalances between its interior and coastal regions. This concern was manifested in the 'Develop the West' framework, which was developed by the Chinese government in the early

---

[16]See Footnote 5, above.
[17]Yan Xuetong, 'From keeping a low profile to striving for achievement', *The Chinese Journal of International Politics* 7(2), (2014), pp. 153–184.
[18]Weifeng Zhou and Mario Esteban, 'Beyond balancing: China's approach towards the Belt and Road Initiative', *Journal of Contemporary China* 27(112), (2018), pp. 487–501.
[19]Mark Beeson, 'Geoeconomics with Chinese characteristics: the BRI and China's evolving grand strategy', *Economic and Political Studies* 6(3), (2018), pp. 240–256; Michael Clarke, 'The Belt and Road Initiative: China's new grand strategy?', *Asia Policy* 24(1), (2017), pp. 71–79; Theresa Fallon, 'The new Silk Road: Xi Jinping's grand strategy for Eurasia', *American Foreign Policy Interests* 37(3), (2015), pp. 140–147; Nadège Rolland, 'China's "Belt and Road Initiative": underwhelming or game-changer?', *The Washington Quarterly* 40(1), (2017), pp. 127–142.

2000s.[20] Moreover, the BRI is a realization of the strategy of 'going out' (*zuo chuqu*) exhibited by Chinese companies, 'the dominant feature of which is outward foreign direct investment, although the concept also covers the export of labour and economic cooperation programs'.[21]

The BRI has attracted a range of scholarship attentive to its scalar dimensions and attendant logics for state and capital, part of which draws our attention to emerging (geo)politics and political economy of connectivity,[22] or towards the broader *global* structures of capital accumulation.[23] Such analyses consider Chinese orientations towards capital accumulation through the BRI and challenge state-centric analysis and related assumptions of inter-state relations. Summers, for example, suggests that 'the Silk Roads vision, with origins in provincial development plans, is a state-led spatial fix [a term elaborated upon below] to provide infrastructure to facilitate the development of networks of capital across the Eurasian continent'.[24]

Flint and Zhu suggest that network capitalism is the structuring logic of BRI undertakings; the latter therefore reproduce contemporary dominant practices of global network capitalism, yielding a hybrid of 1) conventional (Weberian) territoriality, whereby securing national spaces remains the prerogative of nation-states; and 2) 'messy' forms of territoriality, whereby networks obtain at local, regional, national, and even continental levels. Nonetheless, for the authors, such 'hybridity' and messiness do not negate the role of the Chinese state in facilitating a transition towards a Sino-centric world order, in which this networked capitalism and its demands for inter-national and regional cooperation mixes with various 'geopolitical codes,' which are the expression of Chinese national objectives and strategies.[25] One aspect of the geopolitical role embodied by the Chinese state is creating the political conditions through which territory is accessed for the purposes of economic expansion.

Developing the work of Giovanni Arrighi, Zhang considers the Maritime Silk Road Initiative (MSRI) within the context of World-Systems Theory, contending that China's semi-peripheral status enabled rapid economic growth over the latter quarter of the twentieth century and into the 21st; however, this expansion led to over accumulation, overproduction, labor shortages/increased cost of labor, and decreasing return to capital within the Chinese economy. Zhang argues that such stagnation in the Chinese economy was noticeable to Chinese policymakers as early as the late 1990s, and it is this realization that begat the impetus for Chinese firms to focus on 'going out', exploring the possibilities for expansion into foreign markets. Contrary to popular portrayal, Zhang argues, the Chinese state followed the lead of Chinese firms, setting 'going out' as official policy in 2000. The National Commission on Development and Reform, the Chinese state's main economic planning body, cited overproduction as a concern in the Chinese economy first in 2003 and then in subsequent years thereafter.[26] Moreover, the period witnessed the end of the material expansion of the Chinese economy domestically, leading to increasing forms of financialization, which suggests the transition to a period in which financial capital will play a more dominant role in the Chinese economy. Zhang suggests that such realizations culminated in the BRI and associated efforts by multiple Chinese state organs to overcome the mounting structural challenges within the Chinese national economy.

---

[20]Tim Summers, 'China's "New silk roads": sub-national regions and networks of global political economy', *Third World Quarterly* 37(9), (2016), pp. 1628–1643; Yue Man Yeung, *Developing China's West: A Critical Path to Balanced National Development* (Hong Kong: Chinese University Press, 2004).

[21]Summers, 'China's "New silk roads"'; See also: Jean-Pierre Cabestan, 'Beijing's "Going Out" strategy and Belt and Road Initiative in the Sahel: the case of China's growing presence in Niger', *Journal of Contemporary China* 28(118), (2019), pp. 592–613.

[22]Jean-Marc F. Blanchard and Colin Flint, 'The geopolitics of China's Maritime Silk Road Initiative', *Geopolitics* 22(2), (2017), pp. 223–245.

[23]Li Xing, 'China's pursuit of the "One Belt One Road" Initiative: a new world order with Chinese Characteristics?', In *Mapping China's 'One Belt One Road' Initiative*, ed. Li Xing (Cham: Palgrave Macmillan, 2019), pp. 1–27; Li Xing, 'Understanding the multiple Facets of China's "One Belt One Road" Initiative', In *Mapping China's 'One Belt One Road' Initiative*, ed. Li Xing (Cham: Palgrave Macmillan, 2019), pp. 29–56; Justin Van der Merwe, 'The One Belt One Road Initiative: Reintegrating Africa and the Middle East into China's system of accumulation', In *Mapping China's 'One Belt One Road' Initiative*, ed. Li Xing (Cham: Palgrave Macmillan, 2019), pp. 197–217.

[24]Summers, 'China's "New silk roads"', pp. 1637–1638.

[25]Colin Flint and Cuiping Zhu, 'The geopolitics of connectivity, cooperation, and hegemonic competition: The Belt and Road Initiative', *Geoforum* 99, (2019) 95–101. pp. 3–5.

[26]Xin Zhang, 'Chinese capitalism and the maritime Silk Road: A world-systems perspective', *Geopolitics*, 22(2), (2017), pp. 310–331.

Summers considers the BRI as the culmination of sub-national practices and policies concentrating on the development of economic networks before being elevated to the level of national policy.[27] Leveraging the thinking of Manuel Castells, Summers envisions that the BRI, therefore, represents a shift from a concern with 'surfaces', which suggest the control, management and development of national and regional spaces under singular authorities, to networks of connected nodes.[28]

Such networked flows of goods and capital are not immune from state-led efforts to secure and discipline space. Influenced by the now classical formulation of David Harvey, scholars have emphasized the role of the Chinese state in initiating a 'spatial fix' to secure the conditions for capital accumulation for Chinese economic actors in space outside of China itself.[29] Zhang applies Arrighi's twin analytic of a 'capitalist logic' of power (M-T-M'), whereby territory (T) is the means through which material expansion (M-M') is facilitated, and a 'territorial logic' of power (T-M-T'), whereby money (M) serves as the medium to acquire/assert control over further territory (T-T').[30]

The BRI can be thought of as a further expression of a spatial fix, as the Chinese state facilitates a form of territorial expansion (although not necessarily overt control) for the purposes of improving the conditions of accumulation for Chinese capital. Despite the varie-gated scales at which BRI-related projects operate, the Chinese state assumes an organizing role, albeit increasingly through an institutional architecture that involves numerous non-Chinese actors. For a successful state project, such 'material' considerations must be met with corresponding 'ideational' content that asserts the centrality and *legitimacy* of China in the BRI whilst articulating a vision of world order that cultivates consent and buy-in from non-Chinese actors.

The foregoing is useful to approach debates on whether BRI-affiliated governance and institutional mechanisms are reducible to Chinese interests or serve a more broadly multilateral function. Discussions that center on the extent to which China is developing a parallel institu-tional order to challenge Bretton Woods institutions are part of a wider literature which focuses on China's role within global governance mechanisms.[31] This scholarship warrants a longer treatment; however, key themes include China's willingness to socialize, internalize, and per-form in accordance with pre-existing (liberal) institutions[32]; China's ability to benefit from, and hence uphold, liberal institutions,[33] or to achieve regional predominance through adhering to existing norms and collective governance frameworks[34]; and China's propensity to develop parallel (to Bretton Woods) institutions so that its global political power and status is com-mensurate with its economic development.[35]

The BRI has been understood as emerging through this parallel institutional apparatus,[36] including a focus on how BRI-related institutions may achieve such ends in an emerging

---

[27]Summers, 'China's "New Silk Roads"', pp. 1628–1643.

[28]Ibid., pp. 1636.

[29]Blanchard and Flint, 'The geopolitics of China's Maritime Silk Road Initiative', pp. 223–245.

[30]Zhang, 'Chinese capitalism and the maritime Silk Road', pp. 312–313.

[31]Gerald Chan, Pak K. Lee, and Lai-Ha Chan, *China Engages Global Governance: A New World Order in the Making?* (Routledge, 2011).

[32]Gregory Chin and Ramesh Thakur, 'Will China change the rules of global order?', *The Washington Quarterly* 33(4), (2010), pp. 119–138; G. John Ikenberry, Zhu Feng, and Wang Jisi, eds, *America, China, and the Struggle for World Order: Ideas, Traditions, Historical Legacies, and Global Visions* (New York City: Springer, 2015); Yongjin Zhang, 'China and liberal hierarchies in global international society: power and negotiation for normative change', *International Affairs* 92(4), (2016), pp. 795–816.

[33]G. John Ikenberry, 'The rise of China and the future of the West—Can the liberal system survive?', *Foreign Affairs*. 87(1), (2008), pp. 23–37.

[34]Shaun Breslin, 'Understanding China's regional rise: interpretations, identities and implications', *International Affairs* 85(4), (2009), pp. 817–835.

[35]James F. Paradise, 'The role of "parallel institutions" in China's growing participation in global economic governance', *Journal of Chinese Political Science* 21(2), (2016), pp. 149–175.

[36]Mark Beeson, and Fujian Li, 'China's place in regional and global governance: a new world comes into view', *Global Policy* 7(4), (2016), pp. 491–499; Xiao Ren, 'China as an institution-builder: the case of the AIIB', *The Pacific Review* 29(3), (2016), pp. 435–442; Hai Yang, 'The Asian Infrastructure Investment Bank and status-seeking: China's foray into global economic governance', *Chinese Political Science Review* 1(4), (2016), pp. 754–778.

Chinese centered 'multilayered multi-lateral'[37] or 'minilateral' order.[38] Nonetheless, scholars have offered varied assessments of whether the main institutional facilitators of the BRI—the Asian Infrastructure Investment Bank (AIIB), the New Development Bank (NDB), the Shanghai Cooperation Organization (SCO), and the Silk Road Fund (SRF)—are reducible to Chinese interests. Scholars are divided as to whether or not BRI-related institutions primarily augment Chinese national power[39] or serve robust, multilateral functions whereby the public goods and associated products are not reducible solely to the interests of China nor directed by Chinese leadership.[40]

While this article remains agnostic as to a Sino-centric institutional order's ability to deliver 'positive sum' results and public goods for the benefit of non-Chinese actors, it suggests that the 'syncretic' nature of ideational content found in 'state-sanctioned' discourse on the BRI functions to imprint a degree of ideational coherence on the project for the purposes of *external* consumption— that is, by non-Chinese actors. In the process, representations of the BRI cohere to state strategy, offering a picture of an emerging world order under Chinese stewardship that is constituted both by Sino-centric and Sino-deflecting elements.

Embedding the BRI in Chinese State-Sanctioned Discourse

A brief sketch of the undertaking is warranted before considering more elaborate state expressions of the BRI. Preliminary thinking about a new 'Silk Road' initiative began during the tenure of President Hu Jintao. In 2013, Xi Jinping announced plans for two separate but integrated projects: a Silk Road Economic Belt (SREB)—which would link China with Mongolia, Central Asia, Russia, Iran, Turkey, Balkan countries, and Balkans, Central and Eastern Europe, Germany and Netherlands—and a Maritime Silk Road Initiative (MSRI)—which would link South East China South East Asia, Bangladesh, India, the Persian Gulf region, the Mediterranean region, and also up in Germany and Netherlands. Since the 2013 announcement by Xi, the two discrete projects have come to be articulated as one integrated undertaking, 'One Belt One Road' (OBOR) or the 'Belt and Road Initiative' (BRI).[41]

Meanwhile, the initiative has exceeded the initial focus on infrastructure development to become a comprehensive endeavor that incorporates infrastructure financing and development, Chinese economic objectives, geopolitical and 'grand strategy' connotations, and a variety of 'soft power' and public diplomacy components. Initially, the mega-projects were supported by the AIIB and China Development Bank (CDB) and transport and infrastructure focused.[42] First proposed in 2013, the AIIB was launched in October 2014 and has served the BRI as a complementary endeavor from the onset.[43] In 2015, in addition to contributing significantly to the 100 USD Billion initial capitalization of the AIIB, China also created the 40 USD Billion Silk Road Infrastructure Fund and contributed 20 USD

[37]Feng Yuan, 'The One Belt One Road Initiative and China's multilayered Multilateralism', In *Mapping China's 'One Belt One Road' Initiative*, ed. Li Xing (Cham: Palgrave Macmillan, 2019), pp. 91–116.

[38]Xing, 'China's Pursuit of the "One Belt One Road" Initiative'.

[39]Flint and Zhu. 'The geopolitics of connectivity, cooperation, and hegemonic competition,' 95–101; Hong Yu, 'Motivation behind China's "One Belt, One Road" initiatives and establishment of the Asian Infrastructure Investment Bank', *Journal of Contemporary China* 26(105), (2017), pp. 353–368; Zhongzhou Peng and Sow Keat Tok, 'The AIIB and China's normative power in international financial governance structure', *Chinese Political Science Review* 1(4), (2016), pp. 736–753.

[40]Mike Callaghan and Paul Hubbard, 'The Asian Infrastructure Investment Bank: Multilateralism on the Silk Road', *China Economic Journal* 9(2), (2016), pp. 116–139; Bin Gu, 'Chinese multilateralism in the AIIB', *Journal of International Economic Law* 20(1), (2017), pp. 137–158; Shahar Hameiri and Lee Jones, 'China challenges global governance? Chinese international development finance and the AIIB', *International Affairs* 94(3), (2018), pp. 573–593.

[41]Summers, 'China's "New silk roads"', pp.1628–1643.

[42]Peter Ferdinand, 'Westward ho—the China dream and "one belt, one road": Chinese foreign policy under Xi Jinping', *International Affairs* 92(4), (2016), pp. 941–957.

[43]Kevin G. Cai, 'The One Belt One Road and the Asian Infrastructure Investment Bank: Beijing's new strategy of geoeconomics and geopolitics', *Journal of Contemporary China* 27(114), (2018), pp. 831–847.

Billion within the BRICS New Development Bank for the purposes of financing development initiatives outside of China.[44]

Accompanying the development of the BRI itself has been the production of a wealth of information about the initiative by the Chinese state. The state-sanctioned documents and statements offered at various levels of the Chinese state that appear in this section have been chosen for containing detailed elaborations of the parameters of the BRI and for being made available to English reading and speaking audiences. They reflect an intense period of state and academic knowledge production on the BRI (2013–2017). Indeed, the basic parameters of the BRI as a world order vision were established during this period. They combine the comprehensiveness of a bureaucratic mapping exercise, the attempt to demonstrate administrative competency, and the embedding of motifs, language and concepts by which to express the initiative, including those which render analogous the complex mega-project that is the BRI to historical constructions of the Silk Road. In this telling, while historical Silk Roads and the contemporary BRI may have been marshalled by Chinese dynastic authority and Xi's government, respectively, they exceed purely Chinese interests in favor of being to the mutual benefit of diverse peoples and civilizations. Previous iterations of the Silk Road(s) and today's BRI are imagined not as products of Chinese history alone, but rather, a *universal history with Chinese characteristics*.

The argument in this section is that public statements by Chinese officials and state-produced documents present a world order vision of the BRI in accordance with the twin logics of Sino-centering and Sino-deflecting. Publicly oriented documents compiled by the Chinese state and speeches offered by Chinese officials, including President Xi, position Chinese stewardship over the BRI according to two distinct temporal logics. First, they seek contemporary legitimacy from China's prior stewardship over Silk Road(s) that are cast as cooperative, if not cosmopolitan,[45] endeavors yielding benefits for participating peoples, nations, and civilizations. Second, they assert China's *contemporary* ability to facilitate public goods across affected regions via a complex mega-initiative with arguably more mundane (and 'de-politicized') tools of management and governance. A sprawling network of institutions and fora in which the Chinese state plays a pivotal role contributes to the latter.

Early articulations of the BRI by Chinese officials combine these historical and contemporary attributes, presenting past and present iterations of the Silk Road as simultaneously mythisized and routinized. A speech, delivered by President Xi, on 7 September 2013, at Nazarbayev University in Astana, Kazakhstan, titled 'Promote Friendship Between Our People and Work Together to Build a Bright Future,' is an early comprehensive outline of the project.[46] The speech is replete with practical markers of the contemporary belt and road's scope, some basic institutional foundations, and the shared infrastructural, economic and political objectives behind it. Importantly, Xi invokes the Chinese state's historical relations with Central Asian people to set the tone. As such, the statement is imbued with historical and 'civilizational' content. Xi stated:

> Over 2,100 years ago during China's Han Dynasty, a Chinese envoy Zhang Qian was sent to Central Asia twice with a mission of peace and friendship. His journeys opened the door to friendly contacts between China and Central Asian countries as well as the Silk Road linking east and west, Asia and Europe …

> Throughout the millennia, the people of various countries along the ancient Silk Road have jointly written a chapter of friendship that has been passed on to this very day. The more than 2,000-year history of exchanges demonstrates that on the basis of solidarity, mutual trust, equality, inclusiveness, mutual learning and win-win

---

[44]Xiao Ren, 'China as an institution-builder: the case of the AIIB', *The Pacific Review* 29(3), (2016), pp. 435–442.

[45]Recent scholarship places the concept of the Silk Road as born of European aspirations of territorial conquest, an 1877 invention of German geographer Baron Ferdinand von Richthofen (*die Seidenstrasse*), and an early part of a larger German colonial endeavor to map China so as to facilitate the German seizure of Qingdao in 1897. See Chin, Tamara, 'The invention of the Silk Road, 1877.' *Critical Inquiry* 40(1), (2013), pp. 194–219.

[46]'Promote Friendship Between Our People and Work Together to Build a Bright Future. Speech by H.E. Xi Jinping, President of the People's Republic of China at Nazarbayev University', *Ministry of Foreign Affairs of the People's Republic of China*, September 7, 2013, accessed February 8, 2019, https://www.fmprc.gov.cn/mfa_eng/wjdt_665385/zyjh_665391/t1078088.shtml.

cooperation, countries of different races, beliefs and cultural backgrounds are fully capable of sharing peace and development. This is the valuable inspiration we have drawn from the ancient Silk Road.

In October 2013, Xi visited Indonesia on a state visit, and delivered a BRI centered speech to the Indonesian Parliament prior to attending the 21st APEC Economic Leaders' Meeting. Once again, Xi invoked the common linkages between China and its neighbors under previous iterations of Chinese state and economy 'going out,' mixing the historical and civilizational content with the articulation of the desire for mutual economic gain under a common institutional framework (cooperation with ASEAN framework, the development of the AIIB). According to Xi, 'Southeast Asia has since ancient times been an important hub along the ancient Maritime Silk Road.' Moreover,

> As early as the Han Dynasty in China about 2,000 years ago, the people of the two countries opened the door to each other despite the sea between them. In the early 15th century, Zheng He, the famous Chinese navigator of the Ming Dynasty, made seven voyages to the Western Seas. He stopped over the Indonesian archipelago in each of his voyages and toured Java, Sumatra and Kalimantan. His visits left nice stories of friendly exchanges between the Chinese and Indonesian peoples, many of which are still widely told today.

and

> The sea is big because it admits all rivers. In the long course of human history, the people of China and ASEAN countries have created splendid and great civilizations renowned around the world. Ours is a diversified region. Various civilizations have assimilated and interacted with one another under the influence of different cultures, which affords and important cultural foundation for the people China ASEAN countries [sic] to learn from and complement one another.[47]

During a Press Conference for the Third Session of the Twelfth National People's Congress in March 2015, Foreign Minister Wang Yi responded to a question about the comparisons between the BRI and the Marshall Plan by invoking the former's historical antecedents. He stated:

> China's 'Belt and Road' initiative is both much older and much younger than the Marshall Plan. Comparing one to the other would be like comparing apples and oranges. The 'Belt and Road' initiative is older because it embodies the spirit of the ancient Silk Road, which has a history of more than 2,000 years and was used by the peoples of many countries for friendly exchange and commerce. We must renew that spirit and bring it up to date. The 'Belt and Road' initiative is younger because it is born in the era of globalization. It is a product of inclusive cooperation, not a tool of geopolitics, and must not be viewed with the outdated Cold War mentality.[48]

The development of the BRI also has widened the mandate of pre-existing institutions. For example, the SCO has increasingly developed an economic development function, of which the BRI is a central part. Support for the BRI is contained within the Development Strategy of the Shanghai Cooperation Organization Until 2025 (written in 2015), as well as the Ufa Declaration by the Heads of Member States of the Shanghai Cooperation Organization (July 2015). In addition to declaring SCO's main principles, the Tashkent Declaration of the Fifteenth Anniversary of the Shanghai Cooperation Organization, released in June 2016, reaffirms the member states' support for the BRI. Support for the BRI was reiterated in the Joint Communique of The Fifteenth Meeting of the SCO Heads of Government Council (November 2016) and in the Astana Declaration of the Heads of State of the Shanghai Cooperation Organization (June 2017).[49]

The content of such early statements by Chinese officials would be elaborated upon and systematized to a greater degree in subsequent statements and documents. This section will now consider first the Chinese state's most comprehensive BRI document—the 'Vision and Actions on Jointly Building Silk Road Economic Belt and 21st Century Maritime Silk Road.' The

---

[47]'Speech by Chinese President Xi Jinping to Indonesian Parliament', *ASEAN-China Centre*, October 3, 2013, accessed February 8, 2019, http://www.asean-china-center.org/english/2013-10/03/c_133062675.htm.
[48]'Foreign Minister Wang Yi Meets the Press', *Ministry of Foreign Affairs of the People's Republic of China*, March 8, 2015, accessed February 8, 2019, http://www.fmprc.gov.cn/mfa_eng/zxxx_662805/t1243662.shtml.
[49]All documents: http://eng.sectsco.org/documents/.

'vision and actions document'[50] was issued by three key government agencies: the National Development and Reform Commission, the Ministry of Foreign Affairs, and the Ministry of Commerce of the People's Republic of China in March 2015. The document also mobilizes a significant conceptual apparatus through which the 'ideational' components of the BRI are to assume 'world order significance.' It is warranted to review the manner in which it outlines the geographic scope and scale of the initiative, as well as its primary institutional basis.

The vision and actions document proceeds with an emphasis on the international geoeconomic, institutional, and 'ideational' vision contained therein. The document is an explicit attempt at fashioning a Sino-centric vision for world order which both highlights the leading role played by Chinese state and economy and articulates a role and space for mutual gain for non-Chinese actors. For example, the document claims that:

> Accelerating the building of the Belt and Road can help promote the economic prosperity of the countries along the Belt and Road and regional economic cooperation, strengthen exchanges and mutual learning between different civilizations, and promote world peace and development. It is a great undertaking that will benefit people around the world.

The BRI is cast as a collaborative endeavor: interests are not exclusively reducible to that of Chinese state, nation, and capital. Rather, they contain the details of a general vision for Eurasia and beyond, aimed to satisfy the interests of a diverse range of people. The document explicates the guiding principles of the BRI: it 'is in line with the purposes and principles of the UN [United Nations] Charter', including upholding the principles of peaceful coexistence; 'is open for cooperation'; including but not limited to the area of the ancient Silk Road; is 'harmonious and inclusive ... advocate[ing] tolerance among civilizations, [it] respects the paths and modes of development, chosen by different countries'; it 'follows market operation'; and it 'seeks mutual benefit.'

The document envisions the BRI being realized through a number of multilateral dialogue venues, including the SCO, the Association of South East Asian Nations (ASEAN) Plus China (10 + 1), the Asia-Pacific Economic Cooperation (APEC), the Asia–Europe Meeting (ASEM), Asia Cooperation Dialogue (ACD), the Conference on Interaction and Confidence-Building Measures in Asia (CICA), the China–Arab States Cooperation Forum (CASCF), the China-Gulf Cooperation Council Strategic Dialogue, the Greater Mekong Sub-region (GMS) Economic Cooperation, and the Central Asia Regional Economic Cooperation (CAREC). Moreover, the document envisions cultural production and public diplomacy as a significant element of the BRI, including the Silk Road (Dunhuang) International Culture Expo; the Silk Road International Film Festival; and the Silk Road International Book Fair.

The vision and actions document reveals the Chinese state's anticipated scale and scope of the BRI. More specifically, via the Silk Road Economic Belt, China will be linked with Central Asia, Russia and Europe; the Mediterranean Sea (via Central and West Asia); and South Asia/the Indian Ocean. The 21st-Century Maritime Silk Road will connect China's coast to Europe via two routes: 1) the South China Sea and the Indian Ocean; 2) the South China Sea and the South Pacific. The document articulates specific channels of connectivity: the Eurasian Land Bridge; the China-Mongolia-Russia Corridor; the China–Central Asia–West Asia Corridor; the China-Indochina Peninsula Economic Corridor; the China–Pakistan Economic Corridor; and the Bangladesh-China-India-Myanmar Economic Corridor.

The vision and actions document also outlines several cooperation priorities: policy coordination; facilities connectivity; unimpeded trade; financial integration and people-to-people bond. The document lists a number of mechanisms and multilateral institutions through which to achieve financial integration: the AIIB; the BRICS New Development Bank (BRICS-NDB); a (then yet to be

---

[50]All information from the 'Visions and actions document' derived from: 'Vision and actions on jointly building Silk Road Economic Belt and 21st Century Maritime Silk Road', National Reform and Development Commission, Ministry of Foreign Affairs, and Ministry of Commerce of the People's Republic of China, March 28, 2015, accessed January 29, 2019, http://en.ndrc.gov.cn/newsrelease/201503/t20150330_669367.html.

established) financing institution within the SCO; the Silk Road Fund (SRF); the China-ASEAN Interbank Association; and the SCO Interbank Association.

Moreover, the Chinese state has supported new fora through which the BRI is to be articulated and realized as a joint initiative on the part of numerous actors. The inaugural BRI Summit forum was held by the Chinese government in May 2017. Attended by 30 world leaders and with delegates from 68 countries/international organization signing agreements in support of the BRI, the Summit represented an intensification of efforts to by the Chinese government to promote the BRI globally. Importantly, the Summit represented an expansion of the 'soft' supports offered by China in the context of the BRI: RMB 60 Billion to BRI constituent countries for the purposes of food, housing, health care and poverty alleviation.[51]

Furthermore, the BRI is referred to as a civilizational undertaking.[52] In addition to serving as a guide to implementing the BRI, the document serves 'to promote the implementation of the Initiative, instill vigor and vitality into the ancient Silk Road, connect Asian, European and African countries more closely and promote mutually beneficial cooperation to a new high and in new forms.' Moreover,

> For thousands of years, **the Silk Road Spirit**—'peace and cooperation, openness and inclusiveness, mutual learning and mutual benefit'—has been passed from generation to generation, promoted the progress of human civilization, and contributed greatly to the prosperity and development of the countries along the Silk Road. Symbolizing communication and cooperation between the East and the West, the Silk Road Spirit is a historic and cultural heritage shared by all countries around the world.

President Xi's May 2017 speech at the Opening Ceremony of the Belt and Road Forum for International Cooperation[53] similarly elaborates the institutional, material, and ideational markers of the BRI. It provides economic markers of the BRI: 2014–2016 trade between China and BRI countries exceeded US$3 trillion, China's investment in the same countries exceeded US$50 billion, and in 20 constituent countries, Chinese companies created 56 economic cooperation zones, resulting in US$1.1 billion of tax revenue and 180,000 new jobs. Moreover, Xi claims that the AIIB has provided loans of US$1.7 billion for 9 projects in BRI countries, and the Silk Road Fund has facilitated investments worth US$4 billion. Furthermore, Xi signals increased financing for the BRI, including RMB 100 billion to the Silk Road Fund, lending projects via the China Development Bank (RMB 250 billion) and the Export-Import Bank of China (RMB 130 billion).

In the same speech, Xi pledges a number of 'soft' supports: China will provide RMB 60 billion in assistance to 'improve people's well-being' within the sphere of the BRI, including RMB 2 billion in emergency food aid, a US$1 billion contribution to the 'Assistance Fund for South-South Cooperation', and the launching of '100 "happy home" projects, 100 poverty alleviation projects and 100 health care and rehabilitation projects in countries along the Belt and Road.'

Xi's 2017 speech also highlights China's contemporary ability to facilitate public goods across affected regions via the BRI and more mundane tools of management and governance. In such a way does the speech frame the success of the BRI as a matter of technical competency: multiple forms of 'connectivity' (policy, trade, financial, 'people-to-people', land, maritime, air, cyberspace, 'hardware' [transport, infrastructure and energy']; and 'software' [telecommunications, customs, and quarantine]); 'innovation', financing, market integration, infrastructure development, industrial cooperation, 'common, comprehensive, cooperative and sustainable security', and a 'stable and sustainable financial safeguard system,' a 'multilateral trading regime', within which trade and investment are liberalized, ecological stewardship under a 'new vision of green development', amongst others. Such

---

[51]Zhai, 'China's Belt and Road Initiative', pp. 84–92.

[52]For an analysis of 'civilizational discourse' in the post-Cold War global political economy, see Silvius, *Culture, Political Economy, and Civilisation*.

[53]'Work together to build the Silk Road Economic Belt and the 21st Century Maritime Silk Road. Speech by H.E. Xi Jinping, President of the People's Republic of China at the opening ceremony of The Belt and Road Forum for International Cooperation', *Xinhuanet*, May 14, 2017, accessed February 8, 2019, http://www.xinhuanet.com//english/2017-05/14/c_136282982.htm.

goods are to be provided within a framework marked by additional normative dimensions: 'win-win cooperation', a respect for 'sovereignty, dignity, and territorial integrity, each other's development paths and social systems, and each other's core interests and major concerns.'

Moreover, according to Xi's speech, China has worked to provide policy complementarity and harmonization with a number of multilateral institutions and governance initiatives (the Eurasian Economic Union [notably 'of Russia'], the Master Plan on ASEAN Connectivity, Kazakhstan's Bright Road initiative, Turkey's Middle Corridor initiative, Mongolia's Development Road initiative, Vietnam's Two Corridors, One Economic Circle, the UK's Northern Powerhouse initiative, and Poland's Amber Road initiative); countries (Laos, Cambodia, Myanmar, Hungary and others); via cooperation agreements signed with over 40 (unnamed) countries and international organizations; and via 'framework cooperation on production capacity' (with over 30 unnamed countries). In the speech, Xi signals the intention to launch the Belt and Road cooperation initiative on trade connectivity together with 60 countries and international organizations.

Xi Jinping's 2017 keynote address to the Belt and Road International Forum,[54] also marks a crucial development of the 'civilizational' content of the BRI. It reiterates many of the principles and orientations of the 2015 vision and actions document; however, expressly for an international audience, Xi's speech contains a grand narrative of a multi-civilizational world order being integrated under the BRI. Xi states that

> Over 2,000 years ago, our ancestors, trekking across vast steppes and deserts, opened the transcontinental passage connecting Asia, Europe and Africa, known today as the Silk Road. Our ancestors, navigating rough seas, created sea routes linking the East with the West, namely, the maritime Silk Road. These ancient silk routes opened windows of friendly engagement among nations, adding a splendid chapter to the history of human progress.

In the speech, the 'Silk Road spirit', a 'great heritage of *human* civilization' (emphasis added), is characterized by four overarching values: 'peace and cooperation'; 'openness and inclusiveness'; 'mutual learning'; and 'mutual benefit'. The Silk Road (or, rather, multiple silk routes) blossomed in particular epochs, under particular Chinese dynasties (the Han, Tang, Song, Yuan and Ming are directly referenced), and by way of the efforts of particular figures (Han royal emissary Zhang Qian; Tang era explorer Du Huan; Ming navigator Zheng He; as well as Italy's Marco Polo and Morocco's Ibn Battuta). Ancient silk routes connected antiquity's great Eurasian and North African civilizations (the Egyptian, Babylonian, Indian and Chinese) and Buddhist, Christian and Muslim lands and gave rise to major Eurasian trading cities due to a spirit of openness and exchange. They facilitated flows of interaction, capital, technology, people, and knowledge across vast spaces for the betterment of multiple peoples and civilizations.

By attributing concepts and norms to China's historical stewardship of the Silk Road project—which include mutual prosperity, cooperation, Silk Road spirit, inter-civilizational concord—the vision and actions document and Xi's 2017 keynote address articulate a Chinese world order project in real time. That is to say, the Chinese state is framing the undertaking in a way that circumscribes the ideational field within which the BRI, and its attendant politics, are to be understood, as power relations amongst actors and structures comprising the BRI unfold along with the project itself.

While concrete articulations such as the vision and actions document and Xi's 2017 speech offer a specific geographical imagination associated with the BRI, their flexibility suggest a more open-ended initiative, unleashing a range of possibilities that are enabled through deploying the BRI as a cultural metaphor and series of narratives emanating from China.[55] To that end, the document may also be read as that in which Chinese government bodies activate a generic concept of the Silk Road as an historical achievement of a diversity of peoples, yet with China occupying a center role. In the process, the document 'embeds' the ideational content of a 'multi-civilizational' undertaking (the

[54]'Work together to build the Silk Road Economic Belt.'
[55]James D. Sidaway and Chih Yuan Woon, 'Chinese narratives on "One Belt, One Road" (一带一路) in geopolitical and imperial contexts', *The Professional Geographer* 69(4), (2017), pp. 591–603.

civilizational content of the initiative no fewer than seven times in the document) that is centered on, but not reducible to, China. It eschews a more narrow 'national' reading of Chinese history in favor of a universal history in which China is a central, facilitative presence.

Conclusion

The ideas associated with BRI do not exist in a historical vacuum. The complexity of the almost unfathomable BRI—characterized by twenty-first century logics of networked, infrastructural, financialized state capitalism 'with Chinese characteristics'—is rendered intelligible by the use of motifs and concepts associated with the historical Silk Road. Positive assessments of the historical Silk Road maintain that it was an entity that integrated Eurasian space due to its multi-civilizational, cooperative, and mutual gain characteristics. It is rehabilitated and reactivated under twenty-first century Sino-centric world order concepts—whereby the Chinese state is positioned as steward and guarantor of a larger order in which mutual gain is possible—albeit concepts that speak to a *universal* history with China at the center, as opposed to a Chinese history as a *national* Chinese endeavor.

In such a way, historical visions of the Silk Road are refurbished so as to render comprehensible an enormous undertaking that originates in the expansion of contemporary Chinese economic activity, but now is comprised of more complex relationships of capital to scale and territory. The BRI is extolled, and its antecedent concepts conceived, as projects of economic openness under Chinese stewardship but not reducible to Chinese interests. According to a state-sanctioned conceptual apparatus, the BRI offers a cooperative and inclusive form of globalized capitalism in which the Chinese state ensures the production of public goods across Eurasian space and beyond and acts as a responsible global steward, operating via multilateral fora for mutual benefit. The BRI, therefore, functions as a world order concept unfolding in real time, fashioned to speak to the historical achievements of the Chinese nation while being rendered intelligible for non-Chinese audiences.

Through documents and speeches about the BRI, Chinese state organs and officials are seeking to articulate and imprint a world order as the materiality and attendant politics of the components of the BRI are unfolding. As the abstract geopolitical dimensions of the BRI have received considerable scholarly attention, BRI scholarship may now benefit from reconstruction sof the initiative from the ground up, with greater attentiveness to the place-based politics of any given BRI-related project.[56] It is suggested here that BRI scholarship would benefit from scrutinizing the extent to which the BRI coheres as a singular initiative representative of an emerging Sino-centric world order, and examining the politics of cooperation and contestation in zones within which Chinese state and capital are seeking greater influence.

This would involve further analyzing the materiality of the BRI through the politics of production in specific BRI projects. To the extent that the political economy of BRI undertakings has reached the public consciousness in the West, it has been primarily in terms of 'debt-trap diplomacy.'[57] In other words, greater attention towards the BRI as a mechanism for twenty-first century global production through specific sites is warranted. It is precisely to this dialectic—the ideas and practices of BRI at the level of world order and in specific localities vs. the amalgam of productive forces responsible for realizing the BRI in its entirety and in specific projects—that future scholarship on the BRI might turn.

Acknowledgments

The author would like to thank Riley Black for providing exceptional research assistance, and the University of Winnipeg for providing research funding for this project. Furthermore, the author thanks fellow participants at the workshop' 'Global Politics of China's Belt & Road Initiative (BRI)', which was held at Carleton University in February 2019, for their

[56]James D. Sidaway, Simon C. Rowedder, Chih Yuan Woon, Weiqiang Lin, and Vatthana Pholsena, 'Politics and spaces of China's Belt and Road Initiative', Environment and Planning C- Politics and Space, 0(0), (2020), pp. 1–8.
[57]Karen P.Y. Lai, Shaun Lin, and James D. Sidaway, 'Financing the Belt and Road Initiative (BRI): research agendas beyond the "debt-trap" discourse', *Eurasian Geography and Economics* 61(2), (2020), pp. 109–124.

positive reception of an earlier draft of this article and the helpful feedback provided. Finally, the author thanks two anonymous reviewers for providing feedback and Editor Suisheng Zhao for providing guidance for this article.

Disclosure Statement

No potential conflict of interest was reported by the author.

Co-evolutionary Pragmatism: Re-examine 'China Model' and Its Impact on Developing Countries

Tang Xiaoyang

ABSTRACT

There is a gap between the elusive concept of Beijing Consensus and China's effective practices to promote economic growth at home and in other countries. This article aims to expound this phenomenon by examining both the rationale underlying China's structural transformation and the corresponding practices in development cooperation. Using a case study on the evolution of infrastructure construction within China and abroad, this article argues that China's success has little to do with a new pattern of state capitalism, but rather presents a different manner of understanding and facilitating modernization. Target-oriented non-linear synergism can drive comprehensive transformation more effectively in developing countries than model-oriented linear mechanism. With a consistent goal, the pragmatic thinking enables multiple stakeholders to coevolve in diverse contexts through open attitude.

Gap between Practical Effectiveness and Conceptual Elusiveness

During past decades, China's growing influence on developing countries has been as remarkable as its stellar economic rise. The trade volume between China and all the 154 developing economies increased from 50.1 USD billion in 1998 to 1402.2 USD billion in 2017, a 28-fold increase, whereas China's trade with the 39 advanced economies rose just 9.48 fold for the same period.[1] Likewise, the increase in China's outward foreign direct investment (FDI) stock to the developing economies and advanced economies were 87.5 times and 46.8 imes, respectively, between 2003 and 2017 (see Figure 1). Especially, China's 2017 trade volume with Africa was worth more than Africa's trade with the United States, Japan, France, and the United Kingdom combined.[2]

Corresponding to the economic ties, China has developed strong political linkage with the developing countries as well. By August 2019, 117 developing countries have signed agreements of cooperation under the framework of the Belt and Road Initiative (BRI), an ambitious effort by the Chinese government to improve cooperation and connectivity with other countries around the world, however, only 16 advanced economies have signed similar types of agreements.[4] In addition, China has established the association of BRICS together with other major developing economies, namely Brazil, Russia, India and South Africa. The Forum on China–Africa Cooperation (FOCAC) has attracted near-universal participation of African countries to work with China on a broad spectrum of issues since 2000.

---

[1]International Monetary Fund, 'Classification of Advanced Economies and Developing Economies', 2019, accessed January 4, 2020, https://www.imf.org/external/pubs/ft/weo/2019/01/weodata/weoselagr.aspx.

[2]United Nations, 'Commodity Trade Statistics Database', 2017, accessed October 28, 2019, https://comtrade.un.org/db/.

[4]Belt and Road Portal, 'List of countries that have signed cooperation documents with China for the Belt and Road Initiative', April 12, 2019, accessed January 7, 2020, https://www.yidaiyilu.gov.cn/xwzx/roll/77298.htm.

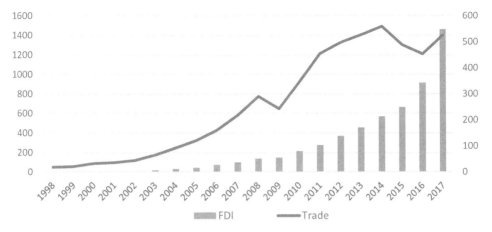

Figure 1. China's trade and investment with the developing economies (in $billion).[3]
[3]National Bureau of Statistics of China, 'Annual Data', 2017, accessed October 28, 2019, http://data.stats.gov.cn/.

Likewise, surveys of public opinions suggest that China has much more popularity in the developing countries than in the developed countries. In 2017, the British Broadcasting Corporation (BBC) conducted polling about China's influence and found that negative opinions on China came mainly from North America and Western Europe, whereas those having positive views were all developing countries.[5] Pew research center's survey confirmed the pattern. The opinions of Latin American, African, Middle Eastern and East European countries were overwhelmingly favorable about China.[6]

Moreover, China's soft power, based on its impressive achievement of poverty reduction, infrastructure improvement and technological advancement, have greatly eclipsed the Western influence in the developing countries.[7] For example, former President of the Philippines Gloria Macapagal–Arroyo praised that China offers an alternative development path to the Western model of Jeffersonian democracy and free market.[8] Rwandan President Paul Kagame argued that while neither European nor American aid delivers sustainable development, Chinese engagements 'bring-[s] greater opportunity for wealth creation in Africa'.[9]

However, researchers have diverging views on what the exact nature of China's model is. Joshua Ramo coined the term 'Beijing Consensus' in 2004.[10] Primarily, the name suggests a competing model vis-a-vis the Washington Consensus, which had been agreed upon by neoliberal-minded policymakers in the West. Interestingly, unlike the Washington Consensus, the 'Beijing Consensus' has never found a consensus among its proponents or its opponents. A dominating view describes the China Model as an authoritarian regime which can steer the economic development through strong state control and mobilization of immense socio-political resources.[11] This interpretation puts

[5]BBC World Service, 'Sharp Drop in World Views of US, UK: Global Poll', accessed January 7, 2020. https://globescan.com/images/images/pressreleases/bbc2017_country_ratings/BBC2017_Country_Ratings_Poll.pdf.
[6]Pew Research Center, 'People around the globe are divided in their opinions of China', December 5, 2019, accessed January 7, 2020, https://www.pewresearch.org/fact-tank/2019/09/30/people-around-the-globe-are-divided-in-their-opinions-of-china/.
[7]Ted Piccone, The Geopolitics of China's Rise in Latin America, Geoeconomics and Global Issues Paper 2, Brookings, November 2016, pp. 6–7, accessed January 7, 2020, https://www.brookings.edu/research/the-geopolitics-of-chinas-rise-in-latin-america/.
[8]'Arroyo hails China development as alternative to Western model', ABS-CBN News, March 31, 2019, accessed January 7, 2020, https://news.abs-cbn.com/business/03/31/19/arroyo-hails-china-development-as-alternative-to-western-model.
[9]Paul Kagame, 'Why Africa welcomes the Chinese', The Guardian, November 2, 2009, accessed January 7, 2020, http://www.theguardian.com/commentisfree/2009/nov/02/aid-trade-rwanda-china-west.
[10]Suisheng Zhao, 'Whither the China Model: revisiting the debate', Journal of Contemporary China (26)103, (2017), pp. 1–17; Minglu Chen and David S. G. Goodman, 'The China Model: one country, six authors', Journal of Contemporary China (21)73, (2012), pp. 169–185.
[11]潘维 [Pan Wei], '当代中华体制' ['Contemporary Chinese system'], in 中国模式: 解读人民共和国的60年 [The China Model: Reading 60 Years of the People's Republic of China] (Beijing: Zhongyang Bianyi Chuban She, 2009), pp. 1, 3–88; Giovanni Arrighi, Adam Smith in Beijing: Lineages of the Twenty-First Century (London: Verso, 2007).

China into the category of state capitalism or developmental state, which challenges the doctrines of democratic capitalism and free market.[12] Yet, a few authors reject such a notion. David Harvey views the China Model as inherently neoliberalist.[13] Similarly, Qin Xiao believes that China's success story is a result of the adoption, albeit incomplete, of certain principles with universal values, such as market economy, democratic polity and rule of law.[14] Scott Kennedy points out that the most competitive economic segment in China, the coastal private sector, actually grew out of a more liberal market system, with little governmental protection and interference. By contrast, sectors in which the Chinese government keeps strong control and provides heavy subsidies, like steel and telecom, remain uncompetitive.[15]

Another perspective to analyze the China Model lays emphasis on the meritocracy of selecting competent technocrats to run the government. Daniel Bell and Eric Li both argue that since Chinese officials are evaluated by their ability to promote economic growth, they can more effectively lead the country to achieve prosperity than those who are elected in Western democracies.[16] However, a growing number of scholars, including Nobel laureate Paul Krugman, criticize Chinese leaders for being incompetent and therefore unable to manage the economic downturn and financial turbulence of recent years.[17] Yuen Yuen Ang further points out that the same personnel system has quite departing outcomes in different regions throughout China's reform period.[18] Consequently, personnel management can hardly explain China's success story.

Another set of literature considers gradualist reform strategy as key to China's success. Instead of completely following the recipes of the Washington Consensus and implementing the shock therapy, Beijing used 'second-best' institutions, like dual-track pricing and hybrid property rights, to stimulate markets in the beginning and eventually forge a mature market with best practice.[19] Yet, this view implies that the gradualist reform is only a 'transitional' step towards the ultimate destination of liberal market institutions. Nonetheless, despite becoming the second-largest economy in the world, China is still fundamentally different from the West regarding its political-economic system. China's incremental adjustments over the past 40 years do not look like transitional measures towards the Washington Consensus.

Remarkably, the Chinese government has kept a consistent stance of non-generalization of China's development model. As early as 1985, Deng Xiaoping told then Ghanaian Head of State Jerry Rawlings, 'Please don't copy our model …. If there is any experience on our part, it is to formulate policies in light of one's own national conditions.'[20] When the debate about the Beijing Consensus heated up in the mid-2000s, Chinese leaders reiterated the position that China does not have a general development model and does not recommend other countries to follow any models.[21] Similarly, Xi Jinping stressed at several occasions that China's unique history and

[3]National Bureau of Statistics of China, 'Annual Data', 2017, accessed October 28, 2019, http://data.stats.gov.cn/.

[12]Ian Bremmer, *The End of the Free Market: Who Wins the War Between States and Corporations?* (London: Portfolio, 2011); David Brooks, New York Times Op-ed, 'The Larger Struggle', June 15, 2010, accessed January 7, 2020, http://www.nytimes.com/2010/06/15/opinion/15brooks.html?_r=0.

[13]David Harvey, *A Brief History of Neoliberalism* (New York: Oxford University Press, 2007), pp. 120–151.

[14]秦晓 [Qin Xiao], '中国道路也须秉承普世价值' ['China's path has to follow universal values'], 金融家 [*Financiers*], May 2, 2013, accessed March 6, 2016, http://www.iceo.com.cn/com2013/138/2013/0502/266616.shtml.

[15]Scott Kennedy, 'The Myth of the Beijing Consensus', *Journal of Contemporary China* (19)65, (2010), pp. 461–477.

[16]Daniel A. Bell, *The China Model: Political Meritocracy and the Limits of Democracy* (Princeton: Princeton University Press, 2015); Eric Li, 'The life of the party: the post-democratic future begins in China', *Foreign Affairs* 92(1), (2013), pp.34–46.

[17]Paul Krugman, 'China's naked emperors', *New York Times*, July 31, 2015, accessed January 17, 2019, http://www.nytimes.com/2015/07/31/opinion/paul-krugman-chinas-naked-emperors.html; Minxin Pei, 'Behind China's woes, myth of competent autocrats', *Nikkei Asian Review*, February 1, 2016, accessed January 15, 2019, http://asia.nikkei.com/Viewpoints/Viewpoints/Behind-China-s-woes-myth-of-competent-autocrats.

[18]Yuen Yuen Ang, *How China Escaped the Poverty Trap* (Ithaca: Cornell University Press, 2016), p 7.

[19]Dani Rodrik, 'Second-best institutions', *American Economic Review*, 98(2), (2008), pp. 100–104; Ling Chen and Barry Naughton, 'A Dynamic China Model: The Co-Evolution of Economics and Politics in China', *Journal of Contemporary China*, 26(103), (2017), pp. 18–34.

[20]中国网[China.com], '2005专题'[2005 Special coverage], September 18, 1985, accessed January 8, 2020, http://www.china.com.cn/zhuanti2005/txt/2004-08/04/content_5627003.htm.

conditions decide a development path only fitting for itself and each country should choose its own path accordingly.[22] The non-generalization makes it even more difficult to define the China Model. Since no universal principles are drawn from the development practices, China cannot provide any model to other countries like Washington Consensus, but only individual experiences.

Thus, there is a puzzling gap between the conceptual elusiveness and the factual effectiveness of the China Model. In spite of China's impressive achievement in both domestic reform and cooperation with the developing countries, why is it so difficult to identify the exact mechanism behind it? While the previous debate about China's experience alone is not sufficient to understand its general implications, a study of China's engagements with other developing countries and their impacts may shed light on the applicability of the China Model on other countries. This paper first aims to find why China can effectively work with other developing countries and how this collaboration influences the development process of these countries. The findings, when compared with China's own experience, are supposed to show the significance of the Chinese development approaches in a broader context. This article argues that the lack of a defined China Model actually reveals the key to China's achievements: development through co-evolutionary pragmatism. This development path distinguishes itself from the Washington Consensus by addressing the circular interactive causality (chicken-egg dilemma) during the socio-economic transformation instead of sticking solely to the linear mechanical causality. The difference between the Chinese approach and Washington Consensus is not caused by conflicting ideological principles, but by different understandings of the development dynamism.

The following section will start with a general analysis of China's tie with the developing countries. Succeeding that, the article will examine the role of pragmatism in China's domestic and international transformation. Following that section, the article will explain the circular interactive causality in the development process and why co-evolutionary pragmatism solves the dilemma. Lastly, the article will use infrastructure construction as a case study to illustrate how China applies the coevolutionary pragmatism in reality.

China's Engagements with Developing Countries

The interpretations of China's growing ties with developing countries are as diverging as the definitions of the China Model. A popular view in the West is that China exploits underdeveloped countries just for resource extraction. For instance, Denis Tull claims that 'there is little doubt that natural resources are at the core of China's economic interests in Africa.'[23] Likewise, Ian Taylor and Giovanni Ortolani argue that interests involving oil and other natural resources dominate China's relationships with other developing countries.[24] However, this view is not empirically supported. Until 2011, for instance, more African oil was exported to the United States than China. Moreover, following 2012, both China and the United States reduced their crude oil imports from Africa.[25] The total FDI stock of China in 63 'resource rich' developing countries 2017 was 105.5 USD billion, whereas that of China in 63 other comparable developing countries was 61.6 USD billion.[26] Although China obviously has interests in resource-related activities, it has significant engagements

[21]Forum on China-Africa Cooperation, 'Speech at the Opening Ceremony of the 4th Ministerial Conference of FOCAC', November 10, 2009, accessed January 18, 2019, https://www.focac.org/eng/zywx_1/zyjh/t627391.htm.

[22]新华网[Xinhuanet], '习近平在莫斯科国际关系学院的演讲' [Xi Jinping's Speech at the Moscow Institute of International Relations], March 24, 2013, accessed January 7, 2020, http://politics.people.com.cn/n/2013/0324/c1024-20892661.html; 新华社 [Xinhua News Agency], '习近平出席中国共产党与世界政党高层对话会开幕式并发表主旨讲话' [Xi Jinping Attends the Opening Ceremony of the High-level Dialogue between the Chinese Communist Party and World Political Parties and Delivers a Keynote Speech], December 1, 2017, accessed January 7, 2020, http://www.gov.cn/xinwen/2017-12/01/content_5243832.htm.

[23]Denis Tull, 'China's engagement in Africa: scope, significance and consequences', The Journal of Modern African Studies 44(3), (2006), pp. 459–479.

[24]Ian Taylor, 'China's oil diplomacy in Africa', International Affairs 82(5), (2006), pp.937–959. Giovanni Ortolani, 'China's Belt and Road poised to transform the Earth, but at what cost?', Mongabay, April 24, 2018, accessed January 8, 2020, https://news.mongabay.com/2018/04/chinas-belt-and-road-poised-to-transform-the-earth-but-at-what-cost/.

[25]UN Comtrade, 'International Trade Statistics Database' 2017.

in other sectors as well. In addition, China offered large amounts of loans and official assistance for infrastructure, education, and healthcare-related projects.[27]

Another interpretation posits that China is taking advantage of its authoritarian political system to seduce corrupt and illiberal governments in other developing countries. Naazneen Barma and Ely Ratner express deep concerns about the challenges posed by China and other authoritarian states. 'China's illiberal capitalism is an attractive alternative, especially for ruling elites eager to tighten their hold on power . . . . . . Through a wide array of bilateral and multilateral arrangements, the Chinese government has begun to build an alternative international structure anchored by these illiberal norms.'[28]

However, when looking at the statistics and data, this argument becomes untenable. China' largest trade partners and investment destinations among the developing countries have a variety of socio-political systems. There are functioning democracies like India, Indonesia and Brazil, former socialist countries like Vietnam, Russia and Lao, as well as fragile states like Cambodia, Pakistan and Myanmar. These countries also have different ranks in the 'Ease of Doing Business' index of the World Bank, which measures regulation burden, business environment and performance of bureaucracy. The result shows that China's comprehensive economic ties with developing countries have little correlation with the political systems and government performance. (see Tables 1 and 2)

Proponents of China's policies also fail to offer satisfactory explanations for the phenomenal growth of its relationship with other developing countries. Chinese scholars often emphasize that China's well-intentioned policies forge long-lasting friendship. For example, Li Anshan asserts that 'the most important element in Sino-African relations' is 'that the development of the relationship over the past 50 years has been based on "equal treatment, respect for sovereignty and common development."'[31] Likewise, Wang Yiwei suggests that BRI is welcomed by other countries because it promotes cooperation rather than confrontation with the spirit of '团结互信, 平等互利, 包容互鉴, 合作共赢'[unity and mutual trust, equality and mutual benefit, tolerance and mutual learning, cooperation and win-win].[32]

These views sound more like political statements than critical analyses. Although China has maintained quite consistent political policies toward developing countries for nearly 70 years, the strong growth of economic ties is a rather recent phenomenon. The statements above cannot explain why an old but lukewarm political friendship has suddenly become a dynamic and comprehensive partnership.

Despite the difficulty in explaining China's strong ties with developing countries, many point out the unique pragmatism of Chinese engagements. Joshua Ramo described China's development approach as flexible and pragmatic for diverse circumstances, in contrast to Washington Consensus's dogmatism as 'prescriptive, Washington-knows-best approach to telling other nations how to run themselves.'[33] More concretely, Barry Sautman and Yan Hairong suggest that China promotes industrialism in the global South more actively than the West without imposing conditions on other countries' policies.[34]

Politicians from China and other developing countries confirm the significance of pragmatism in their collaboration. For instance, South Africa's State Enterprises Minister Malusi Gigaba stated that 'Chinese pragmatism has certainly enabled broader infrastructure and investment in a range of African countries.'[35] China's deputy foreign minister, Zhou Wenzhong put his understanding of the Chinese approach in this manner, 'Business is business. [China tries]to separate politics from

---

[26]Anthony J. Venables, 'Using Natural Resources for Development', *Journal of Economic Perspectives* 30(1), (2016), pp. 161–184. Note: I adopted Venables' classification of resource-rich countries; countries which had no diplomatic ties with PR China and had a population of less than 2.5 million by 2016 are not counted.

[27]国务院新闻办公室 [State Council Information Office], 《中国的对外援助（2014）》白皮书 [China's Foreign Aid (2014) White Paper], July 10, 2014, accessed January 8, 2020, http://www.gov.cn/zhengce/2014-07/10/content_2715467.htm.

[28]Naazneen Barma and Ely Ratner, 'China's Illiberal Challenge', *Democracy: A Journal of Ideas* 2, (2006), accessed January 8, 2020, http://www.democracyjournal.org/2/6485.php?page=all.

[31]Anshan Li, 'China and Africa: policy and challenges', *China Security* 3(3), (2007), pp.69–93.

[32]王义桅[Wang Yiwei], '"一带一路"为何受欢迎？'[Why the 'Belt and Road Initiative' is so popular], 人民日报海外版 [People's Daily Overseas Edition], December 8, 2015, accessed January 7, 2020, http://finance.chinanews.com/ll/2015/12-08/7661576.shtml.

[33]Joshua Ramo, *The Beijing Consensus* (London: Foreign Policy Centre, 2004), p. 4.

[34]Barry Sautman and Yan Hairong, 'Friends and Interests: China's Distinctive Links with Africa', *African Studies Review* 50, (2007), p. 81.

Table 1. China's top 10 trade partners among developing countries[29]

[29]National Bureau of Statistics of China, 'Annual Data', 2017, *Doing Business Report 2018* (Washington: World Bank, 2018), p.4.

Country	Trade volume ($ million) 2017	Doing Business Rank 2018
Vietnam	121,991	68
Malaysia	96,138	24
Brazil	87,808	125
India	84,388	100
Russia	84,221	35
Thailand	80,138	26
Indonesia	63,332	72
Philippines	51,305	113
Saudi Arabia	50,137	92
Mexico	47,709	49

Table 2. China's top 10 investment destinations among developing countries[30]

[30]Ibid.

Country	FDI Stock ($ million) 2017	Doing Business Rank 2018
Russia	13,872	35
Indonesia	10,539	72
Kazakhstan	7562	36
South Africa	7473	82
Lao	6655	141
Pakistan	5716	147
Myanmar	5525	171
Cambodia	5449	135
United Arab Emirates	5373	21
Thailand	5358	26

business... [whereas the West tries] to impose ... market economy[ies] and multiparty democracy-[ies] on ... countries which are not ready for it.'[36]

The practitioners and researchers' comments indicate that the antagonism between the Washington Consensus and 'Beijing Consensus' is very different from the kinds of antagonism prevalent in the Cold War era. China and the West no longer disagree on the value of capitalist markets. To some extent, China attaches even more importance to commerce and economic growth than Western countries do today. Obsessed with economic development, China is often seen as a mainstay of developmentalism.[37] Therefore, China does not differ from the West in its goal of developing a market economy, but rather in its approach to reaching that goal. The Washington Consensus assigned developing countries with restructuring of their sociopolitical systems. However, the diverse and complex sociopolitical conditions particular to each country renders implementation of all the given prescriptions nearly impossible. China was able to develop by promoting market economy and international trade while maintaining a sociopolitical system different from the West. China's own development and its active commercial engagements with other developing countries prove that market-oriented activities can flourish without following the Washington model.

---

[35]Kenneth Kidd, 'China and South Africa: An alliance of "pragmatism"', *The Star*, November 12, 2011, accessed January 7, 2020, http://www.thestar.com/news/world/2011/11/12/china_and_south_africa_an_alliance_of_pragmatism.html.
[36]Howard W. French, 'China in Africa: All Trade and No Political Baggage', *New York Times*, August 8, 2004, accessed January 7, 2020, https://www.nytimes.com/2004/08/08/world/china-in-africa-all-trade-with-no-political-baggage.html.
[37]Arif Dirlik, 'Developmentalism', *Interventions: International Journal of Postcolonial Studies* 16(1), (2012), pp. 30–48.

Pragmatism in Structural Transformation

China's seemingly singular focus on making commercial deals and projects successful, earns its style the label as pragmatism. By comparison, Western countries may have pragmatic attitudes when they implement projects, but these projects are designed under certain frameworks like the Washington Consensus. Pure case-by-case pragmatism is usually criticized for lacking coherent principles. Yet, the Chinese practices at home and with developing countries have sustained rapid development for decades. The effects of these seemingly scattered and incremental activities are more consistent and remarkable than those with a clearly defined ideology. What is the reason for this puzzling contrast?

In this context, we need to examine the Chinese pragmatism more closely to understand its dynamism. Two famous quotes from the architect of the post-1978 reform, Deng Xiaoping, shed light on how the Chinese pragmatism works. The first states, '不管白猫黑猫, 捉到老鼠就是好猫' [It doesn't matter whether the cat is black or white, as long as it catches mice]. It emphasized that increased productivity was the ultimate goal and criterion of social development. Deng did not have a definitive plan to improve production, but rather preferred adjusting the plans based on real effects. This quote is often used interchangeably with another, '摸着石头过河' [cross the river by feeling the stones]. 'Feeling the stones' refers to trial-and-error experiments as well as case-by-case solutions. Failed experiments are to be studied and revised to further align with the concrete, situational reality. In the end, the goal can only be achieved through incremental steps. This attitude also implies openness to various kinds of tools so long as they help to achieve economic growth.

These two interrelated quotes suggest that the pragmatism of the reform is not completely void of principles. 'Catching mice' and 'crossing the river' indicate the unambiguous goal of development and growth. Pragmatism simply leaves the path to this destination wide open and relies on concrete experiments and diverse activities. By comparison, the Washington Consensus and other development policies all attempt to define the path, in addition to the goal, of development. Upon understanding Chinese pragmatism as such, we can also explain why all previous efforts to define Beijing Consensus or China Model have failed, because the essence of China's development experience is indeed to reject *consensus* or *models* for a development path.

However, this explanation raises as many questions as it answers: Can people reap transformation and growth by simply setting a goal for development? How can development work without clear plans for action? Why are all development models, not just some of the failed ones, ineffective? Finally, how can this explanation account for those models that functioned successfully in certain countries and periods, such as institutional reform and developmental states?

Before providing a systematic explanation of the dynamics of Chinese pragmatism, this research needs to first address these questions and clarify the argument.

(1) The rejection of a defined path does not mean only setting a goal but stresses the stimulation of numerous experiments and transformations towards the unwavering goal of productivity growth.

(2) Good plans are of course needed for each experiment but in the case of China, the experiments are so diverse and dynamic that they go far beyond any predesigned master plan. Chinese leadership, meanwhile, is willing to accept those extraordinary attempts as long as they contribute to the goal of productivity growth.

(3) Chinese pragmatism does not deny the value of good development experiences. The Chinese have indeed studied many useful socio-economic models from advanced economies and their developing neighbors. Yet, China refuses to stick to any specific models, as doing so would constrain the possibility of experiments and transformations based on situational

³⁰Ibid.
²⁹National Bureau of Statistics of China, 'Annual Data', 2017, *Doing Business Report 2018* (Washington: World Bank, 2018), p.4.

needs. That being said, we need to investigate why the goal of productivity growth matters and why many diverse experiments and incremental changes are required to reach this goal.

The first question may seem banal at first glance. In today's world, almost every country sets the growth of productivity as its goal. However, such a common pursuit for productivity growth is just a recent phenomenon, and even now not all countries can effectively mobilize their people to strive for this goal in their daily lives. In the 1960s and early 1970s, Deng's view on 'catching mice' was severely criticized by Mao Zedong, who believed that class struggle and pursuit of communist ideology should be the country's top priorities, whereas productivity growth was just a means to support the political agenda of the Chinese Communist Party. Similarly, a number of Third-World countries placed political goals before economic growth in their agenda, particularly during the Cold War era. This order of priorities in China reversed after Deng launched the market reforms. Economic development has since become the central task of the Communist Party, which believes that their political power ought to be used to achieve this goal.[38]

There are also many social and cultural values hindering the prioritization of productivity growth. Confucianism has had a strong tendency to disregard the pursuit of economic and material gain. Confucian classic text *Great Learning* 大学 taught that '国不以利为利, 以义为利也' [a state does not take material gain as its interest, but takes righteousness as its interest] and "德者本也□财者末也 [Virtue is the root, and wealth is the end of the branch.] Taoism expressed similar disdain toward economic and material pursuits, instead placing emphasis on spiritual life. It described an ideal state as follows: '虽有舟舆, 无所乘之 … 甘其食, 美其服, 安其居, 乐其俗' [Though they had boats and carriages, they should have no occasion to ride in them … They should think their (coarse) food sweet, their (plain) clothes beautiful, their (poor) dwellings places of rest, and their common (simple) ways sources of enjoyment].[39] The ideal Taoist state is a state of self-sufficiency and self-contentedness, which rejects any temptations and demands of unnecessary material enjoyment.

It is, in fact, a common phenomenon of traditionalist cultures to emphasize spiritual and ethical values over material wealth. Pre-modern European society attached little importance to the wealth accumulation either. For instance, when St. Thomas Aquinas discussed the fulfillment of a human being's perfection, he quickly rejected the attainment of wealth and concluded that 'perfect happiness can consist in nothing else than the vision of the Divine Essence'.[40] For him as well as for ancient Greek thinkers, a society should primarily be concerned with justice, and in the case of individuals, with their virtues. Unlimited accumulation of wealth was considered the cause of injustice that ought to be reined in.[41] As a result, economists found that the level of productivity in the world did not see any real long-term progress until the 16th century.[42]

Only in the modern era has the constant pursuit of higher profits, both in terms of societies as well as individuals, been popularized and legitimized. This is closely related to the rise of capitalism. As Karl Marx illustrated, the essence of modern capitalism is the endless pursuit of surplus value M-C-M' -C-M"-C-M'"- … …, in which money (M) is invested into commodities (C) for the purpose of generating more and more money (M'). In a pre-capitalistic society, trade usually took place when there were concrete needs for exchange, namely C-M-C. Exchanges occurred as different commodities were exchanged for their concrete utility. By comparison, capitalistic exchange is driven by the desire to increase abstract exchange value.[43]

[38]Rongji Zhu, '1987: One central task and two basic points', *China.org.cn*, September 16, 2009, accessed January 7, 2020, http://www.china.org.cn/features/60years/2009-09/16/content_18535066.htm.
[39]老子道德经注校释[Laozi Daodejing Commentary and Interpretation], comm.王弼[Wang Bi] Beijing: Zhonghua Shuju, 2008), p. 190.
[40]St. Thomas Aquinas, *Summa Theologica* trans. Fathers of the English Dominican Province (New York: Christian Classics, 1948), p. 802.
[41]Tang Xiaoyang, 'Philosophy's Political Duty and Political Practice' (PhD diss., New School University, 2011), pp. 20–21; Hagan, Michael J, 'St. Thomas Aquinas: Economics of the Just Society', Austrian Student Scholars Conference, 2012, pp. 8–9.
[42]Elio Lo Cascio and Paolo Malanima, 'GDP in Pre-Modern Agrarian Economies (1–1820 AD) A Revision of the Estimates', *Rivista di Storia Economica* 25(3), (2009), pp. 391–420.
[43]Karl Marx, *Das Kapital* (Hamburg: Verlag von Otto Meisner, 1867), pp.109–118.

The endless pursuit of value increase consequently stimulates constant productivity growth. With the ever-growing productivity, capitalism has gradually expanded across the world, forcing countries, capitalist or non-capitalist, to attach value to productivity growth, more precisely to continuous productivity growth. Those that neglect productivity growth, because of political ideology or cultural values, face being overwhelmed by other advanced economic and technological powers. China used to rigidly resist the ideas and influences of capitalism in the modern time. In the late Qing dynasty, the government and society put more emphasis on preserving the indigenous old traditions rather than pursuing economic growth. In the Republic period (1911–1949), frequent wars distracted people from focusing on production and development. In the pre-1978 socialist period, the dominating ideology of class struggle put productivity growth only on a secondary role. The occasional pushes of production such as the 'Great Leap Forward' proved to be unsustainable. When Chinese society finally prioritized economic growth as the general target, it signified a fundamental shift to accept the goal of capitalism.[44] As Figure 2 illustrates, the productivity growth rates before 1978 were not merely low, but also violently fluctuating. After 1978, especially after 1992, the consensus on promoting economy and the corresponding reform led to continuous productivity growth.

It is an enormous challenge to achieve sustainable productivity growth, because it requires comprehensive changes of the socio-economic relationship. In the eighteenth century, the division of labor was broadly identified as the cause of 'the greatest [improvement for] the productive powers.'[46] Adam Smith's famous example of a pin factory demonstrates that productivity can increase exponentially through division of labor and specialization. Today, the application of machinery and advanced technology also largely depends on the division of labor into single steps and objects.[47] Yet, elevated production capacity meanwhile creates sales and distribution problems. Adam Smith rightly observed that large-scale division of labor could make sense only when large-scale markets are in place.[48] Sustainable productivity growth must be supported by an expanding and well-functioning market. The production mode, namely M-C (investment to produce commodities), must be coupled with the distribution mode, namely C-M' (sales to realize value increase), so that the production growth can continue. When socialist command

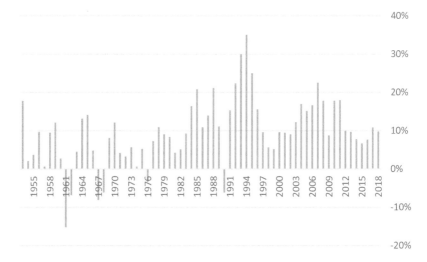

Figure 2. Annual growth rate of labor productivity in China 1953–2018.[45]
National Bureau of Statistics of China, 'Annual Data', 2017. Labor productivity is measured by GDP per labor annually.

---

[44]Although other forms of societies, e.g. the former USSR, may also stress productivity growth sometimes, they only consider the growth as one of their targets, along with other political and cultural goals. By contrast, capitalism takes constant value increase and productivity growth as the primary goal, because the pursuit is the nature of capital by definition.
[46]Adam Smith, *Wealth of Nations* (Edinburgh: Thomas Nelson Press, 1843), p. 3.
[47]Ibid., pp. 14–15.
[48]Ibid., pp. 26–33.

economies intended to increase production through planning instead of through market forces, they caused overproduction in certain sectors and shortages in others. By only stressing the production mode (labor, technology) and neglecting the distributive mode (ownership, market), traditional socialist economies, including pre-reform China, could not sustain growth and failed without exception.[49]

Therefore, comprehensive change must extend to societal structures in order for sustainable productivity growth to occur. The advancement of production methods, such as division of labor, professional specialization, usage of machinery and technological progress, should take place alongside the transformation of societal structure and living style, such as increasing trade activities, rising consumption demands and enhanced distribution channels. Furthermore, improved market regulation, protection of private property, construction of infrastructure, the breakdown of household production, standardization of education, efficient administration and even environmental preservation are also vital. As Max Weber commented, the 'forever renewed profit' of capitalist enterprises is not individual matter, but deals with an order of society.[50] Similarly, Emile Durkheim argued that the complex division of labor led to a new type of social solidarity in the modern world, transitioning from a society with rigid social controls and uniform beliefs (mechanical solidarity) into one with more autonomous individuals, increased differentiation, and frequent interactions between citizens (organic solidarity).[51]

Today, the transition from traditional socio-economic relationship to modern society, which centers on productivity growth, is referred to by development economists as structural transformation. On the one side, this term refers to the expansion of highly productive industries and other modern sectors in the place of subsistence agriculture. On the other hand, it describes the related alterations in economic, political, and social frameworks, including urbanization, secularization and so on.[52] China has experienced effective structural transformation during the rapid growth of the past four decades, significantly reducing its agricultural sector and rapidly increasing urbanization. The trend can be seen through comparison with other developing countries. (Table 3)

In this connection, diverse experiments and incremental changes are crucial to achieving comprehensive structural transformation and sustainable productivity growth. First, because comprehensive transformation touches all aspects of society, policy change must be incremental—no single policy can bring about comprehensive structural transformation. Second, every developing nation must approach structural transformation differently given their unique traditions and societal forms. No uniform models are available. Finally, comprehensive transformation also generates the 'chicken-and-egg' dilemma. When one part, for instance industrial capacity, is growing, it is affected and constrained by many other parts in the society, such as infrastructure and labor force. However, the construction of infrastructure and the development of labor skill are conversely limited by the lack of industrial activities. The sophisticated division of labor and corresponding distributional network requires all the related components to perform their functions appropriately, but it is impossible to enable all actors simultaneously with new skills and knowledge, especially when the collaborating synergism is still new to them. Members of society must be gradually acclimated to their new roles in

Table 3. Percentage of urban population and agriculture in China and other developing countries[53]

[53]World Bank, 'World Development Indicators Database', accessed February 10, 2019, http://wdi.worldbank.org/tables/.

	Agriculture value added (% of Gross Domestic Product (GDP))			Urban Population (% of Total Population)		
	1979	2000	2015	1979	2000	2015
China	30.70	14.68	8.83	18.62	35.88	55.50
Low Income Countries		28.97	25.50	19.85	26.64	31.60
Lower-middle Income Countries	30.30	20.17	15.57	25.59	32.87	38.99

National Bureau of Statistics of China, 'Annual Data', 2017. Labor productivity is measured by GDP per labor annually.
[49]Moishe Postone, Time, labor, and social domination（Cambridge: Cambridge University Press, 2003), pp.10–16.
[50]Max Weber, The Protestant Ethic and the Spirit of Capitalism (London: Routledge, 2001), pp. xxxii ff.
[51]Emile Durkheim, The Division of Labour in Society (London: The Macmillan Press Ltd, 1984), pp. 83–86.
[52]Simon Kuznets, 'Modern Economic Growth: Findings and Reflections', Prize Lecture, NobelPrize.org (1971), accessed January 7, 2020, http://www.nobelprize.org/nobel_prizes/economic-sciences/laureates/1971/kuznets-lecture.html.

order to work effectively and in coordination with their peers. A country must solve the 'chicken-and-egg' dilemma in order to have successful structural transformation. As we will see in the following sections, Chinese pragmatism plays a key role not merely in solving China's 'chicken-and-egg' dilemma, but also in assisting other countries on their own paths toward structural transformation.

Solving the Chicken-and-Egg Dilemma

Some researchers have already noticed the chicken-and-egg dilemma in the structural transformation. For instance, Gunnar Myrdal pointed out that social inertia makes it more difficult for the non-industrialized countries to shift to industrial society than the industrialized countries to continue industrialization. Accordingly, Myrdal was pessimistic about the growth prospect of the Third World and believed that weak institutions in almost all the political, economic, social and cultural frontiers tend to keep these countries in low-level equilibrium.[54] Yuen Yuen Ang also believes that while wealthy capitalist economies are necessarily supported by good institutions, such as protection of private property rights, professional bureaucracy, formal accountability, etc., 'attaining these preconditions also appears to depend on the level of economic growth'.[55] However, China's rise from backward socio-economic conditions to a global industrial powerhouse during past decades offers an invaluable example of how a country can effectively escape the vicious cycle of poverty and bad governance. Ang reveals that, in the case of China, markets and state agencies interacted and adapted to each other. This coevolutionary process manifested itself in diverse forms, over the course of different periods of development. In her view, the practices showed that 'weak' institutions and state capacities actually help build markets when none exist, whereas 'strong' governance preserves existing markets. In particular, improvisation among ground-level agents spurred the coevolution of markets and states.[56] The coevolution on the ground level must be diverse and incremental, as the specific agents need time to undergo mutual adaptation in their own manner. Such a coevolution resonates with Deng Xiaoping's philosophy of 'white cat and black cat' and 'crossing river by touching stones'.

However, Ang investigated solely the interactive relationship between government agencies and market. Structural transformation involves changes in many more aspects of society. As noted before, a modern industrial system with sustainable productivity growth requires not only a functioning market and efficient administration, but also skilled workers and infrastructure facilities. Additionally, entrepreneurship, professionalism, consumerism, and urbanization are also important components. All these factors are interdependent and mutually impact one another. In Adam Przeworski's words, 'In the end, the motor of history is endogeneity. From some initial circumstances and under some invariant conditions, wealth, its distribution, and the institutions that allocate factors and distribute incomes are mutually interdependent and evolve together.'[57]

The revelation of the coevolutionary complexity explains why many previous development programs failed. Since the transformation of a society is not determined by any independent primary cause, attempts to launch a designed program or set definite conditions, either by foreign agents or local authority, cannot shift the entire society rooted in traditional life directly into a new system of modern production. To illustrate how an interdependent system looks like, we may use a football match as an example. A good pass cannot be decided by a single factor but depends on the position and action of the player who passes the ball as well as those of the player who receives the ball. Any change of these elements may turn a good pass to a bad one or conversely. A good pass refers to a harmonious coordination of all the changing factors at the same time, not a definite pattern of actions.

[53]World Bank, 'World Development Indicators Database', accessed February 10, 2019, http://wdi.worldbank.org/tables/.
[54]Gunnar Myrdal, *The Challenge of World Poverty* (London: Allen Lane, 1971), p. 268.
[55]Yuen Yuen Ang, *How China Escaped the Poverty Trap*, p. 1.
[56]Ibid., p.17.
[57]Adam Przeworski, 'The Last Instance: Are Institutions the Primary Cause of Economic Development?', *European Journal of Sociology* 45(2), (2004), pp. 165–188.

The build-up of a football team is thus a chicken-and-egg dilemma too. Only in a strong team can individual players enhance their football skills as solo talent is insufficient. Yet, without skillful players, a team cannot succeed in the field. Everyone learns how to play football by first working within a team. Initially, there must be numerous misunderstandings and miscommunications. Yet, as the experiments continue, the players get familiar with each other and begin to form a cohesive team. They enhance their skills through team practice. A similar approach can be found in China's structural transformation. The market-oriented reform started with incremental experiments in diverse fields such as market liberalization, loosening of price control, establishment of private enterprises, introduction of performance-based bonuses, opening for FDI and so on. A large variety of players; from farmers, workers, technicians to entrepreneurs, officials and foreign investors, were involved in this process. All of them made changes simultaneously and they gradually learned to adapt to each other under the new circumstances. Through trial-and-error, different stakeholders have learned to work with each other to achieve better productivity. Then they continue to evolve and adapt for further productivity growth.

In the co-evolution process, it is critical to ensure all the stakeholders stick to a common target so that synergism can be forged. For a football team, only when all the members strive to score and not be scored on, their training exercises for cooperation and mutual adaptation make sense. Likewise, the stakeholders of structural transformation need to explore the appropriate manner of division of labor and market functioning with the goal of promoting sustainable productivity growth. However, the nature of interdependent co-evolution makes it challenging to achieve the goal. Using the football team again as an example, over 90% of the actions in a match do not directly lead to goals, but the passing and running is necessary preparation for scoring goals. Therefore, instruction and coaching are needed to unite the team and advance towards a single objective. When it comes to structural transformation, most individual actors cannot observe the overall long-term productivity growth, but only local actions and ad-hoc gains, which, albeit necessary for the overall transformation, are likely to deviate from the general goal as well. Strategic direction is thus needed to keep the co-evolving synergism on the track towards structural transformation.

Yet, strategic direction for the co-evolving synergism is not a linear mechanism either. The direction should be an organic component of the co-evolution so that it can effectively guide the constantly changing components. It is not enough to coach the football players on just the basic rules of the game. Similarly, the direction for the structural transformation cannot be limited to mere theories or prescribed instructions, but instead must be absorbed and integrated into the active socio-economic synergism. The Chinese government used the combination of national-level reform design, corporate style evaluation of local cadres, and inter-regional competition to stimulate and coordinate continuous growth.[58] The national-level design is important, as it sets the target and criteria for all the other activities, but it is also relatively broad and flexible, leaving plenty of space for the local officials and enterprises to improvise; with the exception of a few areas marked with 'red lines', e.g. land use. Consequently, although China's market reform was initiated by the central government, the exact outcome of the reform often surprised the central government. This in turn forced the central leadership to learn from the practice and give new policy guidance to keep the development on track.[59] In this manner, the strategic direction and the grass-root changes form a synergism of mutual adaptation, in which the general growth goal gradually merges with the various aims of diverse actors in the country.

To be sure, the relationship between general direction of state strategy and grass-root socio-economic transformation is not a fixed one either. In similar manner that a football team can in some cases develop better through playing actual matches rather than coaching, the structural transformation of a society may also move forward through long-time interactions between diverse capitalist-minded actors with little state intervention. An active state may play a bigger role to

[58]Eric X. Li, 'The Life of the Party'; Yuen Yuen Ang, *How China Escaped the Poverty Trap*, pp.48–68.
[59]Yuen Yuen Ang, *How China Escaped the Poverty Trap*, pp. 73–75, 88–102.

accelerate the learning process in the late-industrialized countries and promote the overall productivity growth. However, no matter which role the state plays, the critical point is that the general direction and grass-root changes should build an interactive co-evolving relationship, not a mechanical linear one.

Case Study: Coevolution of Infrastructure Construction

This section aims to illustrate how China interacts with other developing countries in the spirit of co-evolutionary pragmatism, which grows out of China's own development. The sector of infrastructure construction is an ideal example for this purpose. On the one hand, China has taken part in the construction of numerous infrastructure projects in the developing countries. In 2017 Chinese contractors held a whopping 59.8% share of Africa's entire construction market, 37.7% of Asia's market and 23% of Latin America's market.[60] On the other hand, infrastructure development is critical for the structural transformation. Many countries are unable to advance industrialization because of deficient infrastructure and they hope that China's development experience may help.

China itself had bitter lessons in infrastructure construction both domestically and internationally. Prior to 1980, China's road density, telephone usage rate, and electricity and water supplies were similar to those of sub-Saharan Africa; some indicators were even lower.[61] From 1981 to 1990, when the national economy was growing at an annual rate of nearly 10%, investment in transportation infrastructure increased by only around 1.3% every year, placing a great strain on economic development.[62] The Chinese government at that time was incapable of measuring the exact needs for infrastructure. They either invested too much in a short period of time or radically cut the investment rate after witnessing the economy overheat.[63] Likewise, most of China's early infrastructure projects in other developing countries were economic disasters. For example, the monumental Tanzania-Zambia Railway (TAZARA) in the 1970s has never realized its designed annual capacity. On the brink of bankruptcy, it has to rely on new loans and technical aid from China in order to survive and incurred huge financial burden for all the three countries related.[64]

The challenge of infrastructure construction is caused by the special role of infrastructure in the modern economic development. Infrastructure is not simply a commodity on the market, but also a precondition for the circulation of commodities and industrial production. Whether referring to roadways, water and energy supplies, or waste management, infrastructure builds networks or frameworks that facilitate the efficient flow of people, materials and information. Yet, the exchange and production activities won't immediately start when the infrastructure is ready, because they also rely on the transformation of other parts of the society, such as availability of industrial enterprises, market activeness and habits of consumers and labors, etc. These changes won't happen in short term in underdeveloped rural regions. Hence, infrastructure construction in developing countries usually requires large initial investment, but has slow returns and huge financial risks. Pure marketization might be appropriate in cases where small investments yield quick results and recognizable market returns, e.g. mobile networks, but they cannot be applied wholesale to infrastructure construction.

However, history has taught us how infrastructure construction that neglects economic returns, like TAZARA, can be equally treacherous. Without accompanying economic growth, the facilities built may not generate sufficient revenue to sustain themselves. This forms a chicken-and-egg

---

[60]'The top 250 international contractors', *Engineering News-Record*, August 20–27, 2018, p. 42.

[61]Vivian Foster and Cecilia Briceño-Garmendia, ed., 'Africa's Infrastructure: A Time for Transformation Washington: World Bank, 2010), p. 2.

[62]*World Development Report 1994: Infrastructure for Development* (United Kingdom: Oxford University Press, 1994).

[63]房维中[Fang Weizhong], '20世纪80年代中国经济的发展历程和陈云的经济指导思想'[The Development of Chinese Economy in the 1980s and Chen Yun's Economic Guiding Ideology], 当代中国史研究[Research on Contemporary Chinese History] 12(3), (2005), pp. 27–37.

[64]Tryness Mbale Tembo, 'Tazara records drop in freight', *Zambia Daily Mail*, December 16, 2015, accessed January 8, 2020, http://www.daily-mail.co.zm/tazara-records-drop-freight/.

dilemma in the development process. Market economy requires infrastructure as an enabling condition, but there is not much investment in infrastructure and its maintenance if the market economy is not yet fully developed. Therefore, in developing countries, an unavoidable question emerges as to how infrastructure can be built when commercial prospects are in doubt but there is a potential impact on national economic transformation. It is not easy to achieve a balance between investment return and overall development.

China gradually turned the trend of infrastructure construction within the country during the mid-1990s. From 1998 to 2005, the annual increase in investment for infrastructure soared to 23.3%, almost twice the rate of overall economic growth. In 2006, China's spending on infrastructure accounted for more than 14% of the gross domestic product, the highest of any country in the world.[65] Moreover, increased investment in infrastructure did not derive from state expenditures. Whereas in the 1980s, the proportion of estimated state spending on fixed-asset investment averaged 15–20%, after 1992, it fell to an average of under 4%.[66] The key difference between the 1980s and the years after 1990s is not simply the increase of investment in infrastructure, but the sustainability of such immense investments. Although not every project has been effective, China's infrastructure construction in general has formed a benign synergism with the country's industrialization process and broad economic growth.

Researchers identify local governments and state-owned enterprises as the new driving forces for China's infrastructure construction.[67] On the one hand, in a period dominated by economics, local governments were, like enterprises, evaluated primarily according to economic performance. Local governments had to concern themselves with GDP and fiscal revenue growth. In addition, after the 1990s, most funding for infrastructure came from financial market. Borrowers, namely local governments and state-owned enterprises (SOEs), have had to think about the capability of repayment. On the other hand, China has kept political power highly concentrated in the central government. Beijing has the absolute authority to award or punish local officials. This system prevented local officials from exploiting the huge infrastructure investment for private interests, as happened in Russia.[68] Both SOEs and local governments must strictly comply with instructions from the central government and coordinate with national development strategy. Officials therefore combine economic benefits with overall development goals in their objective for infrastructure investment. Although such a dual identity may sometimes cause confusion, over the past 20 years, this mixed motivation of short-term financial returns and long-term development gains has effectively driven continuous infrastructure development in China.[69]

Drawing upon its domestic experience, China has conducted a series of experiments in infrastructure cooperation with developing countries. Instead of purely offering aid, China has begun to provide commercial financing to other countries on a large scale. One type is the so-called 'resource for infrastructure' agreements. Resource-backed loans were originally used by Western commercial banks to generate hefty profits. Chinese banks, primarily China Eximbank, not only lowered interest rates and extended repayment terms, but also coupled the loans with infrastructure construction. According to the loan agreements, only Chinese companies are contracted to implement the infrastructure projects. In this manner, the profit from the construction contracts can offset the risks and concessions of the loans. For recipient countries, such agreements make it possible to quickly convert future revenue into infrastructure projects which are crucial to the countries'

---

[65]R. Lall, R. Anand and A. Rastogi, *Developing physical infrastructure: A comparative perspective on the experience of the People's Republic of China and India* (Manila: Asian Development Bank, 2010), p. 59. In these statistics, infrastructure included energy, natural gas, transportation, water supply, irrigation, and telecommunications.

[66]Ibid., pp. 64–65.

[67]张军,高远, 傅勇, 张弘 [Zhang Jun, Gao Yuan, Fu Yong, Zhang Hong], 'Why does China have good infrastructure?', 《经济研 究》 [Economic Research Journal] 3, (2007), pp. 9–11; R. Lall, R. Anand and A. Rastogi, Developing physical infrastructure, pp. 63–64.

[68]O. Blanchard and A. Shleifer, 'Federalism with and without Political Centralization: China versus Russia', NBER Working Paper No. 7616 (2000).

[69]Zhang Jun, Gao Yuan, Fu Yong, Zhang Hong, 'Why does China have good infrastructure?', p. 10.

economic take-off. China pioneered the 'resource for infrastructure' deals with Angola in 2004. The outcomes were satisfactory for both sides and received positive evaluation from the World Bank.[70] China later extended similar deals to Sudan, Venezuela, Equatorial Guinea, Congo Brazzaville, and others.

Dealing with different countries, Chinese players do not use any uniform conditionalities, but strive to make projects feasible and sustainable in their respective circumstances. Ethiopia does not produce oil and is usually not considered for resource-backed lending by international banks. Yet, China Eximbank signed a loan agreement in 2006 to allow Ethiopia to use all its exports, mainly sesame, as collateral to secure a loan of 500 USD million, which was mainly spent on improving the country's power transmission network. Democratic Republic of the Congo (DRC) also intended to use resource-backed loans to finance its post-war reconstruction, but unfortunately, the production level of Gecamines, its state-owned mining enterprise, was too low to provide sufficient collateral. China Exim Bank brought in two enterprises, the Chinese Railway Corporation and Sinohydro, to set up a joint venture with Gecamines to extract and sell copper and cobalt from the still undeveloped Kolwezi region. The income from this mining joint venture would then be used to repay the Chinese infrastructure loan.[71] In this case, a pragmatic revision of the original loan deal had been made to allow underground resources to take the place of production resources as loan collateral.

China Exim Bank Chairman Li Ruogu expounded 2007 a comprehensive reflection on the new forms of credit that China has extended to the developing countries in an article: 1) The aim of lending is development. We should not cut off loans to developing countries because of their heavy debt burdens; this would have a negative impact on development, making it even harder for them to make timely repayments and causing them to fall into a vicious cycle. 2) Western institutes neglect to take into account dynamic development and the potential positive impact of new loans. They overly use fixed evaluation criteria that mostly come from hypothetical linear models, whereas the situations of developing countries are often very different. 3) When China Exim Bank assesses loans, it pays more attention to receiving countries' actual situations, and it grants loans for specific projects with the vision of effectively strengthening the countries' ability to pay off debts and establishing a virtuous cycle. 4) Some projects with substantial social welfare benefits may be financially unfeasible. Only in such cases, concessional loans will be employed.[72] These views shed light on the guidelines of a major Chinese institute which distinguishes from the Western institutes with its pragmatism and non-linear thinking.

However, after a period of rapid growth of Chinese financing for infrastructure construction in developing countries, new challenges emerged. Critiques raise the issue of debt sustainability and blame China for giving out excessive loans.[73] Countries including Sri Lanka, Malaysia and the Maldives even threatened to suspend the infrastructure deals with China.[74] Additionally, the socio-environmental sustainability of the China-funded projects is questioned, as they hugely alter the traditional life and natural landscape in the underdeveloped regions. For example, dam projects in Myanmar, Cambodia and Sudan caused numerous protests locally and internationally. Addressing these concerns, Chinese agents have quickly adjusted their approaches. Not only did they renegotiate the deals with Sri Lanka, Malaysia and the Maldives, but they also actively downscaled or delayed a few large projects, for instance, railways in Pakistan, and Kenya.

[70]Håvard Halland, John Beardsworth, Bryan Land, and James Schmidt, *Resource Financed Infrastructure: A Discussion on a New Form of Infrastructure Financing* (Washington: World Bank 2014).
[71]Johanna Jansson, 'China-DRC Sicomines deal back on track', *The Africa Report*, August 4, 2014, accessed May 30, 2015, http://www.theafricareport.com/Central-Africa/chinadrc-sicomines-deal-back-on-track.html.
[72]李若谷[Li Ruogu], '正确认识发展中国家的债务可持续问题' [Correctly Understanding the Debt Sustainability Problems of Developing Countries], 世界经济与政治[World Economy and Politics] 4, (2007), pp. 63–72.
[73]John Hurley, Scott Morris, and Gailyn Portelance, 'Examining the Debt Implications of the Belt and Road Initiative from a Policy Perspective', *CGD Policy Paper* (Washington, DC: Center for Global Development, 2018).
[74]Tom Mitchell and Alice Woodhouse, 'Malaysia renegotiated China-backed rail project to avoid $5bn fee', *Financial Times*, April 15, 2019, accessed January 7, 2020, https://www.ft.com/content/660ce336-5f38-11e9-b285-3acd5d43599e.

However, the reduction of lending is a part of the solution to the chicken-and-egg dilemma rather than a shift of policy model. Based on its own development experience, China does not identify the cause of debt crisis simplistically as over-lending, because Asia and Africa still badly require investments in infrastructure.[75] The real problem is the lower-than-expected growth generated by the infrastructure projects, which derails fiscal consolidations. As a BRI document states, 'productive investment, while increasing debt ratios in the short run, can generate higher economic growth . . . . . . leading to lower debt ratios over time'.[76] Correspondingly, the Chinese government now puts more emphasis on building the 'interactive mechanism between large-scale infrastructure and industrial development'.[77] Industrial projects are developed in coordination with the new railways constructed. For instance, CCECC, a branch of China Railway Construction Corporation, and Ethiopian Ministry of Industry signed agreement 2014 to build a series of industrial parks which would benefit from the Ethio-Djibouti Railway. China Merchants Group was also brought in to build a new port in Djibouti in order to more efficiently handle the expected increased amount of freight from the new railway.[78] For the Mombasa-Nairobi Railway, China and Kenya as well-signed contracts to upgrade the Mombasa port and establish a special economic zone nearby.[79]

The socio-environmental challenges are addressed by Chinese in a similar fashion. China has adopted various approaches to improve the assessment, enhance monitoring and reduce impacts on the environment. Since 2007 China's Ministry of Commerce, Ministry of Environmental Protection and other departments have promulgated several guidelines to encourage Chinese enterprises to fulfill corporate social responsibilities and engage in environmental management. In May 2017 a more encompassing 'Guidance on Promoting Green Belt and Road' was issued by the Chinese government, highlighting the importance of 'ecological civilization and green development' and calling on enterprises to 'promote environmental infrastructure construction'. However, these guidelines stress the importance of 'making sustainable profits' and 'achieving well-balance among the growth of enterprises, social benefit and environment protection' in the meantime.[80] This indicates that the socio-environmental measures ought to serve the goal of sustaining market growth and development. By contrast, some activists in the West demand a complete stop of large infrastructure or industrial projects in the developing countries. The debates on the priority between development need and socio-environmental preservation is not limited to Chinese-funded projects, but also take place within many developing countries. For instance, recently Laos, Cambodia, Ethiopia and Sudan have actively built large dams to boost industrialization in spite of criticism and controversies. China's own experiences make it sympathetic to the needs of other developing countries. Consequently, mega-projects that have not received funding from Western and multilateral institutions often get approved by Chinese financers. By 2015, Chinese firms had been involved in the construction or financing of 375 dams in 74 countries.[81]

---

[75]'Meeting Asia's Infrastructure Needs', *Asian Development Bank*, February 2017, accessed January 7, 2020, https://www.adb.org/publications/asia-infrastructure-needs.

[76]Ministry of Finance of People's Republic of China, 'Debt Sustainability Framework for Participating Countries of the Belt and Road Initiative', April 25, 2019, accessed January 7, 2020, http://m.mof.gov.cn/czxw/201904/P020190425513990982189.pdf.

[77]林松添[Lin Songtian], '在中非智库论坛第五届会议全体会上的发言'[Statement at the plenary session of the fifth session of the China-Africa Think Tank Forum], April 18, 2016, accessed May 18, 2019, http://www.fmprc.gov.cn/web/wjbxw_673019/t1356262.shtml.

[78]'一子做"活"非洲东海岸 中国血统的亚吉铁路今投运'[A step that revivified the East coast of Africa: Yaji railway of Chinese 'descent' put into operation today], 第一财经 [First Financial], October 6, 2016, accessed January 8, 2020, http://www.yicai.com/news/5129772.html.

[79]驻肯尼亚使馆经商处 [Commercial Counsellor's Office of the Embassy of China in Kenya], '中交集团与肯工业化部小签蒙巴萨经济特区开发协议' [China Communications Group and Kenya Ministry of Industrialization Sign Small Mombasa Special Economic Zone Development Agreement], September 24, 2015, accessed January 8, 2020, http://www.mofcom.gov.cn/article/i/jyjl/k/201509/20150901121630.shtml.

[80]State-owned Assets Supervision and Administration Commission, 'Guidelines to the State-Owned Enterprises Directly under the Central Government on Fulfilling Corporate Social Responsibilities', December 6, 2011, accessed January 8, 2020, http://en.sasac.gov.cn/2011/12/06/c_313.htm.

Conclusion

The case study on the infrastructure sector concretely demonstrates how China offers an alternative path for other developing countries. We can also get a clearer idea of the coevolutionary pragmatism after all the discussion above. The term refers to a combination of three parts: 1) the unwavering target to promote sustainable economic development, 2) corresponding transformation towards a market economy and industrialization, and 3) flexible approaches to coordinate multiple aspects and interact with partners during the transformation.

First, the goal of economic growth is a consequence forced by global capitalism as well as a conscious choice of the developing countries. China, like most developing countries, faced the challenge of modernization first as an external pressure. Only after century-long struggle with the Western industrial powers, has China gradually shifted their priority from traditional culture to economic values. Paradoxically, when China accepts the values of global capitalism, its rapid development gives it the capacity to resist foreign influence. Hence, when China stresses the importance of economic growth in its international engagements, it does not completely forget politics. The devotion to the development issues implies both a continuation of China's longtime policy to support movements against Western hegemony and an approach to provide such support. Yet, the political implication is covered and diluted by the economic interests, which are indispensable from global capitalism. The seemingly straightforward goal of China's pragmatism has indeed deep-rooted complexity and ambivalence.

Second, the socio-economic transformation which is required to achieve the goal of continuous productivity growth is even more complex. As traditional, subsistence societies evolve into industrial societies with deepening specialization, extensive division of labor and massive market distribution, almost all social classes and every aspect of social life is greatly affected. Different stakeholders may have differing views on the benefits and losses. Communal gains may need individual sacrifice. Long-term benefits may require high costs in a short period. The transformation inevitably generates numerous controversies and disputes.

Moreover, the changes are highly interdependent. Without industries and markets in place, the society cannot develop expertise on market regulation, entrepreneurship, infrastructure management and others. Yet, without these supporting conditions, industries and markets can hardly sustain. The chicken-egg dilemma is a complex reality of China's own reform and its economic engagements in other developing countries. The interdependent transformation also means that foreign knowledge cannot be simply transplanted. Every society has its unique manner of coordination.

Third, being aware of the complexity in the structural transformation, Chinese lay emphasis on building synergism instead of using linear mechanism or fixed models. Gradualism and experimentalism allow various parties to mutually influence each other. As the case study shows, the Chinese government and enterprises responded to challenges and criticisms in infrastructure construction swiftly and demonstrated remarkable flexibility to adjust to different environment. While China-funded construction projects impact the developing countries, the demands and feedback from these countries also reshape Chinese practices.

It's true that China highlights the role of state in the transformation, but the government has also constantly changed its behaviors and functions to meet the need for market development. The prominence of government in the context of the structural transformation lies in its capability of orchestrating various stakeholders and holding firmly the goal of long-term growth. In comparison to the century-long transformation process in the West, the ongoing industrialization in China and other developing countries takes place within relatively short periods. There is more need for the government to maintain stability and direction amidst the enormous changes and disputes.

---

[81]'China Overseas Dams List', *International Rivers*, November 10, 2014, accessed January 8, 2020, www.internationalrivers.org/resources/china-overseas-dams-list-3611.

Additionally, the Chinese government tries to mobilize multiple actors to facilitate the transformation. For instance, Chinese construction firms, oil importers, banks and industrial investors were all brought together to make infrastructure projects abroad sustainable. Nevertheless, these projects still have to operate according to market mechanism, not political instruction.

To conclude, the co-evolutionary pragmatism, which the author proposes to describe the Chinese development experience, goes beyond the state-market dichotomy. What effectively drives China's phenomenal growth and ever-increasing impacts on developing countries is not any specific political-economic pattern, but a synergism of diverse actors and aspects with clear common vision. The patterns have been constantly changing. Some measures may be painful and occasional reactions may even appear counter-productive. All these challenges should be addressed and corrected quickly, but none of them in itself constitutes the essential cause for the transformation. It's the interaction, mutual adaptation and consensus formation that counts for advancing market economy and industrialization. Paradoxically, the lack of a defined model turns out to be the key to China's success, as it allows diverse practices and flexible adjustments. Therefore, as an alternative to the Washington Consensus, China presents just a different way of understanding and promoting development: target-oriented instead of model-oriented, non-linear circular synergism instead of linear causal mechanism, and experiments with large varieties instead of setting universal rules. The pragmatism opens more possibility for developing countries to transform than the dogmatism.

Disclosure statement

No potential conflict of interest was reported by the author.

From 'Peaceful Rise' to Peacebuilder? How Evolving Chinese Discourses and Self-perceptions Impact Its Growing Influence in Conflict Societies

Pascal Abb

ABSTRACT

Over the past fifteen years, China has turned from a bystander of international peacekeeping operations (PKO) to one of their biggest contributors, often explained in terms of norm adoption or securing Chinese overseas investments.

This article sketches the historical evolution of China's approach to peacekeeping through a role theory prism, explaining policy shifts through changing Chinese self-images and desired roles on the international stage. By studying influential academic and official discourses surrounding Chinese engagement with PKOs, it details processes of role contestation, and how peacekeeping became served to translate newly adopted roles into concrete policies. Finally, the article closes by examining China's growing ambitions as a peace-bringer and the emergence of an indigenous doctrine on the peace/development nexus that could undergird future Chinese agency in conflict settings.

Introduction

Over the past fifteen years, China has turned from a bystander of international peacekeeping operations (PKOs) to one of the biggest contributors to such efforts, with more than 2,000 Chinese military personnel regularly deployed on missions, mainly in Africa, marking a significant shift from China's previous practice of noninterference in foreign countries. China's highly publicized 'Belt and Road' initiative (BRI) seems poised to bolster this approach through a developmental contribution to state-building, as well as providing further incentives for interventions through the expansion of Chinese overseas investments.

The emergence of China as a major actor in peacekeeping and -building is not just significant for its effects on host countries, but has also been closely scrutinized by international observers for information on how China is using its steadily growing military capabilities and clout in regions like Africa.[1] Meanwhile, within China itself, peace-related discourses have shifted—from a largely reactive attempt to counter perceptions of a 'China threat' to highlighting proactive Chinese efforts to provide peace in war-torn societies. Most recently, they have included the development of a concept referred to as 'developmental peace' (*fazhan heping* 发展和平) that is explicitly described as an alternative to Western notions of liberal state-building. This could signal another decisive turn in Beijing's engagement of conflict societies—defined here as countries, or parts thereof, that have

---

[1]Alden, Chris (2005), 'China in Africa', in: *Survival* 47(3), 147–164; Kuo, Steven (2012), 'Beijing's understanding of African security: context and limitations', *African Security* 5(1), 24–43; Rogers, Philippe (2007), 'China and United Nations peacekeeping operations in Africa', *Naval War College Review* 60(2), 73–93.

experienced endemic, organized violence at the level of a civil war—of which there are many among the states that have signed up to the BRI, providing a further point of overlap between Chinese developmental and peace agency.

This article seeks to explain China's expanding activity in the field of peacekeeping and -building with changes in its self-conception as an international actor. It does so by combining an analysis of domestic Chinese expert discourses on these issues with a role theory approach to behavior on the global stage. It tackles the questions of how these debates, and the images developed therein, can explain shifts in policy, and how they relate to domestic and international contestations of Chinese images.

In addition to this historical overview, the article closes with a focus on China's growing international ambitions as a peace-bringer and the emergence of an indigenous doctrine on the peace/development nexus that could undergird future Chinese agency in conflict settings. The article argues that, like earlier historical phases, this discursive shift could signal another change in China's peacekeeping policy, which is why the related academic writings deserve thorough attention.

Role Theory and Its Application to China's International Behavior

Although a relatively, recent addition to the International Relations (IR) repertoire, role theory has a substantial pedigree in Foreign Policy Analysis, mainly because its assumptions are easier to square with approaches that focus on individual agency (e.g., the worldview of top leaders) over structural constraints.[2] Due to its analytical scope—which covers shifts both in a state's external environment, within its political elites, and in domestic debates over the role which the country should play on the global stage—it holds particular promise when applied to the Chinese case, which has seen significant variation in all three factors.

As described in detail by Sebastian Harnisch,[3] China's assumption of international roles has been shaped by three factors: a repertoire of historical experiences that can be selectively used to justify action in the present; the demands and expectations of external 'significant others' that influence Chinese self-images; and the strategic choices of domestic elites that often sought to assume roles that could bridge both influences. This allows for the integration of several strands of literature that have advanced explanations for China's international behaviour based on long-lasting historical or cultural factors (e.g., notions of a 'tianxia' or the experience of victimhood at the hands of colonial nations)[4]; attempts by other states to socialize China into the existing world order[5]; or the elite appropriation of nationalist sentiment.[6] Accordingly, previous applications of this model have proven useful to explain such diverse phenomena as major reorientations in China's foreign relations,[7] the evolution of key bilateral relationships,[8] and as illustrative examples, specific policy choices.

China's engagement with conflict societies, and specifically its embrace of peacekeeping, can be assumed to be shaped by the same factors. Indeed, publications on China's embrace of PKOs in the 00s often focused on similar explanations, most notably Beijing's desire to live up to the role of a 'responsible power' that integrated domestic aspirations with external expectations.[9] Miwa Hirono and Marc Lanteigne use the overlap between three international 'positions' (that of norm maker,

[2]Thies, Cameron and Marijke Breuning (2012), 'Integrating foreign policy analysis and international relations through role theory', *Foreign Policy Analysis*, 8(1), 1–4.

[3]Harnisch, Sebastian (2016a), 'China's historical self and its international role', in: Sebastian Harnisch et al. (eds.), *China's International Roles*, London: Routledge, 2016, 38–39.

[4]Suzuki, Shogo (2007), 'The importance of "Othering" in China's national identity: Sino-Japanese relations as a stage of identity conflicts', *The Pacific Review*, 20(1), 23–47; Wang, Zheng (2014). *Never forget national humiliation: Historical memory in Chinese politics and foreign relations*. Columbia University Press.

[5]Wang, Hongying (2000), 'Multilateralism in Chinese foreign policy: the limits of socialization', *Asian Survey*, 40(3), 475–491.

[6]Weiss, Jessica (2014). *Powerful patriots: nationalist protest in China's foreign relations*. Oxford University Press, 19–24.

[7]Harnisch, 'China's historical self', 39–43.

[8]Thies, Cameron (2016), 'The US and China: altercast roles and changing power in the 20th century'; Maslow, Sebastian (2016), 'China and Japan: partner, rival and enemy?'; both in: Harnisch et al. (eds.), *China's International Roles*, 100–105; 192–195.

[9]Chen, Jing (2009), 'Explaining the Change in China's Attitude toward UN Peacekeeping: a norm change perspective', *Journal of Contemporary Chi*na, 18(58), 157–173; Richardson, Courtney (2011), 'A responsible power? China and the UN peacekeeping

norm taker and developing non-Western country) as a framework to explain the shift.[10] Most recently, He Yin has advanced an explanation based on a changing Chinese identity constructed against an 'other' formed by the entire international system, moving from revolutionary outcast to integrated member.[11]

Other publications have attributed China's embrace of PKOs to more hard-edged strategic and economic calculations. The desire to protect China's expanding business interests (and citizens) overseas has been described as a main driver behind Beijing's increasing engagement in PKOs and other security measures in Africa.[12] This is a plausible contributing factor, but cannot account for the pattern of deployments by itself—for example, some of China's biggest contributions were made to missions in Liberia, Lebanon and Mali, whose economic ties with Beijing are negligible.[13] Another explanation, the desire to gain field experience for the People's Liberation Army (PLA) amid a revolution in military affairs,[14] has difficulty accounting for the initial Chinese reluctance to commit combat troops.

A final explanation, and one that potentially fuses both strands of arguments, can be found in the practicalities of norm entrepreneurship at the international level. Specifically, in order to play a more influential role in the broader debate about interventions and state sovereignty that gripped the international community after the end of the Cold War, China first had to demonstrate its commitment to the United Nations (UN) and credibility as a major security actor.[15] This brings us back to the broader question of self-conception and how it shapes strategic policy choices, underscoring the utility of role theory to investigate China's changing attitude towards peacekeeping.

However, its only formal application, so far, remains a short passage in Harnisch's contribution to a volume on China's international roles.[16] Moreover, Chinese stances on peacekeeping and UN interventions had already undergone several distinct phases prior to the most recent engagement. By relating these to dominant or emergent roles at the time, this article aims to provide a longer-term overview. Additionally, by pointing out the explanatory value such discursive shifts had for previous policy changes, it also stresses the importance of tracing ongoing present debates and provides a brief outlook on the future.

Before presenting this material, it is necessary to sketch a brief model of how the involved actors relate to each other in the Chinese case, and what kinds of dynamics spring from it. Similar to specific policies, international roles will be domestically contested by constituencies and political entrepreneurs that seek to have their own beliefs and values enshrined in the image their country projects on the international stage. Observing such processes and prevalent themes in the related discourses thus offers clues on which role conceptions are waxing and waning. Politically, elites in a Leninist state have a strong ability to defend their preferred roles against bottom-up challenges,[17] and the sizable propaganda apparatus at their disposal also makes it easier to disseminate new, desirable role concepts to the citizenry. At times of especially high centralization of political power—most notably the high point of Mao's personal influence in the 1960s, but to a lesser extent also the Xi Jinping era—roles can be effectively shaped by a tiny group of leaders or even a single figure whose

regime'; Zhao, Lei (2011), 'Two pillars of China's global peace engagement strategy: UN peacekeeping and international peacebuilding'; both in *International Peacekeeping*, 18(3).

[10]Hirono, Miwa, and Marc Lanteigne (2011), 'Introduction: China and UN peacekeeping', *International Peacekeeping* 18(3), 243–256.

[11]He, Yin (2019), 'China Rising and Its Changing Policy on UN Peacekeeping', in: Cedric de Coning and Mateja Peter (eds.), *United Nations Peace Operations in a Changing Global Order*, London: Palgrave MacMillan, 256–258.

[12]Zhao, 'Two pillars'.

[13]Data on specific contributions by country and mission can be found on the UN's peacekeeping portal (www.peacekeeping.un.org/en).

[14]Huang, Chin-hao (2011), 'Principles and Praxis of China's peacekeeping', *International Peacekeeping* 18(3), 257–270.

[15]Tang, Yongsheng (2002), 'China and UN peacekeeping operations (*zhongguo yu lianheguo weihe xingdong*)', *World Economics and Politics* 9/2002.

[16]Harnisch, 'China's historical self'.

[17]Harnisch, Sebastian (2016b), 'Role theory and the study of Chinese foreign policy', in: Sebastian Harnisch et al. (eds.), *China's International Roles*, London: Routledge, 2016, 14.

worldview is seen as authoritative. On the other hand, in times in which power is dispersed or external shocks disrupt a domestic consensus, roles become unsettled and there is more leeway for public dissent with previous orthodoxy. As a result, processes of role setting should become more pluralistic. When selecting and discussing materials that contain Chinese role conceptions over longer periods of time, it is thus important to take the historical, political context into account.

Another point is the emergence of new groups which have a stake in China's international role conception. Crucially, this includes public intellectuals and experts on international issues, who became increasingly involved in the Chinese policy process as a result of a broader trend of professionalization beginning in the 1980s.[18] While their overall influence is debatable and varies significantly between individuals, the increasingly, public presence of such experts makes them a crucial source for information on domestic debates,[19] as well as a powerful indicator for the emergence and adaptation of new roles and self-images.[20]

Accordingly, this article aims to sketch a complex relationship between several factors: first, the development of Chinese international roles that were relevant to engagement with issues of peace-keeping, UN interventions and engagement of conflict societies—which are in turn assumed to be the result of domestic consensus-building and external influences; and finally, the adoption of specific policies like peacekeeping that directly affected these societies.

Methodology

As described above, role development is understood as a social interaction that aims at achieving congruence between self-image and action at the national level, which itself requires the establish-ment of a broad, national consensus. The forging (and breaking) of such a consensus is a public process playing out in the intellectual arena and can thus be observed from the outside. In order to do so, it is necessary to study a large number of documents, both official (definitive statements by top leaders or white papers) and academic (expert discourses on specific policy problems, broader strategic choices or the fundamental role which a country should play on the global stage). Of particular interests are statements containing descriptive notions about China's fundamental char-acter as an international actor, or prescriptive notions about what it ought to be and do.

Accordingly, the methodological approach here is an interpretative 'close reading' of documents that sketches the relationship between general notions of Chinese identity and role in the world with specific attitudes towards peacekeeping. The documents, discussed below, were drawn from three sources: first, statements by key leaders outlining major themes regarding China's role in the world, its overall international strategy and general approach to issues of peace and conflict, drawn from compilations of leaders' speeches, long-form essays and articles. Second, a sample of influential Chinese academic publications identified through a search for key terms like 'peacekeeping', narrowed further down to pieces that were published at important political inflection points or introduced novel arguments and received substantial attention measured by citations.[21] Third, specific policy statements on peacekeeping and its role in China's overall international strategy made either by Chinese representatives in the relevant UN organs like the Security Council and Peacebuilding Commission or outlined in government white papers.[22]

---

[18]Cabestan, Jean-Pierre (2009), 'China's foreign-and security-policy decision-making processes under Hu Jintao', *Journal of Current Chinese Affairs*, 38(3), 63–97; Shambaugh, David (2002), 'China's international relations think tanks: evolving structure and process', *The China Quarterly*, 171, 575–596.

[19]Abb, Pascal (2015), 'China's foreign policy think tanks: institutional evolution and changing roles', *Journal of Contemporary China*, 24(93), 531–553.

[20]Noesselt, Nele, 'China and socialist countries: role change and role continuity', in: Harnisch et al. (eds., 2016), *China's International Roles*, 171–172.

[21]Articles were drawn from the *China Academic Journals* database of Chinese core journals in the social sciences and humanities.

[22]The former can be found on the website of the Chinese permanent mission to the UN (www.china-un.org), the latter are drawn from sections of Chinese defense white papers published through the archives of the State Council or Ministry of Defense.

Chinese Role Conceptions and Shifting Attitudes to Peacekeeping

Since the aim of this article is to shed light on background processes underlying policy changes, it is first necessary to identify crucial turning points. We can roughly divide China's history with peace-keeping missions—and the broader international system supporting them—into four phases: first, a phase lasting from the establishment of the People's Republic of China (PRC) to its official recognition as representing 'China' by the UN General Assembly (UNGA), during which Beijing was locked out of the UN system and often hostile to it (1949–1971); second, a phase of wary rapprochement with its new, elevated position as a UNSC member (1971–1988); third, a shift towards limited contributions to and diplomatic support for PKOs (1988–2003); and finally, China's emergence as a leading troop-contributing country (TCC) and stakeholder in the security of post-conflict societies especially in Africa (2003-present). Each of these will be sketched below, while pointing out connections with broader role debates and/or political shifts going on at the time. Accordingly, this article is mostly organized as a historical overview, but with a particular focus on developments within the last few years. As we will see, these have brought further significant shifts in China's self-image that also may impact its future role in conflict societies, but whose ultimate impact is not yet clear.

Phase 1 (1949-1971)

The newly-established PRC's first engagements with the international system still bore the marks of the civil war from which it had just emerged, and in several ways constituted a continuation of this struggle. Its primary identity (and self-defined role) in world politics was as a revolutionary force, initially firmly aligned with the Soviet Union in a perceived global struggle between socialism and imperialism. This alignment was reinforced by the pattern of official diplomatic relationships emerging after the end of the Chinese Civil War, with nations in the Western camp continuing to recognize the Republic of China (ROC) government on Taiwan as legitimate, while Beijing received backing from the USSR and its allies. Prior to decolonization, the former outnumbered the latter, leaving Beijing shut out of the UN and other international organizations developing in its orbit.

This issue cemented fundamental Chinese opposition to the emerging UN system while deepening the split within it, paving the way for a rapid escalation into armed conflict. The outbreak of the Korean War in June 1950, the deployment of an US-led UN force in response,[23] and China's own intervention in October pitched both sides against each other. This further deepened Chinese hostility towards the UN, leading to its denunciation as an instrument of American hegemony.[24] Instead, China sought integration into the Soviet camp and closer relations with other post-colonial developing countries, a strategy enshrined in the formulation of the 'five principles of coexistence'.[25]

Until the Sino-Soviet split in 1960, Chinese policy towards UN interventions was strongly shaped by its alignment with the USSR, and domestic pronouncements served the associated propaganda needs. For example, when the Suez Crisis in 1956 led to the establishment of the UN Emergency Force (UNEF) by way of an UNGA vote, an editorial in *World Affairs* (*shijie zhishi*) simply mirrored the Soviet position of voicing procedural concerns about this bypassing of the UNSC, but welcomed the initiative as an end to the Anglo-French-Israeli campaign.[26] This attitude reflected Beijing's self-conception as a junior member of the Soviet-led camp, which had been enshrined by Mao in the principle of 'leaning to one side'.[27]

---

[23]In an ironic twist, UNSC authorization of this intervention did not founder on a Soviet veto because the USSR was boycotting the body in protest over its inclusion of the ROC government.

[24]Meng, Wenting (2017), 'A Review of research on China's participation in UN peacekeeping (*zhongguo canyu lianheguo weihe xingdong yanjiu shuping)'*, *Journal of International Studies* 4/2017, 85–102; Zhao, Lei (2011), 'Two pillars'.

[25]Zhang, Shuguang (2007), 'Constructing "Peaceful Coexistence": China's Diplomacy toward the Geneva and Bandung Conferences, 1954–55', *Cold War History*, 7(4), 509–528.

[26]Sun, Nan (1956), „What is UNEF? (*shenme shi lianheguo guoji jinji budui?)"*, *World Affairs*, 10 December 1956.

[27]Zhao, Quansheng (1996), *Interpreting Chinese Foreign Policy: the Micro-Macro Linkage Approach*, Oxford: Oxford University Press, p. 46 f.

With fissures developing in the Sino-Soviet alliance towards the end of the 1950s, China became much more willing to engage the outside world on its own terms, and the same thing applied to conflict societies. While having disavowed interstate wars as a consequence of its own understanding of 'peaceful coexistence' between nations, Beijing remained deeply committed to the cause of world revolution. Revolutionary wars were thus considered both justified and inevitable, particularly in post-colonial areas that were exposed to the twin forces of capitalism and imperialism.[28]

The second norm guiding Chinese behavior, the primacy of national sovereignty, was similarly rooted in China's own experience of colonialist domination (and, more cynically, self-interest in blocking off external 'meddling' in areas like Tibet). This created another significant point of overlap with other post-colonial nations that became more important as China looked for partners outside of the Soviet camp.

Following the outbreak of the Congo crisis and the (Soviet-approved) deployment of the UN operations in the Congo (ONUC) mission, the PRC government issued a proclamation denouncing the intervention as an 'illegal invasion by US imperialists' that 'threatened the independence of the Congo and of African states in general, as well as peace in Africa, Asia and the world'.[29] Reflecting the newly dominant theme of solidarity between post-colonial nations, the statement is also notable for omitting any reference to the position of the USSR—although there were still points of overlap, most notably on the legitimacy of the Lumumba government.

The heated, ideological climate of the 1960s and Mao's return to preeminence led to the formulation of a more extensive and coherent theory on the relationship between revolution and conflict, the resulting global battle lines, and China's own role in this struggle. As perhaps best summarized by Lin Biao,[30] the dominant Chinese thinking of the time understood post-colonial conflicts as analogous to China's own experience of civil war—and not just because they featured nationalist and (sometimes) communist insurrections. Rather, they were seen as a global extension of the old Civil War fronts, constituting an uprising of the 'rural areas of the world' (Asia, Africa and Latin America) against its 'cities' (North America and Europe). World revolution therefore ultimately depended on the victory of the former over the latter, committing China to direct involvement in post-colonial wars. However, intense Chinese support for rebel movements in Angola, Mozambique, Congo, Niger, Ghana and Burundi did not succeed in spreading socialism across Africa, while severely straining China's ties with many African governments.[31] These interventions, conducted entirely outside the UN system, ultimately had to be aborted as the chaos of the Cultural Revolution engulfed China and drastically reduced its international agency.

Phase 2 (1971-1988)

A crucial (and intended) result of Beijing's embrace of post-colonial countries in Africa and elsewhere was its steady gain in recognition as the legitimate government of 'China'. In 1971, the UNGA voted to confer this recognition, and the attendant UNSC seat, on Beijing. This elevated China to the pinnacle of a system it had previously opposed and granted it a prominent voice on global security issues, if initially not much actual influence due to the Cold War gridlock in the UNSC.

Détente with the US led to a significant rhetorical moderation in the 1970s, and references to 'US imperialism' in official documents or published articles quickly receded. Opposition to 'Soviet revisionism' and competition for allegiance in the Third World, however, continued unabated. The Soviet Union served as China's most significant 'other' both in the sense of a contemporary

---

[28]Kim, Samuel (1979), *China, the United Nations and World Order*. Princeton: Princeton University Press, 1979, p. 70.
[29]PRC State Council (1960), „Statement by the PRC government on the situation in the Congo (*zhonghua renmin gongheguo zhengfu guanyu gangguo jushi de shengming*)", *Bulletin of the PRC State Council* 30/1960, 30 September 1960.
[30]Lin, Biao (1965) „The International Significance of Comrade Mao-Tse Tung's Theory of People's War", in: *Long Live the Victory of People's War!*, Beijing: Foreign Language Press, 1965.
[31]Alden, Chris and Ana Cristina Alves (2008), History and Identity in the Construction of China's Africa Policy ", in: *Review of African Political Economy*, 35(115), 43–58.

international foil and for the development of China's own narrative of historical victimhood. In this context, China's reemergent academic historiography began to revisit imperial Russian predations on China,[32] creating a lens through which China's contemporary relations with former colonial powers are still frequently interpreted today.

China's integration into the UN system gave it a global platform on which to expound on its worldview and role, particularly its credentials as a developing country. In 1974, Deng Xiaoping made use of this pulpit to summarize the current line in Maoist thought on international affairs: the so-called 'Three Worlds Theory' which divided the international system into a top tier made up of the two superpowers, a mid-tier occupied by aligned-developed countries, and the bottom rung made up of the world's developing nations.[33] Both superpowers were portrayed as inherently imperialist and exploitative, with countries in the lower tiers being victimized to varying degrees, the heaviest burden falling on resource-rich developing countries. As a self-declared socialist and developing country belonging to the Third World, China's role was to help others in this group to strengthen their political and economic independence, while at the same time reaffirming its support for revolutionary struggle. Crucially, Deng also committed China never to become a 'superpower', although this should not be read as a renunciation of leadership ambitions, but rather of the term's hierarchical and exploitative connotations within this theory.

For the remainder of the decade (and much of the following), China showed little interest in leveraging the influence due a permanent member of the UNSC. China's voting record on UNSC resolutions—including ones that established PKOs in the Sinai, Golan Heights and Lebanon—was one of non-participation and sometimes formal abstention, but refraining from using its veto.[34] The reason, given for this, was invariably opposition to any infringement on national sovereignty, China's normative lodestar as revolutionary ambitions fell by the wayside.

With very little previous indication, however, China suddenly switched its voting stance in December 1981. On occasion of the extension of UNFICYP's mandate in Cyprus, the Chinese delegate to the UNSC announced that his country would, from now on, 'actively support peacekeeping activities, as long as they abided by the UN charter, supported international peace and upheld national sovereignty and independence'.[35] While not establishing any new missions until 1988, the UNSC proceeded to vote unanimously on the extension of existing mandates, a total of 59 times.[36]

Officially, this shift was motivated by vague 'changes in the international environment and in the role of PKOs'[37]; however, the fact that Cyprus was the only developed Western country to host such a mission, while China was primarily concerned with the sovereignty of post-colonial and developing countries, may have played a role as well. Further, this policy shift was very likely the result of a top-down process, as there had been no broader societal debate over it. In fact, the first Chinese article to ever mention the term 'peacekeeping', another *World Affairs* editorial from November 1981, still portrayed it negatively and asserted that 'the position of the Chinese government has always been to oppose peacekeeping on principle'.[38]

For most of the 1980s, China's focus on its nascent reform policy resulted in detachment at the international level, but the decade saw the evolution of a strand of thought that would run through much of its subsequent foreign policy: the link between the concepts of 'peace' and 'development' that was first established by Deng in 1985. In Deng's words, these 'two big issues in the

---

[32]Shi, Zukang (1976), „Good neighbours or predatory invaders? (*shi youhao mulin haishi qinlüe lüeduo?*)", in: *Guoji Maoyi Wenti* 1/ 1976, 37–43; Zhong, E (1976), „The Sino-Russian 'Treaty of Aigun' and the hegemonic logic of Soviet revisionism (*zhong-e 'aihun tiaoyue' yu suxiu baquan luoji*)", *Lishi Yanjiu* 04/1976, 105–120.

[33]Deng, Xiaoping (1974), „Speech at the Special Session of the U.N. General Assembly ", 10 April 1974.

[34]Shichor, Yitzhak (2007), „China's voting behavior in the UN Security Council ", *China Brief* 6(18).

[35]Zhou, Qi (2010), „Changes in China's attitude towards UN PKOs and their causes (*zhongguo dui lianheguo weihe xingdong taidu de bianhua jiqi yuanyin*)", *Human Rights* 02/2010, 54–59.

[36]Query of UNSC voting records and the UN's database on PKOs.

[37]ibid.

[38]Jin, Wanqi, „What are UN peacekeeping forces (*shenme shi lianheguo weichi heping budui?*) ", *World Affairs* 22/1981, November 1981.

contemporary world' had formed a natural point of confluence in China—like the rest of the developing world, China needed peace to pursue its reforms, and in so doing, it would strengthen the global 'peace camp' and make a crucial contribution to world stability.[39] This thought neither amounted to a definitive foreign policy doctrine nor a fully-fledged role at the time, but provided a key theme that subsequent leaders would riff on to far greater consequence.

Phase 3 (1988-2003)

The period of passive acceptance of UN peacekeeping continued until 1988, when China applied for membership in the Special Commission on Peacekeeping Operations, offering up its first explicitly positive appraisal of PKOs as 'effective means to protect international peace and security'.[40] This step slightly predated the end of the Cold War, a structural change of enormous consequence that would clear the way for a rapid expansion of PKOs as UNSC vetoes became much less frequent. From 1988 to 2003, China voted for the establishment of 41 new PKOs (and regular extensions of existing ones), many of which had robust mandates including the use of force.[41] This pattern was broken only on two occasions, when China vetoed the expansion of missions in Guatemala (1997) and Macedonia (1999). However, these votes did not involve objections on principle, but rather China's specific interest in diplomatically isolating Taiwan, which both prospective host states recognized at the time.[42] Generally, the demise of Cold-War-era blocks led to a much more consensual atmosphere in the UNSC, for which peacekeeping votes were an early indication. During the 1990s, China's overall UNSC voting alignment with the US rose to over 90 percent.[43]

Even more importantly, the 1990s also saw the first dispatches of Chinese peacekeepers: by the end of the decade, around 1,200 Chinese troops had participated in a total of nine missions, including a major deployment of military engineers to Cambodia from 1992 to 94.[44] Academic interest in the subject skyrocketed—between 1992 and the end of the decade, 401 articles mentioning the term 'peacekeeping' (weihe 维和) appeared in Chinese core academic journals, whereas the total for 1981 to 1991 had been just nine such pieces.[45]

There was indeed much to discuss—the increasingly intrusive nature of peacekeeping, and the hollowing out of traditional notions of sovereignty, remained a top concern. Academic authors, in the 90s accordingly, tended to focus on issues like the governance of such interventions through the UN system and the danger of its capture by US interests,[46] or sketching key normative principles like host state consent, broad supervision and time limitation.[47] Sometimes, intervention campaigns affected China itself, most notably when the Chinese embassy in Belgrade was hit by NATO airstrikes in 1999. However, despite the domestic outrage over it, this event did not derail scholarly engagement with interventionism and international crisis management.[48] In fact, it seems to have spurred many experts to argue for a greater role in peacekeeping, in order to strengthen the stricter UN

[39]Deng, Xiaoping (1985), 'Peace and development are the two main issues in the contemporary world (heping he fazhan shi dangdai shijie de liang da wenti)', speech dated 4 March 1985, online: http://www.aisixiang.com/data/3403.html.

[40]Zhou, „Changes in China's attitude".

[41]Meng, 'A Review'; UNSC archives.

[42]Chinese statements made during the UNSC debates on draft resolutions S/1997/18 and S/1999/201, see UNSC archives. In the case of MINUGUA in Guatemala, China allowed a follow-up resolution to pass shortly afterwards; it also acquiesced to several missions in Haiti, another Taiwan ally.

[43]Wuthnow, Joel (2013), Chinese diplomacy and the UN Security Council: beyond the veto, London: Routledge, p. 29 f.

[44]Gill, Bates and James Reilly (2000), 'Sovereignty, intervention and peacekeeping: the view from Beijing', Survival 42(3), 41–59.

[45]Based on a query of the CNKI database in August 2019.

[46]Huang, Renwei (1995), 'Impacts of the reform of UN peacekeeping mechanisms after the Cold War and their conflict with national sovereignty (lengzhan hou lianheguo weihe jizhi gaige de yingxiang jiqi yu guojia zhuquan de chongtu)', SASS Quarterly 4/1995, 66–74.

[47]Ji, Xiangxiang (1999), 'Historical study of UN PKOs (lianheguo weichi heping xingdong de lishi kaocha)', Journal of Zhejiang University 3/1999, 1–8.

[48]Carlson, Allen (2004), 'Helping to keep the peace (albeit reluctantly): China's recent stance on sovereignty and multilateral intervention', Pacific Affairs 77(1), 9–27; Pang Zhongying, 'China's changing attitude to UN peacekeeping', International Peacekeeping 12(1), 87–104.

system over US-led multilateral coalitions, warning that the latter would otherwise set the standards for international interventions without any Chinese input.[49]

Despite the controversial nature of this question, many debate participants adopted an attitude described in later reviews as 'learning'[50]—providing descriptions of the UN system that enabled and oversaw deployments, outlining the shifts in international systemic structure, normative beliefs and interpretations of international law that allowed for the expansion of PKOs in the 1990s,[51] or even more specific analyses of PKO performance and 'best practices' established by more experienced TCCs.[52] Common to these contributions was a very positive appraisal of peacekeeping in principle—provided that it strictly followed the UN charter—and the argument that deeper Chinese engagement with the system could help to ensure this.

Given the enormous domestic and international upheaval of 1989–91, it is hard to identify a single causal reason for China's warming towards the expanding UN peacekeeping regime. Multiple factors connecting domestic politics and external expectations arguably formed the nucleus from which a new Chinese role unfolded in the 1990s. Most important among these was the 1989 Tiananmen crackdown and the resulting international condemnation, painting China as an unrepentant and brutally repressive autocracy during a time of sweeping democratization. This characterization, in conjunction with rapid Chinese economic growth and rising tensions over Taiwan, led to the emergence of prominent 'China threat' discourses in the early to mid-90s that cast Beijing as the natural enemy of Western-led liberalization.[53] The necessity to provide a more positive counternarrative of China's international behaviour and undergird it with concrete actions naturally brought a deeper engagement with the UN and PKOs into focus.[54]

Additionally, a thawing in the Chinese ideological climate in the latter half of the 90s allowed for relatively open policy debates, even those which questioned the bedrock norm of sovereignty. Official statements, as well as many scholarly articles, began to acknowledge the need to weigh sovereignty against competing norms, especially the protection of human rights.[55] Chinese voices increasingly reflected international discourses on this issue, thus internalizing outside expectations for how an emerging China should behave in the world.

From a role perspective, the 1990s were a time of profound unsettlement for China—unmoored from the old ideological guidelines, yet not embracing political reform; profiting from globalization, yet flirting with a rising nationalism; still a relatively poor country, yet increasingly seen as a future superpower. Only towards the end of the decade did a new potential consensus emerge around the key theme of 'responsibility', with conceptions of China as a 'responsible country' (fuzeren de guojia 负责任的国家) or even 'responsible great power' (fuzeren de daguo负责任的大国) rapidly gaining traction.[56] As discussed by Richardson,[57] the concept had broad appeal: signaling support for the international order while drawing a clear dividing line with the interventionist practices of the US-led West, and announcing rising Chinese ambitions while assuaging fears about how its growing power may be wielded. It thus neatly integrated domestic influences—exemplified by academic aspirations

---

[49]Gill and Reilly (2000), 'Sovereignty, intervention and peacekeeping'; Mao, Weizhun (2017), 'Debating China's International Responsibility', The Chinese Journal of International Politics 10(2), 173–210.

[50]Feng, Jicheng (2012), 'China's participation in UN PKOs: studying practices and recognizing identity (zhongguo canyu lianheguo weihe xingdong: xuexi shijian yu shenfen chengren)', Foreign Affairs Review 1/2012, 59–71.

[51]Chen, Weidong (1999). 'Discussing the legality of UN peacekeeping forces and related questions (lüelun lianheguo weihe budui de falü xingzhi ji xiangguan wenti)', faxue pinglun 1/1999.

[52]Tan, Yonglei (1994), 'From peacekeeping to peace enforcement—discussing changes in UN PKOs since the end of the Cold War (cong weichi heping dao qiangzhi heping—lun lengzhan hou lianheguo weihe xingdong de bianhua)', lanzhou xuekan 5/1994, 50–54.

[53]Roy, Denny (1996), 'The "China threat" issue: major arguments', Asian Survey 36(8), 758–771.

[54]Chen, 'Explaining the Change in China's Attitude'.

[55]Carlson, 'Helping to keep the peace'; Huang, 'Principles and Praxis'.

[56]Foot, Rosemary (2001), 'Chinese power and the idea of a responsible state', The China Journal, (45), 1–19; Xia, Liping, (2001), 'China: a responsible great power', Journal of Contemporary China, 10(26), 17–25.

[57]Richardson, 'A responsible power?'.

for China to define its own place in the world order[58]—with outside pressure to conform to said order.

Still, there was substantially less domestic agreement about what China's new responsibilities should entail. Many scholars and officials warned that embracing this label risked a rhetorical entrapment, since its specific content could be defined by the US and then used to push China towards compliance with norms not of its own making.[59] The resulting search for areas in which Beijing could demonstrate global responsibility while still advancing its own values, and for a self-defined policy agenda to implement this strategy in practice, quickly led Chinese thinkers to the UN peacekeeping system.

Phase 4 (2003-)

In the early 2000s, Chinese scholars began to suggest deeper engagement with PKOs as a way to demonstrate China's responsibility and integration into the international system, while also enhancing its own security.[60] Other experts embraced PKOs on both normative and strategic reasons: some argued that the UN system was the sole legitimate authority to decide such infringements on national sovereignty, and greater Chinese participation would counterbalance US-led intervention efforts outside of it.[61] China's steadily expanding overseas economic interests, many of which were concentrated in fragile states like Sudan, provided a robust material reason to aid stabilization efforts.[62] The consensus remained strongly favorable of PKOs in general and mainly concerned with procedural constraints like UNSC authorization and host state consent. Chinese operational and diplomatic support was treated as a given, while the focus shifted towards ensuring effectiveness and legality.

On the ground, China set a new precedent by approving and participating in a relatively intrusive mission to East Timor.[63] Deployments significantly expanded beginning in 2003, both in the number of troops and missions: first deployments of combat troops to Liberia and the Democratic Republic of the Congo (DRC) were followed up by missions in Haiti (notably still a Taiwanese ally), Lebanon and Sudan in quick succession. By 2008, China had over 2,000 peacekeepers on active deployments, an average which it has maintained until the present.[64] Rapid expansion went along with professionalization: the Defense Ministry set up a Peacekeeping Affairs Office in 2001 and dedicated riot police and peacekeeper training facilities were opened in 2004 and 2009, respectively.[65] At the operational level, Chinese peacekeepers consistently maintained a strong focus on providing engineering, construction and policing services,[66] a priority that fit in neatly with the contours of the UN's emerging 'peacebuilding' paradigm.

These developments have been directly attributed to China's embrace of responsible power hood just a few years earlier; indeed, the vast majority of publications seeking to explain rising Chinese PKO involvement named it as a key reason.[67] However, while the 'responsible power' role had been highly effective as a domestic rallying point, the same could not be said about its international acceptance. During the 00s, 'China threat' discourses gained further traction as the Chinese economy continued its rapid pace of growth, seemingly putting it on track to overtake the US in relatively

---

[58]Mao, 'Debating China's international responsibility'.

[59]Deng, Yong (2014), 'China: The post-responsible power', *The Washington Quarterly* 37(4), 117–132.

[60]Tang, 'China and UN peacekeeping operations'.

[61]Xu, Weidi (2005), 'Exploration in Vacillation and Hesitation: The Difficulties and Challenges for UN Peacekeeping Operations (*yaobai yu panghuang zhong de tansuo—lianheguo weihe xingdong mianlin de kunnan yu tiaozhan*)', *World Economics and Politics* 5/2005.

[62]Large, Daniel (2008), "China & the Contradictions of 'Non-interference' in Sudan," *Review of African Political Economy*, 35:115, 93–106.

[63]Gill and Reilly, 'Sovereignty'.

[64]ISDP (2018), *China's Role in UN Peacekeeping*, Institute for Security and Development Policy, 2018, online: https://isdp.eu/publication/chinas-role-un-peacekeeping/.

[65]Feng, 'China's participation in UN PKOs'.

[66]Xue, Lei (2018), 'China's development-oriented peacekeeping strategy in Africa', in: Alden, Chris et al. (eds.), *China and Africa*, London: Palgrave MacMillan, 2018, 83–99.

[67]Carlson, 'Helping to keep the peace'; Richardson, 'A responsible power?'; Zhao, 'Two pillars'.

short order. Contrary to earlier versions, these arguments were not so much based on ideological differences, but historical patterns of rising powers challenging the orders built by previous hegemons, thus imbuing them with a structural inevitability while deemphasizing political agency.[68]

These arguments hugely impacted Chinese scholars and policymakers, who devoted an enormous volume of literature and sometimes official statements to their refutation.[69] Since the reality of a power shift between Washington and Beijing could hardly be denied (and was indeed a point of pride for many Chinese observers), their arguments mainly revolved around China's own intrinsical peacefulness or vested interest in maintaining the international status quo.

In 2003, Zheng Bijian—a retired official and scholar with close ties to Hu Jintao—rolled out the concept of China's 'peaceful rise' (heping jueqi和平崛起), soon after recast as 'peaceful development' (heping fazhan和平发展).[70] Its central theme was the interdependence between China's own economic development and a stable international environment, simultaneously committing China to seeking stability and stressing the positive effects of its own growth on world peace.[71] The concept thus provided a positive narrative of China's emerging global role, while domestically serving as a unifying slogan that was relentlessly repeated by political and academic elites and has remained a key parole In China's diplomatic repertoire.[72]

While most of the subsequent attention focused on the commitment to 'peace', this slogan, and its subsequent interpretation, also reaffirmed 'development' as its prerequisite—thus linking up with earlier Deng-era thought on this relationship. Its utility was strengthened further by the near-simultaneous emergence of a similar conceptual and institutional nexus at the UN level, exemplified by the establishment of the Peacebuilding Commission in 2005. Both the roles as a 'responsible power' and a 'peacefully developing' nation had in common that they were rooted at least as much in external expectations as in Chinese self-identification: their adoption cannot be fully explained without taking stock of the 'China threat' narratives they sought to disprove and which acted as a foil for the construction of a more positive counter-image. Accordingly, they can be considered as examples of successful alter-casting on the part of the United States, China's most significant other in the post-Cold-War era.[73] However, these episodes also occurred at a time when there was still a significant gap in status and capabilities between both sides that rendered China receptive to such signals. As the power balance between Washington and Beijing continued to shift, it would also strengthen the hand of domestic actors who held much greater ambitions.

Towards a Chinese Model of Peacebuilding?

Observers of Chinese foreign policy usually trace its shift to a more active or 'assertive' stance to the experience of the Global Financial Crisis in 2007–2008, which hardly left a dent in China's economic growth while signalling an end to the 'unipolar moment' enjoyed by the US since the end of the Cold War.[74] Now acknowledged as a crucial global governance actor and endowed with fresh confidence in its own economic model, China's IR experts entered a new round of debates over the country's international role, in which more ambitious voices pushed the envelope.[75] Within the perennial

---

[68]Chan, Steve (2007). *China, the US and the Power-transition Theory: A Critique*. Routledge. Page #.

[69]Li, Xiaohua (1999), 'Power shifts and the stability of the international system—dissecting the "China threat" theory ("quanli zhuanyi" yu guoji tixi de wending—jianxi "zhongguo weixie lun")', World Economics and Politics 5/1999, 1–5; Sha, Jiguang (2000), 'Discussing the "China threat" theory spread by Western media (dui xifang meiti sanbu "zhongguo weixie lun" pingxi)', Journal of International Studies 3/2000, 113–125.

[70]Glaser, Bonnie and Evan Medeiros (2007), 'The changing ecology of foreign policy-making in China: the ascension and demise of the theory of 'peaceful rise''. *The China Quarterly*, 190, 291–310.

[71]State Council Information Office (SCIO, 2005), *China's Peaceful Development Road*, Beijing: SCIO, online: http://www.china.org.cn/english/2005/Dec/152669.htm.

[72]State Council Information Office (SCIO, 2011), *China's Peaceful Development*, Beijing: SCIO, online: http://english.www.gov.cn/archive/white_paper/2014/09/09/content_281474986284646.htm.

[73]Thies, 'The US and China'.

[74]Swaine, Michael (2010), 'Perceptions of an Assertive China', *China Leadership Monitor* 32.

[75]Pu, Xiaoyu (2017), 'Controversial identity of a rising China', *The Chinese Journal of International Politics* 10(2), 131–149.

debate on China's identity, the balance shifted away from proponents of global integration and engagement with international norms, and towards voices that defined China and its interests as fundamentally distinct from Western or 'universalist' notions.[76] Picking up on this mentality shift, the eminent Chinese IR scholar Wang Jisi argued that it comprised a crucial step towards a new Chinese 'great power role', even more important than the rapid growth of China's hard power resources.[77]

The increasing confidence in China's capabilities and potential rise to the status of global norm-maker is mirrored in writings on PKOs from this period. Two key themes stand out in this literature: first, Chinese assessments of PKOs began to focus much more on their consequences and efficiency rather than their normative and juridical justification. Based on first-hand observations of Chinese PKO deployments in Africa, Chinese analysts began to develop broader critiques of the liberal peacebuilding approach and its focus on political reform, which they saw as unsuited to the situation of poor and developing countries. One influential example from this period stressed the role of economic deprivation in causing conflicts, and accordingly argued for a greater emphasis on government capacity-building, stability and economic and social work over loftier political ambitions[78]; another author pointed out that political reform pressure had triggered resistance from host countries like the DRC and South Sudan, endangering the local missions.[79] The now-traditional role of Chinese peacekeepers in providing infrastructure and health care over combat roles was held up as a positive example for non-controversial developmental work.[80] Notably, some of these arguments dovetailed in part with influential Western critiques of the 'liberal peace' concept and its application,[81] enhancing the likelihood of international receptivity.

Second, there was a strong consensus that China was both obliged to devote greater resources to the peacekeeping system, and that it should use it as a platform to exercise global leadership. In the words of one expert, China must 'not just be an ordinary participant, but in control' of PKOs[82]; others had focussed on the lack of Chinese 'discursive power' in the PKO system compared to the ability of Western actors to shape both the normative guidelines of peacebuilding and narratives over specific crises like Darfur, calling for a greater Chinese representation in UN oversight organs and mission commands.[83] Whether they focused on ideational content or influence within the system, common to these voices is the belief that China could bring PKOs more in line with the needs of host countries, bridging China's own identities as a developing country and an emerging great power,[84] and forming the intellectual nucleus for a nascent 'China model' in peacebuilding.

China's international role was further affected by the handover to the 'fifth generation' of leadership centred around Xi Jinping in 2012, who quickly rolled out his own agenda. Crucially, some of its key concepts like the 'Chinese Dream' and 'new type of great-power relationship'—which promised a sweeping 'national rejuvenation' and peer status with the US, respectively—were early and obvious signals of a growing international ambition. The rollout of China's 'Belt and Road Initiative' (BRI) in 2013

---

[76]Shambaugh, David (2011), 'Coping with a conflicted China', *The Washington Quarterly* 34(1), 7–27.

[77]Wang, Jisi (2010), 'Great powers and the strategic environment: new issues in China's international role (*shijie daguo yu zhanlüe huanjing: zhongguo guoji juese de xin keti*)', *Contemporary International Relations* 4/2010, 1–10.

[78]Li, Dongyan (2012), 'Prospects and pathways for China's participation in UN peacekeeping (*zhongguo canyu lianheguo weihe jianhe de qianjing yu lujing*)', *Foreign Affairs Review* 3/2012, 1–14.

[79]Zhang, Yixiao (2015), 'From conflict management to peace management: the UN peacekeeping and security governance in post-conflict countries (*cong guanli chongtu dao guanli heping—lianheguo weihe xingdong yu chongtu hou guojia de anquan zhili*)', *guoji anquan yanjiu* 1/2015, 136–153.

[80]Zhang, Huiyu (2009), 'Reviewing China's participation in UN peacekeeping (zhongguo canyu lianheguo weihe shuping)', *Contemporary International Relations* 2/2009, 51–57.

[81]Autesserre, Séverine (2010), *The trouble with the Congo: Local violence and the failure of international peacebuilding*, Cambridge: Cambridge University Press; Richmond, Oliver (2009), 'Becoming liberal, unbecoming liberalism: Liberal-local hybridity via the everyday as a response to the paradoxes of liberal peacebuilding', *Journal of intervention and statebuilding*, 3(3), 324–344.

[82]Zhang, 'From conflict management'.

[83]He, Yin (2016), 'UN peacekeeping work and building Chinese discursive power (*lianheguo weihe shiwu yu zhongguo weihe huayuquan jianshe*)', *World Economics and Politics* 11/2016, 40–61; He, Jian and Chen, Cheng (2009), 'Discussing China's discursive power in UN peacekeeping (*lun zhongguo yu lianheguo weihe xingdong zhong de huayuquan*)', *guoji anquan yanjiu* 5/2009.

[84]Hirono and Lanteigne, 'Introduction'; Zhao, 'Two pillars'.

further underlined these aspirations with its promise to kickstart the development of areas that had missed out on globalization and hitch their wagons to the booming Chinese market, thus forming a 'community of common destiny'.[85]

Since many of the areas China seeks to penetrate with the BRI are conflict societies, it is likely that the coming years will see a further increase in engagement and spark another stage in the evolution of China's approach to peacekeeping and -building. While it is too early to tell how the newest role(s) it has claimed will ultimately shape China's approach to conflict societies, a look at emerging academic discourses on the topic can provide some clues. Most notably, recent years have seen a reaffirmation of the fundamental link between peace and development; but where previous applications were mainly concerned with deflecting foreign criticism of Chinese actions, their current iteration is very much outward-looking.

At the normative level, China has championed a 'right to development' since the 1980s and recently reaffirmed it as the 'primary human right' that is a prerequisite for the implementation of all others, as well as a crucial factor in safeguarding peace.[86] The latter point reflects arguments made by Chinese academics during the earlier debates on Chinese PKO engagement.[87]

Meanwhile, conceptually, the link between development and peace has matured into an approach described as the 'developmental peace' (fazhan heping 发展和平) that is explicitly designed as an alternative to Western-championed notions of liberal peacebuilding.[88] According to the most well-known proponent of this approach, He Yin, failures in liberal peacebuilding efforts can be directly attributed to their focus on political and institutional reconstruction in post-conflict societies, at the expense of first providing a solid economic basis. This, he argues, is rooted in a specific Western political experience that prioritizes personal freedom and self-expression, considers a lack of these factors to be the root cause of conflict and hence treats their (re-)establishment as the key to lasting peace. By contrast, China's own experience of moving past a century of turmoil towards economic growth, relative internal stability and steadily rising national strength is cited as proof of the fundamental importance of economic development.

Authors subscribing to this strand of thought argue that the contestation of the liberal paradigm creates a significant gap for China to enter—posing not just as the provider of technical blueprints for post-conflict reconstruction, but as a genuine norm entrepreneur, stressing the principles of sovereignty, political stability and ownership by local governments over the more intrusive Western-led programme of liberal peacebuilding.[89] An expanded and better coordinated Chinese peacekeeping apparatus, had focussed on developmental issues and coupled with the enormous resources being made available under the BRI, could eventually map out a distinctly 'Chinese Way' in global peace agency, separate from the traditional UN system.[90] Other proponents of the theory have suggested that extremely complicated, long-running conflicts in the Middle East can ultimately be attributed to lacking development perspectives, further exacerbated by Western interventionism and political pressure; China, on the other hand, could offer the region a more cautious, stability-oriented approach based on its own model.[91]

---

[85]Zhang, Dehua (2018), 'The Concept of "Community of Common Destiny" in China's Diplomacy: Meaning, Motives and Implications', *Asia & the Pacific Policy Studies* 5(2), 196–207.

[86]State Council Information Office (SCIO, 2016), *The Right to Development: China's Philosophy, Practice and Contribution*, Beijing: SCIO, online: http://www.scio.gov.cn/zfbps/32832/Document/1534707/1534707.htm.

[87]Suzuki, The importance of "Othering"'; Zhao, 'Two pillars'.

[88]He, Yin (2017), 'Developmental peace: China's programme in UN peacekeeping and peacebuilding (*fazhan heping: lianheguo weihe jianhe zhong de zhongguo fang'an*)', *guoji zhengzhi yanjiu* 4/2017, 10–32; Wang, Xuejun (2018), 'Developmental peace: understanding China's Africa policy in peace and security', in: Alden, Chris et al. (eds.), *China and Africa*, London: Palgrave MacMillan, 2018, 67–82.

[89]Kuo, Steven (2012), 'Beijing's understanding'; Meng, 'A Review'.

[90]Li, Dongyan (2018), 'China's international peacekeeping operations: concepts and methods (*zhongguo guoji weihe xingdong: gainian yu moshi*)', *World Economics and Politics* 4/2018, 90–106.

[91]Sun Degang and Zhang Dandan (2019), 'Peace through development: ideas and paths for China's participation in Middle East security (*yi fazhan cu heping: zhongguo canyu zhongdong anquan shiwu de linian yu lujing xuanze*)', *Global Review* 6/2019, 109–129.

These arguments are likely to resonate with Chinese policymakers, whose role ambitions clearly include norm entrepreneurship and who have been seeking to leverage their country's economic weight to this end. The general intellectual climate in Chinese foreign policy circles has in recent years shifted to be far more accommodating to indigenous ideas and solutions,[92] and 'developmental peace' is the first such example in the field of applied conflict theory. Moreover, the growth of China's PKO-related institutional apparatus has also endowed its proponents with positions from which they can influence the practice of global peacebuilding. Notably, He Yin is a professor in the Academy of the People's Armed Police, where he not only trains Chinese staff for overseas deployments, but also organizes courses for international participants.[93]

And while these ideas have not yet been translated into official policy, a quick review of recent official statements, mainly by Chinese representatives in the UN, suggests that they could see significant uptake as China embraces a new, more ambitious role. Conceptually, a developmental peace is very much in tune with the notion of China as an 'engine for development and prosperity' and bringer of development to overlooked corners of the earth,[94] an image that also underlies the BRI and could thus form a logical point of convergence between peacebuilding, economic activities, and other political and diplomatic engagements with conflict societies. Chinese representatives in the UNSC and PBOC have repeatedly described a lack of development as the root cause of conflicts like the one in Sudan[95] and espoused the importance of the BRI in creating peace and stability in Africa.[96] At the same time, Xi Jinping himself had begun to describe the BRI as a 'road of peace' even ahead of its potential economic benefits[97] and suggested that it could help resolve conflicts as intractable as that over Palestine.[98]

Whether the concept will indeed play a major role in China's next major policy shift on peacekeeping is of course not certain. For one, although the concept was first formulated in 2014, its academic uptake has been restricted to a relatively small group of authors. It is also not without its critics within China—in background interviews, two Chinese experts on peacebuilding dismissed the idea that such programs could function without a political component, and one considered its singular focus on economic development to be a regression to an outdated mentality. Historically, this part of Chinese academia has been very receptive to international debates and ideas, and has not shied away from arguing for attunement with them. But whichever way the chips will fall, China's expanding agency in conflict societies will be linked to another round of internal debates over the country's future role.

Conclusion

Studying Chinese attitudes towards peacekeeping through a role theory prism points to a nexus of three interrelated factors that contributed to shifts in the former: domestic policymaking dynamics, the role of scholars as ideational entrepreneurs, and international perceptions and expectations.

---

[92]Shambaugh, 'Coping with a conflicted China'.

[93]Zhang, Yi (2016), 'Training begins in Beijing for UN police missions', *China Daily*, 9 August 2016, online: http://usa.chinadaily.com.cn/world/2016-08/09/content_26397791.htm.

[94]Foreign Ministry of the People's Republic of China (2017a), 'Wang Yi: China will bring to the world greater benefits of peace, development and governance', 22 September 2017, online: https://www.fmprc.gov.cn/ce/cgbelfast/eng/zgxw_1/t1496929.htm.

[95]Foreign Ministry of the People's Republic of China (2017b), 'Statement by Ambassador Liu Jieyi at the Security Council Briefing on South Sudan', 24 May 2017, online: https://www.fmprc.gov.cn/mfa_eng/wjb_663304/zwjg_665342/zwbd_665378/t1481429.shtml.

[96]Foreign Ministry of the People's Republic of China (2017 c), 'Statement by Ambassador Liu Jieyi at the Security Council Open Debate on UN Peacekeeping Operations and Their Potential Contribution to the Overarching Goal of Sustaining Peace', 29 August 2017, online: https://www.fmprc.gov.cn/mfa_eng/wjb_663304/zwjg_665342/zwbd_665378/t1491523.shtml.

[97]Xinhua (2017), 'China Focus: Xi highlights peace, prosperity, opening up of Belt and Road', *Xinhua*, 14 May 2017, online: http://news.xinhuanet.com/english/2017-05/14/c_136281648.htm

[98]China Daily (2017), 'China proposes peace through development in Middle East during Abbas's visit', *China Daily*, 23 July 2017, online: http://www.chinadaily.com.cn/world/2017-07/23/content_30213988.htm.

The process of role adaptation at the domestic level mostly followed the preferences of political elites, with highly influential leaders like Mao, Deng and Xi being particularly effective in shaping subsequent discourses on China's international role and suitable policies. Even domestically weaker leaders like Jiang and Hu were successful in setting down highly influential role markers like the 'responsible power' and 'peaceful development' concepts, although their adoption was the result of collective decision-making and significant input from outside the leadership. This is unsurprising in a system where scholars are judged not just on their expertise, but also on their 'political quality', and where the embrace of slogans issued by the leadership is a way to demonstrate political loyalty.

When roles did become unsettled, it was usually not as a result of domestic challenges, but due to shifting external perceptions and expectations of China on the part of its 'significant others'. Since the 1980s, this has meant an acutely sensitive attunement to American impressions of a rising China, best exemplified by the enormous impact of 'China threat' theories. In this sense, the effects of China's rise on its self-conception were not just rooted in the growth of material capabilities, or indeed the effects this had on the national imagination, but also their reflection among foreign observers.

On the other hand, since Chinese role prescriptions tend to be relatively vague concepts that aim to ensure broad domestic buy-in, the process of translating them into concrete policies has gradually allowed for stronger bottom-up impulses. In large part, this is due to the general trend of professionalization and pluralization that has characterized Chinese policymaking over the last two decades, and which has given experts an increasingly prominent role. China's involvement with conflict societies, and the specific case of peacekeeping, neatly reflects this changing dynamic. Beginning in the mid-1990s, scholarly analysis of the rapidly changing peacekeeping system went hand-in-hand with policy recommendations that proved crucial in filling the new 'responsible power' role with meaning. Likewise, today's proponents of a 'developmental peace' occupy a position where they can influence both elite thinking on China's peacekeeping strategy and the operational doctrines guiding action in the field.

The field of peacekeeping is thus a useful example how processes of role-making tie together diverse domestic and international actors. In setting down these highly visible markers, political elites can simultaneously generate support from domestic constituencies and signal their intentions to other nations, but are subsequently bound to the expectations that come attached with them. In other words, political elites were consistently able to define compulsory new roles, but filling them with meaning was a much more pluralistic process—at least under conditions of a rapidly changing international environment and high pressure to formulate new policies, both of which made expert buy-in crucial.

Accordingly, when trying to gauge China's future role within this field, attention needs to be paid both to high-level statements outlining Beijing's ambitions and the way experts adapt them to concrete policy suggestions. This is especially important when it comes to notions like the 'developmental peace' which, if ever adopted as official policy, could present a potent alternative, and potential challenge, to Western peacebuilding approaches.

Disclosure statement

No potential conflict of interest was reported by the author.

Business is Business: How Does Trade Relationship Fail to Boost Image of China?

Narisong Huhe and Min Tang

ABSTRACT

This study explores how China's increased economic influence shapes its image among foreign audiences. Specifically, it examines the effect of trade relationship with China on the perception of China. A systematic analysis of the data from recent three waves of the Asia Barometer Survey (ABS) consistently shows that, at the country-level, trade exposure to China is associated with a less favorable public view of China. At the individual level, the authors find that trade exposure weakens the positive relationship between individuals' assessment of the domestic economic situation and their perception of China. Meanwhile, political factors such as individuals' political orientation and regime difference correlate with a negative image of China, and trade relationship cannot mitigate this "soft power deficit." In short, trade relationship does not help promote a positive image of China.

Introduction

In the past decades, China has received great attention from both its neighboring Asian countries and other parts of the world.[1] The burgeoning public interest in China is fueled by various factors. The first is China's surging economic influences around the world. Not only has China become the world's second largest economy, it also has been deeply integrated into world economy as the largest exporter in the global trade. Second, benefited from the remarkable economic growth, the Chinese government actively pursues a variety of policies to improve its global image. These 'charm offensives' are exemplified by such activities as hosting the 2008 summer Olympic Games, establishing the Confucius Institutes in foreign universities, and initiating the Asian Infrastructure Investment Bank (AIIB).[2] Third, the Chinese government has adopted a global strategy, Belt and Road Initiative (BRI),

---

[1]Liu Kang, 'Interests, values, and geopolitics: The global public opinion on China', *European Review* 23(2), (2015), pp. 242–60; Liu Kang and Yun-Han Chu, 'China's rise through world public opinion: Editorial introduction', *Journal of Contemporary China* 24(92), (2015), pp. 197–202; John Aldrich, Jie Lu and Liu Kang, 'How do Americans view the rising China?' *Journal of Contemporary China* 24(92), (2014), pp. 203–221; Yun-han Chu, Liu Kang, and Min-hua Huang, 'How East Asians view the rise of China', *Journal of Contemporary China* 24(93), (2014), pp. 398–420; Joseph S. Nye, 'China's soft power deficit', *The Wall Street Journal*, (2012), https://www.wsj.com/articles/SB10001424052702304451104577389923098678842; Peter Hays Gries, H. Michael Crowson and Todd Sandel, 'The Olympic effect on American attitudes towards China: Beyond personality, ideology, and media exposure', *Journal of Contemporary China* 19(64), (2010), pp. 213–231; Barry Sautman and Yan Hairong, 'African perspectives on China-Africa links', *China Quarterly* 199, (2009), pp. 728–759; Christopher B. Whitney and David L. Shambaugh, *Soft Power in Asia: Results of a 2008 Multinational Survey of Public Opinion* (Chicago: Chicago Council on Global Affairs, 2009); Young Nam Cho and Jong Ho Jeong, 'China's soft power: Discussions, resources, and prospects', *Asian Survey* 48(3), (2008), pp. 453–472.

[2]Joshua Kurlantzick, *Charm Offensive: How China's Soft power is Transforming the World*(New Haven, CT: Yale University Press, 2007); James F. Paradise, 'China and international harmony: The role of Confucius institutes in bolstering Beijing's soft power', *Asian Survey* 49(4), (2009), pp. 647–669; Scott Kennedy, 'The myth of the Beijing consensus', *Journal of Contemporary China* 19(65), (2010), pp. 461–477; David Shambaugh, 'China's soft-power push: The search for respect', *Foreign Affairs* 94(July/August), (2015), pp. 99–107.

which involves infrastructure-based development across over 50 countries in Asia, Europe, and Africa.[3] Finally, as a result of the three factors above, China has become a focal point of policy debates in many countries.[4] Particularly, in those with close economic ties to China, policies towards China are framed more often in terms of domestic issues than as mere foreign-policy issues.[5]

All these suggest that 'the rise of China is a complicated phenomenon with a multifarious nature, ... Public opinion, attitudes and perceptions of China's rise are [thus] the outcome of dynamic interactions and assemblage of factors.'[6] Particularly, the recent China–US trade war points to how geopolitical competition, economic interests, ideological underpinnings, and popular sentiments could become all 'intertwined and inseparable' at both the state and individual levels.[7] Moreover, some further argued that the rise of China has triggered the global wave of populism and fueled the public's anxiety and anger against globalization. Voters' support for Brexit in UK, as shown by Colantane and Stanig,[8] was closely associated with the shock of surging imports from China over the past three decades. Similarly, a study of another 15 Western European countries find that exposure to Chinese imports gave rise to popular support for nationalist, isolationist, and radical-right parties.[9]

Despite its critical importance and the burgeoning public interest, there is little consensus on how to assess and explain the foreign mass perception of China. Nye,[10] for instance, argues that the authoritarian rule of the Chinese Communist Party (CCP) induces a 'soft power deficit' for China. Such a deficit makes the returns from its charm offensives quite limited.[11] In contrast, many studies suggest a generally positive image of China.[12] For example, Chu, Kang and Huang argue that 'the overall picture shows that the rise of China has been largely recognized and welcomed by East Asians.'[13] Given these discrepant findings, it becomes imperative to systematically explore how China is perceived by foreign public. Particularly, this study is attempted to examine how China's surging economic influence can or cannot boost its image among the foreign audiences. Focusing on bilateral trade relationship, it addresses the following specific question: how does economic interdependence with China affect the public perception of China?

---

[3]Julia C. Strauss, 'Of silk roads and global transformations: China's rise and its impact on the developing world', *The China Quarterly* 239, (2019), pp. 804–812.

[4]Barry Sautman and Yan Hairong, 'African perspectives on China-Africa links', *China Quarterly* 199, (2009), pp. 728–759; Jeremy W. Peters, 'In Dueling Ads, Candidates Seek to Politicize Issues of China and Manufacturing', *The New York Times*, 15 December 2012; Timothy T. Hellwig, *Globalization and Mass Politics: Retaining the Room to Maneuver* (Cambridge and New York: Cambridge University Press, 2014).

[5]Liu Kang, 'Interests, values, and geopolitics: The global public opinion on China', *European Review* 23(2), (2015), pp. 242–60; see also Italo Colantone and Piero Stanig, 'Global competition and Brexit', *American Political Science Review* 112(2), (2018a), pp. 201–18; see also Italo Colantone and Piero Stanig, 'The trade origins of economic nationalism: Import competition and voting behavior in Western Europe', *American Journal of Political Science* 62(4), (2018b), pp. 936–53.

[6]Liu Kang, 'Interests, values, and geopolitics: The global public opinion on China', *European Review* 23(2), (2015), p. 242

[7]Liu Kang, 'Interests, values, and geopolitics: The global public opinion on China', *European Review* 23(2), (2015), pp. 242–60.

[8]Italo Colantone and Piero Stanig, 'Global competition and Brexit', *American Political Science Review* 112(2), (2018a), pp. 201–18.

[9]Italo Colantone and Piero Stanig, 'The trade origins of economic nationalism: Import competition and voting behavior in Western Europe', *American Journal of Political Science* 62(4), (2018b), pp. 936–53.

[10]Joseph S. Nye, 'China's soft power deficit', *The Wall Street Journal*, (2012), https://www.wsj.com/articles/SB10001424052702304451104577389923098678842

[11]Young Nam Cho and Jong Ho Jeong, 'China's soft power: Discussions, resources, and prospects', *Asian Survey* 48(3), (2008), pp. 453–472; Yiwei Wang, 'Public diplomacy and the rise of Chinese soft power', *Annals of the American Academy of Political and Social Science* 616(1), (2008), pp. 257–273; Mingjiang Li, *Soft Power: China's Emerging Strategy in International Politics* (Lanham, MD: Lexington Books, 2009); James F. Paradise, 'China and international harmony: The role of confucius institutes in bolstering Beijing's soft power', *Asian Survey* 49(4), (2009), pp. 647–669; Christopher B. Whitney and David L. Shambaugh, *Soft Power in Asia: Results of a 2008Multinational Survey of Public Opinion* (Chicago: Chicago Council on Global Affairs, 2009); David Shambaugh, 'China's soft-power push: The search for respect', *Foreign Affairs* 94(July/August), (2015), pp. 99–107.

[12]Matthew Linley, James Reilly, and Benjamin E. Goldsmith, 'Who's afraid of the dragon? Asian mass publics' perceptions of China's influence', *Japanese Journal of Political Science* 13(4), (2012), pp. 501–523; Travis Nelson and Matthew Carlson, 'Charmed by China? Popular perceptions of Chinese influence in Asia', *Japanese Journal of Political Science* 13(4), (2012), pp. 477–499; Julia C. Strauss and Ariel C. Armony, *From the Great Wall to the New World: China and Latin America in the 21st Century* (Cambridge and New York: Cambridge University Press, 2012).

[13]Yun-han Chu, Liu Kang, and Min-hua Huang, 'How East Asians view the rise of China', *Journal of Contemporary China* 24(93), (2014), p. 398.

To answer this question, this study adopts a multilevel and interactive approach. It examines not only the direct effect of economic interdependence at the country level, but also the moderating effect of economic interdependence on the relationship between public perception of China and its correlates at the individual level. The authors of this study conduct a multilevel analysis based on the data of 12 polities included in the recent three waves (2005–2016) of the Asia Barometer Survey (ABS).[14] Their analyses of decade-long public opinion in Asia show that at the country-level, trade exposure to China is associated with a less favorable public view of China in general. At the individual level, stronger economic interdependence does not help boost a positive image of China either. On the one hand, although perception of an improving national economy is associated with a more positive perception of China, trade exposure to China weakens this positive relationship. On the other hand, political factors such as individuals' democratic orientation and the regime difference between China and the surveyed countries still correlate with a negative image of China, and trade relationship cannot mitigate this 'soft power deficit.'

This study advances the understanding of the sources of foreign image of China in several ways. First, it provides a framework to dissect the complexity of the foreign popular perception of China. As Kang and Chu[15] pointed out, foreign attitudes of China are the 'outcome of dynamic interactions and assemblage of factors, a synergy of material interests, ideational and emotional reactions, and values, ideologies, principles.' This study examines the effect of both materials interest and democratic values of individual citizens and, more importantly, explores how the aggregate-level factor (i.e. trade interdependence between countries) shapes the effect of individual-level factors. Thus, the dynamic relationship among these factors exist not only at the same level (e.g., individual level), but across country and individual levels. Such a cross-national and multilevel framework differs from single-country studies and studies that only focus on individual-level sources of foreign image.

This study also helps appreciate the nuanced nature of instrumental sources of China's foreign image in an increasingly globalized world. Scholars have noted that public opinion towards foreign nations (e.g., anti-Americanism) can be strongly shaped by the courses of domestic political competition.[16] For mass perception of China, its instrumental nature is closely associated with China's unprecedented, overseas, economic influences. When the responsibility of national economy is blurred by economic interdependence, how to interpret links with China inevitably becomes the spotlight of national political discourses in many countries.[17] People are embedded in both domestic and international environments. The formation of their perceptions about foreign countries therefore is conditioned by the complex domestic–international interactions.

Finally, the present study points to the fundamental challenges for China's global charm offensive. The findings of this study suggest that while such cultural programs as the Confucius Institute are not delivering desirable returns, more trade and investment deals (e.g., AIIB and BRI) offered by the Chinese leaders can only have mixed, if not counter-productive, impacts on China's foreign image. Tighter economic ties with China would further increase the salience of 'China issue' in domestic political competition. Rather than boosting China's image, such a salience could make more elites and mass to blame China for economic distresses.

---

[14]The polities in ABS that are included in this study are: Japan, South Korea, Mongolia, Philippines, Taiwan, Thailand, Indonesia, Singapore, Vietnam, Cambodia, Malaysia, and Myanmar.

[15]Liu Kang and Yun-Han Chu, 'China's rise through world public opinion: Editorial introduction', *Journal of Contemporary China* 24(92), (2015), pp. 197–202.

[16]See for example Lisa Blaydes and Drew A. Linzer, 'Elite competition, religiosity, and anti-Americanism in the Islamic World', *American Political Science Review* 106(2), (2012), pp. 225–243.

[17]Barry Sautman and Yan Hairong, 'African perspectives on China-Africa links', *China Quarterly* 199, (2009), pp. 728–759; Jeremy W. Peters, 'In Dueling Ads, Candidates Seek to Politicize Issues of China and Manufacturing', *The New York Times*, 15 December 2012; Timothy T. Hellwig, *Globalization and Mass Politics: Retaining the Room to Maneuver* (Cambridge and New York: Cambridge University Press, 2014).

Background: Changing Perceptions of China

Before 'reform and openness' started in 1978, few who study the mass perception of China would be optimistic about China's recognition in foreign public opinion. After tracking mass perceptions of China in the United States for nearly four decades, Hirshberg concludes that the cognition of an authoritarian China fundamentally constrained the development of pro-Chinese sentiments.[18] In addition, pre-reform China lacks the needed grassroots socioeconomic exchanges with foreign countries, and thus the promotion of China image was monopolized by a relatively small number of political leaders and institutions. The early foreign mass perception of China, therefore, has been driven by political motivations, highly consistent with a country's overall diplomatic relationship with China.[19] As Li and Hong noted, the changes of China's national image in the United States have always corresponded to the overall Sino-US relations, which have been known for 'numbers of roller coasters.'[20]

Trade liberalization (i.e., 'openness') has become an integral part of China's post-Mao reform, and China has successfully transformed itself from one of the most closed economies to the largest trading power in the world. China's economic growth is exceptional not only in its rapid growth for a prolonged period, but, more importantly, in its unprecedented integration into the world economy. After its entry of the World Trade Organization (WTO), China was given most-favored nation status among the 153 WTO members, and its foreign trade now accounts for about three-quarters of China's GDP. Moreover, China has dramatically increased its foreign direct investment (FDI). In Africa, for example, the total stock of Chinese investment and aid has grown over fifty-folds since the 1990s.[21] As noted by Shirk, because of a combination of the globalization process and China's unusually high degree of openness, 'the reverberations [of China's economic growth] are felt everywhere.'[22]

China's rapid economic emergence inevitably triggered increasing attention from the citizens in many countries. One of the most important signs has been the mass media coverage on China.[23] Zhang finds that in the past two decades the volume of media coverage of China has experienced a rapid increase in the three major European transnational news outlets (i.e., the *Financial Times*, *The Economist*, and the *International Herald Tribune*).[24] Beyond the increase of the sheer volume, a close examination of the coverage content reveals that, albeit some traditional recurring themes like the CCP's authoritarian regime and alleged human rights abuses, there is a growing and substantial number of reports focusing on such themes as the economic promise of the 'China market,' reform of China's government and economy, and cultural changes.[25] As a result, the ordinary foreign publics have been increasingly exposed to socioeconomic issues related to China.

In summary, the foreign image of post-Mao China is no longer dominated solely by ideological and political concerns. Economic interdependence becomes increasingly important in shaping the

---

[18]Matthew S. Hirshberg, 'Consistency and change in American perceptions of China', *Political Behavior* 15(3), (1993), pp. 247–263.

[19]Warren I. Cohen, 'American Perceptions of China', in *Dragon and Eagle: United States-China Relations, Past and Future*, ed. Michel Oksenberg and Robert B. Oxnam (New York, NY: Basic Books, 1973), pp. 54–86; John King. Fairbank, *China Perceived: Images and Policies in Chinese-American Relations* (New York, NY: Random House,1974); Matthew S. Hirshberg, 'Consistency and change in American perceptions of China', *Political Behavior* 15(3), (1993), pp. 247–263; Ole R. Holsti, *Public Opinion and American Foreign Policy*, Revised ed. (Ann Arbor, MI: The University of Michigan, 2004).

[20]Hongshan Li and Zhaohui Hong, *Image, Perception, and the Making of U.S.-China Relations* (Lanham, MD: University Press of America, eds. 1998), p. 2.

[21]Ali Zafar, 'The growing relationship between China and Sub-Saharan Africa: Macroeconomic, trade, investment, and aid links', *The World Bank Research Observer* 22(1), (2007), pp. 103–130.

[22]Susan L Shirk, *China: Fragile Superpower* (Oxford and New York: Oxford University Press, 2007), p. 22.

[23]Alexander Liss, 'Images of China in the American print media: A survey from 2000 to2002', *Journal of Contemporary China* 12(35), (2003), pp. 299–318; Jiangnan Zhu and Jie Lu, 'One rising China, multiple interpretations: China's 60th anniversary celebration through the lens of the world's printed media', *Journal of Contemporary China* 22(84), (2013), pp. 1067–1088.

[24]Li Zhang, 'The rise of China: Media perception and implications for international politics', *Journal of Contemporary China* 19(64), (2010), pp. 233–254.

[25]Alexander Liss, 'Images of China in the American print media: A survey from 2000 to2002', *Journal of Contemporary China* 12(35), (2003), pp. 299–318; Jiangnan Zhu and Jie Lu, 'One rising China, multiple interpretations: China's 60th anniversary celebration through the lens of the world's printed media', *Journal of Contemporary China* 22(84), (2013), pp. 1067–1088.

mass perception of China. These changes inevitably give rise to an important question: How does China's surging economic power affect its image among the foreign public?

Hypotheses: Trading with China and Perception of China

Public opinion toward foreign-policy issues, though characterized as 'moody' and unstructured in the earlier literature,[26] has been increasingly found consistent,[27] and the centrality of economic concerns has been frequently emphasized.[28] However, much scholarly debate remains concerning the sources of mass perception of a foreign country. The following subsections first explore how trade interdependence could affect public opinions toward China across countries and then examine how it could shape China's image at the individual level.

Trade Interdependence and the China Issue

Trade interdependence has been long advocated, particularly by the 'liberal peace' thesis, as the key remedy for inter-state hostility and conflict. It is argued that international trade not only increases the mutual economic well beings, but also helps foster economic integration between the parties involved. Myriads of quantitative studies also show that trade interdependence, measured usually as trade-to-gross domestic product (GDP) ratio, is associated with a lower likelihood of military conflict.[29] In light of this, China's economic rise could potentially boost its foreign image by promoting common interests and cultivating economic integration with its trade partners.

Yet, trade interdependence has received only limited attention in the extant studies of mass perception of foreign countries. This gap has a lot to do with the fact that historically the global trade impacts of a single foreign country have been small and gradual. China's economic growth, however, is exceptional in its massive size, rapid pace, and heavy reliance on export. Its integration into the global economy has unprecedentedly restructured international trade and thus affected the well beings of massive foreign public. An illustrative case is the bilateral China–US trade. As revealed in Figure 1, since China's 'reform and openness,' particularly after its entry into the WTO, China–US bilateral trade has dramatically expanded. Similarly, based on data of 15 Western European countries, Colantone and Stanig find that the Chinese share of total manufacturing import has grown roughly seven-folds between 1988 and 2007, while the share from other low-income countries remains largely stable.[30]

Despite the huge trade shocks associated with China's integration into the global economy, only recently have scholars started to systematically examine its sociopolitical impacts in foreign

---

[26]See for example Gabriel Almond, *The American People and Foreign Policy* (New York, NY: Harcourt, Brace, 1950).

[27]Christopher J. Anderson, 'When in doubt, use proxies: Attitudes toward domestic politics and support for European integration', *Comparative Political Studies* 31(5), (1998), pp. 569–601; Matthew J. Gabel, 'Economic integration and mass politics: Market liberalization and public attitudes in the European Union', *American Journal of Political Science* 42(3), (1998), pp. 936–953; Jie Chen, 'Urban Chinese perceptions of threats from the United States and Japan', *Public Opinion Quarterly* 65(2), (2001), pp. 254–266; Karl C. Kaltenthaler, Ronald D. Gelleny and Stephen J. Ceccoli, 'Explaining citizen support for trade liberalization', *International Studies Quarterly* 48(4), (2004), pp. 829–852; John H. Aldrich, Christopher Gelpi, Peter Feaver, Jason Reifler and Kristin Thompson Sharp, 'Foreign policy and the electoral connection', *Annual Review of Political Science* 9, (2006), pp. 477–502; Lisa Blaydes and Drew A. Linzer, 'Elite competition, religiosity, and anti-Americanism in the Islamic World', *American Political Science Review* 106(2), (2012), pp. 225–243.

[28]See for example Matthew J. Gabel, 'Economic integration and mass politics: Market liberalization and public attitudes in the European Union', *American Journal of Political Science* 42(3), (1998), pp. 936–953; see also Richard C. Eichenberg and Russell J. Dalton, 'Post-Maastricht Blues: The transformation of citizen support for European integration, 1973–2004', *Acta Politica* 42 (2–3), (2007), pp. 128–152.

[29]See for example John R. Oneal and Bruce Russett, 'The classical liberals were right: Democracy, interdependence, and conflict, 1950–1985', *International Studies Quarterly* 41, (1997), pp. 267–293.

[30]Italo Colantone and Piero Stanig, 'Global competition and Brexit', *American Political Science Review* 112 (2), (2018a), pp. 201–18.

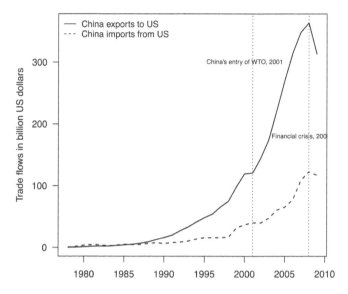

Figure 1. Bilateral China-US trade flows.

countries.[31] First and foremost, it is found that ordinary people do respond to China's economic rise and increasingly perceive China through an economic lens. These findings corroborate with earlier studies on the importance of economic concerns in how the public understand foreign-policy issues. Given the liberal peace thesis and related literature reviewed above, this study proposes the following hypothesis of the direct effect of trade relationship on public perception of China:

> *Hypothesis 1a: Citizens in countries with a greater economic interdependence with China are more likely to view China positively in general.*

However, different from the optimistic expectation of liberal peace thesis, some evidence suggests that an economic view of China does not necessarily mean a positive view. Instead, the China issue has become the new focal point of domestic political debates. The volume and velocity of interdependence with China have markedly blurred and disrupted the boundaries of nation-states' responsibilities for the national economies in many countries. Therefore, the mass perception of China tends to be highly ambivalent. For instance, throughout the most recent US election debates, the China issue has been closely associated with the economic performance. For many, the 2016 US presidential election was marked by the two candidates competing over who would be tougher on China if elected. In Africa, based on surveys in nine countries, Sautman and Hairong also find that national political discourses of China–Africa economic links strongly shape the public's perception of China.[32]

Beyond political debates, the China issue has also been intertwined into actual domestic politics. In their study that tracks the roll-call behaviors and electoral outcomes in the US House, Feigenbaum and Hall find that the localized economic shocks from Chinese import competition cause legislators to vote in a more protectionist direction on trade bills.[33] In issues such as the exchange rate, the China issue has introduced notable domestic cleavages. Galantucci shows that while legislators with

---

[31]See for example David H. Autor, David Dorn and Gordon H. Hanson, 'The China Syndrome: Local labor market effects of import competition in the United States', *American Economic Review* 103(6), (2013), pp. 2121–68; see also Italo Colantone and Piero Stanig, 'Global competition and Brexit', *American Political Science Review* 112 (2), (2018a), pp. 201–18; see also Italo Colantone and Piero Stanig, 'The trade origins of economic nationalism: Import competition and voting behavior in Western Europe', *American Journal of Political Science* 62(4), (2018b), pp. 936–53.
[32]Barry Sautman and Yan Hairong, 'African perspectives on China-Africa links', *China Quarterly* 199, (2009), pp. 728–759.
[33]James J. Feigenbaum and Andrew B. Hall, 'How legislators respond to localized economic shocks: Evidence from Chinese import competition', *Journal of Politics* 77(4), (2015), pp. 1012–1030.

ties to import-competing domestic producers are more likely to introduce and support aggressive bills against the undervaluation of the Chinese yuan, those who represent business interests with stakes in the Chinese economy tend to oppose such bills.[34] Given this discussion, the following competing hypothesis about the direct effect of trade interdependence at the country level can be proposed.

Hypothesis 1b: Citizens in countries that share stronger trade ties with China tend to perceive China more negatively in general.

Winners, Losers, and the China Issue

The lack of consensus on the aggregate impact of trade interdependence indicates important individual variations in how ordinary people orient themselves toward China. From the perspective of political economy, the salient economic concerns in the public opinion can be regarded as people's reactions to the increasing vulnerability of national economy to the globalization process.[35] Specific to international trade, drawing on the Stolper-Samuelson theorem, Rogowski suggests that economic globalization could introduce grave distributive politics to nation-states.[36] Domestic groups endowed with different production factors (i.e., labor, land, and capital) benefit variably from international trade. As a result, varying domestic cleavages and coalitions are formed, influencing a country's foreign policies and even domestic ones.[37] For example, increased trade exposure is found strongly associated with welfare expansion.[38] The globalized production increases people's socioeconomic risks, which in turn decreases their feelings of economic security and leads them to demand more social protection. For instance, after comparing aggregate public opinion across Asian countries, Chu, Kang, and Huang conclude that 'the most important variable predicating a respondent's view on the rise of China is his/her assessment of the overall domestic economic condition.'[39] In light of this, a similar 'economic cleavages' in the mass perception of China can be expected. Economically advantaged citizens tend to feel less threatened by China's economic rise, and thus they are more likely to have a more positive understanding of China.

Hypothesis 2: Individuals with more positive economic perceptions are more likely to orient themselves positively toward China.

In the cross-national context, this micro-positive link between people's sense of economic security and perception of China can be strongly conditioned by the macro trade interdependence. This is because the bilateral economic ties with China strongly affect the salience of the China issue in a given country. The exposure to economic competition from China redefines the responsibility of national economic performance, and the issue linkage between national economy and China tends to change in accordance with the country's economic dependence on China. Considering this,

---

[34]Robert A. Galantucci, 'The repercussions of realignment: United States-China interdependence and exchange rate politics', *International Studies Quarterly* 59(3), (2015), pp. 423–435.

[35]See for example Timothy T. Hellwig, *Globalization and Mass Politics: Retaining the Room to Maneuver* (Cambridge and New York: Cambridge University Press, 2014).

[36]Ronald Rogowski, *Commerce and Coalition: How Trade Affects Domestic Political Alignments* (Princeton, NJ: Princeton University Press, 1989); see also Paul Midford, 'International trade and domestic politics: Improving on Rogowski's model of political alignments', *International Organization* 47(4), (1993), pp. 535–564.

[37]Ethan B. Kapstein, 'Winners and losers in the global economy', *International Organization* 54(2), (2000), pp. 359–384; Michael J. Hiscox, *International Trade and Political Conflict: Commerce, Coalitions, and Mobility* (Princeton, N.J.: Princeton University Press, 2002); Mark Andreas Kayser, 'How domestic is domestic politics? Globalization and Elections', *Annual Review of Political Science* 10, (2007), pp. 341–362.

[38]Kenneth Scheve and Matthew J. Slaughter, 'Economic insecurity and the globalization of production', *American Journal of Political Science* 48(4), (2004), pp. 662–674; Stefanie Walter, 'Globalization and the welfare state: Testing the micro-foundations of the compensation hypothesis', *International Studies Quarterly* 54(2), (2010), pp. 403–426.

[39]Yun-han Chu, Liu Kang and Min-hua Huang, 'How East Asians view the rise of China', *Journal of Contemporary China* 24(93), (2014), p. 413.

people's economic perception of China can be strongly reinforced by stronger bilateral economic ties. In countries under with limited economic influences of China, ordinary people are less likely to perceive China on the economic basis. In contrast, economic concerns matter a lot in China's close economic partners, and people tend to blame China for economic distress.

Such dynamic interactions between the international context and domestic public opinion have been increasingly emphasized in the recent literature.[40] For instance, Alcañiz and Hellwig show that ties with world markets make ordinary citizens often blame policy outcomes on international actors.[41] The responsibility for economic performance thus is shifted from national politicians to foreign actors. The conditioning effects of contextual factors are further supported by carefully designed experimental studies. As an effort to clarify the formation of national image, Eicher, Pratto, and Wilhelm find that group images are far more than a simple function of features of the target group.[42] More important, the collective image is shaped by the relationship between the rater group and the target group. This article, therefore, hypothesizes the conditioning effects of the bilateral economic interdependence as follows:

Hypothesis 3: As the bilateral economic interdependence increases, the positive impacts of people's economic perception on their percpetion of China will decrease.

Values, Trade, and the China Issue

Many studies have shown that individuals' subjective values and predisposition can strongly shape their attitudes toward foreign countries and foreign-policy issues.[43] As argued by Hurwitz and Peffley, one way to understand citizens' foreign-policy attitudes is to conceptualize it as a hierarchical model of constraints.[44] While at the most concrete level are preferences for specific foreign-policy issues, at the foundational tier of the hierarchy are core values, which are more personal statements regarding the individual's priorities and concerns. Mass attitudes of foreign policies, therefore, are an extension of personal core values, learned primarily in domestic contexts and later projected onto foreign-policy issues.[45]

More specifically, value similarity is found critical for the public to form their opinions on foreign-policy issues. For example, Anderson shows that value similarity matters for the European public's support for the membership in the European Union.[46] Due to information deficits, individuals employ proxies like their value similarities with domestic parties (e.g., Left vs. Right) when

---

[40]James A. Caporaso, 'Across the great divide: Integrating comparative and international politics', *International Studies Quarterly* 41(4), (1997), pp. 563–592; Timothy T. Hellwig, *Globalization and Mass Politics: Retaining the Room to Maneuver* (Cambridge and New York: Cambridge University Press, 2014).

[41]Isabella Alcañiz and Timothy Hellwig, 'Who is to blame? The distribution of responsibility in developing democracies', *British Journal of Political Science* 41(2), (2011), pp. 389–411.

[42]Véronique Eicher, Felicia Pratto and Peter Wilhelm, 'Value differentiation between enemies and allies: Value projection in national images', *Political Psychology* 34(1), (2013), pp. 127–144.

[43]Raymond Cohen, *Threat Perception in International Crisis* (Madison, WI: University of Wisconsin Press, 1979); Brett Silverstein, 'Enemy Images: The psychology of U.S. attitudes and cognitions regarding the Soviet Union', *American Psychologist* 44(6), (1989), pp. 903–913; Jie Chen, 'Urban Chinese perceptions of threats from the United States and Japan', *Public Opinion Quarterly* 65(2), (2001), pp. 254–266; Richard K. Herrmann, James F. Voss, Tonya Y.E. Schooler and Joseph Ciarrochi, 'Images in international relations: An experimental test of cognitive schemata', *International Studies Quarterly* 41(3), (1997), pp. 403–433; Michele G. Alexander, Shana Levin and P. J. Henry, 'Image theory, social identity, and social dominance: Structural characteristics and individual motives underlying international images', *Political Psychology* 26(1), (2005), pp. 27–45; Retamero Rocio Garcia, Stephanie M. Müller and David L. Rousseau, 'The impact of value similarity and power on the perception of threat', *Political Psychology* 33(2), (2012), pp. 179–193.

[44]Jon Hurwitz and Mark Peffley, 'How are foreign policy attitudes structured? A hierarchical model', *American Political Science Review* 81(4), (1987), pp. 1099–1120.

[45]Jon Hurwitz and Mark Peffley, 'Public images of the Soviet Union: The impact on foreign policy attitudes', *Journal of Politics* 52(1), (1990), pp. 3–28; Lauren M. McLaren, 'Public support for the European Union: Cost/Benefit analysis or perceived cultural threat?', *Journal of Politics* 64(2), (2002), pp. 551–566; Karl Kaltenthaler and William J. Miller, 'Social psychology and public support for trade liberalization', *International Studies Quarterly* 57(4), (2013), pp. 784–790.

[46]Christopher J. Anderson, 'When in doubt, use proxies: Attitudes toward domestic politics and support for European integration', *Comparative Political Studies* 31(5), (1998), pp. 569–601.

responding to the issue of the European integration. Using experimental studies, Garcia-Retamero, Müller, and Rousseau also confirm that when facing issues in international relations, ordinary citizens tend to compare the ingroup and the outgroup based on abstract values.[47] Their opinions about international relations then are strongly influenced by the perceived value similarity between the two parties involved. Particularly, they show that unsophisticated individuals tend to rely on a single value (e.g., democracy or autocracy). Tomz and Weeks further show that it is the shared democracy that pacifies the public by changing perceptions of threat from other nations.[48] Individuals are substantially less supportive of military strikes against democracies than against otherwise identical autocracies.

Although China has gone through many major social-economic changes since 1980s, the fundamental nature of its ruling regime has not changed much. CCP still imposes a tight control over political domains while it has opened the economy and liberated the society to a great extent. Given this, the following hypothesis can be proposed.

Hypothesis 4: Citizens with a higher level of democratic attitudes have a less favorable perception of China.

How does trade interdependence between countries moderate the negative relationship between one's democratic orientation and his or her perception of China? The answer is not certain. On the one hand, trade exposure to China could mitigate the negative effect of democratic attitudes on China's image. Democratically-minded people who live in a country without much interaction with China are likely to perceive China at its face value. Economic relationship through trade provides opportunities for foreign citizens to know and appreciate the economic changes and societal progress in China. Studies of other countries like US also show that more contacts with foreigners tend to lead to a better popular image of foreign countries. The fact that China can grow as an economic power and conduct businesses in capitalist-style indicates the tremendous progress the country has made. Democratic citizens would thus be less likely to assess China based on the stereotype of an authoritarian regime.

On the other hand, however, trade relationship could also worsen the perception of China among foreign citizens with a strong democratic orientation. For one thing, interactions could make those who otherwise do not know much about China's politics more aware of the value difference between what they hold dear and what the Chinese regime stands for. For another, as revealed in the recent trade war between China and US, when trade with China is portrayed as unfair or when the unfair trade with China is allegedly caused by the wrong-doings by Chinese government, trade could amplify resentment against the China among the democratic citizens and thus further decreases their evaluation of China.

Given the uncertain nature of the effect of trade interdependence on the relationship between democratic attitudes and perception of China, this study has the following undirectional hypothesis:

Hypothesis 5: The negative effect of democratic attitudes on perception of China will be moderated by trade interdependence of China.

[47]Retamero Rocio Garcia, Stephanie M. Müller and David L. Rousseau, 'The impact of value similarity and power on the perception of threat', *Political Psychology* 33(2), (2012), pp. 179–193.
[48]Michael R. Tomz, and Jessica L. P. Weeks, 'Public opinion and the democratic peace', *American Political Science Review* 107(4), (2013), pp. 849–865.

Data and Measurement

Our primary analyses are based on Asian countries. First, the issue about the levels and sources of China's image is particularly important in Asia. Compared to other parts of the world, Asia is the first and foremost region that is markedly affected by China's economic rise as well as its subsequent political and military reemergence. Moreover, Asian countries are also the main targets of China's 'charm offensive.'[49] A scrutiny of the mass attitudes toward China thus can contribute to our understanding of the ongoing interaction between international relations and domestic politics in the region. Second, although international relations in Asia traditionally have been dominated by political hostilities, development and other economic concerns have increasingly become a consensus among Asian governments and the mass public. As regional hostilities have eased and interdependence has grown, China's image has been varying significantly among Asian countries (to be illustrated in Figure 2). This in turn makes the region a perfect laboratory for exploring China's foreign image and its sources. Finally, countries in Asia are substantially different from each other regarding their economic ties with China, levels of economic developments, and paces of economic growth. Such variations provide a perfect pool to examine the complex sources of China's image.

In the main analysis, this study draws individual-level data from the second, the third, and the fourth wave of the Asian Barometer Survey (ABS). The three waves of ABS surveyed citizens in 13 Asian polities beside the Mainland China.[50] Combining the recent three waves of ABS surveys is necessary because more units at the aggregate level are preferred in the model we use (i.e. multilevel model) in this study. After the combination, the effective number of units at the aggregate level

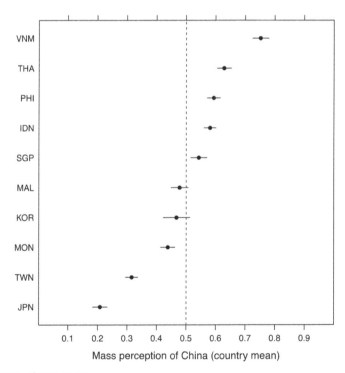

Figure 2. Mass perception of China in ABS.

---

[49]David Shambaugh, 'China's soft-power push: The search for respect', *Foreign Affairs* 94(July/August), (2015), pp. 99–107.
[50]Hong Kong is excluded in this study because it lacks information of key variables.

(country-wave) is 27.[51]

Dependent Variable: The Mass Perception of China

This study measures the mass perception of China by examining whether ordinary foreign citizens orient themselves favorably toward China. In the ABS sample, an index was created based on two general evaluative questions, 'Please let us know about your impressions of China' and 'General speaking, the influence China has on our country is ...' The respondents chose a response on a scale that indicates how positive or negative their views towards China.

Figure 2 presents the country averages of the mass perception of China from the ABS samples. The dots represent each country's average perception of China sorted from highest to lowest, and the lines represent the corresponding standard deviations. The dotted vertical lines represent the pooled mean in the ABS. First, the results in Figure 2 confirm that China is still far from gaining a global recognition.[52] Second, there are considerable variations in how people from different countries view China. For instance, although over 70% of the Vietnamese public have a favorable opinion about China, the corresponding figures for Japan is just around 20%.

Key Explanatory Variables

Earlier discussion of China's foreign image points to a key country-level variable, trade interdependence between China and surveyed countries. It is measured by the sum of the exports and imports between China and the surveyed country, divided by that country's yearly GDP (i.e., $\frac{Export+Import}{GDP}$). This is essentially a measure of trade GDP interdependence controlling for the size of the economy. That is, it gauges the relative importance of China's exports and imports to the economy of a given country.

Figure 3 maps the trade-to-GDP ratios across the recent waves of ABS, and two findings stand out. First, consistent with our expectation, there are marked variations in trade ties between the surveyed countries and China. In Figure 3(a), for instance, while trade with China accounts to roughly 50% of Mongolia's economy, Japan is far less reliant on trade with China with a ratio around 10%. Second, we found that across three waves of ABS, many countries have experienced a steady increase in trade interdependence with China, suggesting China's rising economic influence over the decade. For instance, Vietnam and Mongolia are becoming more reliant on trade with China during 2014–2016 than they are during 2001–2003.

Regarding the individual basis of China's image, this study focuses primarily on the effect of people's economic concerns and value orientations. As for economic concerns, it employs a standard definition of economic assessment,[53] i.e., respondents' evaluation of current economic situation. Scholars usually distinguish between survey items asking citizens to evaluate whether they personally have benefited from economic conditions (i.e., egocentric evaluation) versus evaluating the state of the overall national performance of the economy (i.e., sociotropic evaluation). Recent development in economic voting studies suggests that sociotropic evaluations overwhelm egocentric ones in shaping people's political orientation.[54] This article thus uses sociotropic evaluations.[55]

---

[51]As a robustness check of our findings, in Appendix, we extend our analysis to a global sample. Individual-level data of the robustness check are drawn from the 2012 Pew Global Attitudes Project survey (GAP). Pew GAP conducts its comparative survey in 21 countries. Among these countries, only Japan is also included in ABS. GAP does not contain necessary information for one key variables, democratic values. Therefore, its analysis cannot be only a robustness check for some of the findings of ABS.

[52]Christopher B. Whitney and David L. Shambaugh, *Soft Power in Asia: Results of a 2008 Multinational Survey of Public Opinion* (Chicago: Chicago Council on Global Affairs, 2009).

[53]Beck, Michael S. Lewis and Mary Stegmaier, 'Economic determinants of electoral outcomes', *Annual Review of Political Science* 3, (2000), pp. 183–219.

[54]Beck, Michael S. Lewis and Mary Stegmaier, 'The VP-Function revisited: A survey of the literature on vote and popularity functions after over 40 years', *Public Choice* 157(3–4), (2013), pp. 367–385.

[55]In the ABS, respondents' sociotropic perception of economic situation is gauged as follows: 'How would you rate the overall economic condition of our country today?'

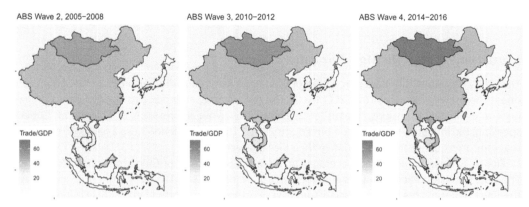

Figure 3. Trade interdependence with China across the recent three waves of ABS.

The value-based explanation, as described above, suggests that respondents' support for democratic principles and their experiences of democracy also may shape how they perceive China. Yet, democracy is an 'essentially contested concept,' which in turn yields great difficulties for cross-national comparison of individuals' commitment to democratic norms. Moreover, given the global acceptance of the ideal, direct questions on democratic commitment are likely to induce socially desirable answers. This study therefore measures one's democratic value based on a set of six questions that ask the respondents' agreement with democratic procedures in the ABS.[56] While these items do not exhaust all the democratic procedures, together they can provide a clear conceptual anchorage and hence serve as a good test of popular democratic commitment across Asian societies. Explanatory factor analysis shows that all six items load to one factor. Thus, an index is created based upon these six items as the measurement of one's support for democratic principles.

This study further gauges the potential impacts of respondents' experiences of democracy by examining the regime (dis)similarity between the surveyed country and China. Specifically, regime dissimilarity is measured as the difference between China and the surveyed countries in the levels of democracy. This study uses the Freedom House (FH) index as the measurement of democracy. The Freedom House index is chosen because it encompasses not only institutional features of democracy but also other political rights and civil liberties. It ranges from 1 to 7, and we calculated the regime differences between the surveyed countries and China.

Control Variables

To control for the effect of 'charm offensive' strategies employed by Chinese government, this study includes a binary variable at the country-level, gauging whether Confucius Institutes have been established in the surveyed countries.[57] For many, the Confucius Institutes are a principle means for the Chinese government to cast its soft power oversea. Paradise argues, 'The best way to think of the Confucius Institute project is as a type of impression management, an effort by China to craft a positive image of itself in a world fraught with danger.'[58]

---

[56]'We should get rid of parliament and elections and have a strong leader decide things;' 'The army should come in to govern the country;' 'When the country is facing a difficult situation, it is okay for the government to disregard the law in order to deal with the situation;' 'Government leaders are like the head of a family; we should all follow their decisions;' 'When judges decide important cases, they should accept the view of the executive branch;' 'If the government is constantly checked by the legislature, it cannot possibly accomplish great things.'

[57]The data is from the Office of the Chinese Language Council International, http://english.hanban.org/node_10971.htm.

[58]James F. Paradise, 'China and international harmony: The role of Confucius institutes in bolstering Beijing's soft power', *Asian Survey* 49(4), (2009), pp. 647–669.

In addition, the analysis controls for the effect of the foreign-policy preferences of the political elites in surveyed countries. Domestic political discourses are strongly affected by the political elites, but their preferences are difficult to capture accurately. This study uses the updated version of the Affinity of Nations Index.[59] The index measures the preference similarity of a given pair of states by examining their voting records in the United Nations General Assembly. Specifically, states with the similar voter patterns (i.e., 'yes,' 'no,' or 'abstain') have a higher score on this index.

At the individual level, this study controls for a variety of factors that are commonly used to predict the mass attitudes towards foreign-policy issues. First, it measures one's nationalist sentiment. In the ABS, the question is straightforward and taps a general notion of national pride. It asks, '[How proud are you of being [your country's people]?' Respondents are asked to select an answer on a 1–4 scale that ranges from 'very proud' to 'not proud at all.' Moreover, it includes necessary sociodemographic factors (i.e., gender, age, urban residence, education attainment, and social trust).

Model and Analysis

To explore the complexity of the sources of foreign perception of China, this study not only tests the direct effect of trade and other factors at both country and individual levels, but also examines how trade relationship at the country-level shapes the effect of individual factors (i.e., economic perceptions and democratic values). Therefore, a multilevel model is appropriate for the analysis. Compared to the no-pooling (i.e., country-based) and pooling analyses, multilevel analysis not only allows for a more accurate estimation of the additive effects of both the individual and contextual correlates, but also examines cross-level interactions between key contextual factors and individual factors.[60]

Table 1 presents the main results of our analyses based on the ABS sample. Model 1 only includes the primary independent variables of this study. The analytical result shows that a more interdependent trade relationship with China at the country level is associated with a more negative view of China among individuals in that country. This confirms H1b, thus rejecting the liberal peace thesis (H1a). The two individual-level factors, economic perception and democratic value, both are a significant predictor of perception of China. A better perception of the national economy is associated with a more favorable perception of China (H2), and a more democratically minded individual is less likely to view China favorably (H4). In addition, at the aggregate level, regime difference matters as well. Individuals who live in a country with a regime that is more different from China in nature (i.e., more democratic) are more likely to have a negative perception of China.

The analyses in Model 2 to Model 5 examine the moderating effect of trade interdependence on the relationship between perception of China and its covariates. The interaction term between trade and economic perception (Model 2), democratic value (Model 3), and regime difference (Model 4) are added to the base model separately, and three interaction terms are then put in one model (Model 5). Together, the results of these three-four models show the negative effects of trade interdependence. On the one hand, the statistically negative sign of the coefficient of the interaction terms between trade and economic perception (−0.022 in Model 2; −0.021 in Model 5) indicates that a closer trade relationship decreases the positive effect of economic perception on the view of China (Hypothesis 3). On the other hand, the statistical insignificance of the interaction term between trade and individuals' democratic values (Model 3) and between trade and regime difference (Model 4) indicates that trade relationship cannot help attenuate the negative effect of these political factors. And the same is true when all three interactions are included in Model 5. Political factors (i.e., individuals' democratic values and countries' democracy level) remain negatively associated with perception of China. In addition, trade interdependence itself is still negatively associated with the

[59]Katherine Barbieri, Omar Keshk and Brian Pollins, *Correlates of war project trade DataSet codebook* Version 2, (2008).
[60]Andrew Gelman and Jennifer Hill, *Data Analysis Using Regression and Multilevel/Hierarchical Models* (Cambridge: Cambridge University Press, 2007).

Table 1. Multilevel regression analysis of mass perception of China (ABS, 2005–2016)

	Model 1	Model 2	Model 3	Model 4	Model 5	Model 6
Primary independent. variables:						
Trade interdependence	−0.14**	−0.071	−0.16**	−0.43**	−0.36*	−0.28
	(0.063)	(0.067)	(0.076)	(0.21)	(0.21)	(0.24)
Regime difference	−4.10***	−4.12***	−4.09***	−6.43***	−6.25***	−5.59**
	(0.78)	(0.78)	(0.78)	(1.74)	(1.75)	(2.37)
Economic perception	1.27***	1.90***	1.27***	1.28***	1.88***	1.82***
	(0.14)	(0.28)	(0.14)	(0.14)	(0.28)	(0.30)
Democratic values	−3.31***	−3.31***	−3.56***	−3.30***	−3.50***	−3.55***
	(0.26)	(0.26)	(0.56)	(0.26)	(0.56)	(0.58)
Interaction terms:						
Trade*econ. perception		−0.022**			−0.021**	−0.031***
		(0.0086)			(0.0086)	(0.0092)
Trade*demo. values			0.0083		0.0065	0.016
			(0.016)		(0.016)	(0.017)
Trade*regime diff.				0.074	0.067	0.051
				(0.050)	(0.050)	(0.059)
Control variables:						
Affinity score						10.5
						(22.6)
Confucius institute						0.31
						(0.28)
Age						0.017*
						(0.0098)
Gender						0.61**
						(0.27)
Education						0.092**
						(0.039)
Urban						0.093
						(0.32)
Interpersonal trust						0.42
						(0.34)
Nationalism						0.76***
						(0.23)
Constant	77.2***	75.6***	77.9***	86.6***	84.7***	66.4**
	(3.76)	(3.81)	(3.97)	(7.26)	(7.45)	(26.7)

$*p < .10, **p < .05, ***p < .01.$

perception of China. This finding falsifies the expected positive effect of trade in terms of its moderating effect on relationship between perception of China and its political determinants.

Finally, Model 6 includes all control variables in the model. The pattern of the analytical result stays like the previous five models. Altogether, these findings demonstrate the overall negative effect of trade interdependence on the perception of China. A set of additional analyses extend this analysis to a global sample, and the results show the same pattern.

Conclusion

The dual processes of economic globalization and China's integration into the world economy have created unprecedented trade interdependence between China and other countries. As China increasingly affects the national economies of these countries, the foreign public inevitably link their perception of China with their assessment of economic situation. More importantly, such responsibility linkage tends to be strengthened by bilateral economic ties. People in countries sharing strong economic ties with China are more likely to blame China for the economic distress. Drawing on data from both the ABS, this study finds strong empirical support for this economic explanation. Overall trade interdependence is negatively associated with mass perception of China. While economically advantaged citizens hold a more positive view of China, this positive link to diminish as trade interdependence increases. Moreover, it is found that China's 'soft power deficit' persists despite its economic rise.

By revealing the complex economic sources of China's foreign image, this study helps highlight the important instrumental basis of foreign-policy issues. Besides traditional value and political concerns, the public also perceives foreign-policy issues based on economic costs and benefits. More important, such economic understandings of foreign-policy issues are strongly moderated by a highly interdependent world economy.[61] More studies are thus called for to improve scholarly understandings of issue linkage between foreign-policy issues and domestic politics in a globalized world.

The findings emerged in our study also have important practical implications. For China, this study points to the inherent problem in China's trade and investment initiatives. Closer economic ties with China are shifting the responsibility of economic performance from the national government to China, and thus drive more political elites and the public to blame China for economic hardship. In other words, China's economic programs like the 'Belt and Road Initiative' do not necessarily deliver an improved foreign image. This study also indicates that China' strategy to develop a positive global image is indeed constrained by the perception of the foreign public about the nature of the political rule. The public moods in many countries are still driven by intrinsic values and political concerns. Trade interdependence and the 'charm offensive' like the Confucius Institute have not altered the soft-power deficit yet.

Disclosure Statement

No potential conflict of interest was reported by the author(s).

Funding

This research has been supported by National Natural Science Foundation of China (Grant No. 71774106)

---

[61]Timothy T. Hellwig, *Globalization and Mass Politics: Retaining the Room to Maneuver* (Cambridge and New York: Cambridge University Press, 2014).

Appendix. Robust analysis using data from the Pew Global Attitude Project (GAP)

This study uses data from the Pew Global Attitude Project (GAP) as a robustness check alongside the main analysis based on data from the recent three waves of ABS. Specifically, the 2012 Pew GAP conducts its comparative survey in 21 countries across the world about the mass perception of China. In GAP, the respondents were asked to assess a general evaluative question: "Please tell me if you have a very favorable, somewhat favorable, somewhat unfavorable or very unfavorable opinion of China?"

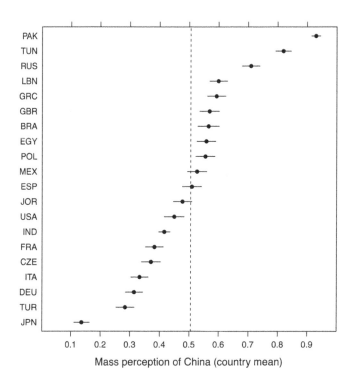

Figure A1. Mass perception of China, pew GAP 2012.

Figure A1 presents the country averages of the mass perception of China from the GAP sample. The dots represent each country's average perception of China sorted from highest to lowest, and the lines represent the corresponding standard deviations. The dotted vertical lines represent the pooled mean in the GAP. We can find that the pattern of a "divided" image about China is consistent across ABS (see Figure 2) and GAP samples.

Table A1. Multilevel analysis of the mass perception of China, GAP (2012)

	(8)	(9)	(10)	(11)	(12)	(13)
Trade interdependence	− 0.13	− 0.25**	− 0.26**	− 0.22*	0.0017	− 0.22*
	(0.13)	(0.11)	(0.11)	(0.11)	(0.0037)	(0.11)
Regime difference		− 0.17***	− 0.17***	− 0.17***	− 0.14***	− 0.16***
		(0.044)	(0.045)	(0.046)	(0.052)	(0.061)
Economic perception			0.20***	0.27***	0.24***	0.28***
			(0.020)	(0.055)	(0.022)	(0.055)
(Trade inderdep.) ×				-0.021	− 0.002***	− 0.021
(Economic per.)				(0.014)	(0.0004)	(0.014)
Confucius Institute						0.67
						(0.51)
Affinity score						0.10
						(1.15)
Gender	0.060**	0.060**	0.043	0.043	0.041	0.043
	(0.031)	(0.031)	(0.031)	(0.031)	(0.031)	(0.031)
Age	− 0.0024**	− 0.0023**	− 0.0024**	− 0.0025**	− 0.0025**	− 0.0025**
	(0.0010)	(0.0010)	(0.0010)	(0.0010)	(0.0010)	(0.0010)
Education						
secondary	0.035	0.039	0.023	0.023	0.025	0.023
	(0.039)	(0.039)	(0.039)	(0.039)	(0.039)	(0.039)
college or higher	0.058	0.061	0.034	0.035	0.035	0.035
	(0.047)	(0.047)	(0.047)	(0.047)	(0.047)	(0.047)
Constant	0.054	2.39***	2.06***	1.93***	0.93*	1.13
	(0.50)	(0.61)	(0.64)	(0.65)	(0.53)	(1.43)

$*p < 0.1; **p < 0.05; ***p < 0.01$

The authors test our main arguments also by examining the GAP sample, and the results are reported in Table A1. Model 9 to 13 exactly replicate Model 1 to Model 5 in Table 1. Overall, the results are highly consistent with those from the ABS sample. Across the globe, trade interdependence is negatively correlated with mass perception of China. While economically advantaged individuals are likely to orient themselves positively toward China, this positive linkage tends to be weakened by higher levels of trade interdependence. The only difference between the ABS and GAP samples is that in Model 11 the interaction term between the unweighted trade interdependence and individuals' economic perception is not statistically significant. But, this set of analyses finds strong interactive effects between weighted trade interdependence and economic perception (Model 12). One possible explanation is that trade interdependence between China and its Asian neighbors is much higher than that in the GAP sample. For instance, Japan, while tops in the GAP sample, is less dependent on China in the ABS sample.

Part II
Domestic Political Economy

Party-state Realism: A Framework for Understanding China's Approach to Foreign Policy

Steve Tsang

ABSTRACT

The author puts forth an analytical framework called party-state realism for understanding how policy makers in the People's Republic of China approach foreign policy. It has four defining characteristics. In order of importance, they are: putting the interests of the Communist Party at the core of China's national interest calculation; and on this basis adopting an instrumentalist approach; adopting a party-centric nationalism; and adhering to a neoclassical realist assessment of the country's place in the international system and its relative material power in advancing national interest. In this conception, the putting of the Chinese Communist Party's interest at the core of national interest is a constant, not a variable, factor. This does not mean the changing international context and relative national power are irrelevant, just that they take secondary importance.

With China emerging as the only other potential superpower in contrast to the United States and its leader Xi Jinping articulating an ambition for the People's Republic of China (PRC) to take centre stage in global affairs, it is useful to have an analytical framework that sets out the drivers of Chinese foreign policy.[1] Notwithstanding Xi's rhetoric that China should take centre stage in world affairs and the fact that Chinese power has been on an uninterrupted upward trajectory for over two decades, it remains reluctant, in comparison to other permanent members of the United Nations Security Council, to take on leadership roles in global affairs where Chinese interests are not immediately at stake. Its unusual approach poses a challenge to mainstream international relations theories. While neoclassical realism seems to apply to how the Chinese approach many foreign policy issues, it falls short as changing relative national power and state to state relations are not the primary driver of Chinese foreign policy. Although Alastair Iain Johnston concludes that China is a status quo rather than a revisionist power, such a distinction is ultimately moot.[2] In reality, Beijing takes 'an à la carte approach to the existing system, supporting those international institutions that serve its interests (…), turning others (…) to its own purposes, and weakening or subverting those (…) that might otherwise pose a challenge to its legitimacy.'[3] A recognition of the limitations of mainstream international relations theories as applied to China has led to attempts to find alternative explanations to explain China's approach to the rest of the world. Quansheng Zhao opted for the micro-macro linkage concept that addresses the interactions between international constraints and domestic determinants at the macro level as well as the approach of decision

---

[1]Xi Jinping, 'Secure a Decisive Victory in Building a Moderately Prosperous Society in All Respects and Strive for the Great Success of Socialism with Chinese Characteristic for a New Era.' (speech, 19th Congress of Chinese Communist Party, October 18, 2017), *Xinhua*, accessed January 29, 2018, http://www.xinhuanet.com/english/download/Xi_Jinping's_report_at_19th_CPC_National_Congress.pdf.

[2]Alastair Iain Johnston, 'Is China a status quo power?', *International Security* 27(4), (2003), pp. 5–56.

[3]Aaron L. Friedberg, Competing with China', *Survival* 60(3), (2018), pp. 24–5.

makers at the micro level.[4] Conceived two decades ago his analysis was based on experience in the transition from the Mao Zedong to the Deng Xiaoping era. China under Xi has changed considerably since then. Feiling Wang puts forth an interpretation that perceptively identifies three key drivers for Chinese foreign policy, namely 'the CPC's political preservation, China's economic prosperity and more Chinese power and prestige'.[5] But he does not explain how they relate to the wider literature on international relations. More recently, June Teufel Dreyer has looked astutely at an indigenous concept, the *tianxia* (all under heaven) trope.[6] While the worldview of China's leaders definitely reveals significant elements of the *tianxia* trope, the PRC's foreign policy is driven by forces more powerful than its Sinocentric worldview.

A striking reality that distinguishes China's approach to foreign policy from that of most great powers is the centrality of domestic politics.[7] Contrary to the pattern in most great powers or the thrust of main international relations theories, which focus on foreign policy considerations, relative capabilities and state to state interaction, consistently the most basic driver of the PRC foreign policy is domestic. The international relations theories that fit this reality best are *Innenpolitik* theories though on their own they are also insufficient to explain Chinese foreign policy as a whole. In general terms *Innenpolitik* theories 'argue that internal factors such as political and economic ideology, national character, partisan politics, or socioeconomic structure determine how countries behave toward the world beyond their borders'.[8]

In the case of the PRC its approach is determined first and foremost by its political system. A focus on the system rather than ideology is important as Communism as the state ideology has essentially been put aside in the post-Mao era, particularly after the Tiananmen Massacre (1989) and the collapse of Communism in Eastern Europe. As this author has explained elsewhere the post-Mao system is a 'consultative Leninist' one, which means the 'Communist Party is obsessively focused on staying in power, for which maintaining stability in the country and pre-emptively eliminating threats to its political supremacy are deemed essential'.[9] This is such an overriding consideration for policy makers in China that it applies as much to foreign policy as it does to domestic policies. As Xi told Chinese diplomats, they must 'uphold the authority of the CPC Central Committee as the overarching principle and strengthen the centralized, unified leadership of the Party on external work'.[10] This is the point of departure for but not the sum total of Chinese foreign policy making.

Being the core of the 'consultative Leninist' system the Communist Party of China (CPC) is much more than the governing party or the party in power. It in effect claims and takes ownership of the country or the state and it asserts a monopoly in national narrative including how national interest is defined. The system in place is a Leninist party-state as the Party exercises a monopoly of the state and military power to an extent unimaginable in democracies or most authoritarian states. Based on this reality this paper puts forth a new analytical framework called party-state realism for understanding how PRC policy makers approach foreign policy in the post-Mao era. (This analytical framework should also be applicable to other Leninist party-states after the collapse of Communism in Eastern Europe and the Soviet Union.) In this conception, the putting of the CPC's interest at the core of national interest is a constant, not a variable, factor that underpins Beijing's foreign policy making. This does not mean the changing international context is irrelevant, just that it takes secondary importance.

---

[4]Quansheng Zhao, *Interpreting Chinese foreign policy: The micro-macro linkage approach* (Hong Kong: Oxford University Press, 1996).

[5]Feiling Wang, 'Preservation, prosperity and power: what motivates China's foreign policy?' *Journal of Contemporary China* 14(45), (2005), p. 694.

[6]June Teufel Dreyer, 'The "Tianxia Trope": will China change the international system?', *Journal of Contemporary China* 24(96), (2015), pp. 1015–31.

[7]Hongyi Lai, *The Domestic Sources of China's Foreign Policy: Regimes, Leadership, Priorities and Process* (London: Routledge, 2010).

[8]Gideon Rose, 'Neoclassical Realism and Theories of Foreign Policy', *World Politics* 51(1), (1998), p. 148.

[9]Steve Tsang, 'Consultative Leninism: China's new political framework', *Journal of Contemporary China* 18(62), (2009), p. 866.

[10]Ministry of Foreign Affairs, 'Xi Jinping Urges Breaking New Ground in Major Country Diplomacy with Chinese Characteristics', June 23, 2018, *Ministry of Foreign Affairs*, accessed August 15, 2018, http://www.fmprc.gov.cn/mfa_eng/wjdt_665385/wshd_665389/t1571296.shtml.

This approach implies that national interest calculation as applied by Chinese policy makers may or may not match a non-partisan evaluation of what would be in China's national interest. Official Chinese foreign policy does not acknowledge that its starting point is the interest of the Party. Instead, it presents foreign policy in terms of promoting Chinese national interest. In the Xi era, this is posed as a revival of the greatness of China encapsulated in 'the China Dream'.[11] To understand Beijing's actual foreign policy one should not start with (though not ignore) what opportunities are on offer as a result of changing relative national power. Instead, one should start with what the CPC sees as the most basic—to protecting and enhancing regime security, which includes maintaining stability, upholding national security and sustaining economic growth. Where such an assessment is at variance with the articulated foreign policy, it is regime security that prevails.

Defining Characteristics

By adapting consultative Leninism to foreign policy making party-state realism serves as an analytical framework for understanding how the Chinese Government in the post-Mao era approaches relations with the outside world. It has four defining characteristics, which are, in order of importance:

- First and foremost, putting the interests in particular the survival of the Communist Party at the core of China's national interest calculation; and on this basis
- Adopting an instrumentalist approach to international organizations, cooperation, law and norm as well as economic ties;
- Adopting a party-centric nationalism that instils in its citizens a belief that the restoration of China's greatness and its rightful place in the world can only be achieved under the leadership of the Party[12]; and finally, taking into account these three factors,
- Adhering to a neoclassical realist assessment of the country's place in the international system and its relative material power in advancing national interest.

Party-first National Interest

Even though Xi Jinping is not attempting a Maoist restoration,[13] he acts as if he were the true heir to the PRC's founding leader, Mao Zedong, as he seeks to reclaim China's place as the most magnificent great power in the world. In the language of the late twentieth and early twenty-first century it means transforming China into a superpower. This is to be achieved by pursuing the China Dream of national rejuvenation, which is to be secured by adhering closely to the leadership of the CPC.[14] While Xi has abandoned Deng Xiaoping's policy of 'hiding capabilities and biding for time', he has merely done what is inherent in Deng's approach, which is for China to assert itself when it is ready. This quest is also complementary to the Party's assertion of core national interests, which came into usage in the mid-1990s and gained general currency in the 2000s.[15] It is reinforced by Xi's instruction to Chinese diplomats that 'they are first and foremost "party cadres".'[16]

---

[11]Honghua Men and Steve Tsang, 'Genesis of a Pivotal Decade', in *China in the Xi Jinping Era*, eds. Steve Tsang and Honghua Men (London: Palgrave Macmillan, 2016), pp. 2–3.

[12]This and the first feature are essentially the same as two of the defining characteristics for consultative Leninism. Tsang, 'Consultative Leninism', p. 866.

[13]A Maoist restoration implies a commitment to reintroduce totalitarianism and to destroy the Party if necessary in order to lead China to achieve its 'revolutionary goal' as defined by the supreme leader. Xi is a Leninist who sees the Party as central to achieving his ambitions for China. Xi freely adopting some Maoist practices—part and parcel of the CPC's heritage—does not amount to a Maoist restoration.

[14]Xinhua, 'Xi urges solidarity for national rejuvenation', *Xinhuanet*, May 20, 2015, accessed February 8, 2018, http://www. xinhuanet.com/english/2015-05/20/c_134256099.htm.

[15]Michael Swaine, 'China's Assertive Behavior Part One: On "Core Interests"', *China Leadership Monitor* 34, (2011), pp. 3–4.

[16]Kevin Rudd, 'Xi Jinping's Vision for Global Governance', *Project Syndicate*, July 11, 2018, accessed August 15, 2018, https:// www.project-syndicate.org/commentary/xi-jinping-has-a-coherent-global-vision-by-kevin-rudd-2018-07.

China's core interests are summed up most succinctly by Dai Binguo in 2009 when he was the State Councilor superintending foreign policy. He defined them as 'foremost, preserving China's basic state system and state security; after this, national sovereignty and territorial integrity; and in third place, sustain stable development of the economy and society' (第一是维护基本制度和国家安全, 其次是国家主权和领土完整, 第三是经济社会的持续稳定发展).[17] Dai's formulation sets the tone and has been adhered to by other Chinese officials and scholars. Indeed, this was reaffirmed by Yang Jiechi who performs a similar role under Xi. Yang said that as Xi Jinping instructed, 'upholding the leadership of the Chinese Communist Party and socialism with Chinese characteristics is the most basic task in foreign policy'.[18] Even though Dai was clear in the order of importance, Michael Swaine argues that in light of the relative frequency in how all three components were mentioned by Chinese officials and media, it was the second component that was most important.[19]

Swaine's relegation of the protection of the party-state to a lower priority reflects a misunderstanding of the original Chinese text, particularly the term *guojia anquan* (国家安全) and the explicit ordering of the priorities—Swaine mistook them for numbered bullet points. This has resulted in a misreading of the Party's intent and Dai's words which, as the rest of this section shows, reflect the reality of Chinese foreign policy. In common with many international relations scholars, Swaine translated *guojia anquan* into 'national security', a term with clear meaning in the English language that chimes with international relations literature. The correct translation should have been 'state security', implying regime security. If Dai or the Party had intended *guojia anquan* to mean 'national security', he would have put it with the number two component where it would have fit in well. Indeed, state or regime security reinforces the first and foremost component, which is about protecting the party-state, essential for the physical security of the leaders and potentially their families.[20] This is the starting point for the Chinese Government view of its core interests. It is about domestic politics which is not contested by external players, and thus does not require regular reiteration by Chinese leaders and officials. In contrast, national security issues like the sovereignty of Taiwan (and other disputed territories) are highly contested internationally, which accounts for the frequency Chinese officials refer to them. Swaine's focus on the frequency and intensity that Taiwan and territorial integrity issues are mentioned thus misses the point. With this key concept of *guojia anquan* mistranslated, Swaine looked pass Dai's statement which put the first component down as the foremost core interest. Being misunderstood by Swaine does not change the reality of China's definition of core interests, which remains that articulated by Dai—the most basic component is regime security. National security, focusing on the upholding of China's sovereignty and territorial integrity, comes second. Sustaining economic and social stability and growth ranks third. This applies all through the post-Mao era, and remains the case under Xi.

Making this distinction enables us to make sense of the PRC's policy towards the Korean Peninsula, particularly as the North Korean regime under Kim Jong-un created a nuclear and missile crisis despite China's declared policy of no nuclear weapons or war on the peninsula.[21] In addition, Xi Jinping publicly affirmed at the 19th Party Congress (October 2017) that he would like China to take centre stage in global affairs. Putting them together it is reasonable to extrapolate

---

[17] '首轮中美经济对话: 除上月球外主要问题均已谈及' ['First round of US-China economic dialogues: Every subjects are covered except landing on the moon'], *www.Chinanews.com*, July 29, 2009, accessed February 9, 2018, http://www. chinanews.com/gn/news/2009/07-29/1794984.shtml

[18] 杨洁篪 '在习近平总书记外交思想指引下不断开创对外工作新局面 [Yang Jiechi, 'Continuously breaking new grounds in external work under the leadership of the diplomatic thinking of General Secretary Xi Jinping'], *Chinese Foreign Ministry*, accessed August 13, 2018, http://www.fmprc.gov.cn/web/zyxw/t1430589.shtml. My translation.

[19] Swaine, 'China's Assertive Behavior', p. 5.

[20] The physical security of top leaders has become an acute issue under Xi who ended the immunity of retired Politburo Standing Committee members against all charges when he violated the post-Mao convention in bringing down and jailing Zhou Yongkang after Zhou's retirement. The overthrown of the CPC can have potential implications for the physical safety for some of its top leaders. The CPC is very mindful of what happened to Nicolae Ceausescu of Romania.

[21] 'Military means not an option for Korean Peninsular issue: spokesperson', *Xinhua*, August 31, 2017, accessed February 21, 2018, http://www.xinhuanet.com/english/2017-08/31/c_136571684.htm.

that it is in China's national interest to find a way to ease tension on the Korean Peninsula and pre-empt escalation into military hostilities. Admittedly, China may not be able to resolve this long-standing thorny issue. But it will earn a place in the centre stage of world affairs if it proactively takes a leadership role in finding a constructive way forward. Instead, Beijing chose passive cooperation with United Nations sanctions and, above all, an insistence that the world, in particular the United States of America (USA), should not see China as the key to a solution on the Korean Peninsula, at least until China appeared to be completely side-lined when South Korean President Moon Jae-in secured a breakthrough with the winter Olympics diplomacy of early 2018.[22] It is noteworthy that China played no active part in bringing this about though its tightening of sanction in 2017 undoubtedly forced Kim's hand. The success of Moon in breaking the ice suggests that there was scope for China to have taken more of a leadership role to get the North Koreans and the Americans to talk. Likewise, there is no evidence that Beijing took any initiative to set up the 2018 Singapore summit between Trump and Kim, in contrast to supporting Kim in preparing for the summit once it had been scheduled.

Why did Beijing choose to avoid taking on a proactive leadership role over Korea, when the changing state to state relations and the relative strength of China's position on the peninsula made it the best placed great power to do so while the Trump Administration's belligerency caused widespread international concern in 2017? This becomes understandable if the party-state realist framework is applied.

In this framework the first and foremost priority for Beijing is not taking centre-stage in global affairs, an articulated goal but not an essential requirement. However the Chinese Government may spin it, resolving the Korean crisis will be seen domestically as working with the Trump Administration, which threatened 'fire and fury' against the Kim regime, a 'fraternal' Leninist state whose survival depended on Chinese support. If the Party should appear domestically as weak *vis-à-vis* the Trump Administration in undercutting the Kim regime, Xi risks being seen as wobbling over his commitment to do whatever it takes to nip in the bud any challenge to the supremacy of the Party within China. The latter was amongst his first major statements of intent after becoming leader in 2012. In his visit to Guangdong late that year he stressed that under his leadership the Party would not made the mistake of the Communist Party of the Soviet Union, in which no one was 'man enough' to stand up against the betrayal of Mikhail Gorbachev in presiding over the collapse of the Soviet Union.[23] Since then Xi has consistently reaffirmed a commitment to pre-empt anyone from doubting his determination to sustain the consultative Leninist system.

Indeed, if the PRC acts solely on neoclassical realism it will have taken on a leadership role to try to resolve the Korean crisis. To China as a nation there are no compelling reasons why it must sustain the Kim regime, since it has largely ignored China's concerns as it pursues its own nuclear ambition. Indeed, the Kim regime has not been a better neighbor to China than South Korea, emphatically since 2011 and arguably for a good deal longer, notwithstanding the existence of a mutual defense treaty between China and North Korea. Given the great disparity in power even in a hypothetical scenario of North Korea being taken over by South Korea, Beijing can expect its uncooperative, unreliable and troublesome neighbor to be replaced by a united Korea governed from Seoul, which has been very friendly to China. A newly united Korea preoccupied with integrating the north cannot afford to take on China and can be expected to continue a friendly and cooperative policy towards China. If China had taken a leadership role to bring about such an eventuality it would be in a good position to enhance its interests.

The alleged concerns that China as a nation may have over the implosion of North Korea—resulting in a massive refugee influx and the loss of a buffer state—are grossly exaggerated. The

---

[22]Kinling Lo, 'US should "do its duty" to resolve North Korea nuclear crisis, China says', *South China Morning Post*, September 15, 2017, accessed February 21, 2018, http://www.scmp.com/news/china/diplomacy-defence/article/2111393/china-says-its-not-key-ending-north-korea-nuclear .
[23]習近平南巡內部講話 [Speech of Xi Jinping during his Southern tour for internal audience]', *www.open.com*, March 8, 2013, accessed February 22, 2018, http://www.open.com.hk/content.php?id=1197#.WpBORRPFLox.

harsh terrain in the China-North Korea borders, the relatively small population on the Korean side of the border region, the Yalu River guarded by the Korean People's Army and the People's Liberation Army on both shores, as well as the prospect of being treated as second class citizens in a much wealthier and human rights respecting united Korea against being at best tolerated as troublemaking refugees in Leninist China should make the risk of a large refugee influx low. This is not to say some Chinese leaders do not want to preempt even a small influx of Korean refugees to an economically degenerating region with a significant Korean minority population, which may pose an unwanted challenge to the Party in the Northeast. Given that the government of a united Korea will inherit the nuclear arsenal of the North while the United States Government will work to remove it from the Peninsula, tension between them will heighten. Furthermore, the USA will have lost the *raison d'etre* for stationing troops in South Korea. The risk that the new Korean government will allow the USA to build new bases in the North while existing ones are underutilized is therefore negligible.[24] China's national interest, in contrast to that of the Communist Party, does not require China to sustain the Kim regime, though both would prefer stability on the peninsula and the elimination of the risk of any accident involving nuclear devices.[25]

Can Beijing be reticent because its scope of influence in North Korea has been significantly reduced since Kim Jong-un came to power in 2011 and purged all Beijing-friendly senior figures from his regime? While this is undoubtedly regrettable to Beijing, it does not change the reality that China still 'provides North Korea with most of its food and energy supplies and accounts for more than 90 percent of North Korea's total trade volume.'[26] This economic leverage is admittedly insufficient to make Kim give up his nuclear program but China does not need to resolve the nuclear crisis to secure a place in center-stage of global affairs. If it takes the lead to do so and uses its economic leverage it will have gone a very long way to achieve this. After all, China recently gained enormous kudos by merely hosting the non-conclusive six-party talks (2003–9). There is much that Beijing can gain in its standing in the world by taking a constructive leadership role in seeking a solution. This is an option dismissed because ultimately the Chinese leadership is, for regime security reasons, unwilling to show a lack of determination to sustain its vexatious Leninist 'little brother'.

China's approach towards the Korean peninsula is not an aberration. The same basic consideration determines how its government tackles foreign policy in general. Xi might have spoken as if China were ready to take a leadership role in economic globalization at Davos (2017) when the Trump Administration advocated 'America first',[27] but his government did not really follow up on such a grandiose gesture. The Chinese Government talks about global common good but acts on Party interests. This attitude is also reflected powerfully in China's support for authoritarian regimes globally.

There is no reason to believe that supporting any type of political system, be it democratic or authoritarian is inherently in the national interest of China, in contrast to that of the Party. The experience of Taiwan, Hong Kong and Mainland China show that Chinese people can flourish in a democracy, a hybrid system or a Leninist party-state. The PRC also maintains good and mutually beneficial relations with countries across regime types. The better relationship Beijing has with

---

[24]The USA has 15 bases in South Korea, of which two are operated by the Air Force and one by the Navy. Of the two Air Force bases, only Osan is home to a combat air wing. With the Kunshan base heavily under-utilized and capable of hosting another air wing, it is hard to see the USAF demanding (and a united Korean government accepting) a new base in northern Korea. President Trump in fact articulated a willingness to withdraw US forces from Korea after he met Kim in Singapore in June 2018. Josh Smith and Phil Stewart, 'Trump surprises with pledge to end military exercises in South Korea', *Reuters*, June 12, 2018, accessed June 15, 2018, https://uk.reuters.com/article/uk-northkorea-usa-military/trump-surprises-with-pledge -to-end-military-exercises-in-south-korea-idUKKBN1J816N.

[25]Ironically, the risk of an accident involving a nuclear device on the Peninsular is more likely to be reduced with a united Korean with no nuclear weapons than a North Korea armed with nuclear weapons.

[26]Eleanor Albert, 'The China-North Korea Relationship', *Council on Foreign Relations*, accessed February 21, 2018, https://www. cfr.org/backgrounder/china-north-korea-relationship.

[27]'Full Text of Xi Jinping keynote at the World Economic Forum', *CGTN*, January 17, 2017, accessed August 20, 2018, https:// america.cgtn.com/2017/01/17/full-text-of-xi-jinping-keynote-at-the-world-economic-forum.

Seoul than with Pyongyang underlines the irrelevance of regime type. Likewise, authoritarian Vietnam does not maintain friendlier relations with the PRC than democratic Indonesia within Southeast Asia.

But Chinese foreign policy is geared to support authoritarian states, even though it is not official Chinese policy to export the consultative Leninist model.[28] The official position, in the language of Xinhua, is that 'the CPC is willing to share its vision, path and experience'.[29] Technically, the policy is not to proactively export the Chinese political system but to assist any government which seeks to learn from its authoritarian development model. Beijing also seeks to ensure its approach to governance in the Internet and other areas prevails globally. But the crux of the matter is to stem the tide of change unleashed by the advent of color revolutions at the end of the Cold War. Supporting authoritarian states makes the CPC less vulnerable to any Western 'conspiracy' inherent in the idea of a 'peaceful evolution'.[30]

In an important sense this Chinese approach both contrasts against and parallels the American commitment to aid democracy abroad. Successive US administrations since President Woodrow Wilson have steadily incorporated this principle into the body politics of US foreign policy—at least until Donald Trump became President.[31] Wilson started the process to 'make the world safe for democracy', a sentiment shared by most Americans. It is true that some national leaders in other political systems, for example Nicholas Maduro of Venezuela, prioritize personal interest above wider national interest. Arguably even Trump does so in the USA, a long-established democracy. But an individual leader pursuing personal interest above national ones is not the same as a political system invariably putting sustaining the Party's monopoly of power above the state and national interest. In China its leader systematically acts on the Party's behalf to make the world safe for authoritarian states. By issuing Document 9 of 2013, Xi has made it clear the Party must resolutely oppose and eliminate any effort to promote 'western' concepts like constitutional democracy or universal values.[32] With sustaining the Party's rule being the starting point of China's national interest, the PRC consistently supports authoritarian states to survive, develop and flourish—as an antidote to post-Cold War color revolutions in recent decades.

Instrumentalist in Cooperation or Confrontation

The Chinese Government regularly underlines the importance of basic principles, such as non-interventionism, projecting an image that it is a principled actor in international affairs. Its proclivity to take a moralistic stance reflects the domestic political reality that as a party-state it enjoys a monopoly of 'the truth' and narrative at home and its policies are always right. But, in reality, it engages with the rest of the world on calculation of interests. Indeed, pragmatism inherent in neoclassical realism modified by party-first national interests means that the Chinese Government's basic approach to cooperation or confrontation is instrumentalist, which is in general terms the second most important defining feature of party-state realism.

This is reflected most clearly in how Beijing views and deals with the international order centered on the United Nations and its ancillary institutions. International organizations or institutions are valued or dismissed depending on how useful they are to Beijing but Chinese rhetoric

---

[28]'President Xi says China will not export its political system', *Reuters*, December 1, 2017, accessed March 23, 2018, https://www.reuters.com/article/us-china-parties/president-xi-says-china-will-not-export-its-political-system-idUSKBN1DV4UM.

[29]Xinhua, 'Commentary: China willing to share, but not to export Chinese model' *Xinhuanet*, December 4, 2017, accessed March 23, 2018, http://www.xinhuanet.com/english/2017-12/04/c_136800287.htm.

[30]For Chinese concern about peaceful evolution, see Russell Ong, '"Peaceful Evolution", "Regime Change" and China's Political Security', *Journal of Contemporary China* 16(5), (2007), pp. 717–727. The CPC leadership is convinced that the West led by the USA is committed to secure the collapse of the party-state. 李慎明,中国和平发展与国际战略 [*China's Peaceful Development and International Strategy*] (Beijing: Zhongguo Shehui kexue chubanshe, 2007), p. 30.

[31]Thomas Carothers, *Aiding Democracy Abroad: The Learning Curve* (Washington: Brookings Institution Press, 1999).

[32]'Document 9: A ChinaFile Translation', *ChinaFile*, November 8, 2013, accessed, August 28, 2018, http://www.chinafile.com/document-9-chinafile-translation.

always presents its approach as based on high-sounding principles. In reality where the international order does not work to the interest of the party-state, the Chinese Government dismisses it or seeks to change it but where it does, it upholds the order. This instrumentalist approach renders efforts to categorize China a status quo or revisionist power moot.

Before the PRC was widely embraced as a near superpower and was able to assert itself strongly, it was highly defensive about the international human rights regime in light of domestic abuse of rights. It largely dismisses this regime as part of the post-war US-centric world order that allowed the West to intervene into the domestic affairs of poorer countries. As it does so it deliberately ignores the history that China actually played a key role in creating this regime. Chinese diplomat P.C. Chang (Zhang Pengchun) served as one of the first vice-chairmen of the Commission on Human Rights and was 'one of the most active and influential participants in the writing of the Universal Declaration of Human Rights'(UDHR).[33] Indeed, Chang made his 'most important contribution' in his 'strong commitment to the universality of the UDHR'.[34]

When the UN regime on human rights was to be revamped in the 2000s Beijing saw a threat and an opportunity. It neutralized the threat by seizing the opportunity. It 'engaged heavily in the institution-building negotiations' and secured a seat at the new Human Rights Council to limit criticism against it.[35] A decade since the Council was established and as China takes a more assertive approach under Xi, it strives to make the Council align closer to its interests. It seeks 'to block or weaken UN resolutions on civil society, human rights defenders and peaceful protests' as well as pushing back against efforts to strengthen some of the mechanisms for country-specific rights advancement.[36] Consequently, the Human Rights Council is no longer a regular thorn on China's side even though the detention of about one in ten of the entire Uyghur population in camps (officially called 'vocational training centers') in Xinjiang means the abuse of rights in China has reached a level unprecedented since the Beijing Massacre of 1989.[37] The same international institution to which Beijing took exception when it put pressure on human rights in China has now been neutralized.[38] Indeed, Beijing's instrumentalist approach has transformed this important UN agency from being a 'hostile' organization into a 'friendly' one.

At the core of the UN itself, China enjoys its status as a permanent member of the Security Council, which carries the obligation to share the 'responsibility for the maintenance of international peace and security', in accordance with Article 24 of the Charter.[39] Unlike the USA, Britain or France, which regularly take on a lead role on difficult peace and security issues China prefers to stay in the backseat.[40] China also conducts itself differently from Russia as it, on balance, does 'not opt for obstructive behavior in the S[ecurity] C[ouncil]' either.[41] It is important not to confuse supporting peace-keeping with taking a leadership role in maintaining international peace and security.

In peace keeping operations China provides more troops than any other permanent member of the Security Council. But then 'developing states … typically compose the top ten troop

[33]Frédéric Krumbein, 'P. C. Chang—The Chinese father of human rights', *Journal of Human Rights* 14(3), (2015), p. 332. The claim that Chang did not represent China as he was not appointed by the Communist Party is highly problematic, as Chang was the official representative of China.
[34]Krumbein, 'P. C. Chang', p. 337.
[35]Sonya Sceats and Shaun Breslin, *China and the International Human Rights System* (London: Chatham House, 2012), pp. 10–15.
[36]'The Costs of International Advocacy', *Human Rights Watch*, May 23, 2017, accessed May 31, 2018, https://www.hrw.org/report/2017/09/05/costs-international-advocacy/chinas-interference-united-nations-human-rights.
[37]This systematic abuse of rights of an identifiable minority of Chinese citizens and the Chinese Government's commitment to make the world safe for authoritarianism raises the question whether they will determine how Beijing sees relations with its neighbours and other states. For the camps, see Adrian Zenz, '"Thoroughly reforming them towards a healthy heart attitude": China's political re-education campaign in Xinjiang', *Central Asian Survey* 38(1), (2019), pp.102–28.
[38]Dave Lawler, 'China's growing influence swallows global criticism on human rights', *AXIOS*, November 9, 2018, https://www.axios.com/chinas-influence-global-criticism-human-rights-9bea0780-90a6-4f65-8899-4aa5ebf714d0.html.
[39]United Nations, 'UN Charter', accessed June 1, 2018, http://www.un.org/en/sections/un-charter/un-charter-full-text/.
[40]Sally Morphet, 'China as a permanent member of the security council October 1971-December 1999 ', *Security Dialogue* 31(2), (2000), pp. 151–166.
[41]Suzanne Xiao Yang, *China in UN Security Council Decision-making on Iraq* (London & New York: Routledge, 2013), p.100.

contributors.'[42] Indeed, UN peace-keeping operations historically did not usually involve troops from the permanent members of the Security Council in order to avoid them dominating such operations. What is noteworthy about the Chinese approach to peace-keeping is how pragmatic it has been in reversing its previous refusal to support it. As it seeks to project a new identity of being 'simultaneously a great power and a Global South member' it proactively provides funding and troops to support peace-keeping operations.[43]

China remains reticent in taking a leadership role on international peace and security generally, and even in its neighborhood. As explained, it has consistently refused to play a more proactive part than hosting the six-party talks (2003–8) over the Korean Peninsula, a significant but essentially passive role.

As a permanent Security Council member China is keen to keep the existing membership and structure unchanged even though it officially supports 'increasing the representation of developing countries' to counter the West's disproportionate dominance.[44] China advocates keeping the Security Council unchanged in order to ensure that Japan cannot gain a permanent seat.[45] It upholds the existing international system as it 'basically serves the interests of China'.[46]

Party-Centric Nationalism

A 'consultative Leninist' system requires a party-directed belief system to give it ideological cohesion in order to operate effectively. When Communism ceased to function as the state ideology after the Beijing Massacre of 1989, the Party adopted nationalism to fill the void, even though it continued to espouse Communism as the official ideology. Strictly speaking nationalism is not a proper ideology like Communism. It was chosen because it was 'the most reliable claim to the Chinese people's loyalty and the only important value shared by the regime and its critics.'[47] It enabled the Party 'to position themselves as the defenders of China's national pride' and unity.[48] In this sense it gives an ideological cohesion to the party-state. Since then the party-state has effectively instilled in PRC citizens the 'my country right or wrong' brand of nationalism. But this also imposes a requirement that any Chinese foreign policy must pass a patriotic test, which generally entails the government not appearing weak under pressure vis-à-vis its international interlocutors. This is the third defining feature of party-state realism.

As Xi makes 'the China Dream' a center piece of Chinese nationalism it takes on an increasingly assertive tone. It is now about 'making China great again'. This passed a significant landmark in the 19th Party Congress (October 2017) when Xi put an end to internal debates on whether China's moment had come. He ended the Dengist strategy of 'hiding capabilities and biding for one's time' and proclaimed a new era in which China expects to take center stage in global affairs.[49] Xi has

---

[42]Courtney J. Fung, 'What explains China's deployment to UN peacekeeping operations?' *International Relations of the Asia-Pacific* 16(3), (2016), p. 415.

[43]Ibid, p. 429. Such operations also enabled Chinese forces to practise deployment overseas.

[44]Permanent Representative of the People's Republic of China on United Nations Reform, 'Position Paper of the People's Republic of China on the United Nations Reforms' *Chinese UN Delegation website*, June 7, 2005, paragraph IV.3, accessed June 11, 2018, http://www.china-un.org/eng/chinaandun/zzhgg/t199101.htm.

[45]Permanent Representative of the People's Republic of China on United Nations Reform, 'Position Paper Clarifies China's Stance on UN Security Council Reform', *Chinese UN Delegation website*, June 7, 2005, accessed, June 15, 2018, www.china-un.org/eng/chinaandun/zzhgg/t199101.htm.

[46]门洪华[Men Honghua], 构建中国大战略的框架 [*Constructing a Framework for a Grand Strategy for China*] (Beijing: Peking University Press, 2005), p. 260.

[47]Suisheng Zhao, 'China's pragmatic nationalism: is it manageable?', *The Washington Quarterly* 29(1), (2005–6), p. 134.

[48]Ibid.

[49]Xi Jinping, 'Secure a Decisive Victory in Building a Moderately Prosperous Society in All Respects and Strive for the Great Success of Socialism with Chinese Characteristic for a New Era' (speech, 19th National Congress of the Chinese Communist Party, October 18, 2017), *Xinhua*, accessed August 13, 2018, http://www.xinhuanet.com/english/download/Xi_Jinping's_report_at_19th_CPC_National_Congress.pdf.

increased the relative weight of nationalism as a defining feature of party-state realism and transformed it into the second most important factor.[50]

At the 19th Congress, Xi also reaffirmed: 'As history has shown and will continue to bear witness to, without the leadership of the Communist Party of China, national rejuvenation would be just wishful thinking.'[51] Under Xi's stewardship, Chinese nationalism is undergoing a further modification—my country right or wrong now implies my party right or wrong, even my leader right or wrong. Criticizing the Communist Party or Xi's leadership is now deemed unpatriotic if articulated by a Chinese person and considered unfriendly if made by a foreigner or foreign government.[52] This imposes an element of ideological rigidity and thus reduces China's foreign policy's ability to take full advantage of the constantly changing international scene.

The implication of this new approach is that cold instrumentalism is increasingly required to make way for the more emotional urge to insist on China and its leadership being duly respected. To be sure, this process started even before Xi became leader. Towards the end of Hu Jintao's tenure, after the West's post-Cold War triumphalism was revealed as hubris when the global financial crisis hit, Hu's hallmark instrumentalist policy of stressing that China's rise would be peaceful had begun to erode. When Hilary Clinton challenged China's salami approach to claim the South China Sea as its newest core interest in 2010, Chinese Foreign Minister Yang Jiechi pushed back. As Yang accused the USA of plotting against China he also threatened Singapore. He said 'China is a big country and other countries are small countries, and that's just a fact', reportedly 'staring directly at Singapore's foreign minister' as he did so.[53] This was unnecessary, counterproductive and not in accord with the instrumentalist approach. It is noteworthy that there is no evidence that Yang did so under Hu's order.

This drift towards emotion driven assertiveness became mainstream after Xi took over from Hu. Yang's successor as Foreign Minister Wang Yi surpassed Yang by publicly lambasting a Canadian journalist during an official visit to Ottawa in 2016. When the Canadian reporter questioned him about China's human rights record, Wang retorted: 'This is totally unacceptable. Have you ever been to China? Please do not ask questions in such an irresponsible manner.'[54] Likewise, when Australian Prime Minister Malcolm Turnbull articulated concern over foreign powers 'making unprecedented and increasingly sophisticated attempts to influence the political process' in Australia in late 2017 the Chinese Foreign Ministry spokesman countered in public: 'We are astounded by the relevant remarks of the Australian leader. Such remarks simply cater to the irresponsible reports by some Australian media that are without principle and full of bias against China.'[55] Neither the Canadian reporter nor the Australian Prime Minister was hostile to China though they questioned the record of the Communist Party in human rights or in infiltrating Australian society and politics. While they reflected discomfort, it was the forceful Chinese responses that caused real concern.

This assertiveness driven by party-centric nationalism further undermines a specific objective of Chinese foreign policy—the cultivation of soft power. Indeed, what the Chinese Government has in reality managed to project, more intensely under Xi than previously, is not soft power but what Christopher Walker and Jessica Ludwig have described as 'sharp power'. Sharp 'in the sense that

---

[50]Party-centric nationalism has not been put as the second defining feature for this analytical framework even though most of the time it is the case under Xi because the framework applies to the post-Mao period as a whole, not only to the Xi era.

[51]Xi Jinping, 'Secure a Decisive Victory in Building a Moderately Prosperous Society in All Respects and Strive for the Great Success of Socialism with Chinese Characteristic for a New Era'

[52]This is not to claim that Xi has completely ended all form of criticism or dissent within China. Xi is restoring a very hard form of authoritarianism that utilises smart technologies, not totalitarianism.

[53]John Pomfret, 'U.S. takes a tougher tone with China' *Washington Post*, July 30, 2010, accessed August 13, 2018, http://www.washingtonpost.com/wp-dyn/content/article/2010/07/29/AR2010072906416.html??noredirect=on&sid=ST2010072906761.

[54]Derek Burney and Fen Hampson, 'When China feels superior, so does its envoys', *The Globe and Mail*, June 6, 2016, accessed August 13, 2018, https://www.theglobeandmail.com/opinion/when-china-feels-superior-so-do-its-envoys/article30277083/.

[55]Bill Birtles, 'China lodges official complaint after Malcolm Turnbull's comments about foreign interference', *ABC News*, December 9, 2017, accessed August 14, 2018, http://www.abc.net.au/news/2017-12-09/china-lodges-official-complaint-after-turnbulls-comments/9242630 .

they pierce, penetrate, or perforate the political and information environments in the targeted countries', which seek 'to manipulate their target audiences by distorting the information that reaches them'.[56] Unlike Russia, which has little choice but to resort to sharp power to make itself relevant globally, China's stunning achievements in the last decade have given it scope for real soft power. As symbols of capitalism like the Lehman Brothers collapsed and Western democracies careened into crisis China's 'consultative Leninist' model looked impressive as it emerged from the global financial crisis. In the Xi era, China is home to world class companies like Alibaba and Tencent and a leader in cutting edge technologies such as artificial intelligence. It now has tremendous scope to generate international admiration without resorting to sharp power. However, party-centric nationalism directs the Xi Administration to project 'soft power' through Confucius Institutes and the Belt and Road Initiative and, in so doing, confuses sharp power with soft power.[57]

Neoclassical Realism at Work

With the Party's interest as the starting point of national interest, neo-classical realism provides a useful guide for understanding China's foreign policy calculation. For this to work well one also needs to factor in the instrumentalist 'magic weapon' of the United Front and party-centric nationalism.

The United Front concept was originally introduced by Vladimir Lenin but Mao modified it to make it much more potent. As the CPC still has a United Front Department, it is easy to assume that the United Front is about the work of this shadowy unit, of which the overwhelming majority of its 12 sub-departments are domestically focused. To do so will miss another, more important, side to the United Front. Mao would not have described it as one of the three 'magic weapons' if he did not think this was highly effective.[58] The United Front needs to be understood as a methodology which the Party uses to guide foreign policy as it does domestic struggles.

The United Front is about ensuring the CPC will come out on top in any contest. Its starting point is to distinguish enemies from friends and treat them in ways to cripple enemies step by step.[59] 'In the simplest terms, the United Front requires the Party to identify a principal enemy, its supporters, and the intermediate zone full of "wavering elements" that can be won over by either the Party or its principal enemy.'[60] The Party is required to exercise strong discipline to focus its attack on the principal enemy and win over, or at least neutralize, as many as possible in the intermediate zone. The Party has no illusion that alliances thus forged would be temporary. They are meant to isolate and thus weaken the principal enemy. Once the principal enemy has been destroyed, the Party elevates one from among the secondary enemies in the intermediate zone to new principal enemy status. It now becomes the focus of attack until it too is defeated. The Party is supposed to repeat the process until no enemy is left and those in the intermediate zone are all converted to 'friends'.[61]

---

[56]Christopher Walker and Jessica Ludwig, 'The Meaning of Sharp Power: How Authoritarian States Project Influence', *Foreign Affairs*, November 16, 2017, accessed August 14, 2018, https://www.foreignaffairs.com/articles/china/2017-11-16/meaning-sharp-power.

[57]Elizabeth C. Economy, *The Third Revolution: Xi Jinping and the New Chinese State* (Oxford: Oxford University Press, 2018), pp. 219–24.

[58]The other two magic weapons were party building and armed struggle. Mao Zedong, 毛泽东选集 [*Selected Works of Mao Zedong*], Vol. 2 (Beijing: Renmin chuban she, 1970), p. 569.

[59]The classic on the subject remains Lyman P Van Slyke, *Enemies and Friends: The United Front in Chinese Communist History* (Stanford: Stanford University Press, 1968).

[60]Steve Tsang, 'China's Grand Strategy and its Rise', in *China Rising: Reactions, Assessments, and Strategic Consequences*, eds. Bo Huldt, Mika Kerttunen, Bo Wallander, Masako Ikegami and Susanna Huldt (Stockholm: The Swedish National Defence College, 2007), p. 52.

[61]Zhonggong zhongyang wenxian yanjiushi (The Documentary Research Office of the CPC Central) (comp.), 毛泽东文集, [*Works of Mao Zedong*], vol.4 (Beijing: Renmin zhubanshe, 1998), pp.196–200; '要胜利就要搞好统一战线'[To secure victory one must get it right with the United Front)—incomplete citation; Liao Gailong,毛泽东思想史 [*A History of Mao Zedong Thought*] (Hong Kong: Zhonghua Shuju, 1993), pp. 187–214.

By harnessing this to foreign policy the Chinese Government takes a hardnosed approach to assess relative strength between itself and its interlocutors, on the basis of 'comprehensive national strength' as well as the relative capacity to make the international environment conducive to its interests.[62] As Anne-Marie Brady rightly observes, the Party takes to heart Lord Palmerston's famous adage—'there are no permanent friends, only permanent interests.'[63] Embedding the United Front approach 'requires Chinese foreign policy makers to stay focused on one primary enemy at any one time.'[64] As they do so they calculate relative strength as well as costs and benefits ruthlessly but this does not imply they always understand the others or the context astutely or maintain the discipline required to secure the desired results. Indeed, party-centric nationalism and/or over-confidence based on nouveau rich hubris can distort or weaken adherence to the United Front methodology.

This approach is exemplified in how China handles the maritime disputes in the South China Sea. While its government laid claim based on a map drawn up by its predecessor government dating back to 1947, it issued 'no legal document ... which formally recognizes the legal status of the nine-dashed line' map.[65] As China's standing in East Asia and its 'comprehensive national strength' reached a new height in 2010, the Chinese authorities allowed or encouraged retired senior officers and affiliates to its national defense educational establishment to put forth the idea that South China Sea and the reefs and rocks China claims should be treated as a kind of proto core interest.[66] If such statements went unchallenged the Chinese would be able to generate incrementally a 'conventional wisdom' that South China Sea should be deemed their core national interest. According to Hilary Clinton, Chinese State Councilor Dai Bingguo mentioned (presumably in private as no public statement can be found) South China Sea as a core interest at the US-China Strategic and Economic Dialogue in May 2010 about which she contested.[67] Clinton's account has been questioned by Michael Swaine who concludes that 'Beijing has not unambiguously identified the South China Sea issue as one of its core interests' and if Clinton's recollection was correct, it 'was done in a decidedly unofficial manner'.[68] Swaine's latter assessment is likely to be on the mark. Up to the end of Hu Jintao's term of office (2012) Beijing had been very careful to not allow any senior official or active service senior officer articulate such a claim formally or publicly, which would have put South China Sea on par with Taiwan or Tibet.[69]

A major development did take place in the summer of 2010, when Clinton, as American Secretary of State, for the first time publicly challenged the salami-slicing approach of the PRC in seeking to change international perception of South China Sea. International recognition that Beijing would use force to defend its core interest gives significance to such Chinese efforts. Clinton put Beijing on the spot by declaring at the July ASEAN Regional Forum meeting that 'The United States has a national interest in freedom of navigation, open access to Asia's maritime commons and respect for international law in the South China Sea'.[70] The Chinese Government pulled back and the demi-official assertion of the South China Sea as proto core interest ceased.

---

[62]For an exposition of 'comprehensive national strength' see Angang Hu and Honghua Men, 'The Rising [sic] of Modern China: Comprehensive National Power and Grand Strategy' (2002), accessed May 30, 2018, https://myweb.rollins.edu/tlairson/china/chigrandstrategy.pdf.

[63]Anne-Marie Brady, *Making the Foreign Serve China* (Latham: Rowan & Littlefield, 2003), p. 21.

[64]Tsang, 'China's Grand Strategy and its Rise', p. 52.

[65]Zheng Wang, 'Chinese discourse on the "Nine-dashed line"', *Asian Survey* 55(3), (2015), pp. 504–8.

[66]Willy Lam, 'Hawks vs Doves: Beijing Debates "Core Interests" and Sino-U.S. Relations' *China Brief* X(17), (2010), accessed May 30, 2018, https://jamestown.org/wp-content/uploads/2010/08/cb_010_86.pdf?x87069. Retired senior military officers and professors in the National Defence University are subject to party discipline and can be reined in by the Party.

[67]US Department of State, 'Interview with Greg Sheridan of the Australian', November 8, 2010, accessed May 24, 2018, https://2009-2017.state.gov/secretary/20092013clinton/rm/2010/11/150671.htm.

[68]Swaine, 'China's Assertive Behavior Part One', p.9.

[69]Alastair Iain Johnston, 'How new and assertive is China's new assertiveness?' *International Security* 34(7), (2013), pp. 17–18.

[70]Mark Landler 'Offering to Aid Talks, U.S. Challenges China on Disputed Islands', *The New York Times*, July 23, 2010, accessed May 24, 2018, https://www.nytimes.com/2010/07/24/world/asia/24diplo.html.

When Premier Wen Jiabao next reiterated China's commitment to defend its core interests in a speech to the United Nations the following month, it was conspicuous by its absence.[71]

But Beijing did not give up. It changed its approach. After Xi became leader China built artificial islands out of reefs and rocks in the Spratly group and put military installations on them notwithstanding Xi's public pledge not to militarize them.[72] Creating new realities on the ground that cannot be reversed without the use of force has replaced the previous approach of getting *de facto* acknowledgement of China's claim. A realistic calculation was made that no Southeast Asian disputant has the capacity and the USA cannot find a legitimate basis and secure international support to reverse its island building.

By embedding the United Front concept, the Chinese approach to foreign policy is governed by a careful calculation of both 'comprehensive national strength' and its ability to win friends and isolate its principal enemy at any one time. This is essentially a realist conception as China seeks to maximize its advantage and push its interests as far as it can go, but it retreats tactically when it meets resistance backed by forces more powerful than what it can muster. But this can be and has under Xi increasingly been distorted where party-centric nationalism is allowed to take precedent.

Conclusions

The defining features of party-state realism consist of two types. The first and foremost feature, systematically putting the Party first, is a constant factor which is the starting point for Chinese foreign policy making. The 'consultative Leninist' system in place is based on the collective leadership at the top but it is a system that can accommodate the rise of a strongman. Since the 19th Party Congress (2017) collective leadership has in effect been replaced by leadership of the core leader, Xi. In such a context, 'Party first' sometimes means 'core leader first', and party directives on foreign policy, as with all policies, now need to dovetail 'Xi Jinping Thought for socialism with Chinese characteristics in a new era'. But the basic political system has not changed, and notwithstanding the concentration of power in Xi's hands China remains a party-state. What distinguishes China's approach is that this is driven by the political system and not the personal whims of its leader who occasionally puts personal interest ahead of national interest, which can happen in any political system. The party-state realism framework applies whether the Party is dominated by a core leader or a collective leadership. What remains essential to understanding Chinese foreign policy is to know what the Party sees as a threat to its monopoly of power in China at any one time.

This basic feature determines how Chinese national interests are defined and distorts how international relations theories can apply in the case of China. It takes precedent over all standard foreign policy considerations of a great power and compels the Chinese government not to pursue policies likely to undermine the capacity of the Party to stay in power. In practical terms, it leads to a policy to make the world safe for authoritarianism and to reject humanitarian interventionism.[73] It also injects an element of pragmatism in external economic relations since the long-term security of the party-state necessitates the maintenance of a robust economy and steady growth. Should economic pragmatism conflict with short-term requirements of the security of the regime, however, it is the latter that prevails. Hence, the signature external policy of Xi, the Belt and Road

---

[71]Ministry of Foreign Affairs, 'Wen Jiabao Attends the 65th General Debate of the General Assembly and Delivers a Speech', September 24, 2010, accessed May 24, 2018, http://www.fmprc.gov.cn/mfa_eng/topics_665678/wenjibaochuxi65jieUNdh_665784/t755848.shtml.

[72]David Brunstrome and Michael Martina, 'Xi denies China turning artificial islands into military bases', *Reuters*, September 25, 2015, accessed March 12, 2019, https://www.reuters.com/article/us-usa-china-pacific/xi-denies-china-turning-artificial-islands-into-military-bases-idUSKCN0RP1ZH20150925.

[73]This undoubtedly is what underpins the concern articulated by George Soros at Davos in January 2019 that China under Xi had become 'the most dangerous opponent of open societies'. Joe Miller, 'China's Xi Jinping "most dangerous" to open societies, says George Soros', *BBC*, January 24, 2019, accessed March 9, 2019, https://www.bbc.co.uk/news/business-46996116.

Initiative (BRI), will remain a flagship policy as long as he stays as core leader, whether it proves to be economically beneficial to China or not. The same thinking also restrains China from taking full advantage of the US withdrawal from the Trans Pacific Partnership (TPP). Given the size of the Chinese economy membership would ensure Chinese domination of TPP, a development that could make the BRI appear like a sideshow and thus highly beneficial to China. Likewise, while broadly defined Chinese national interest should need its government to seek to defuse the 'trade war' with the Trump Administration, this can only happen on the proviso that Xi will not appear to bow under American pressure and, above all, that this would not require changes that can undermine the consultative Leninist system.

The interplay and relative significance of the second and third defining features—instrumentalism and party-centric nationalism—is a dynamic one. They may not always complement each other but they are not inherently mutually exclusive. Chinese foreign policy under Jiang Zemin and Hu Jintao demonstrated how the two worked complementarily under collective leadership. In this period, internal debates and discussions on policies took place on a routine basis, which had the effect of reducing policy swings in favor of one or the other. With the Dengist principle of hiding capabilities and biding for time prevailing, party-centric nationalism merely required foreign policy makers to focus on steering China to rise without overtly provoking pushbacks from others. Before Xi established himself as paramount leader and put priority on making China great again, instrumentalism was the second defining feature of party-state realism.

By prioritizing the 'dignity of China' (and its leader) after Xi's rise to dominance the relative significance of the second and third defining feature by and large changed place. Beijing now places greater emphasis on party-centric nationalism than on instrumentalism. This should not be seen as a permanent shift, as Xi can reverse them. Indeed, in many cases, the two features still complement each other. The transformation of the Asian Infrastructure and Investment Bank (AIIB) from a 'China dominated agency' and 'a blatant agent of Chinese foreign policy' into a respected international development bank reflects instrumentalism at its best—Beijing changed when it realized such changes would enable the AIIB to gain wide international support and participation to secure the coveted credibility.[74] Where the 'dignity of China' is not at stake instrumentalism remains the second defining feature even in the Xi era.

As to the last defining feature, the applicability of neo-classical realism, this works once the peculiarity of the other defining features have been taken into account. It is a 'defining' feature not in the sense that this is new but that this is the international relations theory that applies the most. Starting from the party-first principle neo-classical realism explains Chinese foreign policy, though adjustments need to be made to factor in the relative importance of instrumentalism and party-centric nationalism at any one time. When not put in a party-centric nationalist straightjacket Chinese foreign policy makers are hardnosed realists who mostly seek to maximize the security of the party-state, national security and economic advancement of the PRC, and in that order.

This concept of party-state realism has been developed on the basis of the realities in post-Mao China, but it should not be seen as applicable only to China. It should also be applicable, perhaps with some modifications, to other countries which are a modified Leninist party-state. A notable example is Vietnam. The variant that should work best for Vietnam is likely to be that which prevailed in China before Xi placed party-centric nationalism ahead of instrumentalism as the second most important defining feature. Further research will need to be conducted in Vietnam to assess and verify the applicability of this analytical framework.

---

[74]Suisheng Zhao, 'A revisionist stakeholder: China and the post-World War II World order' *Journal of Contemporary China* 27(113), (2018), pp. 655–6.

Acknowledgments

The author would like to thank Suisheng Zhao, the two anonymous reviewers and Charles Parton for sharing their insights on the paper.

Disclosure statement

No potential conflict of interest was reported by the author.

The Rationale and Effects of China's Belt and Road Initiative: Reducing Vulnerabilities in Domestic Political Economy

Hongyi Lai ⓘ

ABSTRACT

The existing literature suggests that China's rationale for the belt and road initiative was to stimulate infrastructural investment abroad and thus economic growth at home, foster economic ties with Eurasia, and counter the US pivot to Asia. Employing a domestic political economy perspective, this article suggests that the Belt and Road Initiative (BRI) aimed to address China's three following vulnerabilities that could derail its economic growth and threaten its political regime—industrial surplus capacity, massive imports of energy through maritime transport instead of safer land routes, and under-development of the western region. Addressing these vulnerabilities helps to sustain China's economic model characterised by heavy reliance on investment and exports, protection of state firms, and massive energy input. Post-2012 data suggest that the BRI has partially mitigated these three vulnerabilities.

In 2013, China's President Xi Jinping and Premier Li Keqiang announced the belt and road initiative (BRI) in their speeches on China-Kazakhstan and China-ASEAN relations, respectively. The BRI is arguably one of the most ambitious and expensive international strategies China has ever undertaken since 1978. The BRI aims to build two clusters of nations along two economic belts, i.e., namely, the land-based economic corridor along the old Silk Road connecting western China through Central Asia, the Middle East, Eastern, Southern, and Western Europe, and the maritime economic belt connecting southeast coastal China with Southeast Asia, South Asia, the Gulf states, East Africa and Europe. In the following years, the BRI has been incorporated into major political meetings or the most important political documents in China, including the Third Plenary Session of the 18th Central Committee of the Communist Party of China in late 2013 and the amended constitution of the People's Republic of China in October 2017.[1]

Commensurate with these high-profile announcements and declarations have been massive efforts and material inputs into the BRI. According to the Chinese governmental source, in the first five years of the launch of the BRI, more than 100 countries and international organizations inked pacts to foster cooperation with China over the BRI, China's trade with nations along the Belt and the Road surpassed US$5 trillion, and China's foreign direct investment in non-financial sectors in these countries totaled US$80 billion.[2]

The scholarly literature and policy analyses on the BRI have been growing steadily. Much attention has been paid to the motivations of the BRI, as well as its components and projects. The

---

[1]'Chronology of China's Belt and Road Initiative', accessed January 9, 2018, http://www.xinhuanet.com//english/2015-03/28/c_134105435.htm on March 28, 2015.

[2]'Factbox: Belt and Road Initiative in Five Years', accessed January 9, 2019, http://www.xinhuanet.com/english/2018-08/26/c_137420914.htm.

existing literature suggests that three main objectives have motivated China's leaders to inaugurate the BRI—to generate economic growth in China through infrastructural investment, to foster economic, infrastructural and political linkage with Eurasia, and to counter the US pivot to Asia.

While these three motivations are relevant, several other highly significant causes concerning the domestic political economy have not been explored adequately. This article aims to fill the gap in the literature by investigating the linkage between domestic political economy and the launch of the BRI. It suggests that these under-explored domestic considerations behind this ambitious strategy included finding external outlets for China's surplus industrial capacity, securing China's energy importing routes, and augmenting the economy of the western region. It also assesses the accomplishment of these three objectives in the wake of the BRI.

The underlying theme of this article is that China's major foreign policy cannot be simply viewed as a response toward a recent external stimulus (such as the US pressurizing schemes such as the TPP), or merely a remedy to a present domestic economic problem such as a slowdown in economic growth in China. Rather, China's foreign policy needs to be interpreted against a deeper context, namely, its role in reducing major vulnerabilities of political economy and in sustaining the economic regime and eventually the political regime in China.

The subsequent parts of this article are as follows. First, the existing literature on the motivations of the BRI will be reviewed and the gaps will be identified. Second, relevant theories will be briefly reviewed and the analytical perspective will be outlined for the purpose of exploring the structural causes of the BRI. Third, a detailed analysis of the motivations of China's BRI related to its domestic political economy will be offered, followed by an assessment of the fulfillment of these objectives. Finally, the author summarizes the findings of the article.

Literature Review

A stream of literature has emerged on the BRI. The authors ranged from economists, political scientists, and geographers. Much of the literature is devoted to the motivations, the rationale, as well as components of the initiative. In this section, greater attention will be paid to the motivations of the BRI, which are the theme of this article.

Several political scientists, as well as political economists, postulated that China sought greater international economic influences and external security in Eurasia through the BRI and that it attempted to shape the global economic order through its establishment of the Asia Infrastructural Investment Bank (AIIB). Both initiatives served to counter the US initiatives such as the pivot to Asia and the Trans-Pacific Partnership (TPP).[3] A more recent study suggested that the BRI would allow China to reap diplomatic benefits from its proposed networked capitalism and from US President Trump's rejection the TPP.[4] Several studies also coined the BRI as China's scheme for regional integration.[5]

Another most frequently mentioned motivation for the BRI is to maintain economic growth. As argued by Huang (2016), the BRI would allow China to connect closely with economies west to it through infrastructure projects and expand its investment in and trade with these economies, and sustain China's economic growth in the next phrase.[6] Some Chinese sources maintained that the BRI was beneficial to China's industrial upgrade and economic opening.[7]

[3] Michael D. Swaine, 'Chinese Views and Commentary on the "One Belt, One Road" Initiative', *China Leadership Monitor* 47 (Summer), (2015), pp. 1–24; Yong Wang, 'Offensive for Defensive: The Belt and Road Initiative and China's New Grand Strategy', *The Pacific Review* 29(3), (20160, pp. 455–463, DOI: 10.1080/09512748.2016.1154690; Peter Ferdinand, 'Westward Ho—the China Dream and "One Belt, One Road",' *International Affairs* 92(4), (2016), pp. 941–957; Hong Yu, 'Motivation behind China's "One Belt, One Road" Initiatives and Establishment of the Asian Infrastructure Investment Bank', *Journal of Contemporary China* 26(105), (2017), pp. 357–358.
[4] Astrid Nordin and Mikael Weissmann, 'Will Trump Make China great again?', *International Affairs* 94(2), (2018), pp. 231–249.
[5] See Peter Ferdinand, 'Westward Ho', p. 950; Marcin Kaczmarski, 'Non-western Visions of Regionalism', *International Affairs*, 93 (6), (2017), pp. 1357–1376.
[6] Yiping Huang, 'Understanding China's Belt & Road Initiative', *China Economic Review*, 40 (2016), pp. 314–321.
[7] Swaine, 'Chinese Views'.

Another set of relevant economic motivations that partially overlaps the growth imperative is to stimulate the growth of western China and to relocate some of China's excessive capacities to Southeast Asia.[8] In several recent studies, a brief discussion has been made on the domestic political economy of the BRI. De Jonge suggested that concerns with overinvestment (which she did not elaborate on and which she proposed was reflected in low-quality inventory, excess capacity, and ghost cities) and with environmental degradation helped facilitate the setup of the AIIB.[9] Cai briefly described China's intention to overcome domestic 'industrial overcapacity' and to build new transportation lines through Central Asia, Pakistan and the Malay Peninsula.[10]

Two studies echoed the aforementioned economic motivation while pointing to the political rationale. Ye argued that China's leaders used the BRI to mobilize the fragmented authoritarian state. She noted that China's state banks attempted to enhance their international profile through investing in infrastructural projects and by drawing upon local funds from central China.[11] Baogang He observed briefly the rivalry between provinces in China for becoming hubs of external linkage in the implementation of the BRI.[12]

Nevertheless, the aforementioned studies have yet to offer a detailed, empirical and rich database analysis of the role of the BRI in easing surplus capacity, securing rising energy imports and reducing regional inequality in China. Nor is any assessment of the mitigation of these problems by the BRI.[13] This article hopes to fill these empirical gaps, while advancing theoretical analyses by employing a perspective of domestic political economy.

The existing theoretical literature has largely failed to provide a convincing view on the linkages of domestic and international political economy in the launch of the BRI. Mearsheimer, the most prominent neo-realist, argued that China, as a rising power, would try to maximize its power and establish its dominance, especially military preponderance in northeast Asia. He dismissed the argument that economic interdependence among nations would lead to peace,[14] and ignored domestic political motivations. For Mearsheimer, who focused on the relative power, military development and security arrangements in Northeast Asia in discussing China's future in his most important book,[15] the BRI would not effectively cultivate China's hegemony in Northeast Asia, as the main regions covered in the initiative are Central Asia, South Asia, the Middle East, Southeast Asia, and Southern and Eastern Europe, as Northeast Asian economies such as Japan and Taiwan have not participated in the BRI, and as the BRI is first and foremost about trade and investment. Liberals do not provide a unified view regarding the external aspects of the BRI either. In their 2012 edition of their best-known work, Keohane and Nye admitted that inter-dependence and its pacification of inter-state relations applied only to liberal democracies and that they did not heed domestic factors in their analyses.[16] John Ikenberry, a prominent liberal, argued that China has benefited from the liberal international order.[17] Ikenberry and Lim saw elements of institutional statecraft and

[8]Yu, 'Motivation', pp. 357–358.
[9]Alice de Jonge, 'Perspectives on the Emerging Role of the Asian Infrastructure Investment Bank', *International Affairs* 93 (5), (2017), pp. 1061–1084.
[10]Kevin G. Cai, 'The One Belt One Road and the Asian Infrastructure Investment Bank', *Journal of Contemporary China*, 27 (114), (2018), pp. 831–847.
[11]Min Ye, 'Fragmentation and Mobilization: Domestic Politics of the Belt and Road in China,' *Journal of Contemporary China*, 28 (119), (2019), pp. 696–711, DOI: 10.1080/10670564.2019.1580428.
[12]Baogang He, 'The Domestic Politics of the Belt and Road Initiative and Its Implications', *Journal of Contemporary China*, 28 (116), (2019), pp. 180–195, DOI: 10.1080/10670564.2018.1511391.
[13]For example, in a rare mention of China's drive to develop its western region, Ferdinand stated very briefly as follows: 'by 2015 it was estimated that it was still going to need 30–50 years to catch up with the rest of China. The OBOR initiative is partly aimed at speeding up that process.' See Ferdinand, 'Westward Ho', p. 951.
[14]John Mearsheimer, *The Tragedy of Great Power Politics* (New York: Norton, 2001), p. 371.
[15]Ibid, especially pp. 372–402.
[16]For sources of these two views, see Robert O. Keohane and Joseph S. Nye, *Power and Interdependence* (Boston: Longman, 2012), 4th edition, pp. xxxii-xxxiv, 271.
[17]See G. John Ikenberry's updated elaboration of the liberal view, 'The End of Liberal International Order?', *International Affairs*, 94 (1), (2018), pp. 7–23.

multilateralism in the AIIB, an instrument created by China to fund the BRI.[18] Other liberals voiced their concerns that the BRI could become a debt-trap.[19]

The only relevant body of literature would be the domestic impact of internationalization, as exemplified by a landmark volume co-edited by Keohane and Miller.[20] Most relevant to this article is the model of factor endowment-induced trade and domestic coalition by Ronald Rogowski, a contributor to this volume. His powerful theory helped to account for a wide range of events of political economy in the wake of trade expansion or retraction.[21] According to his theory, when China's trade was expanding (which was the case around 2012–2013, when China's trade expanded robustly around 8 percent a year), the political forces championing labor-intensive sectors, where China's factor endowment resided, would have prevailed, causing China to increase exports of these goods, instead of promoting capital-intensive and state firms-dominated infrastructural projects abroad. Therefore, an effective analytical perspective is still needed to expound how the BRI was conceived and how it has served the regime of political economy in China.

Aims and Argument

The aim of this article is to examine and assess China's aforementioned overlooked motivations in launching the BRI. In addition, this author will aim to shed an analytical light on the linkage between domestic and international political economy in the case of China.[22] His analytical perspective goes beyond the usual portray of the BRI as an addition to the rivalry between two of the biggest powers (namely, the USA and China) for the economic dominance of Asia. While there is an element of truth in this depiction, it runs the risks of ignoring the other important elements, namely, how the BRI serves China's political-economic regime. This author will discuss how the BRI could help prevent the bankruptcy of many state firms in sectors harassed by surplus capacity, and help sustain the model of economic growth and ultimately the political regime in China.

Shirk's argument about the pro-reform coalition in China in the 1980s seems applicable to a certain extent. She argued that China's leaders mustered support from a coalition of elites representing coastal provinces and light industry and used their backing to forge ahead with fiscal and state-owned enterprises reforms.[23] Applying her insights to the three vulnerabilities in China's political economy, one could suggest that in launching the BRI, China's leaders catered to the following sectoral, provincial and even ministerial interests. They included 1) a number of industries (mostly extractive and heavy industry) whose survival was threatened by surplus capacity and most of which were dominated by state-owned enterprises (SOEs), 2) the twelve western provinces whose opening had been restricted by their land-locked location and whose favorable share in national allocation of resources in the wake of the western development launched in 2001 seemed to have waded in the later years, 3) a range of powerful national ministries and bureaus overlooking these sectors saddled with surplus capacity and managing its consequences (such as Finance, Human Resources and Social Security, Commerce, People's Bank, State-owned Assets Supervision and Administration Commission, Taxation, Transport, Railway, and Energy), 4) national ministries and bureaus supervising the western provinces (such as Ethnic Affairs and Religious Affairs), and 5) powerful state agglomerates which stood to gain from the BRI, especially transport, railway, and energy. In addition, a number of coastal provinces such as Fujian, Zhejiang, Shanghai, and Guangdong also would benefit from the BRI due to their linkage with the maritime silk road (one

---

[18]G. John Ikenberry and Darren J. Lim, 'China's Emerging Institutional Statecraft', *Project on International Order and Strategy at BROOKINGS*, April 2017.

[19]'Is There a Liberal International Order?', *IISS, Strategic Survey 2018*, November 2018.

[20]See Robert Keohane and Helen Milner, eds. *Internationalization and Domestic Politics* (Cambridge: Cambridge University Press, 1996).

[21]See Ronald Rogowski, *Commerce and Coalitions* (Princeton: Princeton University Press, 1989).

[22]For a book that expounded an innenpolitik theory of foreign policy, see Hongyi Lai, *The Domestic Sources of China's Foreign Policy: Regimes, Leadership, Priorities and Process* (New York: Routledge, 2010).

[23]Susan Shirk, *The Political Logic of Economic Reform in China* (Berkeley: University of California Press, 1993), pp. 129–45.

of the two components of the BRI).However, limited space will allow me to discuss mainly the first two of the aforementioned interests and sketch instead of detailing an analytical framework to explain how the prevailing regime of domestic political economy necessitates a corresponding foreign policy.Rather, this author argues that the interests of these sectors and the catch-up of the western provinces with the coast concern the well-being of China's economic regime, a cornerstone of the ruling party.This is particularly so since most of the industries with surplus capacity are populated with large national and local state enterprises and since the current Chinese leaders especially President Xi Jinping views state ownership as a corner stone of the party-state.

This article postulates that through the BRI China's leaders hoped to reduce economic vulnerabilities and sustain high economic growth, thereby sustaining the political legitimacy of the ruling party. In the reform era 'delivering the economic goods' has been used by the ruling party in China as a key avenue to earn popular support.[24] In the wake of the global financial crisis in 2008, however, China's economic growth has been decelerating noticeably over the years, from 10.6 percent in 2010 to 9.5 percent in 2011, 7.9 percent in 2012, 7.8 percent in 2013, 7.3 percent in 2014 and 6.9 percent in 2015.[25] As a result, in May 2014, the Chinese President Xi Jinping talked about a slower annual growth rate in China below 7 percent as 'the new normal'.[26] As he emerged as China's top leader in early 2013, Xi felt the need to sustain economic growth against the downward trend. Doing so would help to maintain his credibility as an able leader and sustain the party's legitimacy among the Chinese population who has been largely acquiescent toward the one-party rule in exchange for their rising living standard.

As to be detailed later, in order to sustain China's economic growth, Xi would need to address the severe excessive capacity of industrial sectors and find new external and domestic markets. Finally, through the BRI Xi sought to reduce the high reliance on China's growth on its coast and enhance the economic profile of western China. Meeting these objectives would help sustain the present investment-intensive and state-firms-prominent growth model.

A mainly qualitative approach will be adopted in this article. This author will not only outline the official intention of reducing economic vulnerabilities but also examine the data that help to shed light on the effects of the BRI on easing these vulnerabilities. His analysis of the causes and effects of China's BRI will be advanced on the basis of empirical evidence. For this reason, multiple sources of information will be utilized to gain a fuller view of the topic. Firstly, scholarly publications from China, especially economist analyses on the surplus capacity of the industrial sectors before and after the BRI, provide us a valuable academic perspective of problems inside China's political economy. News reports and online commentaries outside and inside China and official publications from China allow us to get up-to-date data and development. Furthermore, data from established western economic websites and organizations, as well as data from China Statistical Bureau on economic conditions over the years or across the provinces, offer us valuable and indispensable evidence on the effects of the BRI on the easing of the domestic economic concerns of China.

China's Rationale of the BRI

Seek New Markets for Surplus Capacity

In the recent two decades, China has experienced severe surplus capacity in the industry, especially in heavy industry. A thorough investigation of the causes of surplus is beyond the scope of this article. Instead, a quick summary of multiple Chinese economic studies will be supplied. Most of the economists authoring these studies seemed to agree on one key and common cause of surplus capacity, namely, the excessive state intervention in the economy. One study in 2015 found that

[24]Yongnian Zheng and Liang Fook Lye, 'Political Legitimacy in China', in *Legitimacy*, ed Lynn White (New Jersey: World Scientific, 2005), pp. 183–203; Tony Saich, *Governance and Politics of China* (London: Palgrave, 2015), p. 250.
[25]World Bank data from https://data.worldbank.org/indicator/NY.GDP.MKTP.KD.ZG?locations=CN, accessed June 1, 2017.
[26]'Fixing Economy, Debt Will Be Xi Jinping's Next Focus', *South China Morning Post*, October 11, 2017.

surplus capacity tended to be associated with heavy industrial sectors such as mining and extraction, public utilities, state ownership, and inland areas.[27] Another study in 2018 suggested that surplus capacity was caused by local officials' zealous pursuit of economic growth in order to claim credits for promotion, as well as by fiscal stimulus responses to the 2008 financial crisis.[28] Echoing these views, a panel data analysis of industrial sectors during 2006–16 revealed an association of high surplus capacity of a sector with soft budget constraints, governmental support, expanding sizes of the firms and sectors, and a lower level of openness.[29]

In most of the years during 2008–2012 prior to the launch of the BRI, investment on average contributed to 59 percent of China's GDP growth, surpassing consumption and net exports to be the largest contributor to growth.[30] Compared to large developed economies such as the United States, investment and net exports have played a larger role and consumption a smaller role in China's economic growth. Take 2017 as an example, consumption's contribution to China's GDP growth reached a decent 58.8 percent, investment's contribution decreased to 32.1 percent and that of net exports went up to 9.1 percent. In the last three quarters in 2017 in the United States, the growth contribution from consumption was 78 percent (nearly 20 percent above China), investment 28 percent (4 percent lower than China), and net exports −12 percent.[31] As economic growth in China relies relatively heavily on investment and net exports and less on consumption, excessive production capacity would arise, creating pressure on the government to seek external markets for the excess capacity. In a wider context, China's heavy-investment driven growth resembles the developmental path traveled by a number of East Asian industrialized economies, such as Japan, South Korea, Taiwan, and Singapore. These economies generated high investment rates through provisioning sound fundamentals such as schooling, sound financial institutions, and public invest- ment in infrastructure and used mild financial repression to encourage investment.[32] However, one noted difference is that if an industry saddled with surplus capacity is dominated by SOEs, it is unlikely that these firms will be decisively shut down in China to ease the surplus, as the state views large SOEs a pillar of its political power and may pressure state banks to lend to these loss-making SOEs. Thus, in 2018, the average industrial capacity utilization (ICU) was a disappointing low 76.5 percent in China, but a whopping 102.5 percent in South Korea and 105.2 percent in Japan (Table 1).

Associated with China's heavy reliance on investment in economic growth is the fact that China's industrial capacity utilization falls far below major developed economies and even some of the emerging markets such as Brazil. As Table 1 suggests, capacity utilization during 2001–11 in China averaged merely 69.3 percent, compared to 76.5 percent in the United States, 83.4 percent in Germany, and 81.5 percent in Brazil. While China's capacity utilization improved to 76.5 percent in 2018, it still trailed behind the USA (78.5 percent), Germany (87.1 percent), and especially Japan (105.2 percent).

As Figure 1 indicates, ICU in China started to decline in 2008–9 after it peaked in 2007, thanks to the global financial crisis. ICU rebounded briefly in 2010–11 after China's government rolled out a fiscal stimulus package. But this effect was short-lived, and ICU decreased in 2012. This might have signaled to China's policymakers the need to arrest its further decline.

---

[27]Minjie Dong, Yongmei Liang, and Qizi Zhang, 2015. 'Zhongguo gongye channeng liyonglv' ['Industrial Capacity Utilization in China'], *Jingji yanjiu (Economic Research)* 1 (2015), pp. 84–98.

[28]Miaojie Yu and Yang Jin, 'Channeng guosheng de xianzhuang, qianyin houguo yu yingdui' ['The Present Conditions, Causes, Consequences and Remedies of Surplus Capacity'], *Changan daxue xuebao (Shehui kexueban)*[*Journal of Chang'an University— Social Sciences Edition*] 20(5) (September 2018), pp. 48–60.

[29]Junlong Chen, Liangzhe Li, and Jing Zhu, 'Zhengfu xingwei yu channeng guosheng de xingcheng zhili fenxi' ['An Analysis of Governmental Behaviour and the Emergence and Remedies of Surplus Capacity'], *Dobei daxue xuebao (Shehui kexueban)* [*Journal of Northeastern University (Social Science)*] 21(4) (July 2019), pp. 360–65.

[30]National Bureau of Statistics of China (NBS), *China Statistical Yearbook 2018*, Beijing: NBS, Table 3–17.

[31]Data on China come from NBS, ibid. Data on the US is based on computation of data from 'Contribution of Components to Real GDP Growth,' accessed April 18, 2019, https://research.stlouisfed.org/datatrends/net/page6.php.

[32]World Bank, *The East Asian Miracle* (New York: Oxford University Press, 1993), pp. 220–242.

Table 1. Average industry capacity utilization in major economies (%)

	2001-11	2018	The Month of Data in 2018
China	69.30	76.5	September
United States	76.50	78.5	November
Germany	83.4	87.1	December
UK	78.9	80.2	December
Brazil	81.5	77.1	October
South Africa		81.2	September
Japan		105.2	October
South Korea		102.5	November

Sources: Dong et al, 'Industrial Capacity Utilization', p. 89; 'Trends in Capacity Utilization Around the World', accessed January 11, 2018, https://fredblog.stlouisfed.org/2018/04/trends-in-capacity-utilization-around-the-world/; 'Capacity Utilization of the World', accessed January 11, 2018, https://tradingeconomics.com/country-list/capacity-utilization.

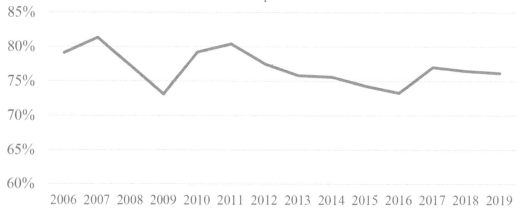

Figure 1. Industrial Capacity Utilization in China, 2006-19
Data source: http://www.qqjisi.com/show 70a6990. Data for 2019 were from the first two quarters.

Figure 1. Industrial Capacity Utilization in China, 2006-19. Data source: http://www.qqjisi.com/showa070a6990. Data for 2019 were from the first two quarters.

As an aforementioned study suggested, heavy industry suffered much greater surplus capacity than light industry. During 2001–11, out of 39 sectors, the ten sectors with the very low capacity utilization ratios belonged to the mining and extraction sectors. Their ratios ranged from 52.5 percent to 61.8 percent. In addition, during this period, among the manufacturing sectors, the average ratio of processing of non-ferrous metal ores, whose key production included electrolytic aluminum and smelting of copper, lead, and zinc, was an abysmal 46.1 percent. In contrast, the following five light industrial sectors, which tended to be labor-intensive sectors where China's comparative advantage rested, enjoyed the highest capacity utilization rate (above 80 percent)—1) textile, 2) culture and education sporting goods, 3) clothes, apparel, shoes and hats, 4) metal products, and 5) leather and feathers. Among the four regions in China, the western region witnessed the most severe surplus capacity as its industrial capacity utilization averaged merely 46.8 percent, followed by the northeast (54.8 percent) and the central region (57.7 percent). The coastal region had no obvious surplus problem, as its utilization rate averaged 81.3 percent.[33]

A large surplus capacity resulted in a host of economic problems in China. As noted by the State Council of China in its Guiding Opinions on Resolving the Problem of a Large Surplus Capacity promulgated in October 2013, continuous surplus capacity would lead to 'mounting financial losses of

---

[33]Dong et al, 'Industrial Capacity Utilization', pp. 89–93.

the sectors, unemployment of employees of the firms, accumulation of bad assets of the banks, degradation of the ecology and the environment, as well as direct endangering of the healthy development of the sectors and even of the improvement of people's livelihood and social stability as a whole'.[34]

As a result, the State Council (the executive arm of the Chinese state) has introduced a series of policy measures to cope with this problem in the recent decade. For example, in 6 out of the 8-year period of 2006–2013, the State Council promulgated policy documents announcing measures to ease surplus capacity.[35] Table 2 presents a picture of the sectors or products targeted by these policy documents. It is not surprising that heavy industrial sectors had been the focus of governmental campaigns to reduce surplus capacity. During 2006–13, the sectors which had been mentioned as those with surplus capacity the most frequently in these five policy documents included steel (4 times), cement (3.5 times), plate glass (3 times), coke (3 times), coal (2.5 times), electrolytic aluminum (2.5 times), electric power (2.5 times), calcium carbide (2 times), iron alloy (2 times), and shipbuilding (1.5 times)(Table 2). In particular, four of these products, namely, cement, iron and steel, aluminum, and plate glass, were inputs for construction.

The Chinese decision-makers were keenly aware of the need to address the industrial surplus capacity and find new external markets for China. At the Central Economic Work Conference convened in mid-December 2012 where all the top national and provincial leaders met to discuss tasks for economic affairs of the nation in 2013 (the year when the BRI was announced), economic slowdown, growing surplus capacity, and unbalanced development (the last one concerned regional disparities) were regarded as among the top domestic challenges for China, whereas a slowdown in the global economic growth and a variety of rising protectionism were identified as top external economic challenges. In response, the meeting demanded adjustment and remedial plans to cope with surplus capacity as well as a proactive strategy to open up China's economy.[36]

China's leaders might well have realized that they could use China's industrial surplus capacity, especially surplus capacity in producing needed products in infrastructural construction and transport equipment, in order to fill the infrastructural deficits across Asia. In 2011, a McKinsey report suggested that in the coming decade Asia would need an investment of US$8 trillion in infrastructure in the order of energy, transport, telecom, and water and sanitation in order to overcome historical underinvestment and meet high growth demand. The report specifically singled out nations such as China and Malaysia as having the greatest capacity to build infrastructure thanks to their adequate 'financial depth in their domestic private-capital markets'.[37] Nevertheless, China

Table 2. Industrial Sectors with Surplus Capacity Named in the Documents of the State Council, 2006-13

	Sectors with Considerable Surplus Capacity Mentioned in the Five Documents
Number of mentions in the documents (Being named as a sector with surplus capacity in one document counts as 1; mention of a sector for possible surplus capacity counts as 0.5)	Steel (4), cement (3.5), plate glass (3), coke (3), coal (2.5), electrolytic aluminum (2.5), electric power (2.5), calcium carbide (2), iron alloy (2), shipbuilding (1.5), coal chemical industry (1), papermaking (1), polycrystalline silicon (1), wind power equipment (1), non-ferrous metal (1), tanning (1), printing, dyeing (1), building materials (1), textile (0.5), and soy squeezing (0.5)

Notes: The official order number of these five documents and the year of promulgation are as follows– No. 11, 2006; No. 15, 2007; No. 38, 2009; No. 7, 2010; No. 41, 2013.
Source: Miaojie Yu and Yang Jin, 'Channeng guosheng de xianzhuang, qianyin houguo yu yingdui' ['The Status, Causes, Consequences and Remedies of Surplus Capacity'], *Working Paper Series of Centre for Economic Research of Beijing University, No.C20128 December 7015*, 2017. The tally is mine.

---

[34]Ibid, p. 84.
[35]See the first source of Table 2.
[36]'The Central Economic Work Conference Held in Beijing', accessed December 17, 2012, http://english.mee.gov.cn/News_service/infocus/201212/t20121221_244093.shtml.
[37]Naveen Tahilyani, Toshan Tamhane, and Jessica Tan, 'Asia's $1 Trillion Infrastructure Opportunity', March 2011, accessed June 1, 2016, https://www.mckinsey.com/industries/private-equity-and-principal-investors/our-insights/asias-1-trillion-infrastructure-opportunity.

enjoyed huge financial assets and manpower for funding massive infrastructure undertaking throughout Asia, whereas Malaysia clearly had far fewer resources. By utilizing China's excess capacity in manufacturing and mining as well as translating its huge holding of foreign reserves into investment abroad, China hoped to help Asia to build up the needed infrastructure in energy, transport, and telecom and helped its firms to find new outlets for their products.

It is no coincidence that the products most frequently mentioned by the capacity-reduction policy documents by the State Council during 2006–13 related closely to the energy, transport, and telecom infrastructural projects identified by the aforementioned McKinsey report. The capital- and resource-intensive sectors were not in China's conventional comparative advantage and tended to be dominated by state firms.

In April 2015, Chinese Premier Li Keqiang hosted a forum on the internationalization of China's equipment manufacturing and international production capacity cooperation where he called on China to go beyond benefiting from trade by helping industrialization and job creation in other countries. A month later, the State Council issued the Guiding Opinions of the State Council on Promoting International Cooperation in Industrial Capacity and Equipment Manufacturing. In this first high-profile State Council document on international production cooperation, 12 key industries were identified as key sectors for international cooperation of production capacity where China would share its excessive production capacity with developing nations.[38] Eleven of these twelve sectors were heavy industry. They included iron and steel, nonferrous metals, building materials, railway, power, chemicals, automotive, communications, engineering machinery, shipbuilding and marine engineering, and aerospace. The first 10 sectors had the obvious excessive capacity and overlapped products in Table 2. Some of these sectors were closely associated with the mining and manufacturing sectors with the lowest rate of capacity utilization mentioned earlier, such as ferrous and nonferrous metals and equipment production. This document specifically suggested that international capacity cooperation would help with the implementation of the BRI.

While the official rhetoric in these documents emphasized free trade and the benefits for the recipient countries which might indeed be materialised, an underlying motivation was to find external outlets for excessive manufacturing and mining capacity. The BRI would thus help China to sustain its investment-driven growth model, while minimizing the hugely unpleasant side-effects, such as massive bankruptcies and lay-offs affecting firms especially SOEs contributing to surplus capacity.

Empirical evidence also suggested that the countries in the BRI became significant export markets of China's steel products in an initial year of the BRI. For example, seven Asian countries included by the Chinese government in the BRI, namely, South Korea, Vietnam, the Philippines, Thailand, Indonesia, Singapore, and India, were among the 10 top export markets of China's steel products in terms of trade value in the first eleven months of 2014, accounted for 36.4 percent of China's exports.[39] Among these nations, only the Indian government has openly resisted the BRI, whereas South Korea has adopted an ambiguous stance due to the US pressure.

Available data on industrial performance shed light on the effects of the BRI in easing surplus capacity. On the bright side, in the wake of the launch of the BRI in the second half of 2013, both the liabilities to assets ratio and the inventories to assets ratio in China's industry declined in a row during 2013–16, thus reducing the financial risks of the industry as a whole. However, in 2017, both ratios edged up very slightly from 2016 (Table 3). The ups and downs of ICU seem less straightforward. As Figure 1 and Table 3 suggest, ICU continued to decline slowly during 2013–16, though its

---

[38]'Premier's "Business Card" Is Global Capacity Cooperation', July 27, 2015, accessed October 20, 2017, http://english.gov.cn/policies/policy_watch/2015/07/27/content_281475155523468.htm. The policy document in May 2015 is posted at http://www.gov.cn/zhengce/content/2015-05/16/content_9771.htm, accessed January 13, 2019. The policy document was mentioned in the first source of Table 2.

[39]Yanling Yu, Yibo Zhu, and Hanbin Li, 'Zhongguo gangtie chanye channeng guosheng huajie yu jiegou shengji wenti yanjiu' ['A Study on the Remedy of Surplus Capacity of China's Steel Industry and Its Structural Upgrade'], *Xiandai shangmao gongye* [*Modern Comercial and Trade Industry*] 6, (2017), pp. 8–10.

Table 3. Capacity Utilization and Liabilities and Inventories to Assets Ratios in Industry

	Capacity Utilization Rate	Liabilities to Assets Ratio	Inventories to Assets Ratio
2006	79.1%	57.5%	12.7%
2007	81.3%	57.5%	12.8%
2008	77.2%	57.7%	12.5%
2009	73.1%	57.9%	11.5%
2010	79.2%	57.4%	11.8%
2011	80.4%	58.1%	11.9%
2012	77.5%	58.0%	11.5%
2013	75.8%	58.1%	11.2%
2014	75.6%	57.2%	10.8%
2015	74.3%	56.6%	10.0%
2016	73.3%	55.9%	9.9%
2017	77.0%	56.0%	10.1%
2018	76.5%		
2019	76.2%		

Sources: http://www.qqjjsj.com/show70a6990; China Statistical Yearbook 2018.

decline was not as steep as during 2011–12. In 2017, ICU staged a spectacular recovery and stayed on a decent level despite a minor drop during 2018–9.

Exports of steel and cement from China to Pakistan and Malaysia, arguably the nations hosting some of the largest projects in Asia, give us a glimpse of the possible effects on these industries in China and the BRI participants. Partly thanks to the demands for steel and cement from the China-Pakstan Economic Corridor (CPEC), a landmark BRI project, Pakistan saw imports of iron and steel from China soaring from US\$0.474 billion to US\$1.18 billion during 2013–17. Under competition from imports, local production with outdated technology contracted by 8.6 percent in the first half of the fiscal year (FY) of 2016 after growing by 31 percent during the same period of the previous FY.[40] Limited data on Malaysia seems to paint a similar picture. During the 2009–2018, Malaysia's imports of iron and steel surged by 107 percent. In 2018, China was the largest importing source of Malaysia's imports of iron and steel, accounting for 26 percent of its imports, and China's exports grew by 14 percent. Imports of iron and steel from China were followed by other Asian producers. Even though Malaysia had 100 steel producing and processing facilities, its exports declined by 43 percent during 2009–18. In order to protect their domestic industries, Pakistan filed five anti-dumping (AD) measures in 2019 and Malaysia four AD measures against China in 2018. In Malaysia, China was the largest AD target.[41]

The picture of cement trade is more benign and even encouraging. The huge demand from the CPEC and the limited capacity in Pakistan stimulated a rapid expansion in production capacity. The capacity grew from 45.6 million tons during 2014–5 to 59.7 million tons during 2019–20, and domestic sales also soared from 28.2 million tons to 40.3 million tons (despite a near 2 percent drop in the last FY). Cement became one of the largest cash cows for the federal government in the FY of 2016. Data on Malaysia's cement imports from China seem lacking. Nevertheless, a recent report suggested that due to tightened environmental restrictions on cement production in China China's cement exports free fell and its imports, especially from Southeast Asia, soared in 2018.[42]

We also can examine the economic performance of the industrial sectors most affected by surplus capacity before and after the launch of the BRI in 2013, especially those mentioned most frequently in the State Council policy documents in Table 2. Figures 2 and 3 illustrate the capacity utilization of three and five, respectively, of the sectors suffering from surplus capacity and mentioned most frequently in Table 2.[43] With a partial exception of manufacture of non-metallic mineral products

---

[40]Shahid Iqbal, 'Steel Imports to Hit \$2.2bn as Local Production Rusts Away', April 16, 2016, accessed January 6, 2020, https://www.dawn.com/news/1252399.

[41]Global Steel Monitor, *Steel Imports Report: Malaysia*, June 2019; Global Steel Monitor, *Steel Imports Report: China*, September 2019.

[42]Information from multiple websites such as https://www.apcma.com/data_history.html and https://oec.world/en, accessed January 6, 2020.

[43]Both figures are based on the data from Chen, Li and Zhu,'Zhengfu xingwei'.

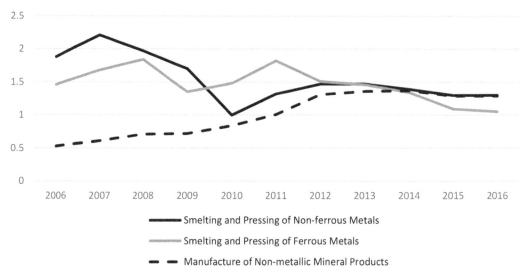

Figure 2. Capacity Utilization Index of Selected Industrial Sectors in China, 2006-16 (Part 1)(Source: Chen, Li, Zhu 2019).

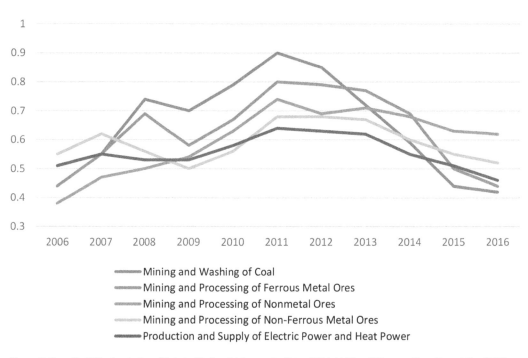

Figure 3. Capacity Utilization Index of Selected Industrial Sectors in China, 2006-16 (Part 2)(Source: Chen, Li, and Zhu 2019).

(which would include cement, plate glass, polycrystalline silicon, and building materials) whose capacity improved in 2013 and 2014, capacity utilization of the other two sectors in Figure 2 and the five sectors in Figure 3 continued to fall to various extents during 2013–16. The only credit we may give to the BRI is that the fall in the following sectors seems to be moderated in 2013–smelting and pressing of non-ferrous metals and ferrous metals (Figure 2), manufacture of non-metallic mineral products (Figure 2), mining and processing of non-metal ores, ferrous metal ores, and non-ferrous metal ores, and production and supply of electric power and heat power (Figure 3).

Overall, the BRI seems to have a detectable effect on easing the liabilities to assets ratio and the inventories to assets ratio of the industry during 2013–16 and on improving the capacity utilization of the industry during 2017–9. Judged by the post-BRI capacity utilization of the sectors identified by the state as top priorities for remedial, however, the positive effects of the BRI seem temporal and limited. The BRI only arrested the decline of the capacity utilization of most of the eight sectors of this kind in 2013, and failed to reverse the decline of all these sectors during 2014–16 (Figures 2 and 3).

Secure Routes for Energy Imports

The BRI also would help China to increase the safety of its strategic sea lanes from the India Ocean, the Straits of Malacca, and the South China Sea. China might even improve the safety of its sea lanes further into the Mediterranean Sea if China could forge good ties with littoral states along these waters. The progression of the land-based New Silk Road, on the other hand, would help ensure the safety of China's energy imports over this land bridge.

The imperative to secure energy importing routes has much to do with China's energy-intensive pathway of economic growth. Fuelled by a rapidly growing number of trucks, passenger cars, and commercial airplanes, as well as the need to build up petroleum reserves, China was responsible for the world's largest growth in demand for petroleum and other liquid fuel nine years in a row since 2009.

As a result of China's rapid demand for energy, China's dependence on imports of crude oil and oil reached a new height into the 2010 s. In 2012 China had a net import of 327.1 million tons of oil, accounting for 57 percent of the oil consumption. The main oil supplying regions were the Middle East, which constituted 44 percent of China's oil imports, followed by Africa (19.7 percent), the former Soviet Union especially Russia and Central Asia (18.3 percent), Latin and North America (10.4 percent), and Asia Pacific (7.7 percent).[44] On the other hand, China started to import natural gas in 2006. By 2012, China imported 42.8 billion cubic meters of gas, accounting for 29 percent of its gas consumption.[45] The top supplying nations were Turkmenistan (51.4 percent of China's imports via gas pipelines), Qatar (16.4 percent via liquefied natural gas or LNG, same for the named nations that follow), Australia (11.7 percent), Indonesia (8.0 percent), Malaysia (6.1 percent), Yemen (2.0 percent), Russia (1.2 percent), Nigeria (1 percent), and Egypt (1 percent).[46]

China's oil imports from the Middle East and Africa had to been transported through sea lines of communication (SLOC) across the Indian Ocean (IO), through the Straits of Malacca (SM) and the South China Sea (SCS)(the IO-SM-SCS SLOC), and these imports amounted to 63.7 percent of China's oil imports in 2012. China's gas imports were far less reliant on the aforementioned SLOC. Only about 34.5 percent of gas imports, that is, those from the Middle East, Africa and Southeast Asia, or at best 46.2 percent if China's imports from Australia were also included, might need to be shipped along the whole or part of the IO-SM-SCS SLOC.

The fact that the majority of the crude oil and oil needs to be imported in order to satisfy China's domestic consumption and that the overwhelming majority of the crude imports have to be shipped through the IO-SM-SCS SLOC heightened the concerns of China's strategic planners. China still does not have the capability of projecting its naval power far away from its coast. China's naval power is dwarfed by the US. The United States has 10 operational aircraft carriers, plus nine potential ones, whereas China has only an operational one plus three being built or tested. Any disruption of this strategic sea lane by external forces (say, the US or Indian navy) could jeopardize the stability of energy imports for China.[47] As

[44]'2006–2012nian Zhongguo shiyou jinchukouliang ji laiyuan' [Amounts and Sources of China's Petroleum Imports and Exports], accessed September 1, 2018, http://www.cnenergy.org/yq/201307/t20130715_44265.html.
[45]'Zhongguo shiyou' [China's Petroleum], January 30, 2018, accessed September 17, 2018, http://www.gov.cn/jrzg/2013-01/30/content_2323461.htm.
[46]'2012nian Zhongguo tianranqi jinkou laiyuanguo ji jinkouliang' [Sources of China's Natural Gas Imports and Amount in 2012], accessed January 13, 2016, https://www.china5e.com/news/news-342770-1.html.
[47]For a survey of China's energy diplomacy and importing routes, refer to Hongyi Harry Lai, 'China's Oil Diplomacy', Third World Quarterly, 28(3), (2007), pp. 519–537.

early as 2004, China started to pay serious attention to its heavy reliance on the IO-SM-SCS SLOC and has been developing alternative routes. As reported by the Chinese and English news sources, the following four routes of energy imports have emerged as alternatives to the IO-SM-SCS SLOC in the recent decades.[48]

1) The Central Asia-China oil and gas pipelines, which this author coins Land Route 1 of China's energy imports. This route includes one oil pipeline and a gas pipeline. The Kazakhstan-China oil pipeline, designed to transport 20 million tons of oil from the largest oil supplying nation in Central Asia (i.e., Kazakhstan) to western China, was put into use in 2004. In addition, multiple lines of gas pipelines of 1,833 km connect the largest gas supplier in Central Asia (i.e., Turkmenistan) with western China, and a further 8,000 km of pipeline transports natural gas all the way to Shanghai and Guangzhou. The gas pipeline was put in service in 2009.

2) The Eastern Siberia-China oil and gas pipelines (Land Route 2). The crude oil pipeline connects Taishet in Siberia with Daqing in northeastern China, stretching 4,770 km and boasting a capacity of 15 million tons a year. The natural gas pipeline (Yakutia–Khabarovsk–Vladivostok-Heihe-Shanghai pipeline) comprises of 3,000 km of pipeline in Russia and 3,371 km in China. With a designed annual capacity of 38 billion cubic meters, it was expected to meet 16 percent of China's gas need in 2017. Its operation has been scheduled in 2019.

3) The Myanmar-China oil and gas pipelines (Land Route 3). This route also comprises an oil pipeline and a gas pipeline, both at a length 771 km inside Myanmar, connecting Kyaukpyu of Myanmar, a deepwater port on the Indian Ocean, with Ruili of Yunnan Province. With a designed capacity of 22 million tons a year, the oil pipeline would run another 1,623 km inside China until it reaches Chongqing. Designed to transport 12 billion cubic meters annually, the gas pipeline would run for another 1,727 km inside China, ending in Guigang in Guangxi. The gas pipeline was in operation in July 2013 and the oil pipeline in January 2015.

4) The China-Pakistan economic corridor (CPEC). Rails, oil, and gas pipelines have been proposed to link up southern Xinjiang with Pakistan's deepwater Gwadar port on the Indian Ocean (Land Route 4). Specifically, rails and highways will be built to link up southern Xinjiang, especially its major city Kashgar with cities across Pakistan as well as Gwadar. Numerous infrastructural and energy projects are underway.

The BRI would not only enable China to expand and consolidate the existing land routes of energy imports and to complete the proposed land route (Land Route 4, or the CPEC), but also would allow it to secure the existing primary route of energy imports through the critical IC-SM-SCS SLOC. It would thus allow Beijing to ease concerns with its energy imports.

First of all, the BRI would further China's infrastructural links through the existing rails, highways, oil and gas pipelines with countries along the three largely completed land routes of energy imports, such as Kazakhstan and Turkmenistan in Central Asia, Russia's Siberia, and Myanmar. China and these nations have proposed and inaugurated additional lines in Land Routes 1–3. For example, Line C of the Central Asia-China gas pipeline was under construction in September 2012 and the construction Line D was started in September 2014 and was scheduled to be completed in 2020.[49] Second, the BRI also enables China to expand energy and infra-structural linkages with nations along Land Routes 1–4. China has furthered energy cooperation through coal-fired, hydro, or renewable power projects in Pakistan, Central Asia and Myanmar. In December 2019, after over seven years of construction, the Eastern Siberia-China natural gas pipeline started operation. Annual delivery of Russian gas to China is expected to soar from 5 billion cubic meters (BCM) in 2020 to 38 billion cubic meters in 2024. Third, through the BRI platform, China and Pakistan have completed several energy projects and could eventually

---

[48]The information below is based on numerous Chinese and English news sources. For a representative overview, see 'Zhonguo sida nengyuan tongdao' [China's Four Major Energy Transport Routes], *Changjiang ribao* [*Yangtze Daily*], June 5, 2013, accessed January 13, 2018, https://www.china5e.com/news/news-340830-1.html.
[49]Information on the Central-Asia gas pipeline and Line D from https://baike.baidu.com/item, accessed January 13, 2019.

complete the CPEC and Land Route 4 for China's energy imports, adding a new alternative route in case of a major disruption of the maritime route. Fourth, China's leaders hoped to forge closer economic linkages with key littoral states along its maritime route of energy imports, such as Indonesia, Malaysia, Singapore, and Sri Lanka, especially when they launched the BRI. China has been pushing forth or has started large-scale infrastructural projects in Malaysia, Indonesia, and Sri Lanka. These projects included the East Coast railway in Malaysia, the Jakarta-Bandung high-speed rail in Indonesia, and an industrial zone in Hambantota, as well as the construction of the Colombo International Container Terminal and the Mattala Rajapaksa International Airport (MRIA) in Sri Lanka. These infrastructural projects were designed to enhance the economic significance of China for these nations and to entice these countries to ensure the safety of China's SLOC.[50]

New reports and data from multiple sources only permit a preliminary assessment of effects of the BRI on China's oil imports. As Figure 4 illustrates, China's crude oil imports grew rapidly from 270 million tons to 462 million tons during 2012–17. In 2017, China surpassed the United States to be the world's largest net importer of crude oil.[51] Among the largest suppliers of crude, Saudi Arabia, whose exports to China rely on the IO-SM-SCS SLOC, saw its share in China's crude imports dwindled from nearly 20 percent to slightly more than 12 percent during 2012–18. In contrast, benefiting from Land Route 2, Russia saw its share of China's crude imports expanded from 9 percent to more than 15 percent. In particular, in 2017 and 2018 roughly 42 percent of Russian crude exports to China was transported by pipelines, which were far more secure than the SLOC. Russian total exports grew to 60 million in 2017 and further to 71 million tons in 2018, eclipsing Saudi Arabia to be China's largest crude supplier during 2016–18.[52]

China-Russia energy partnership is induced not only by the complementary energy relations, but also by their geopolitical and ideological needs. Forged back in the 1990s, their energy partnership is likely to persist, as long as the following circumstances persist–China and Russia do not clash over

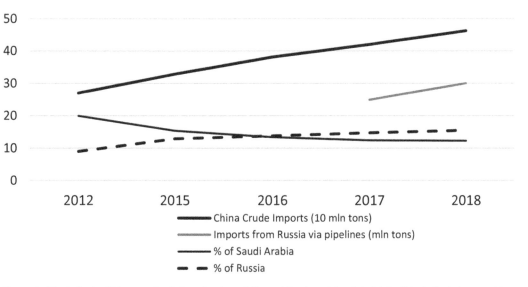

Figure 4. China's Crude Oil Imports, Crude from Russia and Share of Russia and Saudi Arabia in China's Crude Imports. (data sources: multiple news reports located from the Chinese internet baidu)

[50]These motivations do not automically imply their fulfilment. Reports on these projects are too abundant to cite.
[51]'China Overtook the US as World's Largest Crude Oil Importer in 2017', accessed January 10, 2018, https://worldmaritimenews.com/archives/267845/china-overtook-the-us-as-worlds-largest-crude-oil-importer-in-2017/.
[52]Reports on these projects are too abundant to cite. See, for example, 'Shuaikai Shate, E suoding Zhongguo yuanyou zuida jinkouguo diwei' ['Shaking Off Saudi Arabia, Russia Is Locked in the Status of China's Largest Crude Supplying Nation'], accessed January 14, 2019, http://www.guancha.cn/economy/2017_10_25_432254.shtml.

issues of vital importance; they feel the pressure from the US-led unipolar world; they continue to be stung by the West's criticisms of their authoritarianism and assertive external moves.

Enhance the Economic Profile of the Western Region (The West)

Through the BRI China's leaders also intend to expand the trade links and speed up the growth momentum of China's western region, thereby reducing regional inequality. For decades China's economic growth has been primarily driven by the coastal region. Thanks to its proximity to the sea and sea lanes, better infrastructure and technology, higher human capital, earlier opening to the world economy in the reform era, and its vibrant private firms, the coast has been the primary engine of China's phenomenal growth. For example, during 1978–98 the coastal region raised its share obviously in China's GDP from 43.7 percent to 51.1 percent, whereas the share of the western region declined from 20.6 percent to 17.7 percent. Bear in mind that the coastal region had a higher per capita GDP in the early years. As a result, the ratio of per capita GDP of the western region declined from an already alarming 40 percent of that of the coastal region in 1982, to a abysmal 33.8 percent in 1998 (Table 3). Such severe regional inequality had caused discontent from the western region (the west in short, differentiated from the West that represents developed economies especially the US and Europe).

In response, in 1999 Chinese President Jiang Zemin and Premier Zhu Rongji commenced the western region development program (WRDP), aiming to improve the infrastructure and develop the sectors with a comparative advantage in the west (such as resources and energy). A key objective was to address a rising gap in development across regions and to fulfill Deng's pledge to promote shared prosperity among regions by the turn of the 20th century.[53]

After nearly fourteen years of endeavor, the WRDP had registered several noticeable successes. First, the economy in the west had been growing noticeably faster than that in the coastal provinces. The average GDP growth in the western provinces accelerated from 8.8 percent in 1998 to 11.6 percent in 2012, a year prior to the BRI. Meanwhile, the average growth in the coastal provinces decelerated sharply from 10.2 percent to 8.1 percent. As a result, the average growth rate in the western provinces skyrockted from 1.3 percent behind that of the coast to 3.5 percent ahead of it. The west had clearly reversed its relatively disadvantage in the growth pace against the coast. Second and as a result, the ratio of the per capita GDP of western provinces to that of the coast had improved impressively from 33.8 percent to 51.9 percent, cutting the gap from 66.2 percent of the average of the coast to 48.1 percent. Third, thanks to economic catch-up, the share of the western provinces in the national GDP had increased from 17.7 percent to 19.8 percent during 1998–2012 (Table 4). The impressive turnaround in the economic conditions of the west in the wake of the WRDP suggests to China's leaders that a continuous push to develop the west should be fruitful. Finally, the west's share in the nation's foreign trade grew from 4.2 percent to 5.6 percent during 1998–2012, but its share in foreign investment in capital construction fell from 8.9 percent to 5.8 percent (Table 5), indicating a need to stimulate foreign capital inflows into the west.

Table 4. Economic Development of Four Major Regions in China (Provincial Average)

Four Regions	GDP Growth			Per Capita GDP Relative to the Coast (=100%)			Share of Nation's GDP		
	1998	2012	2017	1998	2012	2017	1998	2012	2017
Coastal (10)	10.2%	8.1%	6.9%	100%	100%	100%	51.1%	51.3%	52.9%
Central (6)	9.0%	10.6%	8.0%	40.1%	51.9%	52.6%	21.2%	20.2%	20.8%
Western (12)	8.8%	11.6%	7.7%	33.8%	51.9%	50.4%	17.7%	19.8%	19.9%
Northeast (3)	8.5%	10.5%	5.3%	60.8%	72.4%	55.4%	10.0%	8.8%	6.4%
Coast-west gap	1.3%	−3.5%	−0.8%	66.2%	48.1%	49.6%	33.4%	31.6%	33.0%

Notes: Numbers of provinces in parentheses next to each region. The author's own computation using data from *China Statistical Yearbook* during 1999-2018.

---

[53]A discussion of the rationale of the WRDP is in Hongyi Harry Lai, 'China's Western Development Program', *Modern China* 28(4), (October 2002), pp. 432–40.

Table 5. Trade and Foreign Investment of Four Major Regions in China (Provincial Average)

Four Regions	Share of China's Foreign Trade Volume (by origin)			Share of Nation's Foreign Funds in Investment in Capital Construction		
	1998	2012	2017	1998	2012	2017
Coastal (10)	85.2%	85.6%	83.3%	73.3%	70.2%	56.7%
Central (6)	4.7%	5.5%	7.3%	11.5%	14.0%	20.2%
Western (12)	4.2%	5.6%	6.8%	8.9%	5.8%	11.8%
Northeast (3)	5.8%	3.3%	2.6%	6.2%	10.0%	11.3%
Coast-west gap	81.0%	80.0%	76.5%	64.4%	64.4%	44.9%

Notes: Same as Table 4.

The BRI comprises of two economic belts, namely, the land-based economic belt of nations along the Silk Road, and the maritime economic belt of nations starting from southeast coastal China, through Southeast Asia, South Asia, to the Middle East and Europe. The land-based new Silk Road would commence from Xi'an, the capital of Sha'anxi Province, linking up through China's Gansu, Qinghai, and Xinjiang, into Central Asia, the Middle East and then Europe. This external link would help expand export markets and generate two-way investment flows for western China. Having coined the BRI as a new round of economic opening, President Xi hopes that it could bring prosperity to the west, as China's opening in the preceding decades had done to China's coast.

The economic performance of the west allows us to tentatively assess the effects of the BRI. The BRI apparently has succeeded noticeably in extending the external trade and investment linkages of the west. As illustrated in Table 5, the west increased its share in China's foreign trade from 5.6 percent in 2012, to 6.8 percent in 2017, a clear improvement. More importantly and significantly, the west had more than doubled its share in the nation's foreign funds in investment in capital construction, raising the share from 5.8 percent to 11.8 percent. Meanwhile, the shares of the coastal region in the nation's trade and foreign investment in capital construction declined from 85.6 percent to 83.3 percent and from 70.2 percent to 56.7 percent, respectively. It thus seems that the infra-structural and economic linkages between the western provinces and the nations along the BRI had intensified since 2013, thereby propelling the growth of the economy of the west, while the coast's weight in China's external linkage declined noticeably despite its continuing dominance.

In 2017, the averaged annual growth rate of the twelve western provinces registered 7.7 percent. Even though it was sharply lower than that in 2012 (11.6 percent), it was noticeably higher than that of the ten coastal provinces (6.9 percent). Despite higher growth than the coast in 2017, the average per capita GDP of the 12 western provinces was 50.4 percent of the average of the six coastal provinces in 2017, lower than 51.9 percent in 2012 (Table 4). A possible reason is that the west increased its share in the nation's population from 27 percent to 27.2 percent during 2012–17, suggesting a possible scenario that more people decided to live and work in the booming west instead of moving to the coast. Nevertheless, the share of the twelve western provinces in the nation's GDP improved from very slightly from 19.8 percent in 2012 to 19.9 percent in 2017. Overall, it appears that the BRI has enabled the west to grow faster than the coast and maintain its share in the national economy, though the ratio of its per capita GDP ratio to the coast had declined modestly. As the share of the coastal region in China's GDP also rose from 51.3 percent to 52.9 percent during 2012–17 (Table 4), the coast has apparently also benefited economically from the BRI, likely through active participation in the maritime silk road initiatives.

Xinjiang could be an exception in the west, as it has yet to take full advantage of the BRI. Its economic growth in the recent years might have been hindered by the negative international limelight on the treatment of Uighurs in the so-called re-education centers, as well as extraordinarily tight security. During 2013–2018 Xinjiang economic growth decelerated faster than the nation and the west, and as a result, its annual growth rate deteriorated from 2.2 percent above the national average to 0.6 percent below it.[54]

---

[54]The analysis uses data from http://www.stats.gov.cn/english/, accessed January 26, 2020.

Conclusion

This article, through highlighting the domestic-external linkage, sees the BRI not simply an ad hoc response to China's slowdown in economic growth and to the US intensified strategic pressure. Rather, it regards the BRI as a strategy to help ease economic vulnerabilities and sustain growth, thereby ensuring the survival of the economic and political regimes in China. Economically, China's growth has expediently relied on investment in the recent decade. A heavy reliance on investment and impulsive use of investment by local government, coupled with the continuous protection of state firms in heavy industry and mining, has resulted in a surplus in production capacity in these sectors. In addition, a growing demand for energy, driven by China's manufacturing and growing transport, results in a rising reliance on imported oil and gas and necessitates the construction of land-based routes for energy imports. Furthermore, China's economic growth has been driven by the coast, whose economic slowdown due to external shocks could have derailed the nation's growth.

In launching the BRI China's leaders hoped to ameliorate these three vulnerabilities. The BRI would allow China to devote its surplus capacity to building infrastructural and industrial projects in Eurasia, and to even transfer some of the surplus capacity to other nations in the BRI, thereby sustaining China's economic growth, averting massive bankruptcies and unemployment, and appeasing SOEs in these sectors. Moreover, the BRI would intensify a linkage with Eurasia. This would permit the western provinces to claim a greater share of national economic growth, satisfy the demand from the elites and population from western provinces, and alleviate the risks of over-reliance on the coast. Finally, the construction of land-based energy importing routes through western China would allow China to expand energy imports on the one hand, and ensure their safety on the other, as the land-route imports are less vulnerable to external sabotage and blockades. All these measures would help the survival of China's economic regime and the ruling party.

Evidence and data also allow us to reach a tentative assessment of the accomplishment of the aforementioned three objectives of the political economy. First of all, the BRI seems to have at best moderated the aggravation of surplus capacity in the industry in 2014 and has managed to increase industrial capacity utilization during 2017–19. Nevertheless, the BRI only halted the decline of the capacity utilization of most of the eight sectors identified by the State Council as requiring urgent remedies during 2013–14, but not during 2014–16. Externally, China's sectors with a large surplus and robust export capacities such as iron and steel have found new external markets, but run a risk of aggravating trade disputes and driving out local industries. In contrast, China's declining sectors such as cement create opportunities for imports from other nations. Secondly, the BRI seems to forge a much closer energy partnership between China and Russia and allow the contrusction and operation of land-based pipelines linking these two nations. Russia was thus able to overtake Saudi Arabia as China's largest crude oil supplier during 2016–18, while China's crude imports soar to a world-topping high level. Finally, the BRI has allowed the west to expand rapidly its foreign trade and foreign investment inflows and increase its share in the nation's totals, thereby growing faster than the coast and maintaining its share of the nation's GDP.

In short, this study examines the role of a major external strategy like the BRI in mitigating economic vulnerabilities and in serving the economic regime and political interests of the ruling party. This analytical approach could help us to enrich our understanding of a major strategy in the international political economy well beyond the usual focus on international causes of such a strategy.

Acknowledgments

The author thanks the reviewers for their comments that helped with the revision of the article. He acknowledges the support from his school at UoN in the form of research leave when this article was submitted and revised.

Disclosure Statement

No potential conflict of interest was reported by the author.

ORCID

Hongyi Lai (ID) http://orcid.org/0000-0002-6998-092X

Beaconism and the Trumpian Metamorphosis of Chinese Liberal Intellectuals

Yao Lin🆔

ABSTRACT

This article examines the puzzling phenomenon that many Chinese liberal intellectuals fervently idolize Donald Trump and embrace the alt-right ideologies he epitomizes. Rejecting 'pure tactic' and 'neoliberal affinity' explanations, it argues that the Trumpian metamorphosis of Chinese liberal intellectuals is precipitated by their 'beacon complex', which has 'political' and 'civilizational' components. Political beaconism grows from the traumatizing lived experience of Maoist totalitarianism, sanitizes the West and particularly the United States as politically near-perfect, and gives rise to both a neoliberal affinity and a latent hostility toward *baizuo*. Civilizational beaconism, sharing with its nationalistic counterpart—civilizational vindicativism—the heritages of scientific racism and social Darwinism imported in late-Qing, renders the Chinese liberal intelligentsia receptive to anti-immigrant and Islamophobic paranoia, exacerbates its anti-*baizuo* sentiments, and catalyzes its Trumpian convergence with Chinese non-liberals.

Introduction: The Puzzle of Trump-Idolizing Chinese Liberal Intellectuals

The fact that, throughout his presidential campaign and presidency, Donald Trump owns a large, fervent fanbase in China, '*Chuanfen* [Trump fans]', has received a fair amount of journalistic and scholarly attention. Most reports on, and analyses of, Trumpmania in China have focused on its correlation with 'pro-CCP [Chinese Communist Party]' and/or 'pro-China Model' attitudes, however.[1] For example, according to a *New York Times* report in 2017,

> Mr. Trump's Chinese fans … like the fact that he seems less inhibited than previous American presidents about recognizing China as a superpower and as an equal on the global stage. And after years of American presidents lecturing China on issues like political prisoners and democracy, many also say they are relieved to see a leader who seems to care more about making deals than idealism.[2]

A 2018 article in *The Atlantic* reached virtually the same conclusion, identifying Chinese Trump-cheerers as belonging to either of two categories. On the one hand, there are those who welcomed

---

[1] This was in part attributable to the Western media's lack of interest in sophistication when covering non-Western affairs. For example, when this author was interviewed by an American news outlet before the 2016 U.S. presidential election, he discussed both liberal and non-liberal Trump fandoms in China. The published version, however, omitted the entire liberal part of the story and talked only about Chinese non-liberal Trump supporters. See Louise Liu, 'There Are Tons of Trump Supporters in China —Even Though He Keeps Bashing the Country', *Business Insider*, October 10, 2016, accessed March 11, 2020, https://www.businessinsider.com/why-some-chinese-people-support-trump-2016-10. Later he was told that the editor(s) believed Chinese liberal Trumpian metamorphosis was 'too distant and complicated' a phenomenon to draw the attention of the outlet's American readers.

[2] Javier C. Hernández and Iris Zhao, '"Uncle Trump" Finds Fans in China', *New York Times*, November 9, 2017, accessed March 11, 2020, https://www.nytimes.com/2017/11/09/world/asia/trump-china-fans.html.

him as 'an especially easy president for China to handle', therefore instrumental to the rise of the CCP-led China as a new hegemon in the global arena. On the other hand, there are those who adored him out of shared 'negative impressions of liberalism', and in resonance with his 'nationalist rhetoric and "strongman style" … in China's political culture'.[3]

It has also been noticed that the coming-out of *Chuanfen* as a vocal and influential group is highly correlated with the surge of outright racist, misogynistic, Islamophobic and anti-refugee rhetoric, as well as the popularization, on the Chinese internet, of '*baizuo* [white lefties]' as an epithet for those who care about social justice and speak out against various forms of discrimination.[4] Here again, journalists and researchers looking at the rise of rightwing senti-ments in China have tended to equate those receptive to them with those who favor the 'China model' *vis-à-vis* 'Western' liberal democracy. For example, in Chenchen Zhang's study of rightwing populist discourse on Zhihu, China's largest online Q&A forum, she traces its roots to 'Chinese discontents with liberal hierarchies of the international order', as well as to 'the officially sanctioned campaign against universal values and "Western" ideologies'; accordingly, China's love of Trumpian rhetoric and policies is intertwined with its refutation of 'Western' liberal democratic values and its affirmation of 'the superiority of the "pragmatic" authoritar-ianism of the Chinese regime'.[5]

While it might be true that the vast majority of Trumpian Chinese hold favorable views of the China Model and unfavorable views of 'Western' liberal democratic values, an equivalence between these two groups obscures a curious and crucial component of Trump's fan base in China: a substantial (if not overwhelming) proportion of *Chinese liberal intellectuals*, who are deeply critical of the Party-State, and committed to advocating 'universal values' and China's 'liberal democratiza-tion'. Indeed, as an exiled human-rights lawyer recently admits, 'among outspoken Chinese dissi-dents, … those who are anti-Trump are in a minority'.[6]

It might be tempting to explain away the apparent Chinese liberal enthusiasm about Trump, who assaults liberal-democratic norms and institutions on a daily basis, as *purely tactical* rather than committed or sincere. Thus, some observers have suggested that Chinese liberals support Trump only because they expect, however wishfully, that his trade war against China, commen-cing in early 2018 and reaching Phase-One Deal in January 2020, would have the *effect* of forcing the CCP to 'step back from the economy' and 'loosen its tight grip over the rest of society', *regardless of* his own intentions, beliefs and values.[7] Others have contemplated that given 'the very restricted space to express any kind of political ideas in China under Xi at the moment', Chinese liberals could be speaking about Trump merely as 'a proxy way of trying to speak about generic issues that relate to China, but which are difficult, if not impossible, to speak about in a domestic discourse and context'.[8]

---

[3]Benjamin Carlson, 'Why China Loves Trump, *Atlantic*, March 2018, accessed March 11, 2020, https://www.theatlantic.com/magazine/archive/2018/03/trump-china/550886/.

[4]See, e.g., Chenchen Zhang, 'The Curious Rise of the "White Left" as a Chinese Internet Insult', *Open Democracy*, May 11, 2017, accessed March 11, 2020, https://www.opendemocracy.net/digitaliberties/chenchen-zhang/curious-rise-of-white-leftas-chinese-internet-insult; Chi Zhang, 'WeChatting American Politics: Misinformation, Polarization, and Immigrant Chinese Media', *Columbia Journalism Review*, April 19, 2018, accessed March 11, 2020, https://www.cjr.org/tow_center_reports/wechat ting-american-politics-misinformation-polarization-and-immigrant-chinese-media.php/; Li Luohan, '97% of Chinese Would Reject Receiving Refugees: Online Poll', *Global Times*, June 20, 2018, accessed March 11, 2020, http://www.globaltimes.cn/content/1107731.shtml; Tony Lin, 'After New Zealand Massacre, Islamophobia Spreads on Chinese Social Media', *Columbia Journalism Review*, March 21, 2019, accessed March 11, 2020, https://www.cjr.org/analysis/weibo-new-zealand-massacre.php.

[5]Chenchen Zhang, 'Right-wing Populism with Chinese Characteristics? Identity, Otherness and Global Imaginaries in Debating World Politics Online', *European Journal of International Relations*, OnlineFirst version, (2019), pp. 3, 4, 7, accessed March 11, 2020, doi: 10.1177/1354066119850253.

[6]Zhaoyin Feng, 'Why I Translate All of Trump's Tweets into Chinese', *BBC News*, August 8, 2019, accessed March 11, 2020, https://www.bbc.com/news/world-us-canada-49092612.

[7]Yuan Li, 'Donald Trump, China Savior? Some Chinese Say Yes', *New York Times*, April 16, 2019, accessed March 11, 2020, https://www.nytimes.com/2019/04/16/business/trump-china.html.

[8]The author thanks an anonymous reviewer for articulating this hypothesis.

These 'pure tactic' explanations do not comport with reality, however. Despite censorship and persecution, Chinese liberals who speak about Trump do also speak directly about Chinese politics.[9] Few, if any, of their writings on Trump are intended purely as domestic allegories that do not reflect their appraisal of Trump's politics *per se*. Meanwhile, although the Sino-American trade war's alleged reform-inducing effect might have rendered the Chinese liberal intelligentsia somewhat expectant, it cannot explain why so many of its members have openly confessed their absolute, heartfelt admiration, adoration, and idolization of Trump, and why they have done so both *long before*,[10] and for reasons *beyond*, the trade war.

Whereas written and anecdotal records of Trump-mania are too abundant to compile here, a few examples would help illustrate the point. When Gao Quanxi, a leading liberal legal and political philosopher, gave a talk to Chinese students at Harvard University in December 2017, his effusive adulation for Trump, and rationalization of Trump's flirtation with white suprema-cism, caught the audience off guard and prompted a heated exchange with the invited discussant Huang Yasheng, a Democrat-leaning economist at the Massachusetts Institute of Technology. Months later, Guo Yuhua, a highly regarded liberal sociologist known for her tireless advocacy for human rights in general and workers' rights in particular, lashed out on Twitter at Trump's critics: 'Both Western Lefties and Chinese Lefties insist that Trump is a hooligan, while in fact it is they themselves who are the real hooligans, as is revealed by their words and deeds defaming, vilifying and caricaturing Trump!'[11] More recently, Sun Liping, another renowned liberal sociology professor, applauded Trump for single-handedly initiating a 'profound transformation' of the American society through his 'attack on Political Correctness'; according to Sun, the United States has become 'younger and more vibrant' under Trump's extraordinarily insightful and ambitious leadership, and the 'only political project comparable to Trump's throughout modern history' was China's Reform-and-Opening in 1978.[12] In all three cases Trump was praised for his supposed domestic achievements, rather than for the trade war's supposed reform-inducing effect on China, despite it being looming or already under way.

Nor can 'pure tactic' explanations account for the fact that prominent Chinese liberal intellectuals frequently join the Trumpist choir disparaging black and brown people, Muslims, refugees, feminists, and *baizuo*. For example, when Zhejiang University professor Feng Gang prompted an uproar over his online statement that women are by nature not fit for academia, Xiao Han, a prolific liberal commentator who had been suspended from college teaching due to his criticisms of the Party-State, vehemently denounced feminist activists, whose open letter demanded that Feng apologize, as 'bullying thugs'.[13] Meanwhile, Gao Quanxi, in an exchange with pro-CCP scholar Tian Feilong, defended Brexit by way of claiming that 'many pagan [i.e. Muslim] immigrants are impossible to assimilate through the "melting pot", but will instead only become appropriators of social welfare, saboteurs of the social order, and enemies to

---

[9]For example, when legal scholar Xu Zhangrun was censured for his criticism of Xi Jinping's abolition of presidential term limits, both Guo Yuhua and Gao Quanxi, prominent liberal Trump-admirers, publicly voiced their support for Xu. See 郭于华 [Guo Yuhua], '哪有学者不表达？' ['How Can Scholars Not Be Allowed to Talk?'], *FT Chinese*, March 26, 2019, accessed March 11, 2020, http://www.ftchinese.com/story/001082041; 高全喜 [Gao Quanxi], '清华蛮横处罚许先生有违法治之道与大学自治精神' ['Tsinghua's Capricious Punishment of Mr. Xu Undermines the Rule of Law and Academic Autonomy'], *Weibo*, March 29, 2019, accessed March 11, 2020, http://www.21join.com/index.php?m=content&c=index&a=show&catid=10&id=964.

[10]Chinese liberal Trump-mania grew as early as he led the Republican field of presidential candidates in late 2015 and early 2016; see, e.g., 程凯 [Cheng Kai], '2016美国总统大选, 川普挑战美国的"政治正确"' ['2016 American Presidential Election, Trump Challenging America's "Political Correctness"'], *Boxun*, January 21, 2016, accessed March 11, 2020, https://boxun.com/news/gb/pubvp/2016/01/201601210617.shtml.

[11]@yuhuaguo, *Twitter*, June 17, 2018, accessed March 11, 2020, https://twitter.com/yuhuaguo/status/1019102149437894656.

[12]孙立平 [Sun Liping], '整个世界可能都忽视了这个信号: 谈特朗普对政治正确的冲击' ['The Whole World May Have Missed This Signal: On Trump's Attack on Political Correctness'], *Liping Guancha*, February 17, 2019, accessed March 11, 2020, https://qnmlgb.tech/articles/5c68c064ce56ab804b44e280/.

[13]萧瀚 [Xiao Han], '政治正确与言论自由: 关于"冯钢"事件的几点看法' ['Political Correctness and Freedom of Speech: Remarks on the "Feng Gang" Incident'], *Weibo*, October 23, 2017, accessed March 11, 2020, https://pic2.zhimg.com/80/v2-f526ead9566da1109afca0a7fd9360f3_hd.jpg.

cultural and political orders'.[14] Similarly, in a 2018 panel discussion among four influential liberal intellectuals, only Zhou Lian, associate professor of philosophy at Renmin University, was critical of rightwing demagogy surging in the West, while the other three panelists rushed to its defense, insinuating that the real troublemakers are non-white immigrants and refugees from Africa, the Middle East and Latin America.[15]

To wit, far from making a purely tactical move, many Chinese liberal intellectuals have undergone a *Trumpian metamorphosis* (*Chuanhua*), manifested both/either by idolization of Trump (*Chuanfenhua*, 'becoming a Trump fan'), and/or by internalization of the ideologies he epitomizes (*Chuanpuhua*, 'becoming like Trump'). This is a curious and crucial phenomenon in the development of contemporary Chinese '*sichao* [thought waves]'. It is curious because it defies the conventional (and convenient) narrative in which China's pro-reform, pro-liberal-democracy, pro-universal-values intellectuals fight relentlessly against injustice, authoritarianism and narrow-minded nationalism. Only by comprehending contemporary Chinese liberals' Trumpian metamorphosis can one truly understand what has been going on in the intellectual field of contemporary China.

The curious phenomenon is also a crucial development in contemporary China. While non-liberal intellectuals in China also fall prey to Trump-mania and Trumpism, they do not as much (re)shape public discourses in China as their liberal counterparts, who, upon absorbing raw Trumpian sentiments supplied by ordinary pro-CCP netizens, are able to theorize, systemize and legitimize those sentiments *under the guise of liberal democratic values*. Indeed, such interactions would affect not only the Chinese public but also Chinese liberalism itself, and have profound implications for China's political possibilities in the future.

The rest of this article is divided into five sections. Section 2 provides an overview of liberalism in contemporary China, setting the ground for further analysis. Section 3 discusses and refutes the seemingly straightforward 'neoliberal affinity' explanation of why so many Chinese liberal intellectuals underwent Trumpian metamorphoses. A more plausible and more comprehensive explanation lies in what may be called *the beacon complex* (or *beaconism* for short): the idealization of 'the West', and the United States in particular, as the political and civilizational 'beacon of light' for the rest of the world.

The beacon complex can be further dissected into two interrelated and mutually reinforcing components: *political* beaconism, and *civilizational* beaconism. Section 4 explores the psychology of political beaconism, and argues that the traumatizing experience of Party-State totalitarianism propels Chinese liberals on an anti-CCP pilgrimage in search for sanitized and glorified imageries of Western (especially American) political realities, which nurtures *both* their neoliberal affinity *and* their proclivity for a Trumpian metamorphosis. Meanwhile, the latter proclivity is reinforced by their civilizational beaconism, the subject of Section 5. While less aggressive and less chauvinistic than civilizational vindicativism typical of non-liberal nationalist Chinese, liberal civilizational beaconism shares the former's ideological underpinnings and existential anxieties, which, when triggered under particular sociopolitical and informational conditions, catalyze the convergence between Chinese *liberals and non-liberals* in their Trumpian metamorphosis. The final section concludes with brief discussions on the limits of this article, the derivate questions to be answered by further research, as well as the practical implications of Chinese liberal intellectuals' Trumpian metamorphosis.

---

[14] 高全喜、田飞龙 [Gao Quanxi and Tian Feilong], '归化、自由帝国与保守宪制' ['Assimilation, Liberal Empire and Conservative Constitutionalism'], *Pengpai*, February 4, 2018, accessed March 11, 2020, https://www.thepaper.cn/newsDetail_forward_1976492.

[15] 包刚升、周濂、施展、刘苏里 [Bao Gangsheng, Zhou Lian, Shi Zhan and Liu Suli], '多元主义的陷阱——当代政治的挑战与危机' ['The Pluralism Trap: Challenges and Crises of Contemporary Politics'], *China Strategic Analysis*, December 2, 2018, accessed March 11, 2020, http://zhanlve.org/?p=6356; see also 包刚升 [Bao Gangsheng], '西方政治的新现实——族群宗教多元主义与西方自由民主政体的挑战' ['A New Reality of Western Politics: Ethnic-Religious Pluralism as a Challenge to Western Liberal Democracies'], 政治学研究 [*CASS (Chinese Academy of Social Sciences) Journal of Political Science*] 2018(3), (2018), pp. 103–115.

Delineating Contemporary Chinese Liberalism

Just like any other political label, the meaning of the term 'liberal/ism' varies in accordance with contexts. In order to understand the Trumpian metamorphosis of Chinese liberals, one must first have a grasp of who *count* as 'liberals (*ziyoupai*)' in China, and what their views and positions are. This section offers a brief overview on the disagreements between liberals and their intellectual rivals in contemporary China, as well as the internal diversity within the liberal camp. In a nutshell, Chinese liberals are united primarily through their endorsement of 'universal values' (such as human rights, the rule of law, and political democracy) and the refusal of authoritarian Party-State as a legitimate 'China model', but disagree among themselves on a variety of other political, social and economic issues.

After the 1989 Tiananmen crackdown, public discourses in China were muted until Deng Xiaoping decided to reignite economic marketization (but not political reform) in 1992, thus ushering a new phase in Chinese intellectual history featuring decade-long debates between the 'Liberals' and the 'New Lefts'.[16] Generally speaking, the 'Liberals' were eager to defend the expansion of economic freedom, the deregulation of the market system, and the privatization of state-owned enterprises, not only because they believed in the intrinsic value of market capitalism, but also because they, along the line of the once-influential 'modernization theory', saw economic liberalization as a catalyst for politico-judicial reforms guided by the 'universal values' of human rights, the rule of law and democratic participation, reforms that had stalled since the late 1980s. On the other hand, the 'New Lefts' were deeply suspect of the 'Western' models of market capitalism and liberal democracy. Railing against the economic inequalities and social dislocations introduced by the 'market reforms', especially by the rushed privatiza-tion of state-owned enterprises, the New Lefts took upon themselves to envision a 'non-Western' politico-economic regime informed and legitimated by the 'socialist' past of the pre-reform People's Republic.

In other words, the 'Liberal-versus-New-Left' debates throughout the 1990s and the early 2000s consisted of two interwoven threads of disagreements, one political and the other economic. The economic thread centered around the benefits and costs of market capitalism, economic regulation, privatization, and redistribution. The political thread was about the existence of 'universal values', the desirability of 'Western' liberal democracy, and the possibility of a unique 'China model' that is benignly paternalistic and responsibly authoritarian, economically efficient while socially equitable, and (needless to say) forever led by the CCP.

Entering the 21st century, those two threads started to disentangle in the light of China's economic and political developments, and the intellectual field rapidly diversified beyond the Liberal/New Left dichotomy. On the one hand, the various groups previously lumped together under the 'New Left' label started to assert their own distinctiveness. In addition to accurately labeled New Lefts who remain more or less true to a normative vision of 'socialism with Chinese characteristics' that includes socioeconomic equality, there are now, for example, Neo-Confucians who dream of a homecoming of Chinese politics to its venerable 'cultural tradition' of Confucianism; Chinese 'Straussians' who believe that the state should only be run by those who have mastered the 'esoteric knowledge' taught between the lines by political philosopher Leo Strauss and his (self-styled) Chinese disciples; and unabashed *status quo* apologists who would defend whatever decision made by the CCP leadership as the wisest and the noblest decision possible.[17]

---

[16]See, e.g., Andrew Kipnis, 'Neo-leftists versus Neo-liberals: PRC Intellectual Debates in the 1990s', *Journal of Intercultural Studies* 24(3), (2003), pp. 239–251; Chaohua Wang, 'Minds of the Nineties', in *One China, Many Paths*, ed. Chaohua Wang (London: Verso, 2003), pp. 9–45; Xu Youyu, 'The Debates Between Liberalism and the New Left in China Since the 1990s', *Contemporary Chinese Thought* 34(3), (2003), pp. 6–17.

[17]For discussions on the various early-21st-century Chinese political thoughts, see 陈宣中 [Chen I-Chung], '德意志独特道路的 回声？ ——关于中国"反民权的国族主义"' ['Echoes of the German *Sonderweg*? The Issue of "Nationalism Against Citizenship Rights" in China'], 政治科学论丛 [*Taiwanese Journal of Political Science*] 45, (2010), pp. 107–152; Leiwan Weng,

On the other hand, internal differences within the 'Liberal' camp became more and more salient as well. As China joined the World Trade Organization (WTO), passed the 'hard landing' stage of economic reform, and solidified its domestic control, its skyrocketing ascendance to the status of the second largest economy in the world without signs of foreseeable political reform shattered the expectation that economic liberalization would facilitate democratization, and forced Chinese liberals to confront the question of whether non-instrumental justifications for market capitalism in an authoritarian state are available at all. Some (former) liberals, such as members of the so-called 'Qianbi She [Pencil Society]', subsequently adapted to the reality of authoritarian market economy, and disavowed the ideal of democratic politics as useless or even antithetical to the sanctity of private property.

Others acknowledged that the CCP-led market reform had resulted in the rise of socioeconomic inequality that need to be addressed, but disagreed on the diagnosis and the treatment. Is it because China still does *not* have a full-fledged market economy, as the Party-State still controls key sectors of the economic life and breeds unabashed crony capitalism? Or is it because, in its excessive quest for economic development, the Chinese Party-State has neglected the need for proper regulation and redistribution? This latter strand of liberalism, which concerns itself with not only political freedom but also socioeconomic equality and allows the state to play an active role in providing for the latter, started to gain attraction among younger liberal scholars in early 2010s, culminating in a widely reported conference on 'Chinese leftwing liberalism' in 2014.[18]

That said, market-optimism remains the predominant strand within the broader 'liberal' camp in China. For instance, according to Jennifer Pan and Yiqing Xu, being politically 'liberal' (which they defined as favoring 'more inclusive political institutions such as a multiparty system and universal suffrage' and 'protecting individual rights from state intervention') in contemporary China is highly correlated both with being 'pro-market' (defined as being 'more likely to oppose state intervention in markets[,] more likely to oppose state ownership of assets for protectionism, [and] less likely to believe that China's economic reforms have generated negative outcomes for the working class and peasants'), and with being 'non-nationalist' (defined as being less likely to endorse 'strong defense of territorial sovereignty and adversarial view of the West').[19]

Pan and Xu's results are useful in reminding us of the continuing entanglements and synchronizations among various levels of sociopolitical issues, as well as the dominance of the 'pro-market' strand within the liberal camp in China. Nonetheless, two limits of Pan and Xu's research need to be

---

'The Straussian Reception of Plato and Nationalism in China', *The Comparatist* 39, (2015), pp. 313–334; 陈纯 [Chen Chun], '中国自由保守主义的没落' [The Decline of Liberal Conservatism in China], *Initium*, January 6, 2016 (Part 1), accessed March 11, 2020, https://theinitium.com/article/20160107-opinion-decay-of-conservatism-liberalism-china/, and January 8, 2016 (Part 2), accessed March 11, 2020, https://theinitium.com/article/20160108-opinion-conservatism-liberalism-china-chenchun/; Tang Xiaobing and Mark McConaphy, 'Liberalism in Contemporary China: Questions, Strategies, Directions', *China Information* 32(1), (2018), pp. 121–138; Shi Anshu, François Lachapelle and Matthew Galway, 'The Recasting of Chinese Socialism: The Chinese New Left Since 2000', *China Information* 32(1), (2018), pp. 139–159; Jun Deng and Craig A Smith, 'The Rise of New Confucianism and the Return of Spirituality to Politics in Mainland China', *China Information* 32(2), (2018), pp. 294–314; Dongxian Jiang, review of *Carl Schmitt and Leo Strauss in the Chinese-Speaking World*, ed. Kai Marchal and Carl K.Y. Shaw, *Voegelin View*, June 17, 2018, accessed March 11, 2020, https://voegelinview.com/carl-schmitt-and-leo-strauss-in-the-chinese-speaking-world/; Sebastian Veg, 'The Rise of China's Statist Intellectuals: Law, Sovereignty, and "Repoliticization"', *The China Journal* 82, (2019), pp. 23–45.

[18]See, e.g., 李丹 [Li Dan], '中国左翼自由主义的"香港共识"' [The "Hong Kong Consensus" of Chinese Leftwing-Liberalism'], *Pengpai*, August 6, 2014, accessed March 11, 2020, https://www.gongfa.com/html/gongfaxinwen/201408/06-2649.html; 周保松 [Chow Po Chung], '左翼自由主义的理念' [The Ideal of Liberal Leftism'], 二十一世纪[*The Twenty-First Century*] 149, (2015), pp. 36–54; 林垚 [Lin Yao], '左翼自由主义需要怎样的中国化？' ['What Kind of Sinicization Does Leftwing-Liberalism Need?'], *Initium*, December 4, 2015 (Part 1), accessed March 11, 2020, https://theinitium.com/article/20151204-opinion-liberalism-left-linyao/, and December 5, 2015 (Part 2), accessed March 11, 2020, https://theinitium.com/article/20151205-opinion-liberal-left-linyao/.

[19]Jennifer Pan and Yiqing Xu, 'China's Ideological Spectrum', *Journal of Politics* 80(1), (2018), p. 255. See also Ronggui Huang, Yong Gui and Xiaoyi Sun, 'Beyond the Left-Right Spectrum: A Typological Analysis of Ideologues in China's Weibo Space', *Journal of Contemporary China* 28(119), (2019), pp. 831–847 (dividing 'liberal' Weibo users into three subgroups: pro-market 'economic liberals' who are relatively silent on political issues, 'political liberals' who favor liberal democracy over the Party-State regime but do not say much on economic issues, and 'full-fledged liberals' who are expressive on both fronts).

noted. First, the subjects of their survey were ordinary netizens with average political knowledge, not intellectuals who may have more nuanced views that cannot be captured by oversimplified survey questions. By contrast, this article relies on contemporary Chinese intellectuals' own writings and comments, and attends to the special role intellectuals play in shaping public discourses.

Second, contexts matter. Chinese liberals (including both liberal intellectuals and liberal-leaning netizens) who oppose 'state intervention in the economy' may have in mind the kind of 'planned economy' or 'command economy' practiced in the early days of the People's Republic of China (PRC), and are not necessarily opposed to regulative measures such as anti-monopoly legislation, minimum wage, welfare state, healthcare provision, and so on. Many of them, while receptive to neoliberal talking points, would from time to time chide the Chinese government for being socialist-in-name-only without proper redistribution, and warn against rising economic inequality and social disloca-tion resulted from unconstrained capitalism.[20] The subsequent sections address this complexity.

Neoliberal Affinity: A Coeffect, Not A Cause

Despite the limits of Pan and Xu's research, they plausibly conclude that being politically liberal is highly correlated with pro-market attitudes in contemporary China applies to Chinese liberal intellectuals as well. Indeed, given the fact that China's Reform-and-Opening coincided with the Reagan-Thatcher era, when neoliberalism as an ideology rose to dominance across the globe, it is hardly surprising that the latter has had huge influences on the ways in which most Chinese liberal intellectuals would understand the world and approach political issues. Therefore, a seemingly straightforward response to the phenomenon of liberal Trump-idolization in China might be that it is not *curious* at all.

According to this seemingly straightforward 'neoliberal affinity' explanation, contemporary Chinese liberalism is no more than a local variant of Reagan-Thatcherism, whose hegemony in the globalization era is achieved through 'combining various contradictory agendas within an over-arching neo-liberal framework of ideas,' especially through combining 'extensive marketisation, the commercialization of public services, de-regulation and privatization' with 'other more traditional attachments of the right, notably to patriotism, elitism and a strong commitment to law and order'.[21] Neoliberal elites had used those 'more traditional attachments of the right' as intellectual and electoral allies against the left and the center-left (e.g. 'liberals' in the American sense), but now they could no longer 'tame' those elements, which have been fully mobilized, normalized and legitimized through decades of such alliance. In the United States, for example, self-styled 'libertar-ians' and 'fiscal conservatives' within the Republic Party have, long before the rise of Trump, gradually succumbed to, and internalized, more and more extreme versions of cultural conservatism and rightwing nationalism.[22] By the same token, according to this 'neoliberal affinity' explanation, it is more than natural for Chinese 'liberal' intellectuals, who truly are Reagan-Thatcherite neoliberals deep down, to be captivated by bursting Trumpism.

There might be some degree of truth to this explanation. After all, a substantial proportion of the Chinese liberal intellectuals who fervently defend Trump and his policies are diehard market fundamentalists, such as Liu Junning, former research fellow at Chinese Academy of Social

[20]See, e.g., 孙立平 [Sun Liping], '当前中国的贫富格局' ['Rich-Poor Stratification in Contemporary China'], *Aisixiang*, April 6, 2011, accessed March 11, 2020, http://m.aisixiang.com/data/39821.html; 郭于华 [Guo Yuhua], 倾听底层 [*Listening to the Lower Class*] (Guangxi: Guangxi shifandaxue chubanshe, 2011).
[21]Steven Lukes, 'The Grand Dichotomy of the Twentieth Century', in *The Cambridge History of Twentieth-Century Political Thought*, eds. Terence Ball and Richard Bellamy (Cambridge: Cambridge University Press, 2003), pp. 623–624; see also Daniel Stedman Jones, *Masters of the Universe: Hayek, Friedman, and the Birth of Neoliberal Politics* (Princeton, NJ: Princeton University Press, 2012).
[22]See, e.g., Theda Skocpol and Vanessa Williamson, *The Tea Party and the Remaking of Republican Conservatism* (Oxford: Oxford University Press, 2011); Ian Haney López, *Dog Whistle Politics: How Coded Racial Appeals Have Reinvented Racism and Wrecked the Middle Class* (Oxford: Oxford University Press, 2013); Angie Maxwell and Todd Shields, *The Long Southern Strategy: How Chasing White Voters in the South Changed American Politics* (Oxford: Oxford University Press, 2019).

Sciences expelled for his advocacy of political reform, and Wang Jianxun, associate professor of law at Chinese University of Political Science and Law who received his Ph.D. in political science from Indiana University-Bloomington.[23]

Even those who refuse to call themselves 'Chuanfen' because they disdain Trump's personality or disagree with some of his policy positions have argued that he is a 'lesser evil' for American democracy, compared to the, relatively speaking, socioeconomically redistributive and regulatory Democratic Party. For example, during the 2016 U.S. presidential election, Liu Yu, a Columbia-educated associate professor of political science at Tsinghua University famed for her best-selling *Minzhu de Xijie* [*Details of Democracy*], asked rhetorically: 'As the public opinion in Europe and the U.S. keeps shifting to the left generation by generation, the diversity of opinions quickly vanishing, will there be any force that could prevent Bernie Sanders from becoming Hugo Chavez?' According to Liu, implementation of redistributive policies is the prelude to 'Latin-Americanization': because the majority of the society, a.k.a. the poor, are easily allured by the short-term benefits of redistribution, the left, once in power, would keep winning elections by the 'advantage of sheer number', and gradually transform a "pluralist democracy" exemplified by checks-and-balances into a "monist democracy" in which the winner takes all', ending up with *Chavizmo* authoritarianism. The election of Trump is, therefore, a necessary evil (if an evil at all) to prevent the U.S. from steering towards the wrong direction led by a leftward-moving Democratic Party longing for 'progressivist revolution'.[24]

Nonetheless, explaining the Trumpian metamorphosis of Chinese liberals solely in terms of their neoliberal affinity is inadequate for at least two reasons. First, this explanation fails to establish a plausible *mechanism* pertaining to the social and political contexts of *China*. In a democratic regime such as the United States, self-styled 'fiscal conservative' politicians and intellectuals in the contemporary Republican Party would appease their culturally conservative and white supremacist constituents, whom they have strategically chosen to ally themselves with and to mobilize, in order to win primaries and/or general elections, and would, during those processes of *electoral appeasement*, internalize those voters' views and positions through group conformity, peer pressure, cognitive dissonance and various other psychological mechanisms of adaptation.[25] By contrast, in the authoritarian Party-State China, no such need for electoral appeasement to the 'more traditional attachments of the right' exists for (neo)liberal intellectuals.

Consequently, the 'neoliberal affinity' explanation for the Trumpian metamorphosis of Chinese liberal intellectuals evades the very question it is supposed to answer: Why, in the absence of a pressure for electoral appeasement in China, have those who were initially attracted to the *economic* vision of neoliberalism so easily internalized the rest of the 'contradictory agendas within an overarching neo-liberal framework of ideas', including those 'more traditional attachments of the right', and so quickly fallen prey to the Trumpian demagogue that is so antithetical to the 'universal values' they had held dear? Indeed, not only does the 'neoliberal affinity' explanation fail to explain, it

[23]See 刘军宁 [Liu Junning], '特朗普的胜利是左派的挫败，而非自由的挫败' ['Trump's Victory Is Leftists' Defeat, Not Freedom's Defeat'], *Insight*, November 10, 2016, accessed March 11, 2020, http://www.sohu.com/a/118579005_460385; 王建勋 [Wang Jianxun], '特朗普要做的是回归"美国精神"' ['What Trump Plans Is A Return to the "American Ethos"'], *Aisixiang*, January 25, 2017, accessed March 11, 2020, http://www.aisixiang.com/data/102926.html.

[24]刘瑜 [Liu Yu], '民粹与民主：论美国政治中的民粹主义' ['Populism and Democracy: On Populism in American Politics'], 探索与争鸣 [*Exploration and Contestation*] 2016(10), (2016), p. 74. Notice that her argument is different from Friedrich Hayek's (in)famous 'road to serfdom' argument against socioeconomic redistribution, in that the latter predicts communist totalitarianism at the end of the slippery slope, instead of *Chavizmo* authoritarianism as Liu does.

[25]See, e.g., Janet Hook, '"It Is the Era of Trump": How the President is Remaking the Republican Party', *Wall Street Journal*, August 27, 2018, accessed March 11, 2020, https://www.wsj.com/articles/it-is-the-era-of-trump-how-the-president-is-remaking-the-republican-party-1535380861; Jan Zilinsky, 'Why Didn't More Congressional Republicans Condemn Trump's Racist Tweets About the "Squad": This Graph Explains', *Monkey Cage*, July 20, 2019, accessed March 11, 2020, https://www.washingtonpost.com/politics/2019/07/20/why-didnt-more-congressional-republicans-condemn-trumps-racist-tweets-about-squad-this-graph-explains/. Arguably, this process of electoral appeasement has been greatly accelerated by the fact that Trump's inflammatory rhetoric emboldens the GOP's racially prejudiced voters; see Benjamin Newman, Jennifer L. Merolla, Sono Shah, Danielle Casarez Lemi, Loren Collingwood and S. Karthick Ramakrishnan, 'The Trump Effect: An Experimental Investigation of the Emboldening Effect of Racially Inflammatory Elite Communication', *British Journal of Political Science*, OnlineFirst version, (2020), pp. 1–22, accessed March 11, 2020, doi: 10.1017/S0007123419000590.

is itself in need of explaining: Why are Chinese liberals attracted to, or heavily influenced by, neoliberalism *in the first place*? Even if the neoliberal affinity of Chinese liberals and their Trumpian metamorphosis are *correlated*, the former may not be the *cause* of the latter; instead, they may well be *coeffects* of each other, both to be explained by reference to certain shared root-cause(s).

Second, the 'neoliberal affinity' explanation also fails to connect the dots between the curious Trumpian metamorphosis of Chinese *liberals*, on the one hand, and the relatively well-documented Trumpian metamorphosis of Chinese *non-liberals*, including the so-called New Left intellectuals whose purported socioeconomic agenda has long been a staunch refusal of neoliberalism,[26] on the other hand. To explain the Trumpian metamorphosis of Chinese liberals solely in terms of their neoliberal affinity is to treat it as an isolated intellectual phenomenon, the convergence of which with the Trumpian metamorphosis of non-liberal intellectuals in China is largely accidental. By contrast, the alternative 'beaconism' explanation offered in this article would help explicate the fundamental similarities and deep-rooted connections between those two phenomena, as well as the nuances and complexities of contemporary Chinese *sichao* in general.[27]

In a nutshell, the 'beaconism' explanation contends that the Trumpian metamorphosis of Chinese liberal intellectuals results from the 'beacon complex' widespread among them, which idealizes 'the West', and particularly the United States, as the political and civilizational 'beacon of light' for the rest of the world. Moreover, the beacon complex consists of two interrelated and mutually reinforcing components, *political* beaconism and *civilizational* beaconism. On the one hand, *both* the neoliberal affinity of Chinese liberal intellectuals *and* their Trumpian metamorphoses could be traced back to their *political* beaconism. On the other hand, *civilizational* beaconism not only reinforces Chinese *liberals'* proclivity for Trumpian metamorphoses, but also provides a common denominator between them and their *non-liberal* fellow-Trumpists.

Political Beaconism: Trauma, Struggle and Pilgrimage under the CCP Rule

Political beaconism, the idealization of 'the West', especially the United States, as the political 'beacon of light', is first and foremost an intellectual 'political pilgrimage' in the figurative sense. As Paul Hollander famously observed, intellectuals who are 'critical of their own society [are] highly susceptible to the claims put forward by the leaders and spokesmen of the societies they inspected in the course of [political pilgrimage, are] inclined to give every benefit of doubt to these social systems and [are] successful in screening out qualities that might have detracted from their positive vision'.[28] According to Hollander, Western leftwing intellectuals during the Cold War manifested this mentality of political pilgrimage when they, upon witnessing domestic problems such as the defects of capitalist consumerism and the evils of American racial segregation, sought solace and hope in faraway Communist regimes such as the Soviet Union, China, Cuba and North Korea, idolizing and sanitizing them in their writing and imagination.

---

[26]For example, Cui Zhiyuan, a leading New Left intellectual and allegedly the economic mastermind behind the 'Chongqing Model', has talked approvingly of Trump's 'intention to make American great again' and his assault on 'mass illegal immigration to the United States', as well as Steve Bannon's 'international campaign of economic nationalism and political populism'. See 崔之元 [Cui Zhiyuan], '川普前顾问班农和传说中的普京顾问杜金之思想比较' ['A Comparison Between the Views of Steve Bannon, Former Counsel to Trump, and the Views of Aleksandr Dugin, Rumored Counsel to Putin'], *Aisixiang*, February 23, 2018, accessed March 11, 2020, http://www.aisixiang.com/data/108229.html.

[27]Notice that the 'beaconism' explanation, along with its refutation of the 'neoliberal affinity' explanation as offering a plausible mechanism, does not contend that beaconism is the *only* mechanism underlying the Trumpian metamorphosis of Chinese liberal intellectuals. As subsequent sections show, sociopolitical and informational conditions play important roles in triggering and amplifying beaconist psychologies. Whether further distinctions can be made between different types of mechanisms—for example, between 'causes' and 'conditions'—and whether there are good reasons to categorize beaconism as a (or the) 'cause'—*vis-à-vis* other sociopolitical and informational 'conditions'—of liberal Trumpian metamorphosis in China are important philosophical questions that this article cannot address. The author thanks Chen I-Chung, Guido Parietti and Zhang Chenchen for urging him to clarify on this matter.

[28]Paul Hollander, *Political Pilgrims: Western Intellectuals in Search of the Good Society* (Oxford: Oxford University Press, 1981), p. 6.

By contrast, the *summum malum* for contemporary Chinese liberal intellectuals is, without doubt, the authoritarian Party-State that has committed innumerable atrocities since the founding of the People's Republic and has repeatedly resisted calls for liberal-democratic reform. Consequently, they are drawn to make stark contrasts between China under the insufferable CCP rule, on the one hand, and some other societies in which people supposedly live much happier lives, on the other hand.

Liberal critics of the CCP have tried-and-erred various destinations of political pilgrimage. In early 2000s, for example, they played active roles in cultivating '*Minguore* [the Republic-of-China fad]', a nostalgic narrative campaign portraying China from the 1910s to the 1940s, ruled first by Beiyang warlords and then by the Nationalist Party (Kuomintang), as a 'paradise lost' in which people had enjoyed freedoms of speech and association, as well as other civil and political rights. *Minguore* waned quickly, however, in the face of the intricate question of why, if *Minguo* were so fantastic and beloved, it would have lost the civil war to the CCP in a landslide manner.[29]

On the other hand, a 'journey to the west'—using contemporaneous Western democracies as devices of comparison with the PRC—appears more promising than the nostalgic 'journey to the past' to anti-CCP political pilgrims. After all, not only is it the allegedly 'Western' ideals of human rights and democracy that Chinese liberals are promulgating, but 'actually existing' Western democracies (a.k.a. the 'beacons') are also 'developed countries' presumably more prosperous and well-ordered than China, making it easier to impress upon the general public the attractiveness of liberal ideals and the inferiority of the Party-State regime. Among them, the United States further stands out as the main destination of imaginary pilgrimage, being the 'leader' of the West as well as the only 'worthy' comparison with China in an increasingly 'Chinamerican' world order.

Insofar as nuances do not sell, the imageries of 'actually existing' Western democracies, which Chinese liberal pilgrims popularize as well as internalize, tend to be sanitized and glorified at two levels: internationally, as devoted, omnibenevolent protectors of human rights;[30]and domestically, as near-perfect societies in which, thanks to a series of Whig-historical triumphs in the past, there is no long *systematic*, especially *institutional*, injustice to frown upon. For example, it is typical of a Chinese liberal to deny that, after *de jure* segregation was ended by the Civil Rights movement, institutionalized racism still exists in the United States, that *de facto* segregation, police brutality, mass incarceration and voter suppression are serious institutional—let alone institutionalized-racist—problems, and that contemporary activisms such as Black Lives Matter are legitimate responses to systematic racial injustice. If anything, it is the 'pickier and pickier Political Correctness' and the 'continuous representation of black victimhood by the cultural industry' that are to blame for 'white people's burden of being forever guilty on behalf of their great-great-grandfathers'.[31]

To be sure, Chinese liberal intellectuals' beaconist pilgrimage to their imagined West does not proceed *de novo*, but is shaped by, and interacts with, their own lived experiences through which they perceive and understand politics. In particular, the longstanding appropriation of the left-political vocabulary by the CCP (which, after all, is a self-styled 'leftist' party), and the traumatic horrors and catastrophes of Maoist totalitarianism—the Anti-Rightists Campaign, the Great Leap

[29]See, e.g., 马勤 [Ma Qin], '自由与苦难: 不同的民国记忆' ['Freedom and Suffering: Different Memories of the ROC'], *Huaxia kuaidi*, May 25, 2010, accessed March 11, 2020, http://my.cnd.org/modules/wfsection/article.php?articleid=25892; 梁文道、张鸣、杨奎松、陈丹青 [Liang Wendao, Zhang Ming, Yang Kuisong and Chen Danqing], '民国是历史还是现实?' ['Does the ROC Belong to the History or the Present?'], *Aisixiang*, September 21, 2011, accessed March 11, 2020, http://www.aisixiang.com/data/44487.html; 周怀宗 [Zhou Huaizong], '学者: 怀念民国时代来自于对当前学术环境的不满' ['Scholars: The ROC Nostalgia Reflects Discontents with the Current Academic Environment'], *Beijing Morning Post*, October 21, 2014, accessed March 11, 2020, http://www.cssn.cn/st/st_wybht/201410/t20141021_1370248.shtml.
[30]For example, the late Nobel Peace laureate Liu Xiaobo unequivocally 'support[ed] U.S.-led wars, which he called "all ethically defensible", including the U.S.-led war in Iraq'. Krishnadev Calamur, 'Remebering Liu Xiaobo', *Atlantic*, July 13, 2017, accessed March 11, 2020, https://www.theatlantic.com/news/archive/2017/07/liu-xiaobo-dies/533529/; see also 刘晓波 [Liu Xiaobo], '伊战与美国大选' ['The Iraq War and American Presidential Election'], *Liu Xiaobo Archives*, October 31, 2004, accessed March 11, 2020, http://liu-xiaobo.org/blog/archives/6968.
[31]刘瑜 [Liu Yu], '民粹与民主: 论美国政治中的民粹主义' ['Populism and Democracy: On Populism in American Politics'], 探索与争鸣 [*Exploration and Contestation*] 2016(10), (2016), pp. 73–74.

Forward, the Three-Year Famine, and the Cultural Revolution—committed in the name of 'revolutionary' ideals, have continued to overwhelm liberal critics and mold their political perceptions, aversions and imaginations. Even though few of them would go as far as Liu Junning to assert that all political evils originate from leftism, that the further-on-the-right the better, and that the conventional categorization of Nazism as a far-right ideology is a 'leftist propaganda trick' muddling the water,[32] they are more or less disposed to cram a broad range of political, social and economic agendas in a mono-dimensional, somewhat Procrustean left-right spectrum, and to be more suspicious of apparently further-left ones than their apparently further-right counterparts, as Liu Yu's aforementioned equivalence of Sanders with Chavez exemplifies.

Such a disposition affects how pilgriming Chinese liberal intellectuals see/imagine the West, and is in turn reinforced by what they believe to have seen in the (imagined) West. Indeed, if their neoliberal affinity on *economic* issues has been a natural reaction to self-styled leftism of the CCP and to destitution under Maoist planned economy, it has also been made stronger by their political beaconism, not least owing to the fact that the United States, the 'shiniest of all beacons' and the primary destination of anti-CCP pilgrimage, is socioeconomically much less redistributive and less egalitarian than most of the other Western democracies.

Similarly, the beaconist sanitization of Western (especially American) domestic politics as devoid of systematic injustice, and therefore as in no need for 'radical' rectification, resonates with a kind of 'anti-radicalism' on *sociocultural* issues that has permeated the Chinese liberal intelligentsia in the post-Mao era, which, horror-struck by the Cultural Revolution, hastens to blame political tragedies of the 20th-century China on impulses to radically overhaul the existing social order.[33] The thought that, during the Mao era, techniques of mass mobilization and contentious politics, ideology-critique of traditional cultural norms and implicit biases, and (self-)regulation of speech through social pressure had been relied on to bring forth totalitarian control, full-scale violence and disastrous societal upheaval makes Chinese liberals especially wary of contemporary social justice activisms in the West, which seem to be deploying similar 'radical' tactics while contesting the structures and norms that perpetuate racial, gender and other forms of discrimination and oppression. Projecting their fear of the Cultural Revolution onto the imagined West, beaconist liberals have repeatedly analogized, say, removal of Confederate memorials to '*posijiu* [destroying the Four Olds]',[34] Black Lives Matter activists to '*hongweibing* [Red Guards]',[35] and the MeToo movement to '*dazibao* [Big-Character Posters]' and '*gongshen* [show trials]',[36] and are highly receptive to the idea that the feminist, anti-racist, and anti-colonialist '*baizuo* [white lefties]' are suffocating Western societies with meticulous and inhibitive norms of 'political correctness'.[37]

Meanwhile, rhetorical struggles between liberal beaconists and the CCP help turn the former's wariness of *baizuo* into animosity. To begin with, the Chinese government has always been on the

[32] 刘军宁 [Liu Junning], '纳粹与希特勒: 姓左, 还是姓右？' ['The Nazis and Hitler: Leftwing, or Rightwing?'], *Chinese PEN*, August 8, 2014, accessed March 11, 2020, https://www.chinesepen.org/blog/archives/4380.

[33] See, e.g., 李泽厚、刘再复 [Li Zehou and Liu Zaifu], 告别革命: 回望二十世纪中国 [*Farewell to Revolution: Looking Back upon China of the Twentieth Century*] (Hong Kong: Tiandi, 1995); 林毓生 [Lin Yu-Sheng], 中国激进思潮的起源与后果 [*The Origins and Consequences of Chinese Radical Thoughts*] (Taipei: Linking Publishing, 2019).

[34] For a critical review of this analogy, see 刘波 [Liu Bo], '拆李将军像等于"破四旧"吗？' ['Does Demolishing Statues of General Robert Lee Equal "Destroying the Four Olds"?'], *Tengxun Dajia*, August 19, 2017, accessed March 11, 2020, https://xw.qq.com/iphone/m/category/7cb74407125873315ea8225aacd97e6d.html.

[35] See, e.g. 丛日云 [Cong Riyun], '特朗普反对什么样的多元主义？' ['Which Pluralism Is Trump Against?'], *Aisixiang*, September 13, 2018, accessed March 11, 2020, http://www.aisixiang.com/data/112289-2.html. Cong is a liberal professor at Chinese University of Political Science and Law, and an avowed *Chuanfen*.

[36] See, e.g., 刘瑜 [Liu Yu], '关于metoo' ['On MeToo'], *Matters*, July 27, 2018, accessed March 11, 2020, https://matters.news/forum/?post=16439143-1a75-497a-bad2-875d2fcd5d28-. For a critical response to Liu, see 林垚 [Lin Yao], '"我也是": 作为集体行动的公共舆论运动' ['"Me Too": Public Opinion Movement as Collective Action'], 思想 [*Reflexion*] 38, (2019), pp. 253–326.

[37] See, e.g., 萧瀚 [Xiao Han], '政治正确与言论自由: 关于"冯钢"事件的几点看法' ['Political Correctness and Freedom of Speech: Remarks on the "Feng Gang" Incident'], *Weibo*, October 23, 2017, accessed March 11, 2020, https://pic2.zhimg.com/80/v2-f526ead9566da1109afca0a7fd9360f3_hd.jpg. For a critical response to Xiao, see 孙金昱 [Sun Jinyu], '政治正确"杀死"言论自由: 真实忧虑还是话术陷阱？' ['Political Correctness "Killing" Freedom of Speech: Genuine Concern or Rhetorical Trap?'], 思想 [*Reflexion*] 35, (2018), pp. 115–132.

alert for the subversive power of popularized beaconist imageries. To deflect criticisms and boost legitimacy, it constantly denounces contemporaneous Western democracies as irresponsible, inefficient, corrupt, democratic-in-name-only, deeply unjust, and hypocritical. For example, in the aftermath of the 9 August 2014 police shooting of an unarmed black teenager Michael Brown in Ferguson, Missouri, Chinese propaganda machines promptly seized the opportunity to 'bash the United States in order to create the appearance of moral equivalence', even though 'Beijing has no more interest in advancing racial justice in the United States than it does in safeguarding substantive human rights domestically'.[38] Such official sophistry forces liberal critics into an awkward position when preaching to the public: acknowledging serious shortcomings of 'actually existing' Western democracies complicates the case for the liberal democratic ideal *vis-à-vis* the China Model, and risks being rhetorically taken advantage of by Party-State apologists.

China's rise as a global economic superpower since 2008, and Xi Jinping's tightening grip on the society *à la* Maoist totalitarianism, further intensify liberal intellectuals' anxieties and disorientations in the face of the CCP's self-servicing West-bashing, and reinforce internalized (*vis-à-vis* tactic) beaconism as a coping strategy. In light of this changing discursive dynamic, Western liberal-progressive self-reflections on the systematic injustices within/by their own societies, which seemingly corroborate the cynical 'moral equivalence' rhetoric of Party-State apologists and undermine Chinese liberals' struggle to win over public support for political reform, become increasingly inconvenient and irritating in the eye of demoralized beaconist pilgrims, who, in turn, increasingly resent and despise *baizuo* for presumably spending too much time self-criticizing instead of pressuring China into improving its human rights conditions. Understandably, some Party-State critics would feel energized by the sudden rise of a political figure so blatantly antithetical to *baizuo* in every possible respect, and, instead of merely anticipating his trade war to have reform-inducing *side effects* on China, promptly subscribe to 'a strong belief that Trump is the most *supportive* president in American history for China's human rights', despite all evidence to the contrary.[39]

Civilizational Beaconism, Civilizational Vindictivism, and Civilizational Anxiety

Political beaconism is only part of the story, however. While it gives rise to the wishful thinking among a few Chinese liberals that Trump champions China's human rights, it would be far-fetched to claim that most, if not all, liberal *Chuanfen* in China are subject to that delusion. By contrast, as has been mentioned, they adore and applaud Trump not so much for the ongoing Sino-American trade war as for the racist, sexist, Islamophobic and anti-immigrant rhetoric and policies he espouses. Moreover, insofar as the trauma of Maoism fosters Chinese liberal intellectuals' skepticism of the allegedly '*baizuo*' program of sociocultural transformation in accordance with norms of 'political correctness', it cannot explain how they could leap from such skepticism to endorsing the substances of Trumpist demagogy that are in dire conflict with core liberal democratic values.

This is where civilizational beaconism, the twin of political beaconism, comes into play. Whereas political beaconism worships sanitized imageries of Western (and particularly American) politics, civilizational beaconism is an unquestioning admiration and glorification of the presumably 'advanced' Western 'civilization' that necessitates all of its political achievements and perfections. Though not as menacing as its non-liberal, nationalist counterpart—civilizational vindicativism—that sees 'Western civilization' as the archenemy of resurgent 'Chinese civilization', liberal civilizational beaconism shares some of its genealogical and ideological underpinnings, which, when certain sociopolitical and informational conditions are present, would catalyze the Trumpian metamorphosis of Chinese liberal intellectuals.

---

[38]Nancy Tang, 'Ferguson, Staten Island, and the People's Republic', *Foreign Policy*, December 12, 2014, accessed March 11, 2020, https://foreignpolicy.com/2014/12/12/ferguson-staten-island-china-racism/.
[39]Zhaoyin Feng, 'Why I Translate All of Trump's Tweets into Chinese', *BBC News*, August 8, 2019, accessed March 11, 2020, https://www.bbc.com/news/world-us-canada-49092612; emphasis added.

The Chinese fixation on 'advanced Western civilization (*xianjin Xifang wenming*)' goes a long way back to the late 19th century, when the Qing dynasty was exposed to 'shocks' by Western colonial powers. Startled and awed by the modernizing West's technoscientific and sociopolitical superiorities, and anxious about the 'survival' of the Chinese Nation, *fin-de-siècle* Chinese intellectuals were determined to learn whatever the West had mastered in order to revitalize the '*Dongyabingfu* [Sick Man of East Asia]'. Unfortunately, the era happened to be the heyday of colonialism, 'scientific' racism and social Darwinism in the West. Consequently, by hungrily and blindly absorbing Western 'thought nutrients', they also unwittingly internalized and popularized those ideologies—especially the identification of Chinese as of 'yellow race', the idea that 'all black, red and brown races are far inferior to the white race',[40] the attribution of Western 'civilizational advancement' to racial whiteness (and/or sometimes to Christianity), and the survival-of-the-fittest conception of 'intercivilizational' relations—all of which become firmly ingrained in Chinese public discourses throughout the following century, as many have noticed.[41] Indeed, even the current Internet epithet '*baizuo* [white lefties]' denigrating western liberal/progressive activists is a racialized term, as if only white people were capable of standing up, however naively, for social justice.

Notwithstanding their shared fixation on Western civilization, Chinese intellectuals disagree on what to make of China's '*bainian guochi* [century of humiliation]' and what to aspire for Chinese civilization. In broad strokes, *civilizational beaconism* is the typical view among more liberal-leaning intellectuals, and *civilizational vindictivism* among non-liberal, more nationalist-leaning intellectuals.

Civilizational beaconists aspire that China shall one day join the rank of 'civilized' nations alongside Western developed countries, with 'being civilized' defined more or less in terms of respecting liberal democratic 'universal values' and adopting 'Western' political institutions and norms. To this end, 20th-century liberal intellectuals in China have frequently resorted to certain cultural-essentialist and implicitly racist refrains, such as the 'national characteristics critique (*guominxing pipan*)', in order to 'wake up' the presumably long-complacent Chinese people,[42] even though in dire conditions these 'wakeup calls' would border on fatalism. In mid-1980s,[43] for example, *He Shang* [*River Elegy*], an influential pro-reform documentary, contended that China's repeatedly failed quests for political modernization since the 19th century were but a natural result of the innate 'close-mindedness' of 'land-based' Chinese civilization, *vis-à-vis* the 'ocean-based, enterprising' nature of Western civilization that has enabled its liberal democratization.[44]

Civilizational vindicativists, on the other hand, see Chinese and Western civilizations ultimately as antagonists, and aspire that China shall return to glory not only by replacing the West at the top of

---

[40] 梁启超 [Liang Qichao], '论中国之将强' ['On China's Inevitable Revival'], 时务报 [*The Chinese Progress*], June 30, 1897. Unsurprisingly, Liang (and most of other Chinese intellectuals) refused to accept the 'orthodox' racial hierarchy in which the 'yellow race' is as inferior as other non-white races, and instead maintained that 'only the yellow race is comparable to the white race …, capable of doing anything the white race is capable of'. *Ibid.*

[41] See, e.g., Frank Dikötter, 'Racial Identities in China: Context and Meaning', *China Quarterly* 138, (1994), pp. 404–412; James Reeve Pusey, *China and Charles Darwin* (Cambridge, MA: Harvard University Asia Center, 1983); Michael Keevak, *Becoming Yellow: A Short History of Racial Thinking* (Princeton, NJ: Princeton University Press, 2011); Yinghong Cheng, 'From Campus Racism to Cyber Racism: Discourse of Race and Chinese Nationalism', *China Quarterly* 207, (2011), pp. 561–579.

[42] See, e.g., 袁洪亮 [Yuan Hongliang], '中国近代国民性改造思潮研究综述' ['A Review of Studies on Thoughts about Reforming the National Characteristics in Modern China', 史学月刊 [*Journal of Historical Science*] 2000(6), (2000), pp. 135–141.

[43] Careful readers would notice that the historical overview offered here skips the Maoist era, which arguably saw a brief break from civilizational-beaconist discourses, as the Party-State officially promulgated the ideals of gender, racial and ethnic equality and denounced Western imperialist-colonialist cultural hegemony; see, e.g., Zheng Wang, *Finding Women in the State: A Socialist Feminist Revolution in the People's Republic of China, 1949–1964* (Oakland, CA: University of California Press, 2016); Julia Lovell, *Maoism: A Global History* (New York: Knopf, 2019). Nonetheless, to the extent that the CCP only paid lip services to those ideals, and to the extent that their implementations were inextricably intertwined with the memories of Maoist totalitarianism, the appeal of those ideals soon faded in the Reform-and-Opening era, not least due to the effects of political beaconism as post-Mao pilgrimage. Moreover, the fact that social sciences and humanities in China had stagnated under decades of Party-State disciplination also made intellectuals in the aftermath of the Cultural Revolution, who were thrown into globalization, rapid socioeconomic transformation and the abrupt end of the Cold War, ill-prepared to critique and resist the repopularization of civilizational discourses. The author thanks Wang Chaohua and Zhang Chenchen for pressing him on this point.

[44] See Xiao Xu, 'A Comprehensive Review of the *River Elegy* Debate', *Chinese Sociology & Anthropology* 25(1), (1992), pp. 6–27.

civilizational hierarchy', but also by demonstrating the ingenuity—and intrinsic supremacy—of Chinese civilization to the rest of the world with an alternative 'China model' that is both distinctive from and superior to whatever the West has had to offer. As China rises economically and geopolitically in the early 21st century, non-liberal intellectuals have become more and more confident in asserting their own civilizational aspiration. In a recent article, for example, Peking University law professor Jiang Shigong, an unabashed CCP apologist, flips *He Shang*'s narrative of 'land-civilization versus ocean-civilization' on its head:

> Throughout the confrontation between the Eurasia Continent and the Ocean World, the Eurasia Continent [led first by Napoleon's France, then by Germany twice, and finally by the Soviet Union] had been defeated repeatedly by the Ocean World and had retreated step by step from the west to the east. ... At the end of the day, only China, which is at the eastern end of the land mass, shall be able to stand up on behalf of the Land Force against the Ocean World [led by Anglo-Americans], and eventually tame the power of science and technology [the Ocean Powers] have released [from Pandora's Box].[45]

The affinity between civilizational vindictivism and Trumpism is relatively straightforward. For one thing, they both regard the world as an anarchical might-is-right jungle, in which a 'superior' race deserves to dominate the 'inferior' Others. In the meantime, the 2009 Urumqi ethnic riot and the 2014 Kunming mass stabbing have since fueled the rapid development of Islamophobia in China, a sentiment that is further exacerbated, on the one hand, by the state news media's overwhelmingly negative portrayal of Chinese Muslims that serves to justify the CCP's draconian rule over Xinjiang, where Uyghurs and other Muslim minorities constitute more than half of the population,[46] and, on the other hand, by an active grassroots anti-Muslim community of volunteers who regularly translate and circulate Western alt-right articles and videos for Chinese Internet users.[47] Conveniently, civilizational vindicativists can now ostracize and scapegoat Chinese Muslims as 'uncivilized' and 'uncivilizable' Others who stand in the way of (Han-)Chinese civilization towards its 'great national resurgence (*minzu weida fuxing*)' and triumphant takeover of global hegemony from the West.

Although liberal civilizational beaconists typically do not share the vindicativist eagerness for Chinese hegemony, they are far from immune to Islamophobia permeating the Chinese internet. On the contrary, the latter resonates with their own kind of 'civilizational anxiety', namely, a projected fear that the Western 'civilizational beacon' is being tarnished by a rapidly changing demography, in which the uncivilized and uncivilizable Others will soon overpower the civilizationally superior White Christians. For example, according to Bao Gangsheng, a liberal rising star in political science at Fudan University, 'there is good reason to believe that descendants of Hispanic immigrants in the United States are significantly less attached to democratic values than descendants of white-European Christian immigrants' (even though the single research he ostensibly cites has, in fact, no bearing on this claim); similarly, if the majority of Muslims in 'Egypt, Nigeria, Malaysia and Pakistan' support sharia law, then by extension 'European Muslim immigrants' must also be significantly less attached to democratic values than 'white Christians'; consequently, American and European liberal democracies may have already come to 'tipping points' of demographic suicide, as 'white-European Americans

[45]强世功 [Jiang Shigong], '陆地、海洋与文明秩序' ['Land, Ocean, and the Civilizational Order'], 读书 [*Reading*] 2019(5), (2019), p. 20.

[46]Luwei Rose Luqiu and Fan Yang, 'Islamophobia in China: News Coverage, Stereotypes, and Chinese Muslims' Perceptions of Themselves and Islam', *Asian Journal of Communication* 28(6), (2018), pp. 598–619; see also Human Rights Watch, '*Eradicating Ideological Viruses': China's Campaign of Repression Against Xinjiang's Muslims*, September 9, 2018, accessed March 11, 2020, https://www.hrw.org/report/2018/09/09/eradicating-ideological-viruses/chinas-campaign-repression-against-xinjiangs; Austin Ramzy and Chris Buckley, '"Absolutely No Mercy": Leaked Files Expose How China Organized Mass Detentions of Muslims', *New York Times*, November 16, 2019, accessed March 11, 2020, https://www.nytimes.com/interactive/2019/11/16/world/asia/china-xinjiang-documents.html.

[47]Tony Lin, 'After New Zealand Massacre, Islamophobia Spreads on Chinese Social Media', *Columbia Journalism Review*, March 21, 2019, accessed March 11, 2020, https://www.cjr.org/analysis/weibo-new-zealand-massacre.php.

are now less than 2/3 of the American population while Muslims exceed 5% of the European population'.[48]

This projected paranoia about the 'Fall of Western Civilization' is widely echoed among Chinese liberal intellectuals. Especially since the EU's 2015 refugee crisis, it has become increasingly typical of a Chinese liberal to chide western *baizuo* for being too 'soft' on Muslim and non-white immigrants— for naively providing multicultural accommodations and 'political-correctness' protections to 'inferiors' and 'barbarians' who are flooding into the 'civilized' world and sabotaging it from within by sheer number. Indeed, after the aforementioned 2017 Harvard talk by Gao Quanxi, his disciple came to his defense by invoking a characteristically beaconist analogy:

> Professor Gao is without doubt a 'barbarian visiting Rome' who has a deeper recognition of the greatness of Rome, and defends its civilization more fiercely, than native-born Romans, because it is a civilization that reflects his own ideal, something he yearns [for his own tribe] but could not have. He would not tolerate any barbarian forces that try to destroy Rome.[49]

Consequently, many Chinese liberal intellectuals are more than willing to side with Trump in his 'crusade' against the alleged 'barbarian forces that try to destroy Rome', and against the aiding-and-abetting *baizuo*. Even those who hesitate to take sides are ready to exonerate Trump's manifest racism, deny the role of 'crude "white supremacist" prejudices' in his rise, and assert that it was instead 'the [reverse-discriminatory] racial policies (and immigration policies) by the government [in the past], and the race-talks by [leftwing] cultural elites', that had inflamed white people's legitimate racial resentment.[50]

Concluding Remarks: Individuation, Information, Interaction, and Implication

In sum, the Trumpian metamorphosis of contemporary Chinese liberal intellectuals has deep roots in their beacon complex, which consists of two interrelated and mutually reinforcing components. On the one hand, their *political* beaconism, instantiated in the anti-CCP pilgrimage to an imagined West (and particularly an imagined United States) as a near-perfect political society, gives rise both to their neoliberal affinity on economic issues, and to their latent hostility toward *baizuo*, whom they take to be unappreciative nitpickers of near-perfect Western politics as well as unwitting appeasers of the CCP. On the other hand, having the same *fin-de-siècle* racist, colonialist and social Darwinist underpinnings as non-liberal, nationalistic civilizational vindicativism, the *civilizational* beaconism of Chinese liberal intellectuals makes them receptive to anti-immigrant and Islamophobic 'Fall-of-the-Western-Civilization' paranoia, exacerbates their hostility towards *baizuo*, and facilitates their Trumpian convergence with non-liberal counterparts.

It is worth cautioning that the beaconist dynamic of Trumpian metamorphosis described here is only meant to capture a *general* pattern and mechanism, the precise effects of which on particular Chinese liberal intellectuals may vary *across individuals*.

To begin with, as noted earlier, there are fervently Trump-idolizing Chinese liberals who are characteristically non-Trumpist on certain social and economic issues, as well as Chinese liberals who refuse to identify as *Chuanfen* but whose policy stances are substantially similar to what Trump epitomizes. Potential divergences between political and civilizational beaconisms may help explain this internal variety. One such hypothesis, testable *via* high-profile American political events unfolding at the time of this article's writing, is that the more political (*vis-à-vis* civilizational) one's

---

[48] 包刚升 [Bao Gangsheng], '西方政治的新现实——族群宗教多元主义与西方自由民主政体的挑战' ['A New Reality of Western Politics: Ethnic-Religious Pluralism as a Challenge to Western Liberal Democracies'], 政治学研究 [*CASS (Chinese Academy of Social Sciences) Journal of Political Science*] 2018(3), (2018), pp. 106–107.

[49] 叙拉古之惑 [Xulaguzhihuo], '为高全喜老师一辩——基于古典政治哲学的进路' ['A Defense of Professor Gao Quanxi: An Approach Based on Classical Philosophy'], *Sohu*, December 20, 2017, accessed March 11, 2020, http://www.sohu.com/a/211513053_788167.

[50] 刘瑜 [Liu Yu], '民粹与民主: 论美国政治中的民粹主义' ['Populism and Democracy: On Populism in American Politics'], 探索与争鸣 [*Exploration and Contestation*] 2016(10), (2016), p. 73.

beaconism, the likelier one trusts formal procedures of American constitutional democracy, whereas the more civilizational (*vis-à-vis* political) one's beaconism, the likelier one prioritizes triumph of Trumpist rightwing programs over integrity of the political system. Accordingly, for example, a more-political-than-civilizational beaconist would be less willing to acknowledge Trump's malignancy, corruption and ineptitude (as well as their obsequious enabling by his Republican sycophants) that had been exposed by the impeachment inquiries, insofar as the Republican-controlled Senate has formally 'acquitted' him after blocking witnesses, than would a more-civilizational-than-political beaconist who might gloatingly celebrate the crumbling of institutional checks-and-balances in the face of Trumpism. Conversely, *if* Trump loses the 2020 reelection, the more-political-than-civilizational beaconists' Trump-idolization is more likely to wane, as they could construe the loss as a vote-of-no-confidence by the 'American people' whom they equally idolize, whereas the more-civilizational-than-political beaconists are more likely to blame the loss on *baizuo*'s sabotage of Trump's leadership, and on American voters' acquiescence to *baizuo*'s program of civilizational self-destruction.

In the meantime, there are also Chinese liberal intellectuals who hold true to 'universal values' and rebuke their colleagues for succumbing to the Trumpian temptation. Although numerous anecdotal accounts corroborate the overwhelming presence of *Chuanfen* among contemporary Chinese liberal intellectuals, interested China scholars are welcome to develop quantitative measures to ascertain *Chuanfen*'s percentage, composition, and degree of influence in and out of the Chinese 'Liberal' camp.

For example, one may investigate to what extent age or generation predicts the likelihood of a Chinese liberal intellectual to become Trumpian, as there are at least two reasons for thinking a strong correlation exists in this regard. First, to the extent that *political* beaconism is fueled by enduring traumas of the Maoist era, younger liberal intellectuals who are further away in their experiences may be less susceptible to Procrustean equivalences between the Cultural Revolution and contemporary Western social justice activisms.

Second, it is worth noting that contemporary Chinese liberal intellectuals who are allured by the racist, colonialist and social Darwinist underpinnings of *civilizational* beaconism are, to a large extent, themselves victims of a deteriorating informational ecosystem. The increasingly tightened online censorship, the rise of semi-closed WeChat Moments as the main platform for news dissemination among Mainland Chinese, and the incessant production of anti-black-and-brown, Islamophobic, anti-immigrant, misogynist, homophobic and anti-*baizuo* contents by a group of dedicated 'post-truth' rightwing profiteers on the Chinese Internet,[51] have all made it more and more difficult to perceive the outside world undistorted. Against this background, younger liberal intellectuals growing up in the Internet era, thanks to their greater digital and information literacies, may be more equipped than their older colleagues in discerning misinformation and, consequently, in resisting Trumpian propaganda. Indeed, even well-intended anti-Trump Chinese liberals of older generations have frequently fallen prey to rampant alt-right misinformation on the Internet, and have relied on their younger liberal colleagues for correction.[52]

With regard to younger Chinese outside the 'intellectual circles (*zhishi quan*)', however, things are probably quite different. As a recent study shows, due to the Party-State's vigorous 'patriotic education' since 1989, younger Chinese have become more hawkish than older generations on foreign policy issues.[53] An educated guess, then, is that ordinary younger Chinese are more likely to

[51]See Chi Zhang, 'WeChatting American Politics: Misinformation, Polarization, and Immigrant Chinese Media', *Columbia Journalism Review*, April 19, 2018, accessed March 11, 2020, https://www.cjr.org/tow_center_reports/wechatting-american-politics-misinformation-polarization-and-immigrant-chinese-media.php/; Han Zhang, 'The "Post-Truth" Publication Where Chinese Students in America Get Their News', *New Yorker*, August 19, 2019, accessed March 11, 2020, https://www.newyorker.com/culture/culture-desk/the-post-truth-publication-where-chinese-students-in-america-get-their-news.
[52]See, e.g., 北大飞 [Beidafei], '错误信息导致错误结论——评秦晖老师《欧洲穆斯林政策的两大弊病》' ['Misinformation Leads to Wrong Conclusions: Comments on Professor Qin Hui's "Two Problems with Europe's Muslim Policy"'], *WeChat Public Account*, June 26, 2017, accessed March 11, 2020, http://www.dunjiaodu.com/qizhouzhi/2017-06-26/1389.html.
[53]Jessica Chen Weiss, 'How Hawkish Is the Chinese Public? Another Look at "Rising Nationalism" and Chinese Foreign Policy', *Journal of Contemporary China* 28(119), (2019), pp. 679–695.

dislike Trump because of his 'anti-Chinese' trade war, while at the same time more likely to agree with Trumpist anti-immigrant, anti-black-and-brown, anti-Muslim and anti-*baizuo* messages, as a result of the younger generation's greater receptivity to nationalistic civilizational vindicativism.

Meanwhile, it is likely that their receptivity to those messages would also be enhanced by interactions with liberal *Chuanfen* intellectuals. After all, being more versed in—and hence more capable of appropriating—liberal-democratic terminologies than their non-liberal counterparts, liberal *Chuanfen* intellectuals presumably have a crucial and significant role to play in legitimizing Trumpism in Chinese public discourses. Indeed, whether interactions with liberal *Chuanfen* intellectuals (for example, reading their articles praising Trump) increase one's receptivity to Trumpist ideas more than interactions with non-liberal *Chuanfen* intellectuals do should be an interesting topic for subsequent research.

Finally, not only does the Trumpian metamorphosis of Chinese liberal intellectuals supply novel research materials and topics for scholarly curiosity, but it also raises urgent practical issues that need to be reflected and acted upon. In particular, those concerned with China's political future and uneased by the prospect, however unrealistic in the short term, of having to choose between keeping the Party-State in place, on the one hand, and undergoing political transitions led by a liberal intelligentsia that embraces Trumpist ideologies, on the other hand, should think about how to develop effective countervailing strategies of public engagement and persuasion against the Trumpian metamorphoses of both Chinese liberal intellectuals and the Chinese public at large. In this regard, explicating the mechanisms of the beacon complex establishes the requisite theoretical framework, and thereby makes the first step towards such strategies.

Acknowledgments

The author thanks CHEN I-Chung, Deborah DAVIS, Paul GEWIRTZ, Darius LONGARINO, Andrew NATHAN, Guido PARIETTI, WANG Chaohua, Robert WILLIAMS, ZHANG Chenchen and two anonymous reviewers for helpful feedback on earlier drafts; CHEN Chun, Sechin Yeong-Shyang CHIEN, CHOW Po Chung, Jon ELSTER, LIU Qing, Tenzin Jinba, WANG Yan, WANG Yaqiu, YOU Tianlong, Liya YU, YUAN Yuan, ZHOU Lian and many others for conversations and encouragements that propelled the completion of this project; and LIANG Shan for timely assistance with source materials. The author is also grateful for the organizers and participants of ROUNDTABLE ON CHINESE PERSPECTIVES ON THE AMERICAN PRESIDENTIAL ELECTION (*Xuan Mei* [*iAmElection*] & 706 Youth Space, Beijing, 19 December 2015), FRONTIERS OF DEMOCRACY CONFERENCE (Tisch College of Civic Life, Tufts University, 23 June 2017), WORKSHOP ON LIBERALISM IN CONTEMPORARY CHINA (Weatherhead East Asian Institute, Columbia University, 6 October 2017) and CONTEMPORARY CHINA RESEARCH SEMINAR (Yale Law School, 6 February 2019 & 17 April 2019), where core ideas and precursory versions of this project were presented and discussed. Finally, the author would like to express his gratitude to the contributors, editors, readers and audiences of *Xuan Mei* [*iAmElection*], a civic engagement program the author co-directed with HUA Jianping, HUA Sirui, SHEN Xincheng, YOU Tianlong and ZHUANG Qiaoyi, which, throughout its existence from 2015 to 2019, strived to provide in-depth analyses of American politics for the Chinese-speaking world and to combat Trumpian misinformation on the Chinese Internet.

Disclosure statement

The author reports no potential conflict of interest.

ORCID

Yao Lin 🆔 http://orcid.org/0000-0002-8254-8939

Why Do Chinese Democrats Tend to Be More Nationalistic? Explaining Popular Nationalism in Urban China

Yang Zhong and Wonjae Hwang

ABSTRACT

Popular nationalism remains strong in China. What drives this strong nationalistic sentiment? This is the key question this study attempts to answer. The authors are particularly interested in the connection between domestic politics and outward nationalist feelings among Chinese urban residents, specifically the relationship between democratic orientation and regime support on the one hand and nationalist feelings on the other. Descriptive findings from random survey data on Chinese urban residents in 34 Chinese cities reveal that democracy-oriented Chinese urbanites tend to show stronger nationalistic feelings. A large volume of literature on the relationship between democratic value and nationalistic sentiments, however, generally suggests that people with more liberal democratic values tend to be less nationalistic. How should one, then, reconcile and explain this seemingly contradictory relationship in China? Upon further research, the study finds that system support is a confounding factor affecting Chinese urban residents' nationalistic sentiments. People with more nationalistic feelings tend to be those who show less support for the current system in China. Popular political discontent with the Chinese domestic system may very well have a spill-over effect on Chinese people's nationalist feelings toward the outside world.

Introduction

In recent years the world has witnessed open expression of strong Chinese nationalism both on the street and on the Internet in China.[1] People still remember one of the most recent massive anti-Japan popular protests that turned violent in many parts of China in 2012.[2] Japanese restaurants owned by Chinese citizens and Japanese cars made in China and driven by Chinese citizens were viciously attacked. Popular protests against South Korea over the deployment of **Terminal High Altitude Area Defense** (or THAAD) in South Korea against potential North Korean missile attacks in 2017 dismayed and alarmed many in the international community. The protesting and boycotting targets were South Korean Lotte department stores that were operated in China because Lotte gave up a piece of its lands to the Korean government for the deployment of the THAAD system. Strong nationalistic sentiments are widely expressed on the Internet in China, targeting mostly

---

[1] Jessica Chen Weiss methodically described the nationwide popular nationalist protests in China since the 1980s. Jessica Chen Weiss, *Powerful Patriots: Nationalist Protest in China's Foreign Relations* (Oxford, England: Oxford University Press, 2014); Jackson Woods and Bruce Dickson, 'Victims or Patriots: Disaggregating Nationalism in Urban China', *Journal of Contemporary China* 26(104), (2017), pp. 167–68. The authors do acknowledge that there is a debate among China watchers on whether nationalism is rising in China in the last few decades; Alastair Iain Johnston, 'Is Chinese Nationalism Rising? Evidence from Beijing', *International Security* 41(3), (2016/2017), pp. 7–43.

[2] Min Zhou and Hanning Wang, 'Anti-Japanese Sentiment among Chinese University Students: The Influence of Contemporary Nationalist Propaganda', *Journal of Current Chinese Affairs* 46(1), (2017), p. 169.

western countries and China's neighboring countries that have territorial disputes with China. In fact, the Internet has become a major tool or platform for Chinese nationalists, especially for *fen qings* (angry youth who were born after the 1980s), to express their nationalist feelings.[3]

What drives the popular nationalistic sentiments? This is the key question the authors will attempt to answer in this research. The authors are particularly interested in the relationship between domestic views such as democratic values and regime support and nationalist feelings among Chinese citizens. According to news reports, young people (often referred to as *fen qings*) are often the main participants of popular nationalistic protests in recent years in China.[4] The world learns from the literature on Chinese political culture that young people in China also tend to be more supportive of democratic values and more critical of the Chinese authorities than the older generations.[5] Descriptive findings from the survey research on Chinese urban residents in this article also reveal that democracy-oriented Chinese urbanites tend to show stronger nationalistic feelings. This is contrary to what has been claimed that Chinese nationalists tend to have authoritarian personality.[6]

A large volume of literature on the relationship between democratic value and nationalistic sentiments, however, generally suggests that they are negatively related to each other. In other words, people with more liberal democratic values tend to be less nationalistic. How do we, then, reconcile and explain this seemingly contradictory relationship in China? Studying this relationship carries importance in both theoretical terms and practical implications. Is the Chinese case a deviation with regard to the relationship between democratic values and nationalist feelings? Is popular nationalism indeed a double-edged sword for the Chinese government?

The major findings of this article are summarized as follows. The authors found that strong nationalistic feelings among Chinese urban residents are associated with democratic orientation: support for electoral democracy in China and freedom of expression. These findings seem to contradict the incompatible theory between democratic values and nationalism. The authors further found that system support is a confounding factor affecting Chinese urban residents' nationalistic sentiments. People with more nationalistic feelings tend to be those who show less support for the current system in China. In other words, popular discontent among Chinese urbanites with Chinese domestic politics spills over into their feelings toward Chinese foreign policies. Chinese people who feel they are deprived of their democratic and civil rights at home also expect China to be properly respected by other countries in international affairs.

Relationship Between Democracy and Nationalism

Democracy and nationalism are probably the two most researched and most controversial topics in contemporary political science. Yet, this relationship is not sufficiently studied, and there is much less consensus on the relationship between the two. Modern nationalism started with the Treaty of Westphalia in 1648 which led to the formation of nation-states in Europe. Nationalism in the 18th, 19th and early 20th centuries was perceived as a progressive and positive term describing national independent and liberation movements against imperial control. The rise of Nazism in Germany and aggressive imperialism of Japan in the first half of the 20th century turned nationalism into a somewhat negative term. Nationalism in today's Western lexicon is often associated with narrow-minded parochialism, especially in the age of globalization. Democracy as a functioning political system, on the other hand, occurred much later than

---

[3] See Shameer Modongal, 'Development of nationalism in China', *Cogent Social Sciences* 2, (2016), pp. 1–7, accessed November 16, 2018, https://www.tandfonline.com/doi/pdf/10.1080/23311886.2016.1235749.

[4] See Lijun Yang and Yongnian Zheng, 'Fen Qing (Angry Youth) in Contemporary China', *Journal of Contemporary China* 21(76), (2012), pp. 637–53.

[5] Yongnian Zheng, 'Development and Democracy: Are They Compatible in China?', *Political Science Quarterly* 9, (1994), pp. 235–259; Yang Zhong, 'Democratic Values among Chinese Peasantry: An Empirical Study,' *China: An International Journal* 3(2), (2005), p. 209; Alfred Chan and Paul Nesbitt-Larking, 'Critical Citizenship and Civil Society in Contemporary China', *Canadian Journal of Political Science* 28(2), (1995), p. 308.

[6] Cong Riyun, 'Nationalism and Democratization in Contemporary China', *Journal of Contemporary China* 18(62), (2009), pp. 841–43.

modern nation-state. Earlier democracies such as the United States and some Western European countries were founded in already well-established national boundaries and nation-states.

In general, there are two schools of thought with regard to the relationship between nationalism and democracy: the compatible view and the incompatible view. The compatible view is based upon the following connections between nationalism and democracy. The first compatible connection between the two can be dated back to the revolutionary idea of the nation put forward by French political activist Emmanuel Sieyes.[7] According to Sieyes, the concept of nation is associated with constitutional government and political participation. Democracy, emancipation, political participation and self-determination are all treated as the same. Sieyes also linked the concept of a nation-state with social contract. As Van De Putte puts it,

> The nation is not a body to which one naturally belongs by fate; nationality is not a natural determination. The integration and sense of community which characterize the nation are that of an abstract legal community that does not exist by nature, but is only constitute in and through the mutual recognition of one another's rights ... ... .A nation has no natural borders based on language, race, or ethnicity, but only political-moral borders, and they reach only as far as the principles of the social contract holds.[8]

t seems that the revolutionary concept of the nation is that of modern-day's civic nation. A nation defined as such is more of a political concept than anything else. Furthermore, Liah Greenfeld believed that 'nationalism was the form in which democracy appeared in the world'.[9] Sovereignty and equality are key elements of both nationalism and democracy. The French Revolution symbolized this type of symbiotic relationship between nationalism and democracy.[10] It should be pointed out that Sieyes' conception of the nation also does not exclude diversity because a democratic nation has to be pluralistic and multi-cultural. Obviously, the revolutionary concept of the nation is an ideal type and tends to blur the lines between the concept of a nation and a democracy.

The argument that common national identity or unity is a necessary precondition for a functioning democracy offers another explanation for the positive connection between nationalism and democracy. This view dates back to John Steward Mill who believed that the stronger the national bond the more effective of the democratic system.[11] According to this view, nationalism creates compassion, care, intimacy and solidarity among fellow nationals which provide favorable conditions for democracy and strengthen democratic system. History does show that countries with stronger national cohesion and unity have a better chance for being stable democracies. Moreover, nationalism promotes democracy via political trust and participation. As well researched, political trust and participation are positive factors contributing to functioning democracy. It is easier to establish trust among people with strong national bond and shared identity.[12] Political participation is another key to the success of any democracy. According to Margaret Moore, political engagement strengthens shared national identity and fosters cooperation.[13] It has also been mentioned that common language facilitates political communication and participation among citizens in a democracy.[14] In addition, any democracy has to have territorial boundary, and a nation-state provides that boundary.[15] Therefore, the authors argue that any modern democracy has to be built upon a nation-state.[16]

---

[7]Andre van de Putte, 'Democracy and Nationalism', *Canadian Journal of Philosophy* 22, (1992), pp. 161–195.

[8]Ibid., pp. 167–68.

[9]Liah Greenfeld, *Nationalism: Five Roads to Modernity* (Cambridge, MA: Harvard University Press, 1992), p. 10.

[10]Rogers Brubaker, *Citizenship and Nationhood in France and Germany* (Cambridge, MA: Harvard University Press, 1992), pp. 39–49.

[11]Andre van de Putte, 'Democracy and Nationalism', p. 177.

[12]Russell Dalton, *Democracy and Its Critics* (New Haven, CT: Yale University Press, 1999), pp. 58–59; David Miller, *On Nationality* (Oxford: Oxford University Press, 1995).

[13]Margaret Moore, 'Normative Justifications for Liberal Nationalism: Justice, Democracy and National Identity', *Nations and Nationalism* 7(1), (2001), pp. 1–20.

[14]Dominique Schnapper, 'Lingistic Pluralism as a Serious Challenge to Democratic Life', in *Cultural Diversity versus Solidarity*, ed. Philippe Van Parijs (Bruxelles: De Boeck, 2004), pp. 213–25.

[15]Marc Helbling, 'Nationalism and Democracy: Competing or Complementary Logics', *Living Reviews in Democracy* 1, (2009), p. 8.

[16]Wang Shaoguang, 'Nationalism and Democracy', *China Public Administration Review* 1, (2004), pp. 83–99.

The third positive connection between nationalism and democracy manifests in historical events. Democratization and nationalist movements often occur simultaneously. The world's oldest democracy was born out of a nationalist movement; the American Revolution is an example. Recent examples come from Eastern European countries and the former Soviet republics where democratization coincided with resurgence of nationalism.[17] In fact, regaining national independence became a major goal of the democratization movement among Eastern European countries and the former USSR republics which were controlled by the Soviet empire.

Meanwhile, the opposing view argues that nationalism and democracy are incompatible with each other. First of all, these two concepts fundamentally conflict with each other. Nationalism is about exclusion while democracy emphasizes inclusion and diversity.[18] Nationalism creates 'us' versus 'them' mentality, which may further lead to conformity among members of the same nationality and lack of tolerance. In other words, people of the same national group are expected to think and act alike. Minority or moderate nationalists may be branded as unpatriotic or even traitors by extreme nationalists. Tolerance and open-mindedness are considered essential in a functioning democracy.

Furthermore, it also often happens that non-citizens of a country are treated unfairly and are excluded from participation in the democratic process of the country of their residence. For example, Russians who lived in the former Soviet republics in the Baltics were not offered citizenship after the collapse of the Soviet Union due to resurgent nationalism in those countries. Therefore, nationalism does not promote real democracy. History also shows that extreme nationalism could lead to military aggression against democracies, as shown by Hitler's Germany in the 1930s. Second, it is also argued that there is lack of evidence to show that shared cultural or national identity necessarily facilitates communication and promotes mutual trust among fellow nationals.[19] In fact, shared political ideology, moral values and material interests play much a more important role in fostering inter-personal communication and trust than shared language and skin color. This has been demonstrated time and again by patterns of voting behavior in democratic systems.[20]

What is the relationship between democracy and nationalism in contemporary China? Democratic movements and nationalist movements in China were intricately related to each other prior to 1949 since the two movements shared many of the same ideals, such as national equality, national self-determination, and national liberation.[21] The republican revolution led by Dr. Sun Yatsen was initially a nationalistic movement by Han Chinese to overthrow the Manchu-dominated Qing Dynasty. The birth of the Chinese Communist Party (CCP) in 1921 was directly impacted by the May 4th Movement which was both a popular nationalist movement and a democratic movement.

The argument of this article is that Chinese nationalist feelings toward the outside world are intricately linked to Chinese people's views of Chinese domestic politics. The authors are particularly interested in the relationship between democratic values and system support on the one hand and popular nationalism on the other. As mentioned earlier, much of Western literature on the relationship between nationalism and democratic values suggests that people with stronger democratic values tend to be less nationalistic since an important element of democratic values is tolerance and preference for peaceful resolution of dispute. In fact, this belief leads to the democratic peace theory arguing that it is less likely that democracies fight other democracies.[22] In the Chinese case, however, modern Chinese history indicates that nationalism is often associated with the drive for democracy. More importantly, the authors are particularly interested in the

[17]Peter Rutland, 'Nationalism and Democracy in Armenia', *Europe-Asia Studies* 46(5), (1994), pp. 839–61.
[18]Arash Abizadeh, 'Does Liberal Democracy Presuppose a Cultural Nation? Four Arguments', *American Political Science Review* 96(3), (2002), pp. 495–509.
[19]Ibid.
[20]George Rabinowitz and Stuart MacDonald, 'A Directional Theory of Issue Voting', *American Political Science Review* 83(1), (1989), pp. 93–121.
[21]Wang Shaoguang, 'Nationalism and Democracy'.
[22]Zeev Maoz and Bruce Russett, 'Normative and Structural Causes of Democratic Peace, 1946–1986', *American Political Science Review* 87(3), (1993), pp. 624–638.

relationship between domestic political views and popular nationalism. The authors suspect that people's political dismay or dissatisfaction with domestic politics is contagious and may very well have a spillover effect on their outward nationalist feelings. Therefore, two general hypotheses of this article are that both democratic values and system support among urban residents in China are positively related to their strong nationalist feelings.

The authors base their hypotheses on the intricate connection between domestic politics and foreign affairs. There is extensive literature on the relationship between domestic politics and international relations.[23] Indeed, it is often said that a country's foreign policy is an extension of its domestic politics. Authoritarian China is no exception to the 'two-level game' of interaction between domestic and international politics,[24] even though the focus in this research is on the population level. A number of studies have found that personal values affect foreign policy attitudes.[25] In their study, Rathbun, Kertzer, Reifler, Goren and Scotto found that people in the United States take foreign policy personally.[26] Individuals' basic values define their foreign policy attitudes. People with conservation values are linked to support for more militant and hawkish foreign policies and people holding universalistic values tend to be more supportive of international cooperation.

With a similar logic, the authors argue that people's dissatisfaction and deprivation in domestic politics affect their nationalist feelings toward the outside world. Many Chinese people have become frustrated with the domestic politics and the current political system in China. One of the reasons for this feeling of unhappiness and frustration is that China is not a democratic country. Due to lack of democracy, many Chinese people may feel that they are deprived of their democratic rights and civil liberties. This feeling of deprivation travels to the domain of foreign affairs. Given China's century of humiliation between the 19th and 20th century and the rise of China as an economic power in the last few decades, this same group of people may also feel that China's international status is not well respected and China is deprived of its proper place on the international stage. In this regard, they are likely to strongly support bigger role for China in the international arena and more nationalistic policies with respect to disputes with neighboring countries.

Data

Data for this research were collected in a random telephone survey covering 34 large cities throughout China, most of which are provincial capital cities.[27] The cities represent different regions and different levels of economic development. The survey was carried out between October and November of 2013 by Center for Public Opinion Research of Shanghai Jiao Tong University. The sample size for each city is approximately 100 people, totaling 3,491 observations from all 34 cities. The sampling frame includes both stationary and cell phone numbers in these cities. Computer Assisted Telephone Interview (CATI) system generated random telephone numbers. Trained graduate and undergraduate students at Shanghai Jiao Tong University and several

[23]Robert Putnam, 'Diplomacy and Domestic Politics: The Logic of Two-Level Games', *International Organization* 42(3), (1988), pp. 427–460.

[24]Jessica Chen Weiss, *Powerful Patriots: Nationalist Protest in China's Foreign Relations*, p. 16.

[25]Joh Hurwitz and Mark Peffley, 'How are Foreign Policy Attitudes Structured? A Hierarchical Model', *American Political Science Review* 81(4), (1987), pp. 1218–31; Richard K. Herrmann, Philip E. Tetlock and Penny S. Visser, 'Mass Public Decisions to Go to War: A Cognitive-Interactionist Framework', *American Political Science Review* 93(3), (1999), pp. 553–73; Brian C. Rathbun, 'Hierarchy and Community at Home and Abroad: Evidence of a Common Structure of Domestic and Foreign-Policy Beliefs in American Elites', *Journal of Conflict Resolution* 51(3), (2007), pp. 379–407; William O. Chittick, Keith R. Billingsley and Rick Travis, 'A Three-Dimensional Model of American Foreign-policy beliefs', *International Studies Quarterly* 39(3), (1995), pp. 313–31.

[26]Brian C. Rathbun et al., 'Taking Foreign Policy Personally: Personal Values and Foreign Policy Attitudes', *International Studies Quarterly* 60(1), (2016), pp. 124–137.

[27]The following is the list of the surveyed cities: Beijing, Shanghai, Tianjin, Chongqing, Changchun, Changsha, Chengdu, Dalian, Fuzhou, Guangzhou, Guizhou, Harbin, Haikou, Hangzhou, Hefei, Huhhot, Jinan, Kunming, Lanzhou, Nanchang, Nanjing, Nanning, Ningbo, Qingdao, Shenyang, Shenzhen, Shijiazhuang, Taiyuan, Wuhan, Xian, Xining, Xiamen, Yinchuan, and Zhengzhou.

other surrounding universities in Shanghai conducted the anonymous survey.[28] Surveyees' responses can be influenced by city-level factors such as the level of economic development. To address this hierarchical structure of our data and explain variation across cities, this article employs a multilevel model with varying intercepts.

Research Design

As many scholars have pointed out, nationalism is an ambiguous term lacking a consensus definition.[29] Benedict Anderson's famous definition of a nation as 'an imagined community'[30] implies that national self-identity is at the core of nationalism. National identity involves feelings and passion.[31] Yongnian Zheng argues that there is an international dimension of nationalism. In his view, 'Nationalism [here] is about people's perceptions of China's position in the nation-state system' and 'it is about China's sovereignty, independence and its proper relations with other nation-states'.[32] In fact, Anna Costa points out that, 'The majority of English language literature on Chinese nationalism deals with Chinese foreign policy and China's position in the world politics—often prompted by concerns about the influence of nationalism on China's interactions with the outside world.'[33] In this research, nationalist feelings among Chinese urban residents about China's place in the world and the sovereignty issue of Diaoyu Islands, a disputed territory with Japan, are the dependent variables, and they are measured based on answers to three questions. The first two questions ask the respondents about China's role in Asia and the world, which measure more benign nationalist feelings (see Table 1). Benign nationalism refers to a feeling of national pride not necessarily associated with national prejudice and ill intention against other nations. This type of nationalism is often referred to as 'patriotism'.[34] Majority or close to 70% of the urban residents in the survey either strongly agree or agree that China should play a leading role in Asian affairs. As for China's place in the world, about half of respondents believe that China should play a leading role in world affairs. This may not be the case 20 or even 10 years ago. A third question asks the respondents' support for the government over the Diaoyu Islands dispute: 'Do you support the Chinese government to take Diaoyu Islands back by force even though such an action may cause a war with Japan?' This question measures more aggressive nationalistic feelings. Aggressive nationalism often involves hostile feelings against other nations or countries. Surprisingly more than half of the urban respondents support such an action by the Chinese government (see Table 1). The authors combine answers to these questions to create the variable of Chinese urbanites' nationalism, of which value ranges from 3 (very non-nationalistic) to 13 (very nationalistic). Alternatively, the authors use only answers to the question on Diaoyu to generate the aggressive nationalism variable, ranging from 1 (non-nationalistic), 2 (neutral), to 3 (nationalistic), and answers to the questions on the role of China in Asian and world affairs to generate the benign nationalism variable, ranging from 2 (non-nationalistic) to 10 (very nationalistic). Then, for the purpose of comparison with the aggressive nationalism, the benign nationalism is coded as 1 (non-nationalistic), 2 (neutral), and 3 (nationalistic). The mean value of nationalism is about 9.5, implying that more than half of the respondents are nationalistic.

---

[28]On survey research in China, see Melanie Manion, 'A Survey of Survey Research on Chinese Politics: What Have We Learned?', in *Contemporary Chinese Politics: New Sources, Methods and Field Strategies*, ed. Allen Carlson, Mary Gallagher, Kenneth Lieberthal and Melanie Manion (New York: Cambridge University Press, 2010), pp. 181–200.

[29]Yongnian Zheng, *Discovering Chinese Nationalism in China: Modernization, Identity, and International Relations*, pp. ix–x.

[30]Benedict Anderson, *Imagined Communities: Reflections on Origin and Spread of Nationalism* (NY, U.S.A.: Verso, 1983).

[31]Arthur Waldron, 'Theories of Nationalism and Historical Explanation', *World Politics* 37(3), (1985), p. 417.

[32]Zheng, *Discovering Chinese Nationalism in China*, p. xi.

[33]Anna Costa, 'Focusing on Chinese Nationalism: An Inherently Flawed Perspective? A Reply to Allen Carlson', *Nations and Nationalism* 20(1), (2014), p. 94.

[34]On the concept of patriotism, see Elina Sinkkonen, 'Nationalism, Patriotism and Foreign Policy Attitudes among Chinese University Students', *The China Quarterly* 216, (2013), pp. 1046–1047.

Table 1. Nationalist Feelings of Chinese Urban Residents (%)

	Strongly agree	Agree	Disagree	Strongly disagree	Hard to say	N
China should play a leading role in Asian affairs	33.5	33.2	12.3	4.9	16.1	3491
China should play a leading role in world affairs	23.2	32.7	18.0	7.7	18.4	3491
Hard to say	Support		Not support		Hard to say	N
Do you support the Chinese government to take Diaoyu Islands back by force even though such an action may cause a war with Japan?	54.6		29.4		16.0	3491

Source: *Social and Political Values of Chinese Urban Residents, 2013.*

The explanatory variables in the analysis of nationalist feelings among Chinese urbanites are two democratic value factors. The first factor is public support for freedom of speech. Those who support freedom of speech are likely to be nationalistic. The respondents were asked about their opinions on whether everyone should be allowed to express their political views. Most respondents strongly agreed (59.2%) or agreed (29%). Only a small percent of them disagreed (6.9%) or strongly disagreed (2.4%).

The second factor is public support for electoral democracy in China. Chinese national leaders are currently not directly elected by the population. The survey examined respondents' attitudes toward democracy by asking their opinions on whether central government leaders in China should be directly democratically elected by the people. More than half of the respondents either strongly agreed (33.1%) or agreed (26.7%) with the direct election of Chinese top leaders. About 18.3 and 10.9% of them disagreed and strongly disagreed, respectively, while the remaining 11% of them were neutral. The authors argue that those who support electoral democracy tend to be nationalistic.

Meanwhile, as discussed above, the authors suspect that there exists a confounding variable, *System Support*, in the models of Chinese nationalism. In other words, a respondent's support for the regime could be the real driving factor that affects nationalism through its impact on support for *Democratic Election* and *Freedom of Speech*. This is because people who are not happy with the domestic system are likely to maintain negative views on anything that is being done by the regime, including both domestic and foreign policies. Therefore, it is crucial to include *System Support* as the key variable in the model of nationalism to explore the connection between domestic politics and outward nationalist feelings among Chinese urbanites.

Methodologically, however, if *System Support* works as a confounding variable in the model, this article faces an endogeneity issue that may cause biased estimates. To control for a potential endogenous relationship between *System Support* and *Democratic Election* (along with *Freedom of Speech*), the authors take a two-stage estimation method. In the first stage, the authors formulate a model for democratic election, in which the system support variable along with other theoretically associated variables such as freedom of speech, and education are used as predictors. Similarly, the authors estimate a model for freedom of speech.[35] In this stage, therefore, the authors can generate a residual term of electoral democracy or freedom of speech from each model. Simply, each residual term includes only the remained variation in the variable unaccounted by system support or other control variables. Therefore, the authors can minimize the concern about a potential endogeneity between system support and democratic election or freedom of speech in the model of nationalism.[36] In the second stage, the authors use these two residual terms obtained in the first stage on behalf of their original variables.

---

[35]In these models, the system support variable has a very significant negative impact on the variable of support for democratic election or freedom of speech. The results confirm that those who do not support the regime are very likely to favor democratic election or freedom of speech. The F-statistics of the first-stage regression are 15.52 and 7.7 in each model, which are statistically significantly different from zero. Thus, the instrumentals have a strong first stage.

[36]See Erik Gartzke, 'Preferences and the Democratic Peace', *International Studies Quarterly* 44(2), (2000), pp. 191–210.

As mentioned earlier, people's nationalist feelings and pride are often accompanied and strengthened by the economic success of the country they live in. China has been experiencing rapid economic growth in the last three decades which has made China the second largest economy in the world. It is only natural to expect China's economic achievement has propped up popular nationalism in China. Therefore, in the analyses, the authors also include people's sense of economic achievement or success as a factor affecting Chinese urban residents' nationalistic feelings. Survey respondents were asked what kind of economic success China has made during the reform era. On the one hand, a minority of people either say that China has achieved no economic success (1.7%) or insignificant economic success (13.3%) with 11.9% of them finding it hard to answer this question. On the other hand, close to a quarter (23.7%) of our urban respondents believe that China has achieved significant economic success and about half (49.4%) of them say China has achieved some economic success.

There are several control variables in the analysis. A respondent's personal characteristics can be associated with their support for the regime and nationalism. *Male* is coded '1' for male respondents and '0' otherwise. *Age* is coded '1' for those who are younger than 30, '2' for their thirties, '3' for their forties, '4' for their fifties, and '5' for those who are older than 59. *Education* is coded 1 for those who finish no school education, '2' for elementary school, '3' for middle school, '4' for high school, and '5' for college and above education. *Income* is coded '1' for those who make below 1000 Chinese yuan as monthly income, '2' for between 1000 and 2000, '3' for between 2001 and 3000, and so on. The maximum value is 11 for those who make more than 10000 Chinese yuan monthly. *Han* is coded '1' for Han Chinese and '0' otherwise.

Finally, since surveyees' responses can be influenced by city-level factors, the authors include a control variable at the city level. The level of economic development as represented by GDP per capita for the 34 cities included in our study.[37] Since economic development is positively associated with satisfaction with the system, people living in economically developed cities are less likely to be nationalistic than people in relatively poor cities.

Since this research measures nationalism in three different ways, the authors utilize the ordinary least squares (OLS) regression (Table 2) and the ordered logit (Tables 3 and 4) model for estimation. In the ordered logit models in Tables 2 and 3, it is necessary to check the parallel-lines (proportional odds) assumption that the effects of predictors on the dependent variable are constant across all contrasts. According to Brant test of the assumption, three variables, *System Support, Freedom of Speech*, and *Male*, violate the assumption. To correct the violation of the assumption, therefore, the authors also employ the generalized ordered logit model in Models 7 and 11.

Meanwhile, since surveyees' responses can be grouped based on their living cities, the data have a hierarchical structure. Unless the hierarchical structure of the data is properly addressed, the hypothesis testing results could be misleading. The authors specify the hierarchical structure using a multilevel model with varying intercepts. This specification allows the intercept term to be a function of the city level GDP per capita. Therefore, the city level economic development is assumed to affect the baseline level of nationalism in different cities. In addition, the multilevel model allows us to generate two different disturbance terms: the city level disturbance and the individual level disturbance. By testing whether the city level disturbance term is statistically different from zero, which means that there are no significant variances remained to be explained at the city level, it can be checked whether the city level GDP per capita is a good predictor of varying intercepts across cities. To generate reliable estimates from the multilevel model, the authors employ Markov chain Monte Carlo (MCMC) estimation methods using MLwiN software program (version 3.01). Fifty-thousand iterations along with 10,000 iterations for the burn-in period are simulated for estimation.

---

[37]This variable is the annual GDP per capita of the 34 cities in 2012, obtained from the government websites of the 34 cities.

Table 2. System Support and Nationalism in China (34 cities)

DV: Nationalism†	Model 1 (OLS)	Model 2 (OLS)	Model 3 (OLS)	Model 4‡ (multilevel)
Fixed effects				
Individual level				
System Support		−0.143 (0.056)***	−0.149 (0.055)***	−0.150 (0.056)***
Democratic Election	0.187 (0.032)***	0.223 (0.032)***	0.223 (0.032)***	0.221 (0.030)***
Freedom of Speech	0.240 (0.045)***	0.293 (0.046)***	0.293 (0.046)***	0.291 (0.042)***
Economic Success	0.225 (0.042)***	0.223 (0.042)***	0.227 (0.042)***	0.226 (0.040)***
Male	0.373 (0.084)***	0.368 (0.084)***	0.360 (0.083)***	0.357 (0.084)***
Age	0.266 (0.038)***	0.243 (0.038)***	0.235 (0.036)***	0.230 (0.036)***
Education	0.092 (0.045)**	0.034 (0.045)		
Income	0.039 (0.016)**	0.033 (0.016)*	0.034 (0.016)**	0.036 (0.016)**
Han	0.240 (0.147)	0.244 (0.147)*	0.249 (0.147)*	0.294 (0.145)**
Constant	5.411 (0.371)***	7.726 (0.334)***	7.877 (0.265)***	9.840 (1.586)***
City level				
GDP per capita				−0.180 (0.143)
Random effects				
City level				0.026 (0.019)
Individual level				5.565 (0.134)***
N	3491	3491	3491	3491
F-statistic	23.99***	22.04***	24.72***	
Root MSE	2.370	2.369	2.368	
Deviance				15,912.80

Note: Standard errors are in parentheses. *P*-values: *** *p*< 0.01, ** *p*< 0.05, * *p*< 0.10. The hypotheses tests are based on two-tailed tests.

†The dependent variable is created based on three questions: Diaoyu, the role of China in Asian Affairs and also in the world affairs. Its value ranges from 3 (very non-nationalistic) to 13 (very nationalistic).

‡ Multilevel analysis with MCMC estimation (50,000 iterations, 10,000 burn-in period). Significant credibility intervals: *** 99%, ** 95%, * 90%.

Results and Analysis

In Models 1 through 4 in Table 2, *Nationalism*, the dependent variable, is created based on three questions on Diaoyu, the role of China in Asian affairs and also in world affairs. In Model 1, the authors do not include *System Support* as the key variable to evaluate how exclusion of this variable may affect performance of other variables. Therefore, in Model 2, the authors include *System Support* as the key variable and control for its endogenous relationship with *Democratic Election* and *Freedom of Speech*. It is well known that education and income variables are highly correlated. To control for potential effects that this correlation may generate in the model, the authors also estimate the same model without the education variable in Model 3. Finally, to address the hierarchical structure of the data, the authors utilize a multilevel model in Model 4.

The system support variable has a statistically significant negative impact on nationalism as appeared in Models 2, 3, and 4. The results confirm our expectation that people who do not support the regime are likely to be nationalistic. The two variables, 'support for democratic election' and 'freedom of speech', have strong positive effects on nationalism in Model 1, as expected. Even after the authors include the key variable, *System Support*, and control for the potential endogeneity issue in Models 2, 3, and 4, these variables remain to be statistically significant. However, the sizes of impact of these variables on nationalism become a bit bigger in later models. This implies that, by overlooking the confounding variable and its endogenous relationship with the two variables, the authors are likely to underestimate their impact on nationalism.

In the models involving aggressive nationalism in Table 3, overall the empirical results and their implications remain to be consistent with the ones in Table 2. However, one notable difference is found in Model 7. While *System Support* appears to have significant negative effects on nationalism in all other models, the results in the generalized ordered logit model tell a bit different story. The system support variable does not have significant effects on creating differences between two groups of people, one who chooses to not support the government aggressive action against

Table 3. System Support and Aggressive Nationalism in China (34 cities)

DV: Aggressive Nationalism	Model 5 (ordered logit)	Model 6 (ordered logit)	Model 7† (generalized ordered logit)	Model 8‡ (multilevel ordered logit)
Fixed effects				
Individual level				
System Support		−0.130 (0.047)***		−0.133 (0.048)**
S.S. (1 vs. 2, 3)			0.039 (0.053)	
S.S. (1, 2 vs. 3)			−0.218 (0.049)***	
Democratic Election	0.073 (0.025)***	0.088 (0.026)***	0.088 (0.026)***	0.089 (0.025)***
Freedom of Speech	0.173 (0.033)***	0.192 (0.034)***	0.191 (0.034)***	0.192 (0.034)***
Economic Success	−0.008 (0.034)	−0.015 (0.034)	−0.015 (0.034)	−0.016 (0.034)
Male	0.493 (0.068)***	0.493 (0.068)***		0.502 (0.069)***
Male (1 vs. 2,3)			0.400 (0.078)***	
Male (1,2 vs.3)			0.554 (0.072)***	
Age	0.124 (0.031)***	0.120 (0.030)***	0.120 (0.031)***	0.119 (0.031)***
Income	−0.009 (0.013)	−0.015 (0.013)	−0.016 (0.013)	−0.014 (0.013)
Han	0.130 (0.112)	0.128 (0.113)	0.122 (0.113)	0.160 (0.120)
Constant (1 vs. 2,3)	0.700 (0.242)***	−0.642 (0.215)***	0.354 (0.220)	1.393 (1.466)
Constant (1,2 vs. 3)	1.410 (0.244)***	0.069 (0.214)	0.073 (0.214)	0.675 (1.466)
City level				
GDP per capita				−0.070 (0.131)
Random effects				
City level				0.042 (0.022)***
Individual level				0.746 (0.018)***
N	3491	3491	3491	3491
χ^2	109.26***	113.37***	163.95***	
DIC				6754.67

Note: The dependent variable is created based on the question on Diaoyu. The ordinal variable consists of three values: 1 (non-nationalistic), 2 (indifferent), and 3 (nationalistic). Standard errors are in parentheses. *P*-values: *** $p< 0.01$, ** $p< 0.05$, * $p< 0.10$. two-tailed tests.
† Corrections of the violation of the parallel-lines (proportionality) assumption. A coefficient (1 vs. 2, 3) indicates the effect of the variable on the difference between '*non-nationalistic*' group and the group of '*indifferent* and *nationalistic.*' A coefficient (1, 2 vs. 3) shows the effect of the variables on the difference between '*non-nationalistic* and *indifferent*' group and '*nationalistic*' group.
‡ Multilevel analysis with MCMC estimation (50,000 iterations, 10,000 burn-in period). Significant credibility intervals: *** 99%, ** 95%, * 90%.

Japan over the Diaoyu issue and the other who takes neutral position or choose to support the government on the issue. However, the system support variable is creating significant differences between the group of people who support the government aggressive action over the issue and the others who do not support or take neutral position on the disputed islands issue. In other words, those people who are not happy with the system are very likely to support taking the Diaoyu Islands back by force.

In the models concerning benign nationalism in Table 4, overall the substantive findings remain the same. However, one notable difference found in Model 11 is the system support variable. With respect to benign nationalism, this variable has significant positive impact on nationalism when it comes to the differences between two groups of people, one who do not support the role of China in Asian and world affairs and the other who are indifferent or support the role of China. However, the system support variable has significant negative effects on benign nationalism when it comes to the differences between two groups of people, one who support the role of China and the others. In other words, those people who do not support the system or are indifferent are very likely to link to benign nationalism.

To effectively measure substantive effects of predictors on nationalism, this article simulated Models 3, 6, and 10 using *Clarify* simulation Program[38] and report the simulated results in Table 5. To this end, the authors fixed all dummy variables at their zeros and all other variables at their mean values. Holding all other covariates constant, when the value of the system support variable changes

---

[38]Michael Tomz, Jason Wittenberg, and Gary King, *Clarify: Software for Interpreting and Presenting Statistical Results*, January 5, 2003, accessed July 12, 2017, htttp://gking.harvard.edu/clarify/.

Table 4. System Support and Benign Nationalism in China (34 cities)

DV: Benign Nationalism	Model 9 (ordered logit)	Model 10 (ordered logit)	Model 11† (generalized ordered logit)	Model 12‡ (multilevel ordered logit)
Fixed effects				
Individual level				
System Support		−0.122 (0.044)***		−0.123 (0.045)***
S.S. (1 vs. 2, 3)			0.193 (0.059)***	
S.S. (1, 2 vs. 3)			−0.214 (0.047)***	
Democratic Election	0.135 (0.025)***	0.159 (0.025)***	0.160 (0.025)***	0.159 (0.025)***
Freedom of Speech	0.090 (0.035)***	0.129 (0.036)***	0.191 (0.046)***	0.129 (0.034)***
S.S. (1 vs. 2, 3)			0.106 (0.036)***	
S.S. (1, 2 vs. 3)				
Economic Success	0.214 (0.033)***	0.208 (0.033)***	0.208 (0.033)***	0.211 (0.033)**
Male	0.105 (0.068)	0.113 (0.068)*		0.110 (0.069)*
Male (1 vs. 2,3)			−0.030 (0.100)	
Male (1,2 vs.3)			0.156 (0.072)**	
Age	0.120 (0.030)***	0.120 (0.030)***	0.122 (0.030)***	0.119 (0.030)***
Income	0.032 (0.013)**	0.025 (0.013)*	0.025 (0.013)*	0.026 (0.013)**
Han	0.173 (0.120)	0.170 (0.121)	0.162 (0.120)	0.204 (0.121)**
Constant (1 vs. 2,3)	0.439 (0.254)	−0.730 (0.218)***	0.189 (0.231)	1.717 (1.332)
Constant (1,2 vs. 3)	2.105 (0.256)***	0.940 (0.215)	−0.783 (0.214)***	0.040 (1.332)
City level				
GDP per capita				−0.093 (0.122)
Random effects				
City level				0.013 (0.013)
Individual Level				0.508 (0.012)***
N	3491	3491	3491	3491
χ^2	110.23***	123.71***	174.53***	
DIC				6707.74

Note: The dependent variable is created based on two questions: the role of China in Asian Affairs and also in the world affairs. Its value ranges from 1 (very non-nationalistic), 2 (indifferent), to 3 (nationalistic). Standard errors are in parentheses. P-values: *** $p < 0.01$, ** $p < 0.05$, * $p < 0.10$. two-tailed tests.
† Corrections of the violation of the parallel-lines (proportionality) assumption. A coefficient (1 vs. 2, 3) indicates the effect of the variable on the difference between '*non-nationalistic*' and '*indifferent and nationalistic*' groups. A coefficient (1, 2 vs. 3) shows the effect of the variables on the difference between '*non-nationalistic* and *indifferent*' group and '*nationalistic*' group.
‡ Multilevel analysis with MCMC estimation (50,000 iterations, 10,000 burn-in period). Significant credibility intervals: *** 99%, ** 95%, * 90%.

from 4 (strongly support) to 1 (strongly not support), the value of nationalism increases from 7.29 to 7.74 in Model 3, and the probability of being nationalistic increases from 56.4% to 65.5% in Model 6 and from 74.6% to 80.9% in Model 10. These results imply that the system support variable has a bit bigger substantive impact on aggressive nationalism than benign nationalism.

The two democratic value variables have significant substantive effects on nationalism. The change in the democratic election variable from 1 (strongly disagree) to 5 (strongly agree) increases the value of nationalism from 6.57 to 7.9 in Model 3 and the probability of being nationalistic from 43.6% to 56.4% in Model 6 and from 53.7% to 74.6% in Model 10. An increase of the freedom of speech variable from 1 (strongly disagree) to 5 (strongly agree) also increases the value of nationalism from 6.79 to 8.28 in Model 3 and the probability of being nationalistic from 33.2% to 56.4% in Model 6 and from 60.6% to 74.6% in Model 10.

The authors' findings in this regard are different from what Wenfang Tang and Benjamin Darr found in their study of the association between nationalism and democratic values in China. Their study, based on a nationwide survey, reveals that Chinese nationalists tend to hold anti-democratic values.[39] The differences in findings might be due to the fact that their survey is a nationwide survey and the authors' survey is focused on urban China. In addition, the authors' study measures outward nationalistic feelings while their study focuses on national identity.

[39]Wenfang Tang and Benjamin Barr, 'Chinese Nationalism and Its Political and Social Origins', *Journal of Contemporary China* 21 (77), (2012), pp. 822–23.

Table 5. Substantive Effects of Predictors on Nationalism†

Changes in Predictors	Nationalism (aggressive & benign) (3 = very non-nationalistic, 13 = very nationalistic)	Aggressive Nationalism (Probability of being Nationalistic vs. being non-nationalistic or indifferent)	Benign Nationalism (Probability of being Nationalistic vs. being non-nationalistic or indifferent)
System Support	7.29 [6.78, 7.73] →	56.4 [45.9, 67.1] →	74.6 [65.6, 82.9] →
(4 → 1)	7.74 [7.25, 8.23]	65.5 [55.8, 74.3]	80.9 [74.3, 86.8]
Democratic Election	6.57 [6.04, 7.10] →	43.6 [33.5, 54.5] →	53.7 [42.8, 65.4] →
(1 → 5)	7.90 [7.37, 8.39]	56.4 [45.9, 67.1]	74.6 [65.5, 82.9]
Freedom of Speech	6.79 [6.20, 7.37] →	33.2 [23.4, 44.2] →	60.6 [49.1, 71.1] →
(1 → 5)	8.28 [7.72, 8.77]	56.4 [45.9, 67.1]	74.6 [65.5, 82.9]
Economic Success	8.51 [7.98, 8.97] →	57.7 [46.5, 68.8] →	56.3 [44.0, 67.8] →
(1 → 5)	9.41 [8.94, 9.87]	56.4 [45.9, 67.1]	74.6 [65.5, 82.9]
Male	7.29 [6.78, 7.73] →	56.4 [45.9, 67.1] →	74.6 [65.6, 82.9] →
(0 → 1)	7.64 [7.14, 8.12]	67.8 [58.8, 76.4]	76.7 [68.1, 84.0]
Han	9.41 [8.94, 9.87] →	56.4 [45.9, 67.1] →	74.6 [65.6, 82.9] →
(0 → 1)	9.66 [9.26, 10.04]	59.5 [50.2, 68.4]	77.7 [70.1, 84.3]
Age	9.64 [9.18, 10.10] →	44.8 [35.2, 54.9] →	64.5 [54.6, 73.7] →
(1 → 5)	10.58 [10.11, 11.10]	56.4 [45.9, 67.1]	74.6 [65.5, 82.9]
Income	10.62 [10.15, 11.13] →	60.0 [50.6, 69.0] →	69.6 [60.1, 77.2] →
(1 → 11)	10.96 [10.45, 11.51]	56.4 [45.9, 67.1]	74.6 [65.5, 82.9]

† Simulated results using *Clarify* Program by Tomz, Wittenberg, and King. To obtain theresults, the authors fix all dummy variables at their zeros and all other variables at their mean values using Models 3, 6, and 10. Values in parentheses are 95% confidence intervals.

In addition, the authors did find that people's assessment of China's economic success does have an impact on overall nationalist feelings among Chinese urbanites (as shown in Table 2). However, when examined closely, we find that China's economic success only affects benign nationalism, i.e., people's view of China's role in the world (see Table 4) but not aggressive nationalism, i.e., using force to solve territorial disputes (see Table 3). In other words, economic rise of China may foster normal Chinese nationalism, but not necessarily extreme nationalism. The change in the economic success variable from 1 (no success) to 5 (significant success) increases the probability of being nationalistic from 56.3% to 74.6% in Model 10 of benign nationalism.

As for the control variables, the authors found that male respondents in contrast to female respondents or older people in contrast to younger people are more likely to be nationalistic. High-income earners tend to be more nationalistic than low-income earners in Tables 2 and 4. But, the statistical significance disappears in models in Table 3. In general, there is no statistically meaningful difference between Han Chinese and non-Han Chinese in their nationalistic tendency.

As shown in Models 4 and 8, the hierarchical structure of the data does not generate significantly different outcomes in these models. In other words, even though it matters theoretically, the city-level factor of economic development is not important in explaining variations in nationalism among our Chinese urban respondents.

Conclusion

With rapid economic growth and the fact that China has become the second largest economy in the world, Chinese foreign policy has become increasingly more assertive. Deng Xiaoping's 'staying low' (*taoguang yanhui*) approach to international affairs has been quietly abandoned by the current Xi Jinping administration. The 'one belt, one road' initiative is the latest example that China is trying to expand its international influence and be a leader on the world stage. In fact, China has a unique opportunity to play a leadership role in world affairs due to the decline of the United States and unpopularity of President Donald Trump's policies and his 'America first' international approach around the world. The authors' findings show that this new Chinese assertive foreign policy does have popular support among Chinese urban residents. About half of the urban respondents agree that China should play a leading role in world affairs and even more people support for China's leading role in the region of Asia. A more surprising finding is that more than half of Chinese urban residents are supportive of Chinese government using force to take the disputed Diaoyu islands back from Japan even though such an action risks a war with Japan (and potential with the United States).

What drives popular Chinese nationalism? the analytical findings of this article show that male, older people and higher income earners tend to be more nationalistic. But more importantly, the authors found that people who support for electoral democracy in China and freedom of expression tend also to hold more nationalistic feelings. Upon further research, the authors found that system support is a confounding factor affecting Chinese urban residents' nationalistic sentiments. People who show less support for the current system in China also happen to exhibit more outward nationalistic feelings. China's official position is that Diaoyu islands are historically Chinese territories. However, the Chinese government has been refrained from taking military actions to challenge the *de facto* control of those islands by Japan. Therefore, it may very well be the case that the strong support for military action over Diaoyu islands among Chinese urban residents is a reflection of their popular frustration with the Chinese government over its inaction with regard to its island dispute with Japan. The linkage between views on democratic values and regime support in China on one hand and nationalist feelings among Chinese urbanites on the other may be explained by feelings of deprivation. People who hold democratic values and are not supportive of the current political system in China may feel that they are deprived of their democratic and civil liberty rights. This feeling of deprivation carries over to foreign affairs. They may also feel that China's proper place and power status is also deprived on the world stage.

What are the implications from these findings? First of all, the authors documented strong popular Chinese nationalism, which has the potential of putting pressure on the Chinese government to be more assertive in its foreign policy. Studies have shown that public opinion does influence Chinese foreign policy.[40] Second, nationalism may prove to be a double-edged sword in China since this article found the connection between satisfaction with domestic affairs and feelings toward international affairs among our Chinese urban residents. Popular political discontent may very well have a spill-over effect on Chinese people's nationalist feelings toward the outside world. For both implications, the Chinese government has to be very careful in using nationalistic sentiments in the population to strengthen its political legitimacy. As James Reilly states, 'relying upon nationalism to shore up political legitimacy remains a risky choice, since nationalism identifies the people themselves as the bearers of sovereignty, the central object of loyalty, and the basis for collective security'.[41] Gaining political legitimacy from domestic sources by reducing domestic discontent and granting people more democratic and civil rights might be a good strategy for the Chinese government to lower extreme nationalist feelings. Finally, the authors' findings suggest that the relationship between democracy or democratic values and nationalist feelings is a complicated one. This relationship may be confounded by many other factors, such as domestic regime type and regime support. More studies need to be conducted to explore this complicated relationship in authoritarian settings.

Disclosure statement

No potential conflict of interest was reported by the authors.

---

[40]Suisheng Zhao, 'Foreign Policy Implications of Chinese Nationalism Revisited: the Strident Turn', *Journal of Contemporary China* 22(82), (2013), pp. 535–53; Peter Hayes Gries, Derek Steiger and Tao Wang, 'Popular Nationalism and China's Japan Policy: the Diaoyu Islands Protest, 2012–2013', *Journal of Contemporary China* 25(98), (2016), pp. 246–76.
[41]James Reilly, *Strong Society, Smart State: The Rise of Public Opinion in China's Japan Policy* (New York: Columbia University Press, 2012), p. 38.

Part III

Geopolitics and Geo-Economics

China's Military Base in Djibouti: A Microcosm of China's Growing Competition with the United States and New Bipolarity

Jean-Pierre Cabestan

ABSTRACT

This article analyzes China' and the People's Liberation Army (PLA)'s rationale in opening what it calls a 'logistical support facility' in Djibouti as well as the missions that it is supposed to fulfil. The author also presents this base's activities since its opening on 1 August 2017 and explores the potential role that the Chinese military stationed in Djibouti could play to secure Xi Jinping's Belt and Road initiative and protect Chinese interests and nationals in Africa or the Middle East. Finally, it assesses the PLA base's relations with other militaries present in Djibouti, particularly the US, the French and the Japanese, concluding that Djibouti operates as a microcosm of a multipolar world heading towards a bipolar, though asymmetrical, world order.

Introduction

In November 2015, the Chinese government announced the decision to build a military base in Djibouti, a former French colony and a small territory (974,000 inhabitants, 23,000 km2) strategically located outside the mouth of the Bab el-Mandeb Strait and the Red Sea at the confluence of Africa, the Middle East and the Indian Ocean. This was a surprising decision as China was previously adamantly opposed to the very idea of setting up military bases overseas.

Beijing has argued that its Djibouti outpost is not a military base as such, but a People's Liberation Army (PLA) 'logistical support facility', '*mainly* used to provide rest and rehabilitation for the Chinese troops taking part in escort missions in the Gulf of Aden and waters off Somalia, UN peacekeeping and humanitarian rescue.'[1] Nevertheless, opened in August 2017, China's Djibouti naval base today includes around 2,000 military personnel, not only of the Navy but also the Army and particularly the special forces. In addition, today Djibouti is asked to play a key role in the securitization of Xi Jinping's Belt and Road initiative (BRI), and especially its maritime Silk Road.[2] This initiative underscores

---

[1]Defense Ministry answer to questions, quoted in Andrew Jacobs and Jane Perlez, 'US Wary of Its New Neighbor in Djibouti: A Chinese Naval Base', *The New York Times*, February 25, 2017, accessed May 14, 2018, https://www.nytimes.com/2017/02/25/world/africa/us-djibouti-chinese-naval-base.html?hpw&rref=world&action=click&pgtype=Homepage&module=well-region n°ion=bottom-well&WT.nav=bottom-well.

[2]On the BRI, see Hong Yu, 'Motivation behind China's "one belt, one road" initiatives and establishment of the Asian infrastructure investment bank', *Journal of Contemporary China* 26(105), (2017), pp. 353–368; Jean-Marc F. Blanchard, 'China's Maritime Silk Road Initiative (MSRI) and Southeast Asia: a Chinese "pond" not "lake" in the works', *Journal of Contemporary China* 27(111), (2018), pp. 329–343; Baogang He, 'The domestic politics of the belt and road initiative and its implications', *Journal of Contemporary China* 28(116), (2019), pp. 180–195; Jihong Chen, Yijie Fei, Paul Tae-Woo Lee and Xuezong Tao, 'Overseas port investment policy for China's central and local governments in the belt and road initiative', *Journal of Contemporary China* 28 (116), (2019), pp. 196–215.

China's new international diplomatic and military ambitions as well as growing strategic competition not only with the United States but also with the West-dominated world order.[3]

China's decision to establish a military base in Djibouti has been not only motivated by China's participation in anti-piracy operations in the Gulf of Aden since December 2008 and a growing number of United Nations Peacekeeping Operations but also by Beijing's need to better protect its security interests at large in Africa, the Middle East and the Indian Ocean.

Mainly based on first-hand materials as well as interviews in Djibouti and elsewhere, this article analyzes China's rationale in opening its Djibouti base as well as the missions that it is supposed to fulfil.[4] This article also explores the Chinese government's intentions in presenting the base's activities since its opening. Finally, it assesses the PLA base's relations with the nations that already have a military presence in Djibouti (as France, the USA, Italy and Japan), concluding that Djibouti operates as a microcosm of China's growing competition with the US as well as of a multipolar world heading towards a new bipolar, though asymmetrical, order.[5]

The Background

Since it decided to participate in anti-piracy operations in the Gulf of Aden, the PLA Navy (PLAN) has gradually become more familiar with Djibouti. Its frigates have made regular port calls in this strategic location, for rest and resupplying.[6] Its diplomats posted there have become more active, taking advantage of PLAN visits to establish closer ties with Djibouti authorities.[7] And Chinese companies have become more involved in the local economy.

Djibouti's strategic location is obvious: located at the mouth of the Bab el-Mandeb, a strait that controls any entrance into the Red Sea and the Suez Canal from the Indian Ocean, Djibouti has remained of high value for all maritime nations. The Bab al-Mandeb is the world's fourth most frequented maritime route used by some 30,000 ships every year.[8] Moreover, since the outbreak of the Ethiopia–Eritrea war in 1998, Djibouti has also become a gateway for 90% of The Ethiopia's imports, a trade volume that accounts for 90% of The Djibouti's port traffic.

Although China and Djibouti established diplomatic relations in 1979, 2 years after this former French overseas territory's independence, Chinese economic presence has developed slowly until the late 1990s. Then, pulled by their growing involvement in the Ethiopian economy, Chinese companies started to win a larger number of infrastructure projects in Djibouti.[9] But China's economic presence in this country has really taken off after the PLAN started to participate in anti-piracy operations in the Gulf of Aden and make regular port calls in Djibouti.

Djibouti has directly benefitted from the rapid expansion of Ethiopia–China cooperation. For example, in 2011, Chinese companies started to rebuild the railway from Djibouti to Addis Ababa first laid down by the French a century before. The project which amounted to US$525 million on the Djibouti side, including $514 million Chinese loans (and $3.4 billion on the Ethiopian section), was completed in 2017 and trains have started to operate since January 2018. Simultaneously, Chinese companies have become among the most active in the infrastructure sector, completing the

---

[3] Jianwei Wang, 'Xi Jinping's "major country diplomacy:" a paradigm shift?' *Journal of Contemporary China* 28(115), (2019), pp. 15–30; Andrew Scobell and Nathan Beauchamp-Mustafaga, 'The Flag Lags but Follows. The PLA and China's Great Leap Outward', in *Chairman Xi Remakes the PLA. Assessing Chinese Military Reforms*, ed. Phillip C. Saunders, Arthur S. Ding, Andrew Scobell, Andrew N.D. Yang and Joel Wuthnow (Washington DC: National Defense University Press, 2019), pp. 171–199.

[4] However, the author has been unable to visit the PLA base in Djibouti.

[5] Øystein Tunsjø, *The Return of Bipolarity in World Politics: China, the United States and Geostructural Realism* (New York: Columbia University Press, 2018), ch. 1 and 3.

[6] For example, 23 port visits between 2009 and 2013, Erica Downs, Jeffrey Becker and Patrick de Gategno, *China's Military Support Facility in Djibouti: The Economic and Security Dimensions of China's First Overseas Base* (Arlington, VA: CAN, July, 2017), p. 21.

[7] Interviews with Chinese diplomats, Djibouti, April, 2011.

[8] Geoffrey F. Gresh, 'A vital maritime pinch point: China, the Bab al-Mandeb, and the Middle East', *Asian Journal of Middle Eastern and Islamic Studies* 11(1), (2017), pp. 37–46.

[9] Jean-Pierre Cabestan, 'China and Ethiopia: authoritarian affinities and economic cooperation', *China Perspectives* 4, (2012), pp. 53–62.

construction of the Doraleh Multipurpose Port (DMP, $340 million of Chinese loan), the Ethiopia–Djibouti Water Pipeline ($320 million), Ghoubet Port ($64 million) and Djibouti International Free Trade Zone ($30 million).[10] China has also helped this country setting International Free Trade Zones, first next to the DMP, then in Damerjog, close to Somaliland's border.[11]

These projects have directly contributed to deepening Djibouti's public debt which increased from 50% to 104% of GDP between 2014 and 2018. At the end of 2017, China's loans to Djibouti amounted to $1.47 billion or 77% of Djibouti's annual GDP and consequently represented a large chunk of this country's public debt, leading in March 2018 the IMF to ring the alarm bell about this country's financial situation.[12]

Djibouti is politically stable: while democratic on the surface, it has been dominated by President Ismael Omar Guelleh and his clan since 2001: he was re-elected in 2016 for a fourth presidential term against a fragmented and weak opposition that has little chance of challenging him or his ruling party.

In other words, Djibouti is an island of stability in a troubled region all the way from Somalia to Yemen and Eritrea, troubles that, in spite of the recent reconciliation between Addis Ababa and Asmara, may extend to Ethiopia if the political transition there does not develop smoothly. It is also for China a strategic entry point to the Horn of Africa, a part of the continent where it has decided to invest a lot of diplomatic and financial capital.[13]

But for a few years after the PLA Navy started to participate in anti-piracy operations in the Gulf of Aden, there was no discussion whatsoever among Chinese or Djibouti officials about opening a PLA naval base in this country.[14] Then, the two main foreign militaries present there were the French (around 1,450 personnel including around 1,000 *Légion étrangère* troops in 2019 against 4,300 in 1978) and (since 2002) the Americans (around 4,500 troops including 2,000 marines). The American military base is located in Camp Lemonnier, in the outskirts of Djibouti City, an outpost that shares an airstrip with Djibouti International Airport (DIA), where the French and Japanese Air Forces are also based. Djibouti is the only permanent US military base in Africa. Since 2011, the US military is using an airfield located in the desert nearby (in Chabelley) to fly drones against al-Qaeda in Yemen and al-Shabab in Somalia. Since Djibouti's independence in 1977, France is committed by a bilateral agreement to defend its former 'overseas territory'. France–Djibouti's current security cooperation is enshrined in the 2011 Defense Cooperation Treaty, that 'ensure sustainable peace and security in Djibouti' (art. 2).[15]

Moreover, after the beginning of the European Union anti-piracy operations in the Gulf of Aden (Atalanta), in 2009, Italy opened a small base (80 soldiers) in Djibouti while Spanish and German soldiers from the EU's anti-piracy force make frequent stops in there, hosted in the American facilities. More unexpectedly, in 2011, Japan, a strong Western ally also involved in anti-piracy operations, did the same, turning Djibouti into its only overseas military base since 1945 (180 personnel). More recently, in January 2017, Saudi Arabia signed an agreement with Djibouti to set up a military presence on the territory, but to date, its construction has not started and its location is unknown. Very active economically in Djibouti until February 2018 when the Djibouti government decided to terminate the concession agreement with Dubai Port World (DPW) and nationalize the Doraleh Container Terminal (DCT), the United Arab Emirates (UAE) had also shown an interest to follow suit. However, because of a deteriorating relationship with this country, the UAE has since then privileged Assab in neighboring Eritrea where it already has a military base and Berbera in

---

[10]Downs et al., *China's Military Support Facility in Djibouti*, p. 9.
[11]Thierry Pairault, 'Djibouti et les routes électroniques de la soie' (Djibouti and Electronic Silk Roads), February 4, 2018, accessed January 4, 2019, http://pairault.fr/sinaf/doc/djibouti.pdf; Cf. Djibouti Ports and Free Zones Authority official website, accessed January 4, 2019, http://dpfza.gov.dj/building-region/djibouti-damerjog-industies-development.
[12]Jane.t Eom, Deborah Brautigam and Lina Benabdallah, 'The Path Ahead: The 7th Forum on China-Africa Cooperation', China Africa Research Initiative (CARI), *Briefing Paper* 1, (2018), accessed October 5, 2018
[13]Sonia Le Gouriellec, 'Chine, Éthiopie, Djibouti: un triumvirat pour la Corne de l'Afrique?', [China, Ethiopia, Djibouti: A Triumvir in the Horn of Africa ?], *Études internationales* XLIX (3), (2018), pp. 523–546.
[14]Interviews with Chinese and Western diplomats, Djibouti, April 2011.
[15]Patrick Ferras, 'Djibouti between Opportunism and Realism: Strategic Pivot in the Horn', *Life & Peace Institute*, June 17, 2015, accessed May 5, 2018, http://life-peace.org/hab/djibouti-between-opportunism-and-realism-strategic-pivot-in-the-horn/.

Somaliland where it is currently building another one.[16] Moreover, French, US and other Western militaries have developed among themselves extensive intelligence and logistical cooperation.

Western militaries and particularly NATO (North Atlantic Treaty Organization) countries' dominant role in Djibouti could have dissuaded China from establishing a military base there. Actually, it did not, underscoring Beijing's intention to quietly compete with and challenge the preexisting strategic order in the Horn of Africa.

The Debate around the Establishment of Military Bases Overseas

Since the late 2000s, there has been a debate among Chinese strategists about the necessity to set up logistical supply bases particularly for the PLAN ships on mission far away from China and more generally in order to better fulfil its tasks in terms of securing the sea lanes of communication on which China relies to develop and globalize its economy as well as China's interests and national overseas.

Although little has transpired in open sources, the debate boiled down on two major and somewhat interrelated issues: the rationale of setting up military bases overseas and their main purpose; the location of these bases.

The debate about the first issue was initially triggered as early as 2009 by the PLAN's increasing number of operations and visits overseas and the need to set up a logistical supply base for its ships deployed far from home and for a long period of time.[17] Although this opinion was rapidly contradicted by the Chinese Defense Ministry, discussions continued among experts. But for a long time, the mainstream view in China remained that even a modest facility would send a wrong message and would contradict China's long-held opposition to and criticism of US and other major powers' overseas military bases as symbols of 'imperialism' and 'hegemonism', a stance moreover shared by many African countries. Two major factors have modified the terms of the discussion: the 2011 successful but improvised evacuation of some 36,000 Chinese nationals from Libya and Xi Jinping's arrival to power.

Ghaddafi's sudden fall from power in February 2011 took Beijing by surprise but what shocked even more the Chinese authorities was the unexpected high number of nationals stuck in Libya and that needed to be looked after: short of any precise record, the Embassy in Tripoli estimated the number of Chinese around 10,000 at most. Although the PLA Air Force managed to evacuate some nationals through Khartoum, Sudan, the Chinese government then realized that it had no other choice but to rely on foreign shipping and airline companies to accomplish this task. A prepositioned military facility in the Middle East or in Africa would have helped the Chinese authorities save time and be more self-reliant.

The other factor is Xi Jinping's more assertive foreign policy, including his signature BRI, initially known as One Belt One Road (OBOR) and launched in 2013. We know now that as early as 2013, China's National Defense University submitted a report to the Central Military Commission proposing to establish a military base in Djibouti, a report that was approved by Xi Jinping.[18] The timing is important because, although the exact date of Xi's endorsement remains unknown, it broadly coincides with the Chinese president's BRI initiative. As we will see, since then securing the BRI has become one of the admitted missions of the PLA base in Djibouti.[19]

The other part of the debate focused on the location of China's first overseas military base: reports and speculations all pointed to a port located in the Indian Ocean (the Seychelles[20] or Gwadar, Pakistan) or on

[16]'Ports in the Horn', *The Economist*, July 21, 2018, pp. 33–34.

[17]'China floats idea of first overseas naval base,' *British Broadcasting Corporation (BBC)*, December 30, 2009, news.bbc.co.uk/2/hi/8435037.stm., quoted by Downs et al., *China's Military Support Facility in Djibouti*, p. 21.

[18]Zhang Tao, 'PLA's first overseas base in Djibouti', *Zhongguo junwang* (China Military Online), April 12, 2016, accessed May 7, 2018, http://english.chinamil.com.cn/news-channels/pla-daily-commentary/2016-04/12/content_7002833.htm.

[19]Monica Wang, 'First Place–On the Shores of Bab-el-Manded: Assessing China's First Overseas Military Base in Djibouti and Chinese Grand Strategic Vision for the Horn of Africa and Indian Ocean', *The Yale Review of International Studies*, June, 2018, accessed January 26, 2019, http://yris.yira.org/acheson-prize/2445.

[20]Liu Xiaokun and Li Lianxing, 'Navy looks at offer from Seychelles', *China Daily*, December 13, 2011, accessed May 7, 2018, http://www.chinadaily.com.cn/china/2011-12/13/content_14254395.htm.

the Eastern coast of Africa (Bagamoyo in Tanzania, Lamu or Mombasa in Kenya[21]). Then, the logic was that China would prefer to set up its own base away from Western eyes and military bases. Few observers imagined that Beijing would choose Djibouti, a city-state and port hosting for a long time several Western militaries and, consequently, where the privacy of PLA activities would be seriously challenged.

The Decision to Build a Military Base in Djibouti and Its Initial Official Missions

In retrospect, in making this choice, it appears that China has privileged Djibouti's strategic value and security over privacy.

China's decision to opt for Djibouti was also motivated by a factor that has been often overlooked: the lack of options, as many African countries are opposed to the opening of foreign military bases on their soil. Put differently, in spite of the Chinese government's good relations with the nations listed above and its willingness to present its base as 'dual use logistical facilities', other possible candidates have probably been reluctant to make such a move.

Probably for this reason as well, Beijing decided to move silently. In the early 2010s, China-Djibouti military cooperation expanded and in 2014 Chinese Defense Minister Chang Wanquan signed an agreement allowing PLA ships to make a greater use of Djibouti's ports.[22] But Beijing kept secret until late 2015 its negotiations with Djibouti around the establishment of a logistical military base there.

First publicized by President Guelleh in May 2015, when he announced that discussions were going on for the establishment of a Chinese base in the territory, the decision was only confirmed by the Chinese government and in a much more subdued manner in November 2015, shortly after PLA General Staff Fang Fenghui (now in jail for corruption) visited Djibouti.[23] Then, general Fang's meeting with Guelleh was just presented as the occasion to sign a ten-year contract allowing China to 'use maritime facilities' being built in this country.[24] It was only on 26 November 2015 that the Chinese Foreign Ministry's Spokesperson Hong Lei made the following announcement:

'China and Djibouti are friendly countries. We are consulting with each other on the building of logistical facilities (*baozhang sheshi*) in Djibouti, which will better guarantee Chinese troops to carry out international peacekeeping operations, escort missions in the Gulf of Aden and the Somali waters, humanitarian relief, and other tasks. It will help China's military further carry out its international responsibilities to safeguard global and regional peace and stability.'[25]

While leaving the door open to 'other tasks', this careful statement was the outcome of a third debate among Chinese officials about the nature of their country's military base in Djibouti and, more importantly, the *public discourse* that should be adopted about this new outpost as well as about any future Chinese military facility established overseas.

The same day, the Chinese Ministry of Defense spokesperson, Colonel Wu Qian, was more explicit about the rationale and the main motivations behind this decision:

---

[21]Shermax Ngahemera, 'New Bagamoyo port benefits Tanzania and region', *Africa-China Reporting Project*, May 20, 2014, accessed May 7, 2018, http://africachinareporting.co.za/2014/05/new-bagamoyo-port-benefits-tanzania-and-region/; 'China's New Network of Indian Ocean Bases', *The Lowry Interpreter*, January 31, 2018, accessed May 7, 2018, https://www.maritime-executive.com/editorials/china-s-new-network-of-indian-ocean-bases#gs.WvEg11k.

[22]'Djibouti and China Sign a Security and Defense Agreement', *allAfrica*, February 27, 2014, accessed January 17, 2019, https://allafrica.com/stories/201402280055.html.

[23]Gabriel B. Collins and Andrew S. Erickson, 'Djibouti Likely to Become China's First Indian Ocean Outpost,' *China SignPost* (*Dongcha Zhongguo*), 91, July 11, 2015, accessed May 7, 2018, http://www.andrewerickson.com/2015/07/china-signpost-91-djibouti-likely-to-become-chinas-first-indian-ocean-outpost/.

[24]'Top Chinese General Visits Djibouti Amid Base Speculation,' *Agence France-Presse*, November 10, 2015, accessed May 7, 2018, http://www.defensenews.com/story/defense/naval/2015/11/10/top-chinese- general-visits-djibouti-amid-base-speculation/75527376/.

[25]'Answers to questions by Foreign Ministry Spokesperson Hong Lei', November 26, 2015, accessed May 7, 2018, Chinese: http://www.scio.gov.cn/m/ztk/xwfb/jjfyr/32/wqfbh/Document/1457738/1457738.htm; English: http://www.fmprc.gov.cn/mfa_eng/xwfw_665399/s2510_665401/t1318766.shtml (the words 'and other tasks', translation of '*deng*' in Chinese, do not appear in the official English version).

What needs to be pointed out is that **maintaining regional peace and stability is in the interests of all countries and is also the common aspiration of the people of China and Djibouti and the world at large. China is willing and obliged to make more contributions** in this regard.

Based on relevant UN resolutions, China has sent more than 60 naval ships in 21 batches to perform escort missions in the Gulf of Aden and waters off the Somali coast. The Chinese naval escort ships have **encountered a lot of difficulties** such as personnel recuperation, and food and POL (petroleum, oil and lubricants) replenishment during performing escort missions. It is indeed **necessary** to have effective and near-the-site **logistical support** (*houqing baozhang*).[26]

In other words, the message is that, on the one hand, PLAN sailors need R&R (rest and recuperation) and PLAN ships repair and maintenance facilities: this is the logistic argument. The Gulf of Aden is far away from China and, as a result, some PLAN ships involved in anti-piracy operations have been forced to stay at sea for very long periods of time, up to 124 days, provoking 'physical and psychological problems' among 'a lot of sailors'.[27] Some have seen their power system fails, as in 2010 the destroyer Guangzhou which sailors were rescued by the French Navy.[28] Hence, Djibouti's choice. But it is also that, on the other hand, China is now willing to play a more active security role on the international stage and particularly in Africa, the Indian Ocean and the Middle East regions.

Presented by Chinese officials as a 'logistical support facility' (*houqing baozhang sheshi*) or a 'protective facility' (*baozhang sheshi*) and even as a 'dual use facility' (*junmin liangyong sheshi*), both civilian and military, rather than a military base, the PLA's first outpost overseas was in their eyes very different from any classic Western military bases.[29] As Chinese analysts have also argued, it is not a 'military base in the Western understanding of this term': contrary to Western power, China will not use this base to interfere in other countries' internal affairs; it will only intervene with the endorsement of the United Nations, regional organizations and concerned countries' authorities.[30]

And as China Military Online stated:

'China's base in Djibouti aims to provide logistical supply for China's escort taskforces in the Gulf of Aden and thus it is a logistics base, and is not responsible for combat operations. This is also essentially different compared with bases of other countries in Djibouti as the rest all have operational functions.'[31]

Since then discussion has continued in China about the nature and the mission of this first PLA overseas facility (see below). The initial idea was to portray this base as a defensive facility designed on the same model as Japan's military base in Djibouti and mainly aimed supplying PLAN ships particularly the ones involved in anti-piracy operations and provide logistical support for Chinese peacekeeping troops deployed in Africa or the Middle East. And this approach remains basically valid today. Put differently, it has been less controversial for China to both adopt the same low profile as Japan and build its first overseas military base in a nation where many other countries, including Japan, have a presence, an additional reason for choosing Djibouti.[32]

Nevertheless, in the Defense Ministry's statement, it is already clear that the PLA Djibouti base would fulfil other missions and particularly protect Chinese nationals and interests overseas and play

[26]'Defense Ministry's regular press conference on Nov. 26   , *China Military* News, November 26, 2015, accessed April 25, 2018, http://english.chinamil.com.cn/news-channels/china-military-news/2015-11/26/content_6787702.htm; Chinese: http://www.mod.gov.cn/affair/2015-11/26/content_4630570_2.htm. Bold letters added by the author.

[27]Tao, 'PLA's first overseas base in Djibouti'. Downs et al., *China's Military Support Facility in Djibouti*, p. 21.

[28]Minnie Chan, 'China's navy is being forced to rethink its spending plans as cost of trade war rises', *South China Morning Post* (*SCMP*), May 26, 2019, accessed May 28, 2019, https://www.scmp.com/news/china/military/article/3011872/chinas-navy-being-forced-rethink-its-spending-plans-cost-trade.

[29]Sun Xingwei and Zhou Biao, 'Gonggong tuijin junshi sheshi jianshe junmin ronghe' ['Jointly promote the construction of military facility and military and civilian fusion'], *Zhuhainow.com*, December 18, 2017, accessed April 27, 2018, http://www.zhuhainow.com/zgjq/15652.html.

[30]Wang Lei, 'Jibuji: keyi chengwei ZhongMei junshi hezuo de xinchuangkou' ['Djibouti can become a new window of military cooperation between China and the United States'], *Shijie Zhishi* (World Affairs) (16), (August 2017), pp. 56–57.

[31]Tao, 'PLA's first overseas base in Djibouti'.

[32]Sarah Zheng, 'China's Djibouti military base: "logistics facility", or platform for geopolitical ambitions overseas?', *SCMP*, October 1, 2017, accessed January 19, 2019, https://www.scmp.com/news/china/diplomacy-defence/article/2113300/chinas-djibouti-military-base-logistics-facility-or.

a role in the fight against terrorism, in intelligence gathering as well as in the promotion of closer military and counterterrorism cooperation with African and Arab countries. It is the most obvious manifestation of the PLA' new strategic objectives presented in 2015 which for the first time include the 'protection of the security of (China's) overseas interests' (*weihu haiwai liyi anquan*) and of its 'open seas rights and interests' (*weihu haiyang quanyi*).[33]

It is also part of a broader project aimed at giving teeth to the national security (July 2015) and counterterrorism laws (January 2016), laws that for the first time clearly allow the PLA 'to conduct military operations to protect China's overseas interests'.[34] In addition, it accompanies a more active policy towards the Middle East that emphasizes military and antiterrorism cooperation with Arab countries.[35]

As a result, it is not surprising that China's vocabulary has gradually evolved. In October 2016, while criticizing the West for characterizing the PLA outpost as a 'military base', the Chinese Defense Ministry already referred to it as a 'military logistical support port' (*junshi houqing buji gangkou*) capable of accommodating 10,000 personnel.[36] And at the time of its inauguration in the summer 2017, the PLA referred to its facility as a 'protective base' (*baozhang jidi*).[37] Since then, the word 'base' has been commonly used in the Chinese media even if officially the term 'facility' remains preferred.

The Establishment of China's 'Logistics Support Base' in Djibouti

Announced in November 2015, China's logistical support facility was inaugurated on 1 August 2017, the day of the 90th anniversary of the foundation of the PLA. In July 2017, a flotilla comprising the 25,000-ton Type 071 amphibious transport dock Jinggangshan and the 20,000-ton Donghaidao, a semi-submersible designed to carry equipment and small ships, shipped material and troops to Djibouti.[38]

In November 2015, the Chinese government concluded with Djibouti a 10-year lease to establish this facility and accepted to pay a rent amounting to US$20 million annually, against $63 million for the US, $30 million for the Japanese and 30 million Euros for France ($33 million). Although the facility can accommodate 10,000 personnel, the Chinese authorities have rapidly indicated that it would not deploy more than 2,000 officers and soldiers there.[39] This figure corresponds to the estimates made by local military observers.[40] The PLA base is managed by the PLA Navy and commanded by Senior Captain Liang Yang, former PLAN spokesman.

China's military facility is located on the premises of the DMP, next to the deep-water port, only 8 miles away from Camp Lemonnier. It was built very rapidly, in a year and a half, probably by China State Construction Engineering Company (CSCEC) on behalf of China Merchants, the company in charge of developing the DMP. While the overall cost of the DMP was US$590

---

[33]China's Military Strategy (full text), *Xinhua*, May 27, 2015, accessed May 7, 2018, http://english.gov.cn/archive/white_paper/2015/05/27/content_281475115610833.htm.

[34]English translations of the National Security Law, accessed May 30, 2019, https://www.chinalawtranslate.com/en/2015nsl/; and of the antiterrorism law, accessed May 30, 2019, https://www.chinalawtranslate.com/en/%E5%8F%8D%E6%81%90%E6%80%96%E4%B8%BB%E4%B9%89%E6%B3%95-%EF%BC%882015%EF%BC%89/.

[35]China's first 'Arab Policy Paper' was released in December 2015. Cf. Andrea Ghiselli, 'China's First Overseas Base in Djibouti, An Enabler of its Middle East Policy', *China Brief* 16(2), (January 25, 2016).

[36]Wang Dengke and Shu Chengming, 'Jibuti bei guanwei "junshi jidi", waimei zaichang na chuxi' ['Djibouti crowned "military base", according to the game played by foreign medias'], PRC Defense Ministry, October 25, 2016, accessed May 3, 2018, http://www.mod.gov.cn/jmsd/2016-10/25/content_4752414.htm.

[37]Wu Dengfeng, 'Wojun zhu Jibuti baozhang jidi chengli ji budui chuzheng yishi zai Guangdong Zhanjiang juxing' ['Ceremony held in Zhanjiang, Guangdong for the establishment of China's base in Djibouti and the dispatch of troops'], *Xinhua*, July 12, 2017, accessed April 27, 2018, http://news.xinhuanet.com/mrdx/2017- 07/12/c_136437161.htm.

[38]Minnie Chan, 'Drills show Chinese troops capable of riding shotgun on country's global ambitions'

[39]Kristina Wong, 'China's Military Makes Move Into Africa,' *The Hill*, November 24, 2015, accessed May 3, 2018, http://thehill.com/policy/defense/261153-chinas-military-makes-move-into-africa. It was later confirmed by China: 'Zhongguo shangjiang shouci shecha jibuti jidi nianzujin 2000 wan meiyuan' ['Chinese general inspects for the first time Djibouti base—annual rent US$20 million'], *Xiluwang* (Westland Net), November 25, 2016, accessed May 3, 2018, http://www.xilu.com/jstj/20161125/1000010000970653_1.html.

[40]Interview with Western military official, Djibouti, 14 October 2018.

million, the price of the base was not made public.[41] Military contractors were certainly involved in the construction of the base but no information has been published on them. Thirty-six hectare (or 90 acre) large, the PLA base includes four-story residential buildings, a 1200 m- (and not 400 m-) long helipad, maintenance facilities for helicopters and for military and civilian ships, hangars as well as cargo and logistic areas for pre-position supplies and storage tank for POL.[42] Later a hospital, an hotel and a swimming pool have been built. It is protected by a triple 8-m high-security fence built by PLA Engineer Corps and two roads have been constructed for patrolling between the fences.[43]

Western observers have been both impressed and worried by China's construction work on the naval base: vast and deep underground (23,000 m^2) and likely ordinance facilities were built.[44] The PLA base looks like a highly fortified castle equipped with watchtowers, a drone control facility, a control tower and a fuel storage facility. It is suspected that the base's underground is used for secured transmissions as well as cyber- and electronic warfare.[45] Its helicopter platform is wide enough to land containers parachuted from transport planes; and it is long enough for drones. It is also designed to be protected from air attacks.[46] Its only weakness is the absence of an airport. This said the US base in Camp Lemonnier is five times larger than the Chinese one.

First presented as a modest 'logistical support' and even 'dual facility', China's naval base in Djibouti is actually a complete military and naval base. The naval facility was initially both civilian and military: one of the six berths of the DMP was for the PLA's exclusive use. This berth can accommodate nearly any PLA Navy ship, except the Liaoning Aircraft carrier and the Type 071 Yuzhao-class LDP.[47] However, the berth is too low and strong winds from June to October slow down the port's activities. Besides, badly built, it had to be reconstructed.[48] As a result, very quickly, the PLA decided to build its own deep-water wharf just outside of and directly connected to the base. One difficulty has been the construction since 2018 and next (and east) to the facility of a desalination plant by French company Eiffage with the support of the European Union.[49] The Chinese government tried to convince its Djibouti counterpart to move the plant elsewhere but to no avail. As a result, the PLA decided to build a 600-m long naval pier which can accommodate all types of ships including the Liaoning. Started in February 2018, this new pier became operational in July 2018.[50] Drydock with repair facilities, pier and submarine pens with overhead shelters are likely to be added.[51]

---

[41]'Zhongguo zai Dongfei qidong shouge haiwai junshi jidi jianshe' ['China starts the construction of its first overseas military base in East Africa'], *Initium Media*, February 26, 2016, accessed April 25, 2018, https://theinitium.com/article/20151127-dailynews-china-djibouti-base/.

[42]Actually, according to French defense sources, the Chinese base is over 50 hectare large, interview, Paris, May 31, 2018.

[43]'Zhongguo shangjiang shouci'. Indian Intelligence sources report that there are four layers of security fences, Col Vinayak Bhat, 'China's Mega Fortress in Djibouti could be Model for its Bases in Pakistan', *The Print*, September 27, 2017, accessed May 3, 2018, https://theprint.in/security/china-mega-fortress-djibouti-pakistan/11031/.

[44]'Looking Over China's Latest Great Wall', *Stratford Worldview*, July 26, 2017, accessed May 7, 2018, https://worldview.stratfor.com/article/looking-over-chinas-latest-great-wall; Mike Yeo, 'Satellite Image Offers Cludes to China' Intentions in Djibouti', *DefenseNews*, November 8, 2017, accessed November 21, 2019, https://www.defensenews.com/global/mideast-africa/2017/11/08/satellite-imagery-offers-clues-to-chinas-intentions-in-djibouti/.

[45]Western defense sources, interviews, Djibouti, October 14–15, 2018.

[46]Tang Fei, 'E jinghan Zhongguo Jibuti jidi jianzhao qiaomiao dan rencun yinghuan' ['Russia marvels at the ingenious construction of China's Djibouti base which however hides perils'], *Duoweinews.com*, September 26, 2017, accessed May 3, 2018, http://news.dwnews.com/global/big5/news/2017-09-26/60014848.html.

[47]Downs et al., *China's Military Support Facility in Djibouti*, p. 26.

[48]Interviews, Djibouti, 14–17 October 2018.

[49]Interviews, Djibouti, 14–17 October 2018.

[50]French defense sources, interview, Paris, May 31, 2018; An Indian security expert, retired colonel Vinayak Bhat, has a twitter account, called 'Rajfortyseven' and including many satellite maps that he keeps updating on the Chinese base in Djibouti: *Rajfortyseven*, May 19, 2018, accessed June 6, 2018, https://twitter.com/rajfortyseven/status/998053825268207617?lang=en; *Rajfortyseven*, September 10, 2018, accessed January 21, 2019, https://twitter.com/rajfortyseven/status/1039125456585277440?lang=en.

[51]*Rajfortyseven*, June 4, 2018, accessed June 6, 2018, https://twitter.com/rajfortyseven/status/1003839907373068288.

When it opened on 1 August 2017, 1,000 Navy military personnel who had left Zhanjiang, Guangdong, the seat of China's South Sea Fleet, on 11 July 2017, were already stationed in Doraleh. The personnel then dispatched included some PLA marines and special forces.

Later, Beijing gave more details about its Djibouti base's personnel which rapidly increased to 2,000. According to official sources, in January 2018, the PLA base was made of a brigade (*dadui*) itself constituted of several squadrons (*zhongdui*), including 3–4 support integrated security support squadrons (*zonghe baozhang zhiyuan zhongdui*), 'at least' two security reconnaissance squadrons (*jingwei zhencha zhongdui*), one protection frigate squadron (*huwei jianjing zhongdui*), one helicopter squadron, one intelligence electronic communication squadron (*qingbao dianzi tongxin zhongdui*), one health and medical squadron and one logistics squadron.[52] More importantly, perhaps, the Chinese military includes a special force squadron equipped with heavy-duty Z-8F helicopters that can carry out missions within a few hundred kilometers. The special forces are equipped with light-armored vehicles, modern shooting weapons and LG3 anti-tank rocket launchers.[53] When necessary, air defense systems based on PLA ships can also ensure their own safety.[54]

The type of personnel stationed in Djibouti provides already some indication about the missions that the PLA base may be asked to fulfil in the future. In any event, it is worth indicating that the establishment of China's first overseas military base also coincides with Xi Jinping's decision announced in March 2017 to increase from 20,000 to 100,000 officers and soldiers the PLA's Marine troops.[55]

The Missions of China's Military Base in Djibouti

As early as November 2015, the Chinese civilian and military authorities spelled out the major missions of the PLA base in Djibouti (see above). However, after the base opened in the summer 2017, its missions have been better fleshed out and somewhat expanded. It also aims at helping China implement military cooperation activities, organizing combined exercises and training, conducting non-combatant evacuation operations and emergency rescue as well as protectingstrategic sea-lanes.[56] Counterterrorism and intelligence collections are also part of this new base's missions.[57]

As analyst Wang Lei wrote in August 2017, 'Djibouti's strategic location directly contributes to turning the base into a pivot in the securitization of the maritime silk road', it should better protect commercial exchanges with Africa, large-scale infrastructure projects realized there and Chinese nationals, over a million, residing in Africa. Wang also confirmed that in view of the region's security instability, the Djibouti base can be used as a 'transfer station' (*zhongzhuan zhan*) facilitating evacuation operations similar to the one that China conducted in Yemen in 2015.[58] This viewpoint somewhat echoes retired Admiral Yin Zhuo's comment made in 2016 about the need for China, because of its worldwide economic activities, to establish 'overseas support pivots' (*haiwai zhudian*) where its interests, as well as the risks that it faces, are concentrated.[59]

---

[52]Li Ren, 'Xiangjie Zhongguo haijun diyige haiwai baozhang jidi weihe xuanzai Feizhou zhi jiao' ['Explain why the Chinese Navy's first overseas support base has been established in the Horn of Africa'], *Xinlang junshi* (*New Wave Military*), January 23, 2018, accessed May 3, 2018, http://mil.news.sina.com.cn/jssd/2018-01-23/doc-ifyquptv8834647.shtml.

[53]Dong Xu, 'Bubing zui meng wuqi shouhu Jibuti jidi, neng yi yidibaijiang kongbufenzi mietuan!' ['The infantry's most terrible weapons protect the Djibouti base and can eliminate terrorists on a one to one hundred ratio'], *Sohu Junshi* (*Sohu Military*), January 26, 2018, accessed May 3, 2018, http://www.sohu.com/a/219116457_99893245.

[54]Fei, 'E jinghan Zhongguo'.

[55]Minnie Chan, 'As overseas ambitions expand, China plans 400 per cent increase to marine corps numbers, sources say', *SCMP*, March 13, 2017, accessed January 27, 2019, http://www.scmp.com/news/china/diplomacy-defence/article/2078245/overseas-ambitions-expand-china-plans-400pc-increase.

[56]'Zhongguo jiefangjun zhu Jibuti baozhang jidi chengli ji budui chuzheng yishi zai Zhanjiang juxing' ['Ceremony held in Zhanjiang for the establishment of China's base in Djibouti and the dispatch of troops'], *Xinhua*, July 11, 2017, accessed May 3, 2018, http://www.xinhuanet.com/world/2017-07/11/c_1121302146.htm.

[57]This has been later confirmed by declassified analysis by CNA, a US naval think tank, Zheng, 'China's Djibouti military base'.

[58]Lei, 'Djibouti can become a new window of military cooperation'.

[59]'Zhongguo jiakuai jianshe Jibuti houqing baozhang junshi sheshi' ['China accelerates the construction of the Djibouti logistical base'], *Dongfang Zaobao*, November 28, 2016, accessed May 3, 2018, http://www.zaobao.com.sg/special/report/politic/cnpol/story20161128-695419.

Nonetheless, it remains important for China to present its Djibouti base as mainly concentrating on 'Military Operations other than War' (MOOTW), a concept adopted by China in 2009 (and reasserted in the 2015 Military Strategy White Paper), and, as a result, directly contributing to international security through non-lethal means.[60]

Djibouti Base's Official Missions

The first mission of the Chinese military base in Djibouti has remained to provide logistical support to PLA Navy ships making port calls there, particularly the ones conducting anti-piracy operations in the Gulf of Aden.[61] Between 2003 and 2018, PLAN ships paid not less than 23 visits in Djibouti (against 25 in Oman and 12 in Pakistan).[62] However, as since 2013 piracy has been receding in this area, China's newly established base is likely to be less busy with this task. The drop of piracy activities also shows that anti-piracy operations have been used more as a justification than as a driver of the Chinese facility's construction.

Secondly, the PLA base in Djibouti is to become a 'transit point' for Chinese UN peacekeeping forces deployed in Africa and the Middle East.[63] This mission fits and coincides with Xi Jinping's decision announced in December 2015 to increase to 8,000 the number of Chinese UN peace-keepers. Among other UN peacekeeping missions, China has currently PLA contingents deployed in Mali, South Sudan, the Central African Republic and the Democratic Republic of Congo. Djibouti can become a convenient R&R location for these soldiers. Nonetheless, to date, there has been no report of Chinese UN peacekeepers' transit through the Djibouti base.

Thirdly, the Djibouti outpost helps China participating in humanitarian assistance missions. Actually, this has already been the case. For instance, the PLA Navy has conducted once a year escorts missions of the World Food Program's shipments to Somalia in cooperation with the EU.[64]

Djibouti Base's Other Missions

However, the PLA troops deployed in Djibouti have started other activities that underscore this base's other and more ambitious missions.

Firstly, China's military base in Djibouti enhances the PLA's combat capability in order to be able to evacuate Chinese nationals from non-friendly environments and better protect Chinese facilities in Africa, particularly in the Horn of Africa, a region where more oil and gas has been prospected and has started to be exploited. There are probably 100,000 Chinese nationals in the Horn of Africa (60,000 in Ethiopia alone), a region that includes unsecure countries as South Sudan and Somalia.[65]

More importantly, Djibouti's PLA outpost has a role to play in securing China's Maritime Silk Road, in particular in the Indian Ocean and the Red Sea, halfway between East Asia and Europe. This role goes far beyond anti-piracy operations and is also part of a strategy aimed at increasing China's naval presence in the Indian Ocean and balancing other navies' activities and especially India's own ambitions there. For example, since 2014, Chinese attack and ballistic missile submarines have been regularly conducting patrols in the Indian Ocean.[66]

---

[60]Mathieu Duchâtel and Alexandre Shelton-Duplaix, 'Blue China Navigating the Maritime Silk Road to Europe', *Policy Brief*, ECFR, April 2018, p. 34.

[61]That was the case for instance in November 2018, 'Guofangbu tan Zhongguo zhu Jibuti baozhang jidi: weile genghao lüxing guoji yiwu', *Renminwang Junshi pindao* [people.cn Military Channel], November 30, 2018, accessed January 15, 2019, http://military.people.com.cn/n1/2018/1130/c1011-30434450.html..

[62]Duchâtel and Shelton-Duplaix, 'Blue China Navigating the Maritime Silk Road to Europe', p. 7.

[63]Ibid., p. 32.

[64]These missions were conducted 'on an unequal footing', as European ships ensured most of the escorts, Ibid., p. 34.

[65]Ibid. In 2017, there were around 11,000 Chinese contractual workers in the Horn of Africa, cf. China Statistical Yearbook 2018, accessed January 22, 2019, http://www.stats.gov.cn/tjsj/ndsj/.

[66]Ankit Panda, 'What the Pentagon Thinks of China's Military', *The Diplomat*, May 11, 2015, accessed May 7, 2018, https://thediplomat.com/2015/05/what-the-pentagon-thinks-of-chinas-military/; Ankit Panda, 'The Chinese Navy's Djibouti Base: A "Support Facility" or Something More?', *The Diplomat*, February 27, 2017, accessed May 7, 2018, https://thediplomat.com/2017/

Finally, China has started to offer its good offices to settle or stabilize local disputes. For example, soon after the opening of its military base in Djibouti, it proposed to dispatch PLA troops stationed there along the Djibouti–Eritrea border to replace the Qatari interposition force. In making this offer, China has also wished to demonstrate that it is better positioned than these two countries' neighbors, often in bad terms with each other (as today Saudi Arabia and Qatar), to secure the border.[67]

In other words, China nurtures great ambitions for its Djibouti base. It may be an exaggeration to compare it, as some 'Chinese military fans' (*Zhongguo junmi*) do, to Russia's facility in Syria, and call it 'China's "Tartus"'.[68] Nonetheless, Djibouti military outpost already offers the PLA multiple new missions and options.

PLA's Training in Djibouti

In order to improve its readiness to conduct these missions, the PLA personnel deployed in Djibouti have rapidly started to conduct exercises. The objective is to 'explore a new training model of Chinese overseas garrisons', according to the base commander, Liang Yang.[69] It has been the first time in four decades that the PLA has been training overseas outside of the UN banner. However, regular and publicly reported in 2017 and 2018, these drills seem to have decreased since then, and partly replaced by joint exercises with other armed forces, particularly from Europe (see below).

The first drill took place on 22 September 2017 in Djibouti's own national gendarmerie training range: it was a life-fire exercise that involved 'dozens of officers'.[70] A second, larger-scale exercise was conducted on 23 November 2017 at Djibouti's Maryam Training Area. Then, the PLA showed off some of its materials as Type 095 and Type 90-II wheeled armored fighting vehicles, the most advanced main battle-armored cars according to some Chinese experts.[71] It also conducted live-fire exercises with ZTL-11 amphibious assault vehicles. This particular exercise provoked some surprise because the Djibouti military had not informed on time the French forces, that are 'ultimately responsible for overseeing the Maryam training area', where the PLA held its drill.[72]

A third exercise that mobilized the whole PLA personnel and equipment took place on 9 January 2018: it was a trek in the desert outside of their base (*yewai tubu xingjun*).[73] The objective was to train the Chinese military to desert conditions and prepare them to face both 'enemy planes' and on-land terrorist attacks.[74] The PLA conducted another life-fire exercise on 12 May 2018 'at high temperature' (over 40°C) in order to 'improve the combat capability of troops in regard to dealing with emergencies when in battle with terrorists'.[75]

02/the-chinese-navys-djibouti-base-a-support-facility-or-something-more/; Indrani Bagchi, 'Chinese subs in Djibouti to fight "pirates" worrying: Navy', *Times of India.*, January 10, 2019, accessed January 15, 2019, https://timesofindia.indiatimes.com/india/with-80-news-ships-in-last-5-years-chinese-navy-is-here-to-stay-admiral-lanba/articleshow/67458929.cms.

[67]Roland Marchal, 'Mutations géopolitiques et rivalités d'États: la Corne de l'Afrique prise dans la crise du Golfe' [Geopolitical changes and States' rivalry: the Horn of Africa stuck in the Gulf Crisis], Observatoire Afrique de l'Est, Enjeux politiques et sécuritaires, *Note d'Analyse*, March 4, 2018, p. 13.

[68]Ren, 'Xiangjie Zhongguo haijun'.

[69]Minnie Chan, 'Live-fire show of force by troops from China's first overseas military base', *SCMP*, September 25, 2017, accessed May 6, 2018, http://www.scmp.com/news/china/diplomacy-defence/article/2112780/live-fire-show-force-troops-chinas-first-overseas,.

[70]Chan, 'Live-fire show of force'.

[71]Minnie Chan, 'Drills show Chinese troops capable of riding shotgun on country's global ambitions', *SCMP*, December 18, 2017, accessed May 6, 2018, https://www.scmp.com/news/china/diplomacy-defence/article/2122473/drills-show-chinese-troops-capable-riding-shotgun.

[72]Michael Edward Walsh, 'Major Communication Breakdown During Chinese Live-Fire Exercises in Djibouti', *Island Society*, November 28, 2017, accessed May 7, 2018, http://islandsociety.org/2017/11/28/chinese-live-fire-exercises-expose-need-for-better-coordination-of-foreign-military-activities-in-djibouti/.

[73]Ren, 'Xiangjie Zhongguo haijun'.

[74]Xu, 'Bubing zui meng wuqi'.

[75]'PLA Base in Djibouti Conducts Anti-Terrorism Exercise', *Renminwang*, May 15, 2018, accessed January 24, 2019, http://en.people.cn/n3/2018/0515/c90000-9460275.html.

Clearly inspired by the practice of the French *Légion étrangère* and the US Marines deployed in Djibouti, these drills aim at adapting the PLA to difficult environments and especially preparing it to counter-terrorism operations.[76] However, these exercises have not demonstrated a high level of sophistication. They tend to underscore the long way forward that the PLA needs to go in order to become operational in this part of the world and on that type of terrain.[77]

Yet, Djibouti has become a very useful testing ground for the PLA outside of the UN banner, not only in terms of using new weapons and equipment but also in terms of intelligence gathering and anti-terrorist capabilities. Djibouti's only inconvenience is the presence of other militaries and the need to share with them a 'common operating space' that in Djibouti is rather small.[78]

Cooperation and Frictions with Other Militaries Present in Djibouti

Officially, the PLA wishes to take advantage of its fresh presence in Djibouti to open new avenues of cooperation with the West and above all the United States. However, while opportunities of cooperation have remained limited, frictions with the US and its allies' militaries have quickly emerged, underscoring how much Djibouti has become a microcosm of the growing strategic rivalry between China and the US, and perhaps also between China and the West.

Interactions and Likely Areas of Cooperation

Since the opening of the Chinese base in Djibouti, there have been a number of interactions between Western and Chinese militaries. But these contacts and exchanges of visits have been formal, shallow and have only taken place at the highest level among the three most senior officials of each base.[79] The American military has tried to find ways to enhance communication and avoid frictions with the PLA personnel but without much success: actually, reports indicate that Chinese military officials have been 'overly aggressive' in their interactions with their US counterparts.[80] Contacts with the French military are also scarce and superficial, in spite of the regular invitations issued by the PLA to take part in events and ceremonies on their facilities and the Chinese government's clear strategy to 'play nice' with Djibouti's former colonizer.[81]

Yet, a common involvement of the PLA and other navies in anti-piracy operations in the Gulf of Aden has constituted a proper starting point both for China and Western powers for exploring areas of cooperation. Although the PLA Navy has constantly fulfilled its mission in parallel with but outside of other navies, it has held annual joint exercises with the European Union's Operation Atalanta. For example, in October 2018, the PLAN conducted its first medical evacuation by helicopter—from an Italian ship to the Chinese base in Djibouti—with EU NAVFOR (Naval Force).[82] Two months later the PLAN held a similar joint exercise with the Spanish Navy.[83] More largely, the priority given by the PLA deployed in Djibouti to peacekeeping, escorts and humanitarian assistance can also help developing new forms of communication and cooperation with Western militaries, including the exchange of

[76]Chan, 'Drills show Chinese troops'.
[77]Western defense sources, interviews, Paris, May 31, 2018 and Djibouti, October 14–15, 2018.
[78]Walsh, 'Major Communication Breakdown'.
[79]Arwa Damon and Brent Swails, 'China and the United States face off in Djibouti as the world powers fight for influence in Africa', CNN, May 27, 2019, accessed May 29, 2019, https://edition.cnn.com/2019/05/26/africa/china-belt-road-initiative-djibouti-intl/index.html.
[80]Michael Edward Walsh, 'A Fieldnote on How U.S. Military Officials View the People's Liberation Army Security Base in Djibouti', Asia Maritime Transparency Initiative, November 17, 2017, accessed May 16, 2018, https://amti.csis.org/fieldnote-u-s-military-peoples-liberation-army-djibouti/. Interviews with Western military officials, Djibouti, October 15, 2018.
[81]Interviews, Djibouti, October 14–17, 2018.
[82]EU NAVFOR Somalia, 'EU NAVFOR conducts first exercise with Chinese PLA(N) in Djibouti', European Union External Action, October 16, 2018, accessed January 22, 2019, https://eunavfor.eu/eu-navfor-conducts-first-exercise-with-chinese-plan-in-djibouti/.
[83]'China and Spain conduct joint medical exercise at PLA Djibouti Base', Global Times, December 3, 2018, accessed January 22, 2019, http://www.globaltimes.cn/content/1130154.shtml.

liaison officers and information on threat assessment.[84] Observation of PLA exercises by other militaries (and vice-versa) could be another likely area if not of cooperation and least of confidence-building. But for the time-being, none of these developments have taken place.

Chinese experts have themselves argued in favor of cooperating with the West, particularly the US, underscoring that Africa is not a 'central game area' between both countries. In Wang Lei's view, Djibouti can, on the contrary, become a 'strategic buffer zone' (*zhanlüe huanchongdai*) between the two, giving as an example the possibility for both countries to cooperate on the border dispute between Eritrea and Djibouti.[85]

Nonetheless, few ideas of practical cooperation have so far emerged, a big obstacle being the PLA's proclivity for secrecy and isolation from other militaries. More generally, China's late arrival in a strategic port already occupied by the US and its allies can only draw Djibouti into the great game between the established superpower and the aspiring superpower and, as a result, limit areas of cooperation but rather multiply sources of frictions between them.

Sources of Frictions and Adjustment

Sources of frictions have rapidly emerged between the Chinese and the US militaries. Other countries present there, as France or Japan, have also witnessed some difficulties with the PLA base and its activities. More generally, China's military presence in Djibouti has led other regional powers, as India to adjust.

The US was the first to express in public its concern. Before the PLA outpost's opening, it was already worried about the proximity of China's naval base from Camp Lemonnier and about the fact that Beijing, through China Merchants, might take control of the DMP's management, increasing the insecurity of US and Western military facilities. Djibouti's alarming level of debt to China and inability to reimburse not only the capital but also the interests of the loans granted by this country have deepened these fears.[86]

China Merchants has a 38.8% stake in the Port of Djibouti SA, the holding that also owns DCT.[87] Although Djibouti authorities have dismissed US concerns, China's growing role in this country's port activities clearly gives it an additional leverage over other players.[88] Expressing these fears, US Africa Commander and Marine General Thomas Waldhauser declared in March 2018 to the US Congress, 'if the Chinese took over the port, then the consequences could be significant'.[89]

Some reports already point to deeper problems. According to American military sources, the PLA has been responsible for a number of unspecified 'probing attempts' against the US base, espionage activities that have 'significantly increased' since their first drill in September 2017.[90] As some US militaries already feared in February 2017, the Chinese base 'could provide a front-row seat to the staging ground for American counterterror operations in the Arabian Peninsula and North Africa.'[91]

To be sure, more than any other military already present in Djibouti, the US has also kept a close eye on the PLA facilities and any Chinese activity in this country. Some sources have indicated that by mid-October 2018, taking advantage of the then-existing air corridors around DIA, US surveillance

[84]Duchâtel and Shelton-Duplaix, 'Blue China Navigating the Maritime Silk Road to Europe', p. 40.

[85]Lei, 'Djibouti can become a new window of military cooperation'.

[86]Interviews, Djibouti, October 14–17, 2018.

[87]Initially, 23.5% + 13.3% as a result of a loan of $150 million granted to Djibouti Ports and Free Trade Zone Authority to build a new international free zone, Abdourahim Arteh, 'Djibouti breaks ground on massive Chinese-backed free trade zone', *Reuters*, January 16, 2017, accessed May 9, 2018, https://www.reuters.com/article/china-djibouti-idUSL4N1F649H.

[88]Nizar Manek, 'Djibouti Sees China Involvement in Port as No Threat to U.S.', *Bloomberg*, March 14, 2018, accessed January 26, 2019, https://www.bloomberg.com/news/articles/2018-03-14/djibouti-sees-chinese-involvement-in-port-as-no-threat-to-u-s.

[89]Idrees Ali and Phil Stewart, '"Significant" consequences if China takes key port in Djibouti: U.S. general', *Reuters*, March 7, 2018, accessed January 26, 2019, https://af.reuters.com/article/africaTech/idAFKCN1GJ0RBOZATP?feedType=RSS&feedName=topNews.

[90]Walsh, 'A Fieldnote'.

[91]Quoted by Andrew Jacobs and Jane Perlez, 'U.S. Wary of Its New Neighbor in Djibouti'.

aircrafts had already overflown the Chinese base 80 times.[92] This American curiosity is probably the cause of the 'laser' incident that was reported in early May 2018. Then, the United States formally complained to China for having injured two US airmen by directing high-grade lasers at C-130 US aircrafts in Djibouti. China officially denied the facts.[93] As Shanghai-based military observer, Ni Lexiong recognized a 'quiet contest' to gather information about each other is taking place between China and other foreign militaries present in Djibouti.[94]

After repeated complaints lodged by the PLA through the Chinese Embassy, the Djiboutian government accepted in September 2018 to move slightly away from the Chinese base DIA's air corridors, at least as far as landings and take-offs based on visual flight rules (VFR) are concerned. However, depending on DIA's Air Traffic Control (ATC), instrument flight rules (IFR) have remained unchanged, perpetuating to some extent the PLA base overflights, at least by American planes.[95]

In any event, the 'laser' incident and the more general reciprocal US–China distrust are more the results than the source of a growing worldwide competition between these two great powers. Launched in November 2017 and aimed among other things at reining in Chinese ambitions in the Indian Ocean, the Trump Administration's 'Indo-Pacific Strategy' can only feed this competition.[96]

Yet, the US is not the only power to be worried about the PLA's growing activism in Djibouti.

French military and diplomats also closely observe the PLA's deployment and activities. For training and surveillance purposes, two Mirage 2000 takes-off from DIA every morning. Although since the end of 2016, the French Air Force has stopped flying right over the Chinese base, they have the means to check the PLA's activities. French military officials are in particular afraid of China's 'eviction power' on the Westerners. In spite of their country's close relationship with President Guelleh, they are also concerned by the pressure exerted by the Chinese rent on the amount of the French lease, still relatively cheap in view of France's military presence and multiple facilities there.[97] In their eyes, China is trying to establish with the Djibouti authorities a privileged relationship aimed at gradually weakening, if not marginalizing the French influence there. For example, during his visit in November 2016, general Fan Changlong donated Djibouti police and armed forces various military equipment, including a patrol ship, a Z9 helicopter, a radar and 26 armored vehicles amounting to $80 million, much more that the value of China's arm transfers to this country tracked by SIPRI ($14 million from 2014 to 2016).[98]

Japan is also worried about China's new military base in Djibouti and is obviously keeping a vigilant eye on its activities. In early August 2017, as the PLA base had just opened, it was reported that a Japanese naval ship mooring there at an unspecified date that year had instructed three frogmen to have a closer look at a Chinese warship also docking there. This incident was mentioned in a report on the website of China's *Procuratorial Daily* but was not otherwise made public by Chinese or Japanese media. It was authored by Jian Jiamin, a procurator who had served as a legal counselor to the PLA troops in Africa.[99] The Japanese Defense Ministry rapidly denied the incident.[100]

---

[92]Interview with Western military official, Djibouti, 14 October 2018.

[93]Paul Sonne, 'U.S. accuses China of directing blinding lasers at American military aircraft in Djibouti', *The Washington Post*, May 4, 2018, accessed May 5, 2018, https://www.washingtonpost.com/news/checkpoint/wp/2018/05/03/u-s-accuses-china-of-directing-blinding-lasers-at-american-military-aircraft-in-djibouti/?utm_term=.6874f2ea7649; some Western military observers have doubt that a laser was actually used: US airmen were only 'dazzled', a laser would have blinded them; Interview, Djibouti, October 14, 2018.

[94]Reuben F. Johnson, 'US Warns Pilots of Laser Attacks in Djibouti', *Jane's Defense Weekly*, April 27, 2018, accessed May 3, 2018, http://www.janes.com/article/79630/us-warns-pilots-of-laser-attacks-in-djibouti.

[95]Interview, Djibouti, October 15, 2018.

[96]Michael J. Green and Andrew Shearer, 'Countering China's Militarization Of The Indo-Pacific', *War on the Rocks*, April 23, 2018, accessed May 9, 2018, https://warontherocks.com/2018/04/countering-chinas-militarization-of-the-indo-pacific/.

[97]French Defense Ministry source, interview, Paris, May 31, 2018; Interviews, Djibouti, October 14–15 2018.

[98]Interview, Djibouti, October 14, 2018. *SIPRI Arms Transfer Database*, accessed January 9, 2019, https://sipri.org/databases/armstransfers.

[99]Kinling Lo, 'Japanese frogmen approached Chinese warship at Djibouti, state media say', SCMP, August 2, 2017, accessed January 26, 2019, https://www.scmp.com/news/china/diplomacy-defence/article/2105024/japanese-frogmen-approached-chinese-warship-djibouti.

[100]'Japanese divers neared Chinese warships at Djibouti port: report' *Global Times*, August 4, 2017, accessed May 9, 2018, http://www.globaltimes.cn/content/1059731.shtml.

Since then, the Japanese military seem to have made an effort to improve relations with the PLA. As the French, Japan Self-Defense Forces' aircrafts have stopped overflying the Chinese base since the end of 2016. Later, in order to build confidence, the Japanese military have started to regularly play basketball with their Chinese counterparts.[101] However, Sino-Japanese interactions in Djibouti have remained minimal. In 2017, Japan expanded its base (from 12 to 15 ha) and since then has continued to do so, partly to counter China's growing military presence there.[102]

While not present in Djibouti, India has clearly shown its displeasure about China's naval base, to a point that some have speculated that it is willing to negotiate the opening of its own military facility there.[103] But that is not Delhi's intention. Instead, in March 2018, India and France signed an agreement—a 'strategic pact' for some—that opens up their naval bases to each other's warships across the Indian Ocean.[104] This agreement allows the Indian Navy to make port calls in French-controlled facility in Djibouti (*base navale du Héron*, located north of Djibouti downtown). China has reacted negatively but discreetly to this initiative.[105]

Djibouti government's interest is to make sure that all military powers present on its territory remain in good terms and hopes that everyone, particularly the US, will stay. For instance, in order to demonstrate its inclusiveness, on 27 June 2017, on the occasion of the 40th anniversary of Djibouti's independence, it invited five of the foreign troops present in the territory (France, USA, Italy, China and Japan) to march in the city, which they did in apparent total harmony.[106]

None of the foreign militaries stationed in Djibouti has an interest to see the situation deteriorates.[107] Yet, China's military presence has revealed itself more important in terms of constructions, troops and equipment than anticipated, triggering alarm bells among all Western powers present in Djibouti or in the Indian Ocean. This presence has also deepened this country's financial dependence upon China, the rent of the military base helping the former to reimburse the latter's loans.[108] And the fact that Doraleh Chinese naval base is located next to the landing of undersea internet cables connecting Djibouti both to Europe and Asia has also fed these concerns, particularly after it was learned that this base's underground is equipped with cyber- and electronic warfare facilities.[109]

Conclusion

The establishment of a military base in Djibouti is a turning point in China's foreign and security policy. Conceived and then carried out in less than 4 years, this decision underscores China's as well as its leader Xi Jinping's new international ambitions.

---

[101]Interview with Western military official, Djibouti, October 15, 2018.

[102]Céline Pajon, 'Japan's Security Policy in Africa: The Dawn of a Strategic Approach?', IFRI, Paris, May, 2017, https://www.ifri.org/sites/default/files/atoms/files/pajon_japan_security_policy_africa_2017.pdf; Hinichi Fujiwara, 'Japan to expand SDF base in Djibouti in part to counter China', The Asahi Shimbun, November 15, 2018, accessed January 24, 2019, http://www.asahi.com/ajw/articles/AJ201811150063.html.

[103]Abhijit Singh, 'China's Military Base in Djibouti: Strategic Implications for India', War on the Rocks, 21 August 2017, accessed 2 June 2018, https://warontherocks.com/2017/08/chinas-military-base-in-djibouti-strategic-implications-for-india/; Shashwat Tiwari, 'To counter China, India needs a military base in Djibouti', Wion News, October 6, 2017, accessed May 9, 2018, http://www.wionews.com/world/to-counter-china-india-needs-a-military-base-in-djibouti-21076.

[104]Rod Edens, 'India crafts its own "string of pearls" to rival China's naval jewels in the Indian Ocean', SCMP, March 24, 2018, accessed May 5, 2018, https://www.scmp.com/comment/insight-opinion/article/2138327/india-crafts-its-own-string-pearls-rival-chinas-naval-jewels.

[105]Interview with French and Indian diplomats, October 2018.

[106]Vivienne, 'Djibouti célèbre le 40ème anniversaire de son indépendance dans la communion (REPORTAGE)' [Djibouti celebrates the 40th anniversary of its independence in communion (report)], French.china.org.cn, June 28, 2017, accessed January 27, 2019, http://french.china.org.cn/foreign/txt/2017-06/28/content_41115824.htm.

[107]According to Pierre Razoux, senior research fellow at the Institut de recherches stratégiques de l'Ecole militaire (IRSEM), quoted in 'Pourquoi Djibouti est devenu la "caserne du monde"?' [Why Djibouti has become the 'world's barracks'], Géopolitique, April 8, 2018, accessed January 27, 2019, https://miscellanees01.wordpress.com/2018/04/08/djibouti-caserne-militaire/.

[108]This was revealed by Guelleh to French President Hollande in January 2018, Sébastien Le Belzic, 'A Djibouti, "la Chine commence à déchanter"' [in Djibouti, China is becoming disenchanted], Le Monde, February 5, 2018, accessed January 24, 2019, http://www.lemonde.fr/afrique/article/2018/02/05/a-djibouti-la-chine-commence-a-dechanter_5252153_3212.html.

[109]Interviews, Djibouti, October 14–17, 2018.

Initially cautious, China has become more and more open about its real intentions: from a logistics support facility, the PLA base has rapidly turned into a full-fledged naval and army base able to conduct all sorts of missions. True, it remains to be seen in what kind of operations it will be involved apart from the PLAN's ongoing escorts and port calls. Nonetheless, we can be assured that sooner or later, the Chinese military present in Djibouti will fulfill some of the tasks already publicly listed by their government, for example, extracting nationals from a hostile environment as in the recent popular movies *Wolf Warrior 2* (*Zhanlang Er*) or *Operation Red Sea* (*Honghai Xingdong*). Consequently, contrary to what it was initially announced, the Djibouti PLA base personnel is highly likely to eventually take part in combat operations, potentially compelling the Chinese government to instil additional flexibility in its non-interference principle.[110]

Beyond these important and practical objectives, China's first overseas military base in Djibouti provides that country with an 'entry ticket' to a rather exclusive club. In spite of its official discourse, China is behaving like other great powers: there is not such a thing as a military base with 'Chinese or socialist characteristics'. As a good student of Alfred Thayer Mahan, the Chinese Communist Party leadership knows well that naval power and overseas bases will help China better protect its commerce, trade routes, BRI and interests overseas.

There is no doubt that Djibouti is just the first Chinese overseas military base; China will build other bases. The PLA, particularly China's NRI (Naval Research Institute)'s experts, have already much discussed this issue.[111] Fulfilling UN missions and agreement of the host countries have been invoked as the two main conditions making the construction of such bases possible.[112] Today, Gwadar, or its military extension, Jiwani, is the most likely another potential naval base.[113] Xi's BRI is a strong argument to give priority to Pakistan. However, the PLA is also looking at other parts of Africa where its interests may be at risks, as the Gulf of Guinea (Lomé, Togo, Douala, Cameroon) or Southern Africa (Wallis Bay, Namibia).[114]

In any event, it is likely that Beijing will first test the *modus operandi* and the usefulness of its Djibouti facilities before embarking into establishing another overseas military base. For the time being, it prefers concluding agreements to facilitate access to foreign ports by its Navy ships, as it did with Cambodia in July 2019.

Finally, does China want and hope to kick Western powers and Japan out of Djibouti? China is the seventh nation to have established a military presence in Djibouti and, ironically, the security of its contingent, as well as Djibouti as a whole, largely depends on the presence of other militaries, particularly the US and the French. This environment may be sometimes uncomfortable but basically serves China's interests. However, China's dominant economic influence on Djibouti is giving it an advantage that is likely to have detrimental consequences for other military powers present there.

Yet, the establishment of a PLA naval base in Djibouti has highlighted the growing strategic rivalry between China and the US, and the West in general. In other words, Djibouti operates as a microcosm of a world order which is less and less multipolar and more and more bipolar. In Djibouti as elsewhere, the US–China bipolarity will remain for a long time asymmetrical. Nonetheless, in Djibouti and beyond, this bipolarity is likely to impose limits on cooperation and feed strategic competition between Beijing and Washington.[115]

All in all, Djibouti's PLA military base has become a genuine attribute of China's growing power and global ambitions. It shows that the People's Republic has gone a long way since it denounced

[110]Wang, 'First Place–On the Shores of Bab-el-Manded'.
[111]Li Jian, Chen Wenwen, and Jin Chang, 'Yinduyang haiquan geju yu Zhongguo haiquan de Yinduyang kuozhan' ['Overall Situation of Sea Power in the Indian Ocean and the Expansion in the Indian Ocean of Chinese Seapower'], *Taipingyang xuebao* [*Pacific Journal*] 22(5), (2014), pp. 74–75, quoted by Downs et al., p. 40.
[112]'Additional overseas PLA bases "possible"', *China Daily*, January 10, 2019, accessed January 25, 2019, http://www.china.org.cn/china/2019-01/10/content_74358640.htm.
[113]Duchâtel and Shelton Dupleix, 'Blue China Navigating the Maritime Silk Road to Europe', p. 34.
[114]Marchal, 'Mutations géopolitiques', p. 9.
[115]Tunsjø, *The Return of Bipolarity in World Politics*, Ch. 7.

mperialist' military outposts. The real test in the future will be the operationalization of this facility in ase of an international crisis or even war.

Disclosure statement

No potential conflict of interest was reported by the author.

Funding

This research has been funded by the Research Grant Council of Hong Kong Special Administrative Region (GRF No. HKBU 12400103).

China's Response to Threats to Its Overseas Economic Interests: Softening Non-Interference and Cultivating Hegemony

Yizheng Zou and Lee Jones

ABSTRACT

Chinese firms have acquired enormous overseas interests since 2000. As relative latecomers to global markets, they often invest in territories subject to high political risk, which is often heightened by poorly regulated Chinese practices. This article describes these risks to China's growing overseas economic interests and explores China's response to them. First, the Chinese party-state is gradually softening its insistence on 'non-interference', intervening to secure Chinese economic interests overseas. Second, Chinese actors are seeking to cultivate greater consent among social forces in key states. This partial convergence with the practices of other major capitalist states has important implications for debates on China's rise. These arguments are illustrated through a case study of Chinese engagement in Myanmar after 2011.

Introduction

In 2000, the Chinese government urged private and state-owned enterprises (SOEs) to 'go out': to pursue new overseas markets and investment opportunities. From 2000 to 2016, China's outward direct investment (ODI) flows rose from US$915m to US$183.1bn, taking China's total ODI stock from US$27.8bn to US$1.28tr.[1] Major projects are also frequently accompanied by development finance, estimated at US$354.4bn from 2000 to 2014, just US$40bn less than the United States.[2] Chinese trade has also boomed, from $1.02tr to US$5.92tr from 2000 to 2013.[3] Even Chinese workers have 'gone out', with 970,000 officially posted abroad in 2016 alone.[4]

This dramatic overseas economic expansion shapes the now-extensive debate on the implications of China's rise for global order, much of which is quite negative. Chinese investment is widely seen as poorly governed, with weak social and environmental safeguards, often negatively impacting local communities.[5] Chinese firms and their political backers have often engaged undemocratic governments, including 'rogue' states subject to international sanctions, raising concerns that Beijing is propping up authoritarian regimes.[6] Chinese development financing has been dubbed 'rogue aid'

---

[1]UNCTAD, *World Investment Report 2017* (Geneva: UNCTAD, 2017), pp. 226–32.

[2]Axel Dreher et al., 'Aid, China, and Growth: Evidence from a New Global Development Finance Dataset', AidData Working Paper 46, October 2017.

[3]UNCTAD, 'UNCTADstat', accessed January 26, 2018, http://unctadstat.unctad.org.

[4]Chinese Ministry of Commerce, 'MOFCOM Department Official of Outward Investment and Economic Cooperation Comments on China's Outward Investment and Cooperation in 2016', January 18, 2017, accessed October 18, 2017, http://english.mofcom.gov.cn/article/newsrelease/policyreleasing/201701/20170102503092.shtml.

[5]Yuan Wang and Simon Zadek, *Sustainability Impacts of Chinese Outward Direct Investment: A Review of the Literature* (Winnipeg International Institute for Sustainable Development, 2016).

[6]Julia Bader, 'China, Autocratic Patron? An Empirical Investigation of China as a Factor in Autocratic Survival', *International Studies Quarterly* 59(1), (2015), pp. 23–33; Julia Bader, 'Propping up Dictators? Economic Cooperation from China and Its Impact on Authoritarian Persistence in Party and Non-Party Regimes', *European Journal of Political Research* 54(4), (2015), pp. 655–672.

that undermines Western-promoted 'good governance'.[7] China's illiberal market-authoritarianism is also feared as a more attractive model—sometimes dubbed the 'Beijing consensus'—than Western-backed neoliberalism.[8] Beijing has often rebuffed such criticism by invoking the principle of non-interference in states' internal affairs, raising concern that 'the way is being paved back to Westphalia', reversing liberal gains.[9] The 'Belt and Road Initiative' (BRI), launched in 2013, has provoked fear that Beijing is now using overseas investment and aid as part of a 'grand strategy to re-constitute the Eurasian regional order with new governance ideas, norms and rules'.[10]

Drawing on extensive fieldwork in Myanmar and China, this article contributes to this debate by exploring how China is managing threats to its overseas economic interests. The article's starting point, following more skeptical scholarship,[11] is that China's economic expansion is not an uncomplicated boon for Chinese power and influence, but has actually exacerbated socio-political conflict in many partner countries, creating diplomatic 'blowback' for Beijing. This is a structural, long-term problem: as relative late-comers to international markets, Chinese multi-nationals have been forced into riskier territories shunned by Western firms. Accordingly, over a quarter of China's ODI is located in risky territories (see Table 1), which Chinese analysts have already identified as one of BRI's major challenges.[12] The article's first section discusses the challenges to Chinese economic interests and identifies three responses by the party-state. First, regulations governing overseas investment are tightening, with greater emphasis on social and environmental protection. Second, China is softening its non-interference policy, increasingly intervening to secure overseas economic interests. Third, Chinese elites are seeking to cultivate greater societal consent for China's economic role in foreign countries. Often glossed as a quest for soft power', this is better interpreted as an attempt to build hegemony[13] among subordinated social groups in territories where Chinese business is heavily engaged[14].

The article's second section provides a detailed case study of these dynamics in Sino-Myanmar relations. Since Myanmar's shift in 2011 from a military dictatorship to a constrained electoral regime, Chinese interests have faced serious challenges, including civil and armed unrest threatening Chinese megaprojects and a crisis in bilateral diplomatic and economic relations following the suspension of a major dam project. In response, Chinese party-state leaders have softened their

Table 1. Distribution of Chinese ODI by Recipient-Country Risk Level.

Political Risk Rating	Percentage of Chinese ODI
Very high	13.8%
High	13.4%
Moderate	3.5%
Low	28.9%
Very low	40.4%

---

[7]Moisés Naím, 'Rogue Aid', *Foreign Policy* 159, (2007), pp. 95–96; cf. Axel Dreher and Andreas Fuchs, 'Rogue Aid? An Empirical Analysis of China's Aid Allocation', *Canadian Journal of Economics* 48(3), (2015), pp. 988–1023.

[8]Joshua Cooper Ramo, *The Beijing Consensus* (London: Foreign Policy Centre, 2004).

[9]Daniel Flemes, 'Network Powers: Strategies of Change in the Multipolar System', *Third World Quarterly* 34(6), (2013), p. 1017.

[10]William A. Callahan, *China's Belt and Road Initiative and the New Eurasian Order* (Oslo: Norwegian Institute of International Affairs, 2016), p. 1.

[11]E.g. Bates Gill and James Reilly, 'The Tenuous Hold of China Inc. in Africa', *Washington Quarterly* 30(3), (2007), pp. 37–52.

[12]Ji Miao, 'Expectations and Realities: Managing the Risks of the "Belt and Road" Initiative', *China Quarterly of International Strategic Studies* 1(3), (2015), p. 514.

[13]The authors use 'hegemony' here in a precise Gramscian sense, rather than to denote domineering behaviour, as in common Chinese usage. See below.

[14]Calculated from Carlos Casanova, Alicia Garcia-Herrero, and Le Xia, 'Chinese Outbound Foreign Direct Investment: How Much Goes Where After Round-Tripping and Offshoring?', BBVA Research Working Paper 15/17, June 2015; World Bank 'Political Risk Services International Country Risk Guide', 2016, accessed June 15, 2018, https://info.worldbank.org/governance/wgi/pdf/prs.xlsx.

non-interference policy, intervening in Myanmar's domestic peace process. They have also extended their relationships beyond Myanmar's military and business elites, courting non-governmental organizations (NGOs), monks, trade unions and others, while tightening overseas business regulations, to create a more consensual basis for Chinese investment.

As the article's conclusion discusses, these adaptive strategies indicate a *partial convergence* with the practices of other major capitalist powers, rather than the stark divergence implied by more alarmist accounts. However, this convergence remains limited: Chinese regulation is still weak, compliance remains partial, and not all corporate actors are evolving at the same speed. Moreover, China's cultivation of popular consent is limited by dynamics in target societies and structural constraints emanating from China's own political system.

Investment Blowback and Chinese Responses

This section summarizes the challenges Chinese investments face from socio-political upheaval and regime change and Chinese responses to these. The first part identifies two sets of challenges: rising socio-political conflict in which Chinese investments are directly implicated in and threatened by; and largely unconnected developments like regime instability, collapse and transition. The second part identifies the party-state's threefold response to these challenges: tightening regulation, rising interventionism and efforts to cultivate societal consent.

Political Risks to China's Overseas Economic Interests

The challenges to China's overseas investments are of two broad types. First, Chinese investment has generated or exacerbated socio-political conflict in target states. This is hardly unique to China: it is well understood that foreign investment can intensify unrest, especially in developing countries.[15] However, Chinese investment is particularly problematic for two reasons. First, as noted above, a large portion is concentrated in already-unstable areas. Second, Chinese investment, particularly in developing countries, is concentrated in controversial, high-impact sectors, for example large-scale infrastructure projects, mines, hydropower dams and agribusiness plantations. Third, China's overseas investments are weakly regulated by a highly fragmented governance system, with excessive reliance on host-country regulation—often wishful thinking or simply irresponsible buck-passing in poorly governed developing countries.[16] Accordingly, Chinese 'mega-projects' are often associated with environmental degradation, land-grabbing, forced displacement and militarization, as armed forces move to protect investment sites.[17] These dynamics—again, hardly unique to Chinese investment—are typical of primitive accumulation, or what Harvey calls 'accumulation by dispossession'.[18] The frequent use of imported Chinese labor also generates resentment. Typically, these often-severe costs are borne by subordinated social groups, while benefits flow overwhelmingly to a narrow elite.

Although outcomes vary, depending on how investments interact with local contexts, there are now many instances of these problems, generating challenges for China's overseas interests. Chinese investors' provocation of socio-political unrest has been documented in the Philippines

[15]John M. Rothgeb, *Foreign Investment and Political Conflict in Developing Countries* (Westport: Praeger, 1996).
[16]Friends of the Earth, 'Emerging Sustainability Frameworks: China Development Bank and China Export-Import Bank', January 2016, accessed May 8, 2019, https://foe.org/resources/emerging-sustainability-frameworks-china-development-bank-and-china-export-import-bank; Lee Jones and Yizheng Zou, 'Rethinking the Role of State-Owned Enterprises in China's Rise', *New Political Economy* 22(6) (2017), pp. 743–760.
[17]Transnational Institute, 'Financing Dispossession: China's Opium Substitution Programme in Northern Burma', February 2011, accessed May 9, 2019, https://www.tni.org/en/issues/alternative-development/item/3555-financing-dispossession-chinas-opium-substitution-programme-in-northern-burma; Transnational Institute, 'Access Denied: Land Rights and Ethnic Conflict in Burma', May 8, 2013, accessed May 8, 2019, https://www.tni.org/en/publication/access-denied-land-rights-and-ethnic-conflict-in-burma .
[18]David Harvey, *Spaces of Global Capitalism: A Theory of Uneven Geographical Development* (London: Verso, 2006).

Cambodia, Myanmar, Pakistan, Peru, Ecuador, Ghana and Zambia—to name but a few.[19] Opposition to the China-Pakistan Economic Corridor culminated in fatal attacks on Chinese engineers in early 2017, and China's embassy in November 2018. In Zambia, a negative reaction to Chinese investment spurred the election of a populist government hostile to Chinese investment in 2008.[20] In Ghana, the illegal influx of 50,000 Chinese gold miners, backed by Chinese local government officials, prompted violent unrest, precipitating a major bilateral crisis, endangering China's diplomatic standing and its efforts to access Ghanaian energy resources.[21] In the Philippines, inter-elite struggles over rents flowing from Chinese megaprojects scuttled joint hydrocarbon exploration in the South China Sea in 2005, followed by growing governmental hostility toward Beijing.[22] In Nepal, two Chinese hydropower dam projects worth a combined US $4.3bn were cancelled in 2017–18, following local protests and the election of a pro-Indian government, which turned instead to Delhi for investment.[23] In Myanmar, as discussed further below, ethnic-minority insurgents have abducted and killed Chinese hydropower dam engineers,[24] while protests against the Myitsone dam led to its suspension in 2011, causing a bilateral diplomatic crisis and a 95 percent slump in Chinese investment by 2014.[25]

The second sort of challenge arises from regime changes, which may be unrelated to Chinese actors' behavior. In Libya, for instance, NATO's decision to overthrow Colonel Gaddafi in 2011 plunged China's investment strategy into chaos, endangering over US$10bn-worth of deals.[26] Subsequent attacks on Chinese construction sites led to a 45 percent drop in contracted projects, including the suspension of a major railway project, costing the state-owned China Railways Construction Corporation US$3.6bn, and spurring 36,000 Chinese workers to flee.[27] In 2006, Venezuela's government threatened to nationalize international oil companies unless they established local joint ventures, imposing serious losses on Chinese SOEs.[28] As discussed further below, Myanmar's 2011 transition also generated challenges for Chinese interests.

Given China's political economy, these challenges can rapidly spill over from the economic into the political sphere. Whereas Western investors are largely private, China's largest multinationals

---

[9]Rohit Negi, 'Beyond the "Chinese Scramble": The Political Economy of Anti-China Sentiment in Zambia', *African Geographical Review* 27(1), (2008), pp. 41–63; Pak Nung Wong et al., 'As Wind, Thunder and Lightning: Local Resistance to China's Resource Led Diplomacy in the Christian Philippines', *South East Asia Research* 21(2), (2013), pp. 281–302; Tom Miller, *China's Asian Dream: Quiet Empire Building along the New Silk Road* (London: Zed Books, 2017), pp. 122–23; David Brenner, 'Ashes of Co-Optation: From Armed Group Fragmentation to the Rebuilding of Popular Insurgency in Myanmar', *Conflict, Security & Development* 15(4), (2015), pp. 337–58; Muzaffar Hussain, 'China Pakistan Economic Corridor (CPEC): Challenges and the Way Forward', Unpublished Thesis, US Naval Postgraduate School, 2017, pp. 53–58, accessed May 8, 2019, https://calhoun.nps.edu/handle/10945/55626; Moises Arce, *Resource Extraction and Protest in Peru* (Pittsburgh: University of Pittsburgh Press, 2014); Susana Moreira, 'Learning from Failure: China's Overseas Oil Investments', *Journal of Current Chinese Affairs* 42(1), (2013), pp. 151–52; Frauke Urban et al., 'Chinese Overseas Hydropower Dams and Social Sustainability: The Bui Dam in Ghana and the Kamchay Dam in Cambodia', *Asia & the Pacific Policy Studies* 2(3), (2015), pp. 573–89.
[20]Steve Hess and Richard Aidoo, 'Charting the Roots of Anti-Chinese Populism in Africa: A Comparison of Zambia and Ghana', *Journal of Asian and African Studies* 49(2), (2014), pp. 129–47.
[21]Steve Hess and Richard Aidoo, 'Charting the Impact of Subnational Actors in China's Foreign Relations', *Asian Survey* 56(2), (2016), pp. 301–24.
[22]Caroline S. Hau, 'Entangling Alliances: Elite Cooperation and Competition in the Philippines and China', in *Chinese Encounters in Southeast Asia: How People, Money, and Ideas from China Are Changing a Region*, ed. Pál Nyíri and Danielle Tan. (Seattle: University of Washington Press, 2017), pp. 119–35.
[23]Gopal Sharma, 'Nepal Says to Scrap Hydropower Deal with Chinese Firm', *Reuters*, May 29, 2018, accessed May 8, 2019, https://www.reuters.com/article/china-nepal-hydropower/nepal-says-to-scrap-hydropower-deal-with-chinese-firm-idUSL3N1T04IQ.
[24]Salween Watch, 'Briefing: Current Status of Dam Projects on Burma's Salween River', March 13, 2013, accessed May 8, 2019, https://www.internationalrivers.org/resources/briefing-current-status-of-dam-projects-on-burma%E2%80%99s-salween-river -7868; Grace Mang and Katy Yan, 'China-Backed Dams Escalating Ethnic Tension in Burma', International Rivers, March 26, 2013, accessed May 8, 2019, https://www.internationalrivers.org/resources/china-backed-dams-escalating-ethnic-tension-in-burma-7906.
[25]Jones and Zou, 'Rethinking the Role', pp. 751, 753–54.
[26]Miao, 'Expectations and Realities', p. 511.
[27]Stephanie Erian, 'China at the Libyan Endgame', *Policy* 28(1), (2012), pp. 49–50.
[28]Moreira, 'Learning from Failure', pp. 150–51.

are SOEs. Accordingly, their conduct is widely (though often incorrectly)[29] understood to reflect Chinese government policy, so their mistakes often generate diplomatic 'blowback' for Beijing.

Chinese Responses: From 'Non-Interference' to 'Constructive Involvement' and the Cultivation of Hegemony

Chinese leaders have increasingly noted and sought to address these problems over the last decade.[30] Their efforts are ad hoc and uncoordinated, but three major trends are identifiable.

First, regulators have repeatedly tightened rules governing ODI, particularly by SOEs.[31] Reforms have been piecemeal and largely reactive to crises, the persistent recurrence of which suggests that enforcement remains inadequate. A recent government survey of Chinese firms in BRI countries found that half were neglecting social impact assessments, a third were not conducting environmental impact assessments (EIAs) and ignorance of local regulations was widespread, revealing an extensive violation of basic Chinese laws.[32] Nonetheless, regulatory agencies clearly are seeking to improve companies' overseas conduct. There is also growing evidence that Chinese companies, learning from past mistakes, are embracing 'corporate social responsibility' (CSR), hedging against political risk and engaging better with local communities.[33]

Secondly, Chinese leaders have softened their traditional 'non-interference' policy, increasingly engaging in what is euphemistically called 'constructive involvement'.[34] Beijing's 'non-interference' policy has never been absolute in practice, but there is now growing evidence of Chinese intervention to pacify restive areas and respond to crises. This began in 2004 with the People's Liberation Army's (PLA) 'new historic missions', including counter-terrorism, counter-piracy, and other operations to safeguard overseas Chinese assets, nationals and trade.[35] For example, the PLA navy has joined multinational counter-piracy operations in the Gulf of Aden to protect flows of oil and goods to China, and evacuated Chinese nationals from Libya in 2012.[36] China has also supported counter-piracy efforts around the Malacca Straits, through which much Chinese shipping passes.[37] Following attacks on Chinese vessels on the Mekong River in 2011, the Chinese police established joint law-enforcement patrols with neighboring countries, institutionalized since 2017 in the Lancang-Mekong Integrated Law Enforcement and Security Cooperation Center. Beijing's contributions to UN and regional peacekeeping have also increased sharply. China's UN peacekeeping contribution has risen from 400 troops in 1992 to 2,500 in 2017, the largest among the Permanent Five members of the Security Council. In 2015, Beijing pledged to establish an 8,000-strong permanent standby force for UN peacekeeping (created in 2017), offered to train 2,000 foreign peacekeepers, and extended US$100m in military aid for the African Union's regional peacekeeping.[38] Eighty percent of Chinese peacekeepers are in Africa: around 1,000 in South Sudan, 400 in Mali and 230 in Congo and Darfur. China has a direct economic interest in stabilizing

---

[29]See Jones and Zou, 'Rethinking the Role'.

[30]Gill and Reilly, 'The Tenuous Hold of China Inc. in Africa.'

[31]For a summary see Shahar Hameiri and Lee Jones, 'China Challenges Global Governance? The Case of Chinese International Development Finance and the Asian Infrastructure Investment Bank', *International Affairs* 94(3), (2018), p. 591.

[32]CAITEC et al. *2017 Report on the Sustainable Development of Chinese Enterprises Overseas* (Beijing: CAITEC, 2017), pp. 54, 85, 97.

[33]Li-Wen Lin, 'Corporate Social Responsibility in China: Window Dressing or Structural Change', *Berkeley Journal of International Law* 28(1), (2010), pp. 64–100; Moreira, 'Learning from Failure'; Julian Kirchherr, Katrina J. Charles, and Matthew J. Walton, 'The Interplay of Activists and Dam Developers: The Case of Myanmar's Mega-Dams', *International Journal of Water Resources Development* 33(1), (2016), pp. 111–31.

[34]Zheng Chen, 'China Debates the Non-Interference Principle', *Chinese Journal of International Politics* 9(3), (2016), pp. 349–74.

[35]Mathieu Duchâtel, Oliver Bräuner, and Zhou Hang, *Protecting China's Overseas Interests: The Slow Shift Away from Non-Interference* (Stockholm: SIPRI, 2014); Jonas Parello-Plesner and Mathieu Duchâtel, *China's Strong Arm: Protecting Citizens and Assets Abroad* (Abingdon: Routledge, 2015).

[36]Andrea Ghiselli, 'The Chinese People's Liberation Army "Post-Modern" Navy', *The International Spectator* 50(1), (2015), pp. 117–36.

[37]Nazery Khalid, 'With a Little Help from My Friends: Maritime Capacity-Building Measures in the Straits of Malacca', *Contemporary Southeast Asia* 31(3), (2009), pp. 424–46.

[38]Sarah Zheng, 'China Completes Registration of 8,000-Strong UN Peacekeeping Force, Defence Ministry Says', *South China Morning Post*, September 29, 2017, accessed May 8, 2019, https://www.scmp.com/news/china/diplomacy-defence/article/2113436/china-completes-registration-8000-strong-un.

Sudan and South Sudan in particular, given SOEs' oil investments there. These projects faced fierce Western criticism during Sudan's civil war, compelling Beijing to abandon 'non-interference' and become closely involved in mediating, then implementing, a peace settlement.[39] Likewise, when South Sudan's civil war broke out in 2013, imperiling Chinese oil investments, Chinese diplomats supported the peace process, shaped UN Security Council resolutions, sent peacekeepers and participated in the peace agreement supervision body.[40]

Thirdly, Chinese actors are moving to cultivate societal support for China's growing influence and economic presence in host countries. This is often glossed as a quest for 'soft power' to match China's growing 'hard power'. However, 'soft power' is a problematic concept.[41] It normally contrasts military power to economic and ideological power, which supposedly generate 'attraction'. Thus, some argue that China's rapid economic expansion has increased its 'soft power', generating a so-called 'Beijing consensus'.[42] Yet, as described above, China's economic expansion can generate repulsion, not just attraction. Moreover, 'soft power' is statist, assuming that influence is projected from one state to another. In reality, different social groups may be attracted to/repelled by China and, moreover, because they enjoy unequal access to state power; this will condition political outcomes.[43] If repelled groups are politically marginalized, while attracted groups dominate, this may generate favorable outcomes and vice versa. Moreover, this may shift over time, particularly if social conflict intensifies and/or political transition changes groups' access to state power.

The Gramscian concept of hegemony offers a more nuanced way to understand Chinese behavior. Chinese officials and scholars generally use this term pejoratively to denote domineering behavior by the United States (and previously the Soviet Union). However, this article uses the term very differently. Gramsci argued that ruling-class domination was secured not only through coercion and material concessions but also the cultivation of consent from subordinated social forces, using the ideological apparatuses of 'civil society', including churches, schools, trade unions, media and so on.[44] Gramsci called this collaboration between 'political society' and 'civil society' the 'integral state'. When ideological initiatives were successfully combined with material concessions, 'hegemony' can result, whereby subordinated groups see ruling groups' domination as natural and desirable. International Relations (IR) scholars have scaled up this approach, arguing that dominant powers achieve international hegemony not merely through military and economic power but also when their ruling classes successfully inculcate consent among key social forces within other states.[45] Arguably, this is what China's 'cadre-capitalist' class[46] is attempting today.

This conceptualization shares something with d'Hooghe's notion of '"new" public diplomacy', whereby diverse actors within a state seek to 'influence ... how relevant publics view the entity and its activities, with the objective of winning their sympathy and support.'[47] However, it differs in three ways. First, it is more specific about the 'activities' being legitimated, foregrounding efforts to cultivate support for capitalist domination, which Gramsci identified as the central purpose of hegemony-building.[48] Second, it avoids the potentially misleading term 'diplomacy', which

[39]Daniel Large, 'China and the Contradictions of "Non-Interference" in Sudan', *Review of African Political Economy* 35(115), (2008), pp. 93–106; Aly Verjee, 'Explaining China's Involvement in the South Sudan Peace Process', *The Interpreter*, December 22, 2016, accessed October 18, 2017, https://www.lowyinstitute.org/the-interpreter/explaining-chinas-involvement-south-sudan-peace-process.

[40]abcd.

[41]Shaun Breslin, *The Soft Notion of China's 'Soft Power'* (London: Chatham House, 2011).

[42]E.g. Joshua Kurlantzick, *Charm Offensive: How China's Soft Power Is Transforming the World* (New Haven: Yale University Press, 2007).

[43]Ying Fan, 'Soft Power: Power of Attraction or Confusion?', *Place Branding and Public Diplomacy* 4(2), (2008), pp. 147–58.

[44]Antonio Gramsci, *Selections from the Prison Notebooks*, trans. Quintin Hoare and Geoffrey Nowell Smith (New York: International Publishers, 1971).

[45]Robert W. Cox, *Production, Power, and World Order: Social Forces in the Making of History* (New York: Columbia University Press, 1987).

[46]David S.G. Goodman, *Class in Contemporary China* (Cambridge: Polity, 2014), ch. 3.

[47]Ingrid d'Hooghe, *China's Public Diplomacy* (Leiden: Martinus Nijhoff, 2014), p. 6.

[48]Gramsci, *Selections*, p. 258.

normally denotes inter-state activity between diplomats. Third, and relatedly, Gramsci's 'integral state' concept accounts for the involvement of actors (and targets) beyond traditional diplomatic institutions. Gramscians are unsurprised to see 'policy networks consisting of state and non-state actors' at work[49]; this is expected in the cultivation of hegemony.

This conceptualization also usefully shifts analytical attention away from the usual, rather banal emphasis in the 'soft power' literature on cultural exports and China's 'attractiveness' (e.g. the Beijing Olympics, Confucius Institutes) toward concrete attempts to persuade targeted social groups that China's growing economic might serves their interests, not merely China's. Beijing' provision of development financing—now estimated at around US$5bn annually—clearly reflect this goal. Although aid is usually 'tied' to subsidize Chinese companies, it is also dispensed at recipients' request and without political conditions—so-called 'win-win' cooperation. Similarly, the BRI is depicted as providing global 'public goods', benefiting China and recipients alike. It i accompanied by an extra RMB60bn (US$9bn) of aid for housing, poverty alleviation and healthcare,[50] Targeting poor and marginalized groups that, historically, have benefited little from and have often resisted, Chinese investment. China's BRI masterplan explicitly seeks stronger 'people-to-people bond[s]' by 'promoting extensive cultural and academic exchanges, personnel exchanges and cooperation, media cooperation, youth, and women exchanges and volunteer services, *so as to win public support* for [BRI].'[51]

This involves scaling up activity by Chinese non-governmental organizations (NGOs) and government-organized NGOs (GONGOs). From 2009, Beijing encouraged Chinese NGOs and GONGO to 'go out' to counter African NGOs' mounting criticism of Chinese investments.[52] By 2013, around 100 Chinese (GO)NGOs were operating in Africa.[53] Some engaged African NGOs in dialogue and 'capacity-building' exercises, to try to change their attitudes, while others worked to defuse popular anti-Chinese resentment. The Chinese-African People's Friendship Organization, for example, wa converted into 'a philanthropic charity arm for Chinese private and state-owned enterprises'.[5] Similarly, the China Foundation for Poverty Alleviation (CFPA) built a 'friendship hospital' in Sudan in 2011, heavily financed by China National Petroleum Corporation.[55] CFPA now works in 1: countries, covering healthcare, education and disaster relief.[56] The Global Environmenta Institute, a Beijing-based NGO, has also worked in South and Southeast Asia and Africa to improve the legitimacy of Chinese trade and investment by encouraging Chinese companies, Chinese regulators and financiers, and host-country governments, to adopt stronger environmental and social safeguards.[57]

Case study: Securing Chinese Capitalism in Myanmar

This article now illustrates these trends through a detailed case study of Myanmar, which wa selected for four reasons. First, China now has extensive economic interests there, which are

[49]D'Hooghe, *China's Public Diplomacy*, p. 19.
[50]Xi Jinping, 'Full Text of President Xi's Speech at Opening of Belt and Road Forum', *Xinhua*, May 14, 2017, accessed May 8 2019, http://www.xinhuanet.com/english/2017-05/14/c_136282982.htm.
[51]NDRC et al. 'Vision and Actions on Jointly Building Silk Road Economic Belt and 21st-Century Maritime Silk Road', March 28 2015, accessed May 82019, http://en.ndrc.gov.cn/newsrelease/201503/t20150330_669367.html.
[52]David Brenner, 'Are Chinese NGOs "Going out"? The Role of Chinese NGOs and GONGOs in Sino-African Relations', *Journal c Public and International Affairs* 22(1), (2012), pp. 131–52.
[53]Jennifer Y. J. Hsu, Timothy Hildebrandt, and Reza Hasmath, '"Going Out" or Staying In? The Expansion of Chinese NGOs i Africa', *Development Policy Review* 34(3), (2016), p. 426.
[54]Brenner, 'Are Chinese NGOs "Going out"?', p. 142.
[55]Jennifer Y. J. Hsu, 'The Internationalisation of Chinese NGOs', *Asia Dialogue*, September 9, 2016, accessed October 10, 2018 http://theasiadialogue.com/2016/09/29/gongos-vs-ngos-the-internationalisation-of-chinese-ngos.
[56]CFPA, 'Our International Work', n.d., accessed October 15, 2018, http://en.cfpa.org.cn/index.php?file=article&cmd=list&cid= 12.
[57]Global Environmental Institute, 'Overseas Investment, Trade and the Environment Program', 2017, accessed October 15, 2018 http://www.geichina.org/_upload/file/project_flyer/oite_2017.pdf.

undoubtedly understated even by the following official statistics. By September 2018, 36 percent of Myanmar's approved investment (US$28.12bn) was Chinese.[58] In 2016, 38 percent of Myanmar's trade was with China, while 27 percent of the trade of China's Yunnan was with neighboring Myanmar.[59] Myanmar is also central to China's BRI, especially the proposed Bangladesh-China-India -Myanmar corridor. Secondly, Chinese economic interests in Myanmar have faced many of the challenges described above. Before Myanmar's 2011 regime transition, Chinese investors were criticized by Western states and pro-democracy dissidents for supporting Myanmar's military dictatorship; thereafter, they have encountered mounting socio-political resistance. Third, Chinese government advisors see Beijing's reaction to these challenges as 'globally significant'; it is a 'classroom for China' that will demonstrate to the world whether Beijing can adapt to criticism and lay a secure basis for the BRI.[60] Finally, this recent (indeed, ongoing) case updates the now quite dated literature on this topic and extends its geographical coverage beyond the usual focus on Africa.[61] The following sub-sections identify the nature of the challenge to China's economic interests in Myanmar, then trace the Chinese response.

China's Challenge in Myanmar

Myanmar is one of the world's riskiest investment destinations. It is home to the world's longest-running ethnic conflicts: ethnic-minority rebel groups (EMRGs) in Myanmar's borderlands have struggled against the centralizing, homogenizing state—dominated by the majority-ethnic Bamar—since independence in 1948. Decades of counter-insurgency have cemented a dominant political role for the military (known as the Tatmadaw). Following prolonged military rule, then a military-backed one-party regime, the Bamar heartlands erupted in pro-democracy protests in 1988, prompting another coup. The junta which then ruled Myanmar until 2011 faced Western sanctions, backing Aung San Suu Kyi's National League for Democracy (NLD), but tightened its grip with extensive Chinese military, diplomatic and economic support. The regime tempered ethnic insurgencies through growing repression, ceasefires and 'ceasefire capitalism'[62]—business deals, often focused on natural resource exploitation, which enriched military and EMRG leaders, crony capitalists and foreign investors. Eventually, the military designed a new constitution and staged elections in 2010, leading to a constrained regime transition.[63] Elected civilian governments now share power uneasily with the military, first under ex-general President Thein Sein (2011–16) and now Suu Kyi's NLD government. Ethnic strife remains intense. Indeed, from 2009–15, several longstanding EMRG ceasefires broke down in Kachin and Shan states, bordering China. Conflict also flared in Rakhine state, where long-persecuted Rohingya Muslims endured mounting communal violence from 2012, then a brutal military crackdown in 2017, following attacks by the Arakan Rohingya Salvation Army (ARSA), driving over 727,000 into Bangladesh.

China's economic engagement has exacerbated these deep social conflicts in several ways. Chinese investment has been concentrated in export-oriented natural resource extraction (oil, gas, mining, logging), hydropower dam development and agribusiness, all predominantly in Myanmar's resource-rich borderlands. These investments frequently involved violent land-grabbing, forced displacement and militarization.[64] They were overwhelmingly brokered with—and enriched—a

---

[58]Myanmar Directorate of Investment and Company Administration, 'Foreign Investment of Permitted Enterprises as of 30/9/2018 (By Country)', September 2018, accessed October 16, 2018, https://www.dica.gov.mm/sites/dica.gov.mm/files/docu ment-files/fil_country.pdf. This includes Hong Kong.

[59]UNCTAD, 'UNCTADstat'; Yunnan Department of Commerce, '2017 nian 1–12 yue Yunnan Sheng Jinchukou Qingkuang' ['Yunnan Import and Export Data, 2017   ], January 15, 2018, accessed November 27, 2018, http://www.bofcom.gov.cn/tjsj/jcksj/201805/t20180528_751517.html.

[60]Interview with Experts in a Chinese Think Tank Focused on Sino-Myanmar Relations, Kunming, November 2018.

[61]Cf. Gill and Reilly, 'The Tenuous Hold'.

[62]Kevin Woods, 'Ceasefire Capitalism: Military-Private Partnerships, Resource Concessions and Military-State Building in the Burma–China Borderlands', *Journal of Peasant Studies* 38(4), (2011), pp. 747–70.

[63]Lee Jones, 'The Political Economy of Myanmar's Transition', *Journal of Contemporary Asia* 44(1), (2014), pp. 144–70.

[64]Woods, 'Ceasefire Capitalism'; Jones, 'Political Economy'; Transnational Institute, 'Financing Dispossession'; Transnational Institute, 'Access Denied'.

narrow elite of military commanders, EMRG and militia leaders, and crony capitalists, while ordinary people scarcely benefited. Coupled with the influx of cheap Chinese products and over two million Chinese immigrants since 1988, and with Beijing's economic and political support for the junta, this generated widespread anti-Chinese sentiment. Popular resistance to Chinese mega-projects emerged well before 2011, even under highly repressive conditions, with protests against oil and gas fields and pipelines, and hydropower dams in Kachin state.[65] Even the Tatmadaw has little real affection for China, despite Beijing's patronage, given its previous support for communist insurgency during the Cold War, and its dubious relations with several EMRGs today.[66]

Chinese investment is directly implicated in some of Myanmar's contemporary conflicts, notably the renewed conflict between the Tatmadaw and Kachin Independence Organization/Army (KIO/KIA) after 2011. Through the preceding decade, discontent had mounted among the Kachin ethnic-minority about 'ceasefire capitalism' and rapacious Chinese logging, mining, dam-building and agribusiness investments. The most prominent flashpoint was the SOE China Power Investment's US$3.6bn Myitsone dam project, which threatened to flood a Singapore-sized area of great cultural significance and attracted mounting local resistance from 2004. Alongside other abuses, this rekindled the Kachin resistance and sparked Tatmadaw-KIA tensions, contributing directly to the breakdown of their ceasefire in 2011.[67] The renewed fighting has directly imperiled Chinese investments, beginning at China's Darpein dam and threatening the oil and gas pipelines, which transect Kachin state. Renewed fighting in Shan state has also displaced up to 100,000 refugees into China since 2009, including Chinese nationals. Violence in Rakhine state also imperils Chinese economic interests: its Kyaukphyu township is the starting point of the oil and gas pipelines and was selected in 2014 to host a US$10bn, Chinese-built deep-sea port and special economic zone (SEZ), coupled to a US$20bn China-Myanmar railway and highway.

Myanmar's regime transition has also allowed other societal actors to mobilize openly against Chinese economic projects, including fledgling NGOs, ethnic-minority campaigners and Buddhist monks. Crucially, in 2011 Bamar environmentalists were able to join Kachin activists opposing the Myitsone dam, framing it as an 'existential threat to the people of Myanmar by Chinese colonialism'.[68] Coupled with the Kachin unrest, this prompted President Thein Sein to suspend the project in September 2011, explicitly to demonstrate that the new 'democratic' government was responsive to public opinion.[69] Emboldened, other civil society groups, often led by Paung Ku—an internationally funded NGO founded in 2007—have criticized other Chinese projects, including dams, the oil and gas pipelines, and the US$3bn Laung Lon oil refinery project.[70] Buddhist monks and Kachin and Bamar Christian clergy have also criticized Chinese megaprojects. Farmer- and monk-led protests against the Letpadaung copper mine, a joint venture between a Chinese firm and a military company, were brutally suppressed in 2012 and 2014, while the famed Buddhist monk Zaya Ditha has denounced the BRI.[71] Newly legalized trade unions, led by the Confederation of Trade Unions of Myanmar (CTUM), which comprises around half of Myanmar's unions, are also challenging Chinese

[65]Shwe Gas Movement, 'The Shwe Gas Movement', May 2004, accessed October 15, 2018, http://www.shwe.org/; Kachin Development Networking Group, 'Damming the Irrawaddy', 2007, accessed October 15, 2018, http://burmacampaign.org.uk/media/DammingtheIrr.pdf.

[66]Min Zin, 'Burmese Attitude toward Chinese: Portrayal of the Chinese in Contemporary Cultural and Media Works', *Journal of Current Southeast Asian Affairs* 31(1), (2012), pp. 115–31.

[67]Brenner, 'Ashes of Co-Optation'; see also Laur Kiik, 'Nationalism and Anti-Ethno-Politics: Why "Chinese Development" Failed at Myanmar's Myitsone Dam', *Eurasian Geography and Economics* 57(3), (2016), pp. 374–402.

[68]Tira Foran et al., 'Large Hydropower and Legitimacy: A Policy Regime Analysis, Applied to Myanmar', *Energy Policy* 110, (2017), p. 626.

[69]Debby Sze Wan Chan, 'Asymmetric Bargaining Between Myanmar and China in the Myitsone Dam Controversy: Social Opposition Akin to David's Stone Against Goliath', *Pacific Review* 30(5), (2017), pp. 674–91; Foran et al., 'Large Hydropower and Legitimacy'.

[70]Interview with Kyaw Thu, Director, Paung Ku, Yangon, March 13, 2017.

[71]Zaya Ditha, 'ho ta law le ka a me ri kan than a mat haung' ['Talk with former US Ambassador Days Before'], *Facebook*, April 27, 2017, accessed April 27, 2017, https://www.facebook.com/oozinzero/posts/1960785257491375.

business interests.[72] Strikes, which occurred even under military rule, have intensified, with Chinese factories among those targeted. Most notoriously, from January-March 2017, strikes paralyzed the Hangzhou Hundred-Tex Garment factory, which supplies global brands like H&M. Workers beat their Chinese manager and caused US$75,000 of damage, and the company lost its international contracts.[73]

Aung San Suu Kyi is often hostile to these groups, trying unsuccessfully to block foreign funding and assistance for NGOs and CTUM, apparently seeing them as political rivals.[74] She even warned farmers at Letpadaung to stop protesting or face arrest, arguing that Myanmar 'needed a lot of development'.[75] Nonetheless, even she cannot entirely ignore popular concerns.

These developments seriously challenge Chinese economic interests and pose cross-border security problems. From 2010 to 2014, Chinese investment plummeted from US$1.52bn (68 percent of Myanmar's total) to just US$70.4m (7 percent) and has never exceeded 12 percent since.[76] SOEs' megaprojects, in particular, have faltered. The Myitsone dam remains suspended, with no compensation paid to CPI, and no new dam projects have been approved. An agreement on the China-Myanmar railway lapsed in 2014. Following environmental protests, work on the US$3bn Dawei oil refinery was canceled in November 2017. The Kyaukphyu port and SEZ project, notionally agreed in 2013, was stalled until late 2018.

Chinese experts have widely recognized and lamented this enormous setback, quickly recognizing that China's previous modus operandi—striking cozy deals with military elites, crony capitalists and EMRG leaders without regard to the wider public—was unsustainable. The crisis in Sino-Myanmar relations drove much of the post-2011 tightening of ODI regulation, in addition to the softening of non-interference, and efforts to cultivate popular consent for China's economic presence.

China's Response: (1) From Non-Interference to Intervention

To pacify Myanmar's borderlands and safeguard physical Chinese investments, Chinese elites have softened their traditional 'non-interference' policy, intervening to broker a peace settlement. This was a substantial turnaround. Under the junta, Beijing had prioritized economic engagement beneath the cover of 'non-interference', vetoing Western-sponsored UN resolutions. This served Chinese politico-business interests well for years, but Myanmar's renewed civil war forced China's Ministry of Foreign Affairs (MFA) to change tack.

The MFA has repeatedly intervened to pacify Myanmar's borderlands, first with the KIA, then other EMRGs as the violence spread. Former MFA Vice-Minister Wang Yingfan, appointed Special Envoy for Asian Affairs, brokered KIO/A-government peace talks in Yunnan in February and March 2013.[77] This 'firm intervention' generated Myanmar's first ever multiparty peace talks, followed by a KIA-government truce in May 2013, formally backed by China and the UN.[78] However, sporadic fighting continued. Wang held further talks with the KIO chairman in Kunming in August 2013 and brokered further KIO-government negotiations in November, but

---

[72]Interview with CTUM Executive Committee member, Yangon, March 3, 2017.

[73]'Bosses, Workers Negotiate Return to Work After $75,000 Rampage at Garment Plant', *Frontier Myanmar*, March 10, 2017, accessed May 8, 2019, https://frontiermyanmar.net/en/bosses-workers-negotiate-return-to-work-after-75000-rampage-at-garment-plant.

[74]Interview with a consultant, Myanmar Ministry of Social Welfare, Relief and Resettlement, Yangon, December 2016; Interview with CTUM Executive Committee member.

[75]Lawi Weng and Thet Swe Aye, 'Stop Protests against Copper Mine, Suu Kyi Tells Communities', *Irrawaddy*, March 13, 2013, accessed May 8, 2019, https://www.irrawaddy.com/news/burma/stop-protests-against-copper-mine-suu-kyi-tells-communities.html.

[76]ASEAN Secretariat, 'ASEANstats Database', 2017, accessed October 15, 2018, http://aseanstats.asean.org.

[77]Consulate-General of PRC in Houston, 'Foreign Ministry Spokesperson Hua Chunying's Regular Press Conference on March 12, 2013 ', March 13, 2013, accessed October 15, 2018, http://www.mfa.gov.cn/ce/cght/eng/fyrth/t1021196.htm.

[78]International Crisis Group, 'A Tentative Peace in Myanmar's Kachin Conflict', Asia Briefing 140, June 2013, pp. 1–2, 12–16.

without success. Several similarly fruitless meetings followed through 2014.[79] The conflict escalated in 2015, spreading to Shan state as the Myanmar National Democratic Army, Shan State Army-North, Arakan Army and Ta'ang National Liberation Army all clashed with the Tatmadaw. By then, President Thein Sein had proposed a 'national ceasefire accord' as a precursor to full peace talks—an approach copied by the NLD. Sun Guoxiang, who replaced Wang in September 2015, sought to persuade the EMRGs to sign the accord through early to mid-2016. In August, he also visited the United Wa State Army (UWSA), Myanmar's largest EMRG, urging them to participate in Suu Kyi's 'Twenty-First Century Panglong Conference'.[80] Chinese mediation helped secure several EMRGs' formal participation in September 2016, but the conference ended without agreement, as did two subsequent meetings. In early 2017, Sun visited Wa and Kachin states and hosted further talks in Kunming, urging all parties to implement ceasefires and engage in peace talks.[81] High-ranking officials from China's MFA, Defence Ministry, and PLA have also interceded with the Myanmar government.[82] China has also squeezed the EMRGs by curbing the illicit border trade that sustains them.[83] Agreement remains elusive, but clearly not for want of Chinese intervention.

China has also tried to help pacify Rakhine state, though its intervention here is more tentative, reflecting extreme sensitivity in Myanmar. In April 2017, Sun Guoxiang visited Dhaka, offering to mediate between Myanmar and Bangladesh, where around 300,000 Rohingya refugees were already sheltering.[84] Naypyidaw demurred. But following Rohingyas' mass exodus in late 2017, Foreign Minister Wang Yi flew to Naypyidaw, renewing this offer and outlining a three-stage Chinese plan for a ceasefire, bilateral talks, then steps toward a 'long-term solution'.[85] This apparently pushed Myanmar and Bangladesh into signing a bilateral repatriation agreement. Although Beijing blocked a UN Security Council resolution, it agreed to a presidential statement that largely recapitulated Britain's draft resolution.[86] Beijing thereby condemned the violence in Rakhine and expressed 'grave concern' about human rights violations, calling on Myanmar to cease using 'excessive military force' and halt communal violence. The statement also 'demand[ed]' humanitarian access, urged the involvement of the UN High Commissioner for Refugees, pressed Myanmar to ensure refugees' 'voluntary, safe and dignified return,' and called for swift and full implementation of the domestic reforms specified by Kofi Annan's Advisory Commission on Rakhine State. Finally, the statement called for investigations into human rights abuses, full cooperation with UN bodies and media access.[87] Chinese diplomats reportedly tried to delete

---

[79]Yun Liu, 'Keqin Dulijun Xianzhuang' ['Kachin Independence Army Situation'], *Hanyue Myanmar Commentary*, August 9, 2016, accessed January 29, 2018, http://mp.weixin.qq.com/s/LmhVyc-12KWXswVCXtzRfw.

[80]Wa State Information Bureau, 'Xiao Mingliang fuzhuxi deng lingdao huijian zhongguo Waijiaobu yazhoutéshi Sun Guoxiang yixing' ['Vice Chairman Xiao Mingliang Meets with His Excellency Sun Guoxiang, Special Envoy of the Chinese Ministry of Foreign Affairs and His Delegation'], *Blog of Wa News Bureau*, August 2, 2016, accessed January 29, 2018, http://blog.sina.com.cn/s/blog_9084449c0102wxdu.html.

[81]Wa State Information Bureau, 'Zhongguo Waijiaobu Yazhou Teshi Sun Guoxiang yu Wobang Zhengfu Daibiaotuan zai Kunming Juxing Huitan' ['Asian Special Envoy of the Chinese Foreign Ministry Sun Guoxiang Holds Talks with Our State Government Delegation in Kunming'], *Blog of Wa News Bureau*, March 26, 2017, accessed January 29, 2018, http://blog.sina.com.cn/s/blog_9084449c0102x8ml.html.

[82]'China, Myanmar Hold Consultations on Maintaining Peace, Stability in Border Areas', *Xinhua*, November 26, 2016, accessed May 8, 2019, http://en.people.cn/n3/2016/1126/c90000-9147465.html; Chinese MFA, 'China and Myanmar Hold 2 + 2 High-Level Consultations Led by Ministry of Foreign Affairs and Ministry of Defence', February 7, 2017, accessed January 29, 2018, http://www.fmprc.gov.cn/mfa_eng/wjbxw/t1437166.shtml.

[83]Interview with Yunnan-based expert on Sino-Myanmar border affairs, Kunming, October 2018.

[84]Serajul Quadir, 'China Ready to Mediate between Myanmar, Bangladesh over Rohingya Row', *Reuters*, April 25, 2017, accessed May 8, 2019, https://www.reuters.com/article/us-bangladesh-rohingya-china/china-ready-to-mediate-between-myanmar-bangladesh-over-rohingya-row-idUSKBN17R1UH.

[85]Saibal Dasgupta, 'China to Mediate on Rohingyas Between Myanmar and Bangladesh', *Times of India*, November 21, 2017, accessed May 8, 2019, https://economictimes.indiatimes.com/news/international/world-news/chinese-govt-to-play-mediator-in-sending-back-rohingyas-refugees-from-bangladesh-to-myanmar/articleshow/68788655.cms; 'China Proposed Three-Phase Plan for Rohingya Issue', *Reuters*, November 20, 2017, accessed May 8, 2019, https://www.reuters.com/article/us-china-myanmar-rohingya/china-proposed-three-phase-plan-for-rohingya-issue-idUSKBN1DK00I.

[86]Personal Communication with Senior British Diplomat, January 2018.

[87]United Nations, 'Provisional Verbatim Record of the 8085th Meeting of the United Nations Security Council', November 6, 2017, accessed November 16, 2017, https://www.un.org/en/ga/search/view_doc.asp?symbol=S/PV.8085.

he demands for human rights investigations and accountability.[88] However, this failed, and China nonetheless accepted the forceful statement, further softening Beijing's non-interference posture.

Rakhine aside, China's intervention in Myanmar's ethnic peace talks has ostensibly been welcomed by all sides, notwithstanding period criticism of Chinese 'meddling'.[89] China's motives are clear. As one Chinese expert puts it, unless peace is restored, 'we cannot do the [cross-border BRI] projects.'[90] This is well understood in Myanmar. As UWSA's 'foreign minister' puts it: 'Only when there is peace and stability in the region will the One Belt One Road project [i.e. BRI] be implemented.'[91] Similarly, Myanmar's government reciprocated China's assistance by declaring support for the BRI in 2017.

China's Response: (2) Courting Hegemony in Myanmar's Civil Society

Although political, military and EMRG elites remain crucial interlocutors, Chinese leaders have also moved to cultivate consent for China's economic activities among other social forces. The learning curve has been steep. Following the Myitsone suspension, the MFA initially demanded respect for CPI's interests. However, as malfeasance by CPI and Chinese officials became clearer,[92] Chinese policymakers apparently conceded the validity of some local grievances and recognized that popular opinion could no longer be ignored.

Accordingly, China launched an unprecedented campaign to woo important societal groups, mobilizing national and local government resources but also non-state, 'civil society' actors, that is the 'integral state'. In late 2012, Chinese officials and scholars were sent to investigate how to promote bilateral, non-governmental ties.[93] Diverse initiatives followed in the fields of education, healthcare, disaster relief and the environment. China's embassy sponsored vocational training courses for local businesses and offered Mandarin courses for government bureaucrats.[94] Yunnan University trained NLD leaders, while Yunnan's provincial government sponsored classes for Myanmar's women's organizations.[95] Revealing the economic motives at work, one organizer notes that 'for every training course, we also provide an opportunity to visit [Chinese] hydropower dams.'[96] Beijing has also provided over 100 university scholarships for Myanmar students, and sponsored 16 China-Myanmar 'friendship schools'.[97]

---

[88]Michelle Nichols, 'China Does Not Want UN to Push Myanmar on Accountability', *Channel News Asia*, May 9, 2018, accessed May 8, 2019, https://www.channelnewsasia.com/news/world/china-does-not-want-un-to-push-myanmar-on-accountability-10215530.

[89]Sui-Lee Wee, 'Myanmar Official Accuses China of Meddling in Peace Talks', *Irrawaddy*, October 9, 2015, accessed May 8, 2019, https://www.irrawaddy.com/news/burma/burmese-official-accuses-china-of-meddling-in-peace-talks.html.

[90]Interview with Yunnan-based expert on Sino-Myanmar border affairs, November 2018.

[91]Kyaw Kha, 'The Wa's Zhao Guo An: Suu Kyi Wants to Achieve Peace in Her Lifetime', *Irrawaddy*, May 29, 2017, accessed May 8, 2019, https://www.irrawaddy.com/in-person/zhao-guo-daw-aung-san-suu-kyi-wants-achieve-peace-lifetime.html.

[92]See Jones and Zou, 'Rethinking the Role', pp. 754–55.

[93]Chinese Embassy in Myanmar, 'Gonggong waijiao zhuanjia xiaozu yingyao fangmian' ['Public Diplomacy Experts Invited to Visit Myanmar'], December 21, 2012, accessed January 29, 2018, http://mm.china-embassy.org/chn/xwdt/t999881.htm.

[94]Chinese Embassy in Myanmar, 'Zhongguo zhu miandian dashi Hong Liang chuxi gongfadang hanyu peixunban jieye yishi' ['Chinese Ambassador to Myanmar Attends Chinese Training Course Graduation Ceremony'], September 8, 2017, accessed January 29, 2018, http://mm.china-embassy.org/chn/sgxw/t1499104.htm; Chinese Embassy in Myanmar, 'Shouqi zhongmian fandian lvyou zhiye peixunban qidong yishi zai yangguang juxing' ['First Class of China Myanmar Travel, the China-Myanmar Hotel Tourism Vocational Training Held in Yangon'], September 14, 2017, accessed January 29, 2018, http://mm.china-embassy.org/chn/xwdt/t1493116.htm.

[95]Institute of Myanmar Studies, 'Miandian minmeng qingniandangyuan peixunban wancheng diyijieduan peixun' ['Myanmar National League for Democracy Youth Training Class Completed First Phase'], October 1, 2017, accessed January 29, 2018, http://www.ims.ynu.edu.cn/index.php?route=news/details&id=188&cid=4; Qiang Xiong, '2017 Myanmar Women's Organization Exchange Seminar' Opened in Kunming', *Xinhua*, September 4, 2017, accessed May 8, 2019, http://www.yunnangateway.com/html/2017/guoneixinwen_0904/21300.html.

[96]Interview, November 2018.

[97]Chinese Embassy in Myanmar, 'Zhu miandian dashi Hong Liang wei 2017 nian miandian gongpai fuhua liuxuesheng juxing huansong yishi' ['Ambassador to Myanmar Hong Liang Held a Farewell Ceremony for Students the Myanmar Government Sent to China for 2017], September 1, 2017, accessed January 29, 2018, http://mm.china-embassy.org/chn/xwdt/t1489016.htm; Chinese Embassy in Myanmar, 'Zhu miandian dashi Hong Liang chuxi di shiliusuo "zhongmian youyi xuexiao" jiepai yishi' ['Ambassador to Myanmar Hong Liang Attended the Opening Ceremony of the 16th "China-Burma Friendship School"'], August 14, 2017, accessed January 29, 2018, http://mm.china-embassy.org/chn/xwdt/t1484420.htm.

Meanwhile, the CFPA established an office in Myanmar, creating a new China-Myanmar Paukphaw Friendship Foundation to implement livelihoods projects, enhance Mandarin education and religious exchanges, and promote 'mutual understanding' among youths.[98] The China NGO Network for International Exchange (CNNIE) and the China Foundation for Peace and Development have co-sponsored 'Deep Fraternal Friendship' activities with Myanmar NGOs. These include laptop donations to local schools and the provision of free medical care by Yunnanese doctors, co-organized by Yunnan's provincial government and affiliated NGOs.[99] China also supplied US$2m to help upgrade a women's hospital named after Aung San Suu Kyi's mother.[100] Even the PLA has participated, donating medical equipment and sending its *Peace Ark* to Yangon to provide free healthcare.[101] In the field of disaster relief, China provided RMB100m of aid after serious flooding in 2016 and helped restore pagodas damaged in the 2016 Bagan earthquake.[102] The embassy also initiated a 'China-Myanmar Friendship Forest' program, planting 150,000 trees.[103]

Chinese actors have also sought to improve relations with Myanmar's NGOs and political parties, initiating dialogues and organizing dozens of study tours to China.[104] CNNIE, initially formed in 2005 to target African NGOs,[105] now incorporates 90 Chinese and 76 foreign NGOs, including five from Myanmar.[106] Again revealing the economic motives at work, CNNIE invited a leading Myanmar development NGO, Mingalar Myanmar, to Xi's 2017 BRI Summit, where they jointly launched the 'Chinese Social Organizations' Action Plan for Closer People-to-People Bonds Along the Belt and Road (2017–2020)'. CNNIE's overtly-stated objective is to 'create [a] sound atmosphere and consolidate [the] public opinion foundation' for BRI projects.[107] Politicians and NGOs opposing Chinese projects have also been invited to China for a special charm offensive. For example, Zaw Aung, head of the Myanmar-China Pipeline Watch Committee, was invited to an SOE-NGO dialogue organized by a think tank linked to China's Ministry of Commerce, where the vice-president of China National Petroleum Company promised to address his complaints.[108] Similarly, anti-Myitsone campaigners have been brought to meet CPI and, with NLD delegates,

[98]'China-Myanmar Paukphaw Friendship Foundation Set Up in Yangon', *Xinhua*, June 9, 2016, accessed May 8, 2019, http://www.china.org.cn/world/2016-06/09/content_38634102.htm.

[99]'China-Myanmar Friendship Activities Held in Yangon to Boost Ties', *Xinhua*, May 16, 2012, accessed May 8, 2019, http://www.gov.cn/misc/2012-05/16/content_2138564.htm; Htike Nanda Win, 'China Medical Teams Conduct Free Eye Surgery in Yangon', *Myanmar Times*, August 22, 2017, accessed May 8, 2019, https://www.mmtimes.com/national-news/yangon/27373-china-medical-teams-conduct-free-eye-surgery-in-yangon.html.

[100]Myanmar News Agency, 'Soft Opening of Daw Khin Kyi Women's Hospital', *Global New Light Of Myanmar*, August 6, 2017, accessed May 8, 2019, http://www.globalnewlightofmyanmar.com/soft-opening-of-daw-khin-kyi-womens-hospital/.

[101]Chinese Embassy in Myanmar, 'Zhongguo renminjiefangjun yuanzhu mianjun yiliao shebei jiaojie yishi zai neibidu juxing' ['Chinese People's Liberation Army's Medical Equipment Aid to Myanmar Handover Ceremony Held in Naypyidaw'] August 10, 2016, accessed January 29, 2018, http://mm.china-embassy.org/chn/xwdt/t1388044.htm; 'Chinese Hospital Ship "Peace Ark" Leaves Myanmar', *Xinhua*, September 3, 2013, accessed May 8, 2019, http://www.chinadaily.com.cn/china/2013-09/03/content_16941179.htm.

[102]Chinese Embassy in Myanmar, 'Zhumiandian dashi Hong Liang chuxi zhongguo zhengfu yuanzhu miandian huodongbangfang jiaojie yishi' [Chinese Ambassador to Myanmar Hong Liang Attends Handover Ceremony'], February 22, 2016, accessed January 29, 2018, http://mm.china-embassy.org/chn/xwdt/t1342311.htm; Chinese Embassy in Myanmar, 'Zhongguo zhu miandian dashiguan Yu Bianjiang canzan chuxi pugan dizhen yizhounian fota xiufu guoji yantaohui' ['Counsellor Yu Bianjiang of Chinese Embassy in Yangon Attended the International Symposium of Pagoda Renovation on the First Anniversary of Bagan Earthquake'], September 6, 2017, accessed January 29, 2018, http://mm.china-embassy.org/chn/xwdt/t1490571.htm.

[103]Chinese Embassy in Myanmar, '"Zhongmian youhao shengtai shifanlin" zhishu gongcheng jungong yishi zai miandian maguisheng juxing' ['Completion Ceremony of the "China-Myanmar Friendship Forest" Tree-Planting Project Held in Magu Province, Myanmar'], September 1, 2017, accessed January 29, 2018, http://mm.china-embassy.org/chn/xwdt/t1489172.htm.

[104]Khin Khin Kyaw Kyee, *China's Multi-Layered Engagement Strategy and Myanmar's Realities* (Yangon: ISP, 2018).

[105]Brenner, 'Are Chinese NGOs "Going out"?', p .139.

[106]China NGO Network for International Exchange, 'Jiaru silu yanxian minjian zuzhi hezuo wangluo de zuzhi mingdan' ['List of Network for Cooperation Among NGOs in Countries Along the Belt and Road'], May 17, 2017, accessed January 29, 2018, http://www.cnie.org.cn/WebSite/zlbmj/UpFile/2017/201751716212596.doc.

[107]China NGO Network for International Exchange, 'Silk Road NGO Cooperation Network', May 17, 2017, accessed January 29, 2018, http://www.cnie.org.cn/WebSite/zlbmj/UpFile/2017/20176911853391.doc.

[108]Interview with Zaw Aung, Myanmar-China Pipeline Watch Committee, Yangon, October 8, 2016.

taken to hydropower dam sites in China. Chinese officials have also courted the Arakan National Party, Rakhine state's leading political force, promising to develop local infrastructure and job opportunities if they support the BRI.[109]

Chinese NGOs have even targeted Myanmar's Buddhist clergy, with Xi's support. This has involved large-scale reciprocal visits and donations to help restore Bagan's pagodas.[110] These exchanges seek to assuage the xenophobic nationalism promoted by some prominent Myanmar monks and to enlist Myanmar's influential clergy in the cultivation of popular consent for China's economic projects. This was made explicit by China Buddhist Association president Xue Cheng, who urged Myanmar's monks to 'make contributions to pushing forward the "BRI,"' arguing that cross-border roads would be 'an important channel for the spread of Buddhism'.[111]

Chinese enterprises have also changed their strategies. Alongside tighter domestic regulations, companies have increasingly realized the need to win popular support in post-2011 Myanmar. Accordingly, CSR activity in Myanmar has substantially increased, particularly among hydropower companies.[112] Firms have also engaged more directly with EMRGs when developing megaprojects, seeking to spread material benefits more widely to cultivate consent. For example, PowerChina International Group has worked closely with the Karen National Union on the Tanintharyi hydropower dam and industrial park,[113] and with UWSA leaders on the Mantong dam project, which had previously been agreed only with the central government in 2014.[114] Some Chinese companies have also shown novel willingness to engage with local NGOs opposing their plans. For example, CPI has engaged with NGOs and religious leaders, supporting local schools, and inviting activists to visit the Myitsone site.[115] However, CSR programs are uneven and, as discussed below, limited. Moreover, some firms remain hostile to civil society. PetroChina, for example, an SOE involved in the oil and gas pipelines, has rebuffed approaches from the Paung Ku-backed Myanmar-China Pipeline Watch.[116]

Among Myanmar's emergent socio-political actors, labor unions remain the group that China still deals most awkwardly with, arguably reflecting the Chinese cadre-class's ingrained hostility toward labor militancy. In response to the Hangzhou Hundred-Tex strike, China's embassy issued a highly traditional demarche to Myanmar's foreign ministry, demanding protection for legitimate Chinese business interests,[117] which further alienated CTUM,[118] and failed miserably. Myanmar's government not only failed to suppress the strike; it instructed Hangzhou Hundred-Tex to

[109]Sui-Lee Wee, 'China Courts Hardline Buddhist Party Ahead of Myanmar Poll', *Reuters*, October 15, 2015, accessed May 8, 2019, https://www.reuters.com/article/us-myanmar-election-china/china-courts-hardline-buddhist-party-ahead-of-myanmar-poll-idUSKCN0S90O520151015; Interview with Oo Hla Saw, Member, Central Committee, Arakan National Party, Yangon, October 14, 2016.

[110]China Buddhist Association, 'Xue Cheng huizhang huijian miandian gaoseng fan huatuan' ['President Xue Cheng Meets with Visiting Monks from Myanmar'], March 21, 2017, accessed January 29, 2018, http://www.chinabuddhism.com.cn/xw/jliu/2017-03-21/12685.html; China Buddhist Association, 'Zhongguo fojiao xiehui daibiao tuan jieshu duimian jiaoliu fangwen' ['Chinese Buddhist Association Delegation Completes Exchange Visit to Myanmar'], April 11, 2017, accessed January 29, 2018, http://www.chinabuddhism.com.cn/xw/jliu/2017-04-14/12758.html.

[111]China Buddhist Association, 'Zhongguo fojiao'.

[112]Kirchherr et al., 'The Interplay'.

[113]Su Phyo Win, 'CSOs Call for Greater Transparency in Tanintharyi Developments', *Myanmar Times*, December 16, 2016, accessed May 8, 2019, https://www.mmtimes.com/national-news/24247-csos-call-for-greater-transparency-in-tanintharyi-developments.html.

[114]Wa State Information Bureau, 'Bao Youliang Buzhang huijian Zhongguo Zhongdianjian Shuidian Kaifa Jituan Zongjingli Du Xueze Yixing' ['Minister Bao Youliang Met with China Hydropower Development Group Co. Ltd. General Manager Du Xueze'], August 4, 2017, accessed January 29, 2018, http://blog.sina.com.cn/s/blog_9084449c0102xcxr.html.

[115]Upstream Ayeyawady Confluence Basin Company, 'Sustainable Development Report 2013-15', August 30, 2016, accessed January 29, 2018, http://eng.spic.com.cn/2016SiteEn/Responsibility/report/201612/P020161216528390342984.pdf, pp. 7–11.

[116]Ye Thein Oo et al., 'In Search of Social Justice Along the Myanmar-China Oil and Gas Pipeline: A Follow-Up Report', *Myanmar-China Pipeline Watch Committee*, January 8, 2016, p. vi.

[117]'Zhongguo Dashiguan jiu zhongzi qiy zao chongqi shijian xiang mianfang tichu yanzheng jiaoshe' ['Chinese Embassy Made Solemn Representation to Myanmar Government on Attack on Chinese Enterprise'], *Xinhua*, February 24, 2017, accessed May 8, 2019, http://www.xinhuanet.com//2017-02/24/c_129494969.htm.

[118]Interview with Maung Maung, CTUM Chairman, Yangon, March 3, 2017.

compensate the striking workers.[119] However, even this incident demonstrates China's adaptation. Subsequently, the All-China Federation of Trade Unions was tasked to engage CTUM, and it is now helping to resolve conflicts involving Chinese firms more peacefully.[120]

Conclusion

After 17 years of 'going out', Chinese enterprises and their political backers are now encountering challenges that Western companies and governments have long faced. Unsurprisingly, they are beginning to develop responses similar to those of other powerful capitalist states: they are tightening corporate regulation, becoming more interventionist and seeking to cultivate popular consent in other societies. The case study of Myanmar demonstrated these claims in depth, illustrating a rapid strategic adjustment in just a few years.

These findings have relevance for the debate over China's rise, mentioned in the introduction. As noted, China's economic expansion is often cited by those arguing that China will be a 'revisionist' power, bolstering authoritarian regimes, undermining good governance, and violating norms around environmental and social protection. However, this article's findings suggest that when these practices create destabilizing 'blowback' for Beijing, the Chinese party-state evolves, tightening regulations, moving to improve corporate conduct and intervening to support peacebuilding. This convergence with Western practices should not be exaggerated. Chinese regulations and their enforcement are still weak.[121] And Beijing's willingness to intervene has limits, as its opportunistic, largely pro-government response to the Rakhine crisis shows. Nonetheless, the frequent assumption of stasis in the 'revisionist-versus-status-quo' debate is clearly problematic; scholars more closely attend to China's evolving adaptation to international challenges.

The article's findings also have implications for predicting the fate of China's overseas economic interests. The party-state's adaptive capacity suggests a partial corrective to those who, noting early challenges and 'blowback,' branded China's position in emerging markets 'tenuous'.[122] This was itself an important corrective to the hyperbolic discussion of 'China Inc.' and Chinese 'imperialism'. However, a decade later, it is clear that China's economic engagement has deepened and become more complex and adaptive, with greater emphasis on cultivating consent among subordinated social groups.

Nonetheless, we cannot assume that this process will be smooth or successful; indeed, the Myanmar case suggests significant limitations. China has done enough to secure formal governmental support for the BRI, in 2017, and the China-Myanmar Economic Corridor, in 2018. A framework agreement to proceed with a downsized Kyaukphyu project was finally agreed in November 2018, and a fresh feasibility study is underway for the China-Myanmar railway. Our interviews with Myanmar political *elites* found a generally pragmatic recognition that, especially given Western reactions to the Rakhine crisis, Chinese investment is needed for Myanmar's development.[123] This view was shared by some civil society informants, but they typically expressed considerably greater skepticism about Chinese megaprojects, suggesting that China's attempts to cultivate *popular* consent have been less successful. Indeed, Chinese-commissioned opinion polls have detected only modest improvements in attitudes toward China since 2011, with larger but 'superficial' upticks following China's perceived support over Rakhine.[124] This reflects four limitations.

---

[119]Arbitration Council, 'Order Number (13/2017) for Approval of Litigation in Accordance with the Settlement of Labour Dispute Law', March 23, 2017, accessed January 29, 2018, https://www.facebook.com/pg/ftub.burma/photos/?tab=album&album_id=668408880036884.
[120]Interview with Maung Maung.
[121]Hameiri and Jones, 'China Challenges Global Governance?'.
[122]Gill and Reilly, 'The Tenuous Hold'.
[123]Interviews with Myanmar political elites, Naypyidaw and Yangon, October 2018.
[124]Interview with Experts in a Chinese State-Linked Think Tank, Kunming, November 2018.

The first is the difficulty of the socio-political terrain itself, which will always codetermine the success of any Chinese engagement. As Chinese diplomats have found, Myanmar's domestic conflicts are highly intractable and continue despite China's intensive interventions. Moreover, the Myanmar government remains constrained by political ineptitude, bureaucratic incapacity and excessive centralization: rapid implementation of even notionally agreed projects remains unlikely. Another barrier is the legacy of what civil society actors rightly see as the 'one sided and exploitative' nature of past Chinese investment.[125] As one NGO leader admits, coupled with a chauvinistic, nationalistic and xenophobic political culture, this has generated anti-Chinese attitudes 'verging on racism' among the public and civil society activists.[126]

Second, Chinese engagement remains limited by conspiratorial thinking and patronizing and paternalistic attitudes. The publications of Chinese scholars seeking to understand the Myitsone suspension and the setback in Sino-Myanmar relations are illustrative. Early investigations exposed extensive Chinese malfeasance and tried to convey the need for fundamental change.[127] However, this self-criticism was swiftly replaced by more politically palatable accounts primarily blaming Western governments and local NGOs, CSOs and media.[128] This may partly restrict academic achievements in China. But it also reflects Chinese elites' deep attachment to the idea that economic development (eventually) cures all social ills. This has long legitimized China's overseas economic expansion and still guides Chinese interventions in Myanmar today—despite evidence that capitalist development actually intensifies social conflict.[129] Myanmar participants in Chinese study tours report being pushed to accept this idea, and complain that the Chinese do not understand the deep-seated political and cultural grievances underpinning these conflicts, instead naively believing that actors can be 'bought off'.[130] Recent Chinese attempts to pay Rohingya and Kachin refugees to return to Myanmar are illustrative. This disconnect will obviously undermine Chinese efforts to cultivate consent among marginalized populations. For example, claims that the BRI's road-building will spread Buddhism may enthuse Bamar Buddhists, but not Christian ethnic minorities who have endured years of forced 'Burmanisation'.

The third limitation is the continued weakness of China's ODI governance, which is widely recognized in Myanmar. Myanmar political elites remain concerned about the costs and benefits of Chinese megaprojects, and environmental and social risks, insisting that tough *domestic* regulation is required to avoid junta-era problems recurring.[131] This implies little faith in China's governance reforms. CSOs have even less faith, complaining of China's continued over-reliance on host-country regulation and discerning 'no change in policy or scrutinizing of the companies' on the ground.[132] They claim many SOE managers remain ignorant of China's regulatory changes, while communities are still not being meaningfully consulted, with CSR involving 'charity/bribes' to local headmen or monks 'to tell the villagers to shut up'.[133] CSR along the oil and gas pipelines, for instance, involves donations to schools and clinics, not the action to redress land-grabbing.[134] Moreover, ethnic-minority NGOs still accuse the Tatmadaw of stoking conflict to grab land for Chinese-backed mega-projects, like the Hatgyi hydropower dam.[135]

[25]Interview with Myanmar CSO Executives, Yangon, September 2018.

[26]Interview with Director of a Development-Focused NGO, Yangon, September 2018.

[27]E.g. Qin Hui, 'Behind Myanmar's Suspended Dam', *China Dialogue*, March 28, 2012, accessed October 30, 2018, https://www.chinadialogue.net/article/show/single/en/4832.

[28]E.g. Guangsheng Lu et al. 'Zhongguo dui Miandian de touzi he yuanzhu—jiyu diaocha wenjuan jieguo de fenxi' ['Chinese Aid and Investment in Myanmar: An Analysis of Survey Data]', *South Asian Studies* 2014(1), (2014), pp. 17–30; Song Tao, 'Zhongguo dui Miandian zhijie touzi de fazhan yanjiu' ['Research on the Current Situation and Trends of China's Direct Investment in Myanmar'], *World Regional Studies* 25(4), (2016), pp. 40–47.

[29]Shahar Hameiri, Lee Jones, and Yizheng Zou, 'The Development-Insecurity Nexus in China's Near-Abroad: Rethinking Cross-Border Economic Integration in an Era of State Transformation', *Journal of Contemporary Asia*, 49(3), (2019), pp. 473–499.

[30]Khin Khin Kyaw Kyee, *China's Multi-Layered Engagement Strategy*.

[31]Interviews with Myanmar political elites, Naypyidaw and Yangon, September 2018.

[32]Interview with Deputy Director, Myanmar NGO, Yangon, September 2018.

[33]Interview with Director, rural development NGO, Yangon, September 2018.

[34]Interview with Myanmar Environmental Consultant, Yangon, September 2018.

[35]Mang and Yan, 'China-Backed Dams'; Thu Thu Aung, 'CSOs Say Hatgyi Dam Fuelling Recent Clashes in Kayin', *Myanmar Times*, September 30, 2016, accessed May 8, 2019, https://www.mmtimes.com/national-news/22836-csos-say-hatgyi-dam-fuelling-recent-clashes-in-kayin.html.

Fourth, structural limitations to Chinese NGO engagement stem from China's political system. The organizations engaging Myanmar are mostly GONGOs, and many of their Myanmar interlocutors perceive their mission as information-gathering and advancing China's economic interests. Unlike Western NGOs, Chinese NGOs are barred from doing advocacy work, limiting their ability to address deep-rooted grievances linked to Chinese investment, and they are too small to deliver services to a large population.[136] This reflects the general limitations of overseas Chinese NGOs.[137]

These four problems suggest structural limits on China's capacity to achieve hegemony, stemming from its own socio-political character. Assessments of Chinese 'soft power' have often emphasized the limited extent or appeal of Confucian ideology, for example but this article's Gramscian analysis suggests the constraints go far deeper. The way China governs its companies, the intelligentsia, and civil society are not easily changed, nor is the CCP's developmentalist ideology. These are deeply entrenched aspects of the regime, evolving slowly at best, and subject to growing political constraints and reversals.

Acknowledgments

Both authors contributed equally to this article. They are extremely grateful to Kham Lin Thu, Yiping Zhou and Kejia Yang for excellent research assistance, and to their interviewees. They also thank David Brenner, Shahar Hameiri and the journal's anonymous reviewers for feedback.

Disclosure statement

No potential conflict of interest was reported by the authors.

Funding

This work was supported by the Humanities and Social Sciences Project of the Chinese Ministry of Education under Grant 17YJCGJW013; the Department of Education of Guangdong Province, China, under Grant 2016WTSCX101, and the Australian Research Council, under Grant DP1701102647.

---

[136]Interview with Director, rural development NGO, Yangon, September 2018.
[137]See Li, Xiaoyun, and Qiang Dong. 'Chinese NGOs Are "Going Out": History, Scale, Characteristics, Outcomes, And Barriers.' *Nonprofit Policy Forum* 9(1), (2018), pp. 1–9.

Constructing a U.S.-China Rivalry in the Indo-Pacific and Beyond

Andrew Scobell

ABSTRACT

The Washington-Beijing rivalry of the early twentieth century was neither pre-ordained nor an aberration. It was constructed as domestic constituencies in each country were socialized toward confrontation. Pro-cooperation coalitions, which had emerged in each country to support alignment against a mutually perceived Soviet threat, were undermined by the final chapter of the Cold War. Yet a simmering U.S.-China rivalry was subsumed by an unsustainable accommodation of mutual self-interest by Washington and Beijing during the first two decades of the post-Cold War era. By the 2010s, the rivalry had become quite visible as pro-cooperation coalitions in the United States and China had splintered and been supplanted by pro-confrontation coalitions. U.S. and Chinese geostrategic reassessments also contributed to the emerging rivalry.

Introduction

Until recently, relations between the United States and the People's Republic of China (PRC) were quite cordial, relatively stable, and remarkably resilient. Despite periodic bouts of turbulence since 1971, bilateral relations had always managed to re-stabilize. However, by the 2010s, the underpinnings of U.S.-China comity had come undone, and relations became increasingly confrontational, volatile, and fragile. What explains this dramatic turnabout? What explains the appearance of an overt rivalry between Washington and Beijing after four decades of amity?

Neither of the two dominant theories of international relations—realism or liberalism—provide a satisfactory explanation for the trajectory of U.S.-China relations. According to realists, relations between Washington and Beijing should have come undone much earlier and/or outright conflict was virtually inevitable. Aaron Friedberg, for example, contended that the United States and China were 'locked in a quiet but increasingly intense struggle for power and influence not only in Asia but around the world.'[1] This struggle was all but unavoidable, insisted Friedberg, because 'each [country] has strategic objectives that threaten the fundamental interests of the other side.'[2]

According to liberalism, meanwhile, China should continue to become firmly enmeshed in the global system led by the United States. This reality of 2019 is something different. John Ikenberry, for example, contends that although China is 'not fully embedded into the liberal international order,' Beijing 'nevertheless profit[s] from its existence.'[3] Moreover, Ikenberry insists that while China may never become a 'liberal' state, 'the expansive and integrative logic of the liberal international order

Aaron L. Friedberg, *A Contest for Supremacy: U.S., China, and a Struggle for Mastery in Asia* (New York: Norton, 2012), p. 1.
Friedberg, *A Contest for Supremacy*, p. 2.
G. John Ikenberry, *Liberal Leviathan: The Origins, Crisis, and Transformation of the American World Order* (Princeton: Princeton University Press, 2012), p. 9.

creates incentives for ... [China] to do so.'[4] In any event, Ikenberry argues that Beijing has tremendous incentives to become more embedded into the existing international rules-based system.

What does seem to offer a more persuasive explanation of how and why U.S.-China relation
came off the rails is a combination of constructivism and geopolitics. Constructivism helps explain
the course of U.S.-China relations while patterns in geostrategic thinking in Washington and Beijing
help explain why the two capitals shifted from cooperation to confrontation.

Consistent with constructivism, the course of U.S.-China relations has evolved in accordance with
the positive and negative learning that has occurred in both countries. Specifically, key domestic
constituencies in the United States and China received favorable feedback in terms of accruing
tangible benefits from cooperative ties for an extended period, and these constituencies formed
coalitions in support of continued cooperation. Consequently, bilateral relations remained largely
stable and positive for more than three decades. But, also consistent with constructivism, by the mid
2000s, the benefits of bilateral ties to domestic constituencies in the United States and China were
less tangible. As a result, the feedback among constituencies in each country was more unfavorable
as perceived losses began to outweigh perceived gains of U.S.-China comity. The upshot was that
key domestic constituencies in both countries supporting cooperation unraveled and created
coalitions of confrontation. As the leading proponent of constructivism, Alexander Wendt contends
'[a]narchy is what states make of it.'[5] In other words, states chart their own futures upon the basis of
lessons learned from the conduct of international relations.

Geopolitics also played a central role. Consistent with geopolitical analysis, the trajectory of U.S.
China relations shifted as the two countries adjusted their respective geostrategic thinking. Because
China initially focused solely on internal stability and the country's immediate periphery and the
United States assessed that it was unthreatened by China in the Indo-Pacific and beyond, bilateral
relations remained generally steady for decades. However, by the 2000s, as China became more
focused on the maritime realm and gave greater attention not just to the coastal areas but also to the
open seas, Beijing perceived the U.S. Navy as its major obstacle. The United States, meanwhile, began
to take China's growing military capabilities and intentions far more seriously. Geopolitical analysis—
the influence of geography on international politics—provides a valuable complement to constructivism. Where a state identifies the locations of its primary threat(s)—both target and source—are
important. The geographical proximity of adversaries and allies, as well as the whereabouts of
topographical and maritime features, are of great strategic importance to how a country evaluate
the distribution of international power and assesses its national interests.[6] A state's perception of
another state, its perceptions of the threat environment, and the lessons a state learns are filtered
through that state's history and influenced by cultural insecurities and national security pathologies

Definitions, Periodization, Roadmap

The author defines rivalry as an antagonistic relationship between two states embroiled in 'long
term hostility' with competition manifest in 'multiple disputes, continuing [policy] disagreement
and the threat of the use of force.'[7] States are inherently competitive and tend to view other state
with suspicion, especially major powers that perceive other major powers as threatening or at leas
as potential threats. But the existence of a rivalry does not preclude at least some cooperation
between states. Moreover, the process by which one state identifies another state as a rival is learned

---

[4]Ikenberry, *Liberal Leviathan*, p. 9.
[5]Alexander Wendt, 'Anarchy is what states make of it: the social construction of power politics', *International Organization* 46(2
    (1992), pp. 391–425. See also Alexander Wendt, *Social Theory of International Politics* (New York: Cambridge University Press
    1999).
[6]The approach draws upon the pioneering works of Sir Halford Mackinder (1861–1947) and Nicholas Spykman (1893–1943).
[7]William R. Thompson, 'Identifying rivals and rivalries in world politics', *International Studies Quarterly* 45(4), (2001), pp. 557–8(
    Quote is on p. 574.

nd can evolve, and because the characteristics of any rivalry lie in the eye of the beholder the perception can change over time.[8]

Yet states are not monolithic—they are composed of distinct components—individual leaders, bureaucratic actors, and interest groups. Certainly, this is true in democracies, such as the United States,[9] where multiple voices and actors are clearly discernible—plainly both audibly and visibly—but it can also be at least partly so in authoritarian polities. While the PRC is a Leninist political system—highly centralized and authoritarian—it has never functioned as a unitary actor. Certainly, power has tended to be heavily concentrated in an individual leader or group of leaders at the apex of the system, especially during the tenure of Mao Zedong. However, this has been less true in the post-Mao, era at least until the tenure of Xi Jinping. Of course, a few key individuals—typically those who sit on the Politburo Standing Committee of the Chinese Communist Party (CCP) wield the greatest power. Nevertheless, different factions, bureaucracies, and interest groupings have long existed, albeit with varying degrees of power and influence.[10]

U.S.-China relations since 1971 can be divided into three periods, each corresponding to a discernible phase in the bilateral relationship: first alignment, then accommodation, and finally confrontation.

Anti-Soviet Alignment, 1971–1989: Commencing with the Sino-American rapprochement initiated by President Richard M. Nixon and Henry Kissinger in 1971 and 1972, Washington and Beijing formed an anti-Soviet alignment. This opening ushered in an almost two-decade-long period of generally positive bilateral relations with an emphasis on cooperation and coordination. The period culminated with the fallout from the Tiananmen Massacre of 1989. Yet, the cooperative relationship survived the upheaval between Washington and Beijing.

Unsettled Accommodation, 1990–2007: In the wake of the 1989 brutal crackdown in China and the largely bloodless collapse of communism in Eastern Europe, the United States and China established a new albeit unsettled accommodation. Both Washington and Beijing recognized that heightened bilateral tensions were not in their mutual interests, and each made a pragmatic calculation that resuming cooperative ties served their best interests. But following the Global Financial Crisis—which China weathered remarkably well but shook the U.S. economy to the core—bilateral relations started to deteriorate.

Great Power Confrontation, 2008-present: In the aftermath of the Global Financial Crisis, Beijing began to see itself as much stronger relative to the United States and Washington, too, began to see China as a far more formidable power. The United States and the PRC both became more prone to act assertively in order to promote or defend their respective national interests and against perceived threats from the other. Confrontation is not synonymous with conflict but does signify a heightened state of tension.

This article proceeds as follows. First, it explains how cooperation between the United States and China was constructed and sustained by domestic coalitions between 1971 and 2007 and then how U.S.-China rivalry has been constructed as domestic coalitions transformed from pro-cooperation to pro-confrontation since 2008. This article examines the impact of U.S. and Chinese cultural insecurities and national security pathologies on these domestic coalitions. Third, the article explains how geostrategic shifts contributed to an extended period of U.S.-China cooperation, followed by

[7] For a similar explication, see Andrew Scobell, 'Himalayan standoff: strategic culture and the China-India rivalry', in *The China-India Rivalry in the Globalization Era*, T.V. Paul, ed. (Washington, DC: Georgetown University Press, 2018), pp. 165–186.

[8] For some classic studies focused on the United States, see Graham Allison, *Essence of Decision: Explaining the Cuban Missile Crisis* (Boston: Little Brown, 1971) and Morton H. Halperin with Priscilla Clapp and Arnold Kanter, *Bureaucratic Politics and Foreign Policy* (Washington, DC: Brookings Institution, 1974).

[9] On factionalism see, for example, Jing Huang, *Factionalism in Chinese Communist Politics* (New York: Cambridge University Press, 2000); on bureaucracies see, for example, *The Making of Chinese Foreign and Security Policy in the Era of Reform, 1978–2000*, David M. Lampton, ed. (Stanford: Stanford University Press, 2001); on groups see, for example, *Citizens and Groups in Contemporary China*, Victor C. Falkenheim, ed. (Ann Arbor: University of Michigan Center for Chinese Studies, 1987). See also, Linda Jacobson and Dean Knox, *New Foreign Policy Actors in China* (Stockholm: Stockholm International Peace Research Institute, 2010).

a burgeoning rivalry. Finally, the article summarizes the insights and offers some observations about the future of U.S.-China relations.

From Coalitions of Cooperation ...

During the 1970s, China gradually learned to trust the United States. This was a slow process as Beijing retained considerable suspicion regarding Washington's reliability and intentions. Nevertheless, the gains that accrued to China from the relationship sidelined these suspicions. At the same time, the United States gradually learned to trust China—overcoming its own suspicions— and Washington came to view Beijing as a reliable partner. But in each country, the actual socialization occurred in key constituencies. As David Lampton observes: 'Each [national leader, i.e. Richard Nixon and Mao Zedong] built the domestic *coalition* necessary to create a remarkably durable, four-decade-long period of peace, stability, and growing prosperity for both countries, Asia, and the world. In the United States, eight administrations (Nixon, Ford, Carter, Reagan, Bush, Clinton, Bush and Obama) maintained basic policy continuity, while four did so in China (Mao, Deng, Jiang, and Hu).'[11] Hence the units of analysis are the domestic constituencies that formed the coalition in each state, not the states themselves. But these coalitions of pro-cooperation constituencies were not static across the decades in either country. Indeed, constituencies shifted to form evolving coalitions of pro-cooperation or pro-confrontation constituencies depending upon whether they learned positive or negative lessons about U.S-China relations.

Anti-Soviet Alignment, 1971–1989

Chinese Lessons: Coalition for Cooperation

The U.S.-China relationship provided tangible benefits to PRC domestic constituencies: first in the form of a powerful de facto ally to help counter the Soviet threat, then as a training ground of science and technology for Chinese scholars and students, and then as an economic partner to support China's post-Mao policy of 'reform and opening.' Initially, the coalition was limited to political and military leaders. By the mid-1970s, even radicals, such as the so-called Gang of Four and Mao's immediate successor Hua Guofeng, supported cooperative relations with the United States—or at least did not publicly oppose it.[12] The leadership of the People's Liberation Army (PLA) soon became a key constituency in the pro-cooperation coalition. As Robert Ross observes: 'One of the most significant efforts at institutionalizing support for U.S.-China cooperation involved the development of military relations.'[13] The PLA benefitted significantly from its contact with the highly professional and technologically sophisticated armed forces of a superpower. According to one well-placed analyst: 'China's main purpose for interacting with the U.S. military was to assist with the modernization of the PLA.'[14]

By the early 1980s, Chinese intellectuals also became strong supporters of the relationship because each benefited in some way from China's cooperative relationship with the United States. Between 1979 and 1989, tens of thousands of PRC scholars and students studied in the United States.[15]

---

[11]David M. Lampton, 'Reconsidering U.S.-China relations: from improbable normalization to precipitous deterioration', *Asia Policy* 14(2), (2019), pp. 46. The emphasis is mine.
[12]Robert S. Ross, *Negotiating Cooperation: The United States and China, 1969–1989* (Stanford: Stanford University Press, 1995), p. 259.
[13]Ross, *Negotiating Cooperation*, p. 236.
[14]Frank Miller, 'People's liberation army lessons from recent Pacific command operations and contingencies', in *Chinese Lessons from Other Peoples' Wars*, Andrew Scobell, David Lai, and Roy Kamphausen, eds. (Carlisle Barracks: U.S. Army War College Strategic Studies Institute, 2011), p. 201. Miller emphasizes that the PLA only pursues military to military engagements with the U.S. military when it advances modernization.
[15]Ross, *Negotiating Cooperation*, pp. 242–243.

U.S. Lessons: Coalition for Cooperation

During the 1970s, U.S. political and military leaders began to see China as a useful and trustworthy anti-Soviet ally. By the mid-1980s, senior Department of Defense officials, including Secretary of Defense Caspar Weinberger, paid visits to China. Bilateral security ties strengthened and included security dialogues, military exchanges, arms sales, and intelligence sharing.[16] As Ross notes, ' ... military bureaucracies [developed] an interest in overall stable [U.S.-China] relations.'[17]

During the 1980s, for many ordinary Americans, it seemed as if China was becoming more like the United States—marketizing and liberalizing.[18] The business community became a key constituency supporting cooperation as bilateral trade increased with the United States exporting items such as wheat and timber while importing more Chinese-made clothes and toys. Moreover, by the end of the Reagan administration, the United States had become the PRC's largest foreign investor.[19] One of the most important proponents of an expanded U.S.-China economic relationship in the 1980s was Reagan's Vice President George H. W. Bush.[20]

The Tiananmen Massacre was a great shock to many Americans, and the episode and its aftermath had a 'sharply negative impact' on public opinion. Indeed, twelve months after the massacre, the proportion of the Americans polled having favorable views of China fell to its lowest level since 1979.[21] But in the aftermath of June 1989, then-President George H. W. Bush believed passionately in the importance of trying to 'preserve' U.S.-China cooperation and going as far as to say that because of his firsthand experience and relationships with individual PRC leaders, he took bilateral ties 'very personally.'[22] Other senior U.S. officials, notably National Security Advisor Brent Scowcroft, also firmly believed in the importance of sustaining relations, and it was Scowcroft whom Bush dispatched to Beijing as a secret emissary to meet with PRC leaders in late 1989.

By the early 1990s, Beijing was considered a tremendous economic opportunity that Washington could not afford to ignore, and U.S.-China interactions took off, albeit with greater congressional scrutiny of the relationship.

Unsettled Accommodation, 1990–2007

For decades, in the eyes of most key constituencies in each country, the benefits of cooperation between Washington and Beijing outweighed the detriments. The overarching lesson both sides learned from years of continued cooperation and expanding interaction was that despite multiple headaches and challenges, the relationship continued to be a significant overall net benefit for each country. While the nature of the gains shifted over time—the original Cold War logic of an anti-Soviet coalition evolved into a relationship centered on mutually beneficial economic interactions—key U.S. and PRC constituencies were socialized to believe firmly that the partnership had tremendous value. Moreover, these influential domestic sectors labored hard to sustain the relationship in the face of periodic turbulence.

[16]For an early advocacy of expanding defense ties, see Michael Pillsbury, 'U.S.-China military ties?' *Foreign Policy* 20, (1975), pp. 50–64. Pillsbury was reportedly active in behind-the-scenes efforts to build a pro-cooperation coalition within the U.S. national security community. See, for example, Raymond L. Garthoff, *Détente and Confrontation: American-Soviet Relations from Nixon to Reagan* (Washington, DC: Brookings Institution, 1983), p. 696.
[17]Ross, *Negotiating Cooperation*, p. 236.
[18]See, for example, Harry Harding, *A Fragile Relationship: The United States and China since 1972* (Washington, DC: Brookings Institution, 1992), p. 141.
[19]Ross, *Negotiating Cooperation*, p. 240.
[20]Bush had been an early booster of developing economic ties between the United States and China. This is clear from a discussion Bush had with Kissinger when the former was the senior U.S. diplomat in Beijing in 1974 and the latter was secretary of state. See *The China Diary of George H. W. Bush: The Making of a Global President*, Jeffrey Engel, ed.(Princeton: Princeton University Press, 2008), p. 100.
[21]In May 1990 only 31% of those polled had a favorable impression of China—down from 64% in March 1989. Benjamin I Page and Tao Xie, *Living with the Dragon: How the American Public Views the Rise of China* (New York: Columbia University Press, 2010), p. 99.
[22]Engel, *The China Diary*, p. 461.

Chinese Lessons: Coalition for Cooperation

Following the temporary turbulence of the Tiananmen massacre and the resulting Western sanc-
tions, Beijing determined that Washington was a vital partner essential to stimulating Chinese
economic growth. However, in the aftermath of the 1989 crisis and the collapse of communism in
Eastern Europe and the end of the Soviet Union, many CCP and PLA elites came to perceive
Washington as a major threat to the PRC.[23] Nevertheless, most PRC leaders recognized that the
United States remained an essential partner in sustaining national economic growth and facilitating
China's growing regional and global influence.[24] Moreover, Chinese intellectuals continued to
support and glean benefits from the relationship.[25] In addition, many Chinese entrepreneurs and
workers benefited from the growing economic links with the United States. This pro-cooperation
coalition worked to persuade Washington that Beijing was worthy of joining the World Trade
Organization (WTO), with success finally coming in December 2001. But some economic sectors
were strongly opposed to Beijing joining the WTO. According to Premier Zhu Rongji—the most
senior Chinese official charged with spearheading the PRC's effort to join the WTO—managers, and
workers at State Owned Enterprises were very vigorous in expressing their opposition by 'making
trouble.'[26]

Whereas in previous years PRC officials would spout some hawkish rhetoric, take some largely
symbolic sanctions and then return to business as usual, by the 2000s this was changing as groups of
fiery Chinese nationalists—talking heads, including active duty and retired soldiers, netizens and
other would not only staunchly condemn U.S. actions against Taiwan, for example, but also voice
support for the use of China's military to support territorial claims and go toe-to-toe with the United
States and other militaries—not to resort to combat necessarily but to confront them.[27] PRC public
opinion also became more fiercely nationalistic and more ready to blame the United States for
seemingly using China as a punching bag. Episodes like the accidental bombing of the PRC embassy
in Belgrade in 1999 and the 2001 EP-3 collision in the South China Sea triggered popular outrage
against the United States.[28]

U.S. Lessons: Coalition for Cooperation

In the aftermath of 1989, the United States became more sensitive to the issue of human rights in
China. Nongovernmental organizations become more vocal in the United States, and Congress was
more attuned to the issue.[29] Organizations such as Human Rights Watch became more active in
lobbying members of Congress, and the Clinton administration took human rights in China more
seriously. But different bureaucracies took different stances: the Department of State, for example
tended to take a tougher stance than the Department of Commerce and the White House.[30] The

---

[23]See, for example, *The Tiananmen Papers: The Chinese Leaders' Decision to Use Force Against Their Own People in Their Own Words*
Zhang Liang, compiler (New York: Public Affairs, 2002).

[24]See, for example, David M. Lampton, *Same Bed Different Dreams: Managing U.S.-China Relations, 1989–2000*, (Berkeley
University of California Press, 2001), pp.115–116, 176–188.

[25]Alastair Iain Johnston, 'The correlates of Beijing public opinion toward the United States, 1998–2004', in *New Directions in the
Study of China's Foreign Policy*, Alastair Iain Johnston and Robert S. Ross, eds.(Stanford: Stanford University Press 2006), pp
362–363, 366.

[26]Zhu Rongji is quoted by David M. Lampton, *Following the Leader: Ruling China from Deng Xiaoping to Xi Jinping* (Berkeley
University of California Press), p. 210.

[27]See, for example, Andrew Scobell, 'Is there a civil-military gap in China's peaceful rise?' *Parameters* 39(2), (2009), pp. 4–22. The
rhetoric and action was heartfelt but also calculated to advance professional careers and institutional interests. See also
Lampton, *Following the Leader*, pp. 189.

[28]While this popular emotion was stoked, channeled and controlled by PRC authorities the anti-U.S. ire and nationalistic
sentiments were genuine. See, for example, Peter Hayes Gries, *China's New Nationalism: Pride, Politics, and Diplomacy*
(Berkeley: University of California Press, 2004). See also Johnston, 'The correlates on Beijing public opinion', pp. 364 and 366
Figure 12.7.

[29]Harding, *A Fragile Relationship*, p. 326.

[30]Warren I. Cohen, *America's Response to China: A History of Sino-American Relations* (New York: Columbia University Press, 2010)
p. 253.

.S. business community, meanwhile, remained staunchly in favor of continued economic relations
ith China and sought to blunt or at least mitigate the efforts of the pro-confrontation human rights
)alition. The struggle with the pro-cooperation coalition coalesced in an annual battle in the
ongress to renew Most Favored Nation (MFN) Trade Status for China.[31] By 1994 the pro-
)operation coalition had triumphed as the Bill Clinton administration moved to delink human
ghts from MFN in response to the coordinating efforts of a 'centrist coalition in Congress' and
usiness-oriented departments and agencies.'[32]

Meanwhile, the Taiwan lobby regained some clout as the island democratized. Beijing's anger at
ιe Clinton administration's decision to issue a visa to Taiwan President Lee Teng-hui in mid-1995
ιd its saber-rattling in the Taiwan Strait in late 1995 and early 1996 in the lead up to the island's first
opular election for head of state both served to make China a bully in the eyes of many
mericans.[33] Washington's response to PRC intimidation of Taiwan was to send two aircraft carrier
attle groups to the vicinity. The U.S. view was that relations with Taiwan were unofficial and
merican commitments to end arms sales were conditional on decreased tensions across the
ιiwan Strait. As long as China refused to renounce military force to achieve unification, the
.S. response has been that continued America security support for Taiwan was necessary and
ιstifiable.

Hence the pro-cooperation coalition was engaged in a struggle with a pro-confrontation lobby.
ut the former temporarily maintained an edge as the stronger and more potent alliance.

. to Coalitions of Confrontation

y the first decade of the twenty-first century, the domestic climate in both countries had funda-
ιentally changed. While the evolution was gradual, the trajectory was unmistakable: from near-
onsensus pro-cooperation coalitions at the outset to more potent and vocal pro-confrontation
oalitions. Writing in the mid-1990s, Robert Ross noted: 'Whereas in the 1970s and 1980s, domestic
olitics in Washington and Beijing encouraged compromise solutions to conflicts of interest, ... by
ιe 1990s, domestic politics in both countries impose political costs on leaders suggesting
ompromise.'[34]

reat Power Confrontation, 2008-Present

ι each country, enduring psycho-cultural insecurities and national security pathologies filtered the
:arning process. Although the United States was sincere about wanting to treat China as an equal,
/ashington was unprepared psychologically to embrace Beijing on equal footing. What the United
tates wanted, was a partner willing to support its policies and priorities, or at least not oppose them.
his is essentially what Deputy Secretary of State Robert Zoellick meant when he urged China to
ecome a 'responsible stakeholder' during a major policy address in 2005.[35] The United States was
ot used to being challenged militarily or economically on a global scale since the end of the Cold
/ar. Consequently, while objectively Beijing posed a significant challenge to Washington, this
hallenge was perceived with much greater alarm.

For its part, China was indeed sincere about wanting to be treated as an equal partner by the
Inited States, but Beijing was not psychologically prepared to pull its own weight. China continues

Harding, A Fragile Relationship, p. 260.
Patrick Tyler, A Great Wall: Six Presidents and China: An Investigative History (New York: Public Affairs, 1999), p. 412.
James Mann, About Face: A History of America's Curious Relationship with China: From Nixon to Clinton (New York: Alfred
A. Knopf, 1999), Chapter 17: Crisis over Taiwan. See also Page and Xie, Living with the Dragon, p. 101.
Ross, Negotiating Cooperation, p. 260.
Robert Zoellick's speech to the National Committee on U.S.-China Relations "Whither China: From Membership to
Responsibility, September 21, 2005. Text available at: https://www.ncuscr.org/content/robert-zoellicks-responsible-
stakeholder-speech.

to see itself as a relatively weak state and not as the full equal of other great powers.[36] Beijing wa
worried about overcommitting itself and was reluctant to embrace a greater substantive role i
global affairs.[37]

Moreover, China was also wary because it was fearful that the United States might be luring it int
a trap. For Beijing, the lessons of its past cooperative relationships are largely negative, and many c
these relationships ended badly. China has learned to be extremely wary of its relationships wit
other states, especially with 'the two superpowers.' Beijing was quick to assume that Moscow o
Washington were seeking to take advantage of China.[38] This assumption stems from the PRC bein
an extremely low trust polity.[39] This culture of suspicion and distrust carries over from domesti
politics and into the realm of foreign relations. While this distrust can be overcome, it usually take
considerable time and effort. In the case of relations with the United States, these bonds of trust hav
been built up between individuals over time. While bonds were developed among earlier genera
tions of political leaders, bonds of trust have proved more challenging to build between more recen
generations. This is less a judgement on the quality of newer relationships and more a testament t
the decline intangible benefits accruing from bilateral ties.

Chinese Lessons: Coalition for Confrontation

In Beijing's eyes, the United States posed a heightened across-the-board threat to China: at home, o
its borders, in its Asia-Pacific neighborhood, and to China's interests around the world. From a PR
perspective, U.S. official rhetoric regarding maintaining global leadership and military superiorit
over the armed forces of other countries was interpreted as threatening. Especially concerning t
China are U.S. rhetoric and policy pronouncements regarding Asia-Pacific policy. The Obam
Administration's 'return to Asia' in 2010, followed by its officially declared rebalance or 'pivot' t
Asia in 2012 were all interpreted at being directed against China. From China's perspective, greate
U.S. attention to the Asia-Pacific was signaled both by various assertive actions and high-profil
rhetoric.[40] Intentions to bolster U.S. military capabilities devoted to the Asia-Pacific were viewed a
threatening by China. According to one PRC scholar: 'China was more assertive . . . .[by] 2010 becaus
the United States was more assertive ... announcing a "return to Asia" and building up its militar
posture in the region.'[41] China perceived U.S. Navy activities in the South China Sea as threatenin
and intended to intimidate Beijing.[42]

PRC political and military leaders became increasingly alarmed about the United States an
questioned the value of Beijing's efforts to cooperate with Washington. According to the PRC'
2019 defense white paper: 'International strategic competition is on the rise. The US has adjusted it

---

[36]According to Robert Jervis, China "did not know of . . . relations between equal powers." Jervis, *Perception and Misperception i*
International Politics (Princeton: Princeton University Press, 1979), p. 271. In making this point, Jervis cites John Fairbank an
Immanuel Hsu. Nevertheless, while China continues to consider itself a developing country, it does not just cleave to a singl
identity. According to one scholar, China has seven different national identities. David Shambaugh, *China Goes Global: Th*
Partial Power (New York: Oxford University Press, 2013), chapter 2.

[37]On this point, see Andrew Scobell, 'China's search for security in the Greater Middle East', in *The Red Star and the Crescent: Chin*
and the Middle East, James Reardon-Anderson, ed., (New York: Oxford University Press), 2018, pp. 28–29.

[38]Harry Harding, 'China's co-operative behavior', in *Chinese Foreign Policy: Theory and Practice*, Thomas W. Robinson and Davi
Shambaugh, eds. (Oxford: Clarendon Press, 1994), p. 398.

[39]See, for example, Francis Fukuyama, *Trust: The Social Virtues and the Creation of Prosperity* (New York: Free Press, 1995), chapte
8.

[40]Many Chinese leaders and analysts were especially perturbed by Obama administration rhetoric. See Thomas J. Christensen, *Th*
China Challenge: Shaping the Choices of a Rising Power (New York: W.W. Norton, 2015), pp. 250. America's "return to Asia" wa
trumpeted by Secretary of State Hillary Rodham Clinton in a speech in Honolulu on October 28, 2010 titled: "America'
Engagement in the Asia-Pacific." Accessed at: https://2009-2017.state.gov/secretary/20092013clinton/rm/2010/10/150141.htm
America's "pivot to Asia" was proclaimed by Secretary Clinton a year later also in Honolulu on November 10, 2011 title
"America's Pacific Century." Accessed at: https://2009-2017.state.gov/secretary/20092013clinton/rm/2011/11/176999.htm.

[41]Quoted in Andrew Scobell and Scott W. Harold, 'An "assertive" China? Insights from interviews', *Asian Security* 19(2), (2013), p
120.

[42]Andrew Scobell, 'The South China Sea and U.S.-China rivalry', *Political Science Quarterly* 133(2), (2018), pp. 199–224.

national security and defense strategies and adopted unilateral policies. It has provoked and intensified competition among major countries, significantly increasing its defense expenditure, pushing for additional capacity in nuclear, outer space, cyber and missile defense, and undermined global strategic stability.'[43] This defense white paper is a consensus document, the result of considerable coordination and consultation across PRC national security bureaucracies. Hence it can be read as representing the combined perspective of Chinese military and civilian elites. Chinese public opinion, meanwhile, became more nationalistic, hawkish, and anti-American.[44] A recent manifestation of this occurred in 2019, directed toward the National Basketball Association (NBA) after the general manager of the Houston Rockets NBA franchise expressed his support for demonstrators in Hong Kong on social media. His words prompted a firestorm of criticism within China both from official outlets and China's NBA fans against what is usually one of the most popular American institutions in the PRC. NBA games, which are routinely televised live on Chinese television, were temporarily taken off the air.[45] Furthermore, some Chinese intellectuals have a less positive view of the United States. A growing number perceive the United States as less welcoming because PRC students and scholars now find it more difficult—sometimes impossible—to obtain U.S. visas, and multiple PRC visitors report being interrogated by agents from the Federal Bureau of Investigation when in the United States.[46]

Moreover, the PRC business community and economic sectors were unnerved by the greater turmoil and uncertainty manifest in U.S.-China ties and began to question whether continued beneficial bilateral relations were possible.[47] Some businesses, such as Huawei, perceive Washington to be increasingly hostile because the U.S. Government has been vigorously trying to block the company from the U.S. market and has spearheaded a global effort among allies to restrict the telecommunications company's access to markets around the world.[48] Washington has accused Huawei of being controlled by the PRC and using its technology and telecommunications networks to spy for its government. The most high-profile episode in this ongoing saga to date has been the arrest in Canada of Huawei Chief Financial Officer Meng Wanzhou (Meng is also the daughter of Huawei founder and Chief Executive Officer Ren Zhengfei).[49] Ottawa arrested Meng at the request of Washington. While the PRC has placed considerable pressure on Canada to release Meng, Beijing blames Washington for the incident.

Chinese perceptions of greater U.S. animosity are prompted by enhanced American efforts to target multiple vital national security interests both inside and outside PRC borders. On the domestic front, Beijing has discerned heightened quasi-official U.S. engagement with Taiwan—including expanded security cooperation—as well as U.S. meddling in the latest political crisis in Hong Kong, which emerged in 2019. Externally, Beijing discerns growing U.S. attention to 'the Quad'—composed of Australia, India, Japan, and the United States—which it believes to be a U.S.-led anti-China coalition of Asia-Pacific democracies. Beijing also believes that Washington is now engaged in economic trench warfare with China, and the trade war launched by the Trump

---

[43]*China's National Defense in the New Era* (Beijing: State Council Information Office of the People's Republic of China, 2019), Section I: International Security Situation.

[44]See, for example, Jessica Chen Weiss, 'How Hawkish is the Chinese Public? Another Look at "Rising Nationalism" and Chinese Foreign Policy', *Journal of Contemporary China* 28(119), (2019), pp. 679–695. For views of the United States, see pp. 686.

[45]Laurie Chen, 'NBA in damage-control mode as more Chinese partners cut ties in Hong Kong protest tweet storm', *South China Morning Post*, October 9, 2019, accessed at: https://www.scmp.com/news/china/society/article/3032164/nba-damage-control-mode-adam-silver-lands-china-hong-kong.

[46]Jane Perlez, 'F.B.I. Bars Some China Scholars From Visiting U.S. Over Spying Fears', *New York Times*, April 19, 2019, accessed at: https://www.nytimes.com/2019/04/14/world/asia/china-academics-fbi-visa-bans.html.

[47]Author conversations with Chinese scholars and analysts in Beijing and Shanghai, October 2019.

[48]Anna Fifield, 'Huawei files motion to block U.S. ban, calling it an affront to global human rights', *Washington Post*, May 28, 2019, accessed at: https://www.washingtonpost.com/world/huawei-files-motion-to-block-us-ban-calling-it-an-affront-to-global-human-rights/2019/05/29/fac5ce3e-81bb-11e9-9a67-a687ca99fb3d_story.html.

[49]Emily Rauhala, 'Canada arrested Huawei's Meng for the United States. As China retaliates, it's on its own', *Washington Post*, May 8, 2019, accessed at: https://www.washingtonpost.com/world/the_americas/canada-helped-the-us-arrest-meng-wanzhou-as-it-gets-punished-by-china-its-on-its-own/2019/05/07/c8152fbe-6d18-11e9-bbe7-1c798fb80536_story.html.

administration is just one front—albeit a very important one—in a wider conflict. Part of this larger struggle is American opposition to the Belt and Road Initiative—Xi Jinping's ambitious flagship foreign policy initiative.[50]

U.S. Lessons: Coalition for Confrontation

As China grew stronger economically and militarily, the United States became increasingly concerned about China as a potential threat. In part, this was because China began acting more assertively, but in part, it was because, since the end of the Cold War, the United States is not used to being challenged militarily in the Indo-Pacific and around the world by peer or even near-peer competitors. The U.S. Navy, for example, had become accustomed to operating unchallenged and without significant risk in the oceans of the world. The emergence of the term Anti-Access and Area Denial (A2/AD) in the Pentagon's lexicon in the mid-2000s and its pervasive usage was a key indicator that the U.S. Department of Defense had begun to take the PLA far more seriously.[51]

Furthermore, as China's economy grew ever larger, more technologically capable, and increasingly interconnected with the economies of the United States and other countries, even China's economy came to be interpreted as a national security threat by the United States.[52] The U.S. business community was largely in favor of a tougher China policy. Moreover, a reliable poll of U.S. public opinion taken in mid-2018 found that ordinary Americans viewed China as far more of an economic threat than they did a military threat.[53]

The *National Security Strategy* and the *National Defense Strategy* issued by the Donald J. Trump administration explicitly identify China as the United States' major rival. The Trump administration embraced an adversarial posture toward China across a wide array of bureaucracies, including not just the Department of Defense, the Intelligence Community but also the Department of Justice, the Department of the Treasury, and the Office of the U.S. Trade Representative.[54] In addition, the U.S. Congress was supportive ' ... of the administration's National Security Strategy and National Defense Strategy, establishing a remarkable bi-partisan congressional-executive hardening in US policy toward China not seen [in Washington] since the depths of the Cold War.'[55]

Of course, Russia is also identified, but it is quite clear which country the United States considers its most serious long-term threat. Several respected researchers pithily characterize the difference as follows: 'Russia is a rogue, not a peer; China is a peer, not a rogue.'[56] A U.S. Government analyst recently employed a meteorological analogy to try to capture the greater seriousness with which many in the U.S. national security community view Beijing over Moscow: 'Russia is the hurricane: it comes in fast and hard. China is climate change: long, slow, pervasive.'[57]

In Washington's eyes, China poses a heightened threat at home, on its borders, to its allies and partners, and to U.S. global interests. From a U.S. perspective, the China threat—a combination of

---

[50]See, for example, Robert Sutter, 'Congress and Trump administration China policy: overlapping priorities, uneasy adjustments and hardening toward Beijing', *Journal of Contemporary China* 28(118), (2019), p. 529.

[51]For the report that helped popularize the term, see Andrew Krepinevich, Barry Watts, and Robert Work, *Meeting the Anti-Access and Area Denial Challenge*, Washington: Center for Strategic and Budgetary Assessments, 2003. The text is available at: https://csbaonline.org/uploads/documents/2003.05.20-Anti-Access-Area-Denial-A2-AD.pdf.

[52]*National Security Strategy of the United States* (Washington, DC: The White House, 2017).

[53]By a 2 to 1 margin those polled viewed China as an economic threat over a military threat. Cited in Suisheng Zhao, 'Engagement on the defensive: from mismatched grand bargain to emerging US-China rivalry', *Journal of Contemporary China* 28(118), (2019), p. 507.

[54]This is in keeping with a "whole of government" effort attempted by the Trump administration. See speech by Christopher Ford, Assistant Secretary of State for Security and Nonproliferation "Bureaucracy and Counterstrategy: Meeting the China Challenge," Delivered to a conference at the Defense Threat Reduction Agency, Fort Belvoir, Virginia, September 11, 2019, accessed at: https://www.state.gov/bureaucracy-and-counterstrategy-meeting-the-china-challenge/.

[55]Sutter, 'Congress and Trump administration China policy', p. 527.

[56]James Dobbins, Howard J. Shatz, Ali Wyne, *Russia Is a Rogue, Not a Peer; China Is a Peer, Not a Rogue: Different Challenges, Different Responses* (Santa Monica: RAND, 2019).

[57]Rob Joyce of the NSA cited in Joseph Marks, 'The Cybersecurity 202: U.S. officials: It's China hacking that keeps us up at night', *The Washington Post*, March 6, 2019.

capabilities and intentions—has grown substantially. Growing evidence emerged indicating that China has been conducting influence operations inside the United States and in other countries around the world, including U.S. allies in Europe and Asia.[58] There was also rising alarm over Chinese theft of technology from American companies and growing concern about Chinese penetration of U.S. higher education in pursuit of proprietary scientific and technological information.[59] The worries of the national security community were combined with a U.S. business community increasingly frustrated with China's unwillingness or inability to allow American companies greater access to Chinese markets and a more level playing field within China for U.S. companies vis-à-vis Chinese companies.[60]

While China's increasing military capabilities have played a significant role in U.S. threat perceptions, it is rhetoric and actions that have raised alarm in Washington. Ambitious and strident official rhetoric along with hawkish verbiage by active duty and retired military officers have appeared threatening to many in the United States (and elsewhere). Moreover, assertive—often labeled 'aggressive' by the national security community—Chinese actions, notably this in the South China Sea and the East China Sea, also look threatening. Significantly, whether the actual evidence demonstrates that China had become more assertive, the perception in both the United States and in China was that Beijing was acting more assertively (although Americans preferred the term 'aggressive' while Chinese preferred the term 'assertive').[61]

From Geography of Peace to Geography of Conflict

For the first two and a half decades following the U.S.-China rapprochement (i.e. until 1996), neither Beijing nor Washington perceived each other as a major geostrategic threat. Although when Kissinger met with Mao in July 1971—and when Nixon met with Mao seven months later—the United States maintained a formal security relationship with the Republic of China on Taiwan and U.S. forces remained involved in Vietnam, the PRC considered the United States a new ally and the Soviet Union its most significant long-term adversary. When the United States did withdraw from Vietnam in 1973, then formally severed diplomatic ties with Taiwan in 1978 and officially terminated its alliance with Taiwan a year later, this persuaded Beijing that Washington was delivering on its commitments. Meanwhile, the United States considered China as a de facto ally and the Soviet Union as its primary adversary—a threat to U.S. interests worldwide as well as to the U.S. homeland. China certainly was not perceived as a military threat to U.S. interests in the region, let alone globally. Washington and Beijing maintained these geopolitical assessments of the other until the final years of the twentieth century.

And yet these geostrategic assessments seem at odds with enduring geostrategic priorities. A longstanding U.S. geostrategic priority was to oppose the existence of an unfriendly great power or alignment of great powers in the Pacific and Eurasia.[62] Meanwhile, a Chinese geostrategic default for centuries has been to maintain itself as 'the predominant political, economic, cultural, and military power of East Asia.'[63] What explains the apparent paradox?

---

[58]See, for example, Lampton, 'Reconsidering U.S.-China relations', pp. 55–57.

[59]See, for example, William C. Hannas, James Mulvenon, and Anna B. Puglisi, *Chinese Industrial Espionage: Technological Acquisition and Military Modernization* (New York: Routledge, 2013) and *The Gathering Pacific Storm: Emerging US-China Strategic Competition in Defense Technological and Industrial Development*, Tai Ming Cheung and Thomas G. Mahnken, eds. (Amherst: Cambria Press, 2018).

[60]See, for example, Lampton, 'Reconsidering U.S.-China relations', pp. 54–55.

[61]Research by Iain Johnston suggests that China had not become more assertive. See Alastair I. Johnston, 'How new and assertive is China's new assertiveness?' *International Security* 37(4), (2013), pp. 7–48. However, author conversations with Chinese and U.S. researchers reveal that both perceived this to be so.

[62]Michael J. Green, *By More than Providence: Grand Strategy and American Power in the Asia-Pacific since 1783* (New York: Columbia University Press, 2017), p. 5.

[63]Michael D. Swaine and Ashley J. Tellis, *Interpreting China's Grand Strategy: Past, Present, and Future* (Santa Monica: RAND, 2000), p. 3. The authors identify "a deeply rooted belief in the geopolitical centrality of China to the region." Ibid.

The geopolitical answer is that for this extended period—the 1970s and 1980s—China was predominantly a continental power, and the United States was mainly a maritime one. According to Robert Ross: 'The post-Cold War bipolar regional structure [as of 1999] is characterized by Chinese dominance of mainland East Asia and U.S. dominance of maritime East Asia.'[64] As long as this 'bipolar' balance persisted, Ross argued that the 'geography of the peace' was likely to prevail in the region.[65] Consequently, U.S.-China competitive rivalry was more stable than the U.S.-Soviet geopolitical contest during the Cold War, which had encompassed both significant continental and maritime components.

But the 1995–1996 Taiwan Strait Crisis was a profound shock to Chinese thinking.[66] The U.S. ability to prevent the PLA from successfully coercing the island—let alone seizing Taiwan militarily—proved a dramatic wake up call. It was the dispatch of not one, but two U.S. Navy carrier battle groups to the vicinity of Taiwan prompted a geostrategic and defense policy reappraisal.

Indeed, Ross observed that '... China can only destabilize [the "bipolar structure"] by challenging U.S. maritime supremacy.'[67] Particularly under PRC President Xi Jinping, Beijing has focused more resources on expanded China's maritime capabilities.[68] The rivalry has intensified because U.S. global hegemony in the post-Cold War era is being challenged by China. Specifically, China is contesting America's 'command of the commons' and this is playing out in a very high-profile manner in the South China Sea.[69]

China Rebalances

The realization that the United States could prevent the PLA from accomplishing its Taiwan mission led Beijing to redouble its efforts at sea denial and control inside the first island chain and enhancing its ability to project maritime and air power out toward the second island chain. These efforts included expanding its arsenal of ballistic and cruise missiles and improving their accuracy but also accelerating its aircraft carrier program.

This effort was part of a more ambitious geostrategic maritime roadmap to expand reach of the PLA Navy from a near seas force with a largely defensive mission to a far sea force with greater offensive capabilities. These ambitions, articulated in recent PRC defense white papers, were first outlined in the early 1980s. They are widely attributed to the late Admiral Liu Huaqing (1916–2011). The plan envisioned a phased expansion of PRC sea power.[70] In the first phase, by 2000, the PLA Navy would establish its area of operations in the South China Sea, East China Sea, and the Yellow Sea out as far as the so-called First Island Chain–the Kuril Islands, Japan, the Ryukyus, Taiwan, the Philippines, Borneo, and Natuna Besar. In the second phase, by 2020, the PLA Navy aimed to extend its operational reach out to the so-called Second Island Chain–the Bonins, the Marianas, and the Carolines. In the third phase, by 2050, China would become a global sea power and hence on a par with the U.S. Navy. Indeed, the PLA Navy's activities and power project efforts have so far kept pace with this timeline. China's navy would hence expand its missions beyond China's coastal 'near shore' waters or littoral (*jinan*) and 'near seas' (*jinhai*) and toward the 'far seas' (*yuanhai*).[71]

[64]Robert S. Ross, 'The geography of the peace: East Asia in the twenty-first century', *International Security* 23(3), (1999), pp. 81–119. Quote on p. 84.

[65]Ross, 'The Geography of the Peace'.

[66]Andrew Scobell, 'Show of force: Chinese soldiers, statesmen, and the 1995–1996 Taiwan strait crisis', *Political Science Quarterly* 115(2), (2000), pp. 227–246.

[67]Ross, 'The geography of the peace', 99.

[68]Andrew S. Erickson, 'China's maritime ambitions', in *The Routledge Handbook of Asian Security Studies*, Sumit Ganguly, Andrew Scobell, Joseph Chinyong Liow, eds. (New York: Routledge, 2018), pp. 100–114.

[69]Barry R. Posen, 'Command of the commons: the military foundation of U.S. Hegemony', *International Security* 28(4), (2003), pp. 5–46.

[70]Bernard D. Cole, *The Great Wall at Sea: China's Navy in the Twenty-First Century*, 2nd ed. (Annapolis: Naval Institute Press, 2010), pp. 174–176.

[71]Tang Fuquan and Han Yi, 'Renmin haijun yanzhe dang zhiyin de chuanxiang polang qianjin' ['People's Navy advances along the course set by Party'], *Zhongguo Junshi Kexue* [China Military Science], (4), (2009), pp. 13–14.

Significantly, many PLA strategists have embraced the writings of U.S. naval strategist Alfred Thayer Mahan,[72] who emphasized the central importance of sea power to a nation, notably the link between a state's naval expansion, economic development, and the growth of maritime commerce as Chinese naval thinkers have observed.[73]

China maritime ambitions are explicitly set out in the PRC's 2015 defense white paper:

> The seas and oceans bear on the enduring peace, lasting stability and sustainable development of China. The traditional mentality that land outweighs sea must be abandoned, and great importance has to be attached to managing the seas and oceans and protecting maritime rights and interests. It is necessary for China to develop a modern maritime force structure commensurate with its national security and development interest, safeguard its national sovereignty and maritime rights and interests, protect the security of strategic SLOCs and overseas interests, and participate in international maritime cooperation, so as to provide strategic support for building itself into a maritime power.[74]

While Beijing was very serious about this initiative, there was a recognition that it will be difficult and time-consuming. The United States was unlikely to yield to China without some pushback. Moreover, the United States can count on allies like Japan, South Korea, and Australia to limit or slow China's oceanic advance. By 2011, Chinese analysts were talking about 'Marching West'—strengthening the PRC's economic, diplomatic, and defense capabilities along China's continental frontiers in Central Asia.[75] Rather than intended as a Chinese pivot from east to west, the goal was for China to geo-strategically 'rebalance' so that its economic and military was not so heavily skewed toward the eastern coastal provinces of China.[76] In many ways, the westward initiative was a continuation of the Western Development program effort launched a decade earlier to economically develop China's westernmost provinces and autonomous regions, including Tibet and Xinjiang.[77]

A further continuation of this was Xi Jinping's official launch in 2013 of the Belt and Road Initiative (BRI), which emphasized not just the development of maritime 'roads' but also continental 'belts.' The BRI is all part of advancing a vision of a country that is both a continental as well as a maritime power. In a white paper issued in 2017, Beijing openly declared that the PRC considers the Asia-Pacific its own sphere of influence: 'China has all along taken advancement of regional prosperity and stability as its own responsibility.'[78]

The United States Rebalances

The US began taking China's naval development and assertiveness in the western Pacific more seriously. As a result, by the late 2000s, the U.S. Department of Defense began to talk in grave terms about China's 'Anti-Access/Area Denial' (or A2/AD) and the U.S. Navy began to show a greater respect toward China's maritime capabilities. Then starting in 2011, the Obama administration began promoting a U.S. 'pivot' or 'rebalance' to Asia.[79]

The United States is increasingly concerned about the ability to operate freely in the Western Pacific. A top priority Department of Defense objective is 'to safeguard the freedom of the seas,'

---

[72] James R. Holmes and Toshi Yoshihara, *China's Naval Strategy in the 21st Century: The Turn to Mahan* (New York: Routledge, 2007).

[73] See the discussion in Andrew Erickson and Lyle Goldstein, 'Gunboats for China's new "Grand Canals"? Probing the intersection of Beijing's naval and oil security policies', *Naval War College Review* 62(3), (2009), pp. 49–50.

[74] *China's Military Strategy* (Beijing: State Council Information Office of the People's Republic of China, 2015), Section IV: Building and Development of China's Armed Forces.

[75] Wang Jisi, '"Xijin": Zhongguo diyuan zhanlue dezai pingheng' ['Marching West: China's geostrategic rebalance'], *Huanqiu Shibao* [Global Times], October 17, 2012.

[76] Author conversation with Wang Jisi, Beijing, October 2013.

[77] Barry J. Naughton, 'The Western Development Program', in *Holding China Together: Diversity and National Integration in the Post-Deng Era*, Barry J. Naughton and Dali L. Yang, eds. (New York: Cambridge University Press, 2004), pp. 253–296.

[78] *China's Policies on Asia-Pacific Security Cooperation* (Beijing: State Council Information Office of the People's Republic of China, 2017).

[79] For an articulation the vision and what a strategy to execute the vision would look like see Kurt Campbell, *The Pivot: The Future of American Statecraft in Asia* (New York, Basic Books, 2016).

including 'uses of the sea and airspace ... for military ships and aircraft ... .'[80] The United States is adamant on the matter of the inviolability of the principle of freedom of navigation and the priority of protecting the global commons. The higher principle to which the United States and other liberal democracies subscribe is 'freedom of the seas,' which is enshrined in key documents such as the United Nations Convention on Law of the Sea (UNCLOS). Article 87 of UNCLOS states: 'The high seas are open to all States whether coastal or landlocked.'[81] On a day-to-day basis, the United States tends to emphasize subsets of 'freedom of the seas' (*mare liberum*), namely 'freedom of navigation' and 'freedom of overflight.' Although Washington has yet to ratify UNCLOS, it abides by the convention as a central document of international law. From Beijing's perspective, Washington appears to be biased against China and interfering in a maritime region far removed from U.S. geostrategic core interests and claiming to uphold a document it refuses to formally endorse.

The high-profile freedom of navigation operations (aka 'FONOPS') conducted by the U.S. Navy in waters claimed by Beijing appear to be the arrogant actions of the global hegemon. Officially, the U.S. Navy performs FONOPS in international waters around the world in order to 'demonstrate a non-acquiescence to excessive maritime claims asserted by coastal states.'[82] The U.S. interpretation of UNCLOS is that military vessels can operate unhindered in international waters, meaning anywhere outside of the 12 nautical mile limit of a country's territorial waters.[83] In contrast, China insists that a country has additional rights within its EEZ to deny access to the military vessels of another state unless permission has been granted.[84]

From Asia-Pacific to Indo-Pacific

In early June 2019 U.S. Department of Defense issued an *Indo-Pacific Strategy Report*.[85] The release of this official document by the administration of President Donald J. Trump marks the culmination of burgeoning American attention to a vast geographic expanse once almost exclusively referred to as the Asia-Pacific. This document highlights not only the remarkable rise of the 'Indo-Pacific' as a prominent geostrategic construct in twenty-first century geopolitics, but it also makes plain Washington's growing alarm over China's perceived threat to the United States and the substantial U.S. interests in that region.

Initially, a turn of phrase favored in New Delhi, 'Indo-Pacific' has also been embraced by Canberra, and found favor in Honolulu, before being adopted by Washington, DC.[86] What does the ascendance of the term 'Indo-Pacific' in the national security lexicon of the United States signify about U.S. thinking toward the region and China? There are several possible answers. First, the Trump administration is trying hard to distinguish itself from the foreign and defense policies of its predecessors, but the change in terminology is also a signpost of a geostrategic shift by the United States, which has been in

---

[80] *Asia-Pacific Maritime Security Strategy* (Washington, DC: Department of Defense, 2015), p. 16.
[81] See Article 87 of 'United Nations Convention on the Law of the Sea', accessed at: http://www.un.org/depts/los/convention_agreements/texts/unclos/unclos_e.pdf, September 14, 2019.
[82] 'U.S. Department of Defense Freedom of Navigation Program Fact Sheet', Department of Defense, March 2015, accessed at http://policy.defense.gov/Portals/11/Documents/gsa/cwmd/DoD%20FON%20Program%20–%20Fact%20Sheet%20(March%202015).pdf, September 14, 2019.
[83] *Asia-Pacific Maritime Security Strategy*, p. 2.
[84] Sam J. Tangredi, 'The Maritime Commons and Military Power', in *Conflict and Cooperation in the Global Commons*, Scott Jasper, ed. (Washington, DC: Georgetown University Press, 2012), p. 79.
[85] *Indo-Pacific Strategy Report: Preparedness, Partnerships, and Promoting a Networked Region* (Washington, DC: Department of Defense, 2019).
[86] The earliest contemporary use of the term appears to have been in India although Australia also claims ownership. Indian naval analyst Gurpreet Khurana reportedly coined the term at a conference in 2006. See Mercy A. Kuo, 'The Origin of "Indo-Pacific" as Geopolitical Construct: Insights from Gurpreet Khurana', *The Diplomat*, January 25, 2018, available https://thediplomat.com/2018/01/the-origin-of-indo-pacific-as-geopolitical-construct/ 'Indo-Pacific' was then adopted by Australians and used in reports issued by the Government of Australia starting in 2013. With a few years, the term had found favor at U.S. Pacific Command based at Camp Smith outside Honolulu, Hawaii. By 2018, Washington adopted the term and in mid-2018 the Department of Defense officially changed the name of Pacific Command to Indo-Pacific Command. For an Australian perspective, see Rory Medcalf, 'Indo-Pacific Visions: Giving Solidarity a Chance', *Asia Policy* 14(3), (2019), pp. 79–95.

the offing for a while. Second, the term Indo-Pacific emphasizes the maritime character of the region by combining its two greatest bodies of water—the Indian Ocean and the Pacific Ocean. Third, the term is a nod to the growing importance of India—a rising continental and maritime power—the significance of which is often overshadowed by the greater attention given to the rise of China. Fourth, the Indo-Pacific conception hints at the importance to the United States of another regional power and U.S. ally, which is located at the intersection of these two oceans: Australia. Fifth, Washington's embrace of the Indo-Pacific concept is an indication that the United States has awoken to the seriousness of great power competition in the region and the full realization that China has become America's most significant geostrategic rival. Accompanying this realization is a recognition that to be effective, U.S. rivalry with China will need a concert of regional great powers to stand with the United States. Indeed, Australia and India–along with Japan—are considered key regional allies and/or partners in addressing the challenge of China.

While each of these five answers holds merit, the fifth answer is the most compelling. Noteworthy is that as a concept and turn of phrase, the Indo-Pacific is nothing new to the countries of the region. Significantly, the conception is 'authentically regional rather than narrowly American.'[87] The construct has been embraced by multiple countries, including Australia, India, and Japan. The geographic conception resonates with 'many countries' reportedly because they desire to 'dilute' China's influence across the region."[88] According to Australian academic Rory Medcalf: ' ... given China's strategic weight and temptations toward hegemony, an Indo-Pacific perspective is empowering for other countries, encouraging them to build new defensive and balancing partnerships across outdated geographic boundaries.'[89]

Yet U.S.-China rivalry now also extends well beyond the confines of the Asia-Pacific—or Indo-Pacific. Geographically, Chinese interests are now global in scope. The outcome is that in the second decade of the twenty-first century to whatever corner of the world, American diplomats, military professionals, entrepreneurs, and tourists venture, they encounter some form of PRC presence. While this expanding Chinese presence does not necessarily objectively pose a threat to the United States, when combined with greater U.S. perceptions of a far more ambitious China, the conclusion that many Americans reach is: Beijing is directly challenging Washington.[90] Meanwhile, U.S. reactions of alarm or dismay to this expanding PRC presence beyond the Asia-Pacific fuels a perception among Chinese that Washington is actively seeking to counter or block China's rise.[91]

Conclusion

The Washington-Beijing rivalry of the early twentieth century was neither pre-ordained nor an aberration. It was constructed by the two countries as domestic constituencies were socialized toward confrontation. Pro-cooperation coalitions emerged in the United States and China in support of an alignment to counter a mutually perceived Soviet threat. The viability of U.S.-China cooperative relations was undermined by the final chapter of the Cold War, which witnessed the disintegration first of the Soviet bloc and then of the Soviet Union itself coinciding with the greatest internal challenge to CCP rule in decades—the Tiananmen debacle.

This U.S.-China rivalry was subsumed by an unsettled accommodation of mutual self-interest by Washington and Beijing during the last decade of the twentieth century and the first decade the twenty-first century. By the 2010s, as this rivalry had become far more visible, the pro-cooperation coalitions in the United States and China had splintered and been supplanted by pro-confrontation

---

[87]Medcalf, 'Indo-Pacific Visions', p. 83.
[88]Ibid.
[89]Ibid., p. 90.
[90]On the widespread view that China under the leadership of Xi Jinping has become far more ambitious, see, for example, *Elizabeth Economy, The Third Revolution: Xi Jinping and the New Chinese State* (New York: Oxford University Press, 2018).
[91]See, for example, Andrew J. Nathan and Andrew Scobell, 'How China Sees America: The Sum of Beijing's Fears', *Foreign Affairs* 91(5), (2012), pp. 32–47.

coalitions. The emerging rivalry is also explained by U.S. and PRC geostrategic reassessments. China's expanded geopolitical horizons, notably its greater attention to the maritime realm, collided with a U.S. reconceptualization of the Asia-Pacific.

Significantly each side perceives its own actions as being responses to the provocative or aggressive actions of the other. Chinese officials, as well as analysts and scholars, tend to opine that China is taking hardline actions only as a response to muscular actions by the United States. And U.S. officials, as well as analysts and scholars, often express the view that the United States is merely responding to aggressive Chinese actions. In short, there is an action-reaction dynamic at work or at least the perception of one that seems real to each side.

Indications that this great power competition is broadening both geographically and across domains raise the specter of an intensification and/or escalation of Sino-American rivalry. Is there a path back to US-China comity? Based on the above analysis, the answer is for both countries to reconstruct pro-cooperation domestic coalitions and rethink their geostrategic game plans. Neither effort will be easy, but the level of confrontation and intensity of distrust and suspicion strongly suggests that nothing less than a two-pronged full-bore effort has much hope of success.

Disclosure statement

No potential conflict of interest was reported by the author.

Funding

This work was supported by the Ministry of Education of the Republic of Korea and the National Research Foundation of Korea [NRF- 2018S1A5A2A03037603].

Chinese Multinational Enterprises Operating in Western Economies: Huawei in the US and the UK

Xin Liu

ABSTRACT

Huawei serves as a vehicle for presenting the multiple barriers faced by Multinational Enterprises (MNEs) that happen to be born in China, a non-democratic and non-Western country who now challenges the world's No.1 superpower, thus requires a multi-disciplinary analytical framework by taking much broader contexts into considerations. This comparative case study of its operations in the US and UK aims to develop the old model of examining Chinese MNEs that is heavily economic factor focused by including more variables, such as 'bilateral relations', 'law', 'media influence' and 'cultural proximity' under host country factors, and 'governance structure' under home country factors. The new model will show the increasing complexity in the global competitive landscape and inspire more research to further advance understanding of this new international business phenomenon.

Introduction

As a multinational company operating in over 170 countries, Huawei's international operation is exposed to diverse, conflicting pressures that arise from different business and political environments in the host countries, and in Western economies, in particular, its operations have been plagued by continued uncertainty and distrust. What happened to this Chinese telecommunication giant in 2018–2020 showcased the statement made by Daniels et al. that 'the interplay of political ideologies, conceptions of political freedom, legacies of legality, presumption of fairness, and standards of accountability in each market makes for challenging business environments', in which 'state officials exercise authority, legislate policies, regulate enterprise and punish wrongdoers'.[1] The setbacks Huawei suffered in the US and UK markets made typical examples of how political risks can 'change a country's business environment in ways that force investors to accept lower rates of return, cost them some or all of the value of their investment, or threaten the sustainability of their operation'.[2]

So far, most of the analysis assessing such political risks are about Western MNEs operating in non-democratic host countries like China, with fewer case studies the other way around. In 2016, China was transformed from being a net inward to a net outward investing economy,[3] which has stimulated more academic interests in assessing such risks for MNEs from China, such as Drahokoupil

---

[1] John Daniels, Lee Radebaugh, and Daniel Sullivan, *International Business, Environments & Operations*, 16th ed. (Pearson: Harlow, 2019), p.105.

[2] Ibid, p.118.

[3] United Nations Conference on Trade and Development (UNCTAD), 'World Investment Report 2017: Investment and the Digital Economy', Geneva: UNCTAD, accessed 8 August 2019, https://unctad.org/en/PublicationsLibrary/wir2017_en.pdf.

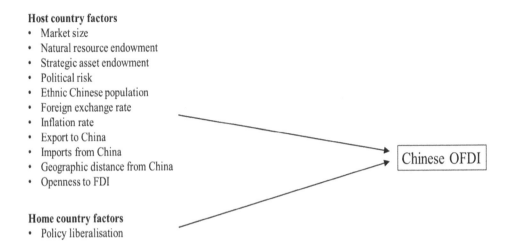

Host country factors
- Market size
- Natural resource endowment
- Strategic asset endowment
- Political risk
- Ethnic Chinese population
- Foreign exchange rate
- Inflation rate
- Export to China
- Imports from China
- Geographic distance from China
- Openness to FDI

Home country factors
- Policy liberalisation

Chinese OFDI

Figure 1. Empirical model, Buckley et al (2007).

et al.,[4] and Buckley et al.[5] The latter was a retrospective of the empirical model for Chinese Outward Foreign Direct Investment (OFDI) they developed back in 2007 (see Figure 1). However, despite emphasizing that the areas for future research 'are best considered as contextual factors', and 'it is necessary to paint as full a picture of context as possible',[6] no new contextual factors were added. Although the model was developed to specifically assess *Chinese* OFDI, most of the factors considered were generic ones that apply to *all* MNEs. Besides, their research mainly looked at the state-owned enterprises (SOEs) from China, and most determinants identified were economic variables.

Today, however, as the world's No. 1 telecom supplier and No. 2 smartphone manufacturer, thus representing an influential Chinese MNE, Huawei is 100 percent employee-owned with no state funding. Its home country of China, as a non-Western and non-democratic state challenging the world's No.1 superpower for the past century in various fronts now, also gives the company more 'liability of foreignness' (LOF). It thus serves as a vehicle for presenting the multiple barriers in business, political, and legal interactions faced by a MNE that happens to be born in China. Yet, so far, most of the Huawei case studies are analyzed in the business framework of internationalisation, and even within this framework, no comparative case studies have been done to analyze the different challenges it faces in unique business environments it encounters globally, let alone within the 'Western economies' that are often treated as a monolithic entity. For example, Mascitelli and Chung's[7] recent PEST analysis involves 'a narrative on the rise of China as a global power alongside the ongoing legacy of the Cold War' and 'strategic mistrust' of China and Chinese firms in 'Western economies'.[8] Plummer argued that Huawei's setbacks in the US market have made 'the company stand out as a case study in the 21st century globalization, specifically in the overarching context of a US–China relationship that is largely defined by competition and distrust'.[9] While agreeing with

[4]Jan Drahokoupil, Agnieszka McCaleb, Peter Pawlicki and Ágnes Szunomár, 'Huawei in Europe: strategic integration of local capabilities in a global production network', in *Chinese investment in Europe: corporate strategies and labour relations*, ed. Jan Drahokoupil, (Brussels: Etui, 2017), pp. 211–229.
[5]Peter Buckley, Jeremy Clegg, Hinrich Voss, Adam Cross, Xin Liu and Ping Zheng, 'A Retrospective and Agenda for Future Research on Chinese Outward Foreign Direct Investment', *Journal of International Business Studies* 49, (2018), pp. 4–23.
[6]Ibid, p.11.
[7]Bruno Mascitelli and Mona Chung, 'Hue and cry over Huawei: Cold war tensions, security threats or anti-competitive behaviour?', *Research in Globalisation*, Vol. 1, (2019), pp. 1–6.
[8]Kenneth Lieberthal and Jisi Wang, 'Addressing US-China strategic distrust'. China Centre at Brookings, Washington DC, accessed 1 August 2019, https://www.brookings.edu/wp-content/uploads/2016/06/0330_china_lieberthal.pdf.
[9]William Plummer, *Huidu—Inside Huawei*. ISBN9781520362007. (Printed in Germany by Amazon Distribution GmbH: Leipzig, 2018), n.p.

these statements, the author sees Huawei stand out as a comparative case study as the US does not represent all 'Western economies'. Huawei has clinched 91 5G contracts all over the world by February 2020,[10] and more than half were from Europe, where the US had explicitly lobbied at the 5G Prague meeting held in May 2019, attended by the US and more than 30 EU and NATO member states. The US National Security Agency was quoted to say that 'allowing Chinese companies in 5G networks is like handing the Chinese government a loaded gun'.[11] However, in a discussion about Germany's 5G roll-out, its Chancellor Angela Merkel said her government would not capitulate to pressure from the US and punish individual vendors 'simply because it's from a certain country'.[12] In January 2020, when the British government announced its long-delayed decision to allow Huawei a limited participation in its noncritical parts of the 5G network as no 'smoking gun' was found, defying Trump' was highlighted in the news headlines of mainstream media.[13] Then, when a dramatic U-Turn was made by Downing Street in July 2020, headlines such as 'Britain may further limit Huawei in 5G, a win for Washington and blow to China'[14] again revealed the triangular nature of the game, while the BBC's announcement of 'Huawei decision: UK "right to stand up to China"'[15] even literally equated Huawei as a symbol for its home country of China.

The factors that have brought Huawei to its contested status are rather complex: its own identity, its domestic and international legal contexts and political environment, the intertwined issue of cyber security and national security, China's policy of technological superiority, the Sino-US trade war and the looming digital Cold War. Therefore, this article argues that the increasing complexity in the intricate global competitive landscape requires expanding the contextual factors identified in the old model. This comparative case study will fill this gap by looking at Huawei in the US and the UK, the two prominent Western markets, where the Chinese telecommunication giant is perceived and received in a similar yet different manner.

In the same year of 2001, Huawei established its European headquarter in Basingstoke, UK and founded a subsidiary company of FutureWei in Texas, US. By 2020, however, amid the intensifying trade war between the US and China, Huawei was first added to the US Department of Commerce's Entity List in May 2019, banning American companies to *sell* components to Huawei. Then, a ban on US federal agencies *buying* equipment and services from Huawei was announced in August. This was further expanded a year later in May 2020 when companies around the world were banned from *using* American technology to design or produce chips for Huawei, a sanction 'narrowly and strategically targets'[16] Huawei, as it is a known fact that both the major alternative 5G equipment suppliers, Nokia and Ericsson, actually manufactured their components in Chinese factories.

Meanwhile, in the UK, Huawei announced new investment in a 550-acre chip plant in Cambridge in March 2019 and completed the first 5G call in the world with Vodaphone in May. In the BBC reports about Trump's UK visit in June, 'Huawei' was listed both among 'the five potential diplomatic flashpoints' prior to his visit and 'the five things we have learned from Trump's state visit', and the

---

[10]Reuters, 'Factbox: Deals by major suppliers in the race for 5G', accessed 5 July 2020, https://www.reuters.com/article/us-telecoms-5g-orders-factbox/factbox-deals-by-major-suppliers-in-the-race-for-5g-idUSKBN23O2G4.

[11]Kara Frederick, 'The 5 G Future Is Not Just About Huawei', *Foreign Policy*, accessed 5 June 2019, https://foreignpolicy.com/2019/05/03/the-5g-future-is-not-just-about-huawei/

[12]Stefan Nicola, 'Merkel Takes a Stand Against U.S. Pressure to Bar Huawei From 5G', *Bloomberg*, accessed 19 March 2019, https://www.bloomberg.com/news/articles/2019-03-19/merkel-takes-a-stand-against-u-s-pressure-to-bar-huawei-from-5g.

[13]'Britain Defies Trump Plea to Ban Huawei From 5G Network', *New York Times*, accessed 29 January 2020, https://www.nytimes.com/2020/01/28/technology/britain-huawei-5G.html.
    'U.K. Allows Huawei to Build Parts of 5 G Network, Defying Trump', accessed 9 April 2020, https://www.wsj.com/articles/u-k-allows-huawei-to-build-parts-of-5g-network-11580213316.

[14]William Boots, 'Britain may further limit Huawei in 5G, a win for Washington and blow to China', *Washington Post*, accessed 6 July 2020, https://www.washingtonpost.com/world/europe/huawei-5g-uk/2020/07/06/7477b862-bf8e-11ea-8908-68a2b9eae9e0_story.html.

[15]BBC, 'Huawei decision: UK 'right to stand up to China', accessed 14 July 2020, https://www.bbc.co.uk/news/uk-politics-53402694.

[16]'Commerce Addresses Huawei's Efforts to Undermine Entity List, Restricts Products Designed and Produced with U.S. Technologies', last modified 15 May 2020, https://www.commerce.gov/news/press-releases/2020/05/commerce-addresses-huaweis-efforts-undermine-entity-list-restricts.

reason why Huawei matters is 'because intelligence is a core element of the UK–US relationship, and any potential threat to that relationship would matter'.[17] The US has been openly using the 'carrot and stick' approach to this relationship: the carrot being the much-allured post-Brexit US–UK free-trade deal, while the stick being the threat of harming their intelligence sharing partnerships. Huawei seemed to have torn open a rift between these two leading Western economies that share 'special relations' as old allies, and also between the UK and Australia, the two allies that share a common language, ancestry and monarch, when a group of Australian MPs canceled a trip to London in protest of Downing Street's Huawei decision in February 2020.[18] As a matter of fact, in a speech at a London conference, the US Secretary of State Mike Pompeo had openly blamed the division as something 'just what China wants—to divide Western alliances through bits and bytes, not bullets and bombs'.[19]

Accusing the division as China's intention is a subjective claim, while objectively, the division shows different business and political environments in the UK and US for Chinese MNEs, particularly in how open they are towards Chinese investment and competition. This article aims to make a comparative analysis of the multiple challenges faced by Huawei both between its host and home countries, as well as between different host countries in the West. After explaining why the old model needs to be reconfigured to assess the complex business environment faced by Chinese MNEs today, it will explore answers to what variables need to be brought into the new analytical framework.

Data and Method

After contacting Huawei's Shenzhen headquarters and its UK company at Reading, the author was directed to a valuable pool of information that are open documents but not readily available to the public without inside sources. For example, *Collection of Interview Transcripts of Huawei Top Management*, Volume 1 & 2, were compiled by Huawei as internal documents, recording 36 interviews carried out with nine members of top management from December 2018 to April 2019. Then, updated English versions of exclusive interviews with Ren Zhengfei were published in two volumes, one from January to May 2019, and one from May to August 2019. More interviews taking place after this were further released on its official WeChat account of Blue Blood Lab. These sources offer a huge bank of 76 interview transcripts in total, with mainstream media from the US, UK, Canada, Germany, France, Italy, Spain, Japan, South Korea, Poland, Austria, Turkey, four Nordic countries, Arab countries in the Middle East, and China. The interview grid, with detailed information, can be found in the Appendix. The author also verified and confirmed fact-based information with her contact person inside Huawei regarding inconsistencies provided by different sources. Other secondary data in this article originate from the existing literature in both Chinese and English, including books about Huawei, academic publications, media reports, government documents, annual reports and information released on its website and official WeChat account.

The case study starts with discussions of Huawei's identity and the LOF it carries, followed by a comparative analysis of its operations in the US and UK, with a view to providing insight to the questions outlined above. If the sustainable and effective operation of Huawei is the dependent variable (DV), then its ability to navigate and manage risks in the host country is the independent variable (IV), and the interactions between Huawei and the host business environment suggest a number of other extraneous variables (EVs) at play in affecting the DV, including bilateral relations, law, media environment and cultural proximity between the host and home countries. These will be mapped out in the enhanced model of Figure 2.

[17] James Landale, 'Five things we have learned from Trump's state visit', *BBC*, accessed 3 July 2019, https://www.bbc.co.uk/news/uk-48531769.
[18] Scott Bade, 'How Huawei is Dividing Western Nations', accessed 3 May 2020, https://techcrunch.com/2020/03/28/how-huawei-is-dividing-western-nations/.
[19] Ryan Daws. 'Pompeo: China wants 'to divide Western alliances through bits and bytes', accessed 2 June 2019, https://www.telecomstechnews.com/news/2019/may/09/pompeo-china-western-alliances-bits-bytes/.

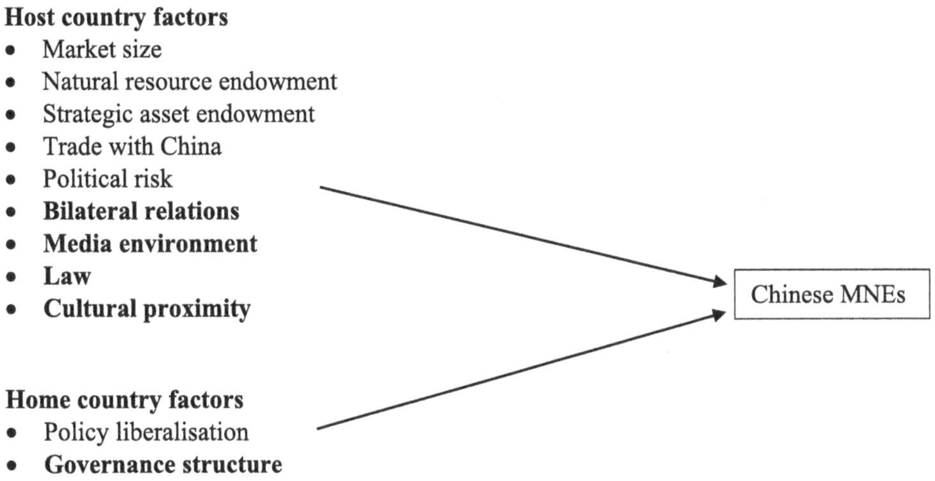

Host country factors

- Market size
- Natural resource endowment
- Strategic asset endowment
- Trade with China
- Political risk
- **Bilateral relations**
- **Media environment**
- **Law**
- **Cultural proximity**

Home country factors

- Policy liberalisation
- **Governance structure**

Chinese MNEs

Figure 2. Expanded model for assessing Chinese MNEs.

Huawei's Identity and Its 'Liability of Foreignness'

All MNEs carry a three-layer identity: as an enterprise of its own, an enterprise with a country of origin (COO) effect, and the overall image of its home country. On top of these, they all suffer from 'liability of foreignness' (LOF)[20] when operating in a host country. LOF is a concept introduced by Hymer in his seminal thesis study to refer to the 'stigma of being foreign' and the discrimination MNEs received. Gaur et al.[21] pointed that there are two sources of LOF: environmentally derived and firm-based; both LOFs are at a higher level for emerging market firms moving to developed market than the other way around, and emerging market firms with state ownership will experience more LOFs than those without.

Now let us unveil Huawei's identity layer by layer. When it was first founded by Ren Zhengfei and six other partners in 1987, it was registered as a 'collective ownership enterprise' and remained as such until 1997, when it was changed to the category of 'private ownership enterprise' to comply with the government's business license regulation. It was a reluctant change due to the more restricted business scope set for private companies, which are also disadvantaged in receiving financial support and government backup. Until today, Huawei is still 100 percent owned by its employees and audited by KPMG, with zero capital provided by the Chinese government.

However, as a private company in a sea of state-owned peers and competitors, the fact that Huawei bootstrapped itself from a start-up to a 120 USD billion, international giant leading the global 5G market over merely three decades invites a lot of speculations on its relationship with the Chinese government, which is often rightfully projected as a source of financial support that gives Chinese MNEs unfair advantages—although those MNEs are mostly SOEs. Huawei did receive as much as 75 USD billion in tax breaks, financing and cheap resources from the Chinese government, but 'it is not justification for accusing Huawei of spying or hacking for the Chinese government'.[22] The Western media often 'obscure the boundaries between state-ownership and state influence, and even state control',[23] and many scholars describe Huawei as operating under some degree of covert government influence. This gives

[20]Stephen Hymer, *The international operations of national firms: A study of direct foreign investment* (MA: MIT Press,1976), pp. 139–155.
[21]Ajai Gaur, Vikas Kumar, Ravi Sarathy, 'Liability of foreignness and internationalisation of emerging market firms', in *Advances in International Management, Volume 24*, ed. Devinney Timothy, Pedersen Torben and Tihanyi Laszlo (Bingley: Emerald Group Publishing Limited, 2011), pp. 211–233.
[22]Chuin-Wei Yap, 'State Support Helped Fuel Huawei's Global Rise', *Wall Street Journal*, accessed, 20 March 2020, https://www.wsj.com/articles/state-support-helped-fuel-huaweis-global-rise-11577280736.
[23]Peter Buckley, 'A Retrospective and Agenda for Future Research on Chinese Outward Foreign Direct Investment', *Journal of International Business Studies* 49, (2018), p14.

Huawei a higher LOF associated with its obfuscated business–government relationship. The fact that Huawei has a Chinese Communist Party committee was often cited as such evidence.

As a matter of fact, Article 19 in Chapter One of the Company Law of the PRC states that 'an organization of the Chinese Communist Party shall, according to the Charter of the Chinese Communist Party, be established in the company to carry out activities of the Chinese Communist Party'.[24] Therefore, not only Huawei as a local company has a CEO and party leader in tandem, other MNEs operating in China such as Motorola, Coca-Cola and Boeing, all host such similar organizations within their companies. This has never caused any questioning, partly because it is not always known, nor is seen as an issue as the committee has no say in the operations or management of the company. Its role was only 'to encourage staff to obey professional ethics and the company's code of conduct' as explained by Ren in his interviews and by Huawei Senior Vice President Ding to the US Congress hearing held in September 2012.[25] In other words, it is part of the governance structure prescribed by Chinese Law that applies to all companies operating in China. However, despite Huawei's repeated explanations, the lack of inside knowledge, or rather, the willingness to under-stand what exactly is going on inside Huawei, means that the existence of a CCP committee itself is taken for granted as a 'red hue' for Huawei's identity. It may be fairer to describe it as a typical 'shade of grey' overshadowed by the 'governance structure' of its home country, where the state role is highly pertinent in its policy environment.

This shade of grey, in the identity of Chinese MNEs, not only often courts mistrust and perceived unfairness, which in turn leads to ill-informed assumptions and decisions, it also could have legal implications. For example, the 'Holding Foreign Companies Accountable Act' (the HFCAA) that the US Senate passed in May 2020 applied the wording of companies 'owned or controlled by a governmental entity', which means if enacted, it will potentially result in a delisting of many Chinese enterprises, not just SOEs, as all Chinese enterprises are perceived to be 'controlled by the government' in one way or the other. Meanwhile, the amended Securities Law of China (SLA) prohibits local auditing firms from turning over accounting documents to foreign regulators. In other words, no Chinese enterprise will be able to both comply with the Chinese law which prohibits them from disclosing certain information, and satisfy the requirements of the U.S. law mandating disclosure of the same information, creating a legal deadlock for Chinese companies to be listed in the US stock market.

True, in a centralized governance structure of China, Huawei as a private company must respond to state strategies to gain government support and assistance. For example, its selection of Russia to establish its first overseas representative office was not entirely a market-driven decision but a result of the signing of the 'partnership of strategic cooperation oriented towards the 21st century' between the two governments in 1998. Huawei's global footprint then expanded into India in 1999, Middle East and Africa in 2000, Southeast Asia, and finally Europe (including the UK) and the US in 2001. This trail seems to show that most of the key factors listed in Buckley's 2007 model, such as 'market size' and 'foreign exchange rate', were not the primary considerations for Huawei. Instead, its decision-making was more driven by the need to overcome the LOFs posed by its next two layers of identity of being a technological firm from China—a developing country with the reputation of 'made in China' as 'a representative of cheap price and inferior quality'.[26] This image is behind the dominant model of Chinese enterprises as 'original equipment manufacturing' (OEM) firms, while Huawei represents the new generation of 'original brand manufacturing' (OBM) firms. Although Huawei has been successful in making the metamorphosis and became a global leader of 5G network by 2018, the extra barrier it faces in securing and expanding Western markets is still related with its heritage in China, the most outer layer of its identity. Despite the transformation from being

---

[24]Company Law of the People's Republic of China (Revised in 2013), last modified 28 December 2013, http://www.fdi.gov.cn/1800000121_39_4814_0_7.html.

[25]See No. 3, 4, Appendix.

[26]Guanjing Zhang, ed., *Providing Global IT Solutions from China: The Huawei Story* (Guangdong: Paths International Ltd., 2013) p. 166.

developing country that can only make cheap products with backward technology into a strong contender of the world's No. 1 economy, what remains unchanged is China's image as an authoritarian state with one-party rule, representing 'the other' ideology. How much does this layer of identity matter for a high-tech company? The answer turns out to be the critical hue to determine whether Huawei is depicted as a red threat or a blue-chip opportunity.

At the inner layer, Ren Zhengfei himself uses the color grey to describe Huawei's identity and culture. 'Grey Balance' is the color between black and white in a layman's term, but technically, it is produced when the equal amounts of the three-light primary colors, namely red, green and blue, are mixed. Ren used it to describe his approach of blending the Chinese culture with both American and British ways to create the unique Huawei's way: the British way for managing the 'stems' of the company with clearly defined rules and standards, and the American way of opening to more initiatives and innovations at the 'tips of branches'.[27] This mentality of making differences comparable is deeply rooted in the traditional, Chinese philosophy of Yin and Yang, which is never purely black and white but contains each other in a dynamic interaction, representing a fundamentally different view of the world from Western culture. For example, Western people often have trouble understanding China's ambivalent economic position as being both capitalist and socialist, and Huawei's status as neither being state-owned nor free from government influence. In multiple interviews, Ren has mentioned that 'outside China, we were labeled communism; inside China, we were labeled capitalism as we gave capital to our employees, they own this company. We don't know what "ism" we are, nor do we want to keep on explaining to the outside world who we are. Instead, we focus our attention on developing our products and improving our management to make Huawei a better company'.[28]

In a way, Huawei's 'grey balance' is an epitome for China as well. When Deng Xiaoping embarked China on the new development road of 'socialism with Chinese characteristics', he applied his famous cat theory: 'No matter if it is a white cat or a black cat, it is a good cat if it catches the mice'. Though still not recognized as a market economy by the European Union, China's economic reform has proved to be a 'good cat' by delivering unrivaled growth and a new development model. Huawei is also such a 'good cat'. True, it is a Chinese company, but it is also a private company with cutting-edge technology, and a fast-growing, international company that operates in over170 countries in the world. It is 'colored red' by those who do not see other colors that blend with red to create the 'grey': it is 'blue' as a top-rated blue-chip company, it is also 'green' for its strong growth, vitality and commitment to sustainable development. But, on the other hand, grey makes things opaque, and needs discerning eyes and inside knowledge to see the mixing hues. Huawei's lack of engagement with media does not help: As admitted by Ren, he has been paying 'more attention to internal management than external communication',[29] until there were too much misinformation and misunderstanding that created and spread the misperception of Huawei. After working as the external Affairs Vice President of Huawei for 8 years from 2010 to 2018, Plummer has clearly elaborated the process of 'mutual feed' between government or government-sponsored reports and media reports:

> The government concerns are mostly based on often-cited, never-substantiated disinformation about Huawei, including purported ties to the Chinese government. The politically-biased government perpetuation of myth was further driven by the immediacy imperative of today's media and the related phenomenon of copy-paste journalism, with few if any bothering to check facts or to question contradictions. In not challenging mis- or disinformation for the better part of a decade, the company had unknowingly allowed fear, uncertainty and doubt (FUD) to become fact. [30]

---

[27] See No.7, Appendix.
[28] See No. 9, Appendix.
[29] Ibid.
[30] William Plummer, *Huidu—Inside Huawei*. ISBN9781520362007 (Printed in Germany by Amazon Distribution GmbH: Leipzig, 2018), n.p.

In February 2019, Huawei published an open letter to the US media on its website: 'Don't believe everything you hear. Come and see us'.[31] It has since then proactively communicated detailed facts about the company, but it takes time to dispel the myth and deeply embedded misperceptions. After 76 interviews with all the mainstream media outlets worldwide, Huawei as the 'Trojan Horse' still appeared as headlines in various news stories,[32] but Ren acknowledged the effect that 'at first Huawei was painted all black in most media reports, after repeatedly opening ourselves to media scrutinize, it's gradually changing color to dark grey, now to light grey'.[33]

The above shows the necessity of including 'governance structure', 'cultural proximity' and 'media influence' as variables in the model as they reveal a more hidden knowledge gap existing in the business environment than what is captured by the International Business-focused model. The following section will discuss other critical variables, including bilateral relations and law.

Huawei in the US

Although Huawei established a joint venture with 3Com in the US in 2003, what has made its name known in the industry was ironically its lawsuit with Cisco, who sued Huawei for infringing upon its intellectual property rights by using stolen technologies. As pointed by Bruce Claflin, former CEO of 3Com, 'most Americans firmly believed that Cisco was right while Huawei was wrong, because a deep root bias towards foreign competitors had misled them',[34] a ready example of the actual effect of LOF. When the two parties eventually reached reconciliation after 20 months, the settlement became an effective advertisement to make Huawei known as an emergent strong competitor even on a par with big names like Cisco. Today, Huawei holds 11,152 core patents registered in the US and in June 2019, it asked Verizon to pay more than 1 USD billion for over 230 patents.[35]

When the Sino-US trade war broke out in 2018, Huawei became the eye of the storm even when it literally had no presence in the US market, that is because the American 'war with Huawei' broke out much earlier than the trade war. In 2008, the US barred Huawei from acquiring 3Com and parts of the wireless division of Motorola. In 2010, it was excluded from the telecommunication contracts for security concerns. Plummer called this 'the model of modern day techno-nationalism', pioneered by the US 'in the context of multiple and opaque market access barriers to China-based telecommunications equipment multinationals, and always based on nebulous, never-substantiated and always prospective national security concerns'.[36] In 2011, the US House of Representatives Permanent Select Committee on Intelligence (HPSCI) launched an investigation into 'national security threat posed by Chinese telecom companies working in the US'. Huawei was charged of being a security risk to the US interests, threatening the sanctity of US intellectual property, and abusing consumers' privacy. Then the 2015 FBI 'SPIN' (Strategic Partnership Intelligence Note) document became a government initiative to distort markets and restrict open competition on the so-called 'national security' grounds. When the American stance became even more vociferous towards Huawei amidst the Sino-US trade war

---

[31]'An open letter to the US media', last modified February 2019, https://www.huawei.com/en/facts/open-letter-to-us-media.

[32]Jessica Bursztynsky, 'Huawei expansion in Western nations may be "a Trojan horse," warns a top GOP senator', accessed 4 July 2019, https://www.cnbc.com/2019/06/28/huawei-expansion-in-western-nations-may-be-a-trojan-horse-warns-a-top-gop-senate-leader.html.

Stephen Chen, 'Could Huawei be using Trojan circuits to help Beijing spy on US?' accessed 2 August 2019, https://www.scmp.com/news/china/science/article/3018057/could-huawei-be-using-trojan-circuits-help-beijing-spy-us.

Richard Heydarian, 'Telecom: China's Trojan Horse? Inquirer columnist', accessed 3 July 2019, https://www.straitstimes.com/asia/telecom-chinas-trojan-horse-inquirer-columnist.

[33]See No. 20, Appendix.

[34]Guanjing Zhang, eds., *Providing Global IT Solutions from China: The Huawei Story* (Guangdong: Paths International Ltd., 2013) p.191.

[35]Omar Marques, 'Huawei asks Verizon to pay more than $1 billion for over 230 patents: Source', *Reuters*, accessed 2 July 2019, https://www.cnbc.com/2019/06/13/huawei-asks-verizon-to-pay-more-than-1-billion-for-over-230-patents-source.html.

[36]William Plummer, *Huidu—Inside Huawei*. ISBN9781520362007 (Printed in Germany by Amazon Distribution GmbH: Leipzig 2018), n.p.

summer named it '21st century politico-mercantilism',[37] while Mascitelli and Chung's analysis also pinpointed that it 'raises the question of whether there are implications for free trade and whether the alleged security concerns are but an ideological way of circumventing market access'.[38] This was elaborated by Sachs' pungent point that 'the Trump administration's conflict with China has little to do with US external imbalances, closed Chinese markets, or even China's alleged theft of intellectual property. It has everything to do with containing China by limiting its access to foreign markets, advanced technologies, global banking services, and perhaps even US universities'.[39]

There are obviously multiple and complex reasons for the rising tensions between the world's two biggest economies. China was referred to as a 'competitor', 'challenger', 'rival power' and 'revisionist power' in the 2017 *National Security Strategy of the USA*,[40] the first national security report issued by the Trump Administration. Reflected in bilateral relations, the long-standing strategic mistrust exacerbates as both sides have increased interactions involving vital national interests and legitimate national security concerns. For example, the US reaffirmed the Taiwan Relations Act amid trade tensions in 2019, and then following the new battlefield over COVID-19 in 2020 were the removal of Hong Kong's special status in response to Beijing's enforcement of the National Security Law there, and the exercising of two US aircraft carriers in the disputed South China Sea, showing the entangled nature of all fronts in the bilateral relations in trade, military, politics and foreign policy. Thus, it was not surprising that the NATO Cooperative Cyber Defence Centre of Excellence (CCDCOE) report on *Huawei, 5G and China as a Security Threat* stated the following:

> Whether the risk of such collaboration is real or perceived, the fear remains that adopting 5G technology from Huawei would introduce a reliance on equipment which can be controlled by the Chinese intelligence services and the military in both peacetime and crisis … …..Eliminating the risk of control over such systems by an adversary state may include the elimination of Chinese products from the supply chain.[41]

This made it clear that since China is defined as an 'adversary state', or a 'malicious actor',[42] even if the risk of collaboration is only 'perceived and not real'—as stated in the report itself: 'to date, there has been no evidence, at least publicly, of significant vulnerabilities in Huawei technology'; and even Huawei is 'the most audited technology company in the world' and 'the only company that can produce 'at scale and cost' all the elements of a 5G network',[43] its products should be banned, leaving Huawei with no chance to disprove the perceived risks or reduce them through collaboration. The report also admitted that 'the fundamental question is one of trust: states need assurances that their critical systems and data—and those of their partners and allies—are safe from foreign meddling, both now and in the foreseeable future, thus cost and speed cannot be the sole or decisive factors in the rollout of innovative infrastructure'.[44] This explains why Huawei's reaction to challenge this move as restricting fair competition and harming the American consumers is useless because national security interests are standard grounds for limiting open competition and this is not about the merit of the product, but its unchangeable identity as being a Chinese company.

The US ban on Huawei can best be understood through the prism of the rapid rise of China, not only economically, but also technologically. As Kang explained, 'it was long thought that we were the number one economy and China just supplied cheap labour … Now it is clear that China has a lot to

Ibid, n.p.
Bruno Mascitelli and Mona Chung, 'Hue and cry over Huawei: Cold war tensions, security threats or anti-competitive behaviour?', *Research in Globalisation*, Vol.1, (2019), p.1.
Jeffrey Sachs, 'The War on Huawei', *Project Syndicate*, accessed 5 July 2019, https://www.project-syndicate.org/commentary/trump-war-on-huawei-meng-wanzhou-arrest-by-jeffrey-d-sachs-2018-12?barrier=accesspaylog.
'National Security Strategy of the United States of America'. December 2017, accessed 3 July 2019, https://www.whitehouse.gov/wp-content/uploads/2017/12/NSS-Final-12-18-2017-0905.pdf.
Kadri Kaska, Henrik Beckvard and Tomas Minarik, 'Huawei, 5G and China as a Security Threat, NATO Cooperative Cyber Defence Centre of Excellence'. CCDCOE, accessed 1 August 2019, https://ccdcoe.org/uploads/2019/03/CCDCOE-Huawei-2019-03-28-FINAL.pdf. p. 4.
Ibid, p.5.
Ibid, p.7.
Ibid, p.5.

offer in terms of innovation and industrial policy and state investment, and now people are scared'.⁴ This was fully recognized in the 2019 Ministry of Defence report on the *5G Ecosystem* that 'in 2009, a the top 10 Internet companies by revenue were American. Today, four of the top 10 are Chinese',⁴⁶ an Trump's reaction is 'the race to 5G is on and America must win'.⁴⁷ However, the US ban also turned ou to have an advertising effect for Huawei as claimed by Ren Zhengfei in his multiple interviews: 'The U Secretary of State has made banning Huawei one of his diplomatic priorities and has been helping u promote our products all over the world'.⁴⁸ He also thanked Trump for giving Huawei the wides' reaching advertisement for free. If Huawei blows its own trumpets, clients may hold reservations; and the Chinese government endorses it, that may even be counterproductive, but the American ba shows the world that putting aside the speculations and fears, Huawei's technology is world-leadinç This also has pushed sales domestically and bred 'patriots' in China,⁴⁹ about which Ren has commente· that 'the media tends to be flag-waving sometimes', leading to some Chinese social media user switching from Apple, but 'Huawei is firmly against the narrow-minded nationalism sentiments c boycotting US products as counter measures'.⁵⁰

This shows internationally, Huawei must manage a whole host of factors posing political risks fror the host country, while back at home, it must guard against media influence in flaming Chines nationalism. Despite his repeated remarks that 'Huawei product is just a commercial product, use it you like it, not if you don't, but do not politicise it',⁵¹ Huawei couldn't escape from its fate of bein· politicalized. Perhaps, already ingrained in its name—Huawei literally means 'China striving' i Chinese—nationalism has been a force at play in both its host and home countries. Of course nationalism is a factor affecting all MNEs, including those from advanced economies entering th· Chinese market, such as the boycotting of Japanese cars and Korean Supermarket when bilatera relations turned sour a few years ago. Microsoft also encountered a three-decade protracted war wit domestic companies like Kingsoft that bears the flag of 'China's national software'. It is thus necessar to recognize nationalism as a factor that falls under both 'political risk' and 'bilateral relations'.

The other two consistent messages that recurred in Ren's multiple interviews include: No. 1, '5G i only a conduit for information transmission, it has nothing to do with the content that goes throug it. Just like a microphone, probably the person who speaks something through it is dangerous, bu how can a tool itself be dangerous?'; No. 2, 'If the lights go out in the West, the East will still shin· And if the North goes dark, there is still the South. The US does not represent the world'.⁵² The fac that Huawei still reported a 13.1 percent year-over-year revenue growth in the first half of 202· despite the pandemic and global campaign waged by the US to blacklist it seems to prov Mahbubani's words: 'even if the US and its allies in the Five Eyes intelligence network completel opt out of dealing with Huawei, most countries in the world will adopt 5G networks based o Chinese technology'.⁵³ In the open letter titled 'China is not an enemy' written by members of th American scholarly, foreign policy, military and business communities to Donald Trump, it state that 'if the United States presses its allies to treat China as an economic and political enemy, it wi

---

⁴⁵Cecilia Kang, 'Huawei's US competitors among those pushing for scrutiny of Chinese tech firm', *Washington Post*, accesse· 3 July 2019, http://www.washingtonpost.com/business/-technology/huaweis-us-competitors-among-those-pushing-fo scrutiny-of-chinese-tech-firm/2012/10/10/b84d8d16-1256-11e2-a16b-2c110031514a_story.html.

⁴⁶Milo Medin and Gilman Louie, 'The 5G Ecosystem: Risks & Opportunities for DoD Defense Innovation Board, 3 April 2019 accessed 10 October 2019, https://media.defense.gov/2019/Apr/03/2002109302/-1/-1/0/DIB_5G_STUDY_04.03.19.PDF.

⁴⁷Todd Haselton, 'President Trump announces new 5 G initiatives: It's a race America must win', accessed 10 October 201· https://www.cnbc.com/2019/04/12/trump-on-5g-initiatives-a-race-america-must-win.html.

⁴⁸See No. 3, 4, 33, Appendix.

⁴⁹Yasheng Huang, 'Trump's Trade War Is Breeding Patriots in China. America goes after Huawei, and Chinese consumers rally · buy from the company', *Financial Times*, accessed 23 August 2019, https://www.nytimes.com/2019/08/09/opinion/china-trade huawei.html.

⁵⁰See No. 6, Appendix.

⁵¹See No. 11, Appendix.

⁵²See No. 3, Appendix.

⁵³Kishore Mahbubani, 'The US strategy is not the best way to deal with Huawei', *Financial Times*, accessed 13 March 2019, https: www.ft.com/content/3d489be2-3e73-11e9-9499-290979c9807a.

weaken its relations with those allies and could end up isolating itself rather than Beijing'.[54] True, if a new Cold War *is* in the making, we can see not only the difference between today's China and yesterday's Soviet Union but also the division within the Western camp, even among The Five Eyes, only Australia government has chosen to follow the US ban. In the case of New Zealand and Canada, when Huawei lost the deal to Ericsson, Nokia and Samsung as 5G supplier of their major telecom companies in March and June 2020, it is important to note the equivocal stance of the government, which tried to keep it separate from the American pressure and the ruling of Meng Wanzhou's case, although it is clear that 'the political tides can be partly credited'[55] for the business decisions.

An important reason for Australia to take side with the US is because both countries have laws allowing their own companies to install 'backdoors': the CLOUD Act (Clarifying Lawful Overseas Use of Data Act), enacted in 2018 by the US to allow federal law enforcement to compel US-based technology companies via warrant or subpoena to provide requested data stored on servers regardless of whether the data are stored in the US or on foreign soil;, and the Australia's Assistance and Access (AA) Bill, a 'controversial law designed to compel technology companies to grant police and security agencies access to encrypted messages'.[56] Actually, Edward Snowden's leaks demonstrated that the Five Eyes alliance allowed a member nation to neatly circumvent its own domestic regulations by allowing another alliance nation to spy on its citizens, and then share that information with the member nation's surveillance organizations. This may explain their manner of 'measuring everybody's corn by their bushel' when they scrutinized and interpreted China's 2017 National Intelligence Law as the Chinese equivalent, ignoring the fact that the American practice of long-arm jurisdiction that allows a court to exercise extraterritorial, adjudicative jurisdiction over foreign defendants does not exist in China. It is clearly reflected in the Preamble to all the Chinese laws that no legislation in China is applied to foreign soil. Besides, 'the Chinese government did not even know that networks could have "backdoors" at first. It was the US accusations against Huawei that raised the Chinese government's level of awareness of cyber security' as disclosed by Ren in his interviews in 2019,[57] he repeatedly said Huawei was ready and happy to sign 'no backdoor' agreements with any country and any company.

This mirrors the example of the none-heard-of Chinese law for companies to have an embedded cell of CPC committee, and the aforementioned legal deadlock created by the HFCAA in the US and SLA in China, all pointing to the necessity of including 'law' as another critical, contextual factor in the model.

Huawei in the UK

As the very first established European partner of Huawei, UK's business environment offers a stark contrast to that of the US, even though Huawei's presence in these two countries started from the same year of 2001. By 2005, Huawei had achieved its first milestone in the UK, being selected as a preferred telecom equipment supplier by both Vodafone and British Telecom (BT). This brought Huawei to the breakthrough point where its international contract orders exceeded domestic sales for the first time. By 2010, Huawei became a significant provider of network gear to several UK service providers.

Regarding Huawei, the UK has long taken a different path to the US. Huawei's hardware has been used in UK telecom networks for years, long before 5G technology was available. BT, the UK government and Huawei worked together in setting up the Huawei Cyber Security Evaluation Centre (HCSEC) in 2011 to deal with the perceived risks of Huawei's involvement in UK critical infrastructure. 'HCSEC has found vulnerabilities that Huawei has subsequently remediated and is improving Huawei's basic engineering and security process and code quality. These efforts have

---

[54]'China is not an enemy', *Washington Post*, accessed 20 July 2019, https://www.openletteronuschina.info/.
[55]Jamie Davies, 'Samsung is the final beneficiary of Canada's Huawei snub', accessed 20 June 2020, https://telecoms.com/505082/samsung-is-the-final-beneficiary-of-canadas-huawei-snub/.
[56]'Australia data encryption laws explained', *BBC*, accessed 3 July 2019, https://www.bbc.com/news/world-australia-46463029.
[57]See No. 25, 27, Appendix.

resulted in a more secure Huawei product'.[58] This reveals the biggest difference between the US and UK stance: while the UK is willing to work with Huawei to mitigate the risk, the US sees no point and shows no intention at all to give Huawei a chance to prove and improve, or any real interest in actually 'solving' the Huawei problem, it has decided to take pre-emptive measures by simply blocking it. Plummer has shared his insight into this difference:

> A variation on the theme was that the CSEC would be Huawei-funded and staffed, but by UK nationals with UK government security clearances. The delta between the way the US and the UK addressed Huawei epitomizes the delta between their approaches to attracting (or discouraging) ever-growing Chinese outbound investment capital, which in turn explains the seeming disproportionality: the UK took a coordinated and comprehensive commercially pragmatic approach to a perceived security concern by employing appropriate technological tools and related disciplines to safeguard the integrity of UK telecom networks while simultaneously adhering to its commitment to free and fair trade and competition and ensuring that UK operators could avail themselves of world-class rationally-priced technology. Huawei and other China-based investment are warmly welcomed. The economy benefits.[59]

Another example to show this difference was the British encouragement of 'China's involvement in the construction of the £56 billion rail line'.[60] In the context of Brexit looming overhead, attraction for overseas investment is staked higher by the UK government, and there was a sincere intent in pursuing solutions among the industry. In multiple interviews, Ren Zhengfei has frankly talked about the 'questioning from the UK', which 'is pushing us to improve our products, we do not regard this as a negative thing, but a chance to improve. We appreciate their pointing of the flaws so that we can work on a solution'.[61] Following the UK announcement that 'Huawei risk can be managed'[62] in February 2019, Ren reiterated that 'one of the reasons why we are doing so well in the UK is its true spirit of an open and free trade. The British sticks to principles of using rule-based supervision to address issues, rather than adopting a simplified Yes or No approach'. He further explained that the British government has made a very clear 5G strategy to keep itself ahead of the field. In order to do so, genuine and open competition are encouraged: as some of the British companies such as EE, Vodaphone and Three chose Huawei, others may choose Ericsson and Nokia, 'then we will compete with each other to see who provides better products, better services and better values'.[63] Then, a more authoritative claim was made by the 2019 NATO Cooperative Cyber Defence Centre of Excellence (CCDCOE) report that 'there is, to date, no public evidence of serious technological vulnerabilities in specific Huawei or ZTE equipment'. Its final section of Recommendations suggested:

> Instead of a blanket ban, the model of inclusive, competent, and transparent oversight embodied in the UK Huawei supervisory board is a good example .... There are as of yet no equivalent alternatives to Huawei 5G technology; the West is neither able nor willing to afford a technological stagnation, and with the expected socioeconomic benefits in the promise of 5G, states will likely remain pragmatic in their approaches.[64]

The CCDCOE report further explained that 'due to different, security cultures, degrees of digital dependency, existing capabilities and different priorities, even Western democracies vary in how they perceive the increasing foothold of Chinese technology'.[65] When the UK government reversed its decision in July 2020, it tried to stick to the technical ground, stating that 'Decision follows

---

[58]Michael Shoebridge, 'Chinese Cyber Espionage and the National Security Risks Huawei Poses to 5 G Networks', *Commentary*. A Macdonald-Laurier Institute Publication, accessed 5 July 2019, http://macdonaldlaurier.ca/files/pdf/MLICommentary_Nov2018_Shoebridge_Fweb.pdf, p.5.

[59]William Plummer, *Huidu—Inside Huawei*. ISBN9781520362007 (Printed in Germany by Amazon Distribution GmbH: Leipzig, 2018), n.p.

[60]Edward Malnick, 'After Huawei, Government turns to China for HS2 line', *Telegraph*, accessed 2 July 2019.https://www.telegraph.co.uk/politics/2019/05/04/huawei-government-turns-china-hs2-line/.

[61]See No. 7, Appendix.

[62]'Huawei risk can be managed, say UK cyber-security chiefs', BBC, accessed 2 June 2019, https://www.bbc.co.uk/news/business-47274643.

[63]See No.1, 3, Appendix.

[64]Kadri Kaska, 'Huawei, 5G and China as a Security Threat, NATO Cooperative Cyber Defence Centre of Excellence'. CCDCOE, accessed 1 August 2019, https://ccdcoe.org/library/publications/huawei-5g-and-china-as-a-security-threat/, p. 21.

[65]Ibid, p.15.

a technical review by the National Cyber Security Centre in response to US sanctions',[66] which means Huawei would have to start sourcing chips from elsewhere, thus no longer can assure the security and reliability of Huawei's products. However, a political interpretation is that the decision is as much in response to pressures from both Washington and domestic politics, as the timeframe of phasing Huawei out by 2024 or 2030 became the hotspot of debate before the final decision of 2027 was reached. Although 7 years may be the best balance Downing Street can strike between the US and China, a more telling move is that the UK turned to pursuing 'an alliance of ten democracies' in order to create an alternative pool of 5G equipment and technologies.[67] After standing up to the politically motivated decision adopted by the US, the UK backed off from its commercially pragmatic approach as well: while keeping the focus on technology merit and encouraging collaboration, this alliance is also ideology-inspired when all the members clearly shared the identity of being 'democracies'. Huawei was excluded due to the outer layer of its identity discussed earlier, the overall image of its home country China, which is a particularly fragile one as shown in May 2020, China's own think tank found that its global image was the worst it had been in 31 years due to COVID19.[68] This outer layer casts a long shadow on all Chinese MNEs, even TikTok, the social media app that is popular among teenagers, was also targeted in the US albeit it is led by an American CEO. The analysis for its being reviewed by the Committee on Foreign Investment in the United States (CFICUS) suggests that while it follows a similar privacy policy, 'TikTok's identity as a company based in the People's Republic of China makes its data access potentially troubling'.[69] Of course, on the flip side, the blocking of US tech companies such as Facebook, Google and Twitter has been etched into the Chinese image as being one of the most restrictive economies in the world.

Comparative Discussions: new Variables Needed in a Multidisciplinary Framework

When asked 'why Huawei managed to establish an effective and feasible communication with the UK, but not able to achieve the same with the US?', Hu Houkun, who has worked as the chair of the Huawei US company, admitted that 'this is what puzzles me as well. In the past decade, our business in the US has shrunk dramatically to almost none, but the questioning and doubts we heard are getting louder and louder. I find it hard to understand, it doesn't make sense for one to blame a product that they never used'.[70] This was echoed by Ding Yun, Huawei's Executive Director and President of the Global Marketing Department: 'there are two kinds of media voices about Huawei: one is from the over 400 clients of Huawei all over the world, the other is from the US. The former has business relations with us for 10 to 20 years, such as BT and Vodafone, who have always trusted and supported Huawei, while the doubts are from the US who has never used Huawei products, I find it ridiculous'.[71]

One after another, from the Confucius Institute to the Belt and Road Initiative, from Huawei to high-speed rail, all flagship projects from China, be it cultural and academic institutions, private or state-owned enterprises, or state-sponsored infrastructure investments, have all triggered similar debates but received different receptions all over the world. China's impact on and engagement with the rest of the world, across the East and West, North and South, along with Trump Administration's 'America First' foreign policy that has alienated some of its traditional allies, have all prevented a formation of a unified 'camp' against China. However, a common feature is to politicize MNEs and projects from China. Just like Huawei

---

[66]'Huawei to be removed from UK 5 G networks by 2027 ', accessed 14 July 2020, https://www.gov.uk/government/news/huawei-to-be-removed-from-uk-5g-networks-by-2027.

[67]Srijan Shukla,'UK wants 5G alliance of 10 countries, including India, to avoid reliance on Chinese Huawei', accessed 1 June 2020, https://theprint.in/world/uk-wants-5g-alliance-of-10-countries-including-india-to-avoid-reliance-on-chinese-huawei/431735/.

[68]James Parsley, 'An influential Chinese think tank warned China its global image is the worst it's been in 31 years and that a worst-case scenario could mean armed conflict with the US', accessed 1 June 2020, https://www.businessinsider.com/chinese-report-global-image-worst-in-three-decades-2020-5?r=US&IR=T.

[69]Shining Tan, 'TikTok on the Clock: A Summary of CFIUS's Investigation into ByteDance', accessed 1 August 2020, https://www.csis.org/blogs/trustee-china-hand/tiktok-clock-summary-cfiuss-investigation-bytedance.

[70]See No. 1, Appendix.

[71]Ibid.

was made a pawn on the chessboard of Sino-US trade war even when it was not directly involved in the bilateral trade, both Chinese government's handling of the COVID-19 and the passing of National Security Law for Hong Kong were mentioned as pressures behind UK's reassessment decision under the 'escalating geo-political tension with China'.[72] Obviously, Huawei's products have nothing to do with the spreading of coronavirus or status of Hong Kong, but in a way, it has become a barometer of bilateral relations, pointing to the importance of including 'bilateral relations' as a crucial variable in the model.

This comparative case study has shown the limitations of the old model that fails to capture the variables unique and critical to Chinese MNEs, particularly those entering Western markets. While generic economic factors that apply to *all* MNEs were listed separately, such as 'market size', 'foreign exchange rate', 'inflation rate', 'exports,', and 'imports', other key factors such as 'law' and 'media influence' that have significant influence on Chinese MNEs are missing. The huge impact of 'bilateral relations' is also worthy of being listed as a separate factor, particularly when the bilateral relations between different host countries also would have significant bearing on the market entry of a Chinese MNE as showcased by Huawei. The factor of 'openness to FDI' in general could well be at a different level from the host country's 'openness to *Chinese* FDI' due to the politicization of any investment from China. Previous researches have already found that 'Chinese investors appeared to be attracted towards risky environments when and where strong bilateral political relations existed between China and the host country, since political ties may reduce potential risk'.[73] Such risks exercised a profound effect on the amount, direction and operation of Chinese MNEs. Huawei's global footprint also shows that 'ethnic Chinese population' and 'geographic distance' do not matter as much as 'cultural distance', or 'cultural proximity'[74] that was mentioned in Buckley et al.'s 2018 retrospective but not added to the model. Meanwhile, more importance should be given to 'home country factors' such as 'governance structure' that were under-recognized before in the IB research but exert strong influence on Chinese MNEs. Therefore, amendments to the 2007 model (see Figure 1) are suggested in Figure 2 to incorporate unique features that are highly pertinent to Chinese MNEs. While shedding light on previously overlooked gaps, the juxtaposition of contextual factors included in the reconfigured model generates new insights, offers meaningful theoretical nuance from an interdisciplinary perspective, thus helps develop a multidimensional understanding of the complex environment Chinese MNEs face.

Host Country Factors

- Market size
- Natural resource endowment
- Strategic asset endowment
- Trade with China
- Political risk
- Bilateral Relations
- Media Environment
- Law
- Cultural Proximity
- Home Country Factors
- Policy liberalisation
- Governance Structure

---

[72]Dan Sabbagh, 'Boris Johnson forced to reduce Huawei's role in UK's 5 G networks', *Guardian*, accessed 22 May 2020, https://www.theguardian.com/technology/2020/may/22/boris-johnson-forced-to-reduce-huaweis-role-in-uks-5g-networks.

[73]Alisa Amighini, Roberta Rabellotti and Marco Sanfilippo, 'Do Chinese SOEs and private companies differ in their foreign location strategies?', *China Economic Review*, 27, (2013), pp. 312–325.
    Jing Li, Klaus Meyer, Hua Zhang and Yuan Ding, 'Diplomatic and Corporate Networks: Bridges to Foreign Locations', *Journal of International Business Studies* Vol. 49, Issue 6, (2017), pp. 659–683.

[74]Peter Buckley, 'A Retrospective and Agenda for Future Research on Chinese Outward Foreign Direct Investment', *Journal of International Business Studies* 49, (2018), p 6.

Conclusion

Huawei stands out as a multifaceted case study that calls for an interdisciplinary framework of analysis to address the much broader contexts that are outside the International Business field. The success of a Chinese MNE is determined by a combination of exogenous (host country) and endogenous (home country) factors and the inherent interactions of the two, which was inadequately captured by the old model.

The comparative analysis of Huawei's story in the UK and US shows an overall different business environment in these two host countries due to the combination of the variables, especially those five new factors added to the revised model. In Ren's own words, the contrast is that 'the US is too closed and tends to politicize everything. The UK is a lot more open than the US'.[75] The British environment is generally more open because the government approach is more balanced between principles and pragmatism, however, its on-and-off decisions regarding Huawei also show how precarious and fragile such balance is and suggests the dynamic and volatile nature of the environment.

On a broader context, this comparative case study of Huawei represents how China as a rising power is perceived: as an ideological entity of 'red' China, or even a red threat to hegemony in the eyes of the US, which leads to hostility and wariness ingrained with fear and deep mistrust; or a complexity produced by the mixing of multi-colours that requires a much more measured reaction. Just as the Belt and Road Initiative represents such a division on the geo-political front and the Confucius Institute on the cultural front, Huawei represents the divided views of China on the technological front, but 'being politicized' is a common challenge faced by Chinese organizations, red or grey, they are always perceived with more hues than simply being black and white, making the interdisciplinary analytical framework all the more necessary and important. However, since this new framework is mainly derived from case studies, its contribution is less with pronouncing definitive conclusions of a universally applicable framework than illustrating the importance of developing a more complex model for Chinese MNEs and generating new directions of inquiry to inspire more research in this field.

Acknowledgments

The author would like to thank the anonymous reviewers for their insightful comments and constructive suggestions.

Disclosure Statement

No potential conflict of interest was reported by the author.

Tao Tian and Chunbo Wu, 下一个倒下的是不是华为？ [*Huawei: Leadership, Culture and Connectivity*] (China CITIC Press: Beijing, 2012), p.116.

Appendix: Interview Grid*

No.	Interviewee	Interviewer	Date	Available at:
1	Seven members of top management of Huawei	A collection of 18 interviews with domestic and international media groups	Dec. 2018-Feb. 2019	Transcripts of Huawei Top Management with Media (Huawei gaoguan meiti fasheng shilu), Volume 1, https://www-file.huawei.com/-/media/corp/facts/pdf/on_the_record_huawei_executives_speak_to_the_public_volume_i_cn.pdf?la=en
2	Nine members of top management of Huawei	A collection of 18 interviews with domestic and international media groups	Mar. 2019-Apr. 2019	Transcripts of Huawei Top Management with Media (Huawei gaoguan meiti fasheng shilu), Volume 2, https://www-file.huawei.com/-/media/corp/facts/pdf/on_the_record_huawei_executives_speak_to_the_public_volume_2_cn.pdf?la=en
3	Ren Zhengfei	A collection of 13 interviews with domestic and international media groups	Jan. 2019- May. 2019	In His Own Words, Dialogues with Ren. https://www-file.huawei.com/-/media/corp/facts/pdf/in_his_own_words_dialogues_with_ren_en.pdf?la=en
4	Ren Zhengfei	A collection of 11 interviews with domestic and international media groups	May. 2019- Aug. 2019	In His Own Words, Dialogues with Ren. https://www-file.huawei.com/-/media/corp/facts/pdf/in-his-own-words-dialogues-with-ren-volume-ii.pdf?la=en
5	Ren Zhengfei	Mobile World Live, Financial Times, Associated Press, The Wall street Journal, Bloomberg News, CNBC, Fortune	15 January 2019	https://www.scmp.com/tech/big-tech/article/2182367/transcript-huawei-founder-ren-zhengfeis-responses-media-questions
6	Ren Zhengfei	CCTV, Face to Face	15 January 2019	https://www.jqknews.com/news/129290-CCTV_interview_full_text_%7C_Ren_Zhengfei_Learning_from_the_United_States_to_absorb_scientists_into_China.html
7	Ren Zhengfei	BBC, UK	18 February 2019	https://www.huawei.com/en/facts/voices-of-huawei/ren-zhengfei-interview-with-bbc
8	Ren Zhengfei	CBS, US	19 February 2019	https://www.cbsnews.com/news/huawei-president-ren-zhengfei-says-he-would-defy-chinese-law-on-intelligence-gathering/
9	Ren Zhengfei	CNN, US	13 March 2019	https://www.huawei.com/en/facts/voices-of-huawei/ren-zhengfei-interview-with-cnn
10	Ren Zhengfei	CNBC	14 April 2019	https://www.cnbc.com/2019/04/15/cnbc-transcript-ren-zhengfei-huawei-founder-and-ceo.html
11	Ren Zhengfei	Dong Qian, CGTV, China	21 May 2019	https://www.jqknews.com/news/129290-CCTV_interview_full_text_%7C_Ren_Zhengfei_Learning_from_the_United_States_to_absorb_scientists_into_China.html
12	Ren Zhengfei	Bloomberg News	24 May 2019	https://www.bloomberg.com/news/articles/2019-06-01/huawei-s-ren-zhengfei-interviewed-by-bloomberg-news-excerpts
13	Ren Zhengfei	George Gilder, Forbes, & Nicholas Negroponte, Wired, the US	17 June 2019	Coffee with Ren, https://www.huawei.com/en/facts/voices-of-huawei/a-coffee-with-ren
14	Ren Zhengfei	CNBC, US.	19 June 2019	https://www.cnbc.com/video/2019/06/21/watch-cnbcs-full-interview-with-huawei-founder-and-ceo-ren-zhengfei.html

(Continued

(Continued).

15	Ren Zhengfei	James Kynge, Financial Times, UK	24 June 2019	https://www.huawei.com/en/facts/voices-of-huawei/ren-zhengfeis-interview-with-the-financial-times
16	Ren Zhengfei	The Globe and Mail, Canada	27 June 2019	https://www.huawei.com/ca/facts/voices-of-huawei/ren-zhengfeis-interview-with-the-globe-and-mail
17	Ren Zhengfei	Akiko Fujita, Yahoo Finance, US	17 July 2019	https://uk.finance.yahoo.com/news/exclusive-interview-with-huawei-ceo-tech-204320046.html
18	Ren Zhengfei	BBC Story Workshop Documentary Film	23 July 2019	https://www.firstxw.com/view/238049.html
19	Ren Zhengfei	SKY	15 August 2019	https://www.huawei.com/en/facts/voices-of-huawei/ren_zhengfeis_interview_with_sky_news
20	Ren Zhengfei	The Associated Press	20 August 2019	https://www.huawei.com/uk/facts/voices-of-huawei/ren-zhengfeis-interview-with-the-associated-press
21	Ren Zhengfei	Los Angeles Times	8 September 2019	https://video.sina.cn/finance/2019-09-10/detail-iicezueu4747421.d.html?cre=wappage&mod=r&loc=2&r=9&rfunc=73&tj=none&cref=cj&wm=3236
22	Ren Zhengfei	New York Times	9 September 2019	https://www.huawei.com/en/facts/voices-of-huawei/ren-zhengfeis-interview-with-new-york-times-op-ed-columnist-thomas-l-friedman
23	Ren Zhengfei	Economist	10 September 2019	https://www.economist.com/business/2019/09/12/a-transcript-of-ren-zhengfeis-interview
24	Ren Zhengfei	Fortune	19 September 2019	https://www.huawei.com/my/facts/voices-of-huawei/Ren-Zhengfeis-Interview-with-Fortune
25	Ren Zhengfei	Jerry Kaplan and Peter Cochrane	26 September 2019	https://www.mobileworldlive.com/featured-content/top-three/a-coffee-with-ren-zhengfei-huawei-founder/ https://www.youtube.com/watch?v=UcFEicRisgM
26	Ren Zhengfei	CNBC	4 October 2019	https://www.cnbc.com/2019/10/04/cnbc-transcript-ren-zhengfei-founder-ceo-huawei.html
27	Ren Zhengfei	Northern European Media Roundtable	15 October 2019	https://www.huawei.com/en/facts/voices-of-huawei/Ren-Zhengfeis-Northern-European-Media-Roundtable
28	Ren Zhengfei	Kyodo News	16 October 2019	http://www.guancha.cn/economy/2019_10_21_522109.shtml
29	Ren Zhengfei	Arabic media from the Middle East countries	20 October 2019	https://www.guancha.cn/ChanJing/2019_11_04_523846.shtml
30	Ren Zhengfei	Euronews	22 October 2019	https://www.huawei.eu/index.php/press-release/transcript-mr-rens-euronews-interview
31	Ren Zhengfei	Wall Street Journal	5 November 2019	https://www.huawei.com/en/facts/voices-of-huawei/ren-zhengfeis-interview-with-the-wall-street-journal
32	Ren Zhengfei	German media roundtable	6 November 2019	https://www.huawei.com/ke/facts/voices-of-huawei/ren-zhengfeis-german-media-roundtable
33	Ren Zhengfei	Los Angeles Times	18 November 2019	https://www.huawei.com/en/facts/voices-of-huawei/ren-zhengfeis-interview-with-the-los-angeles-times

(Continued)

(Continued).

34	Ren Zhengfei	CNN	26 November 2019	https://www.huawei.com/en/facts/voices-of-huawei/ren-zhengfeis-interview-with-cnn
35	Ren Zhengfei	Globe and Mail	2 December 2019	https://www.huawei.com/en/facts/voices-of-huawei/ren-zhengfeis-interview-with-the-globe-and-mail
36	Ren Zhengfei	Roundtable with media from Latin America and Spain	11 December 2019	https://www.huawei.com/en/facts/voices-of-huawei/ren-zhengfeis-roundtable-with-media-from-latin-america-and-spain

Note: *The first two volumes of interview transcripts, from Dec. 2018 to Apr. 2019, published by Huawei, are only available in Chinese. However, two more compilations in English were published, covering interview transcripts from Jan. 2019 to Aug. 2019. The author has added the individual web links available for further interviews taken place from Sept. to Dec. 2019. This grid provides access to a complete collection of 76 interviews in total, taken place from Dec. 2018 to Dec. 2019. Individual web links are provided for some key interviews included in collections No. 3 and No. 4 for easy access.

The Tenuous Co-Production of China's Belt and Road Initiative in Brazil and Latin America

Gustavo de L. T. Oliveira⬥ and Margaret Myers

ABSTRACT

China's Belt and Road Initiative (BRI) evolved from promotion of Eurasian connectivity into a catchall for Chinese foreign policy and infrastructure investments worldwide. Although usually portrayed as a top-down geopolitical project of the Chinese central government, this article argues the BRI is actually shaped by converging and diverging interests of a wide variety of actors within and outside China. In order to conceptualize the relational, contingent, and unstable emergence of the BRI in Latin America, the article emphasizes the process of co-production as a theoretical framework. It first analyzes how the BRI incorporated Latin America through policy and discourse analysis, then examines the multi-scalar and multi-sited co-production of Chinese-funded port and railroad infrastructures through interviews and public documents in Brazil.

Introduction

China's Belt and Road Initiative (BRI) has evolved considerably since its inception in 2013, from an effort to reinvigorate Eurasian connectivity to a catchall for Chinese foreign policy and infrastructure investments worldwide. The BRI's newfound place in the Chinese constitution suggests that it is being orchestrated at the highest levels of the Chinese government. Although it is usually and understandably framed as a top-down geopolitical project 'from Beijing', most literature on the BRI in general, and on its tenuous extension to Latin America in particular, lacks analysis of *how* the initiative is constructed and implemented around the world.

The article demonstrates how the recent but tenuous incorporation of Latin America into the BRI results largely from growing interest in the Initiative among Latin American political and economic elites, illustrating the co-production of the BRI among various actors and locations. This interest in expanding the Initiative to encompass Latin America, however, coexists in tension with concerns in China about their investments in the region and over-extension of the Initiative, and geopolitical resistance from the United States to China's growing international influence. The result has been a rather piecemeal application of the BRI framework across the region, largely rebranding pre-existing infrastructure construction initiatives and development cooperation projects as part of the BRI, yet so far lacking substantial disbursement of political or economic resources for large-scale infrastructure construction in Latin America.

There are two common frameworks for discussion of China's BRI and its loans and investments in Latin America. The first are narratives about the 'Beijing Consensus', a state capitalist or authoritarian developmental state approach that successfully industrialized China, and is now being deployed internationally through soft power, development bank loans, and foreign investments led mainly by

China's state-owned enterprises.[1] This theoretical approach emphasizes the coherence of Chinese international investments and development cooperation with its own domestic path of modernization, and their strategic direction under the leadership of the central government in Beijing. As will be shown, however, it thereby obfuscates the crucial role of non-Chinese actors in facilitating, foreclosing, and reshaping Chinese endeavors abroad. Moreover, it also overstates the unity of interests among Chinese actors, overlooking how distinct Chinese companies and/or government agents may compete with each other in their international activities. The second set of theoretical approaches presents another side of the same coin, assuming a relatively homogenous and coherent 'China', and seeking explanations for variations in Chinese foreign investments and development cooperation projects in endogenous characteristics of foreign countries alone.[2] In this view, whether a foreign country is targeted for mergers and acquisitions aiming at technological upgrading, or direct investments in infrastructure to export raw materials, turns basically upon the economic characteristics of each place, while conformity with environmental best practices and corporate social responsibility results from the relative strength or weakness of local legal and political institutions.[3] But once again, the agency of foreign governments, companies, and social movements as well as the competition among Chinese actors and disputes between them and other international actors remain largely concealed.

Unlike these approaches, this article emphasizes the process of co-production as our theoretical framework. Rather than assuming a homogeneous 'China', and that its foreign investments and international development projects follow a coherent strategic direction 'from Beijing', or assuming that local political and economic characteristics inevitably determine the specific form and consequence of Chinese investments and development projects, the authors seek to more adequately capture the highly varied, contingent, and tenuous emergence of the BRI in Latin America from the relations among multiple actors, Chinese and non-Chinese alike. What the authors mean by 'co-production' has been elsewhere called the practice of assembling—'the on-going labor of bringing disparate elements together and forging connections between them.'[4] Theorizing the emergence of the BRI in Latin America as a result of co-production recognizes both the multiplicity of actors involved in the process and also the 'provisional socio-spatial formation' that results from their engagements, emphasizing the 'emergence, multiplicity and indeterminacy' of such relations.[5]

This approach has proved particularly useful for studying transnational infrastructures, technologies, institutions, and social formations that transcend and destabilize the traditional territoriality of nation-states. Thus, this article understands the BRI as a collection of intertwined discourses, policies, and projects promoted by a variety of actors within and outside China, who leverage them for numerous interests of their own, which sometimes align and are sometimes contradictory. Focusing on these entanglements inverts analysis of the BRI from a top-down coherent strategy 'from Beijing' to a relational, contested process of co-production that occurs both transnationally and in specific places. By 'relational' it is meant that the 'same' project that might be characterized as 'part of the BRI' in one place also might not be so characterized in another place, where it is subject to a different set of socio-economic and political relations. And by 'contested' it is meant that such projects emerge, are transformed, and ultimately become implemented (or not) due to the convergence

[1]Suisheng Zhao, 'Whither the China Model: Revisiting the Debate', *Journal of Contemporary China* 26(103), (2017), pp. 1–17.
[2]Enrique Peters, Ariel Armony, Shoujun Cui, *Building Development for a New Era: China's Infrastructure Projects in Latin America and the Caribbean* (Mexico City: Red ALC China/University of Pittsburgh, 2018); May Tan Mullins, 'Smoothing the Silk Road through Successful Chinese Corporate Social Responsibility Practices: Evidence from East Africa', *Journal of Contemporary China* 29(122), (2020), pp. 209-211.
[3]Mullins, 'Smoothing'; Rebecca Ray, Kevin Gallagher, Andres López, Cynthia Sanborn, *China and Sustainable Development in Latin America: The social and environmental dimension* (London: Anthem Press, 2017).
[4]Tania Li, 'Practices of Assemblage and Community Forest Management,' *Economy and Society* 36(2), (2007), p. 263; Gustavo Oliveira, 'Boosters, Brokers, Bureaucrats, and Businessmen: Assembling Chinese Capital with Brazilian Agribusiness', *Territory, Politics, Governance* 7(1), (2019), pp. 22-41.
[5]Ben Anderson, Colin McFarlane, 'Assemblage and Geography', *Area* 43(2), (2011), 124.

ıd divergences of interests that contest the resources, purposes, and benefits (or harms) associated ith each project.

The authors argue a methodological focus on co-production contributes to efforts in critical eopolitics to de-center nation-states and government-to-government relations. This is particularly nportant for studying the BRI and China's global integration as a whole since the prominent role of ıe Chinese state tends to weigh debates down to discussions of the geopolitical and/or collabora-ve aspects of the inter-governmental and macroeconomic phenomena at hand, even when framed y notions of the co-production of space.[6] Thus, the article contributes to the emerging literature on ıore relational, grounded, and critical approaches to the study of China and globalization.[7]

In the following sections, the article begins with policy and discourse analysis to outline how the ₹I represented at first a turn away from Latin America as a priority for Chinese finance and foreign vestments. Then, it demonstrates how it was through the proactive lobbying of Latin American ites that the BRI evolved to contemplate the continent. Thirdly, it outlines the Chinese concerns ıat including Latin America in the BRI will overextend the Initiative, negatively affecting its iplomatic and economic framework through high-risk investments in the region and provoking ɔo much geopolitical resistance from the United States. In the fourth section, it examines the ɔntested co-production of BRI-related infrastructure projects in Brazil—competing railroad projects ıd port infrastructures—revealing the multi-scalar and multi-sited production of Chinese-funded frastructure initiatives by heterogeneous and often discordant actors and interests. The article ɔncludes with a discussion of the significance of the BRI for Latin America and vice-versa, the sefulness of this approach for critical geopolitics, and a critical assessment of the political, :onomic, and ecological basis upon which the BRI is being co-produced worldwide.

ıe BRI as a Pivot Away from Latin America

ıe BRI is the conjunction of two separate Asia-based initiatives—one land-based, webbing across ıe Eurasian continent, along with a set of maritime linkages connecting the dispersed nations of ɔuth and Southeast Asia. Both emerged through high-profile speeches delivered by Chinese ˈesident Xi Jinping in the months after assuming power. First, a much-referenced address in ızakhstan in September 2013, where Xi first mentioned developing a 'Silk Road Economic Belt' to ·eate greater connectivity across Eurasia. One month later, in a speech to the Association of ɔutheast Asian Nations (ASEAN), the Chinese president unveiled the second component, the '21st entury Maritime Silk Road', which would build on the maritime portion of the original.[8] Yet the eginning of Xi's administration was also marked by a notable retrenchment in subsidized credit and ɔvernment support for foreign investments in projects and regions considered to be 'high risk.' ˈhina's controversial (and often failing) direct investments in natural resources across Latin America ıd Africa—widely criticized as 'neocolonial' or 'neoimperialist' incursions,[9] 'land grabs' with detri-ıental socio-ecological impacts,[10] and 'extractivist' (as opposed to 'productive') endeavors that

ˈaximilian Mayer, Dániel Balázs, 'Modern Silk Road Imaginaries and the Co-production of Space', in *Rethinking the Silk Road: China's Belt and Road Initiative and Emerging Eurasian Relations*, ed. Maximilian Mayer (Singapore: Palgrave MacMillan, 2018), 205.

ustavo Oliveira, Galen Murton, Alessandro Rippa, Tyler Harlan, Yang Yang, 'China's Belt and Road Initiative: Views from the Ground,' *Political Geography* (2020), DOI 10.1016/j.polgeo.2020.102225; Julie Klinger, Tom Narins, 'New Geographies of China and Latin America Relations,' *Journal of Latin American Geography* 17(2), (2018), 6.

Veifeng Zhou, Mario Esteban, 'Beyond Balancing: China's Approach Towards the Belt and Road Initiative', *Journal of Contemporary China* 27(112), (2018), pp. 487-88; James Sidaway, Chih Yuan Woon, 'Chinese Narratives on 'One Belt, One Road' (一带一路) in Geopolitical and Imperial Contexts,' *Professional Geographer* 69(4), (2017), p. 591.

ˈairong Yan, Barry Sautman, 'Chinese Farms in Zambia: From Socialist to 'Agro-imperialist' Engagement?,' *African and Asian Studies* 9(3), (2010), p. 307.

Deborah Brautigam, *Will Africa Feed China?* (Oxford: Oxford University Press, 2015); Ray et al., *China*; Gustavo Oliveira, 'Chinese Land Grabs in Brazil? Sinophobia and Foreign Investments in Brazilian Soybean Agribusiness', *Globalizations* 15(1), (2018), pp. 114-133.

deepen Latin America's economic dependence on exporting natural resources[11]—were curtaile
even while the BRI was being launched.

Indeed, at the end of 2012, during the transition of power to Xi's administration, the Chines
central government undertook a broad revision of policies and strategies. It circulated an intern
report that showed about 60 percent of foreign investments announced since 2008 failed t
materialize, while another 25 percent were delayed or operating at a loss, and called for more caref
approach to future investments, particularly in natural resources and sensitive regions, such as Lati
American countries were political resistance to perceived Chinese 'land grabbing' was taking plac
The report was not made public, but it was referenced in several of interviews Oliveira undertoc
with Chinese agribusiness executives, policy-bank officials, and government bureaucrats famili
with the topic in Brasília, São Paulo, Rio de Janeiro, and Beijing from 2013 to 2015.

The BRI emerged as a singular concept in 2014. Notably, however, Xi Jinping did not mention it a
all during his high-profile state visits to Latin America that year, even though he explicitly promote
the participation of Chinese financiers and infrastructure construction companies in the Brazil-Per
Bi-Oceanic (or Trans-Andean) Railway, among several other smaller infrastructure construction an
investment projects across the continent. BRI discourse also didn't feature in Chinese addresses a
the founding of the China-CELAC (Community of Latin American and Caribbean States) Forur
ministerial meeting in 2015, which addressed multiple investment projects and economic cooperá
tion initiatives with ministers from nearly every Latin American and Caribbean nation.

In a foundational Chinese government document of 2015, the BRI was defined with 'five links' a
core features, all intended to improve connectivity and accelerate economic growth: policy coord
nation, infrastructure development, trade facilitation, financial integration, and cultural and socia
exchange.[12] These 'five links' and their ultimate goal are broad enough that, presumably, they coul
have applied to China's engagement with Latin America. Yet the key document only formal
extended the reach of the Initiative to include Asia and some portions of Europe and Africa—leavin
Latin America notably absent, despite the sharp rise in Chinese funding and investments since 201
in the continent's natural resource sectors and related infrastructure.[13]

That document did not explicitly rule out the inclusion of Latin American countries and othe
regions in the BRI, noting 'the construction of the Belt and Road is open and inclusive,' and welcome
'the active participation of all the world's countries, and international and regional organizations'.
This combination of focus on Eurasian connectivity with openness to global participation wa
particularly instrumental in Chinese state efforts at assembling international political and financia
support for the creation of the Asian Infrastructure Investment Bank (AIIB), a multilateral develop
ment bank clearly led by China, which serves as one of the BRI's principal engines.[15] Despite th
increasing number of state investors in the AIIB and official BRI bilateral agreements, and the gradu
increase in their scope and scale, it is also worth noting that investment may be diverted away fror
non-BRI countries, as both Chinese and other investors seek gains from the opportunities created th
BRI's structures of finance and political support.[16] This appears evident with the relative de
prioritization of Latin America in the first five years following the establishment of the BRI.

---

[11]Ruben Gonzales-Vicente, 'Development Dynamics of Chinese Resource-based Investment in Peru and Ecuador,' *Latin America
    Politics and Society* 55(1), (2013), 46.
[12]National Development and Reform Commission of the People's Republic of China (NDRC), *Vision and Actions on Jointly Buildir
    Silk Road Economic Belt and 21st-Century Maritime Silk Road*, March 28, 2015, https://reconasia-production.s3.amazonaws.con
    media/filer_public/e0/22/e0228017-7463-46fc-9094-0465a6f1ca23/vision_and_actions_on_jointly_building_silk_road_ec
    nomic_belt_and_21st-century_maritime_silk_road.pdf.
[13]Ray et al., *China*; Margaret Myers, Ricardo Barrios, 'LAC's not Part of the Belt and Road, but does that Matter?' *Voces, Inte
    American Dialogue. January 26, 2018.
[14]NDRC, *Vision*.
[15]Hong Yu, 'Motivation behind China's 'One Belt, One Road' Initiatives and Establishment of the Asian Infrastructure Investmei
    Bank', *Journal of Contemporary China* 26(105), (2017), p. 353.
[16]Jean-Marc Blanchard, Colin Flint, 'The Geopolitics of China's Maritime Silk Road Initiative', *Geopolitics* 22(2), (2017), 229.

A second official document two years later specified the routes that comprise the BRI and their corresponding core projects, all limited to Eurasia and extending only into the Pacific and Indian Oceans.[17] These five routes assemble 'Six Corridors, Six Ways (which include railways, roads, seaways, airways, pipelines, and space integrated information networks), Many Countries, and Many Ports'. 'Many Countries' refers explicitly to an '*initial* group of cooperating countries' with the keyword here being 'initial.' After all, this 'useful fuzziness'[18] avoids ossifying commitments that may become troublesome but allows for pragmatically expanding the scope and scale of the BRI.

The Co-production of the BRI in Latin America

According to Inter-American Dialogue accounts,[19] over 150 Chinese infrastructure projects were proposed in 28 countries in the region between 2002 and 2018, with particular focus on Bolivia, Jamaica, Brazil, and Ecuador. Like most BRI projects in Asia and elsewhere, more than half of China's total proposed projects in Latin America are focused on improving transportation, mainly from resource-rich regions to ports. In addition, proposed investment in the Agua Negra Tunnel (Argentina, Chile), Bi-Oceanic Railway (Brazil, Peru, Bolivia), Mid-West Integration Railway (Brazil, Peru); and the bridge across Corentyne River (Guyana, Suriname), all aim to achieve some cross-border connectivity. Nevertheless, Latin America hardly factored in the Initiative's official geography, which remained focused exclusively on Asia and adjacent regions until recently, when Latin American political leaders began to lobby the Chinese government for international cooperation efforts under the banner of the BRI.

It is evident that these efforts have been driven by actors from outside China, as there were no high-profile voices in the Chinese government advocating for the inclusion of Latin America in the official scope of the BRI during the early years of the Initiative. The few who pushed early on for the BRI's formal inclusion of the region were Chinese scholars of Latin America, and some journalists like Ding Gang at the *Global Times*, who alluded to the trade routes that brought together Mexico and China in the 16th century to suggest a contemporary extension of the BRI to Latin America.[20] Yet, these were very few and relatively weak voices among the key state and non-state actors producing public discourse about the BRI in China.

In Latin America itself, however, discourse that Latin America should be (or was already) included in the BRI emerged merely months after the Belt and Road came into being as a singular concept. The global political economic context was certainly relevant. Despite important unevenness, the Latin American continent, as a whole, faced a decade-long drop in GDP growth, so a new influx of foreign investments and capital for development projects became highly prized.[21] Hence, Latin American leaders and diplomats unabashedly attempted to control the narrative that China's massive infrastructure investments should flow into their own countries. In 2015, for example, Bolivia's ambassador to China stated that the BRI is 'extremely important to Bolivia's future development'.[22] Months later, Peru's former Foreign Minister and the ambassador to China both published articles in the Chinese media expressing hope the BRI extends to Latin America, thus promoting mutual reliance, economic complementarity, and technology transfers between China and Latin America,' as well as 'connecting both the Atlantic and the Pacific.' In 2016, Ecuador's

---

[17]Office of the Leading Group for the Belt and Road Initiative (OLGBRI), *Building the Belt and Road: Concept, Practice and China's Contribution*, May 2017, https://eng.yidaiyilu.gov.cn/wcm.files/upload/CMSydylyw/201705/201705110537027.pdf.

[18]Tom Narins, and John Agnew, 'Missing from the Map: Chinese Exceptionalism, Sovereignty Regimes and the Belt Road Initiative', *Geopolitics* 25(4), (2020), 809-837 .

[19]Margaret Myers, "China's Transport Infrastructure Investment in LAC: Five Things to Know," *Voces*, Inter-American Dialogue. November 13, 2018. https://www.thedialogue.org/blogs/2018/11/chinas-transportinfrastructure-investment-in-lac-five-things-to-know/

[20]Gang Ding, "China Trade Thrives Again in Latin America," *Global Times*, January 4, 2015, http://www.globaltimes.cn/content/899845.shtml.

[21]Brian Winter, "Latin America's Decade-long Hangover," *Americas Quarterly*, April 9, 2019, https://www.americasquarterly.org/content/latin-americas-decade-long-hangover.

[22]Guillermo Chalup, "Ambassador of Bolivia to China: 'One Belt, One Road' Helps Alpacas Leave Bolivia," *Huanqiu*, June 19, 2015, http://world.huanqiu.com/exclusive/2015-06/6727446.html.

Ambassador to China went so far as to credit the Belt and Road with having *already* boosted Ecuador's trade to the Asian region, even though there are still no official BRI projects in that country at all.[23]

More recently, Chile's Ambassador to China praised the Initiative's intent to unite the world through infrastructure and called on Latin America to join.[24] During the 2017 Belt and Road Forum an official in Brazil's federal tax bureau indicated that Brazil was willing to actively participate in all aspects of the BRI.[25] A former Argentine Foreign Minister was similarly quoted as saying that the Initiative is 'a crucial multilateral integration project that goes beyond the traditional Silk Road to reach Latin America,' and that Argentina 'is willing to actively participate in the building of the Belt and Road'.[26] During Deputy Foreign Minister Qin Gang's visit to Suriname in 2017, that country's government also expressed its interest in participating in the Initiative. As will be illustrated with the case study on Brazil below, government and corporate elites in Latin America are soliciting Chinese infrastructure (and other) investments—outlining concrete investment opportunities, facilitating corporate forums for Chinese and Latin American firms to establish partnerships, and attempting to overcome the Chinese government's hesitation to formally include Latin American countries in the BRI.

This lobbying by Latin American elites began to shift Chinese public discourse around 2017, when a wider variety of scholars, such as Wang Lei of Beijing Normal University's BRICS Center, began considering the extension of the Initiative to the Latin American region. Wang predicted that the BRI would become a new platform for cooperation between China and Latin America, noting, as official policy documents also did at the time that the BRI is 'global, cooperative initiative proposed by China,' guided by the principles of openness, inclusiveness, cooperation, and win-win scenarios that are not limited geographically.[27] More importantly, in April 2017, Xu Shicheng, one of China's top Latin America experts, voiced his support for including Latin America in the Initiative, demonstrating that the incorporation of the region into the BRI was finally becoming mainstream among Chinese intellectuals.[28]

Consequently, the region also began to appear with more frequency in official documents beginning in 2017. The BRI Leading Small Group's 'Building the Belt and Road' document was the first to mention the region by name, stating, 'China welcomes the participation of Latin America and the Caribbean in the building of the Belt and Road,' and that 'China is committed to coordinating development strategies with countries in these regions … and expanding common interests based on the [BRI] ideas, principles and approaches.'[29] This language is very revealing of how tenuously Chinese officials still considered Latin America's role in the BRI, welcoming its *participation* in the BRI much in the same way they welcomed their participation in the AIIB, without however making any commitments to *extend* BRI funds or investments to the region itself.[30]

Facing continuous Latin American efforts to deepen China's commitment to infrastructure and other investments in the region, high-level Chinese officials began to reference Latin America's role in the BRI, however distant, with growing frequency in 2017. During the May 2017 Belt and Road Forum, Xi Jinping stated that '[all] countries, from Asia, Europe, Africa or the Americas, can be

---

[23]Zhenfeng Wang, "Xi Jinping's Visit to Latin America to Expand the New 'One Belt, One Road' Cooperation," *People.cn*, April 5 2017, http://ydyl.people.com.cn/n1/2017/0405/c411837-29190711.html.

[24]Xinhua, 'Chilean Ambassador to China: The "One Belt, One Road" International Cooperation Summit was held at the Right Time' May 12, 2017. http://www.xinhuanet.com/world/2017-05/12/c_129603466.htm.

[25]Ruifang Wang, 'Brazilian officials: Brazil, as a Latin American power, is Willing to Join the "Belt and Road" Cooperation in Various Fields', *International Online*, May 15, 2017. http://news.cri.cn/2017-05-15/a211e102-efdb-8914-2f59-f5c4d348b9af.html.

[26]Hui Lu, 'Spotlight: Chinese Infrastructure Capabilities Help Promote Regional Interconnectivity, Global Growth', *Xinhua*, June 22 2017. http://www.xinhuanet.com/english/2017-06/22/c_136386664.htm.

[27]Qianwen Chen, '"Latin American Young Politicians Dialogue" Summary', *SOHU*, April 24, 2017. www.sohu.com/a/136194457_ 740082

[28]Ni Zhang, "Scholar: The "Belt and Road" Initiative Should Include Latin America," *Xinhua Silk Road Information Service*, April 25 2017, http://www.sh-"beltandroad.net/article/llyjnew/201704/1419253_1.html.

[29]OLGBRI, *Building*.

[30]Yu, 'Motivation'.

nternational cooperation partners of the Belt and Road Initiative', and mentioned his intention to nk the BRI to various multilateral consultation bodies and mechanisms, including CELAC.[31]

Also in 2017, according to Cuba's *Granma*, the Director General of the Department of Latin merican and Caribbean Affairs at China's Foreign Ministry said the BRI is 'an inclusive project, ith neither limits nor frontiers, in which Latin America and the Caribbean can take part.'[32] He added hat 'while it is true that the core of the project ... is concentrated on Asia, Europe, and Africa, nrough the AIIB, all parties may participate and aspire to infrastructure plans in Asia, as well as ithin their own borders.'[33] Despite growing frequency of such statements, however, almost all nerely alluded to Latin America's possible participation in the Initiative, or to the BRI as an inclusive latform, rather than to formal incorporation of the region or any specific countries in the Initiative's eographic purview.

It is evident that active lobbying by Latin American corporate and government officials has closely orresponded with increasingly warmer characterizations by Chinese government officials of Latin merica's role in the BRI. Indeed, there are some indications that the highest levels of the Chinese tate have taken Latin American interests into account when making decisions about the BRI and its pplication to the region. According to a Chinese official familiar with these arrangements, Argentine resident Mauricio Macri and Chilean President Michelle Bachelet were invited to attend China's 017 Belt and Road Forum only after expressing interest in doing so.[34] Though not on the initial uest list, the two leaders left with bilateral communiqués, and the China-Argentina Communique in articular states that both parties will strengthen linkages 'under the BRI framework.' The authors are ot suggesting that Chinese foreign policy simply results from interest group bargaining, but ndicating that the emergence of the BRI *in Latin America* is co-produced by Chinese actors *and* atin American actors as well.

Moreover, the authors also not simply echoing assessments by Latin American elites that inflate neir own importance in the making of Chinese foreign policy. The key turning point for the entrance f Latin America in the BRI is documented in the strategic thinking of top-tier Chinese government fficials themselves. This occurred during the months preceding the January 2018 China-CELAC linisterial Forum in Santiago, Chile, and during the Forum itself, when Chinese officials began eferencing the region's (and specific countries') significance to the Initiative. In late 2017 and 2018, hinese Foreign Minister Wang Yi and other officials referred to the region as a 'natural extension' of ne Maritime Silk Road, for example, while adding that the region is an 'indispensable participant' in ne construction of the BRI.[35] China also alluded to Mexico's, Panama's, and Trinidad and Tobago's ey roles in the BRI, calling all three 'important nodes of the natural extension of Belt and Road onstruction in Latin America.'[36]

Unlike similar events just a year before, the Belt and Road took center stage at the 2018 China-ELAC Forum—it was mentioned at least 16 times during Wang Yi's opening remarks. According to hinese Foreign Ministry reports, the Initiative was also discussed in Wang's meetings with Latin merican foreign ministers, including Mexico, Chile, Bolivia, and Trinidad and Tobago. In addition, Vang's five proposals for China-LAC cooperation closely resemble the BRI's 'five links' and explicitly all for establishing bilateral agreements under the framework of the BRI. More concretely, Wang roposed transportation networks 'connecting lands and oceans,' with specific reference to bi-

Xi Jinping, "Speech at the Dialogue on Strengthening Connectivity Partnership," *Xinhua*, May 14, 2017, http://www.xinhuanet. com//english/2017-05/14/c_136282982.htm. "Opening Remarks at the Belt and Road Summit Roundtable," *Xinhua*, May 15, 2017, http://www.xinhuanet.com//politics/2017-05/15/c_1120976082.htm.
Iramsy Forte, "Las relaciones entre Cuba y China están en su mejor momento," *Granma*, May 31, 2017, www.granma.cu/mundo/ 2017-05-31/las-relaciones-entre-cuba-y-china-estan-en-su-mejor-momento-31-05-2017-21-05-50.
Forte, 'Las relaciones'.
Personal interview by Myers on condition of anonymity, March 2018, Beijing.
Ministry of Foreign Affairs of the People's Republic of China, "Wang Yi: The Belt and Road Initiative Becomes New Opportunity for China-Latin America Cooperation," September 18, 2017, https://www.fmprc.gov.cn/mfa_eng/zxxx_662805/t1494844.shtml.
Embassy of the People's Republic of China in the Republic of Ghana, "Wang Yi meets with Secretary of Foreign Affairs Luis Videgaray Caso of Mexico," January 23, 2018, http://gh.china-embassy.org/eng/zgyw/t1528753.htm.

oceanic rail and tunnels, facilitating trade through an export-import exposition, and broadening financial channels to 'break developmental bottlenecks.' This language and Wang's approach during the Forum are clear departures from previous treatment of the BRI in Latin America.

Beyond merely framing its cooperation with Latin America with the same principles of the BRI, the Chinese government has gradually begun to execute formal BRI agreements in the region. Panama was the first to sign a formal BRI agreement and to be featured on China's BRI website. As a result Panama's vice-minister of foreign affairs held a meeting with the vice-minister of China's National Development and Reform Commission in January 2018 to discuss a feasibility study for the Ciudad de Panamá-David railway for both cargo and passengers, which would connect Panama's Pacific and Atlantic coasts in parallel with the US-controlled Panama canal.[37] This echoes the same logic of overland roads and pipelines across Central and South Asia to bypass the Suez Canal and the strait of Malacca and Hormuz.[38] After all, Panama's inclusion reflects the importance of the Panama Canal for global trade, and the Chinese government's similar interest in reducing dependence on this US controlled chokepoint for shipments from East Asia to Latin America, west Africa, and western Europe as well.

After Panama, a series bi-lateral BRI agreements were signed across Latin America, including Antigua and Barbuda, Trinidad and Tobago, Bolivia, Guyana, Uruguay, Costa Rica, Dominican Republic, and Venezuela.[39] Venezuela's case above all illustrates why certain Latin American political elites are so enthusiastic about joining the Initiative. Facing dramatic economic crisis domestically and increasingly rigorous economic sanctions from the US, the Venezuelan government sees in the BRI the possibility of restructuring its preexisting loans with the Chinese government, and possibly leveraging additional commitments for infrastructure investments that may enable it to reverse the downward spiral of its economic crisis. Yet its inclusion in the BRI remains largely discursive and diplomatic, as the Chinese government provided no concrete guarantees of any infrastructure investments in Venezuela, or any substantial restructuring of its outstanding loans besides payment extension.[40]

Moreover, Venezuela's case is not unique, as Chinese officials have done little beyond formalizing participation of some Latin American countries in the Initiative. Most significantly, there has been no extension of financing to the region from the AIIB and Silk Road Fund, or invitations for Latin America-based projects to apply for such funds. This may reflect Chinese government concerns about overextension and political resistance to their flagship foreign investment and international cooperation project.

Concerns about Overextension and Political Resistance

The inclusion of Latin America in the BRI was not simply co-produced by elite actors across China and Latin America in a clear, linear fashion. Its emergence has been a relational, contested process that involves Chinese government concerns about possible overextension, and both Chinese and Latin American elite anxiety about mounting political resistance to BRI-related projects, including project specific protests by those marginalized or displaced by infrastructure construction, regional- and

---

[37]Priscilla Perez, "Panamá, país estratégico para la iniciativa china la 'Franja y la Ruta'," *El Capital Financiero*, January 22, 2018 https://elcapitalfinanciero.com/panama-pais-estrategico-para-la-iniciativa-china-la-franja-y-la-ruta/.

[38]Blanchard and Flint, 'Geopolitics'. David Brewster, 'Silk Roads and Strings of Pearls: The Strategic Geography of China's New Pathways in the Indian Ocean', *Geopolitics* 22(2), (2017), pp. 269-291.

[39]Ricardo Barrios, "China's Belt and Road Lands in Latin America," *China Dialogue*, July 11, 2018, https://www.chinadialogue.net article/show/single/en/10728-China-s-Belt-and-Road-lands-in-Latin-America. Katherine Koleski, Alec Blivas, *China's Engagement with Latin America and the Caribbean*. Staff Research Report. October 17, 2018. Washington, DC: US-China Economic and Security Review Commission, 16.

[40]Teddy Ng, "China Says Promise of more Money for Venezuela Part of 'Mutually Beneficial Cooperation'," *South China Morning Post*, September 14, 2018, https://www.scmp.com/news/china/diplomacy/article/2164321/china-says-promise-more-money venezuela-part-mutually.

ational-level political competition for investments and votes that may be leveraged with pro- or nti-Chinese rhetoric, and geopolitical competition with the United States.

First, consider how concerns about the Initiative's possible overreach are articulated in China nce these are the most public justifications for previously excluding Latin America. Xue Li, director f the Institute of World Economics and Politics at the Chinese Academy of Social Sciences, uggested that establishing close economic links with all countries in the region is beyond China's apacity and responsibility, and that China should focus on a few central partners.[41] China's financial sources may be abundant, but they are still finite, and prioritization is certainly necessary. But the eer scale of the BRI, or distance to investment targets, is certainly insufficient to explain what onstitutes 'overextension', as the incorporation of the Arctic in the BRI suggests.[42] Rather than king the BRI's continued focus on Asia at face value, this article calls attention to the manner that oncerns about overextension are dialectically intertwined with the characterization of Latin America 5 'too risky' for Chinese investments.

Many Chinese policymakers and intellectuals who call attention to investment risks in Latin merica bear recent high-profile 'failures' closely in mind. Here is an important moment in which theorization of co-production is particularly useful. After all, environmentalist, labor, and other ocial movements are rarely examined as part of the process of globalization of Chinese capital and evelopment interventions, yet their interests also structure and shape whether, where, and how the RI becomes produced in Latin America. Above all, they have resisted transnational capital expan-on in general, sometimes directly undermining or reshaping Chinese investments and international ooperation projects. Prominent cases include the collapse of attempted farmland investments in razil and Argentina due to resistance among various sectors of society, which triggered government strictions on acquisition of farmland by foreigners, and even the occupation of a Chinese-owned rm by landless peasants.[43] In infrastructure construction as well, disappointing experiences for ninese investors in Latin America are marked by social resistance. A private Chinese entrepreneur tempted but failed to launch the Nicaragua canal, for example, because local resistance outpaced e apparent attempt 'from Beijing' to lure the Nicaraguan government into diplomatic relations ith China instead of Taiwan.[44] Railroad projects failed in both Venezuela and Mexico.[45] The collapse f the Venezuelan project was attributed to poor economic planning rather than active resistance, ut the collapse of the agreement in Mexico resulted primarily from political competition over public ontracts and kickbacks among various Mexican politicians and infrastructure construction xecutives.[46] For China, which seeks to export increasingly high-tech products and services, exico's about-face was an awkward development, especially since this deal was highly publicized the Chinese media.[47] Nonetheless, Mexican lobbying for Chinese investments in the country's undering railroad transportation sector has been reignited in 2018 by a new administration that me to power with a major anti-corruption drive, explicitly arguing this new constellation of olitical forces within Mexico may dispel Chinese hesitation.[48] Most significantly still, the new railway

_i Xue, "China should not overestimate Latin America's strategic significance," _FT_中文网, January 21, 2015, www.ftchinese. com/story/0010602237?full=y&archive.

Huirong Liu, 'The Arctic Shipping Route and its uses Under the One Belt, One Road Context', _China Engineering Science_ 18(2), (2016), p. 111.

Nicolás Perrone, 'Restrictions to Foreign Acquisitions of Agricultural Land in Argentina and Brazil', _Globalizations_ 10(1), (2013), p. 205. Oliveira, 'Chinese land grabs', pp. 118-119.

Shoujun Cui, 'The Chinese-backed Nicaragua Canal: Domestic Rationale, Multiple Risks, and Geopolitical Implications', In Peters et al., _Building_, 144.

Haibin Niu, 'Strategic Analysis of Chinese Infrastructure Projects in Latin America and the Caribbean', In Peters et al., _Building_, 180. Enrique Peters, 'Chinese Infrastructure Projects in Mexico: General Context and Two Case Studies,' In Peters et al., _Building_, 58.

bid.

Wei Chen, "Chinese High-Speed Rail's First Order 'Goes Out': Heading Towards Latin America," _People's Daily_, November 5, 2014, http://military.people.com.cn/n/2014/1105/c1011-25977114.html.

Jude Webber, "Mexican 'Silk Road' Trade Corridor is Set to Spice up US Tension," _Financial Times_, June 6, 2018, https://www.ft. com/content/93f1efda-6966-11e8-b6eb-4acfcfb08c11.

project showcased for Chinese investment is no longer high-speed rail for passenger transport, bu
the Trans-Isthmus Corridor Railroad for cargo, a century-old proposal that is being reformulated nov
as perfect candidate for the BRI, given Chinese interest in reducing dependence on the Panam
Canal chokepoint.[49]

The notion of risk that characterizes the Chinese government's tenuous, hesitant, and limite
inclusion of Latin America in the BRI is not limited to the possibility that investments may fail t
materialize due to political resistance within recipient countries. It also pertains to concerns tha
loans may not be repaid, or investments may fail to yield profitable returns.[50] In 2014, engineerin
contracts for Chinese companies in Latin America already totaled over 100 USD billion, which som
interpret as posing too much risk to China, noting uncertainties surrounding China's oil-backed loar
to Venezuela as example of this risk, and the collapse of the railroad project there.[51] Despite it
enormous oil reserves, the economic and political crisis in Venezuela is indeed limiting its ability t
repay debts already incurred with Chinese lenders, and the threat of regime change, compounde
by volatility in international energy markets, is certainly cause for alarm from the perspective of th
Chinese government and its state-owned banks and oil companies.[52] On the other hand, Venezuela
recent inclusion in the BRI involves very limited financial commitments from China, as describe
above, and the Chinese state has leveraged it for significant propaganda purposes in demonstratin
how the BRI is not a geopolitical imposition by Beijing, but rather a much-desired framework fc
international development cooperation. Venezuelans 'call the Chinese "good older brothers" an
actively support the BRI proposal,' claimed a Chinese newspaper discussing the Venezuelan pre
sident's visit to China to sign the BRI agreement.[53] Venezuelans 'are eager to truly join the ranks an
become a hub for the extension of the BRI to Latin America,' emphasized the paper.[54]

There is some discrepancy, therefore, about how 'risk' is conceptualized and measured in bot
economic and political terms. In the case of Venezuela, for example, political gains outweighe
a (limited) extension of economic risks. Yet the profit-seeking nature of Chinese infrastructu
construction companies remains at the foundation of the 'overextension' thesis, as exemplifie
once again by Xue Li's statements: 'Beijing is not expecting to make a fortune on China-Lati
America economic and trade relations, but neither can it suffer a big loss ... when it comes t
Latin America, China has the money, but must be cautious when it comes to spending.'[55] Similarl
a recent study by Oxford University questioned the BRI's economic viabilities, noting that China
infrastructure projects feature cost overrun, lack real economic benefit in the areas where th
projects are built, and provide minimal returns to investors.[56]

Nonetheless, an official at the Chinese embassy in Brazil and an investment broker involved wit
these negotiations both explained in interviews with Oliveira (undertaken in Brasília during 201!
that the economic rationale of China's international infrastructure construction ventures must b
understood as part of a longer-term strategy for market access, where short-term risks are justifie
for long-term gains. 'When Brazil was awarded the [2012] Olympics, our [infrastructure constructio
companies tried to get any contracts they could even if they made no profits,' explained the Embass
official, 'because they wanted to promote and showcase their work so they could make money i

---

[49]ibid.

[50]Pin Zuo, "Thoughts on the Construction of the Belt and Road and the Deepening of Sino-Latin American Cooperation," Chir Think Tanks, October 26, 2015, http://www.chinathinktanks.org.cn/content/detail/id/2902266.

[51]Zuo, 'Thoughts.' Cf. Niu, 'Strategic Analysis.'

[52]Although no quantitative evidence was presented, such as insurance prices or operational losses, such risks were explicit mentioned by a director of the China-Latin America and Caribbean Cooperation Fund, managed by the China Export-Impc Bank. Personal interview by Oliveira, Beijing, May, 2019.

[53]Shen Liu, "Does China agree with Venezuela's Request to Replay 5 Billion USD Loan with Oil? China's Response," Guanchazr Network, September 14, 2018, https://www.guancha.cn/politics/2018_09_14_471996.shtml.

[54]ibid.

[55]Li Xue, Yanzhuo Xu, "Why China Shouldn't Get Too Invested in Latin America," The Diplomat, March 31, 2015, https: thediplomat.com/2015/03/why-china-shouldnt-get-too-invested-in-latin-america/.

[56]Atif Ansar, Bent Flyvbjerg, Alexander Budzier, Daniel Lunn, 'Does Infrastructure Investment Lead to Economic Growth Economic Fragility? Evidence from China', Oxford Review of Economic Policy 32(3), (2016), p. 360.

future contracts with the [2014] World Cup and even bigger projects.' Similarly, the investment broker explained that 'our [Chinese] clients were willing to outbid anyone because they knew their government would support them even if they lost money when opening up a new market.' Nonetheless, Chinese firms ultimately did not secure any infrastructure construction contracts associated with the Olympics or World Cup in Brazil. These interviewees attributed this more to the inexperience of Chinese firms with Brazilian public-bidding bureaucracy and weak ties to Brazilian construction companies, than to risk aversion. The source of the 'risk', therefore, is not necessarily endogenous to Latin America, but a relational dynamic between various Chinese, Latin American, and other actors.

Crucially, this relational dynamic extends to the United States as well. The sense of risk that surrounds continued Chinese restraint also results from US anxieties about China's growing role in the region, and the Chinese central government's desire to avoid entrapment in discourses of geopolitical competition. Indeed, Chinese scholars consistently and explicitly identify the historically strong and continued US influence in the region as one of the top factors shaping China's own relations with Latin America, alongside weak economic interconnectivity, and cultural differences.[57] Significantly, the Chinese government accepted US requests for bilateral dialogue on their relationship to Latin America from 2006 to 2016, attempting to build trust for its engagement in the region with the US even while this process simultaneously raises mistrust among Latin American governments themselves.[58] It appears, therefore, that China has hesitated to link major infrastructure projects in Latin America with the BRI, even though similar projects in Asia and Africa are affiliated with the Initiative, in order to limit what might be perceived as geopolitical provocations against the US in 'its own backyard'.

In other words, even if Chinese officials and firms are not backing down from massive infrastructure construction projects that advance their interests in Latin America, they are still careful about the discourses utilized to describe it. The recent but tenuous official incorporation of Latin American countries into the BRI, therefore, conforms with the widely acknowledged process of gradual transformation in China's foreign policy discourse from 'keeping a low profile' as oriented by Deng Xiaoping, and denying that massive infrastructure proposals for Latin America are part of its 'grand strategy', towards the recent but tenuous establishment of bilateral agreements explicitly framed under the BRI, that yet remain largely non-committal with financial resources and concrete projects.[59]

Discursive transformations like this are not insignificant for Chinese foreign policy.[60] The literal translation of China's foreign policy framework at hand is 'One Belt, One Road' (一带一路), and it is frequently discussed as a 'grand strategy' for China's geopolitical advancement, which evokes fears and intentionally so, for Western actors seeking to destabilize international support for the BRI) that other countries risk becoming ensnared in China's growing geopolitical ambitions. This led the Chinese government to consciously and consistently promote an alternative English translation of 一带一路 as 'the Belt and Road Initiative', displacing connotations of a singular strategy with more open ended discussions of infrastructure initiatives.[61]

Nonetheless, US officials in particular still seize on these discursive techniques to criticize the BRI and dissuade other countries from collaborating with China: 'In a globalized world, there are many belts and many roads, and no one nation should put itself into a position of dictating "one belt, one

[7]Xue, 'China Should not.' Niu, 'Strategic Analysis.' Zhenshing Su, 'How to Face the Future of China–Latin America Relations', *Journal of Latin American Studies* 2, (2009), pp. 1-8.

[8]Evan Ellis, 'Cooperation and Mistrust Between China and the US in Latin America,' In *The Political Economy of China-Latin America Relations in the New Millennium*, eds. Margaret Myers, Carol Wise (New York: Routledge, 2017), pp. 36-42.

[9]Suisheng Zhao, 'Chinese Foreign Policy as a Rising Power to Find its Rightful Place', *Perceptions* 18(1), (2013), 101. Zhou and Esteban, 'Beyond balancing,' 500-1.

[0]Sidaway and Woon, 'Chinese Narratives,' 591.

[1]Wade Shepard, "Beijing to the World: Don't Call the Belt and Road Initiative OBOR," *Forbes*, August 1, 2017, https://www.forbes.com/sites/wadeshepard/2017/08/01/beijing-to-the-world-please-stop-saying-obor/. See also the explicit orientation on English translations of 一带一路 on the Chinese government's official BRI online portal: https://eng.yidaiyilu.gov.cn/ztindex.htm.

road",' asserted the US Secretary of Defense Jim Mattis in testimony before the Senate Armed Services Committee on October 2017.[62] Secretary of State Rex Tillerson saw fit to 'warn' Latin America about its growing ties to the Asian nation, stating that 'China's offers always come at a price,' and describing Beijing's ambitions as imperialistic.[63] According to a major US government report on China's engagement with Latin America, China's expanding infrastructure investments in the region can 'reinforce the region's overreliance on highly cyclical exports and create unsustainable debt burdens for some LAC countries, which China could use for political leverage.'[64] Additional notes of caution frequently warn that Chinese investments may aggravate environmental conditions in Latin America, encourage further corruption of political and corporate elites, and facilitate new channels for drug cartels to move contraband and launder money.[65] Underlying everything is the fact that Chinese finance for Latin America has allowed certain governments (particularly in Venezuela, Bolivia, Ecuador, Honduras, and Argentina) some relief from US government sanctions and restricted lending by financiers from the Global North.

> The rise of China as an alternative source of trade, investment, and finance for the nations of Latin America and the Caribbean has provided both anti-U.S. governments and other nations with alternatives to the US for loans, investments, and markets, indirectly weakening US leverage for advancing its policy goals.[66]

Chinese policymakers are by no means beholden to Washington's whims, but they continue to take the risk of accentuating US opposition into account when formulating their Latin America policy which leads to a relatively hesitant and fragmentary approach. The complex manner that the BRI and BRI-related projects are assembled in Latin America, including their co-production by multiple Chinese and non-Chinese actors, and the relational and contested dynamics of competing visions and interests, will be further exemplified with the case study in the next section.

Chinese-backed Ports and Railroads in Brazil

On 23 May 2019, the vice presidents of Brazil and China signed an agreement 'recognizing the possible synergies' between infrastructure investment policies in both countries, 'including the Belt and Road Initiative.'[67] Although still not officially listing Brazil in the roster of the BRI, and even though many infrastructure projects discussed here emerged prior to the Chinese extension of BRI discourses to Latin America, this remains a useful case study. After all, key pillars of the BRI in Asia itself are actually preexisting projects that were reframed as BRI. Such re-labeling is not reducible to mere branding exercises without material effects. As shown in previous sections, the gradual expansion of the BRI articulates with institutional transformations and shifts in socio-material practices ranging from finance to resistance. Thus, this case study will demonstrate how, since the BRI (and BRI-related projects) are assembled through such co-production, they inevitably gather multiple actors who leverage it for numerous interests of their own, which sometimes align and are sometimes contradictory.

The vast majority of Chinese financing and infrastructure construction in Brazil has gone to the petroleum and energy sector.[68] Since 2010, State Grid and China Three Gorges have acquired multiple large-scale transmission lines in Brazil, and secured contracts to build new ones associated

[62] Anjit Panda, "Is the Trump Administration about to Take on China's Belt and Road Initiative?" *The Diplomat*, October 19, 2017 https://thediplomat.com/2017/10/is-the-trump-administration-about-to-take-on-chinas-belt-and-road-initiative/.
[63] Robbie Gramer, Keith Johnson, "Tillerson Praises Monroe Doctrine, Warns Latin America of 'Imperial' Chinese Ambitions," *Foreign Policy*, February 2, 2018, https://foreignpolicy.com/2018/02/02/tillerson-praises-monroe-doctrine-warns-latin-america-off-imperial-chinese-ambitions-mexico-south-america-nafta-diplomacy-trump-trade-venezuela-maduro/.
[64] Koleski and Blivas, *China's Engagement*, p. 3.
[65] Ellis, 'Cooperation', pp. 33-42.
[66] Ellis, 'Cooperation,' p. 38.
[67] Minutes of the Third Plenary Session of the High-Level Sino-Brazilian Commission on Concentration and Cooperation (COSBAN), Beijing, May 23, 2019.
[68] Kevin Gallagher and Margaret Myers, "China-Latin America finance database," Inter-American Dialogue, March 2020, https://www.thedialogue.org/map_list.

vith dam construction in the Amazon, where Chinese companies also have gained a foothold. nergy generated from these projects is often supportive of the mining sector, which also receives :hinese investments and has in China its largest export market.[69] Yet many high-profile diplomatic, ournalistic, and academic discussions of Chinese infrastructure construction projects in Brazil have entered recently on the Bi-Oceanic Railway, a project for linking Brazil's Atlantic littoral to ports on 'eru's Pacific coast.[70]

The idea of a transcontinental railroad across South America is as old as railway construction itself. 3razilian intellectuals proposed it along the east-west axis for South American integration as early as 874, while the US proposed it on the north-south axis in 1890 to facilitate, of course, US hegemony cross the whole continent.[71] Yet Brazilian railway construction only extended from the coast to the outheastern edge of the Central Plateau, while smaller stretches across the Amazon only reached nineral deposits in eastern Pará state, and connected a few waterways, without establishing an interconnected network across Brazil, much less stretching towards and across the Andean nations. tail construction halted in the mid-20th century, and new proposals only began to gather interest fter the end of the military dictatorship in 1988. Construction on a few projects finally began in the 000s, featuring most prominently the North-South Railroad and the West-East Integration Railway Ferrovia de Integração Oeste-Leste, FIOL), linking the soy/corn belts of central Brazil to ports on the oasts. The impending inauguration of these railroads during the early 2010s was used by Brazilian ureaucrats to boost Chinese agribusiness investments along their routes, only to leave Chinese nvestors sorely disappointed when construction of FIOL was stalled, and the North-South Railway vas inaugurated but left un-operational due to multiple technical problems.[72]

So far, the closest a Chinese company has come to building a railroad in Brazil is also an illustrative isappointment. The China Railway Construction Company (CRCC) partnered with Camargo Corrêa, ne of Brazil's leading infrastructure construction companies, to bid for the construction of the Mid-Vest Integration Railway (Ferrovia de Integração Centro-Oeste, FICO), a project that would tap Mato irosso state's soy/corn belt as an east-west branch of the North-South Railway. As a Brazilian xecutive and government official who participated in the process indicated to Oliveira, the joint id was ready and about to be approved by the Brazilian government for about 5 billion BRL in 2012, vhen Camargo Corrêa insisted on withdrawing the proposal unless the Brazilian government raised he price to 7 billion BRL.[73] CRCC executives disagreed since their interest was not to maximize rofits but simply to gain exposure and experience for additional Brazilian projects in the future. But he divergence of interests remained, the proposal was withdrawn, and within two years Camargo orrêa was disqualified for bidding on public projects due to its involvement in a massive corruption candal.

Nevertheless, Xi Jinping seized upon the idea of a transcontinental railroad across Brazil and Peru ɔ his visit to the continent during July 2014, drawing upon a proposal drafted in 2008 by the ɔrazilian government but immediately abandoned due to the onset of the global financial crisis. Four nonths later, he was signing memoranda of understanding with the presidents of Brazil and Peru luring their follow-up visits to China, agreeing to initiate feasibility studies in collaboration with :hinese financiers and railway construction companies.[74] Unlike previous incarnations of 'South .merican integration' projects, however, the goal now was explicitly to facilitate the export of ɔrazilian soy and iron ore to China from South America's Pacific coast. So even though feasibility tudies were launched upon premier Li Keqiang's visit to Brazil in 2015, the impetus for

ᵞCelio Hiratuka, 'Chinese infrastructure projects in Brazil: Two case studies,' In Peters et al., *Building*, pp. 130-134.
ᵞCesar Azevedo, 'Reflections on the South American Transcontinental Railway,' *Revista Brasileira de Políticas Públicas e Internacionais* 3(1), (2018), pp. 254-285.
ᵞAzevedo, 'Reflections', pp. 254-255.
²Gustavo Oliveira, "The South-South Question: Transforming Brazil-China Agroindustrial Partnerships" (PhD dissertation, University of California, Berkeley, 2017).
³Personal interview on condition of anonymity, August, 2014, Brasília.
⁴Hiratuka, 'Chinese infrastructure', pp. 134-138.

a transcontinental railroad reduced Peru's role to a mere *entrepôt*, and placed the project in direc
competition with other routes for the export of Brazilian agroindustrial commodities to China.[75] Thi
arrangement would harness divergent interests that are ultimately forestalling the projec
altogether.

This divergence was aptly illustrated during a Corporate Seminar co-organized in Brasília, on th
occasion of premier Li Keqiang's state visit in 2015, by the Brazilian National Federations o
Transportation (CNT), Agriculture (CNA), and Industry (CNI), the most representative national-leve
business associations. Brazilian boosters, brokers, bureaucrats, and businessmen (mostly men
collaborated in making detailed presentations about Brazil-China economic relations and opportu
nities for investments, elaborating particularly on the process of consortium bidding for the con
struction and concession of public infrastructure projects, and showcasing above all the EF-17(
railway project, dubbed 'Ferrogrão' or 'Grain Railroad' (Figure 1).

The Grain Railroad is a project that runs on a north-south axis from the soy/corn heartland in Matc
Grosso to the new fluvial ports of Itaituba/Miritituba on the Tapajós river, where soy/corn can shift t
barges for much cheaper waterway navigation to the deep-water ports at the mouth of the Amazo
river. With a load of 20 mmt by 2020 (rising to 42 mmt by 2050) and total cost of 4 billion USD, th
Grain Railroad is anticipated to transport about the same amount of soy/corn as the Bi-Oceani
Railway, but at less than one-third the total estimated cost. Moreover, the Grain Railroad is not onl
far shorter than the transcontinental alternative, it also follows an existing federal highway, an
consequently does not pose nearly as much social and environmental concern for its construction
Unsurprisingly, the agribusinesses that stand to benefit the most from either project have sidec
unequivocally with the more topologically feasible Grain Railroad over the more ambitious trans
Andean vision, including not only Brazilian, US, and European firms, but also at a later moment a ke
Chinese state-owned agribusiness company, the China National Cereals, Oils, and Foodstuff
Corporation (COFCO), that is investing in this region.

Interestingly, feasibility studies and proposals for public bidding on the Grain Railroad wer
already being undertaken by a consortium of US and Brazilian agribusiness companies, when th
project was showcased as a 'model for Chinese investment' during the Corporate Seminar held o
the occasion of Li Keqiang's visit. This prompted highly critical and unenthusiastic responses fron
the Chinese infrastructure construction executives hosted at the seminar. Oliveira was present at th
event and noted a visibly frustrated Chinese businessman questioning the official from Brazil'
Ministry of Transportation after his presentation on the topic: 'Why do you invite us to a projec
that is already controlled by a Brazilian alliance with the ABCDs?', utilizing the acronym for the majo
US agribusiness trading companies against which Chinese agribusinesses are in harsh competitior
The Brazilian official fumbled a response about highlighting models merely as example, but th
frustration of Chinese executives was self-evident in the fact that the side rooms prepared fo
business-to-business negotiations were left empty after the seminar.

Furthermore, Oliveira visited several Brazilian maritime ports from the southeastern states of Sant
Catarina and São Paulo to the northeastern states of Bahia, Pernambuco, Maranhão, and the norther
state of Pará during 2014 and 2015, and consistently documented how local- and state-level official
and port management executives lobbied Chinese executives to invest in new terminals or expansio
of their own ports, sometimes even referencing the maritime extension of the BRI as justification. Suc
boosterism finally paid off in 2017, when the China Merchants Port Holding acquired Brazil's secon
largest container terminal (in Paranaguá, Paraná state), and the China Communications Constructio
Company (CCCC) acquired a mid-sized Brazilian construction company and its 51 percent share of th
Port of São Luis (in Maranhão state). CCCC also began negotiations for port construction projects i
Bahia and Santa Catarina states (Porto Sul and TGB), and for a stake in the operational port of Suape i
Pernambuco state.[76] However, previous negotiations for Chinese construction of Brazilian ports rais

[75]Azevedo, 'Reflections', p. 254.
[76]Koleski and Blivas, *China's Engagement*, pp. 33-34.

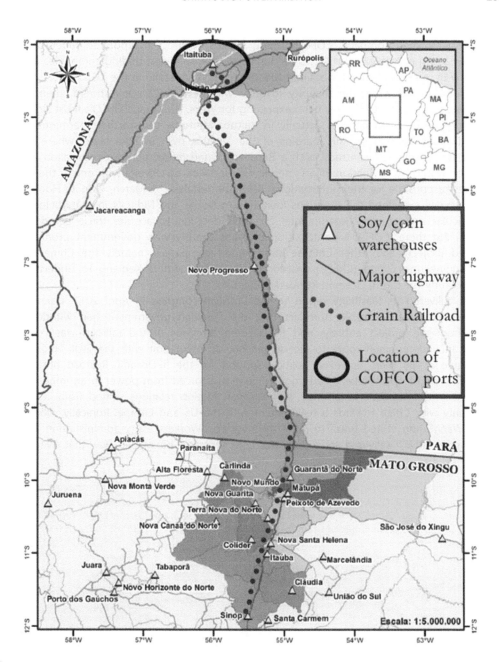

Figure 1. The EF-170, dubbed 'Ferrogrão' or 'Grain Railroad'. Source: Adapted from the Brazilian Federal Government's Investment Partnership Program, 2016.

caveats that such deals may fall through or become significantly delayed. Chinese agribusiness trading companies negotiated for participation in Brazilian grain terminals since 2006 without any success, and when a private company finally secured a 20 percent stake in a new grain terminal in São Francisco do Sul (Santa Catarina state) in 2010, it only managed to start construction in 2015.[77]

Gustavo Oliveira, 'The Battle of the Beans: How Direct Brazil-China Soybean Trade was Stillborn in 2004', *Journal of Latin American Geography* 17(2), (2018), pp. 113-139; Oliveira, 'South-South Question', pp. 211-215.

If CCCC does implement the TGB port project, it will effectively converge with another majo Chinese state-owned company, COFCO. This is because COFCO incorporated Nidera and th agribusiness arm of Noble in 2014, two medium-sized transnational trading companies expanc ing rapidly in Brazil, and thus it obtained Nidera's 20 percent stake in the TGB project. But th project soon stalled when the majority investor withdrew. CCCC's investment, then, woul finally realize a project COFCO has been expecting for years. However, COFCO's most significan participation in Brazilian ports is actually in Itaituba/Mirituba, the northern terminus of th projected Grain Railroad on the margins of the Tapajós river in Pará state, where COFCC inherited its subsidiaries' contracts with a Brazilian-owned infrastructure construction start-u focused on waterway navigation. In an interview undertaken by Oliveira with one of the COFCC executives responsible for their international M&As undertaken on March, 2015 in Hong Kong the interviewee explained the synergies identified in Noble and Nidera's joint participation i this particular project were instrumental for their decision to acquire these companies i particular. But there, COFCO's participation diverges sharply with government promotion c BRI-related projects and other Chinese state-owned companies, namely the China Railwa Eryuan Engineering Group (CREEC), tasked by Xi Jinping and Li Keqiang to undertake th feasibility study for the Bi-Oceanic Railroad project.

CREEC delivered its feasibility report to the Brazilian congress in April 2017, claiming th project remains viable—despite the fact that the Peruvian government had withdrawn it support from the project entirely, and the eastern terminus of the railroad was conteste between an undetermined route to Rio de Janeiro, or integration with the FIOL across Bah state (Figure 2). By then, however, political support for the Bi-Oceanic Railroad project ha dissipated in Brazil. The Workers' Party government was forced from power in an impeachmen by a right-wing congressional alliance, and Brazilian foreign relations shifted from cultivatin multipolarity with China towards a realignment with the US and Europe. Ironically, when vic premier Wang Yang visited Brazil to meet the new post-Workers' Party administration just fiv months after CREEC delivered its report, the core message he carried was that 'we remai

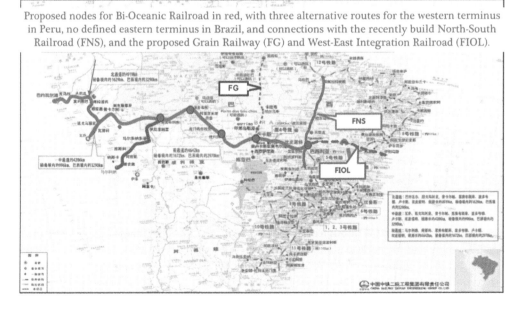

Proposed nodes for Bi-Oceanic Railroad in red, with three alternative routes for the western terminus in Peru, no defined eastern terminus in Brazil, and connections with the recently build North-South Railroad (FNS), and the proposed Grain Railway (FG) and West-East Integration Railroad (FIOL).

Figure 2. CREEC's viability study on the Bi-Oceanic railway to the Brazilian government, 2017. Source: Adapted from CREE 'Presentation of the basic viability study of the Brazil-Peru Transcontinental Railway,' Document presented at public hearing Brasília: Federal Senate of Brazil, April 2017.

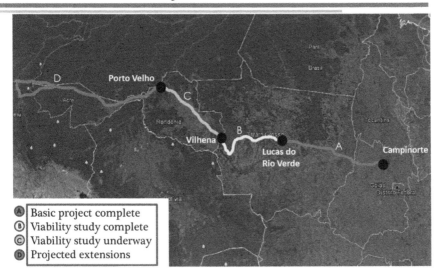

Figure 3. Path of the EF 354 (Bi-Oceanic Railroad) in national territory. Source: Adapted from presentation by the Ministry of transportation to the Brazilian Federal Senate, 8 August 2017

interested in participating in the bids for infrastructure projects' under the new administration's priority program, which includes the Grain Railway but no transcontinental projects anymore, supporting the priorities of COFCO over CREEC.[78] The shift was not the result from divergences between Xi and Li, or direct competition between CREEC and COFCO, but rather from the underlying transformation of agribusiness priorities within Brazil itself, including the localized interests of COFCO.

The Brazilian Ministry of Transportation now effectively reduced discussion from a transcontinental railway to the central stretch that overlaps with the FICO connection lost by CRCC in 2012 (Figure 3). Moreover, the new president of Brazil, Jair Bolsonaro, gained office through a fervently anti-China campaign and increased anti-China rhetoric during the COVID-19 pandemic. So it is unlikely that Brazil will formally join the official roster of the BRI in the near future. Nonetheless, Brazilian agribusiness elites are lobbying hard to temper Bolsonaro's anti-China turn, hoping to sustain exports to Brazil's largest market for agricultural and mineral exports, and seek further investments that may alleviate logistical bottlenecks by expanding export-oriented infrastructure, especially now that a global depression seems at hand.[79] Given the convergence and divergence of interests in the co-production of Chinese infrastructure projects in Brazil, the ventures that may roll into this framework do not follow the Chinese central government's visions and pronouncements, nor a cohesive government and elite strategy within Brazil, but are tenuously co-produced by multiple converging and conflicting actors across China and Brazil, responding to opportunities and pressures emerging from multiple locations around the world.

[8]Cristina Campos, "Temer Tells Chinese that Brazil is Getting 'Back on Track' for Development," *Agência Brasil*, September 2, 2017, http://agenciabrasil.ebc.com.br/economia/noticia/2017-09/temer-diz-chineses-que-brasil-esta-voltando-para-o-trilho-do.
[9]Diário do Comércio & Indústria (DCI), "Infrastructure Continues to be the Main Demand on the Agenda for Agribusiness," *Brazil Modal*, January 10, 2019, http://brazilmodal.com.br/2015/jornalmultimodal/infraestrutura-segue-como-principal-demanda-na-agenda-do-agronegocio/. This was also noted by Oliveira in several interviews with members of the Brazilian Minister of Agriculture's delegation to China, Beijing, May 16, 2019.

Conclusion

Latin American countries are gradually and tenuously joining the official roster of the BRI. A general interest of the Chinese government in projects that allow for trade to bypass the Panama Canal is an evident cornerstone of BRI-related proposals for the region, yet divergent Chinese and Latin American interests have largely curtailed the emergence of any cohesive set of investment projects. Thus, the region remains largely outside the scope of the Initiative's framework, receiving relatively limited financial disbursements and infrastructure construction projects directly aligned with the Chinese government's vision for the internationalization of its infrastructure construction companies, and the reshaping of global politics and economics in its favor. Certainly, some of China's over 150 proposed infrastructure projects in Latin America will proceed with or without BRI-specific discourses and backing, while others are likely to stall or even collapse. This article demonstrated, however, that the tenuous emergence of BRI discourses and projects in Latin America is not simply an advancement of Chinese investments, diplomacy, and geopolitics, but rather a co-produced bundle of diplomacy and lobbying efforts, financial and technical resources, and both converging and conflicting interests across China, Latin America, and beyond.

Consequently, the article also illustrates the usefulness of a relational approach to theorize the BRI and China's global integration, and advance critical geopolitics more generally. In particular, the authors reveal the process of multi-sited and multi-scalar co-production to de-center nation-states and inter-governmental relations, and emphasize instead the dispersed agency of Chinese and non-Chinese actors alike in the formulation and contestation of the BRI. Evidently, the authors do not claim there is anything unique or special about this process involving the BRI in Latin America, but rather that this common approach to critical geopolitics—emphasizing co-production rather than top-down decisions and unidirectional impacts—should gain more space in studies and narratives about Chinese foreign investments and international development cooperation in general.

Finally, in a context of deepening economic crisis across the world due to the novel coronavirus pandemic, limited foreign investment, and slim pickings for multilateral credit to support infrastructure—especially of the cross-border variety—China remains a vital source of capital in a region in need of sustained investment. Latin American governments and multiple think tanks frame the challenge as generating project proposals that match China's interests, with plans for such projects that can reboot economic growth in a manner that minimizes negative social and environmental impacts. In other words, finding a way for Latin American governments to shape investment from China more effectively, with or without BRI-specific backing. Whereas some projects will deliver much-needed connectivity and related economic gains, others will likely fall short of expectations.

The normative implications of this argument pertain to how the BRI in Latin America should be conceived and critiqued: not as a geopolitical imposition 'from Beijing', nor as a necessary result of 'local characteristics', but rather as a tenuous, contingent, and unstable arrangement of discourses, policies, and projects promoted by a variety of actors within and outside China, who leverage them for numerous interests of their own, which sometimes align and are sometimes contradictory. Attending to the BRI in Latin America in this way, it becomes possible to better examine new and crucial research questions such as the following: Should the BRI continue to focus upon infrastructure projects that facilitate the export of Latin American agricultural and mineral commodities to China, relegating social benefits to a possible (but questionable) ancillary outcome of 'economic growth', or could priorities be reimagined for infrastructure construction that addresses intra-regional connectivity and social inclusion more directly? Must health costs and environmental protection continue to be seen merely as an impediment for the advancement of infrastructure projects, or could China-Latin America cooperation in areas such as agroecology, renewable energy, and public health be reimagined as part of the BRI? Last but not least, can the discourse of the BRI as a framework for international development cooperation be sustained when so many of its projects and proposals advance primarily the interests of corporate and government elites in China and partnered countries, but largely at the expense of the indigenous peoples, peasants, and workers who are displaced or exploited by its pharaonic infrastructure construction projects?

Acknowledgments

The authors would like to thank Yang Yang, Alessandro Rippa, Suisheng Zhao, and the anonymous reviewers for helpful feedback on this manuscript.

Disclosure Statement

No potential conflict of interest was reported by the authors.

Funding

Oliveira's research was supported by the Inter-American Foundation, the BRICS Initiative for Critical Agrarian Studies, and the University of California Berkeley's Graduate Division, Center for Chinese Studies, and Institute for International Studies – Simpson Fellowship. The arguments and analysis do not necessarily reflect the views of any of these institutions.

ORCID

Gustavo de L. T. Oliveira (iD) http://orcid.org/0000-0002-1800-227X

A Role Model for Africa or Exceptional Engagement? Assessing China's South Sudan Experience

Malte Brosig

ABSTRACT
China's engagement in South Sudan has been branded a crucial test case for the country's foreign and security policy in Africa. Investment in the oil sector is significant, and Chinese political engagement in conflict mediation and peacekeeping are unparalleled. Will the experiences gathered provide China with reasons to extend its engagement, is South Sudan a model or exceptional case? In this context three sectors will be explored: the economic, political and security sphere. This article finds that there are few reasons to assume that South Sudan is a role model. Access to oil was never critically important, and oil revenue is fuelling the conflict. The Chinese model of developmental peace and conflict mediation preferring non-punitive diplomacy are problematic. The peacekeeping mission could not stop the fighting but succeeded in setting up civilian protection sites. In sum, the South Sudan engagement has not produced favorable outcomes and is unlikely to be replicated.

The literature on China-Africa relations continues to burgeon. While early studies focused mostly on trade relations, Chinese investment in large scale infrastructure projects, and access to natural resources, the latest wave of publications also examines the field of peace and security activities.[1] Many studies connote either an end of the non-interference policy, a gradual shift away from the classical but also dogmatic application of the famous five principles of co-existence (territorial integrity, non-aggression, non-interference, equality in relations, peaceful cooperation), or China becoming a norm shaper in international affairs including conflict management.[2] While nuances in evaluation exist, the majority of studies implicitly assumes a more proactive role of China in African security policies, using examples such as the opening of a military base in Djibouti, increasing number of Chinese peacekeepers including combat troops, or China's support for the African Peace and Security Architecture (APSA).[3] However, the limits of more engagement are less focused on, the rising power discourse is dominating the literature, implying that with continuing Chinese economic expansion the security field will rather mechanistically follow. In fact, China's 2015 Military Strategy issued the same assumption.[4]

In contrast to this mainstream perspective, this article aims to evaluate the potential limits of Chinese proactive engagement in African conflicts by exploring the one case in which China is most

---

[1]Chris Alden et al. eds., *China and Africa Building Peace and Security Cooperation on the Continent* (Cham: Palgrave Macmillan, 2018).
[2]Obert Hodzi, *The End of China's Non-Intervention Policy in Africa* (Cham: Palgrave Macmillan, 2019); Chris Alden and Daniel Large, 'On Becoming a Norms Maker: Chinese Foreign Policy, Norms Evolution and the Challenges of Security in Africa', *The China Quarterly* 221, (2015), pp. 123–142.
[3]Reuters, 'China formally opens first overseas military base in Djibouti', August 1, 2017, accessed July 3, 2019, https://www.reuters.com/article/us-china-djibouti/china-formally-opens-first-overseas-military-base-in-djibouti-idUSKBN1AH3E3.
[4]The State Council Information Office of the People's Republic of China, 'China's Military Strategy,' Beijing, May 2015, accessed July 16, 2019, http://english.gov.cn/archive/white_paper/2015/05/27/content_281475115610833.htm.

ctively involved in conflict management and has been characterized by Chinese leadership and academics as an exploratory test case.[5] This article evaluates to which extent the South Sudan example either forms an exceptional case or a potential role model that Chinese foreign policy can e replicated. In the end, it is argued, that the South Sudan experience is unlikely to serve as a role model. Experiences made are rather sobering, neither have economic profits been stable nor has an increased Chinese engagement in peacekeeping and mediation delivered favorable outcomes. China has also not come up with a clearly formulated concept for conflict resolution apart from general concepts such as developmental peace. In sum, the case of South Sudan might actually provide for arguments more in line with classical Chinese foreign policy principles which favor reluctance over activism than a major shift toward radically different principles. In this regard, South Sudan might rather be a case of atypical engagement.

Chinese Rise and Its Foreign (Security) Policy toward Africa

There is no doubt China is gradually playing a more active role in global affairs and a particularly influential role on the African continent. The sheer size of China's economy, its demographics, and economic outreach make it a global player in any case. In Africa, it has become the largest trading partner (single country) for the continent which pledges multi-billion investments through the Forum on China-Africa Cooperation (FOCAC), the Belt and Road Initiative (BRI), the BRICS New Development Bank (NDB), or bi-laterally, through private investments. China has amassed quite considerable economic power within a fairly short amount of time. This has placed its traditional foreign policy concept based on the above mentioned five principles of coexistence under pressure. While the coexistence doctrine originated from the times of Mao Zedong, the emphasis on keeping low profile propagated by Deng Xiaoping has been replaced by a more proactive, arguably assertive position Xi Jinping is favoring.[6] China's foreign and security policy becomes more proactive. It also tries to disperse concerns over its use of power by displaying itself as a responsible power which rejects hegemonic ambitions.[7]

The pressure to become more engaged in African security issues emanates from a number of conditions. The most relevant one is China's economic expansion on the continent. With an estimated over a million Chinese citizens living in Africa, a trade volume of 148 USDbn in 2017 and multi-billion investments in hundreds of infrastructure projects, China is exposed to nearly every violent conflict that breaks out, especially as Chinese businesses tend to operate in high risk environments from which Western firms have stayed away.[8] The frequent targeting of Chinese business people by criminals, the risk of losing large scale investments due to insurgencies against governments, the reputational risk of propping up suppressive and autocratic regimes as well as illegal business activities of its nationals all pose a direct risk to China. Although not an existential one topping the national security agenda which prioritizes mainland China, the Asia-Pacific region and its relations with the US, it remains a considerable one.

Under these circumstances the traditional position of staying aloof of political conflicts, abstaining in UN Security Council voting and watching events unfold from distance clearly becomes untenable and needed to be rectified. However, restraint still remains an important point of

---

Daniel Large, 'Sudan and South Sudan: A Testing Ground for Beijing's Peace and Security Engagement' in *China and Africa Building Peace and Security Cooperation on the Continent*, ed. Chris Alden et al. (Cham: Palgrave Macmillan, 2018), pp. 163–178; Crisis Group International, 'China's Foreign Policy Experiment in South Sudan', Asia Report N°288, July 10, 2017, accessed November 24, 2018, https://www.crisisgroup.org/africa/horn-africa/south-sudan/288-china-s-foreign-policy-experiment-south-sudan.

Angela Poh, and Mingjiang Li, 'A China in Transition: The Rhetoric and Substance of Chinese Foreign Policy under Xi Jinping', *Asian Security* 13(2), (2017), pp. 84–97.

Xi Jinping, 'China's Peaceful Development Road, State Council Information Office of China. Secure a Decisive Victory in Building a Moderately Prosperous Society in All Respects and Strive for the Great Success of Socialism with Chinese Characteristics for a New Era', 19th National Congress of the Communist Party of China, October 18, 2017, pp. 53–54.

The Observatory of Economic Complexity. 'China', July 4, 2019, https://atlas.media.mit.edu/de/profile/country/chn/accessed.

guidance as it is deeply ingrained in key strategic interests China has. These are non-intervention and state sovereignty as the most important principles in foreign relations keeping the CCP in power and shielding external unwanted interferences from it (one China policy, fierce rejection of secessionis movements: Tibet, Xinjian).

However, despite China's conservative and essentially non-liberal approach to state sovereignty its foreign policy went through a number of transformations. Sovereignty is now not perceived from a dogmatic position or fundamental opposition to external intervention. There now appears to b considerably more conceptual flexibility but no moving away or complete giving up of classica foreign policy principles.[9] China has not actively rejected concepts such as the Responsibility t Protect (R2P) but fiercely opposes regime change in the name of protecting civilians.[10] Interventior and the use of force are accepted if they are authorized by the UN Security Council and applied a last resort and with member state consent.

South Sudan is a case in point in which China sent around 700 combat ready troops to an UP mission with a civilian protection mandate. Increasingly China gets involved in maintaining interna tional peace and security far beyond its own borders. Its Military Strategy from 2015 promise a gradual increase of China providing more global public goods and engaging more in organization such as the UN. China is now the largest troop contributor to UN peacekeeping missions of the P and makes the second largest monetary contribution to the peacekeeping budget.[11] While at th beginning of the Millennium China hardly deployed any peacekeepers in May 2019 it has 2,53 military and police serving under the UN banner.[12] Additionally China participates in the interna tional military operations against Somali pirates, also deploys combat troops to a UN mission in Ma and has opened a military base in Djibouti in 2017 which is designed to host up to 10,000 troops.

While the signs of a more pro-active China in Africa are clearly visible and do form a significar shift in emphasis, adjustment in foreign policy principles and use of instruments it is equall important to ask how far will China adjust and will it become an ever more relevant political an security actor? The assumption that China inevitably will need to protect its economic expansio with political and military robust engagement is rooted in realist thinking. It is based on the logic c great power rivalry and doubtful of a peaceful rise of China. Especially offensive realists lik Mearsheimer see a more power conscious China emerging.[13] While China could use significantl more of its power resources it is not self-evident that it will do. Getting more involved in conflic management through using political and military resources is not an end in itself but very likel results from experiences made in specific settings such as the conflict in South Sudan.

The following sections will explore if Chinese engagement in South Sudan can be treated as a ro model or constitutes as an exceptional case. The question is of relevance for both China and Afric Chinese investment in natural resources and infrastructure projects continues to grow while Afric remains the continent with fragile statehood and many armed conflicts. While China needs access t natural resources, Africa needs to grow out of poverty. From this perspective the South Suda example could be of crucial importance either as a role model for other cases or as turning point fc a more limited or nuanced Chinese engagement on the continent. Although the mainstrear literature implies an ever growing Chinese involvement in Africa as a consequence of the country economic expansion a degree of caution needs to be applied if increased security and politica engagement is actually leading to favorable results?

---

[9]Benjamin Barton, 'China's security policy in Africa: A new or false dawn for the evolution of the application of China's non interference principle?', *South African Journal of International Affairs* 25(3), (2018), pp. 413–434.

[10]Tiewa Liu and Haibin Zhang, 'Debates in China about the responsibility to protect as a developing international norm: a gener assessment', *Conflict, Security & Development* 14(4), (2014), pp. 403–427.

[11]UN DPKO website, Troop and Police Contributors, accessed July 3, 2019, https://peacekeeping.un.org/en/troop-and-polic contributors.

[12]Ibid.

[13]John Mearsheimer, 'China's Unpeaceful Rise', *Current History* 105, (2006), pp. 160–162.

A role model function can be assumed to emerge when the applied foreign policy instruments have been perceived positively, and the situation in South Sudan is somewhat representative for a number of other cases. What positive evaluation means in the context of Chinese foreign and security policy requires some discussion and might not be straightforwardly clear. Foreign policy decision-making in China is notoriously difficult to assess from the outside and official evaluative statements are carefully crafted intending to portray China in a favorable light. When it comes to decision-making with regard to South Sudan one is to distinguish between a mixture of different actors ranging from the Chinese Communist Party (CCP), the Peoples Liberation Army (PLA), the Ministry of Foreign Affairs (MFA), State owned Enterprises (SOE), and the presidency. Central to the process is the CCP and the role of the secretary-general of the party and president of the country. However, SOE and the PLA are fairly independent actors and the decision-making system within the CCP is not designed in a monolithic manner but allows for inner-institutional competition for decision-making across various committees.[14]

This leads to a situation in which different priorities and standards for evaluation can be applied. While the PLA might prioritize effective execution of peacekeeping mandates within the UN mission and gaining operational experience in an active war zone, the MFA might concentrate on portraying China as a non-partisan conflict mediator and partner for African countries. SOE would favor uninterrupted business and monetary profits and the CCP might emphasize China's developmental benefits for Africa. The Party might also be interested in nurturing a rhetoric on developmental peace as being ideologically different from the Western liberal peace model.[15] These goals are not necessarily standing in contradiction to each other, but they are not forming a coherent picture and can portray conflicting or isolated interests. This in itself makes it difficult to craft and design a role model because partly atomized decision-making undercuts the endeavor to create such models in the first place. Despite this situation one can still go through individual bits and pieces of assessment and evaluate if more narrow goals have been reached, out of which the sum of experiences might be either positive or negative and in this regard either more or less suitable for model building.

The following sections try exactly this. They are forming an assessment of individual sectors within China's foreign and security policy toward South Sudan. Accordingly the article distinguishes between three macro sections. The section on economics is primarily focusing on the oil business and its relevance for China, exploring to which extent oil exports from South Sudan remain critical or disposable. The section will also briefly look into other investment such as infrastructure and developmental support. The politics section in which issues of conflict mediation and conceptual thinking around developmental peace predominates explores what role Chinese diplomacy is playing for conflict resolution. In this context the critical question is, what results is the unusual direct involvement in mediation actually delivering? Is it helping to protect Chinese investments, has it helped to solve the conflict? Lastly the security section is looking into matters of peacekeeping in South Sudan. Operating in a high risk environment with a sizable number of combat troops outside of China's direct regional neighborhood is novel for the PLA. One can thus assume that a performance evaluation will bear some relevance if this endeavor will be perceived as a worthwhile project to be replicated in similar contexts.

Table 1 provides a quick overview of the mentioned assessment sections. While it is not possible to do an in-house evaluation for the respective actors involved given the rather secluded mode of operation it is still possible to evaluate outcomes as displayed in the table above. The study distinguishes between sector specific outcomes and their respective narrow or wider focus. Finally one can assume that activities and outcomes in one sector can have an impact on other sectors. The prevalence

---

[14]Linda Jakobson and Ryan Manuel, 'How are Foreign Policy Decisions Made in China?' *Asia & the Pacific Policy Studies* 3(1), (2016), pp. 101–110; See also Nector Gan, 'Who are the players behind China's foreign policy?' *South China Morning Post*, March 8, 2018, accessed July 3, 2019, https://www.scmp.com/news/china/diplomacy-defence/article/2136248/how-does-china-formulate-its-foreign-policy.

[15]Linda Benabdallah, 'China's Peace and Security Strategies in Africa: Building Capacity is Building Peace?' *African Studies Quarterly* 16(3–4), (2016), pp. 18–19.

Table 1. Evaluating South Sudan

		Outcomes	
Sector	Actors	Narrow focus	Wide focus
Economics	SOE	Individual profits	Access to critical resources
Politics	CCP/MFA	Facilitating peace talks	Promoting Chinese approach
Security	PLA	Achieving peacekeeping mandate	Ending conflict or cushioning its impact

of armed conflict can be negatively associated with economic activities while the success of peace talks would potentially lead to positive outcomes in both the security as well as economic sector.

The selection of South Sudan as a single case is warranted for two reasons. First, it displays the most advanced case in which China has moved beyond its traditional foreign policy principles of strict non-interference and for the first time in the post-revolutionary period engaged in conflict mediation, and peacekeeping as a visible actor. In this regard it is important to ask if this role is likely to be replicated elsewhere. Second, while the South Sudan conflict certainly has its own unique trajectory and stands out as one of Africa's most violent conflict of recent times, it shows some typical features which can be found in other African countries. China's concentration on investments in extracting natural resources in high risk or post-conflict countries is rather typical. In a number of African countries governments are challenged by insurgents or rebel groups. Thus the South Sudan case might in fact stand for a wider group of fragile but resource rich countries which are the target of Chinese investment.

Conflict in South Sudan

Even before the outbreak of the civil war in South Sudan in December 2013, the country had a trajectory of violent conflict reaching back decades ago and before the secession of the South from Sudan. Uninterrupted peace is rather the exception but not the rule for the two countries. At the core of the conflict in South Sudan is a leadership contest within the ruling party the Sudan People's Liberation Movement (SPLM), between President Salva Kiir and his deputy Riik Machar. However, what started as a personal dispute over power has since 2013 morphed into a complex layered conflict which involves rivaling militias, ethno-politics, regional proxy interest and has generally seen an increase in factionalism and decentralization.

South Sudanese independence in July 2011 resulted from decades of political and military struggle. In 2005 a Comprehensive Peace Agreement (CPA) was adopted which laid the foundations for self-administration and a referendum on independence.[16] Sudan and South Sudan were forming a government of national unity and the South received half of the revenue Sudan was gaining by selling its oil.[17] Before formal independence and after the signing of the CPA some 13 USDbn in oil revenue were allocated to the South. These funds were mainly spent to extend the payroll of the Sudan People's Liberation Army (SPLA) creating a network of patronage based on oil rents which is dominating the political economy. In 2011 the SPLA enlisted a staggering 240,000 soldiers and 90,000 militia and policemen in a country with a population of just around 12 million.[18]

With the independence of South Sudan, oil became an issue of contestation between Juba and Khartoum. Large parts of the oil production were placed in independent South Sudan but the pipeline transporting the oil out of the country and to international markets goes through Sudan.

---

[16]See the full text of the CPA at: 'The Comprehensive Peace Agreement between The Government of The Republic of The Sudan and The Sudan People's Liberation Movement/Sudan People's Liberation Army', January 5, 2005, accessed March 6, 2020, https://reliefweb.int/report/sudan/comprehensive-peace-agreement-between-government-republic-sudan-and-sudan-peoples.

[17]Luke Patey, *The New Kings of Crude China, India, and the Global Struggle for Oil in Sudan and South Sudan* (London: C. Hurst & Co, 2014), p. 210.

[18]Alex De Waal, 'When Cleptocracy becomes Insolvent: Brute Causes of the Civil War in South Sudan', *African Affairs* 113(452), (2014), p. 355.

Additionally a clear border demarcation was missing. Before the outbreak of the civil war, military encounters between the North and South intensified in 2011 and 2012. South Sudan temporarily occupied the oil fields in Heglig, in Sudan. The quarrel over pipeline transmission fees escalated and led South Sudan to shut down its entire oil production in early 2012. Later the civil war interrupted oil production again. In fact, oil revenue never reached pre-independence levels which peaked in 2009.[19] In 2016 oil covered 99% of South Sudan's total export practically all of it going to Chinese companies and accounted for 1.34 USDbn of revenue.[20]

The link between oil rents and violent conflict is well documented, it has best been articulated by Alex de Waal.[21] In his research he describes how the SPLM/A is built upon a kleptocratic and neo-patrimonial system of rule, effectively looting the country's resource wealth by converting it into political and military gains which in the end is contributing to violent conflict. While the oil wealth was important to gain independence from Sudan, the dwindling revenue and the oil shutdown fueled internal conflict between Kiir and Machar which turned violent in December 2013. Internal leadership rivalry could turn violent relatively easily because politics in South Sudan are militarized, party and army structures are deeply interconnected. Furthermore, the SPLM has a long history of divisions and is no unitary political party but also builds on ethnic loyalties.[22] This makes it vulnerable for leadership competition. International mediation efforts have mostly not tried to address the root cause of conflict (resource loot and neo-patrimonial politics) but are concentrating on power-sharing agreements aiming to re-establish the *status quo ante* before December 2013 with Machar and Kiir occupying top leadership positions.

Conflict mediation started immediately with the outbreak of violence. Leadership was assumed by neighboring countries such as Ethiopia and regional organizations like the Intergovernmental Authority on Drought and Development (IGAD) and the AU. Several multinational mediation efforts had to be coordinated.[23] There was no shortage on mediation attempts and ceasefire agreements but most if not all of them failed. As violence continued to intensify while a peacekeeping mission was located in the country the UN agreed to increase its mission size to a maximum of 17,000 troops including 2,000 police and a regional protection force of up to 4,000 troops under IGAD as well as adding a civilian protection mandate.[24] In addition to regional organizations and the UN the so-called Troika of the US, UK and Norway got involved in conflict mediation. Thus Chinese involvement was meeting an already crowded field. While in the past this situation would rather likely lead to China leaving other actors the floor, this time it decided to also facilitate peace talks.

The issue of South Sudan also came up in the UN Security Council. After the February 2015 power sharing agreement collapsed, the Council agreed unanimously on targeted sanctions.[25] Later in that year an important peace deal could be reached the Agreement on the Resolution of the Conflict in the Republic of South Sudan (ARCSS).[26] It was again a power sharing agreement which foresees the return of Machar to Juba to become the country's vice-president in April 2016. In order to accompany the agreement a Joint Monitoring and Evaluation Commission (JMEC) was established of which China was a member. Despite successful mediation attempts violence did not stop in 2016.

[19]Alex De Waal, *The Real Politics of the Horn of Africa Money, War and the Business of Power*. (Cambridge, Malden: Polity, 2015), p. 102.

[20]Data drawn from: The Observatory of Economic Complexity, August 13, 2018, https://atlas.media.mit.edu/en/profile/country/ssd/accessed.

[21]Alex De Waal, *The Real Politics of the Horn of Africa Money, War and the Business of Power*, pp. 91–108.

[22]Douglas Johnson, 'Briefing: The Crisis in South Sudan', *African Affairs* 113(451), (2014), pp. 300–309.

[23]Dimpho Motsamai, 'Assessing AU mediation envoys The case of South Sudan', Pretoria: Institute for Security Studies, East Africa Report, Issue 10, February, 2017.

[24]See UN Security Council Resolutions, 2132, 2155, 2252, 2416.

[25]UN Security Council resolution March 3, 2015, 2206.

[26]IGAD, Agreement on the Resolution of the Conflict in the Republic of South Sudan, Addis Ababa, August 17, 2015, accessed August 14, 2018, http://www.sudantribune.com/IMG/pdf/final_proposed_compromise_agreement_for_south_sudan_conflict.pdf.

Instead of taking his place in a unity government, Machar escaped an assassination attempt and fled the country.[27] He ended up under house arrest in South Africa which he only left in late 2018.[28]

In 2018 IGAD and the UN increased diplomatic pressure by extending the sanction regime including an arms embargo in order to revitalize the ARCSS. On the issue of sanctions China abstained in the Security Council arguing that punitive measures can be counter-productive for peace talks. This turned out not to be true. Increased pressure in combination with regional neighbors leading mediation efforts resulted in the signing of a power sharing agreement in August 2018 which was mainly built on the ARCSS and until today remains the main reference document for negotiated peace.[29] By mid-November 2019 Machar is supposed to return to government fulfilling his part in the ARCSS. It is not clear if the peace deal will last.

China's Stakes in the South Sudan Conflict

This section evaluates Chinese engagement within the conflict in South Sudan looking into three segments: economics, politics (conflict mediation) and security (peacekeeping). The overall aim is to assess what impact and consequences Chinese engagement was having on the conflict and for China itself in order to inform a debate around the relevance of South Sudan as an exemplary test case for Chinese foreign and security policy in Africa. It is implicitly assumed that a role model character is broadly able to link up with key Chinese interests such as stable and secure access to essential natural resources, crafting a positive image of China as responsible great power and advancing the Chinese model of peace and development and finally making a contribution to end hostilities in South Sudan. If these goals are met South Sudan might indeed be a model worth replicating elsewhere.

Economics

Chinese economic engagement in South Sudan dates back long before independence. The first investment into the oil sector occurred in the mid-1990 s at an early stage of Chinese economic outreach to the continent. As such China sought investments in areas in which there are low levels of competition with Western companies. Sudan appeared as a promising ground as oil had been discovered some time ago but was not exploited systematically. Most Western companies left the country because of the fragile security situation and increasing political pressures (NGO campaigning) not to prop up the rule of Al Bashir and become complicit to war crimes. China's investment and therewith support for Bashir turned out to be a major political issue when the Darfur crisis erupted and the Olympic summer games were taking place in Beijing. Given Chinese dynamic economic growth rates and the priority on rapid development at home this meant that China became a net oil importer from 1993 onwards with the share of foreign oil increasing continually.[30] In 2017 China became the largest crude oil importer worldwide.[31] Thus foreign direct investment into the oil sector became a strategic target for China, with Sudan as one of the pioneering cases.

Sudan was primarily important because it provided the chance of investing in the oil sector opening up opportunities to expand into other ventures globally. Indeed, while at the beginning the Sudan investment China got very little international experience, it is now drilling for oil in 42

---

[27]Kate Almquist Knopf, 'Ending South Sudan's Civil War. Council on Foreign Relations', Council Special Report No. 77 November 2016.

[28]Simon Allison, 'Riek Machar's lonely 'exile' in SA', *Mail & Guardian*, July 21, 2017, accessed August 17, 2018, https://mg.co.za. article/2017-07-21-00-riek-machars-lonely-exile-in-sa accessed.

[29]BBC News, 'South Sudanese celebrate peace deal signed by Kiir and Machar', August 6, 2018, accessed August 14, 2018, https://www.bbc.com/news/world-africa-45077389.

[30]Luke Patey, 'Learning in Africa: China's Overseas Oil Investments in Sudan and South Sudan', *Journal of Contemporary China* 26(107), (2017), p. 758.

[31]US Energy Information Administration, 'China surpassed the United States as the world's largest crude oil importer in 2017 December 31, 2018, accessed July 5, 2019, https://www.eia.gov/todayinenergy/detail.php?id=37821.

ountries.[32] After 1999 and until independence of South Sudan, the Sudanese investment made up
.5% of China's oil imports and 2.6% of its overall consumption.[33] While Chinese demand and import
of crude oil continued to rise from about 5 million barrel a day in 2011 to over 9 million 2018,
production in South Sudan declined to only 130,000 barrel per day in 2018 and thus its overall
elevance for China was declining too.[34] During the oil standoff between Sudan and South Sudan
vhich followed its independence production was even lower. When considering its overall quantity,
outh Sudanese oil has never been of critical importance for China Sudan and South Sudan could
never rival inner African oil exporting nations such as Nigeria or Angola and were significantly behind
the Middle East.

Despite this, the investment in the two Sudans was of greater importance for the China National
Petroleum Company (CNPC). CNPC being one of the big three Chinese oil companies the Sudan
investment was not a small or unimportant one. Until 2007 7 USDbn were invested and it was one of
the company's early investments at times making up 40% of the company's overseas production.
Patey finds 'Sudan was more than just another investment on the company's portfolio: it was
a venture of crucial strategic importance for CNPC's international expansion.'[35] Although Chinese
investment in South Sudan is the most important in the oil sector around 100 Chinese companies
from various sectors were operating in the country before the civil war broke out.[36]

Independence from Sudan brought more insecurity for Chinese investors not only through the oil
shutdown. Oil contracts held by Sudan had to be transferred and renegotiated with Juba. The
historically good relations of China with Khartoum were treated with suspicion at times. Newly
agreed contracts with China ruled out any restitution payments in case of a stop of oil production.
outh Sudanese Chinese relations reached a low point with the oil shutdown in 2012.[37] Juba accused
Chinese oil firms to side with Khartoum in the quarrel over pipeline fees and expelled a top manager,
iu Yingcai leading Petrodar, a consortium also including the CNPC.[38]

When looking at international trade stats, oil exports are dominating South Sudan's economy and
provide the most important source of income. Thus Chinese investment is critical for the political
economy of South Sudan. While the Chinese economy can operate fairly well without South
Sudanese oil, revenue from oil exports are a critical part of the political system. Politics of neo-
patrimonialism, fractured political parties and an excessively militarization characterize this system
which runs without having established a functioning state or providing basic services for its
population. Revenue from oil exports is used mostly to feed a system of patronage to exert political
power. The linkages between oil revenue and violent conflict are increasingly documented by NGOs
and investigative journalist.[39] Dar Petroleum Operating Company (DPOC) an international consor-
ium dominated by Chinese state-owned enterprises today is the main institution through which the
oil wealth is generated. CNPC and SINOPEC each own 41% and 6% of DPOC (see Figure 1). DPOC has
supplied the government militia Padang with fuel in 2014 and 2015 which has been involved in
ttacks on UN protection sites and is financing the elite lifestyle of government ministers for example
686,056 USD hotel bill was paid for the petroleum minister.[40]

[2]Patey, 'Learning in Africa: China's Overseas Oil Investments in Sudan and South Sudan', p. 757.
[3]Patey, The New Kings of Crude China, India, and the Global Struggle for Oil in Sudan and South Sudan, p. 118.
[4]Data drawn from https://www.ceicdata.com/en/indicator/china/crude-oil-imports accessed July 5, 2019; Sudan Tribune, 'South
Sudan oil production to resume in September: minister', July 30, 2018, accessed July 5, 2019, http://www.sudantribune.com/
spip.php?article65949.
[5]Patey, The New Kings of Crude China, India, and the Global Struggle for Oil in Sudan and South Sudan, p. 111.
[6]Crisis Group International, 'China's Foreign Policy Experiment in South Sudan', Asia Report N°288, July 10, 2017, p. 8.
[7]Patey, The New Kings of Crude China, India, and the Global Struggle for Oil in Sudan and South Sudan, p. 229.
[8]BBC News. 'South Sudan expels Chinese oil firm boss', February 22, 2012, accessed July 8, 2019, https://www.bbc.co.uk/news/
world-africa-17126340.
[9]Fueling Atrocities Oil and War in South Sudan, The Sentry, March 2018, accessed November 4, 2019, https://cdn.thesentry.org/
wp-content/uploads/2018/03/FuelingAtrocities_Sentry_March2018_final.pdf.
[0]The Taking of South Sudan The Tycoons, Brokers, and Multinational Corporations Complicit in Hijacking the World's Newest State,
The Sentry, September 19, 2019, pp.12–16, 18, accessed November 4, 2019, https://thesentry.org/reports/taking-south-sudan/.

41% CNPC (China)
40% PETRONAS (Malaysia)
8% NILEPET (South Sudan)
6% SINOPEC (China)
5% TRIOCEAN (Egypt)

Figure 1. DPOC ownership structure.
Source: https://africaoilandpower.com/about/sponsors/dpoc/accessed 4 November 2019

The war itself has not stopped Chinese businesses from acquiring new licenses for exploration. In 2016 Fortune Minerals and Construction Limited was set up.[41] The discovery of new oil fields was announced in August 2019 with the prospect to more than double the current output to over 350,000 barrels per day.[42] New concessions have been issued to established partners such as DPOC. While the findings are important for South Sudan and the companies involved in drilling the overall importance for China of South Sudanese oil is only affected peripherally as the country consumes around 9 million barrel per day and not all of the oil is likely to be sold to China alone. How profitable the Chinese oil investment is cannot be objectively assessed. However, the significant fall of production levels the evacuation of most of the CNPC staff since the outbreak of the war are surely limiting factors.

While the oil sector is the most important business component of Chinese investment it is not the only one. In 2012 140 Chinese owned mostly smaller businesses were operating. These numbers have halved. The number of Chinese expatriates fell from around 10,000 to just 500.[43] In essence, most economic activities have been negatively affected by the war. This also includes infrastructure projects. While China also increased funds for humanitarian relief and developmental projects these remain far behind the amount and scale of traditional donors. The oil investment far out-performs other sectors. What is interesting to observe is that although South Sudan is of declining importance to China Chinese engagement in the conflict is relatively increasing in the political and security sphere.

With its beefed up political and security engagement China was surely following its long-standing involvement in Sudan long before partition. If Chinese foreign and security policy is mainly driven by Chinese economic outreach measured by today's relevance South Sudan would not top the priority list in Africa and the over the average engagement in mediation and peacekeeping would hardly be justified. Investment in the oil and gas sector is considerably less risky in countries such as Angola, Mozambique or Nigeria but provides better economic returns. The combination of high risk environment and above the average political and security engagement in South Sudan appears as rather exceptional. However, most problematic might be that investment in the oil sector is a contributing factor to the war and thus the initial economic motivation for investment is undermining its very operation.

Politics

The Sudan and South Sudan venture is not only a purely economic enterprise. The term test case refers much more to Chinese political and security involvement than its economic activities. From the beginning security issues and with them politics became an integral feature of Chinese engagement independent of any non-intervention rhetoric. A political dimension was unavoidable as both Sudan and South Sudan were involved in armed conflicts toward which the UN Security Council had

[41]Ibid., pp. 24–25.
[42]Radio Tamazuj, 'Petroleum minister says new oil discovery "significant"' August 23, 2019, accessed November 4, 2019, https://radiotamazuj.org/en/news/article/petroleum-minister-says-new-oil-discovery-significant.
[43]Lily Kuo, 'There's at least one place in Africa where China's "win win" diplomacy is failing', *Quartz Africa* 21, November 2017, accessed November 5, 2019, https://qz.com/africa/1111402/south-sudan-china-win-win-diplomacy-struggles/.

o respond. Today three peacekeeping missions are deployed to the Sudans, in Darfur, South Sudan nd Abyei. Chinese political influence on conflict parties is not clear cut. However, given the nvestment in the oil sector (an essential source of income), China's permanent seat at the UN ecurity Council and the willingness to cooperate even with autocratic leaders and wanted war criminals (Bashir was indicted by the ICC but travelled to China) made China an important political player in Sudanese politics. However, in comparison to economics the international political playing ield is much more crowded. The UN, US, African regional organizations, neighboring countries and Western donors are all active. There is no shortage of political interests and ambitions in the region. China is not the only or most important actor but this might have rather enabled more pro-active nvolvement as political risks and opportunities were shared among many actors.

China's activism in South Sudan stands in line with a certain legacy of Chinese engagement with udan. The UN peacekeeping mission in Darfur which was resisted by Bashir could finally be eployed also because of Chinese diplomatic involvement. Through the independence war relations o South Sudan were difficult given Beijing's close links to Bashir. This changed over time and SPLM adres established better relations with the CCP for example by inviting them to training programs. However, China had very little influence on events happening on the ground. The oil shutdown and utbreak of the civil war severely impacted China's oil installations. It therefore actively supported N Security Council resolutions 2135 and 2155 and did not abstain as it often did in the past. Resolution 2155 mentions the protection of oil installations and foreign nationals twice and thus can e assumed to be drafted by the Chinese delegation.[44] A key rationale for becoming politically ngaged in conflict mediation certainly also emerged from the need to protect its nationals and ssets as the conflict escalated and showed little signs of a rapid solution.[45]

In the dispute between Kiir and Machar, China did not take a position for either candidate, instead ollowing its classical emphasis on political neutrality. China repeatedly called for a peaceful resolu-ion of the conflict. Both parties the SPLM of Kiir and Machar's SPLM-IO visited Beijing for diplomatic alks. The initiative for conflict mediation came from IGAD members with Chinese support. China layed the role of a facilitator but did not become an active mediator itself. Regarding the IGAD-led eace process African Affairs representative Zhong Jianhua noted: 'We are not the party to propose ur own initiative, at least at this stage. So, we urge all parties concerned to respect an African olution proposed by African parties.'[46] However, early mediation attempts collapsed as quickly as hey were started and thus China increased its engagement. Foreign minister Wang Yi in anuary 2015 presented a four-point peace plan alongside IGAD peace negotiations.[47]

These explicit mediation attempts are exceptional for China which often avoided getting directly nvolved in conflict mediation. In this case as well as in others Chinese foreign policy prefers crisis nanagement based on non-punitive instruments, mentioning the primacy of developmental peace nd portraying China as responsible power.[48] This approach is rather different from the Western emplate which often operates with sanctions and links up to concepts of peace which are rooted in he liberal tradition of governance. In this context the increased Chinese engagement in the case of outh Sudan can be seen as a testing ground for a Chinese approach.

The continued failure of conflict mediation let to a gradual toughening of responses to the crisis. n resolution 2206 in early 2015 the UN Security Council agreed to targeted sanctions. The resolution vas adopted by consent. Later in the year a power sharing agreement was reached, the ARCSS. China

---

⁴UN Security Council, Resolution May 27, 2015, 2014, para. 21.
⁵Hodzi, *The End of China's Non-Intervention Policy in Africa*, p. 191.
⁶Michael Martina, 'South Sudan marks new foreign policy chapter for China: official' *Reuters*, February 11, 2014, accessed August 17, 2018, https://www.reuters.com/article/us-china-southsudan/south-sudan-marks-new-foreign-policy-chapter-for-china-official-idUSBREA1A0HO20140211.
⁷UN Security Council 7396th meeting March 3, 2015. Liu Jieyi.
⁸Ministry of Foreign Affairs, Peoples Republic of China, Foreign Minister Wang Yi Meets the Press, March 8, 2015, accessed August 20, 2018, http://www.fmprc.gov.cn/mfa_eng/zxxx_662805/t1243662.shtml.

became a signatory to the deal forming part of an international monitoring mechanism. The agreement collapsed as well.

A general arms embargo which the US and other members of the Security Council favored often failed because China and Russia were against it arguing it would be a too interventionist instrument disrupting peace mediation. While the argument falls neatly within traditional Chinese foreign policy rhetoric it should also not be forgotten that the US and China are in politically different camps when it comes to questions of the two Sudans with the US pushing for tougher sanctions.[49] More coercive means of diplomacy such as sanctions are perceived by China as a form of power politics which it does not simply agree with. Consequently the October 2015 resolution 2241 only mentions the willingness of the UN to use sanctions against peace spoilers and also condemns attacks against oil installations.[50]

In the end, lack in tangible progress in the peace process forced the Security Council to consider tougher sanctions such as an arms embargo. Given Chinese interest in conflict resolution in South Sudan but its skepticism toward punitive instruments such as sanctions, there is a tension between the preferred method on engagement (non-punitive) and the need to sanction peace spoilers. While hard sanctions might run counter to traditional Chinese foreign principles a dogmatic non-interference policy was not bearing any tangible results in peace talks. Ultimately, China voted in favor of resolution 2206 and 2241 (targeted sanctions) it abstained on resolution 2428 adopted in July 2018 implementing an arms embargo. The Chinese representative to the UN voiced principled concerns. It was argued that 'sanctions should serve only as a means, not an end in themselves.'[51]

In this situation China has to weigh in two perspectives. On the one hand, global order questions and the use of selective punitive politics, and on the other, progress in peace talks. The latter was desperately needed, as the civil war continued, for saving Chinese investments in the country. Additionally Chinese diplomatic engagement in the conflict identified as a test case by Chinese diplomats was receiving international attention but not leading to any positive results. China abstained in the voting likely because regional African organizations such as the AU and IGAD did not lobby for tougher sanctions. The resolution was only adopted with a minimum of nine affirmative votes. However, after tougher sanctions were adopted peace talks started to progress leading to a so called revitalized ACRSS signed on September 12 2018 after which violence until today (November 2019) decreased visibly.[52] Despite this it is still too early to proclaim a definite end to the civil war.

The South Sudan case is not only relevant because we can observe a shift away from dogmatic non-interference but also because it is testing Chinese conceptual (doctrinal) thinking around war and peace. While the adjustment from non-interference policy might just be a pragmatic move reorganizing foreign policy principles the supposed greater challenge might in fact be too simplistic and missing conceptual thinking of how peace can be achieved.

For China one of the bigger problems when becoming more active in peace mediation and conflict resolution is the relative absence of workable, realistic and normatively attractive standards for bringing and maintaining peace. The problem lies within Chinese foreign policy positions and opinions on issues of global governance in our case a peace order. Shaun Breslin argues:

> If there is a normative position underpinning China's official approach to reform of global governance, it is perhaps that there should be no normative basis. For the time being at least, China is less interested in promoting a clearly articulated grand strategy and a new set of universal values than it is in finding pragmatic solutions: primarily solutions to problems that it itself faces, but also at times solutions to problems facing others.[53]

---

[49]US Department of State, 'U.S. Arms Restrictions on South Sudan' February 2, 2018, accessed August 20, 2018, https://www.state.gov/r/pa/prs/ps/2018/02/277849.htm.

[50]UN Security Council, Resolution October 9, 2015, 2241, para.34.

[51]UN Security Council 8210th meeting, July 13, 2018, Ma Zhaoxu.

[52]For conflict data on South Sudan see ACLED: https://www.acleddata.com/dashboard/#728 accessed November 9, 2019.

[53]Shaun Breslin, 'China and the global order: signalling threat or friendship?' *International Affairs* 89(3), (2013), p. 633.

onceptually China endorses the idea of developmental peace. This rather rudimentary concept merges out of Chinese domestic experience assuming that at the heart of most societal conflicts is conomic underdevelopment.[54] In contrast to liberal peace models, the developmental peace genda operates under the premise of state-led economic growth. State building is important not ecause of the necessity of good governance, democracy or human rights but because state capacity , needed for developing a country's economy.[55] This rather top down and state centric approach isplays a number of flaws.

The scientific literature gives no indication that economic development alone is a sufficient ondition for providing sustainable peace. To the opposite a vast literature exists pointing to the roblem of resource abundance, war economies and poor governance standards contributing to iolent conflicts in Africa.[56] While development is an important condition helping to ease political ressure and inner societal tension it is no stand-alone instrument but needs to be contextualized nd integrated into conflict mediating structures such as accountable governments to lead to ustainable peace. It is highly doubtful if the Chinese developmental peace concept is suitable for outh Sudan. Given the militarized nature of the South Sudanese political system which is built on eo-patrimonial patronage, income from oil revenues South Sudan's single most important source of ncome, is primarily not used to develop the country and provide its population with better life pportunities but is feeding the civil war.[57] As Patey finds with regards to Sudan: 'Oil revenues in udan reinforced longstanding practices of economic mismanagement, political patronage, militar- :ation and corruption of the Sudanese ruling elite in Khartoum, and oil companies became targets or disenfranchised groups to undermine the Sudanese government's main source of wealth.'[58] imilarly, South Sudan's oil revenue feeds a small kleptocratic military elite which rules through fear, iolence and distributing oil wealth to its supporters. State structures primarily exist for distributing il loot but not for effectively improving living conditions of the population. In 2017 South Sudan nked 187 out of 190 countries in the UN human development index.[59] The notion of develop- ental peace is not only conceptually simple, de facto Chinese investment was feeding a war conomy. The continuous fighting was bringing the oil production almost to a complete stand :ill harming Chinese economic interests.

At the political front the venture into conflict mediation in South Sudan was not leading to clearly ositive results but was rather displaying weaknesses in the conceptual approach. China played the ole of an active facilitator within multilateral structures and was positively received for that role by fricans. Its overall contribution to peace talks and the ARCSS was more indirect as multiple actors ere active in conflict mediation and China did not assume a domineering role. Conceptually more roblematic for China is the fact that more coercive diplomatic instruments actually led to resumption of peace talks and a peace deal which finally reduced violence. While China welcomes n end of hostilities and views punitive diplomacy with more skepticism. In South Sudan it could not ave the one without the other.

Equally problematic is the developmental peace rhetoric. Even when viewed most favorably (who ould be against development?), Chinese investment in the oil sector was not only risky but is contributing factor to the many wars in Sudan and South Sudan. The South Sudan case illustrates tension between China's diplomatic efforts to reduce violence through mediation and its inability

---

Xuejun Wang 'Developmental Peace: Understanding China's Africa Policy in Peace and Security' in *China and Africa Building Peace and Security Cooperation on the Continent*, ed. Chris Alden et al. (Cham: Palgrave Macmillan, 2018), pp. 67–82.
Romain Dittgen, et al., 'On Becoming a Responsible Great Power: Contextualising China's Foray into Human Rights and Peace & Security in Africa', *SAIIA, Policy Insights* 27, (2016).
'Some examples from the literature referring to Africa: Kathryn Nwajiaku Dahou, 'The Political Economy of Oil and "Rebellion" in Nigeria's Niger Delta', *Review of African Political Economy* 39(132), (2012), pp. 295–313. Eghosa Osaghae, 'Resource Curse or Resource Blessing: The Case of the Niger Delta "Oil Republic" in Nigeria', *Commonwealth and Comparative Politics* 53(2), (2015), pp. 109–129.
Alex De Waal, 'The Political Marketplace and the roots of persistent conflict', *Fletcher Security Review* 1(1), (2015), pp. 10–14.
'Patey, 'Learning in Africa: China's Overseas Oil Investments in Sudan and South Sudan', p. 764.
UNDP: South Sudan profile. Accessed July 9, 2019, http://hdr.undp.org/en/countries/profiles/SSD.

to address the structural deeper laying causes of conflict to which its investment and political orientation concepts have contributed. In this context part of the problem might be that China still lacks first-hand experience and expertise on African conflicts, the absence of comprehensive strategic thinking in conflict resolution is not helpful either.[60]

The Security Dimension

As such China has no direct or urgent security interests in South Sudan. They exist only in conjunction with its investment in the oil production. In a narrow sense security of its nationals and protection of oil installations are the most direct interests. Reference to them would not automatically explain Chinese rather exceptional contribution to the UN peacekeeping mission, as in the case of Libya China was more heavily invested and decided to just evacuate its nationals. As the civil war escalated China along with the UN increased its military presence. While in December 2013 it provided 340 soldiers it tripled its contribution to reach 1,062 staff in May 2019.[61] The UN Mission to South Sudan named UNMISS consists of 16,468 civilian and military staff. The Chinese contribution while being remarkable for China which in the past only sent smaller contingents and hardly combat troops it still only makes up 6.44% of all personnel.[62] Chinese nationals also occupied higher ranking positions within UNMISS such as the position of a deputy force commander (Gen. Zhang Yijun) or acting force commander (Maj. Gen Chaoying Yang). By international comparison the troop contribution somehow falls within the expected range of a larger country and is not out of proportion. The largest troop contributing countries in South Sudan remain Rwanda and India with around 2,300 to 2,700 troops.

Has Chinese participation paid off in UNMISS? How effective the mission is depends on the expectations one has. It is unusual that a civil war breaks out while peacekeepers are on the ground. Unlike in other situations the mission was already located in South Sudan and had to be reinforced. This made it easier for troop contributing countries to prop up numbers. However, it can hardly be a sign of mission success if violence intensifies while peacekeepers are in the country. Obviously the mission had no preventive effect. The determination with which Kiir and Machar were fighting each other left little room for the UN and thus it rather opted for limiting the effects of the war than actually ending it. As such this must be a somewhat frustrating experience but it is not fundamentally different from other conflict settings in Africa. In countries like Mali, DRC or the Central African Republic we can see the deployment of peacekeepers into active wars with often unclear exit options and little tangible progress in peace negotiations.[63] It remains to be seen how China is evaluating this kind of situation. It is rather clear that returns in terms of a quick and sustainable peace deal are difficult to achieve in most of Africa's recent conflict zones.[64]

What is interesting with regard to China's participation in UNMISS is also that the mission operates with an explicit civilian protection mandate creating protection sites for civilians. Peacekeepers are not only expected to passively protect civilians in and around UN camps but also 'to deter violence against civilians, including foreign nationals, especially through proactive deployment, active patrolling ... '[65] Given the fragile situation in the country, Chinese peacekeepers are exposed to considerable risks. Indeed a small number of Chinese soldiers got killed in service and had to handle conflictive situations.[66] In 2016 heavy fighting broke out in the capital Juba in which

---

[60]Chun Zhang and Mariam Kemple-Hardy, 'From conflict resolution to conflict prevention: China in South Sudan. Saferworld accessed August 20, 2018, https://www.saferworld.org.uk/downloads/pubdocs/from-conflict-resolution-to-conflict prevention—china-and-south-sudan.pdf.

[61]Data drawn from https://peacekeeping.un.org/en/troop-and-police-contributors, accessed July 9, 2019.

[62]Ibid.

[63]John Karlsrud, The UN at War (Cham: Palgrave Macmillan, 2018).

[64]Malte Brosig and Norman Sempijja, 'Does Peacekeeping Reduce Violence? Assessing Comprehensive Security of Contemporary Peace Operations in Africa', Stability: International Journal of Security & Development 7(1), (2018), pp. 1–23.

[65]UN Resolution March 15, 2019, 2459, para.7.

[66]Katrin Huang, 'Chinese peacekeepers in tense stand-off with armed militants in South Sudan', South China Morning Post January 6, 2018, accessed July 9, 2019, https://www.scmp.com/news/china/diplomacy-defence/article/2127140/chinese peacekeepers-tense-stand-armed-militants-south.

so UN civilian protection sites are located. The UN's response to the renewed violence was investigated and deemed 'chaotic and insufficient'. As a consequence the China trained Rwandan force commander was removed from his post. During the event Chinese peacekeepers have left their positions on several occasions.[67]

More controversial and catching widespread attention are arms deals with South Sudan. Months after the civil war broke out Kiir received arms and ammunition from the China North Industries Corporation (Norinco) worth 20.7 USD m.[68] Providing one party of the conflict with weapons, if intentional, could be interpreted as one-sided support and certainly expands far beyond political neutrality and non-interference. In this case the order for the shipment is likely to have been placed before the outbreak of hostilities and China declared a moratorium on arms deals with South Sudan. A UN expert panel on South Sudan monitoring arms sales has since not reported Chinese arms shipments to the country.[69] However, Chinese weapons played a role in various armed conflicts in the two Sudans over the years. The fragile political and security situation was well known and China tends to support incumbent governments in Khartoum and Juba. Thus China has either willingly or through neglecting Sudanese politics indirectly contributed to conflict. Arms shipments to Sudan have a longer history. Oil exports led to larger imports of Chinese weapons in the past.[70]

The PLA has also not been fully in compliance with UN sanctions on leading military staff which included a travel ban for some individuals. South Sudanese chief general Jok Riak banned by the UN to travel attended a two week workshop in Beijing.[71] While his attendance falls within what can be called military diplomacy China entertains with many African countries, at war times these relations become a political statement rather quickly.[72]

In sum, the value added of peacekeeping in South Sudan might have less to do with tangible progress on the ground which is difficult to generate as peace deals are notorious fragile and conflict dynamics are difficult to influence from the outside.. Combat experience in South Sudan is also limited to get as the UN does not apply a peace enforcement strategy. With the still unusually (for China) large contribution to the peace mission China can demonstrate that it is not only interested in extracting natural resources but also acts as a responsible large power.[73] Domestically China tries to promote Chinese peacekeeping and military operations in Africa as a tool to install a sense of national pride by sponsoring war movies such as Wolf Worrier 2, Operation Red Sea or Chinese Peacekeeping Forces.[74] In the end, the evaluation of stronger than usual Chinese participation in peacekeeping is mixed. While it cannot be expected to simply end a protected war and there has been critique against Chinese peacekeepers it is also true that without UN protection sites the humanitarian situation would have been much more strained.

Conclusion

South Sudan has been declared a test case for Chinese foreign and security policy but will it turn out to be a role model which is worth replicating? While the mainstream literature implies an ever

South Sudan peacekeeping commander sacked over "serious shortcomings"' The Guardian, November 2, 2016, accessed November 5, 2019, https://www.theguardian.com/global-development/2016/nov/02/south-sudan-peacekeeping-chief-sacked-alarm-serious-shortcomings-ondieki.

Interim report of the Panel of Experts on South Sudan established pursuant to Security Council resolution 2206 (2015), August 21, 2015, para.70.

For an overview of reports please see: https://www.un.org/sc/suborg/en/sanctions/2206/panel-of-experts/work-mandate.

'China's Arms Sales to Sudan, Fact Sheet', Human Rights First, (2007), accessed August 20, 2018, https://www.humanrightsfirst. org/wp-content/uploads/pdf/080311-cah-arms-sales-fact-sheet.pdf.

Joseph Oduha, 'South Sudan army chief defies UN travel ban with visit to China' The East African, August 16, 2018, accessed July 10, 2019, https://www.theeastafrican.co.ke/news/ea/South-Sudan-army-chief-defies-UN-ban-with-China-visit/4552908-4715152-m84ct/index.html.

Shen Zhixoing, 'On China's Military Diplomacy in Africa' in China and Africa Building Peace and Security Cooperation on the Continent, ed. Chris Alden et al. (Cham: Palgrave Macmillan, 2018), pp. 101–122.

Courtney Fung, 'What explains China's deployment to UN peacekeeping operations?' International Relations of the Asia-Pacific 16, (2016), pp. 409–441.

Yu Fengsheng, 'Chinese Peacekeeping Forces': Latest domestic war film debuts in China', CGTN, November 26, 2018, accessed July 10, 2019, https://news.cgtn.com/news/3d3d674e3459444f30457a6333566d54/share_p.html.

Table 2. Chinese experience in South Sudan

Sector	Actors	Outcomes	
		Narrow focus	Wide focus
Economics	SOE	Individual profits:	Access to critical resources
		Reduced economic activity, oil sector contributing to conflict	Less relevant today. South Sudanese oil is not of critical importance
Politics	CCP/MFA	Facilitating peace talks	Promoting Chinese approach
		ACRSS was agreed but fragile peace	Developmental approach and preference for non-punitive measure have not paid off
Security	PLA	Achieving peacekeeping mandate	Ending conflict or cushioning its impact
		Protection sites have saved some	Mission could often not actively stop continuing violence and war
		Operational but no combat experience	

growing role of China in Africa's security politics following its economic expansion into the continen
a close evaluation of the Chinese experiences in South Sudan cautions against a too ambitioni
perspective. The article was exploring three sections: economics, politics and security, analyzin
narrower and wider effects of China's engagement.

In three sectors of analysis: economics, politics and security the overall assessment of relevanc
and achievements is somehow sobering (see Table 2). Based on a narrow economic focus on Sout
Sudan profits for China are rather unassuming. There is no critical need for South Sudanese c
because Chinese companies have internationalized their explorations globally and the global marke
supply covers even growing demand. Today South Sudan is not needed any more as a launching pa
for its oil industry. More problematic is the effect of oil revenue on the conflict. The oil wealth
a contributing factor to the armed conflict which undercuts Chinese investment as oil productio
was severely impacted by the war.

At the political sphere positive returns are also difficult to identify. A tension remains betwee
traditional Chinese foreign policy preferences for non-punitive diplomacy and the reality that harde
sanctions played a positive role in the peace negotiations finally leading to the revitalized ACRSS i
2018 which since then led to a visible drop in violence. Potentially more problematic is the absenc
of a durable peace concept. The notion of developmental peace is too simple and one-sided whi
liberal peace models are not compatible with the CCP's ideological position. In other worlds, th
South Sudan experience challenges key Chinese rhetoric and at the same time is not producin
favorable outcomes.

Finally security. China did increase its troop contribution considerably but will the South Suda
experience motivate it to do so elsewhere? The peacekeeping mission itself could not do much t
stop the fighting but did set up protection sites for civilians. At the same time the war continue
unabated. Only recently there is a drop in casualty numbers. South Sudan is still far away fron
addressing the root causes of conflict which is based on its political system operating with resourc
rents and elite patronage. However, the instable security situation is likely to remain for the foresee
able future which is also typical for other African conflicts zones.

In the end, there are a number of strong indicators which combined make it less likely that China w
use its South Sudan experience as a role model. On the security front success is highly unstable but risk
for soldiers are high. On the political front South Sudan is an example for the problems concepts suc
as developmental peace can create. Considering all this Chinese engagement in South Sudan is rathe
exceptional but not very likely to be replicated. Naturally foreign policy is not only based on rational c
coherent decision-making but if it bears some relevance the South Sudan case does not deliv
undisputable positive results but rather calls for recalibration of applied policies.

Disclosure statement

No potential conflict of interest was reported by the author.

Index

For Product Safety Concerns and Information please contact our
EU representative GPSR@taylorandfrancis.com Taylor & Francis
Verlag GmbH, Kaufingerstraße 24, 80331 München, Germany